A COMMENTARY ON
HOMER'S ODYSSEY

A COMMENTARY ON
HOMER'S ODYSSEY

VOLUME II
BOOKS IX–XVI

🙢

ALFRED HEUBECK
ARIE HOEKSTRA

CLARENDON PRESS · OXFORD

OXFORD
UNIVERSITY PRESS

Great Clarendon Street, Oxford OX2 6DP

Oxford University Press is a department of the University of Oxford.
It furthers the University's objective of excellence in research, scholarship,
and education by publishing worldwide in

Oxford New York

Athens Auckland Bangkok Bogotá Buenos Aires Cape Town
Chennai Dar es Salaam Delhi Florence Hong Kong Istanbul Karachi
Kolkata Kuala Lumpur Madrid Melbourne Mexico City Mumbai Nairobi
Paris São Paulo Shanghai Singapore Taipei Tokyo Toronto Warsaw

with associated companies in Berlin Ibadan

Oxford is a registered trade mark of Oxford University Press
in the UK and in certain other countries

Published in the United States
by Oxford University Press Inc., New York

Originally published in Italian under the title Omero: Odissea
© Fondazione Lorenzo Valla
English edition © Oxford University Press 1989

First issued in Clarendon Paperbacks 1990

British Library Cataloguing in Publication Data
Data available

Library of Congress Cataloging in Publication Data
Heubeck, Alfred, 1914–1987.
A commentary on Homer's Odyssey.
Revised English edition of: Omero: Odissea.
Vol. 2. by Alfred Heubeck, Arie Hoekstra.
Contents: v. 2. Books IX–XVI.
1. Homer. Odyssey. 2. Odysseus (Greek mythology)
in literature. I. Hoekstra, A. II. West, Stephanie.
III. Hainsworth, J. B. (John Bryan) IV. Title.
V. Title: Homer, Odyssey.
PA4167.H48 1988 883'.01 87–18509
ISBN 0–19–872144–7

5 7 9 10 8 6

Printed in Great Britain on acid-free paper by
Biddles Ltd., Guildford and King's Lynn

CONTENTS

BIBLIOGRAPHICAL ABBREVIATIONS

The abbreviations used for ancient authors correspond to those employed in the ninth edition of Liddell and Scott, *Greek–English Lexicon* (LSJ) and in the *Oxford Latin Dictionary*, for periodicals to those of *L'Année philologique*.

Editions of the *Odyssey* referred to in the Commentary:

Allen	T. W. Allen, *Homeri Opera*, iii², iv² (Oxford Classical Text), Oxford, 1917, 1919.
Ameis–Hentze–Cauer	*Homers Odyssee* f. den Schulgebrauch erklärt von K. F. Ameis u. C. Hentze, bearbeitet von P. Cauer, i 1¹⁴, 2¹³, ii 1⁹, 2¹⁰, Leipzig, 1920, 1940, 1928, 1925.
Hainsworth*	*Omero, Odissea, libri v–viii: Introduzione, testo e commento* a cura di J. B. Hainsworth, Fondazione Lorenzo Valla, Rome, 1982.
Heubeck*	*Omero, Odissea, libri ix–xii; xxiii–xxiv: Introduzione, testo e commento* a cura di Alfred Heubeck, Fondazione Lorenzo Valla, Rome, 1983, 1987.
Hoekstra*	*Omero, Odissea, libri xiii–xvi: Introduzione, testo e commento* a cura di Arie Hoekstra, Fondazione Lorenzo Valla, Rome, 1984.
Merry–Riddell	W. W. Merry and J. Riddell, *Homer's* Odyssey: *Books i–xii*, Oxford, 1886.
Monro	D. B. Monro, *Homer's* Odyssey: *Books xiii–xxiv*, Oxford, 1901.
Russo*	*Omero, Odissea, libri xvii–xx: Introduzione, testo e commento* a cura di Joseph Russo, Fondazione Lorenzo Valla, Rome, 1985.
Stanford	W. B. Stanford, *The* Odyssey *of Homer²*, Macmillan, London, 1959.
van Leeuwen	J. van Leeuwen, *Homeri Carmina, cum prolegomenis, notis criticis, commentariis exegeticis, Odyssea*, Leiden, 1917.
von der Mühll	P. von der Mühll, *Homeri Odyssea³*, Basel, 1961 (Stuttgart, 1984).
S. West*	*Omero, Odissea, libri i–iv: Introduzione generale di Alfred Heubeck e Stephanie West, introduzione, testo e commento* a cura di Stephanie West, Fondazione Lorenzo Valla, Rome, 1981.

* The present volume is the second in the English edition (introductions and commentary only); the first volume (Books i–viii) was published in 1988, and the third (Books xvii–xxiv) is forthcoming (both from OUP).

Works mentioned by abbreviated title:

Ameis–Hentze, *Anhang* K. F. Ameis and C. Hentze, *Anhang zu Homers Odyssee*³, Leipzig, 1889, 1895³.

Archaeologia *Archaeologia Homerica: Die Denkmäler u. das frühgriechische Epos*, ed. F. Matz and H. G. Buchholz, Göttingen, 1967.

Arend, *Scenen* W. Arend, *Die typischen Scenen bei Homer*, Berlin, 1933.

Austin, *Archery* N. Austin, *Archery at the Dark of the Moon: Poetic Problems in Homer's* Odyssey, Berkeley–Los Angeles, 1975.

Bechtel, *Lexilogus* F. Bechtel, *Lexilogus zu Homer*, Halle, 1914.

Beekes, *Laryngeals* R. S. P. Beekes, *The Development of the Proto-Indo-European Laryngeals in Greek*, The Hague–Paris, 1969.

Besslich, *Schweigen* S. Besslich, *Schweigen–Verschweigen–Übergehen: Die Darstellung des Unausgesprochenen in der Odyssee*, Heidelberg, 1966.

Bethe, *Homer* E. Bethe, *Homer: Dichtung und Sage*, i–iii, Leipzig–Berlin, 1914, 1922, 1929².

—— *Odyssee* —— ibid. ii: *Odyssee, Kyklos, Zeitbestimmung*², Leipzig, 1929.

Bolling, *Evidence* G. M. Bolling, *The External Evidence for Interpolation in Homer*, Oxford, 1925.

Bowra, *HP* C. M. Bowra, *Heroic Poetry*, London, 1952.

Burkert, *Religion* W. Burkert, *Greek Religion: Archaic and Classical*, trans. John Raffan, Blackwell, 1985.

Cauer, *Homerkritik* P. Cauer, *Grundfragen der Homerkritik*³, Leipzig, 1921–3.

Chantraine, *Dictionnaire* P. Chantraine, *Dictionnaire étymologique de la langue grecque*, Paris, 1968–80.

—— *Formation* —— *La Formation des noms en grec ancien*, Paris, 1933.

—— *Grammaire* —— *Grammaire homérique* i³, ii², Paris, 1958, 1963.
—— *Morphologie* —— *Morphologie historique du grec*, Paris, 1967.

Clay, *Wrath* J. S. Clay, *The Wrath of Athena: Gods and Men in the* Odyssey, Princeton, 1983.

Companion *A Companion to Homer*, ed. A. J. B. Wace and F. H. Stubbings, London, 1962.

Delebecque, *Télémaque* E. Delebecque, *Télémaque et la structure de l'Odyssée*, *Annales de la faculté des lettres d'Aix-en-Provence*, NS xxi, 1958.

Denniston, *Particles* J. D. Denniston, *The Greek Particles*², Oxford, 1954.

Ebeling, *Lexicon* H. Ebeling, *Lexicon Homericum*, Leipzig, 1880–5.

Eisenberger, *Studien*	H. Eisenberger, *Studien zur Odyssee*, Wiesbaden, 1973.
Erbse, *Beiträge*	H. Erbse, *Beiträge zum Verständnis der Odyssee*, Berlin–New York, 1972.
Fenik, *Studies*	B. Fenik, *Studies in the* Odyssey, *Hermes* Einzelschriften, xxx, Wiesbaden, 1974.
Finley, *World*	M. I. Finley, *The World of Odysseus* (second revised edn.), Harmondsworth, 1979.
Finsler, *Homer*	G. Finsler, *Homer*, i 1–2, ii, Leipzig, ²1918, ³1924.
Focke, *Odyssee*	F. Focke, *Die Odyssee*, Stuttgart–Berlin, 1943.
Fränkel, *Gleichnisse*	H. Fränkel, *Die homerischen Gleichnisse*, Göttingen, 1921.
Frisk, *GEW*	H. Frisk, *Griechisches etymologisches Wörterbuch*, Heidelberg, 1954–73.
Germain, *Genèse*	G. Germain, *Genèse de l'Odyssée*, Paris, 1954.
Goodwin, *Syntax*	W. W. Goodwin, *Syntax of the Moods and Tenses of the Greek Verb*, London, ²1889, repr. London, 1965, 1966.
Guthrie, *Gods*	W. K. C. Guthrie, *The Greeks and their Gods*, London, 1950.
Hainsworth, *Flexibility*	J. B. Hainsworth, *The Flexibility of the Homeric Formula*, Oxford, 1968.
Heubeck, *Dichter*	A. Heubeck, *Der Odyssee-Dichter und die Ilias*, Erlangen, 1954.
Hoekstra, *Modifications*	A. Hoekstra, *Homeric Modifications of Formulaic Prototypes*, Amsterdam, 1965.
Hölscher, *Untersuchungen*	U. Hölscher, *Untersuchungen zur Form der Odyssee*, Leipzig, 1939.
Kirchhoff, *Odyssee*	A. Kirchhoff, *Die Homerische Odyssee und ihre Entstehung*, Berlin, 1879.
Kirk, *Commentary*	G. S. Kirk, *The* Iliad*: A Commentary*, i. *Books 1–4*, Cambridge, 1985.
—— *Homer*	——*Homer and the Oral Tradition*, Cambridge, 1976.
—— *Myths*	——*The Nature of Greek Myths*, Harmondsworth, 1974.
—— *Songs*	——*The Songs of Homer*, Cambridge, 1962.
Kl. Pauly	*Der Kleine Pauly: Lexicon der Antike in 5 Bänden*, ed. K. Ziegler and W. Sontheimer, Munich, 1964–75, DTV Munich, 1979.
Kühner–Gerth	R. Kühner, *Ausführliche Grammatik der griechischen Sprache*, i–ii. *Satzlehre*³, besorgt v. B. Gerth, Hanover, 1898–1904, repr. Leverkusen, 1955.
Kurt, *Fachausdrücke*	C. Kurt, *Seemännische Fachausdrücke bei Homer*, Göttingen, 1979.
Leaf, *Iliad*	W. Leaf, *The* Iliad², London, 1900–2.

Lejeune, *Phonétique* M. Lejeune, *Phonétique historique du mycénien et du grec ancien*, Paris, 1972.

Lesky, *Homeros* A. Lesky, *Homeros*, *RE*, Supplementband xi, Stuttgart, 1967.

Leumann, *Wörter* M. Leumann, *Homerische Wörter*, Basel, 1950.

LfgrE *Lexicon des frühgriechischen Epos*, ed. B. Snell and H. Erbse, Göttingen, 1955– .

Lord, *Singer* A. B. Lord, *The Singer of Tales*, Cambridge, Mass.–London, 1960.

Lorimer, *Monuments* H. L. Lorimer, *Homer and the Monuments*, London, 1950.

Ludwich, *AHT* A. Ludwich, *Aristarchs Homerische Textkritik*, i, ii, Leipzig, 1884–5.

Marzullo, *Problema* B. Marzullo, *Il problema omerico*², Milan–Naples, 1970.

Mattes, *Odysseus* W. Mattes, *Odysseus bei den Phäaken*, Würzburg, 1958.

Meister, *Kunstsprache* K. Meister, *Die homerische Kunstsprache*, Leipzig, 1921, repr. Darmstadt, 1966.

Merkelbach, *Untersuchungen* R. Merkelbach, *Untersuchungen zur Odyssee*², Zetemata, ii, Munich, 1969.

Meuli, *Odyssee* K. Meuli, *Odyssee und Argonautika* (= Gesammelte Schriften (Basel, 1975), ii. 593–676), Berlin, 1921.

Monro, *Homeric Dialect* D. B. Monro, *A Grammar of the Homeric Dialect*², Oxford, 1891.

Moulton, *Similes* C. Moulton, *Similes in the Homeric Poems*, Hypomnemata, xlix, Göttingen, 1977.

Nickau, *Untersuchungen* K. Nickau, *Untersuchungen zur textkritischen Methode des Zenodotos von Ephesos*, Berlin, 1977.

Nilsson, *Geschichte* M. P. Nilsson, *Geschichte der griechischen Religion*³, i, Munich, 1967.

Onians, *Origins* R. B. Onians, *The Origins of European Thought*, Cambridge, 1951.

Page, *Folktales* D. L. Page, *Folktales in Homer's* Odyssey, Cambridge, Mass., 1972.

—— *Odyssey* —— *The Homeric* Odyssey, Oxford, 1955.

—— *PMG* —— *Poetae Melici Graeci*, Oxford, 1962.

—— *SLG* —— *Supplementum Lyricis Graecis*, Oxford, 1974.

Palmer, *Interpretation* L. R. Palmer, *The Interpretation of Mycenaean Greek Texts*, Oxford, 1963, 1969².

Parry, *Blameless Aegisthus* Anne Amory Parry, *Blameless Aegisthus*, Leiden, 1973.

—— *Homeric Verse* Adam M. (ed.), *The Making of Homeric Verse: The Collected Papers of Milman Parry*, Oxford, 1971.

Powell, *Lexicon*	J. E. Powell, *A Lexicon to Herodotus*, Cambridge, 1938, repr. Hildesheim, 1966.
Radermacher, *Erzählungen*	L. Radermacher, *Erzählungen der Odyssee*, SAWW clxxviii, Vienna, 1915.
RE	*Paulys Realencyclopädie der classischen Altertumswissenschaft*, ed. G. Wissowa, W. Kroll, K. Mittelhaus, and K. Ziegler, Stuttgart, 1893– .
Reinhardt, 'Abenteuer'	K. Reinhardt, 'Die Abenteuer des Odysseus', in id., *Von Wegen und Formen*, Godesberg, 1948, 52–162 = *Tradition und Geist*, Göttingen, 1960, 47–124.
Risch, *Wortbildung*	E. Risch, *Wortbildung der homerischen Sprache*[2], Berlin, 1973.
Roscher, *Lexikon*	W. H. Roscher–K. Ziegler, *Ausführliches Lexikon der griechischen u. römischen Mythologie*, Leipzig, 1884–1934.
Rüter, *Odysseeinterpretationen*	K. Rüter, *Odysseeinterpretationen. Untersuchungen zum ersten Buch u. zur Phaiakis*, Hypomnemata, xix, Göttingen, 1969.
Ruijgh, *Élément*	C. J. Ruijgh, *L'Élément achéen dans la langue épique*, Assen, 1957.
——*Études*	——*Études sur la grammaire et le vocabulaire du grec mycénien*, Amsterdam, 1967.
——τε *épique*	——*Autour de 'τε épique': Études sur la syntaxe grecque*, Amsterdam, 1971.
Schadewaldt, *Welt*	W. Schadewaldt, *Von Homers Welt und Werk*[4], Stuttgart, 1965.
Schulze, *Quaestiones*	W. Schulze, *Quaestiones epicae*, Gütersloh, 1892.
Schwartz, *Odyssee*	E. Schwartz, *Die Odyssee*, Munich, 1924.
Schwyzer, *Delectus*	E. Schwyzer, *Dialectorum Graecarum exempla epigraphica potiora* (P. Cauer, *Delectus*[3]), Leipzig, 1923, repr. Hildesheim, 1960.
Schwyzer, *Grammatik*	E. Schwyzer, *Griechische Grammatik*, i–iii, Munich, 1939–53.
Severyns, *Homère*	A. Severyns, *Homère*, i[2], ii[2], iii, Brussels, 1944, 1946, 1948.
Shipp, *Studies*	G. P. Shipp, *Studies in the Language of Homer*[2], Cambridge, 1972.
Simpson–Lazenby, *Catalogue*	R. Hope Simpson and J. F. Lazenby, *The Catalogue of the Ships in Homer's* Iliad, Oxford, 1970.
Snodgrass, *Armour*	A. M. Snodgrass, *Early Greek Armour and Weapons*, Edinburgh, 1964.
Stella, *Ulisse*	L. A. Stella, *Il poema di Ulisse*, Florence, 1955.
Thompson, *Birds*	D'Arcy W. Thompson, *A Glossary of Greek Birds*, London–St Andrews, 1936.

Thompson, *Motif Index* — Stith Thompson, *Motif Index of Folk Literature*, Copenhagen, 1955–8.

Thornton, *People* — A. Thornton, *People and Themes in Homer's Odyssey*, London, 1970.

Thumb–Scherer, *Handbuch* — A. Thumb and A. Scherer, *Handbuch der griechischen Dialekte*, ii, Heidelberg, 1959.

Touchefeu-Meynier, *Thèmes* — O. Touchefeu-Meynier, *Thèmes odysséens dans l'art antique*, Paris, 1968.

Trümpy, *Fachausdrücke* — H. Trümpy, *Kriegerische Fachausdrücke im griechischen Epos*, Basle, 1950.

van der Valk, *Textual Criticism* — M. van der Valk, *Textual Criticism of the Odyssey*, Leiden, 1949.

van Leeuwen, *Enchiridium* — J. van Leeuwen, *Enchiridium dictionis epicae*, Leiden, 1918.

Ventris–Chadwick, *Documents* — M. Ventris and J. Chadwick, *Documents in Mycenaean Greek*[2], Cambridge, 1973.

von der Mühll, 'Odyssee' — P. von der Mühll, 'Odyssee', *RE*, Supplementband, vii, 696–768, Stuttgart, 1940.

von Kamptz, *Personennamen* — H. von Kamptz, *Homerische Personennamen*, Göttingen, 1982.

Wackernagel, *Untersuchungen* — J. Wackernagel, *Sprachliche Untersuchungen zu Homer*, Göttingen, 1916.

Wathelet, *Traits* — P. Wathelet, *Les Traits éoliens dans la langue de l'épopée grecque*, Rome, 1970.

Webster, *Mycenae* — T. B. L. Webster, *From Mycenae to Homer*, London, 1958.

Werner, *H u. ει vor Vokal* — R. Werner, *H u. ει vor Vokal bei Homer*, Fribourg, 1948.

West, *Papyri* — S. West, *The Ptolemaic Papyri of Homer* (Papyrologica Coloniensia III), Cologne and Opladen, 1967.

Wilamowitz, *Heimkehr* — U. von Wilamowitz-Moellendorff, *Die Heimkehr des Odysseus*, Berlin, 1927.

—— *Glaube* — —— *Der Glaube der Hellenen*, i–ii, Berlin, 1931–2, reiss. Darmstadt, 1959[3].

—— *Untersuchungen* — —— *Homerische Untersuchungen*, Berlin, 1884.

Woodhouse, *Composition* — W. J. Woodhouse, *The Composition of Homer's Odyssey*, Oxford, 1930, repr. Oxford, 1969.

Wyatt, *Lengthening* — W. F. Wyatt, jun., *Metrical Lengthening in Homer*, Rome, 1969.

BOOKS IX–XII

Alfred Heubeck

The late Alfred Heubeck's Introduction *was translated for this volume after his death by Jennifer Brooker and Stephanie West, and likewise his* Commentary *by Jennifer Brooker.*

INTRODUCTION

In Books ix–xii Odysseus tells the Phaeacians of his adventures in the course of the wanderings which brought him from Troy to Scheria. We cannot fail to admire the poet's skilful use of this device to unify his composition. Narration in the first person, by the hero, allows the events of several years to be encompassed retrospectively within the period covered by the epic, the forty days between the divine assembly on Olympus (i) and Odysseus' vengeance on the suitors (xxii). The influence of the *Iliad* on the poem's structure is here unmistakable. The poet of the older epic, whom we may call Homer, likewise confines himself to representing a relatively short period within the ten-year conflict: the action of the *Iliad* covers only fifty days (of which only four or five are described in any detail), but the poet manages to convey a complex picture of the whole Trojan War. By treating his material in this way Homer evidently established his own conception of epic composition against the tradition of the oral heroic lay which, almost certainly, is to be envisaged as a chronologically constructed narrative recounting a simple succession of events. The poet of the *Odyssey* has, in turn, made this Homeric conception his own, and achieves its realization in a new and no less distinctive form, corresponding to the unusual character of his subject-matter.

Use of first-person narrative also gives the poem a new depth of internal unity. Earlier epics, including the *Iliad*, centred on a story of heroic action set in a mythical, idealized past. But the wanderings which the poet of the *Odyssey* imposes on his hero take us into a very different environment; Odysseus moves in a distant world where the normal heroic values, the values of human society and Greek civilization, simply do not apply; Odysseus is confronted not with heroic antagonists but with supernatural beings, giants, witches, and sea-monsters, figures inhabiting the world of the folk-tale, of the irrational and the magical, of the remote and the mysterious. A direct, third-person, account of Odysseus' experiences in this territory would have been a departure from the conventions of epic composition, and would also have impaired the work's internal equilibrium. The events of the wanderings are set on a different narrative plane and yet integrated with the overall narrative structure by being presented from the hero's standpoint as he tells his story to the Phaeacians, the only figures from the world of folktale whom the poet

3

invests with human characteristics, portraying them, indeed, as an idealized human community, stripped of all irrational traits. The poet's consummate skill in handling material from the two quite distinct worlds of heroic saga and folktale on two correspondingly different narrative planes and in integrating these first- and third-person narratives so as to preserve the internal unity of the whole poem has been well discussed by W. Suerbaum (*Poetica* ii (1968), 150–77, esp. 163, 177).

The unusual subject-matter of Odysseus' tales involves a further problem. On his wanderings Odysseus encounters beings which, in one way or another, are alien or positively hostile to men, and indeed are on occasion represented as the negation of human values; accordingly, these beings are set in a world which not only lies beyond the world of experiential reality assigned to the heroes by the poets but also has a different internal structure. This 'monde imaginaire' (Germain) and its landmarks are not to be found on a map—unlike the stopping-places of Menelaus' wanderings round the Mediterranean (iv 81–9 *et passim*). They lie somewhere and nowhere, in the unattainable distance; after the storm off Cape Malea (ix 80–1) Odysseus has crossed a fundamental boundary, normally closed to mortals, which separates the real and the unreal worlds; he can pass back across it only with the help of the godlike Phaeacians. It is true that this unreal world is, like its real counterpart, bounded by Oceanus; the winds blow in the familiar directions of north, south, east, and west; and there are countries and islands, mountains and rivers, caves, houses, and cities. But how remote this landscape is from reality may be judged from the fact that a traveller can sail directly from the far east to the extreme west without having to cross any intervening continent.

It is in these circumstances a quite pointless undertaking, and one based on completely false premises, to try to plot on a map the route taken by Odysseus. This pastime was already popular in antiquity: the earliest evidence for it is offered by Hesiod's *Theogony* (1011–1016), where the heroes Agrius and Latinus, lords of the remote Tyrsenians, are called sons of Odysseus and Circe. Evidently as early as the seventh century Circe's island was thought to lie in the direction of Central Italy (and this view was maintained later: see x 133–9 n.); we may be sure that even at that early date the identification of Aeaea was not enough to satisfy the desire for localizations. Thus the *Odyssey*'s account of its hero's wanderings seems to have suffered a fate comparable to that of the pre-Homeric, eighth-century, oral Argonautic epic, which had Jason's band of heroes journeying to an imaginary, mythical, east (cf. Meuli, *Odyssee*): perhaps as early as the seventh century attempts were made to relate the Argo's voyage too to real geography and to pinpoint its route from the Hellespont to Colchis at the far end of the Black Sea. This misguided activity continues even now, despite the tart comments of Eratosthenes (Strabo i 2, 12–14); its pointlessness is clearly demonstrated by the lack of agreement as to the reconstruction of the route as a whole, or even as to the identification of individual sites. Eratosthenes' warnings have been reiterated by many modern scholars, notably by Albin Lesky ('Aia', *WSt* lxiii (1948), 22–68 (= *Ges. Schriften* (Zürich, 1966), 26–62)); they effectively discourage serious consideration of the innumerable attempts to trace Odysseus' itinerary on the map. The interested reader may consult the work of H.-H. and A. Wolf, *Der Weg des Odysseus* (Tübingen, 1968; cf. review by W. Marg, *Gnomon* xlii (1970), 225–37), which has at least the merit of providing a brief history of the various localizations and assembles a useful bibliography.

Other lines of enquiry are more profitable, and far more important. We must investigate the sources of Odysseus' narrative, drawing as it does on ancient folktales found worldwide, on prehistoric mythological conceptions, on primitive superstition, and on the fantastic tales of early seafarers; we should likewise enquire into pre-Homeric forms and adaptations of the material. We must also try to elucidate the narrative structure, and seek to understand the spirit and conception which the poet wished to impart to the *nostos*-story which he chose to handle in this particular way.

For the extremely diverse motifs to be found in ix–xii research has assembled an immense mass of comparative material from every period and from all over the world: see further Radermacher, *Erzählungen*, Germain, *Genèse*, Page, *Folktales*. From this it has become clear that in Odysseus' adventures we only rarely have to do with a single tradition; in general we are faced with a complex of multifarious elements, combined and adapted to the epic composition with the utmost versatility.

There has been much scholarly debate as to the form and the context in which the tales related in ix–xii might have been treated in the pre-Homeric period of epic composition. The advocates of an analytical approach to Homer included these tales in their earliest speculations about the genesis of the Homeric epics, and came to very different conclusions. We may, for example, recall Kirchhoff's famous thesis (revived in a different form by Wilamowitz (*Untersuchungen*, 230)) that the account given by Odysseus to Alcinous

5

represents the adaptation of an older narrative poem in the third person. Wilamowitz (*Untersuchungen*, 115–98) sees this section as a conflation of several earlier poems of travel and adventure, while among more recent scholars Focke, for example, believes that in ix–xii he can clearly distinguish large parts of an older travel poem A, expansions by a later poet O, and, finally, interpolations by the last poet T (*Odyssee*, 156–269; summarized 239–47).

However, if we reject the notion of poetic 'strata' somehow inserted ready-made into the new context, while accepting that there are old 'elements', we must try to deal with the problems before us in another way. Settling the much-disputed question of Odysseus' origins is only of secondary importance in interpreting ix–xii. Odysseus has been variously seen as a pre-Greek god (E. Bickel, *Homer* (Bonn, 1949), 120, with bibliography), a shaman (Meuli, *Hermes* lxx (1935), 164–76 = *Gesammelte Schriften* (Basel, 1975), 865–79), a figure from popular folktale (G. Patroni, *Commenti mediterranei all'Odissea di Omero* (Milan, 1950), *passim*), an ancestral hero (Wilamowitz, *Heimkehr*, 187–97), and so on. More important is what the *Iliad* has to say about Odysseus. There we see him as one of the leading spirits in the Pan-achaean expedition against Troy, and as the father of Telemachus (ii 260, iv 354). The *Iliad* gives him, as later the *Odyssey* does, the epithets πτολίπορθος (ii 287), πολύμητις (i 311), and πολύτλας (viii 97), the last two being associated exclusively with Odysseus. All this suggests that in pre-Homeric poetry Odysseus was already established not merely as a heroic chieftain who fought at Troy but as the city's real conqueror (because he was responsible for the stratagem of the Wooden Horse). It also implies that in this earlier poetry Penelope and Telemachus already played a certain part, and that a harsh fate was imposed on the hero. This last inference, suggested by the epithet πολύτλας, has been connected with the vicissitudes of the hero's return, the subject of the *Odyssey* and surely, in some form or other, of earlier narrative.

It is not, however, at all certain that pre-Homeric epic associated any of the adventures related in ix–xii with the figure of Odysseus, so as to provide a direct model for these books. There is much to suggest that the poet of the *Odyssey* was the first to send his returning hero on the route with which we are familiar. He may of course have adapted and attached to Odysseus current travellers' tales, stories of fabulous voyages (like Sindbad's) undertaken by figures who bear different names or none at all. The idea of sending his hero to the underworld as well may have been suggested by a tale of necromancy already linked with Odysseus, but may also have been inspired by the old story of Heracles' *catabasis* (descent to Hades), since Odysseus should not prove inferior to Heracles. The adventures of Jason related in the pre-Homeric Argonautic epic may have provided, at least in part, the poetic model for relating Odysseus' experiences. All this is not the systematic exploitation of earlier work (*Quellenbenutzung*) envisaged by the analysts; rather, the poet sought and found inspiration for his own composition in the subject-matter and motifs of older poetry and story-telling. The creative process which controlled the form of expression, the adaptation of heterogeneous material and motifs to the hero, the order and scale of the several adventures, and, finally, their integration in what may be called the poet's view of the world—all this is exclusively his own.

The way to a proper appreciation of this section was pioneered by Reinhardt in his masterly essay 'Die Abenteuer des Odysseus' (*Von Wegen und Formen* (Godesberg, 1948), 52–162 = *Tradition und Geist* (Göttingen, 1960), 47–124). His interpretation, which completely undermines the credibility of an analytical approach, shows that these stories are an essential and indispensable part of the extended epic treatment of Odysseus' return, a part in which the poet remains as true to himself as in the Telemachy or in the Massacre of the Suitors. By the felicitous device of making the hero himself relate his adventures in the folktale-world, the poet distances these episodes from the third-person epic narrative in which they would have seemed out of place, and at the same time links them tightly to it through the figure of the narrator, who has himself experienced all this. The poet's skill in dovetailing these stories with the narrative context and the mythical-heroic world familiar to his audience from countless oral heroic poems and, above all, from the *Iliad* is manifested both in the main lines of his treatment and in a wealth of significant detail.

Stories of the type related in ix–xii are, in their original form, primarily associated with men whose motivation to sail the furthest seas is a pure love of adventure and a thirst for action, or perhaps the fascination of the unknown and a desire to make their fortunes. But Odysseus, as the poet portrays him, is not at all like that. Only once does curiosity impel him into a situation of danger which could have been easily foreseen and avoided, when, quite unnecessarily, he ventures from the Island of Goats to the Land of the Cyclopes (ix 170 ff.); he has to pay cruelly for his curiosity. All his other adventures are setbacks which delay his safe and happy return to his much desired home, obstacles set in the way of his goal by a cruel fate, heaven's will, and divine wrath, inextricably combined with faults on his own part and on the part of his companions. For all their intrinsic fascination, the colourful variety and exotic character of these adventures cannot conceal the fact that in them is worked out the destiny of a man who must pass through the lowest depths of human existence, through unspeakable hazards and humiliations, through disappointment and despair, in order to become again, at last, what he once had been. A man capable of surmounting all these terrors and dangers must be made of quite different stuff from his adventurous 'predecessors'; and so the poet has endowed him, above all, with patience and determination, with the power to endure stoically the very worst. Odysseus' adventures lead us on a long journey during which the proud commander and conqueror loses first his fleet and most of his men, then the rest of his companions and his last ship together with his possessions, and, finally, even his own identity; a nameless Nobody stands naked and defenceless before Nausicaa, lacking rights or possessions, more like an animal than a man (vi 127 f.). But here, at the lowest point in his fortunes, when his human personality has been virtually obliterated, there are the seeds of renewed life; this is the starting-point for a final arduous journey which, set in a world very different from that of the hero's tales and in the reverse direction, leads to a recovery of identity, to a re-establishment of existence in human society, as the king is restored to his family, his community, and his kingdom. Thus the poet has made these adventures a crucial element in this epic of a soldier's return. The descent from pride of place to the utmost humiliation and despair is the pre-condition for an ascent to the old splendour which is, at the same time, new. Κάθοδος and ἄνοδος: these are two aspects, complementing and almost mirroring each other, of the one long journey on which the hero must go in accordance with the poet's will.

The function assigned to the adventures within the overall framework has determined their form and, above all, their sequence. The fantastic experiences, when they formed part of the tales told by seafarers (then as now), required no particular ordering, either external or internal, being, indeed, freely interchangeable in their sequence. These now had to submit to the poetic constraint of significant arrangement. For the first adventure, the sacking of the city of the Thracian Cicones, we have Odysseus as commander of the fleet of twelve ships with which he had once come to Troy (*Il.* ii. 637) and still wholly the sacker of cities, accustomed to victory, that he had been in pre-Homeric tradition; likewise, this military action is set in the clear light of the world which epic poetry had assigned to the mythical heroes of the past as their proper sphere. But already at this first stop on the homeward journey there are ominous signs of trouble to come. For the first time Odysseus' men in their folly fail to obey his orders, and we hear of the evil fate imposed by Zeus; the morning's brilliant success has turned by evening to disaster. The beginning thus foreshadows the terrible end: on Thrinacia the companions will by their folly provoke the anger of Zeus, and the loss of seventy-two of his men (six from each of the twelve ships) in the land of the Cicones prefigures the loss of everything that had once been Odysseus' in the storm which is the instrument of Zeus' vengeance. But Odysseus is still in possession of his entire fleet when he crosses the boundary separating the heroic world from the world of the imaginary and fantastic. It is as commander of a fleet that he undergoes his adventure in the land of the Lotus-eaters, and the poet has made it possible for him to continue in this role, even after the nightmarish days which he must endure with a small band of his men in Polyphemus' cave, by the brilliant invention of the Island of Goats, where the other eleven ships can lie at anchor during the hero's visit to the land of the Cyclopes. The fatal consequences of the visit to Aeolus show the hero still in possession of his fleet; the poet was skilful in disguising the difficulty that the internal logic of this story really requires it to be told by the captain of a single ship. The first series of adventures thus features Odysseus in command of a fleet; it is brought to an end by the bloody encounter with the Laestrygonians, which introduces a decisive change. The form of the narrative here is dictated by the function which the poet has given the episode within the structure as a whole. The encounter with these man-eating giants is narrated with surprising brevity; only one point matters. The Laestrygonian harbour, at first a refuge for the fleet, turns into a fatal trap, and only the flagship escapes destruction as the natives send down a hail of rocks; Odysseus is now left in command only of his own ship.

The second stretch of the journey begins, like the first, in a relatively harmless manner, with Circe; it ends in horrible disaster, corresponding to the destruction of the fleet in the Laestrygonian harbour, as a devastating storm robs Odysseus of his last ship, and thus of all his remaining companions. He is exposed to Charybdis' maelstrom a naked, pitiable figure, clinging with difficulty to the keel of his shattered ship. Nothing remains of the splendour, the power, and the riches of the former commander of a fleet and conqueror of Troy.

The order of the adventures and their individual configuration cannot be the result of compilation, or of the mechanical juxtaposition

9

of inherited materials, or of gradual accretion. Every detail points to
the controlling hand of the poet who deliberately employed every
conceivable means of unifying his composition and thus created a
whole designed with reference to a definite purpose. There are
innumerable connective devices of various kinds between the individual scenes: we have references forward in the form of warnings,
premonitions, and advance announcements, and references to earlier
events by way of reminiscence and reflection; there are correspon-
dences and parallels, and likewise contrasts; there are links between
pairs of episodes and unifying themes which serve as guidelines; and so
on. Thus, to take only one example, we may note as highly
characteristic the consistent way in which the relationship between
Odysseus and his men is developed. In the encounter with the Cicones
there is disobedience due to lack of understanding: cracks in the
leader's authority have already begun to appear. In the confrontation
with the Cyclops the companions hold back and hesitate when their
leader remains determined on action. Then there is a second case of
disobedience in the Aeolus-episode, with more serious consequences
than the first. Their poor morale is barely concealed at the beginning
of the Circe story—and now from the ranks of the hitherto nameless
companions there emerges a spokesman, Eurylochus, who becomes
more and more clearly delineated; developing as a rival to Odysseus'
leadership he reacts to the latter's plans first with defeatist mistrust,
then with bitter reproaches and self-confident counter-proposals, and
finally with a successful appeal to his comrades to mutiny and break
their solemn oath. There is thus a clear line of development from the
encounter with the Cicones to the destruction of the offending
company in the final storm. This is the bitter fruit of the seed already
sown in the first episode; what anyone with ears to hear could already
have predicted at the outset has now finally come to pass.

Not only does the complex of the adventures form an internally
well-unified whole; as has already been indicated, it has also been
made to serve a vital function in the whole epic of return. Much
might be said on this topic, but we may continue with the case of
Odysseus' companions. We can hardly overlook a certain similarity
between what the poet tells us of Penelope's suitors and the actions
and fate of Odysseus' men during their wanderings. In both cases we
have a group of men envisaged as rivals to Odysseus, on the one hand
the companions who gradually change from loyal followers to
perjurious mutineers, on the other the suitors who propose to rob the
hero of his wife, his son, his possessions, and his right to rule. Both
groups are subject to folly and blindness: the companions' own

wickedness brings about their destruction (as the proem tells us in advance (i 7–9), and the actions and fate of the suitors are from the outset marked by the same spirit. Odysseus' warnings to his companions fall on deaf ears; the suitors likewise prove impervious to the repeated calls to mend their ways, from the first such admonition in the assembly in ii until the final warning delivered by the divinely inspired seer Theoclymenus, whose role cannot be properly appreciated unless we take account of the part played by the dead Tiresias in this section (cf. xii 394–6 n.). Odysseus' account of his adventures ends, as does the work as a whole, with the punishment ordained for evil-doers by the gods. In both cases it is severe, indeed it may appear excessively severe for a punishable offence which arose 'beyond what was originally fated' from folly and human weakness. The fate of the companions prefigures the fate of the suitors; the poet shows how much importance he attached to this parallel at the very beginning when he makes Zeus, the final arbiter, cite the example of Aegisthus in support of his argument. From Aegisthus, who despite explicit warning sinned ὑπὲρ μόρον and justly suffered ὑπὲρ μόρον, a train of thought leads both to the companions and the suitors.

To summarize: Books ix–xii are pervaded by the same spirit, the same poetic, human, and theological conceptions as govern the rest of the epic, Telemachy and Tisis alike. This section is not a foreign body within the work as a whole, certainly not a piece of earlier adventure-poetry incorporated with minimal alteration into a new context; the form in which Odysseus is made to tell his story is entirely in harmony with the narrative style elsewhere. We shall better understand these tales if we observe how they are shaped and sustained by the tension between their individual life and their function in the poem. They form a composition complete in itself, which also serves as the means to a larger purpose; they are a part of the whole, essential for its life, and they in turn derive from the whole their meaning, their significance, and their justification.

In addition to studies of this section already mentioned see also (in chronological order): W. Kranz, 'Die Irrfahrten des Odysseus', *Hermes* l (1915), 93–112; Bethe, *Odyssee*, 109–35; Schwartz, *Odyssee*, 28–54; Wilamowitz, *Heimkehr*, 115–226; Woodhouse, *Composition* 41–5; von der Mühll, *Odyssee*, 719–32; W. Theiler, 'Vermutungen zur Odyssee', *MH* vii (1950), 102–22 (cf. xix (1962), 1–27); F. Eichhorn, *Homers Odyssee* (Göttingen, 1965), 63–84; G. Bona, *Studi sull' Odissea* (Turin, 1966), 91–105; J. A. Davison, 'The foam of perilous seas', *WSt* lxxix (1966), 13–20; Lesky, *Homeros*, 108–77. For discussions of individual episodes see nn. ad loc.

BOOK IX: COMMENTARY

1. (= v 214 etc.): links Alcinous' last speech (viii 536–86) and Odysseus' reply, which after a sort of proem (5–38) serves as a vehicle for the account of his wanderings (ix 39–xii 453).

2. = viii 382 etc.

3–4. (~ i 370–1): Odysseus' response to viii 536–41. He can well appreciate the talent of a bard as gifted as Demodocus, who has just given proof of his skill (viii 499–520).   ἦ τοι: on the spelling (ἦτοι, not ἦ τοι) and syntax see Ruijgh, *τε épique*, 198–200; here it anticipates 12–13 (σοὶ δ').

5–11. 'There is no fulfilment (τέλος; cf. P. Ambrose, *Glotta*, xliii (1965), 38–62, esp. 59–61), which brings greater joy (J. Latacz, *Zum Wortfeld "Freude" in der Sprache Homers* (Heidelberg, 1966), 100–1) than when ...' Odysseus praises as ideal the situation of a people filled (ἔχῃ κατὰ = κατέχῃ) with joy as they listen to a bard while feasting and drinking (μέθυ = οἶνος) to their hearts' content: the joyful, lavish banquet is an outward and visible sign of a stable and peacefully ordered community as exemplified by the Phaeacian utopia. Here we are indirectly reminded of the disorder at present prevailing in Ithaca. Odysseus is referring to himself in his comment that only an ordered and peaceful society can accord the bard his rightful place. Odysseus' story, which will rival the tale of Demodocus, will be sympathetically received by the Phaeacians. 5–11 are parenthetic (κάλλιστον refers back to χαριέστερον); 12 ff. follow on from 3–4.

12–13. 13 ~ xi 214, xvi 195. Odysseus means: although it is indeed lovely to hear a bard perform (3–4), if your heart is now moved (ἐπετράπετο), Alcinous, to ask me to sing of my own misfortune (viii 572 ff.), it may bring you joy, but it will increase my sorrow still further.

14–15. 15 = vii 242. Odysseus begins with a rhetorical question: he does not know where to begin or where to end (καταλέγειν suggests a methodically ordered account; cf. W. Kühlmann, *Katalog und Erzählung* (diss. Freiburg im Breisgau, 1973), 23–8). The scale of his suffering adds to the difficulty of his task.

16–18. Odysseus prepares to reveal the secret of his identity and so satisfy the long-awakened expectation. When answering Arete (vii 241 ff.) he had deliberately ignored (see Besslich, *Schweigen*, 60–9) the question about his identity (vii 238–9). Only now, in response to Alcinous' demand (viii 550–5), is he ready to give his name, family and home. In 19–36 he makes good that promise; in 37 ff. he complies with Alcinous' other request (viii 572 ff.). In giving his name Odysseus hopes not only to satisfy the Phaeacians' curiosity, but also 'in time to come, if he should have (ἄν) escaped the pitiless day (for νηλεὲς ἦμαρ see viii 525), to be a ξεῖνος to them, although his home is far away'. The meaning behind this passage (ἐγὼ ...

17–18) is not entirely clear. It may refer to the idea that a ξενίη cannot exist until both parties have introduced themselves (W. Nestle, *Hermes*, lxxvii (1942), 49). Alternatively, by naming himself Odysseus means to offer the Phaeacians the possibility of enjoying his hospitality one day.

19–20. Beginning with an emphatic εἴμ', Odysseus identifies himself by name and patronymic, as the hero whose most successful stratagem (ἵππος δουράτεος: viii 492–3) has just been, at his own request (viii 493–4), recounted by Demodocus (viii 500–20). He thus has every right to start with the proud claim that his δόλοι have made him world famous; many other δόλοι will feature in his story.

21–7. Odysseus briefly describes the geographical position and topography of his native island of Ithaca (cf. also xiii 242–7 and iv 605–8). The difficulties of reconciling the details given in the poem with geographical reality were already felt in classical times: Strabo's discussion (x 451–8) of the Ionian islands and their Homeric names presupposes earlier treatments. He identifies the islands named in 24 (cf. also i 246–7 and xvi 247–51) as follows: Doulichion as the islet later known as Dolicha, in the Echinades; Same as Cephallenia; Zacynthus and Ithaca as having retained their Homeric names; and Leucas as not having been an island for Homer, but 'a peninsula of the mainland'. Certain features of the Homeric description of Ithaca led W. Dörpfeld (first in 1902; for more detailed discussion see *Alt-Ithaka. Ein Beitrag zur hom. Frage* (Munich, 1927); cf. H. Rüter, *Zeit und Heimat der hom. Epen* (Berlin, 1937)) to formulate his well-known theory that by Ἰθάκη Homer meant the island now known as Leucas, by Δουλίχιον modern Cephallenia, and by the name Σάμη the island later renamed Ithaca (Ithaki, Thiaki). The suggestion is that the island now known as Thiaki changed its name at the time of the Dorian invasion: the people migrating from the old Ἰθάκη (Leucas) to Same renamed their new territory after their old home. The debate has continued ever since. J. F. Leutz-Spitta, *Korfu-Ithaka* (Neidenburg, 1920) and 'Corfu-Ithaque', *REG* xlii (1929), 288–98; later R. Hennig, *Die Geographie des hom. Epos* (Berlin, 1934), 85–101, and P. B. S. Andrews, *BICS* ix (1962), 17–20, proposed the identification of Homeric Ithaca with Corfu. They encountered vigorous opposition from F. Ott, *Korfu ist nicht Ithaka* (Würzburg, 1934). More recently K. Völkl, *Serta Philol. Aenipontana* (1962), 65–8, has advanced the theory that by Ἰθάκη Homer meant modern Cephallenia. Another suggestion, from D. Mülder, *RhM* lxxx (1931), 1–35, is that by Ἰθάκη the poet meant all the territory ruled by Odysseus. Most scholars today support the older view that Homeric Ἰθάκη is modern Thiaki; cf. V. Burr, ΝΕΩΝ ΚΑΤΑΛΟΓΟΣ (Leipzig, 1944), 72–80, and Germain, *Genèse*, 560–9, who also cite the older literature. F. H. Stubbings, in *Companion*, 398–421, gives a prudent discussion of the whole question, and his solution, followed by Simpson–Lazenby, *Catalogue*, 103–6, is attractive: Homeric Ἰθάκη is identified as Thiaki, Σάμη as Cephallenia, Ζάκυνθος as Zacynthus, and (tentatively) Δουλίχιον as Leucas. The descriptions of Ithaca as κραναή, τρηχεῖα, παιπαλόεσσα, λυπρή (approx. 'poor, barren'), αἰγίβοτος, βούβοτος, οὐχ ἱππήλατος, and the mention of wooded Mt. Νήριτος as a landmark, etc. all correspond to geographical reality. The only difficulties are posed by the details χθαμαλή and πανυπερτάτη πρὸς ζόφον (αἱ δέ τ᾽ [ἄλλαι νῆσοι] ἄνευθε πρὸς ἠῶ τ᾽ ἠέλιόν τε). The gloss on χθαμαλή as πρόσχωρον τῇ ἠπείρῳ, approved by Strabo, is without doubt incorrect: χθαμαλός means 'low', while the rest of the description can only mean 'the most remote and furthest towards the west (the other islands extending out towards the east)'; cf. E. Risch, *MH* xxv (1925), 209, who refers to *Il.* xii 239–40, *Od.* iii 335, x 190–2, xiii 240–1. As one look at a map shows, these details are not easily reconciled with geographical reality; but see Simpson–Lazenby, op. cit., 105. The poet cannot have been writing on the basis of first-hand knowledge or even with map in hand: for information he must have depended on the reports of those who had sailed that way. On the excavations of Thiaki and Leucas, which support the identification of Thiaki as Homeric Ithaca, see Stubbings, loc. cit.

21. ναιετάω (used in a different sense at 23): see Leumann, *Wörter*, 191–4. **εὐδείελον:** cf. ii 167.

22. Νήριτον: Crates' reading Νήϊον is pure conjecture, depending as it does on identifying this mountain with the Mt. Νήϊον of i 186. The place name Νήρικον, xxiv 377, (for which Νήριτον is an old variant reading) has no connection with the Νηριτο- root. Leumann, op. cit., 243–7, sees a connection between the name and νήριτος, 'countless' (< *νᾱ́-ριτος < *n̥ᵒ₁ri-tos) (cf. Ruijgh, *Élément*, 161–2; M. Lejeune, *BSL* lix (1964), 74, who takes a different line; and Webster, *Mycenae*, 124); but his analytical conclusions are hardly cogent. We may perhaps think here in terms of old formulaic phrases such as ν. ὕλη ('forest of countless trees'; cf. Hes. *Op.* 511) and ὄρος ν. εἰνοσίφυλλον. Νήριτος has already appeared in *Il.* ii 632 as a place-name, and other such instances of transferred meaning are also to be found at *Od.* ix 22 and xiii 351, although here too we might take ν. as an adj. But this interpretation is ruled out by the personal names Ἴθακος and Νήριτος (xvii 207), formed after the place-names. On εἰνοσίφυλλον cf. Chantraine, *Grammaire*, i 100–1; Wyatt, *Lengthening*, 115–19.

27–8. Odysseus' reference to his love for his country, underlined in 29–33 (his determination to return home has survived even the blandishments of two goddesses) and repeated in 34–6, which express the idea in the form of a generally accepted maxim, taken in conjunction with 38, invites the Phaeacians to think of him not as an adventurer for the sake of adventure, but as one whose sole aim is to see his home again. Only the will of Zeus has forced him into the role of wanderer. **ἧς γαίης** (= ἐμῆς γ.): 'than one's own country'.

29–36. The correspondingly constructed references to Calypso (29–30) and Circe (31–2), introduced by an ἦ μέν which anticipates the ἀλλ᾽ of 33, are evidence for rather than against the authenticity of lines which (in whole or in part) have been suspect since Kirchhoff. Even 30 (= i 15) can be justified. 34–6 resume and develop 27ᵇ–8.

14

30. On the orthographical problems of σπέος see Werner, *H u. ει vor Vokal*, 36–40.

32. Circe's title Αἰαίη is the same as the name of her island (x 135). Philologically we might have expected to find a title derived from the island's name here, 'the lady of Aeaea'.

33. (= vii 258, xxiii 337). ἔπειθεν (sg.) is to be preferred to the (logically more exact) pl. ἔπειθον.

35. καί qualifies πίονα: 'however grand the house in which one lives'.

37–8. Odysseus' interjection in the first person, 'Come now, let me tell', links the introductory 2–36 with the opening lines of the account of his wanderings (39 ff.) and thus has a similar function to e.g. 10 (Rüter, *Odysseeinterpretationen*, 33). Like his creator, Odysseus is an epic poet: the grand saga of his *nostos* is comparable to the poem in which it is set.   καί νόστον: Odysseus will tell of his 'journey home too' and so meet Alcinous' third request (viii 573 ff.) now that the other questions, about name (viii 550) and home (viii 555), have been answered.

39–61: the Cicones. On leaving Troy Odysseus encounters first the Cicones, who are named in the *Iliad* (ii 846, xvii 73) as allies of the Trojans. According to Hdt. (vii 110), they lived on the Hebrus; Pi. (fr. 169. 9–10 Snell) calls the Thracian king Diomedes μόναρχος of the Cicones. In his first adventure, then, Odysseus is still in the familiar world of the Aegean. His tale is in many ways similar to the stories he fabricates for Athena (xiii 256–86), Eumaeus (xiv 199–359), and Penelope (xix 172–307), for these too lack any element of the fantastical or folk-tale, and the events are set in a geographical context regarded as familiar to the heroes. The realism of the events is matched by their topicality: the poet here presents neither a legendary past nor a fairy-tale world, but his own time, the age of colonization, in which events such as those described in 39–61, marauding campaigns and the sacking of cities (particularly on the coast of Thrace), must surely have been nothing unusual. Particularly striking is the correspondence with Odysseus' yarn to Eumaeus about his experiences in Egypt (xiv 240–84), which also features an attack on a coastal area, mass destruction, the division of booty, mutiny, a battle with kinsmen intent on revenge, and defeat; the similarity even extends to the phraseology (ix 43: xiv 259). The fighting is described in the language of the *Iliad*, thereby reinforcing the link with the events around Troy; ix 51:*Il.* ii 468; ix 54–5:*Il.* xviii 533–4; ix 56–7:*Il.* xi 84–5 (= vii 66–7); ix 58–9:*Il.* xvi 779–80. Here, however, the description of a day's fighting from morning till late afternoon (*Il.* xi 84–xvi 778) is compressed into a few lines. The Ciconian episode prepares the way for the action to follow in two important respects: first it is a foil to subsequent events set in a wholly unreal world; second—and more important—reference to the grim αἶσα of Zeus overshadowing the travellers (52) places the whole journey in a quite specific theological context (cf. 38): just as now, so throughout the following nine years the will of Zeus is fulfilled; the hero's sufferings are inflicted by fate. This theme, however, is intertwined with another: by their folly men make themselves the victims of fate; men bring their appointed fate on themselves by their own deeds. Purely on this human level Odysseus' companions are responsible for their own downfall by their folly and insubordination (43–6). Here the poet first introduces a theme which will reappear often, and indeed prefigures the eventual fate of the crew. They may have escaped lightly once again on this occasion, but the outrage on Thrinacia (xii 260 ff.), which is also caused by human inadequacy, brings death to the whole crew. There is a clear link between the Ciconian and Polyphemus episodes, for the wine which Odysseus takes to the Cyclops' cave came from Maron, the priest of Apollo, whom Odysseus had protected in the land of the Cicones (196–211). The poet withholds the additional detail until the point where its introduction will advance the action on the principle of παραλείπειν καὶ ὕστερον φράζειν. See further Focke, *Odyssee*, 161 ff.; Reinhardt, 'Abenteuer', 60 ff.

40. πόλιν ... αὐτούς: 'the city ... its male inhabitants'.

42. = 549. Modelled on *Il.* xi 705. **ἀτεμβόμενος:** ἀτέμβεσθαι with gen., 'to lose/be cheated of a thing' (Chantraine, *Dictionnaire* s.v.). **ἴσης:** Fick's conjecture ἴσσης (~ αἴσης), accepted by Bechtel, *Lexilogus*, 182, is implausible; μοίρας is to be understood; cf. Chantraine, *Dictionnaire* s.v. ἴσσασθαι; Beekes, *Laryngeals*, 128.

43. ἦ τοι μεν (ἤτοι μεν): a 'coordonnant préparatif' (cf. 3 n.; Ruijgh, τε épique, 197–200). On διερός (here approx. 'swift, agile') see Chantraine, *Dictionnaire* s.v.

44. ἠνώγεα: from the original pres. pf. ἄνωγα was formed ἀνώγω, and from that an impf. ἤνωγον and plpf. ἠνώγεα; (the form is attested elsewhere only at x 263, xvii 55; -εα with synizesis always in arsis) cf. Ruijgh, *Élément*, 128–30. δέ is long here before μ-; the phenomenon is common, especially before μέγας or μέγαρον. On νήπιος see Heubeck, *SMEA* xi (1970), 70–2.

45–6. Modelled on *Il.* ix 466–9; cf. W. Diehl, *Die wörtlichen Beziehungen zwischen Ilias und Odyssee* (Greifswald, 1938), 76. **46ᵇ:** cf. i 93ᵇ.

47. From plpf. ἐγεγώνει (pres. pf. γέγωνα) were formed ἐγεγώνεον (xvii 161) and γεγώνευν (attested only here and xii 370); see Chantraine, *Grammaire*, i 347–8.

48. For a detailed discussion of ἀρείων (pl. ἀρείους < -ohes) see Chantraine, *Dictionnaire* s.v. (with bibliography); Mycenean a-ro₂-a (n. plur.).

49. The Cicones living inland (ἤπειρος) are as skilled fighting from chariots (ἀφ' ἵππων) as on foot.

51. Modelled on *Il.* ii 468; cf. Schwartz, *Odyssee*, 29. 1.

52. ἠέριοι appears four times in Homer; here as in the *Iliad* (i 497, 557, iii 7) it looks as if it means 'at dawn' (cf. Bechtel, *Lexilogus*, 151; Chantraine, *Dictionnaire* s.v.); cf. the root ἠερι- in Ἠερίβοια and ἠριγένεια, and the Mycenean names a-e-ri-qo-ta and a-e-ri-qo/Āeriquhontās, -quos. Risch, on the other hand, *Wortbildung*², 113–4 prefers a derivation from ἀήρ (cf. Att. ἀέριος, Hom. ἠερόεις, ἠεροειδής).

54. (~ *Il.* xviii 533–4): scarcely an interpolation; cf. Merkelbach, *Untersuchungen*, 182. 2.

55. χαλκήρεσιν ἐγχείῃσιν: cf. Myc. *e*]-*ke-a ka-ka-re-a*/*enkheha khalkāreha* (KN R 1815).

56. ἱερὸν ἦμαρ: on the meaning cf. C. Gallavotti, *AC* xxxii (1953), 399-428; P. Wülfing–v. Martitz, *Glotta*, xxxviii (1960), 272-307, esp. 292 ff.; J. P. Locher, *Untersuchungen zu* ἱερός *hauptsächlich bei Homer* (Bern, 1963), 61.

58. μετενίσσετο: -νῖσ-, which is also to be found in Ionian inscriptions, is to be preferred to -νισσ-; cf. discussion by Schwyzer, *Grammatik*, i. 287, 690: νῖσομαι < *νι-νσ-ομαι (~ *nes- in the case of νέομαι and νόστος) like μίμνω (~ *men- in μένω), despite certain difficulties which suggest to Chantraine a different explanation, *Grammaire*, i 313, 440). **βουλυτόν**: literally 'the time when oxen are unyoked', -δε: 'towards evening'.

62-3. 62 = 105, x 77; 62-3 = 565-6, x 133-4. Bechtel's explanation, *Lexilogus*, 66 ff., of the somewhat unusual use of the word ἄσμενος (here approx. 'saved'), is surely correct, although one cannot agree with his highly individual approach to *Il.* xx 350 or with his conclusion that 63 is interpolated. On the disputed etymology of ἄσμενος cf. Chantraine, *Dictionnaire* s.v.

64-5: 'before we had all (τινα) cried out three times to each one of our fallen comrades (ἕκαστον τῶν ἑτάρων, οἳ ...)'. This is a reference to the religious practice of saluting the dead by name to help their spirits to find rest; cf. Verg. *A.* vi 506.

67. Cf. v 109; 68-9 = xii 314-15 ~ v 293-4.

70. ἐπικάρσιαι: ἐπικάρσιος, 'sidelong', may be derived from *ἐπί-καρ-τος (<κείρω); cf. Frisk, *GEW*; Chantraine, *Dictionnaire* s.v. Bechtel's explanation, *Lexilogus*, 132, is surely incorrect; cf. B. Forssman, *Glotta*, xlv (1967), 2. 1.

73. αὐτὰς δ' (the ships) contrasted with τὰ μὲν (i.e. ἱστία, 72); for the form of expression cf. *Il.* i 3-4, ψυχὰς ... αὐτοὺς δέ (the bodies of the fallen), *Il.* viii 182, νῆας, ... δὲ καὶ αὐτοὺς (the men).

74-8. For 74 cf. v 388, x 142; 75-6 = x 143-4; 76 = v 390.   **συνεχὲς αἰεί** is merely a connective between one formulaic phrase (cf. v 388) and the equally formulaic 75-6 (Shipp, *Studies*, 39). On the unusual lengthening of σῦν (as at *Il.* xii 26; Hes. *Th.* 636) cf. Chantraine, *Grammaire*, i 100; Wyatt, *Lengthening*, 237. 3.

77. =xii 402. On the history of this formulaic phrase see Hoekstra, *Modifications*, 48. 1.

78. =xi 10, xii 152, xiv 256.

80-1. Cape Malea, on the SE coast of Laconia, was always feared by mariners. The prevailing currents and winds, so accurately described in 81-2, drive seafarers off course. Both Menelaus (iii 287) and now Odysseus begin their wanderings at this point.   **Κυθήρων:** Κύθηρα (neut. pl.) is an island to the SW of Malea. Cf. Myc. *ku-te-ra₃* (PY Aa 506; -*ra-o* Ad 390) and *ku-te-re-u-pi* (abl. pl.: PY An 607. 2), perhaps ethnics derived from the name of the island.

82-104. After a 'nine-day' (i.e. unusually long) voyage, Odysseus encounters a people named from their staple crop: the Lotus-eaters. Contrary winds have driven him across the border separating the reality of the familiar Mediterranean world from the realm of folk-tale. There is significance in Odysseus' meeting the Lotus-eaters first: the λωτός plant, with its magical properties of suppressing the desire to return home, is symbolic of the insecurity of human existence poised precariously between the spheres of empirical reality and mythical unreality. It is, therefore, pointless to attempt, as so many scholars, both ancient and modern, have done, to identify either the λωτός plant itself or the country where it grows. In identifying the country as the Little Syrtis (iv 176 ff.) Hdt., and scholars after him, showed no understanding of the nature and function of poetry. How the story of the Lotus-eaters is to be understood genetically has been shown by Page, *Folktales*, 3–21, who cites some illuminating parallels; cf. Bethe, *Odyssee*, 175, and Radermacher, *Erzählungen*, 10–13. The poet knows a type of story found in folk-tales throughout the world and based on mythological concepts, in which tasting a certain magic food makes return impossible for one who has crossed the boundary of the world of men; the strange world may be the realm of fabulous beings or, more commonly, the kingdom of the dead. An example is the story of Persephone, banished to Hades by her eating of a pomegranate seed (κόκκος ῥοιῆς *h.Cer.* 372). The poet's reshaping of his material removes much of the fairy-tale element: Odysseus' close encounter with another realm of existence is not a descent into Hades, but the acceptance of normal hospitality from a people who are in most respects entirely ordinary, and not in the least malign. The offer of lotus to their honoured guests is not intended to weave any magic spell. Indeed the very name 'Lotus-eaters' is itself intended as a link with the real world, since the poet appears to have heard tales of a real people who lived almost exclusively off one crop, known to the Greeks only as λωτός. We may think here of the two species of *Nymphaeaceae* mentioned by Hdt. (ii 92). The encounter with the Lotus-eaters marks a decisive turning-point; now Odysseus is in another world but he will not remain subject to it; he will succeed in crossing the fundamental boundary between the two worlds in the reverse direction. See, most recently: M. Rosseaux, 'Ulysse et les mangeurs de coquelicots', *Bull. Ass. Budé*, lxxi (1971), 333–51.

83. ἀτάρ is to be preferred to αὐτάρ; cf. Ruijgh, *Élément*, 46.

84. ἄνθινον (*hapax*) εἶδαρ: the relative clause explains Λωτοφάγοι: not only are they—unlike others—vegetarian, but they also restrict themselves to one plant in particular, the lotus; cf. J. M. Aitchinson, *Glotta*, xl (1963), 273; B. Mader, *LfgrE* s.v. ἄνθινος, takes a slightly different view.

85–7. = x 56–8.

87. ἐπασσάμεθ': from πατέομαι; see Bechtel, *Lexilogus*, 273–4.

88–90. = x 100–2.

89. On opt. εἶεν see Chantraine, *Grammaire*, ii 224.

94–5. There is a difference between ἤθελεν, 'he no longer wished to', and βούλοντο, 'they preferred'.

97. The use of the word ἐρέπτομαι, which normally refers only to animals

feeding, is to be explained as a catachrestic use of the phrase λωτὸν
ἐρεπτόμενοι, used of Achilles' horses, *Il.* ii 776.

99. ὑπὸ ζυγὰ: lit. 'under the deck beams', i.e. 'below deck'.

100. ~193. **ἐρίηρας:** cf. ἐρίηρον (i 346 n.).

101: cf. *Il.* viii 197.

103. ~xi 638, xv 221, 549; 103–4 ~ iv 579–80, ix 179–80, 471–2, 563–4, xii
146–7.

105–566. After the Lotus-eaters Odysseus comes to the Cyclopes, presumably on the same day. The adventure with Polyphemus is among the most
elaborately developed but for no other episode are there so many parallels
in folktale; cf. O. Hackmann, *Die Polyphemsage in der Volksüberlieferung*
(Helsinki, 1904). Polyphemus legends were told and retold almost
throughout the ancient world; modern scholarship has identified well over
two hundred different versions; cf. most recently J. Glenn, 'The Polyphemus Folktale and Homer's Kyklopeia', *TAPhA* cii (1971), 133–85, who
gives an extensive bibliography; Germain, *Genèse*, 55–129 gives the North
African parallels. It is of course possible that some of the other versions,
which were of course recorded only relatively late, are ultimately dependent on Homer; see e.g. K. Meuli, *Odyssee und Argonautika* (Berlin, 1921),
65–70. Most scholars, however, quite rightly reject this view; cf. Radermacher, *Erzählungen*, 13–16; Glenn, loc. cit. Analysis of the folk-tale
material shows that the poet was using two originally unconnected stories,
the first about a hero blinding a man-eating giant. Consistent features of
this story are the hero's use of an animal, usually a sheep, or at least an
animal skin, to effect an escape and the giant's attempt to bring the hero
back with the help of a magical object. The second story concerns a hero
outwitting a monster by giving a false name, usually 'I myself'. The fusion
of these two stories is surely the work of the poet himself. Analysis of form
and motifs of the older fairy-tale material demonstrates his achievement in
synthesizing a new story by introducing variations in his old material,
expanding some themes and abbreviating others. The result reflects the
same attitude to life and poetic genius as distinguishes all his work. The
organization of the episode is determined by his wish to adapt the role of
the traditional story's hero to his Odysseus and to give the Cyclopeia a well
defined place and a clear function in the overall structure of the poem. The
story is rationalized, its more barbaric aspects suppressed, and the whole
set in a clear moral/theological context; cf. Reinhardt, 'Abenteuer', 78–85;
R. Dion, *Les Anthropophagues de l'*Odyssée (Paris, 1969). There is no need to
consider here the analytical approaches to the story; cf. Schwartz, *Odyssee*,
28–38; Focke, *Odyssee*, 164–81; Merkelbach, *Untersuchungen*, 212–15. Nor
need we consider attempts, begun in classical times, to place the land of the
Cyclopes on a map, except to note that Th. (vi 2) knew of an old tradition
that the Cyclopes had lived in Sicily, that the localization became widely
established (cf. E. *Cyc.*; Theoc. vi and xi), and that in our own century
attempts have been made to place the Cyclopes in Tunisia (A. Klotz,
Gymnasium, lix (1952), 293; H.-H. and A. Wolf, *Der Weg des Odysseus*

(Tübingen, 1968), 39–42). The Homeric treatment of the story was widely influential. The oldest pictorial representations of the blinding are on a vase from Eleusis discovered in 1954 (K. Schefold, *Frühgriechische Sagenbilder* (Munich, 1957), 32, pl. 16) and the seventh-century Caeretan krater of Aristonothus. Particularly impressive are the remains of a group of monumental figures found in Tiberius' grotto at Sperlonga, and based on a late Hellenistic (II sec.) bronze; cf. G. Iacopi, *L'antro di Tiberio* (Rome, 1963); H. Sichtermann, *Gymnasium* lxxiii (1966), 220–39, illust. For a general discussion see D. Fellmann, *Die antiken Darstellungen des Polyphemabenteuers* (Munich, 1972). In literature the epic material was reworked into dramatic form (Cratinus' comedy Ὀδυσσῆς and Euripides' satyr play *Cyc.*); and the figure of the Cyclops has undergone a remarkable transformation in the works of Philoxenus of Cythera and Theocritus.

105. = 62.

106–15. Hes. *Th.* 144–45 has surely given the correct explanation for the Cyclopes' name: οὕνεκ' ἄρα σφέων κυκλοτέρης ὀφθαλμὸς ἔεις ἐνέκειτο μετώπῳ. This conveys the conception underlying the Homeric narrative (the account of the blinding presupposes a one-eyed Cyclops), even though the poet, surely intentionally (Glenn, op. cit. (105–566 n.), 154–6), omits any direct reference to this detail. Already in classical times scholars speculated on the reason behind the omission; see e.g. Servius ad *Aen.* iii 636: *multi Polyphemum dicunt unum habuisse oculum, alii duos, alii tres.* It is certain that κύκλωψ originally indicated someone with a round eye or face, not a μονόφθαλμος; cf. Chantraine, *Dictionnaire* s.v. Lines 139–46 of Hes. *Th.* however refer to the three sons of Uranus and Gaia, who forge thunder and lightning for Zeus, and are also called Κύκλωπες. The exact relationship between these Hesiodic and the Homeric Cyclopes has not yet been established, despite many attempts; cf. for example Meuli, *Odyssee*, 75–8; and Wilamowitz, *Glaube*, i 277 ff. It is hardly possible to see how these figures can be derived from a single source in view of the profound difference between the three Titans and the man-eating monsters of folktale. The feature of having only one eye, so essential to the story of blinding, is a common folklore motif (cf. Hdt.'s legendary Arimaspeans, iv 27). It is conceivable that the old title of the Titans was transferred to the Polyphemus-figure of the folk-tale at a relatively late stage, and with a shift of meaning from 'round-faced' to μονόφθαλμος; Hes. then adapted his account of the Cyclopes to fit the Homeric pattern. The poet also requires that Polyphemus is only one of a whole community of Cyclopes for the hero's device of naming himself Οὖτις to be fitted into the story of blinding, which of itself requires only the one monster; without the presence of others of his kind the trick with the name cannot work. The poet's description of the Cyclopes' way of life deserves particular attention. They have no θέμιστες (106, 112) and no ἀγοραὶ βουληφόροι; they neither sow nor plough (108–9), but rely entirely (πεποιθότες 107) on the fact that the gods let everything grow that is needed. (This is not meant to imply any particular faith in the gods, or any contradiction to 275–6.) They live in natural caves, each for himself without regard for the others (113–15). This initial description is supplemented in 125–30: the Cyclopes know nothing of shipbuilding and seafaring. Other details, given later, complement the picture: Polyphemus knows no αἰδώς (269, 272–3); and he respects neither the gods nor the sacred laws of hospitality (275–6). The sociological implications are clear: the poet has painted a picture of a people on the lowest cultural level, devoid of all that gives human life its distinctive quality. The Cyclopes know nothing of life in a community ordered by laws and decrees, of piety and morality, or of nature made to serve man by 'ratio' and τέχνη (agriculture, building, and seafaring). They are a negation of human values, and a negative counterpart to the Phaeacians who enjoy all the benefits of civilization; they are the embodiment of the non-human. The impression of unsociability is reinforced by the isolation of Polyphemus from his kinsmen who are quite unconcerned about him despite his power and position (κράτος i 70–1); cf. G. Bona, *Studi sull'Odissea* (Turin, 1966), 72–8, who rightly opposes Page, *Odyssey*, 6. We are not, therefore, surprised that this race, the embodiment of inhumanity, is endowed with non-human characteristics and is capable of acts of extreme barbarity. Polyphemus himself is more beast than man, and in fact we are told that he has a particular affinity with his flocks.

106. ἀθεμίστων: the Cyclopes have no θέμιστες, 'divinely appointed ordinances'; cf. Myc. *te-mi/themis*.   **ὑπερφιάλων:** cf. i 134.

109. All the crops grow without sowing (σπείρω: ἄσπαρτα) or ploughing (ἀρόω: ἀνήροτα).

110–11. =358. The ἄμπελοι yield (= allow to grow) wine from excellent grapes (ἐρισταφύλος). It is doubtful whether we are to think of the Cyclopes as skilled in viticulture. Certainly οἶνος cannot mean 'grapes' (as Stubbings supposes, in *Companion*, 524). It is also significant that the relative clause here refers not to the Cyclopes' country specifically, but is meant as a general statement (τε); cf. Ruijgh, τε *épique*, 370. The lines are relevant to 357–8.

112. ἀγοραὶ βουληφόροι: 'assemblies to take counsel'. 112–15 are quoted in Pl. *Leg.* 680 b 5–c 1.

114. θεμιστεύω with gen. (dat. only at xi 569): 'rules (as upholder of the θέμιστες) over'. The irony is intentional: the Cyclopes do not recognize any θέμιστες. The word is seldom used in its Homeric sense in later literature. An exception is in the Gyges fragment (*POxy* xxiii (1956), 2382, 2. 13 λαοῖς θεμιστεύσοντα). More usually it means 'to give an oracle' (*h.Ap.* 253). Cf. H. Frisk, *Kleine Schriften* (Göteborg, 1966), 414; Shipp, *Studies*, 103.

116–36. The fleet anchors by an island off the coast of the Cyclopes' territory. This island represents a necessary invention by the poet: Odysseus can come to Polyphemus with only *one* ship, and the rest must be kept at a distance; cf. Reinhardt, 'Abenteuer', 63 ff. The poet has Odysseus describe the island in enthusiastic appreciation of its ideal situation. What he sees is an uninhabited island (the Cyclopes have no ships to reach it), with extensive forests (118) and herds of wild goats

(124), fertile (131) with soft water-meadows (132–3), and furnished with an excellent harbour (136–9) with a fresh-water spring nearby (140–1). Like a prospective settler he thinks of how the land can be cultivated (130), where to plant more vines and what rich harvests could be expected (133–5). This portrait of the island inhabited only by goats echoes the description of the Phaeacians' island. The similarity lies in their respective geographical position, natural resources, and climate. The contrast lies in what the Phaeacians have made of their land (cf. vii 112–31): on the one hand we see an untamed wilderness; on the other, a landscape made to serve man.

116. λάχεια is the reading given by all the MSS and Aristarchus. Zenodotus' ἔπειτ' ἐλάχεια is surely pure conjecture; see van der Valk, *Textual Criticism*, 98. Leumann, *Wörter*, 54, gives a convincing account of its genesis from ἐλάχεια as a result of incorrect word-division of an earlier (pre-Homeric) expression like *νῆσος δελαχεια*. x 509 suggests that the new word acquired the meaning 'flat'.

117. ἀποτηλοῦ (*hapax*): 'at a distance'.

118. ἀπειρέσιαι: 'innumerable'; ἀπειρέσιος (alongside ἀπερείσιος: both with metrical lengthening ε > ει) is prob. < *ἀ-περετος; cf. Schulze, *Quaestiones*, 245; Bechtel, *Lexilogus*, 49.

119. πάτος: 'comings and goings'.

120–1: rejected by Fick; cf. Schwartz, *Odyssee*, 314; Shipp, *Studies*, 331. 2. κυνηγέτης (for θηρητήρ) is indeed *hapax*, but in view of Myc. *ku-na-ke-ta-i/kunāgetāhi* (dat. pl.) PY Na 248 is not evidence for interpolation.   **μιν** (120): νῆσον.

122–4. καταΐσχεται (*hapax* for κατίσχεται): 'is covered by'.   **ἀρότοισιν:** ἄροτος here means 'tilled field'; cf. Chantraine, *Dictionnaire* s.v. ἀρόω. On 123 see 109 n.   **χηρεύει** (*hapax*): from χῆρος with gen., 'bereft'; χηρεύει ἀνδρῶν: 'is devoid of men'.

125. μιλτοπάρῃοι (poss. cpd. from μιλτο- and παρειά, < *παρᾱϝά), 'cheek'; cf. Myc. *pa-ra-wa-jo/parāwajō* PY Sh 737, 'cheek piece'; O. Szemerényi, *SMEA* iii (1967), 63–5. The ships are 'red-cheeked' because their bows are painted vermilion.

128–9. οἶά τε πολλὰ ... θάλασσαν: 'as often men ... cross the sea'.

130: 'such men would also have made the island good to live in'.   **ἐϋκτι-μένην:** cf. Myc. *ki-ti-me-no, -a/ktimeno-, -ā*, formed from the athematic *κτεῖμι; Chantraine, *Dictionnaire* s.v. κτίζω.

131. κακή: here, 'barren'.   **ὥρια** (Att. ὡραῖος, predic. of πάντα): 'in season'; cf. εἰς ὥρας 135.

134–5. ἄροσις: 'land which can be ploughed'; cf. H. Jones, *Glotta*, li (1973), 17–18.   **μάλα ... οὖδας:** 'one would always reap a good crop at harvest, since there is great richness (nourishment for the plants) below the ground'. On ἀμῶεν see J. Irigoin, *LfgrE* s.v. ἀμάω. *H.Ap.* 60 ἐπεὶ οὔ τοι πῖαρ ὑπ' οὖδας, is modelled on 135[b].

136–41. These lines amplify the adj. εὔορμος. There is no need here for πεῖσμα (neither for εὐναί, 'anchor-stones', nor for πρυμνήσια, 'mooring

22

ropes' (thrown from the πρύμνη)): it is possible to beach a ship on the flat shore (καταπλέειν; cf. 142). ἐποτρύνῃ (139): sc. ἀποπλέειν. The nearby source of fresh water (140–1) is of particular importance to seamen. On the form of σπείους see R. Werner, *H u. ει vor Vokal* 36–40.

142–5: see J. Bechert, *Die Diathesen von ἰδεῖν und ὁρᾶν bei Homer* (Munich, 1964), 183–7. **ἔνθα** (loc.) refers us back to 136–41; Odysseus and his crew landed at this point. The circumstantial details are worth closer examination: a benign deity guides them through the pitch-black night, without however revealing himself ('he did not show himself, so that a glimpse of him could be seen'); for a thick fog (ἀήρ) enveloped the ships. The moon did not light up the scene (προφαίνω is used absolutely here) because it was covered by cloud. **περὶ:** to be preferred to παρά, despite van der Valk, *Textual Criticism*, 117–18, 176.

146. ἔνθ': 'in these circumstances' (referring back to 143–5.

148. νῆας: subject of ἐπικέλσαι (here intr., 'come ashore').

149. κελσάσῃσι ... νηυσὶ: ethic dat., almost equivalent to dat. abs.; cf. Chantraine, *Grammaire*, ii 324.

150–2. = xii 6–8. 150 = 547, ~ xv 499, *Il.* i 437; 152 = ii 1 etc., *Il.* i 477. (ἀπο-)βρίζω (etym. unknown): 'fall asleep'.

154. αἰγιόχοιο: cf. iii 42 n.

155. ὀρεσκῴους: 'mountain-dwelling' (cf. *Il.* i 268); in the second element we have the *o*-grade of the root κει- (κεῖμαι), but the form -κωιο- is not easy to explain; see Frisk, *GEW* s.v. A. Fick, followed by F. Bechtel, prefers the spelling -κοίους; Risch, *Wortbildung²*, 198, suggests a shift -κοιός > -κώιος as with ζῷον.

156. αἰγανέας δολιχαύλους: an αἰγανέη is a particular kind of spear used in hunting; its range and effectiveness are increased by use of a sling (ἀγκύλη) held by one finger or two. δολίχαυλος: 'with a long socket'; for a detailed description see H.-G. Buchholz, *Archaeologia* J, 88 ff., pls. 25–32); on the linguistic aspects see Frisk, *GEW*, S. Laser, *LfgrE* s.v. αἰγανέη.

157. The hunters divided themselves (διακοσμέω) into three groups; cf. *Il.* ii 653.

158. θήρην ('hunt'): here 'bag'. **μενοεικέα:** cf. v 166 n.

159–60. This is the first time that the number of ships is given; cf. *Il.* ii 637; Reinhardt, 'Abenteuer', 61–7. Nine goats fell to each ship by lot (λάγχανον), except (οἴῳ) to Odysseus (i.e. his ship), who was allotted ten.

161–2. = 556–7, x 183–4, 476–7, xii 29–30; 161 = *Il.* i 601. Leumann, *Wörter*, 98–9, gives a convincing explanation of πρόπαν ἦμαρ.

163–5. The passage refers us back to 39–81 (μέθυ 45), but the lines also anticipate 196–215 and 345–74. This double function, far from proving that the lines are spurious (as Schwartz supposes, *Odyssee*, 314), in fact proves their authenticity. **ἀμφιφορεῦσιν** (164): ἀμφιφορεύς, 'two-handled jar'. On the form and derivation cf. F. Schuh, *LfgrE*, and Chantraine, *Dictionnaire* s.v. There are two parallel forms in Myc.: *a-pi-po-re-we/amphiphorēwes* (pl.) KN Uc 160. 1 (the Homeric form); and *a-po-re-we/amphorēwe* (dual; an example of haplology) MY Ue 611. 1.

COMMENTARY

166–7. During the day which the heroes spend on the Island of Goats their gaze is attracted to the nearby land of the Cyclopes (ἐλεύσσομεν ... φθογγὴν: zeugma). The lines prepare us for the action to follow.

168–70. = 558–60, x 185–7; 170 = 152. The lines are taken from *Il.* i 475–7 (with slight alteration in 476ᵇ).

171. = x 188, xii 319.

172–6. Odysseus briefs his companions on his plan to cross over to the land of the Cyclopes with just his ship and its crew (ἐμοῖς ἐτάροισιν). In 173 he uses the same words as Agamemnon (*Il.* i 183). His plan is to find out what the inhabitants are like. 175–6 (the answer to which we know from 106–15) occur also at vi 120–1 and xiii 201–2, except that in those two instances they are preceded by the despairing cry, 'Alas, whose country have I come to now?' (vi 119, xiii 200), and are indeed a question of life and death, which destiny will answer. Here, however, Odysseus is prompted merely by curiosity, and in testing whether the inhabitants are φιλόξεινοι is still acting as a hero accustomed to receiving hospitality as an honoured guest or, where necessary, by a show of strength. His encounter with Polyphemus exposes his attitude as shallow, and thereafter he shows no curiosity or interest in πεῖραι except when advised by Athena (xiii 363 ff.) to use πεῖραι as a tactical measure on his return home (xvi 305–6). 176 gives the first reference to the theme of ξείνια, which is a leitmotif throughout the episode; see A. J. Podlecki, 'Guest-gifts and Nobodies in *Od.* 9', *Phoenix*, 15 (1961), 125–33.

177. ἀνὰ νηὸς (cf. ii 416): 'up on to the ship' (gen. of place); cf. E. Hermann, *Sprachwissenschaftlicher Kommentar zu ausgewählten Stücken aus Homer*[2] (Heidelberg, 1965), 103.

178. ἀνά ... λῦσαι (tmesis): 'loose and take on board the hawsers'.

179–80. = 103–4.

181. τὸν (demonst.) χῶρον: 'the place mentioned before' (166).

182–92. Odysseus describes what can be seen from that point on the coast (Bentley's cj. εὕρομεν (182) is incorrect). The details given are also those, of course, which will be significant in the further development of the story. They include some which the hero in fact noticed only later: the flocks spent the night in the cave; the wall (the only other instance of this secondary meaning of αὐλή is at *Il.* v 138; cf. Shipp, *Studies*, 193) made, presumably very crudely, of stones, pines and oaks; and for that matter all the information given here (187–92) on the Cyclops himself. These details are given not from the perspective of the hero at the time, but from that of the narrator looking back. On the interwoven perspectives of poet and character see W. Suerbaum, 'Die Ich-Erzählungen des Odysseus', *Poetica*, ii (1968), 150–77, esp. 156 ff. On the description of the cave see F. Müller, *Darstellung und poetische Funktion der Gegenstände in der Odyssee* (diss. Marburg, 1968), 109–15.

182. ἐπ' ἐσχατιῇ: 'at the most outlying point of the Cyclopes' territory'; 187–9 amplify.

184. ἰαύεσκον (cf. ἐνίαυε 187): 'they would spend the night'. On the

24

connection between 184–5 and vi 262–7 see B. Marzullo, *Il problema omerico* (Florence, 1952), 450–1.

187. τὰ μῆλα is the correct reading (τε F); cf. Ruijgh, τε *épique*, 443.

188–9. The Cyclopes' unsociability (cf. 112–15) is accentuated in Polyphemus' case: οἷος, ἀπόπροθεν ('set apart from'), οὐδὲ μετ᾽ ἄλλους πωλεῖτ᾽, ἀπάνευθεν; ἀθεμίστια ἤδη refers back to 112–14. All the details given reinforce the image of humanity negated in the Cyclops. The cave-dwelling, a traditional feature of giant stories, is here a pointer to the Cyclopes' lack of τέχνη. We are not told that Polyphemus has only one eye, but his size is emphasized with a simile. The description is thus sparing in its use of the fantastical, and concentrated more on the sociological side.

191–2. σιτοφάγῳ: an important anticipation of the giant's other outstanding characteristic, ἀνδροφάγος (x 200). θαῦμ(α) ... πελώριον (190) is amplified by the comparison of Polyphemus with a solitary (οἷον) wooded peak standing out above the other mountains in a range. ῥίῳ: ῥίον, attested also as a place-name, is already found in Myc.: *ri-jo-/Rhijon* PY An 1 etc., < *sri-yon; on IE **sēr-*, 'above', see Heubeck, *Orbis*, xiii (1964), 266–7.

193. = 100.

194. = x 444, ~ xiv 260, xvii 429.

196–215. Odysseus describes how he went provided with a skin of wine, and digresses at length on its quality and how he had come by it. There are similar digressions in the *Iliad*, and they too are devoted to descriptions of objects which are to play an important part in the action to follow (Agamemnon's sceptre *Il.* ii 101–8; Pandarus' bow iv 105–11). The lines, anticipated by 163–5, are also a kind of supplement to the Ciconian material: we now learn that Odysseus had protected Maron, the priest of Apollo, and been rewarded with a number of gifts including a quantity of fine wine; this detail will now become unexpectedly relevant; cf. F. Müller, loc. cit. (182–92 n.).

197–8. The name Μάρων is derived from Maroneia, a town on the S. coast of Thrace famous for its wines (cf. οἶνος Ἰσμαρικός Archilochus, fr. 2), just as many ἥρωες κτίσται and ἐπώνυμοι are named after their towns; the father's name is likewise invented and intended to indicate a connection with viticulture. The Hesiodic Catalogue (fr. 238 M–W) names Maron as a great-grandson of Dionysus. Maron serves as priest of Apollo among the Cicones (the only mention of a ἱερεύς in the *Odyssey*). Apollo is named as Lord of Ismarus in similar terms to his designation as Protector of Chryse, Cilla, and Tenedos (*Il.* i 37–8).

199–201. The pious dread (ἀζόμενοι) which leads Odysseus to spare the priest and his family (παιδὶ is probably an Alexandrian conjecture; see van der Valk, *Textual Criticism*, 143) is due to Maron's cultic position; he lived in the god's sacred grove. ἄλσεϊ: ἄλσος is already attested as a place name in Myc.: cf. *a-se-e/Alsehē* PY An 18. 4; 852. 4; cf. Heubeck, *Kadmos*, i (1962), 60.

202–5. Odysseus received, besides the Ciconian wine, wrought gold to the value/weight of 7 talents and a κρατήρ (cf. Myc. *ka-ra-te-ra/krātēra* MY Ue 611; acc.?). 204 read in conjunction with 159 and 164 would appear to indicate that Maron had filled 12 amphorae with wine, one each for the twelve ships. **ἀκηράσιον** (ἀκη-ράσιος): 'pure, unmixed'; < ἀκήρατος. On 205 Bechtel, *Lexilogus*, 24–5 compares ἄκρητον θεῖον ποτόν ii 341. On the form see Chantraine, *Dictionnaire* s.v. ἀκήρατος.

205–7. In Maron's household (as in the palace at Ithaca) only the ταμίη, besides the king and queen, has access to the θάλαμος; cf. ii 337–53.

208–11. When mixing wine Maron added one δέπας to twenty μέτρα of water. Scholars have generally concluded that this means the ratio of wine to water was 1 : 20 (2 : 3 was the more usual ratio in later times), but this of course presupposes that a δέπας and a μέτρον are equal measures, which is by no means certain. A further complication is the fact that in Homer δέπας can mean a very large vessel (e.g. the δέπας of Nestor, *Il.* xi 632–5; Myc. *di-pa/dipas* is also large), but it can also refer to a cup (e.g. x 316); see Chantraine, *Dictionnaire* s.v. (with bibliography). It is clear, however, that Ciconian wine is unusually strong and therefore ideally suited to the purpose in hand.

212–14. Odysseus resumes the tale after his digression (ἀσκὸν ἔχον 196: φέρον ἀσκὸν 212). He suspects that he will meet a man of gigantic strength (ἐπιειμένον ἀλκήν; cf. *Il.* vii 164, *Od.* iii 205). 215, on the other hand, continuing from 106–15, 175, 189, gives once more the perspective of the narrator looking back on events.

217. νομὸν κάτα: 'in the pastures' (νόμος, 'law', is not attested in Homer).

219. ταρσοὶ ('flat baskets for drying cheeses') are presumably the same as the πλεκτοὶ τάλαροι of 247, into which the fresh soft cheeses are forced; cf. O. Panagl, *ZAnt.* xxii (1972), 78–9. **τυρῶν**: for τυρός cf. Myc. *tu-ro₂* PY Un 718 etc.

221–3. ἔρχατο: 'they were penned in'; the explanation of this and related forms is difficult and much disputed; cf. Leumann, *Wörter*, 179–80, Chantraine, *Dictionnaire* s.v. εἴργω, Beekes, *Laryngeals*, 62–3, who suggests a root *sergh-*. πρόγονοι, μέτασσαι, and ἔρσαι must surely refer to older, younger, and new-born sheep respectively. Bechtel, *Lexilogus*, 227, derives μέτασσαι (*hapax*) from *meta-tyo-*; it is thus comparable with other IE *-tyo*-forms derived from prepositions or adverbial forms; cf. R. Gusmani, *AION* iii (1961), 41–58. This would give it the meaning 'those born later' (after the πρόγονοι); cf. Frisk, *GEW* s.v. ἔρσαι is usually identified with ἔρση, ἐέρση, 'dew' (Bechtel, *Lexilogus*, 139; Chantraine, *Dictionnaire* s.v.); but cf. Leumann, *Wörter*, 258. 11; Beekes, *Laryngeals*, 64.).

222–3. ναῖον (van der Valk, *Textual Criticism*, 137, prefers νᾶον): prob. 'they flowed'; presumably a metrically convenient alternative to νάει (vi 292 etc, both derived from *nau̯-yo: Chantraine, *Grammaire*, i 167. Less convincing: Bechtel, *Lexilogus*, 234–5; Schwyzer, *Grammatik*, i 686. **γαυλοί** and **σκαφίδες** amplify ἄγγεα ('vessels'): the milking pails in which the milk curdles (cf. θρέψας 246) and the whey (ὀρός) separates; cf. Panagl, loc. cit. (219 n.).

224–7. πρώτιστα: with αἰνυμένους (the latter contains the subject, sc. ἡμᾶς, to ἰέναι; cf. Chantraine, *Grammaire*, ii 312), and likewise αὐτὰρ ἔπειτα with ἐξελάσαντας. **ἰέναι πάλιν:** anticipatory.

228–30. Odysseus persists in his original intention (174–6); with the observation that it would have been better to yield to his companions (228 is taken from *Il.* v 201) he turns his attention to what is to come: 'in fact the Cyclops when he appeared (φανεὶς) would not prove ἐρατεινός' (a bitter understatement; δεινός would be more accurate). It is not easy to defend Odysseus here from the charge of folly: he is still consumed by curiosity, heedless of danger; cf. Bona, op. cit. (106 n.), 82 n. 39, 102; Eisenberger, *Studien*, 135.

231. The men make a burnt offering, and themselves also (i.e. like the gods to whom they sacrifice) eat some of the cheese. This is no abuse of hospitality (Germain, *Genèse*, 68 ff.). On alternatives κήαντες/κείαντες (cf. x 533, xi 46, 74) see Werner, *H u. ει vor Vokal*, 25–6.

233. ἦος: ibid., 71. **νέμων:** 'driving in his flocks' (cf. n. on νομός 217). Polyphemus regards the dry wood as ποτιδόρπιον, lit. 'useful at supper', i.e. to keep the cave warm and give light; he does not use it for cooking.

235–9. ἔντοσθεν: The reading ἔκτοσθεν should be retained: Polyphemus throws in the ἄχθος 'from outside the cave'. The beasts to be milked (ἤμελγε) are driven inside the cave, while the males are left ἔκτοθεν αὐλῆς ('outside the enclosed courtyard'); cf. Chantraine, *Grammaire*, ii 38; F. Eichhorn, *Homers Odyssee* (Göttingen, 1965), 67. 38; Focke, *Odyssee*, 171, argues (mistakenly) for ἔντοσθεν.

240–3. 240 = 340. The lines refer to the rock used as a θυρεός to close the entrance to the cave. The emphasis is on the great size (μέγαν; ὄβριμον cf. 233), although the comment that the rock could not be moved by twenty-two four-wheeled waggons is an indication of the stone's weight (rather than its size) and Polyphemus' strength. The account lingers over this point because it is one which will figure prominently in Odysseus' plans (320 ff.); F. Müller, op. cit. (182–92 n.), 43–5. We are reminded also of Hector's feat (*Il.* xii 445–9) in lifting a rock which two of the strongest men today could hardly have hoisted on a ἄμαξα (ix 242 ∼ *Il.* xii 448). A four-wheeled cart (ἀπήνη, ἄμαξα, as opposed to a two-wheeled chariot, δίφρος, ἅρμα, ὄχεα) was used for transport (cf. *Il.* xxiv 150–1, *Od.* vi 37–8); the comparisons here and at *Il.* xii 445–9 indicate its use also in building-operations; cf. J. Wiesner, *Archaeologia* F, 5–11. **ἠλίβατον:** the exact meaning and derivation are unknown.

244. = 341.
245. = 309, 342.
246–9. Polyphemus leaves half the milk in buckets to curdle (θρέψας) at once (presumably with the addition of some fermenting agent, e.g. ὀπός, 'fig juice'; cf. *Il.* v 904; Panagl, loc. cit. (219 n.); W. Richter, *Archaeologia* H, 62–4). He then gathers together (ἀμησάμενος) the curds and puts them in the woven ταρσοί (see 219 n.). On the disputed etymology of ἀμάομαι cf. Chantraine, *Dictionnaire* s.v. 2 ἀμάω, J. Irigoin, *LfgrE* s.v. ἀμάο(μαι), (with bibliography).

COMMENTARY

248–51. 250 = 310, 343. The milk poured into ἄγγεα is intended for immediate use (οἱ ... αἰνυμένῳ, 'when he wanted to drink some of it'), and is thus available for his δόρπον (ποτιδόρπιον). The wood which he collected (233–5)—likewise ποτιδόρπιον (249 ~ 234)—is lit, and now Polyphemus sees the Greeks who had hidden in the darkest corner of the cave (236).

252–5. Polyphemus uses the same words as Nestor to Telemachus (iii 71–4), although Nestor first justifies his questions (iii 69–70): now (νῦν δή) that his guests have enjoyed his hospitality he has a right to learn their identity. Polyphemus demands immediately to know who the strangers are, which does not bode well: he is obviously ignorant of the laws of hospitality. On the parallels and contrast between the ἄξεινος Polyphemus and the Phaeacians, the φιλόξεινοι par excellence, see Besslich, *Schweigen*, 33–6, 69.

256–8. The Greeks panic (δεισάντων gen. abs. despite 256 ἡμῖν) at the thundering voice and the massive figure before them (πέλωρον is subst., 'before the monster in person'); cf. Bechtel, *Lexilogus*, 274–6. Nevertheless (ἀλλὰ καὶ ὥς) Odysseus dares to answer (258 = iv 484).

259–71. Odysseus first answers Polyphemus' questions (259–65): they are victorious Greeks returning from Troy (Τροίηθεν: πόθεν 252) to their own country; they are not wanderers travelling μαψιδίως (cf. 253), but towards a particular destination (κατὰ πρῆξιν). Odysseus does not, however, give his name (cf. his reply to Arete, viii 241 ff.). The observation that they have been driven off course by the will of Zeus prepares the way for 266–71; they are αἰδοῖοι, and so deserve respectful treatment (αἰδεῖο 269). In spite of his fear (256–7), Odysseus still has his pride in his heroic origins; conscious of his fame and status as a hero (263 εὐχόμεθ᾽ εἶναι) he does not ask for pity (cf. his very different attitude at vi 175). He comes as a suppliant (266–9), but emphasizes the status and rights of the ἱκέτης; in fact he claims the right to hospitality (ξείνων θέμις 268) and a gift (W. Burkert, *Zum griechischen Mitleidsbegriff* (diss. Erlangen, 1955), 136). He is still unaware that he is outside the heroic milieu, and confronted by a being as unimpressed by the deeds and status of heroes as by the moral order of the heroic world. Odysseus' pathetically proud words, grotesquely inadequate to the matter in hand, are exposed as mere posturing as Polyphemus' reaction severely disillusions the hero.

261–2. ἄλλην ὁδόν, ἄλλα κέλευθα: they have travelled a great distance on a false course of many stages (κέλευθα); cf. O. Becker, *Das Bild des Weges und verwandte Vorstellungen im frühgriechischen Denken* (Berlin, 1937), 20. For 262 cf. 67–81.

264: cf. *Il.* x 212–13; S. Laser, *Hermes*, lxxxvi (1958), 399.

269. On αἰδώς, αἰδοῖος, αἰδεῖσθαι cf. W. J. Verdenius, 'Αἰδώς bei Homer', *Mnemosyne*, S. 3, xii (1945), 47–60; A. Beil, 'Αἰδώς bei Homer', *Der Altsprachliche Unterricht*, v 1 (1961), 51–64.

271. ἅμ᾽ ... ὀπηδεῖ: 'he is with them as protector'. As Ξένιος and Ἱκέσιος Zeus is responsible for the safety of ξεῖνοι and ἱκέται and punishes their oppressors. For ξεῖνος and ἱκέτης cf. Myc. *ke-se-nu-wo/ksenwos* PY Cn 286. 1; *i-ke-ta/Hiketās* (a name) KN B 799. 8.

28

272. νηλέϊ θυμῷ (cf. iv 743, viii 507) anticipates the response.

273–80. Polyphemus replies in fact only to the appeal to fear the gods (266–71). If he spares them it will not be out of piety, but because his θυμός so inclines him. The strangers' request is not refused in as many words, but the equivocal nature of the reply underlines the precariousness of the Greeks' position. The Cyclops does not react at all to Odysseus' summary of his status, his achievements, and his claim to fame, because he inhabits a quite different world. The names of Troy and Agamemnon obviously mean nothing to him: a vast gulf separates his world from that of Odysseus (τηλόθεν εἰλήλουθας 273). It is characteristic of Polyphemus, and not unimportant for the development of the episode, that he does not notice that Odysseus has failed to answer (except in vague general terms) his first question, τίνες ἐστέ; (252). The cunning (πειράζων 281) and the danger behind his last question (279–80) are emphasized by the concealment of the Cyclops' purpose behind the reason stated, ὄφρα δαείω. On this speech see W. Nestle, *Hermes*, lxxvii (1942), 60–5.

273. = xiii 237: Besslich, *Schweigen*, 35, against Schwartz, *Odyssee*, 35, gives a correct interpretation of the line repetition.

280. ἐπ' ἐσχατιῆς (slightly different from 182) belongs with ἔσχες (279), 'you anchored'.

281–2. Odysseus, sensing danger in the Cyclops' question responds with deceit himself. οὐ λάθεν sc. πειράζων.

283–6. Odysseus claims that Poseidon has wrecked his ship on the coast (ἐπὶ πείρασι; cf. ἐπ' ἐσχατιῆς 280). The details are given in reverse order: κατέαξε–βαλὼν–προσπελάσας–ἔνεικεν. There is dramatic irony in the lie Odysseus chooses: we know (from i 72–3), but the hero does not, that Poseidon is Polyphemus' father, and he will take on an important part at the end of the episode; moreover, (as we have known since bk. v) what is here invented is to become reality (admittedly in a somewhat different form). **Νέα:** either variant νέα/νῆα would have to be scanned as a monosyllable; both have been condemned by Chantraine, *Grammaire*, i 36–7, as suspect. But the alternatives proposed by, among others, Ahrens, van Gent, Schulze, and von der Mühll (cf. Ameis–Hentze, *Anhang*, iii 64) are hardly convincing. M. D. Petruševski's solution, νῆν, ZAnt. xvii (1967), 96, is ingenious, but surely incorrect nevertheless. The late epic form νέα is acceptable (van der Valk, *Textual Criticism*, 137); Hoekstra, *Modifications*, 57, sees in νέα μέν μοι the modification of a prototype *νᾶϝα δέ ϝοι κατέϝαξε.

291. Polyphemus tears his victims to pieces (μελεϊστί 'limb from limb'); cf. F. Bader, *BSL* lxv (1970), 85–136; E. Risch, *MH* xxix (1972), 69. The mutilation (ταμὼν explanatory) is to prepare the bodies for δόρπον (cf. 234, 249 nn.).

295. The mention of ἀμηχανίη (*hapax*), despair of having any μῆχος against Polyphemus, in fact prepares the reader to expect a μῆχος (299 ff.) from Odysseus, who is never short of ideas (πολυμήχανος).

297. For a recent discussion of ἀνδρόμεα see E. Risch, *Acta Mycenaea*, ii (Salamanca, 1972), 299; on κρέ' see Chantraine, *Grammaire*, i 210.

Polyphemus washes down his horrible meal with ἄκρητον milk (the word is otherwise used only of wine): there may be intentional contrast with the Hellenic custom of adding water to milk as well as to wine; but the main function of the detail is to point to the later use of ἄκρητος οἶνος; cf. S. L. Schein, 'Odysseus and Polyphemus in the *Odyssey*', *GRBS* xi (1970), 73–83, esp. 79.

299–305. Odysseus' first, impulsive plan (βούλευσα ingressive) is that of a warrior; cf. Achilles' reaction to Agamemnon's insult, *Il.* i 189–92 (300 uses the vocabulary of epic warfare; cf. *Il.* xxi 173, again with Achilles as subject). But ἕτερος θυμός ('a further impulsive thought'; cf. Schein, op. cit., 78. 13, with bibliography) holds him back: consideration of the massive door-stone (ὄβριμον 305 as in 241; cf. 240–3 n.). The obvious parallel is *Il.* ix 458–61. The main difference between this episode and the several 'deliberation scenes' in the *Iliad* is the division of the scene into two phases (199–305; 316–18); cf. C. Voigt, *Überlegung und Entscheidung*[2] (Meisenheim, 1972), 27 ff. The epic elements in the episode are of course unparalleled in the folklore material, and serve to characterize Odysseus as a true hero of the Trojan War.

301. ὅθι ... ἔχουσι: 'where the midriff contains the liver', a vulnerable spot.

302. χείρ' (i.e. χειρί) **ἐπιμασσάμενος:** 'feeling for the right place with my hand' (the cave is now dark).

303. καὶ ἄμμες: 'we too (like our dead comrades) would have perished there (αὐτοῦ)'.

306. = 436: cf. 151.

307. = 152; **309** = 245; **310** = 250.

311. ~ 344: cf. 289, 291 (with significant alterations: αὖτε and δεῖπνον ('morning meal') for δόρπον.

312–14: these lines are a counterpart to 237–43. Both passages illustrate the size and strength of the Cyclops, but the first emphasizes the weight of the rock, while the second concentrates on the ease with which Polyphemus moves it. ὡς εἴ τε (epic τε used in simile), i.e. like an archer or hunter.

316–18. These lines continue the 'deliberation scene' from 299–304. Odysseus is thinking how he can (εἴ πως) successfully (emphasized by the paratactic clause δοίη ... Ἀθήνη; cf. xxi 338, *Il.* vii 454) take revenge when a viable plan suddenly becomes clear to him (φαίνετο).

316. κακὰ βυσσοδομεύων: 'planning (δέμω, lit. "building") evil in the depths (βυθός, βυσσός) of my heart'. In parallel passages (xvii 66, 465 = 491 = xx 184) βυσσοδομεύω is used without further specification of the κακά concerned; here it means 'violent actions' against Polyphemus. We are reminded of the μερμηρίζειν episodes of the *Iliad* (ii 3–4; ii 5 ~ *Od.* ix 318 = 424, xi 230 etc.). Obviously two formulaic expressions have been combined here. On βυσσοδομεύω cf. Bechtel, *Lexilogus*, 85; Chantraine, *Dictionnaire* s.v. βυθός.

317. εὖχος: 'an achievement of which one can boast'; cf. M. Greindl, κλέος, κῦδος, εὖχος, τιμή, φάτις, δόξα (diss. Munich, 1938).

319–39. The βουλή is not explained immediately, but the detailed description of the ῥόπαλον indicates that it will play a decisive part (cf. 167–211 and 240–3 nn.). The purpose of the stake is not given until 331–2.

320. The stake is of olive-wood (ἐλαΐνεον for -ϊνον 378) that is still green (χλωρός); olive-wood is particularly hard (cf. Ar. *Lys.* 255). ἔκσπασε, the reading of the ἀκριβέστεραι, accepted by Meuli, *Odyssee*, 74. 2, is a late attempt to 'improve' on the poet perhaps inspired by Theoc. xxv 210; see further van der Valk, *Textual Criticism*, 24, who also cites AR i 1118. **φοροίη:** L. R. Palmer, in *Companion*, 95, 127, sees here an Atticism for *φορείη (similarly with φιλοίη iv 692). Chantraine, *Grammaire*, 464, takes a different and more correct view, but does not exclude the possibility of interpolation.

321–2. ἐΐσκομεν (<*ϝε-ϝικ-σκω, caus., cf. ἔοικα): 'compare to'. On the construction see Ruijgh, τε épique, 558: *ἐΐσκομεν τόσσον εἶναι ὅσσος θ' ἱστός ἐστιν. **ἐεικόσοροιο:** 'twenty-oared' with root *ἐρε- in the second element; cf. ἐρέ-της (Myc. *e-re-ta*/eretas; *e-re-e*/erehen, 'to row' PY An 724. 4) etc.; cf. Risch, *Wortbildung*, 8, Chantraine, *Dictionnaire* s.v. ἐρέτης.

323. λαῖτμα, sc. θαλάσσης: cf. v 174, ix 260.

325. On the construction see Ruijgh, τε épique, 558: *κόμμα ὅσον τ' ὄργυιαν. On ὄργυια (cf. x 167, xi 312, *Il.* xxiii 327) see Beekes, *Laryngeals*, 37–8.

326. ἀποξῦναι (from ἀπ-οξύνω): the only variant is the reading of W, ἀποξῦσαι (from ἀπο-ξύω; -ξύσσαι Schulze); cf. vi 269 (Ameis–Hentze, *Anhang*, i 154–5). E. *Cyc.* 456 (ἐξαποξύνας) supports -ῦναι.

327. ὁμαλόν (*hapax*, from *sem-/som-/sm̥-): 'smooth'. ἐθόωσα (θοόω, *hapax*): 'sharpen'.

328. ἐπυράκτεον (*hapax*): the meaning is clear from E. *Cyc.* 457 (ἐς πῦρ καθήσω); it is an expressive development of πυράζω; cf. Frisk, *GEW* s.v. The object is not to dry the wood to make it easy to kindle, as Bechtel, *Lexilogus*, 288–9, supposes, but to harden the point (Focke, *Odyssee*, 169) for use as a weapon. Spears made in this fashion were one of the earliest inventions of prehistoric man (W. Burkert, *Technikgesch.* xxxiv 4 (1967), 281–99) and continued in historical times to be used by primitive tribes in war (see e.g. Hdt. vii 71; 74: Libyans, Mysians; further examples cited by Burkert, loc. cit. 284.6), and by more sophisticated peoples for religious purposes (cf. the Romans' 'hasta praeusta', Livy i 32. 12). It is significant that Odysseus escapes the man-eating monster by using the very invention which secured the future of primitive man (Burkert, op. cit., 285). The sword, of which Odysseus still thought at 300–1 and which could equally have served the same purpose, is now forgotten: Odysseus can find a way out of the most difficult situation; cf. Glenn, op. cit. (105–566 n.), 164–6.

330. On κατά (with gen.) see Chantraine, *Grammaire*, ii 113. On the unusual use of μεγάλ'(α) (adv., 'high') see Ameis–Hentze, *Anhang*, i 113.

331–5. Only now are we told how exactly the stake will be used. It is reasonable to suppose that at this point in the traditional story the drawing of lots determined who should next be eaten (Page, *Odyssey*, 12–13). The poet here has in mind the heroic scene of *Il.* vii 170–9. In order to be fair

Odysseus must let the lot decide which of his comrades is to help him; cf. Bona, op. cit. (106–15 n.), 82. It is a good omen that the lot falls on those whom Odysseus would have picked out himself. πεπαλάσθαι (331): the MS-reading πεπαλάχθαι/πεπάλαχθαι (cf. *Il.* vii 171) suggests an expanded form παλάσσομαι from πάλλομαι; then κλήρῳ π. means 'to draw lots, let the lot decide' (Bechtel, *Lexilogus*, 266–7). But since we would not expect a pf. here, it may be more prudent to adopt Doederlein's cj. πεπαλέσθαι (aor.); cf. Aristarchus' reading πεπαλάσθαι (an inexplicable form); Chantraine, *Grammaire*, i 396.

334. τούς: the use of the article as a relative where the antecedent is itself an article (οἱ) is unusual; see Chantraine, *Grammaire*, ii 167. ἄν κε is hardly possible; perhaps it should be emended to τοὺς ἄρ κε (ibid., ii 345).

335. ἐλέγμην: ibid., i 384.

336–43: cf. 231–50. 337 ~ 237; 338 ~ 238–9; 340 = 240; 341–2 (~ 308–9) = 244–5; 343 (= 310) = 250; 344 (= 311) cf. 291.

338–9. There is one significant change from 238–9: on this occasion Polyphemus drives the male animals into the cave as well. Odysseus leaves open the question as to whether this is the giant's own idea (ὀϊσάμενος, cf. 213) or if he is inspired by some god. The lines contain a hint of what is to come; the effect of the Cyclops' action is to give the Greeks the means of escape, which is scarcely possible without divine assistance.

345. = 474.

346–52. Only now is there any suggestion as to the function in Odysseus' plan (332–3) of the Ciconian wine (196–211) which, by a sound premonition (213), he brought with him. He offers the giant a cup of wine, ironically described as a λοιβή ('libation' usually offered to gods), and pleads for ἔλεος; this represents an advance on Odysseus' position in 259–71. But in accusing Polyphemus of madness (μαίνεαι, 350) he displays the same attitude as characterized his first speech: to break the ground-rules of hospitality is to go against self-interest because it leads to social isolation (351–2). The wine is not, however, an essential element of Odysseus' plan, which might suggest that it was already present in the old folktale; but it might also come from other stories dealing with the intoxication of a daemonic being by a mortal: examples in Meuli, *Odyssee*, 71–3.

353. δέκτο: cf. Chantraine, *Grammaire*, i 296, 384; A. Debrunner, *Gedenkschrift f. P. Kretschmer* (Vienna, 1956), i 77–84, esp. 78; O. Szemerényi, *Gnomon*, xliii (1971), 664; J. Narten (who takes a different view), *Festschrift f. F. B. J. Kuiper* (The Hague, 1969), 15–43.

354. ἡδὺ ποτὸν refers us back to 205, 208–10; Polyphemus drinks the strong wine as he drinks milk (295), unmixed. On ἡδὺ ποτὸν written as one word (ii 340, iii 391, xv 507) see Leumann, *Wörter*, 68.

355–9. Polyphemus asks for another cup of wine and makes a second attempt to find out Odysseus' name having got only a vague answer at his first attempt (252 ff.). The parallel with the Phaeacians is intentional; see Besslich, *Schweigen*, 69. There too the first question (Arete's vii 237) must be repeated (by Alcinous, viii 550–5). There Odysseus' name must be given as a pre-condition for his conveyance home, here if he is to receive the ξείνιον which he claimed at 267–8. This time Polyphemus is adhering to the conventions, for a ξεινίη does require the exchange of names (W. Nestle, *Hermes*, lxxvii (1942), 49), but in 369–70 we learn the cynical motivation behind, and the nature of, the proposed ξείνιον. The introduction of the exchange-of-names motif eases the combination of the two legends of blinding and outwitting by giving a false name (cf. 105–566 n.).

358. = 111.

359. ἀπορρώξ (from ῥήγνυμι: cf. Risch, *Wortbildung*, 194): here it has a transferred meaning, 'equal to the food of the gods'; cf. D. Motzkus, *LfgrE* s.v.

360. αὖτις πόρον: αὖτις ἐγὼ is the better attested reading; cf. van der Valk, *Textual Criticism*, 68; Stanford ad loc. is unconvincing; Ruijgh, *Élément*, 46.

362. οἶνος περιήλυθεν Κύκλωπα φρένας, lit. 'the wine stole around the Cyclops and in particular his senses'; cf. xvii 261, *Il.* x 139; S. Laser, *Hermes*, lxxxvi (1958), 395–7.

364–7. Odysseus gives his name as Οὖτις, 'No one' (οὔ τις) and thus happens on a means to trick the Cyclops (414). The invention of this name (the folk-tale generally has 'Myself' or 'Myself-I-did-it') is explained by the subsequent course of events, especially the scene 399–412; cf. 408–12 n.). On the trick itself see E. Heitsch, *Die Entdeckung der Homonymie*, Abh. Ak. Mainz, xi (1972), 8 f. n. 3; N. Austin, 'Name Magic in the *Odyssey*', *CSCA* v (1972), 1–19, esp. 13–15. The name given is not, as K. Ziegler, *Gymnasium*, xlix (1962), 396–7, supposes, a disguised form of Odysseus' real name.

366. On acc. Οὖτιν see Leumann, *Wörter*, 48.

368. = 272; cf. 287.

369–70. With the specification of the ξείνιον the theme of ξεινίη (cf. 176, 229, 267–71, 356, 365) is brought here to a climax (cf. 517–21 n.). The cynicism with which Polyphemus apparently conforms to the demands of *themis* and at the same time shamefully ignores them confirms the picture of the Cyclopes given earlier (106–15) and justifies the blinding; this is not only necessary if Odysseus and his men are to escape, but also proper punishment for one who so outrageously offends against the most basic moral precepts. **πύματον** ('last') has never been satisfactorily explained; cf. Frisk, *GEW* s.v.

372–3. κὰδ ... πανδαμάτωρ: modelled on *Il.* xxiv 4–5. On φάρυ(γ)ξ, 'throat', cf. Bechtel, *Lexilogus*, 327; Frisk, *GEW* s.v.

374. οἰνοβαρείων: from οἰνοβαρής (cf. *Il.* i 225); see Risch, *Wortbildung*, 73–4.

375–94. Here the poet uses (with obvious modifications) essential elements in the *Iliad*'s descriptions of heroic *aristeiai*: the 'arming' of the hero (375–6); the exhortation to his followers (375–7); the divinely inspired μένος (381); and the double comparison (384–8; 391–4). See further R. Schröter, *Die Aristie als Grundform homerischer Dichtung* (diss. Marburg, 1950), 98 ff.

375–9. τὸν (demonst.) **μόχλον**: 'the μόχλος already mentioned' (319–30). The tip of the stake, still green (χλωρός περ ἐών 379; cf. 320) despite its previous treatment by fire, is re-heated until it glows (ἧος θερμαίνοιτο 376) and almost catches fire (ἅψεσθαι; cf. G. Busch, *Glotta*, xxxiv (1955), 309). Focke, *Odyssee*, 170–1, has refuted the technical objections raised by, among others, Merkelbach, *Untersuchungen*, 313. Page, *Odyssey*, 10–11, and C. M. Bowra, in *Companion*, 53, have raised the possibility (and it is no more than that) of an earlier version of the story which featured a metal spit which glowed red-hot, διεφαίνετο (379).

382–90. The men seize the μοχλός and drive it (ἐνέρεισαν 383) from above into the eye of the Cyclops while he lies on his back (371–2). Odysseus, lifted up (ἀερθείς, see 383 n. below), twists the pole like a shipwright (νηῶν τέκτων, cf. 126) wielding a τρύπανον (*hapax*; a large auger as opposed to the smaller gimlet, τέρετρον, v 246). The difference is that he does the job of ἐνερείδειν, while his men twist the pole round (δινεῖν = ὑποσσείουσιν) with the aid of a thong (ἱμάντι) held at both ends (ἁψάμενοι ἑκάτερθε 386) and pulled back and forth; cf. E.-M. Voigt's somewhat different explanation, *LfgrE*, 1120.

383. ἐρεισθείς (Arist.) does not match what Odysseus is doing; ἀερθείς (Vulg.) must be accepted, cf. E. Bornemann, *Odyssee-Interpretationen* (Frankfurt-on-Main, 1953), 104–5; van der Valk, *Textual Criticism*, 281. 1.

384. τρυπῶ̣: τρυπᾷ (subj; Ps. Draco, La Roche) is to be preferred to opt. τρυπῷ (codd.); cf. von der Mühll, ad loc., Chantraine, *Grammaire*, ii 260, Ruijgh, τε ἐπique, 639.

387. The μοχλός is πυριήκης (*hapax*) because it has a point (*ἄκος) made glowing by the fire; for the cpd. cf. τανα-ήκης, πυρί-καυστος, etc.; Frisk, *GEW* s.v. **ἑλόντες:** ἔχοντες ('holding') corresponds to the situation, unlike the alternatives ἑλόντες (Aristarchus and many MSS.) and ἑλῶντες (proposed by Schwartz, *Odyssee*, 314).

389–90: 'the fiery smoke singed the eyelids and eyebrows all round as the pupil (γλήνη) burned.' **σφαραγεῦντο** (only here and 440): 'the roots (sc. γλήνης) crackled, hissed.'

391–4. Another simile describes the effect of the red-hot stake. The eye hisses (σίζ' 394) like a hatchet or σκέπαρνον (v 237) plunged by a χαλκεύς (Myc. *ka-ke-u*/*khalkeus*) into cold water to harden. φαρμάσσω (*hapax*) is a technical term ('treat with a φάρμακον (here, liquid to temper the metal); harden'). **τὸ γὰρ ... ἐστίν** (cf. *Il.* ix 706): 'for the strength of iron depends on this hardening process'. While the poet elsewhere consistently archaizes (he equips his heroes exclusively with bronze weapons and tools) he includes in the similes pictures of the contemporary world. The technique here described was introduced in Greece around the ninth century BC (R. Forbes, *Archaeologia* K, 26, 32).

395. The striking juxtaposition of σμερδαλέον and μέγα is perhaps due to combining two expressions such as σμερδαλέον δ' ᾤμωξεν (*Il.* xviii 35) and μέγα δ' οἰμώξας (*Il.* xxii 34; cf. vii 125); see West, *Papyri*, 237.

398. χερσίν surely belongs with ἔρριψεν (T. Rüsing, *LfgrE* s.v., who refers to *Il.* xx 418) rather than ἀλύων. On the latter and Aeol. ἀλυίω cf. Chantraine, *Grammaire*, i 111, 372; *Dictionnaire* s.v.

399–414. The other Cyclopes (113–15) come to ask Polyphemus why he is shouting (ἤπυεν 399). They suppose that someone is trying to do him harm (ἀρή): ὅττι ἑ κήδοι (402) and ἀρημένος (403; cf. vi 2; D. Mader, *LfgrE* s.v. ἀρή II and ἀρημένος). This is the first mention of the name Polyphemus.

400. σπήεσσι: cf. 30 n.

406. κτείνει: conative pres.   **δόλῳ ἠὲ βίηφιν:** the Cyclopes unwittingly hit on the right answer: Odysseus uses both.

408–12. Polyphemus replies with a slight variation in the words of the questions of 405–6 (ἦ μή τις ... ἦ μή τις ...): he means 'Οὖτις is trying to kill me by treachery, not by violence'. The other Cyclopes mistake him to mean "οὔ τις ... οὐδὲ ...": 'there isn't anyone trying to kill me by treachery, and there is no violence being used against me'; (cf. Ruijgh, τε *épique*, 190–1). They respond on the assumption εἰ ... μή τίς σε βιάζεται, 'if there is no one assaulting you ...' To highlight the misunderstanding, εἰ οὐ, which we would normally expect with an indic. protasis, is replaced by εἰ μή τις (Chantraine, *Grammaire*, ii 333–4, Shipp, *Studies*, 145) and there is a word-play, already prepared with 405–6, in μῆτις (414); cf. A. J. Podlecki, loc. cit. (172–6 n.), S. L. Schein, loc. cit. (297 n.) 79–81. In fact it is the μῆτις of the πολύμητις which overpowers the giant. 410–11 are elliptical: 'If no one is attacking you then the only reason for your cries can be a νοῦσος ('madness'?) sent by Zeus, and there is no way (οὔ πως ἔστι; on the construction see Chantraine, *Grammaire*, ii 305) anyone can escape that. We cannot help you. Pray to your father Poseidon!' 411 indicates trouble to come. On 412a (an interpolation modelled on 519) see West, *Papyri*, 238–9.

416. ψηλαφόων: 'feeling around'; Frisk, *GEW* s.v., discusses this expressive form (with bibliography). It is odd that Polyphemus has already removed the θυρεός, although it is not yet day. For a discussion against the analytical trend exemplified by Merkelbach, *Untersuchungen*, 214, see latterly Eisenberger, *Studien*, 140. 34; cf. 420–4 n.

418. On the artificial form ὄεσσι (found only here and *Il.* vi 25, xi 106) see Chantraine, *Grammaire*, i 219, (for *ὄισσι?); Shipp, *Studies*, 48.

419. The expression is somewhat strange ('suspecta': von der Mühll), but the meaning is clear: Odysseus is trying to rationalize Polyphemus' behaviour (417) ('perhaps he thought I would be stupid enough (to attempt to run out alongside his sheep)').

420–4. The new circumstances require a new plan. As in the first deliberation scene 299–318 (constructed along similar lines: 420 ~ 299, 316; 421–3 ~ 317; 427 = 318) the aim is not in doubt. The frantic thought (ὕφαινον is a graphic metaphor from weaving) goes into devising the means of achieving it. Then suddenly the fully fledged plan is there (cf. C. Voigt, op. cit. (382–90 n.), 21, 28–9). On λύσις (421) see H. Jones, *Glotta*, li (1973), 15. On ὥς τε περὶ ψυχῆς (423, 'as is usual in matters of life and death') see Ruijgh, τε *épique*, 583.

425–36. In the folk-tale versions the hero generally wraps himself in an animal skin. The more unusual device used here allows for the Cyclops' address to his sheep (444–61).

35

425. The emphatic initial position of ἄρσενες ὄιες reminds us of Polyphemus' unusual measures in 338–9. On ὄιες/οἴιες (perhaps the reading of Aristarchus: van der Valk, *Textual Criticism*, 137–8) see Chantraine, *Grammaire*, i 219, and Wyatt, *Lengthening*, 178–9.

426. ἰοδνεφές: cf. iv 135. εἶρος (< *ϝερϝος; cf. Myc. *we-we-e-a/werweheha*, neut. pl.), 'wool'.

427–31. Odysseus uses withes (λύγος, fem.) to lash together three rams for each of his men: 'in each case the middle one carried one of my companions' (429). Exactly how is not revealed until 443: 'each of the men was tied to the underbelly of his ram' (which explains how it can also be stated (431) that each man was carried by three animals).

428: cf. 189.

429. σύντρεις αἰνύμενος: i.e. σὺν τρεῖς αἰ.; cf. σὺν δὲ δύω μάρψας (289) 'taking them three at a time'; on the development of the distributive-iterative meaning see Leumann, *Wörter*, 75–6.

430. σώοντες (< *σαόοντες): see Leumann, *Kleine Schriften* (Zurich, 1959), 266–72.

433–5. Odysseus grasps with one hand the back of the leader of the flock and curls up (ἐλυσθείς) under its shaggy belly, and then hangs there, clinging with both hands (χερσὶν) to the fleece (στρεφθείς is difficult to understand precisely; cf. West, *Papyri*, 240), and thus holds on tightly (ἐχόμην).

435. νωλεμέως: cf. iv 288.

436–7. = 306–7. The repetition is deliberate: to draw our attention to parallels with the previous situation. A difference then becomes immediately apparent: yesterday Polyphemus milked the females κατὰ μοῖραν, today they are left unmilked and suffer alongside their ἄναξ (440).

439. ἐμέμηκον (plpf.): cf. Chantraine, *Grammaire*, i 438.

440. σφαραγεῦντο: 'were full to bursting' (in contrast to 390).

443. εἰροπόκων (only here and *Il.* v 137; possessive cpd.), 'having a woolly fleece'; cf. εἶρος (426); Hoekstra, *Modifications*, 68. 3.

445. The MSS are divided between λαχμῷ (supported by the lexicographers) and λάχνῳ (supported by Seleucus *Et.Magn.*). Masc. λάχνῳ (*hapax*: the usual form is fem. λάχνη) may be a cj. by Seleucus to replace λαχμῷ (cf. van der Valk, *Textual Criticism*, 44–5). λαχμῷ finds some support in the reading of P 31, βληχμῷ (τ' ἀχθόμενος), behind which λαχμῷ may lurk. Analysis of the sound-effects leads G. Scheibner, *Miscellanea Critica* (Leipzig, 1965), i 260, to conjecture λαχμῷ ἀχθόμενος; cf. also West, *Papyri*, 241.

446–61. Polyphemus addresses a speech full of pathos to the ἀρνειὸς μήλων (κριός 447; cf. 432). With Odysseus underneath it leaves the cave last. The Cyclops wonders why his favourite ram, usually at the head of the flock, should now be last (πρῶτος is given three times, between ὕστατος (448) and πανύστατος (452)), and supposes that he is mourning his master's loss of sight. Then he is overwhelmed by helpless rage against his tormentors. The speech reveals the danger inherent in the situation and heightens the dramatic tension; it also rounds off the Odyssean picture of the Cyclops.

The monster, who passes his savage life cut off from society and is impervious to any sense of obligations towards others, is capable of feelings and friendship, but they are directed only towards an animal; indeed he has more in common with his flock than with his fellow giants. The poet delicately balances the reader's feelings of revulsion towards the Cyclops with the pity aroused by these lines.

450. μακρὰ βιβάς: used in the *Iliad* formulaically (cf. *Od.* xi 539) to describe heroes proudly striding out.

451. ἀπονέεσθαι: Wyatt, *Lengthening*, 84–7, attempts an explanation of the unusual lengthening of ἀ- as in ii 195 (cf. *Il.* ii 113); the variant εὐνηθῆναι (cf. *Il.* xiv 331) given in P 31 is an attempt to eliminate the metrical difficulties of the line.

453–4. κακός: here 'cowardly' (cf. λυγρός 454); amplified by 454[b].

456. ὁμοφρονέοις: usually 'to be of the same mind', as in vi 183; here 'if you could think like me' (cf. variant ὁμὰ φρ., P 31; and emendation ὁμοῦ φρ. proposed by I. Bekker and P. Cauer); cf. Schwartz, *Odyssee*, 314; in support of ὁμοφρονέοις see van der Valk, *Textual Criticism*, 55.   **ποτιφων-ήεις** is an unusual formation from the formulaic προσεφώνεε (perhaps modelled on φωνή: φωνήεις (Hes. *Th.* 584) or αὐδή: αὐδήεις (*Il.* xix 497), also of an animal; cf. Risch, *Wortbildung*, 153–4). The meaning of the line as a whole, however, is clear: 'if only you could speak to me (as I can to you)'.

457. ἠλασκάζει (only here and *Il.* xviii 281) was originally intr., 'flit from place to place' (cf. ἠλάσκω *Il.* ii 470, xiii 104), but here with acc. μένος, 'flee from' (cf. perhaps ἀλυσκάζω with acc., 'avoid', v.l. xvii 581).

459. θεινομένου gen. (abs.) despite οἱ (458): cf. 257. Duentzer's cj. ῥαίνοιτο produces an unusual construction (in place of ῥαίνω τί τινι, 'sprinkle with'); ῥαίω, 'shatter', retains a normal construction. The similarity to ῥαίνεσθαι is perhaps intentional (cf. ἄλλυδις ἄλλη).   **κὰδ δέ κ':** the transmitted text is sound, cf. Ruijgh, τε *épique*, 702–3.

459–60. κὰδ ... λωφήσειε (καταλωφάω, *hapax*; with gen.): 'rest from'; cf. Frisk, *GEW* s.v. λωφάω.   **οὐτιδανός:** cf. *Il.* i 293, xi 390; cpd. with suffix -ανος from old neut. *οὔτιδ (W. Schulze; Bechtel, *Lexilogus*, 263; Chantraine, *Grammaire*, i 281); effective word-play on Οὖτις.

462. ἠβαιόν in the *Iliad* always preceded by negation, οὐδ' ἠβαιόν; result of wrong division of pre-Homeric *οὐ δὴ βαιόν; Leumann, *Wörter*, 50.

463: anacoluthic after ἐλθόντες.

464–6. The crew's wish, refused by Odysseus earlier (224–8), is now fulfilled. The reason for stealing the animals is not entirely clear (cf. Merkelbach, *Untersuchungen*, 214, Page, *Odyssey*, 14, Glenn, op. cit. (105–566 n.), 172–3). It is surely derived from the conventional schema of a heroic *aristeia* (cf. 375–94 n.): the defeated enemy is regularly despoiled; Schröter, op. cit. (375–94 n.), 107–8.

464. ταναύποδα (*hapax*): meaning and derivation unclear (Chantraine, *Grammaire*, i 33; Risch, *Wortbildung*, 168); μῆλα τ. parallels the equally obscure βόες εἰλίποδες (i 92).

465. περιτροπέοντες (cf. *Il.* ii 295; *h.Merc.* 542): perhaps here 'turning round frequently'.

468-9. ἀνὰ ... ἑκάστῳ: amplifies οὐκ εἴων κλαίειν. ἀνανεύειν, 'to throw the head back; to deny, refuse, forbid' (opp. κατανεύειν, 'to nod; agree'; cf. 490); the prohibition here is indicated not verbally, but ὀφρύσι, 'with the eyebrows'.

471-2. = 103-4.

473. = v 400, xii 181; cf. vi 294.

474-9. Odysseus' jeers (κερτόμια (474), neut. pl.) are also to be understood by reference to the *Iliad*'s *aristeia*, in which the victor addresses his rival (whether still alive or already dead). Odysseus emphasizes his own strength (ἀνάλκιδος: cf. 463) and the moral justification of his actions (τίσις): he feels himself to be the agent of the vengeance of Zeus ξείνιος, in whose name he had requested hospitality (269–271); his action is the answer to Polyphemus' impious words (273–7).

476. ἔδμεναι: ἔδομαι has no fut. infin. and so the pres. is used instead of the fut. to be expected after ἔμελλες (cf. 477 κιχήσεσθαι); Chantraine, *Grammaire*, ii 309.

476. On the form of σπῆϊ see Werner, *H u. ει vor Vokal*, 36–40.

477. The κακὰ ἔργα have found out their perpetrator; their consequences have fallen upon him.

478. οὐχ ἅζεο (here with inf.): 'you did not scruple to ...'

480-4. Polyphemus, stung to even greater fury by 475–9, breaks off a great pinnacle of rock and hurls it after the ship; this is surely a motif taken from the folklore versions of the story. The Cyclops throws the rock so far that it lands (κατέβαλε) in front of the ship. 483 was rejected even before Aristarchus; it belongs to the parallel scene 537–42, (481 ~ 537–8; 482 ~ 539; 484 = 541; 485–6 ~ 542), and makes sense only at 540.

482. νεὸς κυανοπρῴροιο (formulaic); Hoekstra, *Modifications*, 125–6.

485. The wave made by the rock drives the ship back to the shore. **παλιρρόθιον:** cf. v 430. ἂψ ἠπειρόνδε (Aristarch.) is preferable to αἶψ'; cf. αὖτις ἐς ἤπειρον (496). At 542 πρόσω corresponds to ἂψ. van der Valk, *Textual Criticism*, 131. 4, however, disagrees.

486. πλημυρίς (*hapax*; from πλήμη): 'flood'; Bechtel, *Lexilogus*, 278–9. **θέμωσε** (*hapax*): here 'drive'; Bechtel, *Lexilogus*, 162; Chantraine, *Dictionnaire* s.v. θεμός.

487-8. κοντόν (*hapax*): 'pole'. **ὦσα παρέξ**: 'I thrust it in at the side'.

489. = x 129. There is no reason to doubt the authenticity of the line, as do van Leeuwen and von der Mühll. We would expect an infin. after ἐκέλευσα (cf. xii 193–4); in 490 the order ἐμβαλέειν κώπῃς (cf. *remis incumbere*, Verg. *A.* v 15) is carried out.

490. For security reasons the order ἐποτρύνειν is not given in words, but by κατανεύειν κρατί (like the command 468–9).

491. The apparent contradiction with 473 was already noted in classical times (von der Mühll, *Odyssee*, 720). The question is whether Odysseus could be heard at over twice the distance. There is no need, however, to turn to the analytical approach offered by Merkelbach, *Untersuchungen*, 214, because the formulaic 473 is not intended to give an exact distance; cf. van Leeuwen and Ameis–Hentze–Cauer ad loc.; Focke, *Odyssee*, 158–9; Bona, op. cit. (106–15 n.), 35–6, 2; Eisenberger, *Studien*, 141, 35. πρήσσοντες: cf. ii 213.

493. =x 442. This time (contrast 224–7) the warning is given in direct speech; this emphasises the extreme danger.

497. φθεγξαμένου: 'uttering a sound'.   αὐδήσαντος: 'speaking'.

500–5. In his first speech (475–9) Odysseus describes his action as the vengeance of Zeus and does not give his own name; now, in the moment of relief and to further his own κλέος, Odysseus claims authorship of the deed and gives his own name. The two speeches thus complement each other. By identifying himself Odysseus exposes himself to the curse which follows (528–35); we have here the ancient belief that knowledge of a man's name bestows some kind of magical power over him. Odysseus does provoke the curse laid on him; but it is carelessness, not ὕβρις or a breach of a law which requires punishment (Focke, *Odyssee*, 168; Bona, op. cit. (106–15 n.), 45–6).

501: cf. 282.

503. ἀλαωτύν (*hapax*; archaizing *nomen actionis* in -τύς): 'the blinding'.

505. = 531; **506** = xi 59.

507–21. At the mention of Odysseus' name Polyphemus remembers the almost forgotten words of a seer who had predicted just such a fate for him. The poet likes such inventions, which have no basis in tradition; Circe (x 330–32) and Alcinous (xiii 172–8) similarly recall relevant predictions. The complaint that the prophecy has been fulfilled in a quite unexpected way leads to the second half of the speech (517–21), in which Polyphemus attempts to lure Odysseus back with a promise of ξείνια.

507. =x 172.

509. Τήλεμος and Εὔρυμος are invented names, short forms of, e.g. Τηλέμαχος and Εὐρύμαχος.

512. ἁμαρτήσεσθαι: here, by a most unusual shift in meaning, 'lose, be robbed of'; Naber's emendation ἀμερθήσεσθαι (*Mnemosyne*, iv (1888), 212) nevertheless cannot be accepted. ἁμαρτήσαντα (P 31): see West, *Papyri*, 243.

513. ἐδέγμην: see 353 n.; δέχομαι here 'expect that'; both meaning and construction are unusual.

514. The parallel between 513–14 and 213–14 is intentional. Odysseus' expectations have been dreadfully fulfilled, while those of Polyphemus have been dashed. A small (ὀλίγος), worthless (οὐτιδανός; cf. 460) weakling (ἄ-κικυς) has overcome him by a trick (οἴνῳ 516).

517–21. After the monologue (506–16), Polyphemus addresses Odysseus directly: he offers ξείνια and the promise to pray to his father Poseidon for a fortunate πομπή (cf. viii 545 n.: πομπὴ καὶ φίλα δῶρα). The situation of the previous evening repeats itself with significant variation: after a name has been given (there a false one), the offer of a ξείνιον (364–70). What gift the Cyclops has in mind on this occasion is not stated. But 517 thus resumes (for the last time) the leitmotif of the Cyclops episode. Polyphemus promises a ξείνιον at the point where, in the folk-tales, the giant, supposedly out of remorse, gives the hero a magic object (usually a ring) which in fact either forces the wearer to return to the giant, or makes him give away his position (for example by calling out, 'I'm here'). The hero generally escapes the spell, when he discovers that the ring cannot be removed from his finger, by sacrificing the finger. The poet must surely have been aware of these traditional features of the tale (Page, *Odyssey*, 19; C. S. Brown, 'Odysseus and Polyphemus. The name and the curse', *Comp. Lit.* 18 (1966), 201; Glenn, op. cit. (105–566 n.), 177–9), but chooses to substitute a solemn curse (528–35) as the fateful ξείνιον; cf. the similar substitution of Althaea's curse for the magic brand in the story of Meleager *Il.* ix 566. 520–1 do not contradict 275–8: Polyphemus is still unconcerned about the gods, but he relies on the help of his divine father.

519a: the extra line given in P 31 is a gratuitous addition to the text.

522–5. Odysseus has only scorn for the Cyclops' hopes (520). He wishes that he could be as certain of being able to rob Polyphemus of his life (ψυχῆς τε καὶ αἰῶνος) and send him to Hades (πέμψαι is an ironic echo of πομπή 518), as he is that Poseidon can not heal his eye. Odysseus' conduct here is no more reprehensible than in 503–5 (Bona, op. cit. (106–15 n.), 45–6). **εὖνιν** (elsewhere only *Il.* xxii 44): see Bechtel, *Lexilogus*, 144.

526–35. Polyphemus addresses a formal prayer to his father: after the conventional plea to be heard (κλῦθι) and the solemn listing of the god's titles come the justification of the request (529) and finally the request itself (cf. for example *Il.* i 37–42, 451–6), in this case that Odysseus should not be permitted to see his home again, or at least, if he should be allowed to return to his home, that it should be in the least favourable circumstances possible. The curse itself and the preceding lines (518 ff.) have long since been regarded by analysts as a secondary addition (Duentzer); it is seen as an interruption to the natural flow of thought (B. Marzullo, *Il problema omerico* (Florence, 1952), 107) etc., and critics note that the wrath of Poseidon invoked in this prayer is practically ignored in ix–xii (see however Bethe, *Odyssee*, 116–17; J. Irmscher, *Götterzorn bei Homer* (diss. Berlin, 1950), 56 ff.). However we must note the close connection between Odysseus' giving his name and the curse (Focke, *Odyssee*, 159; Bona, op. cit. (106–15 n.), 35–51), and indirect preparation for the curse at 412. On the wrath of Poseidon see 532–5, 536 nn.

527. = *Il.* xv 371.

528. γαιήοχε: cf. i 68 n.   κυανοχαῖτα: cf. iii 6 n.

529: cf. 519.

531: the line is not, as some critics have supposed (van Leeuwen, von der Mühll), to be suspected as a secondary repetition of 505. The curse attains its full effect only when a victim's full name and identity have been given: name, father's name and country (Schwartz, *Odyssee*, 211, van der Valk, *Textual Criticism*, 268, Merkelbach, *Untersuchungen*, 183. 1, Brown, op. cit. (517–21 n.), 201, Bona, op. cit. (106–15 n.), 41. 21).

40

532–5. The petition is qualified in accordance with the Homeric conception of fate: if fate decrees that Odysseus shall return to his home, not even a god can alter that fact. Within these limitations, however, the god has the power to exercise a considerable influence on events. In fact we already know what Odysseus' eventual fate will be from the speech of Halitherses (ii 174–6) and the words of Zeus (v 41–2; ~v 114–15 ~ ix 532–3); it is restated in the prophecies of Tiresias (xi 100–37; xi 114–15 ~ ix 534) and Circe (xii 140–1).

536. For the formal conclusion to the prayer cf. *Il.* i 43 (=457), xvi 248. Poseidon hears the petition and decides on revenge for his son's mutilation (cf. i 69; xi 103 = xiii 343). He is as little interested in the motivation and circumstances of the deed as in Odysseus' bold words (523–5); Bona, op. cit. (106–15 n.), 45–6.

537–42. Polyphemus throws a second rock; cf. 481–6 (538 = *Il.* vii 269; 537: cf. *Il.* vii 268). **ἐπιδινήσας:** περιστρέψας, originally written in P 31 for ἐπιδινήσας, is certainly not authentic, but clarifies ἐπιδινήσας. ἐπιδινεῖν (intrans.), 'to swing round', refers to the movement of the trunk in throwing. **ἐπέρεισε ... ἵν':** extra force is added as the previously bent arm is straightened; cf. H. Lutz, *Beiträge zur Frage der Leibeserziehung und zur Erklärung einzelner Stellen der Odyssee* (diss. Erlangen, 1927), 45–6. **ἀπέλεθρον** (only here and *Il.* v 245, vii 269, xi 354): ἀ- privative and πέλεθρον; cf. Ion./Att. πλέθρον; 'immeasurably wide'; Frisk, *GEW* s.v.

539: cf. 482. This time the rock falls short, μετόπισθε νεός, very near in fact (τυτθόν). The comment given in 540 (=483) suits only this context as the missile only just misses the rudder (οἰήϊον, found only here and xii 218; cf. οἴηξ *Il.* xxiv 268).

541. = 484.

542: cf. 485ᵃ (ἄψ: πρόσω) and 486ᵇ. χέρσον refers here to the Island of Goats.

546. = xii 5 (cf. xi 20). Variant ἐλάσαντες given by P 31 is improbable, in view of the parallel passages.

547. = 150, xii 6. The line's authenticity has been questioned by von der Mühll, who compares xi 20. But the exact correspondence of 546–9 and xi 20–2 is evidence of authenticity; cf. Merkelbach, *Untersuchungen*, 183. 1.

549. = 42.

550–5. Odysseus sacrifices the ram given to him as a special honour (ἔξοχα 551) at the division of the μῆλα. The sacrifice is in honour of Zeus, invoked as protector (271–2) and, in the last adventure to have befallen them, saviour (479). The god does not, however, accept it. Many scholars have found this strange and have regarded the allegedly 'duplicated divine wrath' of Zeus and Poseidon as resulting from secondary reworking of an older version in which only one god was angry. But there is no question here of Zeus being hostile to Odysseus; we are simply told that he did not accept the offering. He must let events take their course in accordance with Moira, which has ordained that Odysseus should return only after twenty years, and so he gives thought to destroying Odysseus' fleet and companions. (μερμήριζε: impf., because Zeus is concerned with this purpose both before and after this episode; the weakly attested variant μερμήριξε would give the wrong sense. On μερμηρίζω see 316 n.). Poseidon's desire for revenge is in accordance with fate, and we must therefore expect Zeus to fulfil Poseidon's wishes, although he has just saved Odysseus; cf. Eisenberger, *Studien*, 144–5.

552. = xiii 25.

556–7. = 161–2. 557: cf. *Il.* vii 268–9.

558–60. = 168–70.

561: cf. 488.

562–4. = 178–80.

565–6. = 62–3.

BOOK X: COMMENTARY

1–79. Odysseus comes to the floating island of Aeolia (3), home of Aeolus, appointed by Zeus as ταμίης of the winds (21), and his family. During the events related in 1–27 Aeolia is stationed in the furthest, mythical, west; with a prevailing west wind it takes Odysseus nine days to travel to within sight of Ithaca (25, 28). The function of the episode within the narrative of Odysseus' wanderings is clear: the crew's frustration of Aeolus' kindly intention and his subsequent curse bring home to Odysseus what previously he could at most suspect: Poseidon will fulfil his son's prayer (ix 526–36) as far as possible, and Zeus intends the destruction of the ships and their crew (ix 550–5; cf. 52). Aeolus himself tells Odysseus that he is hated by the gods (74–5), and his words are confirmed by his reception from the Laestrygonians. It is interesting to note that the portrayal of Aeolus emphasizes his human aspects: his palace stands in a city (3) and he himself is imagined as a king who like other kings is a favourite of the gods (2); his name (cf. Myc. a_3-wo-ro/Aiwolos KN Ch 896, although not a personal name but given to a bull) and patronymic (son of Ἱππότης) are Greek; and the (Greek) idea that winds are minor deities is suppressed. The custodianship assigned to Aeolus need not be inconsistent with the notion that the gods can control the winds (cf. e.g. Poseidon, v 291–2), but there is a clear difference from the conception found in *Il.* (xvi 150, xxiii 200) and in Hes. (*Th.* 379–80, 870), and in certain later cults (see Wilamowitz, *Glaube*, i 265–6; Nilsson, *Geschichte*, 116–17; R. Hampe, 'Kult der Winde in Athen und Kreta', *Sitz.-Ber. Heidelberg* 1967, 1). The latter originated in much earlier times (cf. Myc. a-ne-mo i-je-re-ja/Anemōn hijerejāi KN Fp. 1. 10 etc.; Hampe, op. cit., 24–5). The poet uses elements of popular belief, particularly sailors' lore, rather than motifs from mythology and formal religion. The floating island is a common feature of seamen's tales (Germain, *Genèse*, 154), and Aeolus' essential function of binding the winds corresponds to the activities of wind-sorcerers, who feature in sea-folklore of every period the world over; cf. Radermacher, *Erzählungen*, 18–21; R. Strömberg, 'The Aeolus Episode, a Greek Wind Magic', *Acta Gotoburg.*, lvi (1950), 71–81; Page, *Folktales*, 73–8; the Schleswig story, Radermacher, 20–1, and Page, 77, is of particular interest. Modern Cretan wind magicians (Hampe, 16–17) are in the tradition of the Corinthian ἀνεμοκοῖται, Attic εὐδάνεμοι, and Empedocles κωλυσανέμας (DK 31 A 1, 278. 33–5). Aeolus' imprisonment of winds in a bag (κατέδησε 20), although there are no accompanying magic rites, corresponds to the sorcerer's laying of a wind (καταδεσμός); cf. Germain, *Genèse*, 179–91. On the poet's transformation of his traditional material see Reinhardt, 'Abenteuer', 91–4; Eisenberger, *Studien*, 147–9. The whole Aeolus episode is in many ways a foil to the encounter with the Phaeacians.

43

1–4. The *Αἰολίη νῆσος*, named after Aeolus, has sheer cliffs (4ᵇ: cf. v 412) and a bronze wall (cf. Alcinous' palace, vii 82–7) round the coast. As a floating island (3) it has no fixed location (see above and 55 n.), so there is little point to the attempts, from classical times onwards, to place it on the map (Thucydides sets it among the Lipari Islands (iii 88)). On the basis of P 31 (see West, *Papyri*, 247–8) G. Scheibner, op. cit. (ix 445 n.), 260, reconstructs as the original form of 3 *πάντη δέ τέ μιν*.

5: cf. *Il*. xxiv 603.

6. = *Il*. xxiv 604.

7. **ἀκοίτις** (P 31: -εις): see Chantraine, *Grammaire*, i 217. Marriage between brother and sister (cf. vii 54–68) adds a touch of the exotic.

10. **κνισῆεν**: 'full of steam from cooking'.   **αὐλή**: the transmitted *αὐλῇ*/ *αὐδή*/*αὐλή* are all questionable. *αὐλῇ* cannot be read as dat. loc. (K. F. Ameis); and *αὐδή*/*αὐλή* cannot be understood as the subject. We would expect a dat. belonging with *στεναχίζεσθαι*, along the lines of *δῶμα περιστεναχίζετο ποσσίν* (xxiii 146), and so various emendations have been proposed: *αὐλῇ*, i.e. *αὐλῷ* (Ernesti, Allen), *αὔλη*, i.e. *αὐλήσει* (Schäfer), *αὐλῷ* (Rochefort), *αὐδῇ* (Nitzsch), *ἀοιδῇ* (Duentzer), *ἀϋτῇ* (Agar), *οὔμη* (von der Mühll). They are all questionable in view of the meaning of *(περι-)στεναχίζεσθαι* ('groan'; cf. *Il*. ii 95, *Od*. x 454, xxiii 146); cf. Ameis–Hentze, *Anhang*, ii 78; Stanford ad loc. *ἄλμηι* (P 31) is no help (West, *Papyri*, 248).

12: see S. Laser, *Archaeologia* P, 4–5, 12–13, 31.

13. Odysseus resumes the narrative. *ἱκόμεσθα* refers back to 1 *ἀφικόμεθ'*.

14–18. **φίλει**: 'gave hospitality'. Everything is done *κατὰ μοῖραν* (16): the friendly welcome; the host's questions and the guest's reply; the request for *πομπή*; and the bestowal of a *ξείνιον*. We are reminded of the Cyclops' neglect of such ceremony (cf. ix 252–78, 527 ff.) and the contrasting entertainment on Scheria.

16. = xii 35.

19–24. Aeolus hands over (*μ'* = *μοι*) the wind-bag made from the skin of a nine-year-old ox, without, however, giving any indication of how and when Odysseus may use it. The bag is not in any case required for the homeward journey, since Aeolus sends the west wind. These oddities are to be explained by the poet's having reshaped traditional material from stories in which precise instructions played an important part. Here the mysterious bag serves to awaken the curiosity of the crew.

20. **βυκτάων** (*βύκτης, hapax*) has never been satisfactorily explained (cf. Chantraine, *Dictionnaire* s.v.): it could mean 'howling'.   **ἀνέμων ... κέλευθα**: 'the winds blowing in different directions'; on *κέλευθα* (for -ους cf. v 382) see West, *Papyri*, 250. *καταδέω* is a technical term from wind magic; the meaning is amplified in 23–4 as Aeolus seals the bag with a silver tie, so that no breath of wind can escape.

24. On the MS.-variation between subj. and opt. in purpose clauses see Chantraine, *Grammaire*, ii 269.

26–7. **οὐδ' ἄρ' ἔμελλεν** (sc. *ζέφυρος*) **ἐκτελέειν** (pres. or fut.): 'it was not our

44

fate that Zephyrus should complete his work'. 27 anticipates the outcome of the episode and the reason for it: they fail not because of another's fault, but through their own folly (cf. i 7).

28. =80; cf. xv 476.   ὁμῶς: here 'without stopping'. Odysseus arrives within sight of his homeland in nine days, exactly the length of time it had taken to travel from Cape Malea to the fairy-tale land in the west.

30. πυρπολέοντας (*hapax*; πέλομαι, πολέω): 'keep up, keep alive a watch-fire'. It is difficult to decide between ἐόντας and -ες (Aristarchus).

31. =xiii 282.

32. πόδα (cf. v 260): sheet, rope for tightening sails.

34-5. His companions appear throughout the *nostos* in opposition to Odysseus; that opposition takes various forms. Their failure to heed his warning nearly led to disaster in the Ciconian adventure (ix 43-61); and his failure to heed their anxious warning was equally fatal in the encounter with the Cyclops (ix 224-228; 228 ∼ 44); similarly, but with a happy outcome, at the end of that episode (492-500). Here the crew once more play a fatal role: mistrust, envy of their captain's supposed wealth (41-2), foolish anger, and plain curiosity impel them to open the bag. They do not break any moral laws here, or disobey an order from Aeolus or Odysseus: their actions are merely ἀφραδίαι (27), but bring to an end the happy journey home nevertheless.

36. Αἰόλου (codd.): the metrical difficulties are removed if we follow Payne Knight and others (cf. Ameis–Hentze, *Anhang*, ii 81) in assuming that the poet intended Αἰόλοο; cf. Chantraine, *Grammaire*, i 46-8; L. R. Palmer, in *Companion*, 95, H. Geiss, *LfgrE* s.v.; van der Valk, *Textual Criticism*, 66, disagrees.

37. =viii 328; xiii 167 etc.

38. 40-4 expand on φίλος καὶ τίμιος. Everywhere he goes Odysseus enjoys τιμή and hospitality (cf. 14), as is shown by his generous share of booty from Troy and his collection of valuable presents indicating the respect in which he is held by his hosts.

41. Zenodotus' reading ἐκτελέοντες is incorrect; see Chantraine, *Grammaire*, ii 168.

42. σὺν ... ἔχοντες: tmesis.

43. χαριζόμενος φιλότητι: 'showing kindness for friendship's sake'; cf. J. Latacz, op. cit. (ix 5-11 n.), 112-13.

46. νίκησεν (absol.): 'prevailed'.

50-3. The decision facing Odysseus here (μερμήριξα, ἠὲ ... ἦ) is radically different from the Iliadic deliberation scenes presenting an ethical choice between two alternatives. Here the delineation of Odysseus' options serves instead to illustrate his desperate plight, and his mood; the resolve to bear patiently the burden imposed on him (ἔτλην 53) characterizes the hero, whose outstanding quality of τλημοσύνη is increasingly manifested during these adventures; he is on the way to becoming πολύτλας; cf. ix 299-305 n. It cannot reasonably be said (but cf. von der Mühll, *Odyssee*, 721) that the lines reflect badly on the character of Odysseus; K. Rüter, *Odysseeinterpretationen*, 86.

45

51. πεσών ... ἐνί: here 'throw myself in'. On opt. ἀποφθίμην see Chantraine, *Grammaire*, i 381.

54-5. The released winds return to their ταμίης and take the fleet with them back to the island which has in the meantime moved: in the following six days' travel Odysseus reaches the Laestrygonian land, and from there moves on to Circe's island, which lies in the extreme east (cf. 80–132 n.).

56-8. = ix 85–7. Wilamowitz, *Untersuchungen*, 127, drew attention to the fact that these lines are less suitable here than in ix. His suspicions were confirmed by P 31. It is not certain, however, that the one line offered there is in fact the correct reading (Wilamowitz, *Heimkehr*, 2; G. Jachmann, *NAWG* (1949) 7, 209–10; D. del Corno, 'I papiri dell'Odissea anteriori al 150 a.C.', *RIL* 95 (1961), 39); cf. von der Mühll, *Odyssee*, 721.

59-76. The narrative concentrates on the contrast with the first visit to Aeolus. The gods' favourite, who had earlier received Odysseus and set him on his way with every honour, now dismisses him with a curse. Aeolus recognizes the wrath of heaven behind the crew's stupidity and its disastrous consequences, and will have no contact with those who incur that wrath (75). This double episode is probably an addition of the poet's to his traditional material.

59-60. On this occasion Odysseus takes only two companions with him (ὀπάζομαι: 'take as a companion') when calling on Aeolus. The scene is otherwise unchanged from 13 ff., except that their reception will be very different.

64-6. The content and tone of the questions (ἐξερέεινεν 14: ἐκ ... ἐρέοντο 63) are much altered. There is no concern here for the visitors' identity and fate, only surprise (tempered by suspicion) at their ill-success, despite Aeolus' generous assistance, and the inference that a δαίμων must have fallen on them (like a wolf attacking a flock of sheep; cf. *Il.* xvi 352, 356). For 64 cf. v 396.

66. = vii 320.

68-9. ἄασαν: here 'injured'; the reading of P 31, ἔβλαψαν, gives the right interpretation. It also suggests the complex of meanings surrounding the word ἄτη, from which it is derived; G. Müller, *Navicula Chilonensis* (Leiden, 1956), 6; J. Gruber, *Über einige abstrakte Begriffe des frühen Griech.* (Meisenheim, 1963), 60. On πρὸς τοῖσι ('and in addition') see Chantraine, *Grammaire*, ii 132. **ἀκέσασθε** ('heal'): here 'set right'.

70. = ii 240; iii 345. Zenodotus' ἀμειβόμενος is a secondary alteration: see van der Valk, *Textual Criticism*, 27.

71. ἄνεῳ: cf. ii 240, vii 144.

72-5. Aeolus refuses Odysseus further help, and sends him away. (ἔρρ': cf. v 133. θᾶσσον: cf. vii 152.) It is not θέμις for him (the favourite of the gods 2) to continue to be ξεινοδόκος (κομιζέμεν, ἀποπέμπειν) to a man hated by the gods. 75 not only repeats the order to leave (72), but also gives the explanation, and is scarcely dispensable (though it is missing in P 31). According to Payne Knight (cf. Schwartz, *Odyssee*, 314, and von der

Mühll, ad loc.) 75 was a late addition to the text, intended to replace 72–4, considered defective because of a supposed contradiction between οὐ ... θέμις ... ἀποπέμπειν and ἀπέπεμπε (76); cf. also West, *Papyri*, 255. In fact ἀποπέμπειν (73) in conjunction with κομίζειν signifies the πομπή required by θέμις, whereas ἀπέπεμπε δόμων (76) means 'he chased (us) out of the palace'.

74. κε (codd.) is to be preferred to τε (Doederlein, P 31; von der Mühll); see also Ruijgh, τε *épique*, 429.

77. = ix 62.

78–9. εἰρεσίης: (abstract from ἐρέτης, 'rower', with metrical lengthening of ἐρ-): 'rowing', caused by the crew's own ματίη (*hapax*; created for metrical convenience from μάτη; cf. adv. μάτην) or ἀφραδίη (27), by which they have lost their πομπή. When Aeolus sent the west wind (25) all that was necessary was to steer.

80–132. Several elements in the Laestrygonian episode belong to a widespread type of folk-tale: man-eating giants who attack travellers by pelting them with rocks; a girl showing the way; the absence of the master of the house, and the subsequent flight on his return (Radermacher, *Erzählungen*, 16–18; Page, *Folktales*, 25–31; Germain, *Genèse*, 415–17, refers to the scorpion-people of the Gilgamesh epic). It is, however, possible that here (unlike the Cyclops episode) the poet did not draw directly on folktale, but had as a model a pre-homeric Argonautica, in which Jason may have undergone a similar experience and from which he perhaps took the names Lamus and the spring Artakie (108) (Meuli, *Odyssee* 58, 90–1; for objections see Eisenberger, *Studien* 149–51). Of the folk-tale elements of earlier treatments, in which magic and sorcery may well have played a prominent part, only the superhuman size and cannibalism of the inhabitants are retained. And a number of realistic elements are introduced: the Laestrygonians are ruled by a king (110) with a Greek name; the centre of the community is a city (ἄστυ 104, 108, 118), from where the king is summoned, from the ἀγορή in fact (114); and the harbour is ideally situated (cf. 87–94 n.). Ironically it is the latter feature which proves to be Odysseus' undoing: the eleven ships of his companions fall an easy prey to the Laestrygonians in the harbour-basin and only Odysseus manages to escape with just the one ship, admiral of a fleet no longer. The importance of the episode is not so much its content as its function in the structure of the poem, as Odysseus' status is reduced (Reinhardt, 'Abenteuer', 95–6). Attempts were already made in classical times to identify the land of the Laestrygonians: the pseudo-Hesiodic *Catalogue* places it in the west (fr. 150. 25–7 M–W); Th. (vi 2) identifies the Cyclopes and Laestrygonians as the earliest inhabitants of Sicily (where later a Λαιστρυγόνιον πεδίον was pointed out). Theopompus, Strabo, Pliny, *et al.* followed Thucydides; some believed that the Laestrygonians had come to Sicily from Central Italy (Horace, *Carm.* iii 16. 24). However Crates of Mallus (Schol., x 86) inferred from 82–6 a localization in the extreme north; cf. van der Valk, *Textual Criticism*, 113–14. Modern scholars have either inferred a situation on the Propontis from A.R.'s location of the spring Artakie near Cyzicus (cf. 108 n.) or proposed locations even further afield (from Morocco to the Black Sea). There is, of course, no such country, and the story belongs in the realm of folktale. It is, however, clear that at this point Odysseus is in the mythical east, like his fore-runner Jason (cf. 54–5 n.), since it is not far to his next stop, the island of Circe. 82–6 do not conflict with this interpretation.

80: (cf. 28) = xv 476.

81–2. Λάμου ... Λαιστρυγονίην: the difficulties of interpretation may be due to the poet's presupposing knowledge in his audience of an older Argonautica (Page, *Folktales*, 31–2). Λάμος is probably meant to be understood as the name of the city founder (the king is Antiphates); it is by no means certain whether the following phrase should be read as Τηλέπυλον Λαιστρυγονίην 'the Laestrygonian town Telepylus' or as τ. qualifying Λ. as the name of the town; the meaning and morphology of τηλέπυλος are quite obscure.

82–6. The herdsmen bringing their animals in greet those who are on their way out with theirs: 'someone who did not need his sleep could earn double wages, one for tending herds and another for keeping watch over white sheep; because the paths taken by Nyx (Night) and Hemere (Day) are in the vicinity' (ἐγγύς 86; for a different interpretation see O. Becker, *Das Bild des Weges* ... (Berlin, 1937), 18, 213; Page, *Folktales*, 40). Crates' explanation, that the scene is set in the far north with its bright summer nights (F. Gisinger, *RE* Suppl. iv (1924), 534; Merkelbach, *Untersuchungen*, 201. 1; Lesky, *Homeros*, 111) is untenable (cf. R. Hennig, op. cit. (ix 21–7 n.), 79–85; H. Vos, 'Die Bahnen von Nacht und Tag', *Mnemosyne*, xvi (1963), 18–34). The other explanation offered in classical times, that the Laestrygonians drove their cattle to pasture after nightfall because of an infestation of gadflies, the sheep left to graze during the day being protected by their wool, (Hennig, loc. cit., A. Klotz, *Gymnasium*, lix (1952), 294–5) cannot be reconciled with the text. Nor are the difficulties removed by deleting 84–5 (Schwartz, *Odyssee*, 314–15, Germain, *Genèse*, 517–25). The lines convey a sense of the topographical strangeness of the legendary country in the far east (cf. H. Vos, loc. cit., L. Woodbury, *TAPhA* xcvii (1966), 60–1, W. Karl, *Chaos und Tartaros in Hesiods Theogonie* (diss. Erlangen, 1967), 104–6, R. Rebuffat, *Mél. d'archéologie et d'histoire*, lxxvii (1965), 336). The Laestrygonians live in a land of perpetual light just as the Cimmerians live in a country of unbroken darkness (xi 14–24); the east is home of the dawn (xii 3–4) while the sons of night, Hypnos and Thanatos, live in the west (Hes. *Th.* 758–9). The idea that in the land of the Laestrygonians the κέλευθοι of Night and Day are near is drawn from the same mythological conception as inspired Hes. to describe the regular meeting of the two goddesses in the mythical west (*Th.* 746–57).

85. ἄργυφα (only here and *Il.* xxiv 621): cf. Bechtel, *Lexilogus*, 58.

87–94. The description of the harbour emphasizes its perfect natural situation (not unlike a fiord). The bay is surrounded by cliffs which offer shelter; and the projecting ἀκταί leave only a narrow channel for access. Conditions within the harbour are, therefore, always calm (93–4). The similarity with the natural advantages of the Phaeacians' country (vi 262–4) is obvious (cf. B. Marzullo, op. cit., 449–50 (analytic)). But here the ideal berth for the fleet is the cause of its destruction; 87–94 prepare for 121–4.

88. τετύχηκε (here 'continues, extends') is remarkable for its form, corresponding to Attic; cf. plpf. ἐτετεύχεε (Hdt.); Shipp, *Studies*, 113.

91–6. οἵ γ' ... πάντες (cf. αἱ μὲν, i.e. νῆες, 92) is explained by αὐτὰρ ἐγὼν οἶος (95): while the main fleet shelters in the harbour Odysseus' flagship remains outside.   ἐπ' ἐσχατιῇ (96): cf. ix 180, 280. The apparent safety of the harbour leads to the fleet's destruction, while the relatively exposed position of the flagship, which Odysseus has chosen out of a sense of responsibility proper in a commander, allows escape (Eisenberger, *Studien*, 151).

97. = 148. **παιπαλόεσσαν:** cf. iii 170.

98–9. There is no sign of human habitation except for (οἶον) a wisp of rising smoke.

100–2. = ix 88–90.

103–7. The reconnaissance party (by heroic convention authorized to act as ambassadors; cf. 89) follow a path which looks (λείην) as if it is used for bringing down (καταγίνεον) wood (ὕλην) from the mountains to the city. On the way they meet the king's daughter who is drawing water from a spot lower down (cf. κατεβήσετο 107; on the form cf. i 330 n.).

108. The name of the spring Artakie is almost certainly drawn from an older Argonautica. The transfer of the Argonauts' journey from mythical to real geography in post-Homeric saga, which moved Jason's objective from the eastern limit of the world to Colchis, placed the Laestrygonian episode on the Propontian coast. The spring Artakie (AR i 957, still called Artaki) in Cyzicus was so named by the inhabitants when the Argonaut legends set the goal of Jason's quest at Colchis; naming the Laestrygonian spring Artakie is therefore not intended to place the action on the Propontis (R. Hennig, op. cit. (ix 21–7 n.), 84–5, refutes among others Wilamowitz, *Untersuchungen*, 168–9). The problem has been the subject of much discussion: cf. Ameis–Hentze, *Anhang*, ii 84–5, Schwartz, *Odyssee*, 264, Focke, *Odyssee*, 183; von der Mühll, *Odyssee*, 722. The best treatments remain K. Meuli, *RE* Suppl. v (1931), 533, Lesky, *Homeros*, 111.

110–11. (111 = xv 424). The messengers ask who rules the country and who his people are. On the unusual combination of οἶσιν with the indirect ὅς τις (Shipp, *Studies*, 80) and the remarkable use of the opt. see Chantraine, *Grammaire*, ii 224; on Aristarchus' variant τοῖσιν cf. Ameis–Hentze, *Anhang*, ii 85, van der Valk, *Textual Criticism*, 31. Only the first question is answered immediately as the girl shows the landing party the way to the palace (ἐπέφραδεν; cf. vii 49). The other is answered by the events which follow.

112–16. The similarity between the Laestrygonians and Cyclopes is emphasized by verbal parallels: the comparison (112–13) recalls ix 191–2 (on the

COMMENTARY

construction ὅσην ... κορυφήν see Ruijgh, τε épique, 556–7); the cannibalism of the king (115) is described in the words used of Polyphemus, ix 289–91, 311, 344). The metrically irregular ἕνᾱ is explained by the correct δύω at ix 289 (Shipp, *Studies*, 333). For other parallels see 118–19, 121–4, 129 nn. On Ἀντιφατῆα for -ην see K. Witte, *Glotta*, iii (1912), 110–11.

115: cf. iii 194.

117. On φυγή (only here and xxii 306), 'escape' (as opposed to φόβος, 'flight') see J. Gruber, op. cit. (68 n.), 30.

118–19. The Laestrygonians come on hearing their king's cry; cf. the Cyclopes, ix 399–401, except of course that the Laestrygonians come out of their houses, not caves.

120. Γίγασιν: cf. vii 59.

121–4. From the cliffs, i.e. above the harbour, the Laestrygonians hurl rocks at the Greek fleet. Unlike the Cyclops they are successful: the fleet is obliterated. There are echoes of the language of the *Iliad*: for κακὸς κόναβος (*hapax*) ... ἀγνυμενάων cf. *Il.* ix 573–4 ὅμαδος καὶ δοῦπος ὀρώρει | πύργων βαλλομένων; iv 450–1, viii 64–5 ἀνδρῶν | ὀλλύντων τε καὶ ὀλλυμένων; xvi 769 ἀγνυμενάων (verse end), etc. The brief simile at 124 is drawn from fishing: the Laestrygonians spear their prey, and then carry the bodies home for food (cf. n. below).

121. ἀνδραχθέσι (*hapax*) is almost certainly a neologism (K. Witte, op. cit. (112–16 n.), 126): the stones are so large that they are a weight (ἄχθος) too heavy for a man (ἀνήρ) to throw.

124. φέροντο: On the reading πένοντο, given by most MSS, see van der Valk, *Textual Criticism*, 178.

125–32. The section framed by ὄλεκον (125) and ὄλοντο (132) gives the main point of the story: the loss of the fleet. Odysseus saves only himself and the crew of his own ship, cutting the cable with his sword (for 127 cf. 96). The ironic contrast, as the Greeks cut and run to save their lives, is in the drawn sword, in the *Iliad* a heroic gesture (for 126 cf. *Il.* i 190). Odysseus' own retreat (criticized by Focke, *Odyssee*, 192) is hardly culpable since the odds are overwhelming. This is no time for heroics; there is no alternative to the cold-blooded decision to escape and patient acceptance (τλῆναι; cf. 50–3 n.) of the fate behind which Aeolus recognized the anger of the gods (72–5).

128: cf. ix 488.

129. = ix 489.

130. Comparison with vii 328 (ἀναρρίπτειν ἅλα πηδῷ; cf. also xiii 78) would appear to confirm the reading ἅλα (Rhianus and Callistratus) against ἅμα (codd.); cf. Nauck's cj. ἅλα πηδῷ (cf. Ameis–Hentze, *Anhang*, ii 85–6); on ἅμα see van Leeuwen ad loc. and van der Valk, *Textual Criticism*, 108. ἀναρρίπτειν may be a technical term, as is ἐμβάλλειν.

133–574. The encounter with Circe is also founded in folk-tale and magic. Witches who turn people into animals are found in numerous widely diffused folk-tales (Radermacher, *Erzählungen*, 4–9, Germain, *Genèse*, 130–50, 153–91, R. Wildhaber, 'Kirke und die Schweine', *Festschrift f.*

K. Meuli (Basle, 1951), 233–61, Page, *Folktales*, 49–69) as are magic wands, magic plants, magic formulae, antidotes to magic (amulets etc.), helpers in the fight against magic, the breaking of magic spells, and the release of captives from enchantment. There are two basic types of enchantress: the wicked witch, who simply transforms her victims into animals and destroys them, but who is herself finally overcome by a man, and meets her just deserts; and the beautiful, but no less dangerous seductress, who entices mortals into her bed, and metamorphoses them when she is tired of them—until she too meets her match (cf. the story of Bedr Basim and Queen Lab in the tale from the *Thousand and One Nights*; Page, *Folktales*, 60–2). Traits from both types are to be seen in Circe, but, as is characteristic of the epic treatment, the central elements of the folktale are restricted to a minimum. Pure magic is to be found only in the few lines which deal with the companions' actual metamorphosis and transformation back into human form. We are not told how, or indeed if, the magic plant Moly works on Circe. The action is set on as realistic a level as possible, and transferred from the alien realm of magic and irrational fantasy to the epic world: Circe does indeed live, as the traditional witch does, in a forest, but in a palace with a host of servants; the benign supernatural helper is replaced by the youthful god Hermes; and Odysseus is not the traditional folktale hero, who, whether by force or by cunning, applies a stronger magic, but the cautious, resourceful leader, caring for the welfare of his men, meeting sorcery with the drawn sword of the epic warrior. But the greatest advance on the traditional story is the depiction of Circe herself. She is a highly individual character, full of contradictions, yet no less convincing or compelling. Indeed part of her fascination lies in the multi-faceted nature of her character: daemonic and threatening on the one hand; on the other, offering aid and protection. She can glory in her terrible deeds, and then prove full of solicitude for those who have been rescued; both deceitful, and sincere, she is a passionate woman, who can also coolly give up the man she desires without protesting; a goddess, cold, distant, majestic, and at the same time a woman, warm, caring, and direct (cf. C. Segal, 'Circean Temptations', *TAPhA* xcix (1968), 419–42). In the poem, of course, we see these various aspects of her character appearing one after another: a different side of her nature appears after Odysseus' bold intervention, but this does not mean that there is any fundamental change in her at this point in the story. On the contrary, she remains the same until the last. The episode owes little, then, to traditional folk-tale (the encounter with Hermes and the description of the preparation of the feast (348–72) are purely epic); the poet draws more on *Il.* xxiv, and the debt is emphasized by several verbal echoes (G. Beck, 'Beobachtungen zur Kirkeepisode in der Odyssee', *Philologus*, cix (1965), 1–29). It is doubtful (Eisenberger, *Studien*, 152–67) whether there was a Circe episode in the old Argonautica (as suggested by Meuli, *Odyssee*, 97–114, and Merkelbach, *Untersuchungen*, 202). That epic, however, in telling of Aeetes and his daughter Medea, and their magic arts, may have mentioned Aeetes' sister

Circe. The poet may have given the anonymous witch of the folktale the name, genealogy, and country of the Circe of the Argonautica. The connection between Circe and Calypso and between the relevant scenes in bks. x and v is much disputed. Reinhardt ('Abenteuer', 96–111) argues convincingly against any analytical interpretation (cf. *inter al.* Wilamowitz, *Untersuchungen*, 115–16, Schwartz, *Odyssee*, 53); we can at most ask which of the two figures is morphologically the earlier (Woodhouse, *Composition*, 46–53). W. Bauer finds a clue to Circe's antecedents in her name (κίρκος, hawk, falcon): he argues that the story has its roots in seafarers' tales of destructive birds of prey (*Festschrift f. K. J. Merentitis* (Athens, 1972), 41–4). A. Stassinopoulos-Skiadis, *Der Kirkemythos. Dichterische Behandlung und allegorische Deutung* (diss. Kiel, 1962), and B. Paetz, *Kirke und Odysseus: Überlieferung und Deutung von Homer bis Calderon* (Berlin, 1970), discuss the post-Homeric treatments of the Circe episode: in Greek and Etruscan art (E. Lessing, *Die Odyssee* (Freiburg im Breisgau, 1965), pls. 69–71, 74, 75, O. Touchefeu-Meynier, 'Ulysse et Circé', *REA* xciii (1961), 264–70), and Roman poetry (Verg. *A.* vii 10–24, Ovid, *Met.* 14; cf. Segal, op. cit., 428–42).

133–4. = ix 82–3, 565–6.

135–9. Circe and Aeetes are both children of Helios and Perse, daughter of Oceanus; cf. Hes. *Th.* 956–62, which gives Medea's name as well, and Perse's as Περσηΐς. In the old Argonautica Helios' palace was in Aea (cf. Mimnermos fr. 11. 2 D, 11a West) in the extreme east; here Helios' daughter lives on the island Αἰαίη ('belonging to Αἶα'; Wilamowitz, *Untersuchungen*, 165; cf. Αἰήτης, 'the man from Aea'), which likewise lies in the east, xii 3–4) and indeed very near to Oceanus (507–8). Odysseus is therefore following in the footsteps of Jason. Only after Homer was the Argonauts' goal identified as Colchis (= Αἶα, Hdt. vii 193), while Circe's island was at an early date set in the western Mediterranean. According to Hes. (*Th.* 1011–15) the sons of Odysseus and Circe, Agrius and Latinus, ruled over the Τυρσηνοί; this view was widely accepted in the ancient world, and can be seen in the name of Capo Circeo (north of Naples). See further the fundamental study by A. Lesky, 'Aia', *WS* lxiii (1948), 22–68.

135: cf. 1.

136. (= xi 8, xii 150). **αὐδήεσσα:** cf. v 334, vi 125.

137. Aeetes is described as ὀλοόφρων ('meaning mischief, baleful') for his part in the Argonaut story. The epithet also hints at the danger to come; cf. δεινή (136).

138. On φαεσίμβροτος (prob. with shift of meaning from 'seeing mankind' to 'giving light to men'; cf. xiv 502) see T. Knecht, *Geschichte der griech. Komposita vom Typ τερψίμβροτος* (diss. Zurich, 1946), 9.

141. (141^b = ix 142^b). The formulaic ναύλοχον λιμένα (cf. iv 846) gives a clue to the happy outcome of the episode.

142: cf. ix 74; Shipp, *Studies*, 331. 1.

143–4. = 75–6.

145–50. The episode begins as the Laestrygonian venture did, with Odysseus seeking from a high vantage point to learn something of the country; again, smoke is the first evidence of habitation (ἔργα βροτῶν 147: ἀνδρῶν ἔργα 98). The parallel with 97–9 is intentional; A. Rüdiger's doubts as to the authenticity of 148 (= 98; cf. Schwartz, *Odyssee*, 315) can therefore be dismissed (Ameis–Hentze, *Anhang*, ii 86).

145. ἔγχος and φάσγανον are mentioned because they are soon to play an important part (158–71, 321–45).

149. εὐρυοδείης: cf. iii 453 n.

150. The narrative perspective changes once more to that of Odysseus looking back with hindsight. The style here is much closer to that of the epic poet; cf. W. Suerbaum, op. cit. (ix 182–92 n.), 150–77; 150ᵇ = *Il.* xi 118ᵇ.

151–5: Some have objected to the formulation of this deliberation scene (cf. ix 299–318, 420–4): E. Kapp (ap. C. Voigt, op. cit. (ix 299–305 n.), 37–8) proposed deletion of 153–6; see also Merkelbach, *Untersuchungen*, 183–4. μερμήριξα (aor.) with inf. does not here mean 'I considered whether to, I was undecided', but that at the sight of the smoke 'a plan suddenly came to me'. Then Odysseus thinks of a second, better plan, expressed with the formulaic line 153, which elsewhere (*Il.* xiii 458, xiv 23, xvi 652, *Od.* xviii 93, xxii 338, xxiv 239) concludes consideration of alternatives; it is thus used untypically here, but makes good sense. The second plan, introduced by ὧδε, is explained in 154–5: Odysseus decides to see that his men are fed before sending out a reconnaissance party (πυθέσθαι 155: cf. πυθέσθαι 152, with a change of subject). For further discussion see Erbse, *Beiträge*, 201; Eisenberger, *Studien*, 153. 16.

156–63. Some god (cf. 141) ensures the success of Odysseus' plan by providing the δεῖπνον in the form of a stag sent across Odysseus' path (εἰς ὁδὸν αὐτήν 157).

156. = xii 368.

157: cf. iv 364. The line is hardly surprising as G. Beck, op. cit. (133–574 n.), 4–5, supposes; cf. Eisenberger, *Studien*, 153. 17.

158. On the accentuation of ὑψίκερων see Chantraine, *Grammaire*, i 189.

160. ἔχεν: here 'tormented'.

161. On the correct reading κατὰ κνῆστιν ('on the spine') see Bechtel, *Lexilogus*, 27; Leumann, *Wörter*, 49.

162–5. The stag's death is described in the terms used in the *Iliad* for the death of heroes in battle: 162 = *Il.* xvi 346; 163 (= xix 454) = *Il.* xvi 469; 164 ~ *Il.* vi 65; 164ᵇ = *Il.* xvi 862ᵇ. πλήττειν ἔγχει (cf. 145)/δουρί (only here and *Il.* xvii 294–6): in both cases the fatal blow is struck at close quarters (cf. 158ᵇ; αὐτοσχεδίην *Il.* xvii 294), surely with a spear-thrust; inaccurately explained by Trümpy, *Fachausdrücke*, 100.

167–8. ὅσον τ' ὄργυιαν ('a fathom long'): cf. ix 325 n. πεῖσμα belongs with ἐϋστρεφές, ἀμφοτέρωθεν ('from both sides', i.e. 'from both ends, with both hands') with πλεξάμενος.

169. καταλοφάδεια: (*hapax*; 'hanging from my neck') prepositional *Rektionskompositum*; the form in -ῖα (with metrical lengthening) is used adverbially; cf. Bechtel, *Lexilogus*, 188, Chantraine, *Grammaire*, i 101, 176.

170–1. The unusual size of the beast (δεινοῖο πελώρου) requires an unusual method of carrying: Odysseus ties the animal's legs together and puts his head through, so that the carcass hangs down forward (κατὰ λόφον); Odysseus can then lean on his ἔγχος with both hands; cf. Heubeck, *ZAnt* xxiv (1974), 37–41; inaccurately explained by H.-G. Buchholz and G. Jöhrens, *Archaeologia* J, 121–2.

172: cf. ix 482.

173. = 547, xii 207. On παρασταδόν (adv., 'approaching') see Risch, *Wortbildung*, 365–6.

174–7. Odysseus tells his crew that they are not yet fated to die, so they should feast while there are still rations on board. (The actual words used ('to go down to Hades') are dramatic irony: in xi they do indeed go down to Hades, although not as Odysseus means here.) His words are somewhat strange in view of his successful hunt (Beck, op. cit. (133–574 n.), 4–5); his intention is, apparently, to surprise his men, and in this he succeeds (θηήσαντο 180). 174–5 (γὰρ) explain the invitation to eat (ἀλλ' ἄγετ' ... 176). On βρῶσις, πόσις, βρώμη see P. Chantraine, *BSL* lix (1964), 11–23.

178. = 428, xii 222.

181. = iv 47.

182: cf. ii 261ᵃ, iii 66ᵇ.

183–7. = ix 556–60.

188. = ix 171, xii 319.

189–97. The structure of the speech is that of 174–7 (other examples: xii 154–64, 208–21, 320–3, xxii 70–8): the γὰρ sentence (190–2ᵇ) explains the proposal which follows (ἀλλὰ φραζώμεθα ... 192ᵇ). The formulaic line 189 (=xii 153a, 271, 340) was already rightly suspected by the Alexandrians (probably on account of the duplication involved 189–90); it comes from a different type of speech altogether (found at xii 271–6, 340–51) and in fact no more belongs here than it does after xii 153 (see xii 153a n.). The comment that they do not know which way east and west lie (190, amplified 191–2) is strange coming after 187, and also in view of xii 3–4 (A. Lesky, *WS* lxiii (1948), 66). On the other hand 187 is merely a standard formula for daybreak, and Odysseus at this point does not yet know the exact position of Aeaea. His intention in emphasizing the difficulty of their situation (on a lonely island in the vast ocean (195), with no bearings for the next stage of their journey) is to reinforce his appeal for a μῆτις (an idea on how to save the situation). His claim to be bankrupt of ideas himself is however mere pretence: in reality the grounds he gives (γὰρ 194) for his alleged perplexity (including the report of his own reconnaissance (146–50)) indicate his own μῆτις, without explicitly stating it. They must get their bearings again, exploiting an observation which promises success: the smoke indicates that the island is inhabited. Thus his speech achieves exactly the effect needed for a plan which he has good reason not to present *expressis verbis*. Analytical objections to his speech (as in Ameis–Hentze, *Anhang*, ii 87–9, and latterly Merkelbach, *Untersuchungen*, 184–5) are thus unjustified; see van der Valk, *Textual Criticism*, 274–5 and Eisenberger, *Studien*, 154.

190. On variants γάρ τ' and γάρ cf. van der Valk, *Textual Criticism*, 46, Hoekstra, *Modifications*, 30, and Ruijgh's extensive discussion, τε *épique*, 737 ff.

192. ἀννεῖται: i.e. ἀνα-νέεται.

194: cf. 148.

195. ἀπείριτος (*hapax*) should probably be distinguished from ἀπειρέσιος (cf. xi 118 n.), and seen as derived from *ἀ-περ(ι)-ι-τος; cf. Schulze, *Quaestiones*, 116. 3, Bechtel, *Lexilogus*, 49, Chantraine, *Dictionnaire* s.v. ἀπειρέσιος. ἐστεφάνωται: 'is set around like a crown'.

196–7: cf. 149–50.

198–201. The reaction of the crew (they break down and cry) shows that they have understood all too well their captain's intention to send out another reconnaissance party: they remember what happened when shore parties encountered the Cyclopes and Laestrygonians; and they also know that on this occasion there is no option available, and so raise no objection.

198. (= 566, xii 277): cf. iv 481 n.

200. The authenticity of the line has been doubted (Kirchhoff, V. Bérard, Schwartz, Focke); it is, however, required by the logic of 198–201 (cf. n. above; Marzullo, op. cit. (ix 526–35 n.), 16; Merkelbach, *Untersuchungen*, 183. 1).

202. (= 568). The line incorporates a commonplace on the futility of weeping: cf. οὐ γάρ τις πρῆξις πέλεται κρυεροῖο γόοιο (*Il.* xxiv 524), ἀλλ' οὐ γάρ τις ἔστιν πρᾶξις τάδε μυρομένοις (Bacchylides, *Epin.* v 162–3); for κατὰ πρῆξιν cf. *Od.* iii 72 = ix. 253. Here the aphorism is incorporated in the narration (ἐγίγνετο): 'but in vain (cf. J. C. B. Lowe, *Glotta*, li (1973), 39) for their tears did not help them'.

203–9. Odysseus proceeds with his plan without further explanation. He divides his crew into two groups (δίχα ἠρίθμεον) of 22 men, led by himself and Eurylochus respectively. The lot falls on Eurylochus' party to explore the country. There are ironic echoes of the *Iliad*, where decisions on a much grander heroic scale are also taken by lot (205 ∼ *Il.* iii 316; 207[a] = *Il.* vii 182[a], cf. iii 325).

210–43. Again the narrative perspective is that of Odysseus telling the story after the event (cf. 150 n.; F. Müller, op. cit. (ix 182–92 n.), 107). Odysseus learned about what is here related only later, from Eurylochus' report, the advice of Hermes (cf. 233–40 n.), and his own experience. The description of Circe's palace is brief and stereotyped to concentrate attention on what happens there. The account of the animals' strange behaviour is augmented by a brief reference to their 'past'. Everything from the beginning of the passage serves as preparation for the encounter with Circe.

211. περισκέπτῳ (cf. 426 n.): 'elevated' (cf. W. Richter, *Archaeologia* H, 29).

212. ὀρέστεροι: see M. Wittwer, *Glotta*, xlvii (1970), 60–1. μιν belongs with δώματα (or χώρῳ) rather than with Circe.

213. κατέθελξεν: (κατα-)θέλγειν always means an activity producing the alteration (usually temporary) of normal thought and consciousness, not magical transformation of the outward form or appearance. It can be brought about by words (i 57), songs (xii 40), trickery (*Il.* xxi 604), ἔρως (xviii 212), a magic staff (*Il.* xxiv 343), etc. The passage must refer then to animals whose normal behaviour has been altered by Circe's θέλγειν: thus lions and wolves behave like dogs (216). ἐπεί is probably explicative ('by her φάρμακα') rather than temporal ('after application of the φ.'); cf. 236–7, 290–1, 318. This is supported by the simile, 216–17: here μειλίγματα (*hapax*; cf. μειλίσσω) take the place of φάρμακα as 'the means by which the ἄναξ makes gentle (μειλίσσει) the dogs' θυμός'. Though it may be natural to interpret these lines in terms of the familiar folk-tale motif of men transformed into beasts (cf. 239), in fact the poet has at this point deliberately excluded that traditional element of magic from his story. φάρμακον is Mycenaean (*pa-ma-ko* PY Un 1314).

220. ἐν προθύροισι/εἰνὶ θύρῃσι: the choice of reading is difficult because πρόθυρον/-α can mean either the palace door or the gate to the courtyard; the majority of MSS gives εἰνὶ θ. in 310, which describes a parallel situation, so that reading is probably to be preferred here also. The poet appears not to allow anything more than θύραι to the dwellings of these figures drawn from folk-tale (cf. ix 417 (Polyphemus), xii 256 (Scylla)), even though Circe's home is particularly magnificent (210–11). The dwellings of heroes and gods are described in quite different terms; see for example i 103, viii 304, 325 (cf. nn. ad loc., Ameis–Hentze, *Anhang*, ii 90, van der Valk, *Textual Criticism*, 129).

221–3. (cf. v 61–2). Here for the first time the similarity between Circe and Calypso is brought out by parallelism in the language; cf. also 223 and v 231. **λεπτά:** already in Myc. an epithet for λίνον: *re-po-to/lepton* PY Un 1322.

224. The line is formulaic; cf. iii 417 etc., iii 400 etc.

225–7. The singing gives the hearers some idea of the activity of the occupant. **ἀμφιμέμυκεν** ('echoes round') is a departure from the usual sense of μυκ-. On 225 cf. Hoekstra, *Modifications*, 116. After 225 a few MSS add ὅ σφιν ἐὺ φρονέων ἀγορήσατο καὶ μετέειπεν, which van der Valk (*Textual Criticism*, 278) regards as perhaps authentic.

230. (= 256, 312). These and similar parallels between 220–37 and 310–20 highlight the difference in Odysseus' reactions. Thus 220–37 prepare for the later scene; cf. C. Segal, *TAPhA* xcix (1968), 427.

231. κάλει: here 'invited them inside'.

233. The second half of the line is formulaic (cf. i 145 etc.); Heubeck, *Acta Mycenaea*, ii (Salamanca, 1972), 78.

234–43. The lines are modelled on *Il.* xi 638–40, where Hecamede prepares a κυκεών with Pramnian wine (κύκησε οἴνῳ Πραμνείῳ) in Nestor's δέπας; that mixture too contained τυρός and ἄλφιτα (cf. μέλι χλωρόν 631). The crucial difference is the addition of φάρμακα which give the invigorating mixture its magical power. Later references to Pramnian wine in Hippocrates and comedy show that it is not a Homeric invention; the name, which came to indicate a particular type of wine, probably originally referred to origin (cf. W. Richter, *Archaeologia* H, 129–30). The magical events and the witch herself originate in different conceptions; cf. Radermacher, *Erzählungen*, 4–5, 10–11; Eisenberger, *Studien*, 154. The first motif, the offer of food which makes the eater forget his previous life, has already been used in the Lotus-eaters episode (236 ~ ix 92–7), the difference being that there the λωτός (~φάρμακα 236) is not given for evil purposes. The second motif, metamorphosis into animal shape, in which magic wands or ointments traditionally feature prominently, is combined here with the first to form a highly complex scene. After taking the φάρμακα Odysseus' companions forget their home, i.e. their memory of their previous life and their sense of identity are lost. This amnesia is not a loss of νοῦς (this is retained: ἔμπεδος 240). The antidote (φάρμακον ἄλλο 392) restores their sense of identity, whereupon they recognize their master once more (396). The transformation proceeds from 237; here the ῥάβδος plays a role which certainly goes beyond that of a goad for driving herds, (as claimed by W. B. Stanford, *Hermathena*, lxvi (1945), 69–70), as in 319–20, where a magic formula accompanies the touch of the ῥάβδος. In Circe's malevolent activity we have a counterpart to the help proferred by two female characters in the heroic world: Helen, who adds a φάρμακον to wine (iv 219–32) to induce forgetfulness (κακῶν ἐπίληθον ἁπάντων iv 221), and Athena who with her ῥάβδος transforms Odysseus into a beggar (xiii 429–38) and then again restores him to his former state (xvi 172–6).

238. On συφεοῖσιν (and συφειοῦ 389) see Wyatt, *Lengthening*, 225.

239–43. φωνήν, τρίχας, and δέμας are *acc. limit.* (acc. of respect), dependent on κεφαλάς; κεφαλή here must mean something like 'body form' (cf. *Il.* iii 168, ix 548, xi 72, xxiii 348; H. Krafft, *Vergleichende Untersuchungen zu Homer und Hesiod* (Göttingen, 1963), 41–2). The impf. ἔχον is striking; it is presumably intended to mark the process of metamorphosis. καὶ πόδας (240) is a cj. of Zenodotus; cf. Krafft, op. cit., 41. 4. On the problems of 239–43 see Schwartz, *Odyssee*, 315–17 (with far-reaching analytical conclusions; cf. also von der Mühll, ad loc., Merkelbach, *Untersuchungen*, 185. 1). He objects to the following: τε remains short before τρ- in τρίχας (239), (but see Schwyzer, *Grammatik*, i 168), the contraction of νοῦς guaranteed by metre (240) (but see Meister, *Kunstsprache*, 181), and the acephalous beginning πὰρ ἄκυλον, which is however surely modelled on πάρειπών *Il.* xi 792 etc. (cf. πάρέχῃ xix 113); see Wyatt, *Lengthening*, 237. 3.

241. ὣς οἱ μὲν ... is formulaic, but has the particular function of rounding off 239–40. On ἔερχατο (regular plpf.) as basis for the artificial forms ἔρχαται (283) and ἐρχατόωντο (xiv 15), see Leumann, *Wörter*, 180–1.

242–3. ἄκυλον: fruit of the Quercus ilex (πρῖνος). βάλανον: here perhaps the fruit of the Quercus aegilops (φηγός). κρανείης: 'cornel tree'. On χαμαιευνάδες (only here and xiv 15) and χαμαιεῦναι (*Il.* xvi 235) see Risch, *Wortbildung*, 210.

244. The line of the story broken off at 232 is here resumed; Εὐρύλοχος δ' is prepared by ὣς οἱ μὲν ... (241); on αὖψ' (which is preferable to ἄψ) see Ameis–Hentze, *Anhang*, 23.

245. ἀδευκέα (cf. iv 489 n.) πότμον: amplifies ἀγγελίην ἑτάρων.

246. On δύνατο see Meister, *Kunstsprache*, 40–2.

247. The line is modelled on *Il.* ix 9 and *Od.* vi 131; on βεβολημένος see Chantraine, *Grammaire*, i 435.

248. δακρυόφιν: cf. vi 152 n. 'His heart foreboded γόος': i.e. he guessed that his experience (of the disappearance of his companions) would be cause for mourning.

249. ἀγασσάμεθ' (von der Mühll accepts the alternative reading ἀγαζόμεθ'): Eurylochus' behaviour gives his comrades cause to ἀγάσασθαι, and so he is bombarded with questions. On the complex meaning of ἀ. cf. J. Irmscher, *Götterzorn bei Homer* (Leipzig, 1950), 19–20; H. J. Mette, *LfgrE* s.v. ἄγαμαι; W. Schadewaldt, *SHAW* (1959), 2. 18. 14. The companions are shocked and disturbed, but also frustrated by Eurylochus' long silence (246), and anxious to know further details.

250. ὄλεθρον is how the situation appears to Eurylochus: the men did not return, and so are presumed dead. κατέλεξεν: as in 16 (cf. ix 14 n.).

251–60. The phraseology of Eurylochus' report draws extensively on the preceding account: 252 ~ 210 (with the necessary adaptation καλά); 253 = 211 (missing in most MSS and Eust.; perhaps inauthentic); 254 ~ 221–2; 255 ~ 229; 256–7 = 230–1; 258 ~ 232.

261–2. The lines are written in the style of the Iliadic arming scenes, and in fact the sword does play an important role later (294, 321). ἀμφὶ ... (βαλόμην) τόξα: 'I girded myself with all my archery equipment', i.e. the γωρυτός, complete with strap and carried on the back, containing both bow and arrows; cf. *Il.* xxi 490–504, *Od.* xxi 23–60, *h.Ap.* 6–8, L. Deubner, *SPAW* (1938), 24. 28–9.

263. αὐτὴν (= τὴν αὐτήν; cf. R. Renehan, *Glotta*, l (1972), 161). ὁδόν: on the construction see L. R. Palmer, in *Companion*, 130. ἠνώγεα: (with synizesis) cf. ix 44 n. αἶψ' is probably to be preferred to ἆψ (only in P); see van der Valk, *Textual Criticism*, 131. 5.

265. (= ii 362 etc.). The line is surely an interpolation (Ameis–Hentze, *Anhang*, ii 91–2); the strongest evidence against authenticity is the parallel of *Il.* vi 45–6.

266–9. There are numerous verbal parallels with *Il.* xxiv; the following scenes are based on Priam's journey to Achilles; cf. M. Groeger, *Philologus*, lix (1900), 222–3, G. Beck, loc. cit. (133–574 n.). Eurylochus' warning and advice to flee parallel the speech of Idaeus, *Il.* xxiv 354–7.

268. σῶν: 'tuorum'; apparently misunderstood by Aristarchus as σόον; cf. Ameis–Hentze, *Anhang*, ii 92.

272ª. = *Il.* xxiv 476ª.

274–9. Like Priam, Odysseus meets Hermes in the form of a youth, which is striking because the god was normally seen in the archaic age as bearded. In the *Iliad* the youthful appearance of Hermes is justified by the poet's intention to contrast youth with honourable old age. Here there is no such justification; the poet is merely following his model (K. Reinhardt, *Die Ilias und ihre Dichter* (Göttingen, 1961), 479–82). Kirchhoff's rejection of 278

(= *Il.* xxiv 348), *Odyssee*, 219, mistakes the poet's intention. It is significant
that in the different world of the *Odyssey* Odysseus who does not need a
guide is here met by Hermes with instruction and guidance (Eisenberger,
Studien, 155). Wilamowitz, *Untersuchungen*, 125-6, refutes the explanation
given by Kirchhoff (*Odyssee*, 305; followed by Merkelbach, *Untersuchungen*,
203-4, Page, *Folktales*, 56) for Odysseus' immediately speaking of Hermes,
although at this stage he cannot know the stranger's identity, as the
remnant of an earlier third-person narrative.

277. χρυσόρραπις: as in v 87.

279. On ὑπηνήτης see Risch, *Wortbildung*, 35.

280. = ii 302 etc.

281. On I. Bekker's correction δὴ αὖτε (cf. ix 311) for δ' αὖτ' see Ameis–
Hentze, *Anhang*, ii 92.

283. ἔρχαται: cf. 241 n.   **ὥς τε σύες:** see Ruijgh, *τε épique*, 577 (who refers
also to *Il.* xviii 518, 539). Hermes means that the crew, who have been
metamorphosed into pigs, are kept in pens like real pigs; Odysseus, who as
yet does not know of their transformation, understands him to mean that
the men are being treated like animals.

285. νοστήσειν: here 'return safely'.

286. ἐκλύσομαι (not the same as λύσομαι 284) **κακῶν** here almost means 'I
shall protect you from harm'.

287. Hermes puts into Odysseus' hand a φάρμακον (cf. τῇ, τόδε); the nature
of the φ. is not revealed until 302-6.

289–301. Hermes' intention is to instruct Odysseus in all of Circe's ὀλοφώϊα
δήνεα, but the promised account is in fact somewhat curtailed after 290 by
the directions on the use of the φάρμακον. With the words ἐρέω δὲ ἕκαστα
(292), picking up πάντα ἐρέω (289), Hermes proceeds to advise Odysseus on
how to deal with further δήνεα. Schwartz's objections, *Odyssee*, 317, to the
authenticity of 289-301, can hardly be sustained; it is no detraction from
Odysseus' μῆτις that he follows the advice of the god.

289. ὀλοφώϊα: cf. iv 410 n. On δήνεα (only here and xxiii 82, *Il.* iv 361) see
Chantraine, *Dictionnaire* s.v. On 289 ~ iv 410 cf. W. Theiler, *MH* vii
(1950), 104; Merkelbach, *Untersuchungen*, 179. 1.

290–2. Circe will prepare a κυκεών with φάρμακα (cf. 234–6), but Hermes'
ἐσθλὸν φάρμακον will prevent the λυγρὰ φ. from having their usual effect
(θέλγειν: cf. 236).

293–301. To counteract Circe's second ploy (the touch of her ῥάβδος:
293 ~ 238) Odysseus must take the initiative himself, draw his sword and
make as if to kill her (295; cf. Ruijgh, *τε épique*, 577). Here he must stand as
the heroic man of action against a figure from the non-heroic world of
magic (cf. ix 299–305 n.). Circe will be shocked into inviting Odysseus to
share her bed, an action which she intends as preparation for a third
assault. Hermes shows Odysseus how to foil this attempt and achieve a
decisive success. He instructs him to accept the goddess's invitation: it is his
only chance to gain access to the palace as a guest (κομίζειν, cf. 73) and to
free his companions. He must, however, impose a condition: a solemn oath

59

not to attempt against him personally (τοι αὐτῷ) 'any other evil trick' (as opposed to the πῆμα that has befallen the crew), i.e. not to take advantage of him when he has laid aside his armour, to rob him of his manhood (to make him κακός and ἀνήνωρ). 301 explains the concept πῆμα. 300 and 301 therefore operate on different syntactic levels: 300, dependent on κέλεσθαι, gives the content and wording of the oath; 301, dependent on ὁμόσσαι, gives the reason for it. The oath obviates the danger of sleeping with the witch, and prepares the way for rescuing the crew. 289–301 are not contradictory: on the contrary, in the following lines everything happens as explained here. The parallels with the Calypso episode (300–1 = v 178–9, 342 ~ v 177) do not allow of analytical conclusions either (Focke, *Odyssee*, 266–9, and Reinhardt, 'Abenteuer', 106–7, 501. 19, rightly oppose Wilamowitz, *Untersuchungen*, 121, on this point).

299. The oath demanded here, in contrast to Eurycleia's oath by the gods (θεῶν μέγαν ὅρκον ii 377) is that which the gods themselves swear (cf. *Il.* xiv 271 ff., xv 36 ff., *Od.* v 184 ff.). μακάρων as a substantive (without θεῶν) is noteworthy; the line is based on formulae such as those found in ii 377 and x 343 (=v 178).

301. The motif of the danger here only obliquely indicated appears to be oriental in origin (cf. Gilgamesh and Ishtar; Germain, *Genèse*, 263–4).

302–6. The φάρμακον, described at 287 as a φ. ἐσθλόν, which Hermes had picked while speaking and now gives to the hero, has a black root and milk-white petals; we are also told that the gods call it μῶλυ. There are several difficulties with the passage. φύσιν (here only in Homer; its earliest occurrence) is generally explained with reference to 304–6: Hermes is thought to show Odysseus the 'natural form of the plant' (equating φύσις with φυή; cf. Stanford, ad loc., F. Heinimann, *Nomos und Physis* (Darmstadt, 1965), 16–17); H. Jones, *Glotta*, li (1973), 16–17, explains it a little differently as the 'process of growing'); but δεικνύναι may mean not only showing something visible, but also giving instruction (cf. xii 25, Hes. *Op.* 502), so that φύσιν ἔδειξε refers to Hermes' explanation of 287–92; φύσις would thus mean the hidden power within the plant. The name of the plant is an example of the so-called 'language of the gods' (cf. H. Güntert, *Von der Sprache der Götter und Geister* (Halle, 1921), Heubeck, *WJA* iv (1949/50), 197–218, P. Kretschmer, *AAWW* iv (1947), 13–26); but unlike the *Iliad* (i 403–4, ii 813–14, xiv 291, xx 74), the *Odyssey* (here and at xii 61) does not give the name in the language of mortals as well; the object thus belongs exclusively to the world of the immortals (cf. J. Clay, *Hermes*, c (1972), 127–31). μῶλυ may be related to Sanskrit *mūlam* ('root'), which would mean that it was an early technical term in the practice of magic. The idea that it is impossible (or at least very difficult) for a mortal to dig up the plant is to be connected with ideas widespread in folklore. The ancients endeavoured to identify μῶλυ botanically (following Ps.Theophrastus e.g. Pliny *HN* xxv 26; for further details see H. Rahner, *Griech. Mythen in christlicher Deutung* (3rd edn., Zurich, 1966), 164–96; English edition *Greek Myths and Christian Mystery* (London, 1963),

179–222); for a modern attempt see H. Philipp, 'Das Gift der Kirke', *Gymnasium*, lxvi (1959), 509–16; on the later allegorical tradition, expounding μ. as logos (Stoic) or παιδεία (Neo-platonist), and Christian development of the idea, see Rahner, op. cit., 232–83.

307. (= *Il.* xxiv 694): cf. 266–9 and 274–9 nn.

309. = iv 427, 572.

310. (= 220; cf. n. ad loc.). The difference between Odysseus' meeting and his crew's encounter with Circe is highlighted by a number of parallels in the language here and in the following lines.

311. ~ 229, 255; 312 = 230, 256; 313 ~ 231 = 257; 314 ~ 233 (with an important variation).

315. (= 367 = i 131). There is no cogent argument against this line, despite its omission by Aristarchus and the suspicions of some modern critics; cf. van der Valk, *Textual Criticism*, 271.   θρόνου (314) and θρῆνυς: cf. Myc. *to-no*/*thornos*, *thr̥nos*, *ta-ra-nu*/*thrānus*; Ventris–Chadwick, *Documents*, 342–3.

316–20. 316–17 are a variation on 234–6, but the first significant deviations from the previous scene are in 318–19 (cf. 237–8). As Hermes promised (291–2) the φάρμακον fails to have any effect on Odysseus (οὐδέ μ' ἔθελξε); the μῶλυ, which is not actually mentioned at this point, appears to be effective simply by being carried about the hero's person. Striking the companions with her ῥάβδος Circe had driven them into the sties (cf. 238); her attempt to treat Odysseus in the same way fails, and she vainly utters a kind of spell (320; there is no parallel to this in 238–9). It is significant that this spell, intended to force Odysseus to join his companions, contains no explicit reference to metamorphosis. On δέ τε/δὲ τὸ (317) see Ruijgh, τε *épique*, 697.

320. On μετά with gen. see Chantraine, *Grammaire*, ii 119.

321–4. Odysseus acts as instructed by Hermes (321–2 correspond to 294–5). The effect of the heroic gesture is described in the language of the *Iliad*: 323ᵃ = *Il.* v 343ᵃ; 323ᵇ = *Il.* xxi 68ᵇ; 324 = *Il.* xi 815 (cf. 265 n.).

324. The reading μ' ὀλοφυρομένη is to be preferred to με λισσομένη; cf. van der Valk, *Textual Criticism*, 104; Schwartz, *Odyssee*, 317, takes a different view.

325–35. Here as elsewhere (325 ~ vii 238; viii 550–5) the enquiry after the guest's name and country follows the offer of food. But here Circe asks out of surprise at the failure of her magic (326–9), and then answers the question herself, remembering a prophecy of Hermes' (330–2). She concludes with the invitation (333–5) of which Hermes had warned Odysseus (296).

328. καὶ ... ὀδόντων amplifies ὅς κε πίῃ. Comparison with *Il.* ix 409 allows only the explanation given in the scholia, which involves a change of construction καὶ οὗ ἕρκος ὀ. (obj.) φάρμακα (subj.) ἀμείψεται; cf. H. Erbse, *LfgrE* s.v. ἀμείβω; Stanford, ad loc., is quite wrong here.

329. The line is modelled on *Il.* iii 63. Its authenticity has been disputed, both by Aristarchus and by modern critics, but there is no contradiction with 240, as often supposed. κηλέω is almost synonymous with θέλγω (cf. 213 n.; Odysseus' νόος remains ἀκήλητος in spite of the φάρμακα (318), unlike his companions', which Circe was able to bewitch (θέλγειν, κηλεῖν) but not destroy (it remains ἔμπεδος (240); cf. 235–42 n.).

330–1. The recollection of a prophecy parallels Polyphemus' recalling παλαίφατα θέσφατα (ix 507–8). Such references to oracles (familiar enough in the world of men but not found in the traditional folk-tale) bring the story closer to the heroic world. πολύτροπος refers to Odysseus' behaviour in 320–1; its force is, then, not the same as in i 1; cf. Marzullo, op. cit. (ix 526 n.), 58. 3.

333. κολεῷ: cf. viii 404.

335. πεποίθομεν: short-vowel subj.; see Chantraine, *Grammaire*, i 406. Circe's hope is that the εὐνή will bring about a relationship of mutual trust; this agrees with what Hermes said about εὐνή as a pre-condition for the release of the crew (298).

336. = iv 375 etc.

337–44. The reply is in accordance with Hermes' instructions (297–301; cf. n. ad loc.). Odysseus does not refuse Circe (μὴ ἀπανήνασθαι 297), but in view of his companions' transformation and his own danger (343 = 301) demands first an oath as advised by Hermes (343–4 ~ 299–301). On the correspondence between 342–4 and v 177–9 cf. 297–301 n.

345. Cf. xii 303. **ἀπόμνυεν:** cf. ii 377. Circe 'forswears', i.e. swears not to do what Odysseus had feared she would (344). The wording is taken from the similar situation, v 184–7.

346. = ii 378 etc.; 347 = 480. As Hermes had foreseen, the release of the companions follows after the consummation of the relationship between Odysseus and Circe and the preparations for a feast. It is, however, odd that concern for the crew should delay their eating together (373), but not their sleeping together (cf. Page, *Folktales*, 56): it is the other way round, as we might expect, in the version of the tale from Ceylon (Page, op. cit., 62–3). The poet probably meant to show the freeing of the men as the consequence of joint action from Odysseus and Circe (πεποίθομεν 335).

348–74. The unusually detailed account of the preparations for the meal, gratuitous for the time being, while Odysseus refuses to eat, serves to build up suspense before the decisive moment, Circe's actions of 375 ff. (Note the anaphora 352, 354, 356, 358.)

348–9. = xix 345. While Odysseus and Circe retire to the bedchamber and afterwards (τῆος), four ἀμφίπολοι are busy preparing for the feast; in Circe's palace they serve as δρήστειραι, i.e. house servants. On the terminology and sociological implications see G. Ramming, *Die Dienerschaft in der Odyssee* (diss. Erlangen, 1972), 101–2 *et passim*. On τῆος/τέως cf. R. Werner, *H u. ει vor Vokal*, 71.

350–1. The origins of the ἀμφίπολοι are in keeping with the divine rank of their mistress (they are water and wood nymphs). On τ' εἰς ἅλαδε (Zenodotus has τε ἅλαδε) cf. Ameis–Hentze, *Anhang*, ii 95; van der Valk, *Textual Criticism*, 45.

352–3. The first nymph lays out purple rugs over a protective undercover (λῖθ'; cf. i 130; S. Laser, *Archaeologia* P, 38–41). On λῖς, originally an adj., 'smooth', then also subst. (here and i 130; *Il.* viii 441), 'smooth cloth', see Bechtel, *Lexilogus*, 217-18; Frisk, *GEW* s.v.; it does not mean 'linen'.

354-5. The second nymph sets before each θρόνος (there are only two here) a τράπεζα, a (small) serving table. τιταίνειν (τανύειν 370) shows that these τράπεζαι were originally folding tables (cf. Laser, op. cit., 56-68). The κάνεια are left empty at first (cf. 371-2).

356-7. The third nymph mixes wine and water in the κρητήρ, and sets on each table a cup to be filled.

358-63. The fourth nymph warms water in a bronze cauldron over a fire; ἰαίνεσθαι means not so much 'heating up' as 'boiling' (360 = *Il.* xviii 349; cf. J. Latacz, op. cit. (ix 5-11 n.), 225). Then she (not Circe!) invites Odysseus to step into a bath; she adds cold water to the hot until it is just the right temperature (θυμῆρες κεράσασα: 'so mixing the water that it is θυμῆρες, well suited to the θυμός'; Bechtel, *Lexilogus*, 169), and pours this water from the cauldron over Odysseus' head and shoulders; H. Lutz, op. cit. (ix 438 n.), 18-19, gives the correct explanation. The lines are also remarkable for the many words attested in Myc.: θρόνος and θρῆνυς (367): cf. 315 n.; τράπεζα: *to-pe-za/torpedza*, *tr̥pedza*; κρητήρ: *ka-ra-te-ra/krātēra* (acc.?); τρίπους: *ti-ri-po/tripōs*; ἀσάμινθος: *a-sa-mi-to/asaminthos*. The fourth servant acts as a *re-wo-to-ro-ko-wo/lewotro-khowos*; cf. λοετροχόος (xx 297).

364. = iii 466 (cf. viii 454); 365 = viii 455 (cf. iii 467); 366-7 = 314-15; cf. also *Il.* xxiv 587-8.

368-72. = i 136-40, vii 172-6, xv 135-9, xvii 91-5. The lines have been suspected by many scholars: Köchly, Kirchhoff, Nauck, Nitzsch, Ameis–Hentze; and, later, Schwartz, *Odyssee*, 301, 317; G. Beck, op. cit. (133-574 n.), 13. But van der Valk, *Textual Criticism*, 278. 3, Eisenberger, *Studien*, 158. 27, and particularly H. Lutz, op. cit. (ix 438 n.), 14-17, argue in favour of their authenticity. The inclusion of these formulaic lines does indeed make for some weakness in the sequence of 348-74, but no essential contradiction with 348-67. After his bath Odysseus is dressed by the fourth servant and led to his θρόνος (364-6; cf. 352-4), where another nymph (presumably the second servant from 354-6) gives him water for the ritual washing of hands (368-9; this is not superfluous after taking a bath), and draws up the table (370), which has already been set (364). Finally the fifth and most important servant, the housekeeper, brings in the food (371-2); the κάνεια (355) are still empty. Now at last the invitation to eat may be given.

373-4. The unusually lengthy description (25 lines) of a 'typical' scene is matched here by the equally unusual 'negation' of the typical: where we would normally expect the guest to fall to (cf. οἱ δ' ... χεῖρας ἴαλλον xv 142) Odysseus has no appetite (373; οὐδ' ἐπὶ σίτῳ | χεῖρας ἰάλλοντα 375-6). From 373 onwards we are reminded again of *Il.* xxiv 552-3, where Priam refuses the invitation to sit down because he is preoccupied with concern for Hector's body. On ἀλλοφρονέω (only here and *Il.* xxiii 698; here 'my thoughts were elsewhere') see M. Treu, *LfgrE* s.v.; Chantraine, *Dictionnaire* s.v. ἄλλος (with bibliography). 374[b] (= xviii 154[b]; cf. *Il.* xviii 224), 'I saw evil things (in the mind's eye)', is amplified in 384-7.

378–81. The tension has not been removed by 345–7. It is significant that it is Circe, who is a changed character after 321–2, who takes the initiative to relieve it. Genuinely concerned, she asks the hero the reason for his lack of appetite (377[a]) and supplies one possible answer herself (380), although she must know the real reason.

378. (κατ' ...) ἕζεαι: both form and meaning ('you sit there') are most unusual for Homer: Wackernagel, *Untersuchungen*, 231, suspects textual corruption; cf. Chantraine, *Dictionnaire* s.v. ἕζομαι, (with bibliography).

383–7. Again we are reminded of *Iliad* xxiv, and again we are aware of the changes in the material. Odysseus, like Priam (*Il.* xxiv 553–8), asks for a 'release'; unlike Achilles, however, Circe fulfils the wish at once; in both episodes the agreement is sealed with a meal shared. The parallel is underlined by the correspondence of 387[a] to *Il.* xxiv 555[a]. The use of λύειν, which is properly used of the release of a corpse, but suffers a change of meaning when applied to the restoration of Odysseus' companions to their proper form (but cf. λύεσθαι 284, 385), shows that the Circe episode derives from *Il.* xxiv (not *vice versa*, as W. Thieler, *MH* xix (1962), 8, supposes).

383. ἐναίσιμος: cf. ii 122.

385. On ἐν ὀφθαλμοῖσιν ἰδέσθαι and ὁ. ἴδω (387) see Bechert, op. cit. (ix 142–5 n.), 75–6.

386. πρόφρασσα: cf. v 161.

388–99. Circe drives from their pen the metamorphosed companions, who have the appearance of nine-year-old boars, and smears each one in turn with a φάρμακον ἄλλο (like a salve), whereupon each loses his bristles (τρίχες), finds his human shape restored, and indeed made more beautiful than before, and recognizes Odysseus. The reunion is so emotional that even Circe is moved (ἐλέαιρε 399) by the γόος. The relationship of this transformation scene to the first metamorphosis (234–40) is problematic. It is clear that an antidote (φάρμακον ἄλλο) in the form of a χριστόν (cf. E. *Hipp.* 516) is used to counter the effect of φάρμακα λύγρα (236) which were administered as ποτά; and the recognition of Odysseus does not contradict 236–40 (cf. 235–43 n.). But whereas the effect of the φάρμακα λύγρα was explicitly said to be only λαθέσθαι πατρίδος (and we are left to supply the complementary effect of the ῥάβδος), here the φάρμακον ἄλλο is sufficient by itself to reverse both the physical metamorphosis and the loss of memory: the ῥάβδος is only briefly mentioned in passing (389). The greatest difficulty lies in 393–4, which attribute the original metamorphosis to the effect of the φάρμακον οὐλόμενον. We should not allow ourselves, however, to be drawn to analytical conclusions by this contradiction. The inconsistencies in the passage are caused by the fusion of the conception of a female figure adept in producing altered states of consciousness by administering mysterious φάρμακα and that of the sorceress who uses her wand and incantations to metamorphose her victims, together with the poet's desire to suppress the crudely irrational from his story (a point which can be fully appreciated only by those familiar with older treatments of the material). But, despite its slight inconsistencies, the passage leaves the impression of a homogeneous whole.

389. συφειοῦ: cf. 238 n.

390. σίαλοι here replaces σύες (239, 283, 338) for variety; cf. Myc. *si-a₂-ro/sihalons* (acc. pl.) PY Cn 608.

395. αὖψ' (codd.) is probably to be preferred to the less graphic ἂψ (Bechert, op. cit. (ix 142–5 n.), 403).

398–9. ἱμερόεις γόος is an unusual expression; cf. the meeting of Odysseus and Telemachus, xvi 215 τοῖσιν ὑφ' ἵμερος ὦρτο γόοιο, where both parties are so overcome by emotion that they weep unrestrainedly. ἱμερόεις γόος appears to be almost synonymous with ἵμερος γόοιο. **σμερδαλέον κονάβιζε** a formula coined for warfare (cf. *Il.* ii 466 etc.) is here transferred to a different context, although not as boldly as in xvii 541–2. 399[a] is exceptional. Elsewhere when a god is moved to pity, it provides the motive for decisive action; here, however, the point is simply the effect on Circe's own state of mind; she is moved to pity almost against her will on a tide of more general emotion as a witness to the feelings of others who have escaped the evil she intended; 'she was disturbed'; cf. Burkert, op. cit. (ix 259–71 n.), 143.

400. = 455: cf. 377.

401. = v 203.

402: cf. 154, iv 779.

403: cf. 423, iv 780.

404: cf. 424.

406. = 471: cf. ii 103.

407. = iv 779: cf. 402.

409. 409[a]: cf. iv 719. 409[b] = 201[b].

410–15. A simile drawn from everyday life in the country is used to heighten the drama of the reunion-scene: with tears of joy the men surround their captain (δακρυόεντες ἔχυντο) just as calves gambol around their mothers when they return from the fields to the stall, frisking round them and mooing (μυκώμεναι ἀμφιθέουσι) continually (ἀδινόν).

410. ἄγραυλοι: properly 'remaining out in the fields at night' (Risch, *Wortbildung*, 186), here means approx. 'living at a country steading' because the calves are obviously kept in the σηκοί (411–13). **πόριες:** For the alternative reading πόρτιες cf. Myc. *po-ti-pi/porti-phi* (instr. pl.) PY Ta 707. **βοῦς ἀγελαίας** (from ἀγέλη): 'cows of the herd'. The construction begun with ὡς δ' ὅτ' ἂν is abandoned after the parenthetic 411; at 412 the poet continues as if he had begun with ὡς δὲ, and so uses σκαίρουσιν instead of -ωσιν. The conjectures of von der Mühll (ὡς δ' ὅτε) and Bekker (σκαίρωσι) are unnecessary; cf. Ruijgh, τε *épique*, 637; Chantraine, *Grammaire*, ii 356.

414–15. ἔχυντο (on which ἐμὲ depends, as well as on ἴδον) is striking; the construction is explained by the continuing effect of περὶ βοῦς from 410 and ἀμφιθέουσι μητέρας (413–14); the passage should be understood as περὶ ἐμὲ ... ἔχυντο.

415–21. The simile and the situation it describes are both characterized by overwhelming joy. Again the poet turns to a comparison to convey the intensity of emotion: 'their minds were in the same state, they felt as if (δόκησε) they had arrived home'. The poet's intention is made clear by the direct speech of the companions: 'We were made as happy at your return as if we had arrived back in Ithaca' (419–20); on the diction cf. Latacz, op. cit. (ix 5–11 n.), 55–6. The crew not only compare their joy with that which they hope to experience at their home-coming; the return of Odysseus also renews that hope of seeing their homes again, which we know will not be fulfilled. 419–20 and the episode as a whole thus play on the ultimate fate of the crew: the solidarity now so intensely felt between Odysseus and his companions will soon collapse as the crew break their oath on Thrinacia, mutiny, and pay for it with the loss of their lives and homecoming; cf. H. Fränkel, *Gleichnisse*, 95; Reinhardt, 'Abenteuer', 98–9; D. N. Maronitis, *EEThess.* ix (1965), 269–93, esp. 278–80.

415–17. There is no reason to doubt the authenticity of these lines (as do Kirchhoff, Fick, van Herwerden, von der Mühll).

416. αὐτὴν is probably a cj. by Aristarchus for αὐτῶν; van der Valk, *Textual Criticism*, 132.

418. = 324 (with pl. -ηύδων for -ηύδα; this formulaic phrase is not found elsewhere in the plur.).

421. Seeing Odysseus appear alone, and remembering the words of Eurylochus (259–60), the men assume their comrades are dead.

423–4. = 403–4.

425–7. 427 = vii 99. The order also answers the question of 421.

428. = 178.

430. The line, which is attested only late and not found in Eust., must be a late interpolation based on iv 77, to introduce Eurylochus' speech.

431–7. Eurylochus attempts to hold the companions back with a warning of the possible dangers. His previous experiences (207–44) make this a fitting rôle for him, but his particular fear, of metamorphosis, is surprising in view of the fact that at this point he knows nothing of Circe's witchcraft (Page, *Folktales*, 54); we are left to assume that Eurylochus has drawn the right conclusions from his previous observations (212 ff., 259 ff.) and forebodings (232, 258). He reminds his listeners of what happened on Polyphemus' island in similar circumstances: one group who followed a misguided order from Odysseus has already found itself trapped, and perished. Reinhardt ('Abenteuer', 500. 16) has convincingly demonstrated the authenticity of 435–7 (doubted by Kirchhoff and Fick; cf. Schwartz, *Odyssee*, 318, Focke, *Odyssee*, 254, Marzullo, *Problema*, 59). Odysseus' reaction (modelled on *Il.* i 189–92) can only be in response to an insult from Eurylochus such as the charge of recklessness (ἀτασθαλίῃσιν 437). 435–7 refer back to the Cyclops episode and also look forward to the action on Thrinacia, where the companions, including Eurylochus, lose their lives by their own ἀτασθαλίαι (cf. i 7). On this occasion Eurylochus' attempt to stir up mutiny fails; on Thrinacia the companions are provoked to rebel against Odysseus' authority, and the rebellion costs the mutineers and their leader their lives.

432. καταβήμεναι amplifies κακῶν τούτων (431).

434. οἵ κεν ...: 'as which we then ...'. **καὶ ἀνάγκη**: cf. v 154.

435. ὥς περ Κύκλωψ ἔρξ': 'exactly as the Cyclops did when he trapped our comrades when they ...'. **μέσσαυλον** (the only occurrence in the *Odyssey*; morphology uncertain; cf. Frisk, *GEW* s.v.): here 'an enclosed courtyard at the entrance to the cave' (cf. W. Richter, *Archaeologia* H, 30–1); perhaps originally 'grounds containing a courtyard'.

436. ὁ (demonstr.!) **θρασὺς Ὀδυσσεύς**: this is the only occasion on which the word θρασύς is used of Odysseus; it is meant, of course, in the pejorative sense ('rash, over-bold'), referring to ix 224–30.

438–42. This 'deliberation-scene' is typologically comparable with 151–5 n.: Odysseus 'considers whether' to kill the would-be mutineer. The intended comparison is with *Il.* i 188 ff., where Achilles does seriously consider killing his man, and is restrained by Athena; here Odysseus' own crew dissuade him.

439. = xi 231, *Il.* xvi 473. **τανύηκες**: see Risch, *Wortbildung*, 190.

440. τῷ (i.e. ἄορι): 'to bring his head to the ground'.

442. = ix 493.

444. = ix 194.

445. The crew obey Odysseus' order of 425–6.

446: cf. 274.

448. ἐνιπήν: ('rebuke'); here (as v 194) approx. 'angry outburst'.

449. τόφρα: 'meanwhile'.

450: cf. 346.

451. = iv 50: cf. 365.

454: cf. 398–9; 10 n.

456. = 401. The line is missing in most MSS (and Eust.), and is usually considered to be an interpolation on the model of 400–1 because a speech addressed to the general company (cf. ἡμῖν 466) could hardly begin with an address to Odysseus; cf. Ameis–Hentze, *Anhang*, ii 99. But 456 is prepared by μευ ἄγχι στᾶσα, and the poet wanted to underline the parallelism between Circe's three speeches (456–65, 488–95, 504–40) by beginning them all in the same way (456 + μηκέτι νῦν ... 457; 488 + μηκέτι νῦν ... 489; 504 + μή τί τοι ... 505).

457. We need not wonder how Circe (a goddess) knows.

459. ἀν-άρσιος: here 'hostile'; on the form see K. Matthiessen, *LfgrE* s.v.; Chantraine, *Dictionnaire* s.v. ἄρτι. **ἐδηλήσαντ'** cf. viii 444 n.

460. = xii 23.

462. οἶον: sc. ἔχετε.

463. ἀσκελέες: this is the only example of its use as an adj.; elsewhere it is adv. (i 68, iv 543) and used with a transferred meaning ('obstinately, stubbornly'); cf. *Il.* xix 68. Here the etymology and meaning are uncertain; cf. Bechtel, *Lexilogus*, 66; Chantraine, *Dictionnaire* s.v. The meaning must be related to ἄθυμος, something like 'weak, lacking strength'.

464–5. 'Your heart is not in εὐφροσύνη.' The reason is not so much their suffering in itself (465ᵇ) as the continual remembrance of it (464; cf. a similar thought in 374). **εὐφροσύνη** ('joy, unencumbered high spirits'): cf. Latacz, op. cit. (ix 5–11 n.), 163–4. **πέπασθε** (Aristarchus): *πέποσθε* (attested by most sources) is probably to be preferred; Chantraine, *Grammaire*, i 25; van der Valk, *Textual Criticism*, 134–5, Scheibner, op. cit. (ix 445 n.), 255.

466. = xii 28; cf. 406.

467. The length of the *δαίνυσθαι* matches the unusually elaborate preparation (348–72), but is also determined by the refusal in 373–4: after Odysseus' initial rejection the meal is accepted all the more enthusiastically. 467[b]: cf. iv 86.

468. = ix 162.

469–70. 469[a]: cf. i 16; 469[b]: cf. ii 107: 'when the seasons had run their course'. 469–70: cf. Hes. *Th.* 58–9 (with *πόλλ' ἐτελέσθη* for *μακρὰ τ.*), *Od.* xix 152–3, xxiv 142–3, ii 107, 107a). 470 is missing from many MSS and Eustathius and is generally considered to be an interpolation from Hes. *Th.* 59; on the other hand a similarly full form of expression is to be found in *Od.* xi 294–5, and 469–70 themselves largely consist of old formulae (cf. van der Valk, *Textual Criticism*, 275–6). *μακρά*, however, for *πόλλ'*, is strange; the substitution may be explained by the easterly position of the island (cf. 82–6 n.).

472. The companions do not understand Odysseus' delay, and so address him as *δαιμόνιε* (cf. E. Brunius-Nilsson, *δαιμόνιος* (Uppsala, 1955)); they think he must be possessed by a *δαίμων*.

475–9. 475 = 406; 476–8 = 183–5, ix 556–8, xii 28–30. The lines are missing from most MSS and Eust., and are considered suspect (either wholly or in part) by a number of modern critics (Ameis–Hentze, *Anhang*, ii 99, Schwartz, *Odyssee*, 318, von der Mühll, ad loc.). In fact the passage does not fit the context as well here as it does elsewhere, but it is not superfluous for the development of the narrative. *ὥς* (476) refers to the changed situation, and so serves to introduce the following scene. 477 prepares indirectly for the fall of Elpenor (555), and 480 is inconceivable without 478–9; cf. G. Beck, loc. cit. (133–574 n.), 17–18, Eisenberger, *Studien*, 165, 43, W. Theiler, *MH* vii (1950), 105 (an analytical discussion).

480: cf. 347.

481. 481[a] is loosely modelled on *Il.* xxiv 357 and ix 451; cf. Erbse, *Beiträge*, 228. 481[b] = 311[b], although with a slight shift of meaning.

482: *λιτανεύω* (481) introduces direct speech: 482, missing from most MSS and Eust., is probably an interpolation; cf. *Il.* i 15, *Od.* vii 145.

483–6. Odysseus asks Circe to fulfil a promise she has not in fact given in so many words (Merkelbach, *Untersuchungen*, 203). But she has formally recognized the Greeks as guest-friends (456–65), and this act implies an obligation to facilitate the next stage in their journey (*πομπή*); see Eisenberger, *Studien*, 160.

484. θυμὸς … ἔσσυται: here 'θ. is eager'.

485. φθινύθουσι: cf. *Il.* i 491, *Od.* i 250.

486. ὅτε with subj.: here iterative.

487. = iv 382 = x 503, xii 113.

488–95. Circe assents, but unexpectedly tells Odysseus that before his final departure he must journey to Hades to consult Tiresias (although she does not yet say what question is to be put to the prophet). The divine authority of Circe (who knows the future as well as the past, 457–9) provides convincing motivation for the journey to Hades, which could not be omitted from the series of adventures, but which—unlike Odysseus' other adventures—could come about only as a result of direction and planning.

491. = 564. ἐπαινῆς: the secondary development of the adj. ἐπαινός, correctly explained in principle by Buttmann and Bechtel (*Lexilogus* 128–9), has been set in a wider context by Leumann (*Wörter*, 72).

492. = 565, xi 165, xxiii 323. The character of Tiresias is drawn from older oral epic; the function of the living seer in the Theban epics is transferred to the ψυχή of a dead prophet.

493–5. μάντιος: μάντηος (given only in M), preferred by G. Hermann, is shown to be the linguistically correct form by R. S. P. Beekes, *Glotta*, li (1973), 244; the metrical difficulties posed by μάντιος are thus avoided. 493ᵃ is probably formulaic; older versions may have given *μάντηος (ϝ)αλα(ϝ)οῖ'(ο); cf. also Schwyzer, *Grammatik*, i 572, Chantraine, *Grammaire*, i 218–19, Scheibner, op. cit. (ix 445 n.), 258. Tiresias is the only one of the dead to have retained his φρένες ἔμπεδοι (cf. νοῦς ἔμπεδος 240): 494 explains that Persephone has granted him the unique privilege of νόος after death; πεπνῦσθαι belongs with and explains νόος ('capacity for intelligent thought'). The others (τοὶ δέ, i.e. ἄλλοι ἄνδρες τεθνεῶτες) flit around as σκιαί (so devoid of φρένες). Tiresias, then, enjoys φρένες ἔμπεδοι as the living do, just as Odysseus' bewitched companions (240) retained along with their corporeal existence their mental faculties with the exception of their memory of the past. On the construction of 495ᵇ see Chantraine, *Grammaire*, ii 159. Plato quotes the line twice (*Men.* 100 a 5; *R.* 386 d 7); see G. Lohse, *Untersuchungen über Homerzitate bei Platon* (diss. Hamburg, 1960), 58, 80–2. On the orthography of τεθνηώς/-ειώς cf. R. Werner, *H u. ει vor Vokal*, 52–4, 62 f.; on the linguistic problems C. J. Ruijgh, *Lingua*, xxviii (1971), 164. Schwartz (*Odyssee*, 318) sees 493 as a redundant counterpart to 494–5.

496–9. Odysseus' reaction is described in the same lines as Menelaus' reaction to the news of his brother's death (iv 538–41). It is not certain which passage is earlier: Kirchhoff (*Odyssee*, 222), von der Mühll (*Odyssee*, 723–4), Reinhardt ('Abenteuer', 503. 27) and Theiler (*MH* vii (1950), 105; xix (1962), 13–14) give priority to iv, Focke (*Odyssee*, 201) to x, while Merkelbach is undecided (*Untersuchungen*, 179. 1). The verbal parallel is, however, certainly intentional: it underlines the similarity of the fates of the two heroes with the longest νόστος, and is not to be explained in terms of analytical discussion. On the other hand, the lines do suit the context of iv better, and acquire a strange twist in meaning in x: the hero has lost the will to live (498) i.e. he wishes to go to Hades, just at the moment when he is ordered, to his horror, to go to Hades. The irony is quite intentional.

501. ἡγεμονεύσει: cf. vi 261, vii 30.

69

502a (=xi 156) is given only in P, and is certainly inauthentic: van der Valk, *Textual Criticism*, 268, Bechert, op. cit. (ix 142–5), 413.

503. =487.

504. (here surely authentic) = 400 etc.

505. ποθή (cf. *Il.* i 240): 'Do not let your lack of a ἡγεμών to accompany you be an anxiety'.

506: cf. ix 77, viii 54.

507–8. ἧσθαι (inf. with imperat. force): 'Stay sitting in the ship (and do nothing)'; the crew need neither row nor steer; the North Wind will guide the ship to their destination. On subj. + κε with fut. sense see L. R. Palmer, in *Companion*, 151. On the mythological geography cf. xi 14–19 n.

509–12. At the end of the voyage (505; cf. xi 13) Odysseus will come to Persephone's grove (ἄλσεα). There he should leave the ship at anchor and proceed on foot to Hades' δόμος. It is strange that when the Greeks carry out these instructions there is no mention of ἄλσεα: the ship is anchored off the land of the Cimmerians (xi 20, cf. x 511), and from there the Greeks proceed to the place described by Circe (xi 22, cf. x 512–15). It is questionable whether this discrepancy can be adequately explained by analytical theories, such as that xi 14–19 are a late addition to the text (Eisenberger, *Studien*, 168), Page, *Odyssey*, 21–2, A. Dihle, *Homer-Probleme* (Opladen, 1970), 151. The details given in xi do not necessarily contradict the account of x; Circe's silence about the Cimmerians may have a purpose. 509–10 and 513–15 may be based on an epic katabasis of Heracles (von der Mühll, *Odyssee*, 727, Merkelbach, *Untersuchungen*, 190); this cannot be proved, but it is a possibility that such lines are pre-Homeric.

509. λάχεια: cf. ix 116 n. The grove with αἴγειροι is reminiscent of Athena's ἄλσος αἰγείρων (vi 291–2).

510. ὠλεσίκαρποι (*hapax*): 'shedding their fruit (so that it perishes)'. As Theophrastus *HP* iii 1, 3 explains, this fits well the ἰτέα, which sheds its fruits before they are fully ripe. On the metrical lengthening of ὀ- to ὠ- (instead of οὐ- as in οὔρεα etc.) see, most recently, Wyatt, *Lengthening*, 61–3. On the later symbolism of the ἰτέαι ὠ. cf. H. Rahner, op. cit. (302–6 n.), 245–80 (Engl. edn. 286–327), on the willow in Christian tradition.

511. βαθυδίνη (the only occurrence in the *Odyssey*): 'with deep eddies'; cf. Risch, *Wortbildung*, 185, 210; E. Rüedi, *Vom Ἑλλανοδίκας zum ἀλλαντοπώλης* (diss. Zurich, 1969), 41–3.

512. εὐρώεντα: 'abounding in εὐρώς (mould, decay)'; cf. Chantraine, *Dictionnaire* s.v. εὐρώς.

513–15. Circe describes the immediate surroundings of the entrance to Hades (ἔνθα 513). The Pyriphlegethon and Cocytus (the latter a branch of the Styx) flow into Acheron (which is perhaps a lake). 515 completes the picture of a spot from which a rock and the confluence of the two (δύω gen.) rivers can be seen; i.e. the rivers probably converge shortly before they discharge into Acheron as a waterfall over the rock. The lines have been rejected as interpolation by Hennings, Nitzsch, and Schwartz (*Odyssee*, 318) without adequate reasons.

514. ἀπορρώξ (here approx. 'branch of a river'): cf. ix 359 n. The whole line is modelled on *Il.* ii 755.

515. πέτρη is perhaps the λευκὰς π. of xxiv 11. **ξύνεσις** (*hapax*): see H. Jones, *Glotta* li (1973), 8. **ἐριδούπων**: cf. iii 399 n.

516–40. 516–37 are partially repeated, xi 25–50. Circe gives Odysseus exact instructions on what to do at the entrance to Hades (χριμφθεὶς πέλας (516): on its only occurrence in the *Odyssey* used in a different sense from the *Iliad*, 'approaching close'). Odysseus is to dig a βόθρος (its significance becomes clear after 527) and then (517–25) offer to the dead a threefold χοή (μελίκρητον, 'milk with honey'; followed by wine; followed by water) with a threefold vow (to sacrifice on his return to Ithaca a heifer, a burnt offering, and, for Tiresias alone, a black sheep). Second (526–34) he is to sacrifice in the βόθρος a ram and a ewe with a prayer to Hades and Persephone. Finally (535–40) he is not to allow the other souls to approach the blood of the sacrifices until he has spoken with Tiresias. This threefold injunction is a complex of ideas drawn from many religious and cultic sources. The intention is partly to signal that Odysseus' descent will be very different from the journeys of Heracles and Theseus, which inspire the episode. Its principal purpose is the consultation of Tiresias, in other words, necromancy: the difference is that here the seer is not conjured up from Hades to the world of the living, but the enquirer goes to Hades himself. By this expedient the poet can enable his hero to meet many others who have died. Odysseus has, then, to perform a ritual which has its closest analogies in the practices of the festivals of the dead, during which spirits summoned and appeased by sacrifice were thought to mingle with the living (the second and third days of the Attic Anthesteria, which were dedicated to the departed, were known as Χόες and Χύτραι, and featured offerings of water as in hero-cult); cf. Reinhardt, 'Abenteuer', 143. The sacrificial blood allows the spirits to converse with Odysseus because on tasting it they recall, for a time, their previous existence. The poet thus combines very ancient conceptions drawn from different spheres to create something quite new, which can have had no precedent in earlier epic.

517. The trench, usual in the cult of the dead (M. P. Nilsson, *Geschichte* i 173–4) is to be about (ὅσον τε) a cubit each way; cf. 113 (Ruijgh, τε *épique*, 556–7).

518. ἀμφ' αὐτῷ: 'round the edge of the βόθρος'.

521. Most unusually, γουνοῦσθαι is here followed by a fut. inf. (Chantraine, *Grammaire*, ii 311). **νεκύων ἀμενηνὰ κάρηνα:** 'the powerless heads of the dead', i.e. the ψυχαί. On the use of κάρηνα cf. κεφαλαί (239 and n.). On ἀμενηνός (ἀ- priv., μένος) see Risch, *Wortbildung*, 100.

522. στεῖραν (only fem.): 'barren'; latterly H. Eichner, *Die Sprache*, xx (1974), 26–42.

523. ἐσθλῶν (neut.): 'with good, i.e. costly gifts'.

525. (ὄϊν) **παμμέλαν':** cf. *Il.* iii 103 ἄρν' ... μέλαιναν (for Gaia) contrasted with (ἄρν') λευκόν (for Helios).

526. The prayers just mentioned are εὐχαί (xi 34 εὐχωλαί, λιταί), combining

71

petition (for protection, and, in that addressed to Tiresias, a favourable oracle) with the promise to repay the help given with further sacrifice at a later stage.

527–9. μέλαιναν: the sense demands that this be read in conjunction with ὄϊν ἀρνειόν; cf. 625 n. Odysseus is to turn the heads of the sacrificial victims towards Hades (ἐς βόθρον xi 36), but to face away himself (τραπέσθαι for -όμενος) 'looking towards the streams of the river' (ἱέμενος ποταμοῖο ῥοάων), i.e. towards the Ocean, from which he arrived (cf. *Il.* iii 5 Ὠκεανοῖο ῥοάων).

531–7. When the victims have been slaughtered the companions are to skin and burn the animals and offer prayer, while Odysseus sits with drawn sword, warding off approaching spirits from the sacrificial trench. **ἀνῶξαι:** aor. from ἄνωγα.

531. ἐποτρῦναι: only here in the *Odyssey* with dat. (as *Il.* xv 258).

535: cf. ix 300.

539–40. Tiresias will tell Odysseus the ὁδόν, μέτρα κελεύθου, and νόστον; ὡς ... ἰχθυόεντα serves to define the complex of ideas contained in these expressions. There are considerable difficulties involved in the lines, although the intended parallel with iv 389–90 (Reinhardt, 'Abenteuer', 120–4), as of 496–499 with iv 538–41 (cf. n. ad loc.), is clear, underlining the similarity between the fates of the two heroes whose return is long delayed. Menelaus, trapped on the island of Pharos excites the compassion of the goddess Eidothea (iv 364: x 399), who approaches him (iv 370: x 455) when he is away from his companions (iv 367), refers him to her father Proteus for directions on his νόστος (iv 389–90 = x 539–40), and explains how he is to extract the information from the god. After a struggle Menelaus forces an answer from Proteus: he will return to his home after he has returned to Egypt and made a sacrifice of atonement to the angry gods. The parallel figures of Proteus and Tiresias give comparable answers to the same question (iv 475–80: xi 100–36) in that neither gives the information we might expect: a route. Both name an important inter-mediate destination (Egypt and Thrinacia respectively), and make the return home dependent on the fulfilment of a condition: both heroes are required to sacrifice hecatombs (iv 478–9: xi 132–3). The answer expected of Tiresias (x 539–40) is only given by Circe (xii 37–141). Analytical discussion has largely dealt with the question of priority with the assumption that bk. x served as a model for bk. iv (see e.g. Merkelbach, *Untersuchungen*, 181; W. Theiler, *MH* vii (1950), 105, however, disagrees). But the fact that Circe gives the answer we might have expected from Tiresias has also attracted analytical discussion (see e.g. Focke, *Odyssee*, 202–4) on the assumption that xi is a late addition which does violence to the close connection between x and xii (for the older literature see Erbse, *Beiträge*, 24. 48). The development of the narrative as it stands, however, is both satisfying and well-considered. The poet needs to provide a motive for his hero's descent into Hades, and a visit to consult the prophet fulfils that need. Prophets do not conventionally give detailed answers to petitioners; it is therefore not so surprising that Tiresias does not give Odysseus a detailed route for his journey home. Instead he reveals to Odysseus the background to events past and future, and by naming Thrinacia as a critical point on the voyage gives Circe the clue she needs to supply details of Odysseus' route (van der Valk, *Beiträge zur Nekyia* (Kampen, 1935), W. Büchner, *Hermes*, lxxii (1937), 104–22, Erbse, *Beiträge*, 24–6). If the predictions of 539–40 and iv 389–90 are fulfilled in an unexpected, though comparable, way in the pronouncements of Tiresias and Proteus, this surely indicates that ὁδὸν ... νόστον θ' mean nothing more than is implied by the explanatory ὡς ... ἰχθυόεντα. The expression μέτρα κελεύθου can thus hardly mean 'stages of the journey' (O. Becker, *Das Bild des Weges* (Berlin, 1937), 19–20) or 'legs of the journey and halts' (Focke, *Odyssee*, 202); we find the expression as obscure as μέτρα θαλάσσης (Hes. *Op.* 648), and it may be necessary to think of μέτρον as 'goal' (cf. xiii 101 μέτρον ὅρμου, 'the goal which is the mooring-place', i.e. the harbour).

541. = xii 142, xv 56, xx 61.   **χρυσόθρονος:** cf. v 123.

542. = xiv 320.

543–5. (= v 230–2; cf. A. J. B. Wace, in *Companion*, 499). Focke, *Odyssee*, 261–2, argues that 542–5 are an interpolation by his T-poet (cf. also Wilamowitz, *Untersuchungen*, 117), but the objection cannot be sustained: Circe dresses herself to continue her support for Odysseus outside (571–4); cf. Calypso (v 233 ff.). It is striking that Circe is only here called a νύμφη, as Calypso often is, but the word can mean simply 'young woman').

541. = xii 206.

547. (= 173) = xii 207.

548. ἀωτεῖτε: ἀωτέω (only here and *Il.* x 159) has never been adequately explained; it may be connected with ἄωτος (ix 434); ὕπνον a. originally meant 'I pluck sleep' (cf. Chantraine, *Dictionnaire* s.v.).

549. ἐπέφραδε: here 'gave me a direction' (explained 561–5).

550. = xii 324, xix 148: cf. x 406.

551–60. Odysseus tells the story of Elpenor, who had been asleep on the palace roof when woken by the noise of his comrades preparing to depart, and fell to his death. The incident is related from the point of view of the poetic narrator; Odysseus himself learns what happened only later, on meeting the spirit of Elpenor in the Underworld (xi 51–6). The incident, related in three sections (x 551–60, xi 51–80, xii 8–15) is thought by some (incl. Wilamowitz, *Untersuchungen*, 145, 167, Merkelbach, *Untersuchungen*, 205) to be based on an aetiological legend; Reinhardt, 'Abenteuer', 134, rightly argues against this. Other scholars are of the opinion that the episode is based on the old epic Argonautica (Meuli, *Odyssee*, 91. 1, Merkelbach, *Untersuchungen*, 204). There is, however, at least an element of truth in the suggestion (argued most recently by Kirk, *Songs*, 239–40) that the episode is a late addition to the story to bind in the Hades episode more closely with the other material, for the Elpenor episode does closely connect x, xi, and xii. Elpenor himself, the youngest member of the crew, about whom nothing of significance is known except the manner of his death and his lack of the qualities which distinguish his captain (552–3), is a characteristic invention of the poet; cf. Reinhardt, 'Abenteuer', 132–4, G. Strasburger, *Die kleinen Kämpfer der Ilias* (diss. Frankfurt-on-Main, 1954), 112–14, R. Spieker, *Der altsprachliche Unterricht*, viii 3 (1965), 57–80.

553. ἀρηρώς: here by extension 'well furnished, well endowed in his φρένες'.

554. Following Blass, W. B. Stanford (*CR* lix (1945), 138–9) and Merkelbach (*Untersuchungen*, 185. 1) would read ἄν δώμασι for ἐν δ., while Bérard prefers ἐπὶ δ.; a change here would involve altering x 62 (ἐν μεγάρῳ).

555. οἰνοβαρείων: cf. ix 374n. κατελέξατο is used with plpf. force.

556. Elpenor is woken with a start by the sounds of his comrades carrying out Odysseus' order of 546–50.

558–90. = xi 63–5. **ἐκ ... ἐάγη:** lit. 'his neck was broken from the vertebrae'; cf. M. Bertheau, *LfgrE* s.v. ἄγνυμι. The unheroic death of Elpenor is ironically described in heroic terms (560ᵇ = *Il.* vii 330ᵇ).

561–65. The narrative is resumed from 550; in true epic style the poet has marked the passage of time between summoning the crew and their mustering by inserting the Elpenor incident. Odysseus must now disappoint their hopes (562–3) raised by 471 ff. The repetition of Circe's exact words (564–5 = 491–2) arouses the same response from the men as earlier from Odysseus (496 ~ 566).

567. γόων: cf. Leumann, *Wörter*, 186–7, who would read γόον.

568. = 202 (cf. n. ad loc.).

569: cf. 402.

571. τόφρα δ' introduces the main clause after ὅτε ('while we ...').

572. The animals are for the sacrifice prescribed in 527.

573–4. ῥεῖα is amplified by what follows: 'without our noticing'.   **οὐκ ἐθέλοντα:** 'when he wishes not (to be seen)'.

BOOK XI: COMMENTARY

Odysseus' journey to the Underworld is given particular prominence. It occupies an entire book, is carefully introduced into the story (by means of Circe's instructions), and affects the subsequent narrative in various ways, (in particular by the prophecy of Tiresias (xi 100–37)); the story of Elpenor, divided between x 551–60 (see n.), xi 51–83, and xii 8–15, serves to link the underworld journey closely with events on earth; and there is no mistaking the mastery displayed in the organization of the heterogeneous material into a lucid and coherent whole. The peculiarities of material, structure, and treatment reflect the unusual character of the episode; no other adventure is so dangerous or comes so near to the limits of human experience. In his encounter with the Lotus-eaters Odysseus has already crossed the boundary between the heroic world and the realm of fantasy and folk-tale; now, however, he approaches the borderline between life and death itself.

The very complexity of the episode has been sufficient to attract a multitude of analytical interpretations and attempts to reconstruct its original form. The variety of incident in the book, the apparent lack of cohesion, and the juxtaposition of elements drawn from quite disparate mythological and religious sources (a hero's descent into Hades, sacrifices to and conjuration of the dead, necromancy, a parade of heroes) have suggested to many that the book may be made up of a number of layers of material composed at different times, and that the genesis of the story may provide the key to its interpretation. Attempts to provide such an analysis have, however, led to widely differing accounts, and agreement on one point only: that the two catalogues (235–327 and 568–629) are the latest, possibly post-Homeric, additions to the book (see e.g. Germain, *Genèse*, 329–70, esp. 330 ff.; cf. Lesky, *Homeros*, 811 ff.). We can give here no more than a brief indication of the various analytical approaches. Some scholars, for example, have suggested that the descent into Hades was originally an entirely independent work, a poem only later incorporated into the epic series of adventures (Page, *Odyssey*, 21–51; cf. Webster's critical approach, *Mycenae*, 245–8). Others see the descent into Hades as one of the oldest elements in the cycle of adventures associated with the figure of Odysseus (R. Carpenter, *Folk Tale, Fiction, and Saga in the Homeric Epics*[2] (Berkeley, 1956), for example), an element which is perhaps to be explained from the hero's origins in shamanistic conceptions, a journey to the underworld being an essential qualification for the shaman (Meuli, *Odyssee*, 114 ff. and *Hermes*, lxx (1935), 164–71; Thornton, *People*, 32 ff.). Another hypothesis is that an account of necromancy as practised at a sanctuary where there was an oracle of the dead has been transposed to a setting in Hades, in other words, an older *nekuomanteia* has been conflated with the poetic conception of a heroic *katabasis* (Merkelbach, *Untersuchungen*, 185–91, 209–30, Kirk, *Songs*, 236 ff., G. Steiner, 'Die Unterwelts beschwörung des Od. im Lichte heth. Texte', *Ugarit-Forschungen*, iii (1971), 265–83). There have been many such attempts at analysis (cf. also Wilamowitz, *Untersuchungen*, 140–62, Schwartz, *Odyssee*, 137–49, von der Mühll, *Philologus*, xciii (1938), 4–11, Focke, *Odyssee*, 199–247, Theiler, *MH* vii (1950), 104–7). However, no sure results have emerged, nor can any be expected.

If, as we suppose, the poet of the *Odyssey* was the first to transform the setting for the wanderings of a victor of the Trojan war from the heroic world to the realm of folk-tale, and to model his protagonist's adventures partly on the exploits of legendary seafarers, and partly on the deeds of other mythical heroes (like the Argonauts), then it was quite natural for him to send his hero down into Hades in the footsteps of such predecessors as Heracles (and Theseus), whose fearless descent to the world of the dead represents the climax of a heroic career; cf. xi 601–27 n. The difference lies in the motivation: Odysseus is seen by the poet as undergoing adventures inflicted by fate, against his will: he could not, therefore, undertake the journey to Hades on his own initiative with a view to some bold feat. His katabasis required an order which brooked no refusal, and so the poet made the consultation of Tiresias in Hades an essential pre-condition for Odysseus' safe return home. But this in itself does not explain why he chose to send Odysseus to Hades. What Tiresias tells Odysseus could equally well have been relayed by Circe, if a prophecy appeared necessary. The author's underlying intention must, therefore, lie elsewhere; and in fact we can see the attraction of confronting Odysseus with the shadowy images of those to whom, in his heroic existence, he had stood nearest, precisely at that point where he is furthest from the world of the living. Even at the furthest limit of the world of the miraculous, at the boundary between being and not-being, Odysseus has remained the same: the King of Ithaca, the hero of the Trojan War.

It is significant that the theme of an actual descent into the Underworld appears only once, at the beginning of the episode. In fact Odysseus does not cross the threshold into Hades or appear before the thrones of the gods of the Underworld. The souls of the dead approach him, or are seen in the distance. The sacrifice at the entrance to the Underworld is reminiscent of purification and atonement rituals performed in Greek culture at any point where men felt themselves near the world of the dead. Even the solemn invocation and consultation of dead seers at the many supposed entrances to Hades, which were considered sacred ground, may have followed rituals similar to that described in xi. When Odysseus comes into contact with the hosts of the dead, the emphasis shifts from necromancy to a tradition equally powerful in popular religion: the concept behind the Attic-Ionian Anthesteria, in which the souls of the dead were believed to mingle with the living and to be entertained by them.

The various gaps and inconsistencies in the narrative discovered by the analysts are not in fact evidence for any long genesis of the story, multiple authorship, redaction, or process of interpolation. Consideration of the episode as a whole leads rather to the conclusion that the poet has succeeded admirably in combining motifs from religious practice, folk-tale and saga, and subordinating each to the overall concept of the poem. The internal unity of the story is underlined externally by the clear arrangement of the material:

(a) the first three encounters (Elpenor, Tiresias, Anticleia, 51-224)
(b) the fourteen heroines (225-332)
(c) the so-called 'intermezzo'
(d) the three encounters with heroes from the Trojan War (Agamemnon, Achilles, Ajax, 385-565)
(e) the six heroes from the distant past (566-630).

The essential unity of the episode has been defended by, among others, van der Valk, *Beiträge zur Nekyia* (Kampen, 1935), W. Büchner, 'Probleme der hom. Nekyia', *Hermes*, lxii (1937), 104-22, Reinhardt, 'Abenteuer', 118-44, M. Untersteiner, *Omero-Odissea libro XI* (Florence, 1948), Heubeck, *Dichter*, 33-5, F. Eichhorn, *Homers Odyssee* (Göttingen, 1965), 73-80, Rüter, *Odyssee-interpretationen*, 220. 14, Erbse, *Beiträge*, 23-33, Eisenberger, *Studien*, 164-91. For ancient writers' views on the subject see J. G. Petzl, *Antike Diskussionen über die beiden Nekyien* (Meisenheim, 1969). To gauge the influence of xi on later writers it is necessary only to think of Verg. *A.* vi and Dante's *Inferno*.

1. ~viii 50.
2. =iv 577.
3. =iv 578, 781, viii 52.
4. τὰ μῆλα: cf. x 527, 572.   ἐν .:. ἐβήσαμεν transitive.
5. ~x 570.
6-10. =xii 148-52.   ἴκμενον οὖρον: cf. ii 420.   πλησίστιον (*hapax*): 'filling the sails'; cf. Risch, *Wortbildung*, 192.
8. =x 136.
9: cf. ii 390.
10. =78, xiv 256; cf. Reinhardt, 'Abenteuer', 58-9.   ἥμεθα: fulfils the promise made by Circe in x. After their routine duties the crew have nothing further to do, while the north wind and the helmsman do all the work.
11. While the ship continues on its course throughout the day (πανημερίης predicative), the sails stay fully inflated. For a full discussion of the linguistic peculiarities of 11-12 (incl. ποντοπορούσης with the 'late' contraction -εου-〉-ου- for the formulaic ποντοπόροιο, e.g. *Il.* i 439) see F. Sommer's article in *Sybaris, Festschrift für H. Krahe* (Wiesbaden, 1958), 146-63.
12. =ii 388 etc. The use of the formulaic line is criticised by, among others, Schwartz, *Odyssee*, 138. 1, and rightly defended by Focke, *Odyssee*, 207-8. Cf. also A. Lesky, *WS* lxiii (1948), 66.
13. The ship reaches at last the πείρατα Ὠκεανοῖο, home of the Cimmerians (14-19); cf. x 509-12 n.
14-19. The location and identity of this people have never been satisfactorily resolved. The ancients, and some modern scholars, generally connected or

identified the inhabitants with the historical Cimmerians of the 8th/7th centuries (described in J. Wiesner, *Die Kulturen der frühen Reitervölker* (Frankfurt-on-Main, 1968/73), 9–12, 28–35), and set their country in the far north on account of the long wintry nights (14–19); see e.g. Lehmann-Haupt, *RE* xi, 427. For the counter-arguments see R. Hennig, op. cit. (ix 21–7 n.), 73–9, who argues the case for Britain; cf. A. Klotz, *Gymnasium*, lix (1952), 296 ff. Both the people and their country do, of course, belong to the realm of folk-tale: they are part of the irrational world which lies beyond the confines of the real world and surrounds it, itself being bordered by the circumambient Oceanus. Helios rises at the eastern shore of the river which encircles the world (xii 4) and sets at the western edge, where we find the πύλαι of Helios (xxiv 12) and the entrance to the Underworld (xxiv 11–14). The account of Odysseus' journey to the land of the Cimmerians reflects the same conceptions of mythical geography. The hero sets out at dawn (x 541) from the east (xii 3–4), and travels with a north wind (x 507, xi 7–8). The journey is a περᾶν δι' Ὠκεανοῖο (x 508), which leads to the πείρατα Ὠκεανοῖο (xi 13). This cannot be conceived as crossing the river to a (non-existent!) far shore: Odysseus travels along Oceanus following the rim of the earth from east to west via the southern perimeter, as on the return journey (κατ' Ὠκεανοῖο xi 639). His destination is the point furthest away from the place where his journey began (πείρατα Ὠ. from the perspective of the man beginning his journey); here the entrance to the Underworld is situated. The nocturnal return journey is from west to east via the northern edge of the world, so that Odysseus accomplishes in one day a complete (clockwise) circumnavigation of the earth; see W. Karl's convincing account, *Chaos und Tartaros in Hesiods Theogonie* (diss. Erlangen, 1967), 65–106. The mythological location of the Homeric Cimmerians' country at the entry to the Underworld in fact excludes any possibility of connecting them with the historical Cimmerians. (The Assyrian sources call the country Gamir and the people Gimirrai; the Bible (Gen. 10: 2–3, etc.) gives the name of the people as Gomer.) The Cimmerians of history crossed the Caucasus towards the end of the eighth century as migrants from further north. In 714 they achieved two swift and spectacular victories, over King Rusa of Urartu and King Midas of Phrygia respectively, and for the next century terrorized the whole of Asia Minor. The similarity of names between the Homeric Cimmerians and the historical Gimirri has given rise to much speculation, and in attempts to date the *Odyssey* this passage has been cited as evidence both for a *terminus ante* and for a *terminus post*, (as well as being rejected as a later interpolation); cf. e.g. von der Mühll, *MH* xvi (1959), 145–51, A. Dihle, op. cit. (x 50 n.), 512, 155 ff., and Eisenberger, *Studien*, 169 (with bibliography). It is scarcely credible that the poet has taken the name and identity of a tribe of invading horsemen from the north, and transferred them to a mythical homeland in the far west which is continually shrouded in darkness. It is much more probable that the Greeks transferred the name of a mythological people to the trans-Caucasians who came to their notice *c.* 700 because it sounded rather like the northerners' own name for themselves, known to us only in the various forms in which it was reproduced by others; cf. R. Hennig, op. cit. (ix 21–7 n.), 85. The concept of a land in the dark west (ζόφος means 'west' as well as 'darkness'), veiled in thick mists and cloud (near to Hades εὐρώεις x 512) which the light of the sun never penetrates (16), corresponds to the concept of a mythical country situated in the bright east, bathed in perpetual light (x 81–6). 14–19 are therefore intended primarily as contrasting material to the descriptions of such people as the Laestrygonians and the Ethiopians of mythology (A. Lesky, *Hermes* lxxxvii (1959), 27–38), who as friends and hosts of the gods live happily in unbroken sunshine (*Il.* i 423, xxiii 205, *Od.* i 22). The descriptions of Olympus (vi 41–7) and Elysium (iv 565–8) are also formulated, even in points of detail, to contrast with 14–19, as has been demonstrated by R. Spieker, *Hermes* xcvii (1969), 136–61. Olympus and Elysium provide their inhabitants with all things necessary for a happy existence. The unfortunate Cimmerians possess no such advantages: the δειλοὶ βροτοί experience the negation of the qualities of the realms of the blessed (μάκαρες). 'Normal' men live between these two extremes, sharing, in differing proportions, aspects of life in either. All this supports the supposition that 'Cimmerian', like 'Ethiopian', is a 'speaking' (significant) name: Cimmerians may mean 'those living in foggy darkness' (A. Heubeck, *Hermes* xci (1963), 490–2; against this view see C. Nylander, *Hermes* xciii (1965), 131–2). Alternatives to the Κιμμέριοι given in our Homeric MSS are known from elsewhere: Κερβέριοι (Crates), Χειμέριοι, Κεμμέριοι; they are merely learned conjecture, designed to distinguish the Homeric from the historical tribe, or to give a name with a suitable meaning (with some success in echoing the poet's intention). Χειμέριοι requires no comment. On Κεμμέριοι see *Etymologicum Magnum* s.v. Κιμμερ-ιούς: ἔνιοι δὲ Κεμμερίους· κέμμερον γὰρ λέγουσι τὴν ὁμίχλην. Crates evidently saw a connection with Cerberus, the hound of Hades.

15. ∼ viii 562. κεκαλυμμένοι: with δῆμός τε πόλις τε.

16. ἐπιδέρκεται is given in most MSS and in Hes. *Th.* 760, which is an obvious Homeric 'quotation'; καταδέρκεται is almost certainly an Alexandrian conjecture (van der Valk, *Textual Criticism*, 38). The rays of Helios cannot reach the earth's surface, evidently because of the ἀήρ and νεφέλη. This explanation is not given in Hes.; but with his 'quotation' he clearly indicates the 'proximity' of the homes of Hypnos and Thanatos (758–61) and the Cimmerians (in the mythical West); cf. 17–18 ∼ *Th.* 761.

17–18. On the striking, and surely intentional repetition of ἄν see Chantraine, *Grammaire*, ii 258, 347.

19. νὺξ ὀλοή: used only once in Homer; cf. Hes. *Th.* 224.   δειλοῖσι βροτοῖσι: formulaic for 'mortal men'; used with individualizing force here.

20. Cf. ix 546, x 20.   μῆλα: cf. 4 and x 527.

21. παρὰ ῥόον: 'beside the stream'.

22. Cf. x 509–15.

23–4. The companions Perimedes (named here for the first time; xii 195) and Eurylochus (x 205, 429 etc.) seize the sacrificial animals, the repeatedly mentioned μῆλα. Odysseus digs the βόθρος with his sword—a heroic gesture (cf. ix 300, x 294, 321) introduces an action which is banal even though based in ritual.

25–34. 25–33 recall Circe's instructions (=x 517–25) as Odysseus follows her words exactly. 34–6, however, leave out some details of x 526–9 in favour of emphasizing ἐς βόθρον and above all ῥέε δ' αἷμα, a pointer to the scene to come. 37 (~x 530) is amplified by 38–43, erroneously regarded by the Alexandrians and some modern critics as late interpolation (Ameis–Hentze, *Anhang*, ii 104–5, von der Mühll, *Odyssee*, 725, Merkelbach, *Untersuchungen*, 189; Focke, *Odyssee*, 208, gives a different view).

36. αἷμα κελαινεφές: cf. Leumann, *Wörter*, 202–6.

39. παρθενικαί here distinguished from νύμφαι (38): 'brides, young women'. ἀταλαί: on ἀταλός (used only once in the *Odyssey*) see Leumann, *Wörter*, 139–41, E. Heitsch, *Aphroditehymnus, Aeneas und Homer* (Göttingen, 1965), 46–56. νεοπενθέα: νεοπενθής (hapax) is probably meant in contrast to πολύτλητοι (38), 'enduring sorrow when young' (i.e. dying young), rather than 'enduring fresh sorrow'.

41. ἀρηΐφατοι (ἀρηΐ-φατος; its only occurrence in the *Odyssey*): 'killed in war' (φόνος, θείνω). βεβροτωμένα (hapax): 'spattered with blood', from βροτόω, derived from βρότος, 'blood' (Leumann, *Wörter*, 124–7). The idea of the spirits of the dead appearing as they did at the moment of death is not in itself as surprising (they are after all called εἴδωλα) as the notion that the dead warriors appear in their bloodied armour.

42. Variant ἔνθα καὶ ἔνθα is preferred by Schwartz, *Odyssee*, 318.

43. The line dismissed as inauthentic by Wilamowitz (*Untersuchungen*, 142. 3, cf. Schwartz, *Odyssee*, 318) corresponds to 633 (with θ. ἰαχῇ for ἠχῇ θ.); the opening and end of the uncanny scene are thus clearly marked. ἰαχή and ἠχή are synonymous, and signify the fluttering and whirling rather than the cries of the ghosts (cf. 605, xxiv 9, Focke, *Odyssee*, 208).

44–50. Cf. x 531–7.

51–83. Odysseus' meeting with the ghost of Elpenor is the first of a long series of encounters with the dead; but it is also a link with the preceding Circe episode (cf. x 551–60). Elpenor was one of Odysseus' closest circle of associates: even in Hades Odysseus is confronted by figures crucial to his fate; cf. R. Spieker's fundamental study, op. cit. (x 551–60 n.), 57–60. The episode, which has so often been seen as a late addition, is an essential element in the *Nekuia*.

51–4: criticized by Wilamowitz (*Untersuchungen*, 144; cf. Focke, *Odyssee*, 209–12) on the grounds that many spirits had already approached (36–43). πρώτη virtually means 'before'; Elpenor's spirit appears before the other spirits named (49), and is in fact still on a different level from them. While the body remains unburied (52–4) the spirit must wait at the entrance to Hades, and still enjoys an unimpaired memory. He is therefore able to address Odysseus directly. Only on burial will his soul be able to enter Hades, whereupon he will lose both νόος and φρένες, as is the fate of the other ghosts (Tiresias being an exception). This accords perfectly with the conceptions presupposed at *Il.* xxiii 71 ff. The draught of blood, for which the other spirits clamour, temporarily restores memory, and permits them to recognize Odysseus. The form of words confirms what we have hitherto only suspected (from x 551-60), that Elpenor's burial had been postponed due to the 'pressing need' (54) to undertake the visit to the Underworld; cf. W. Büchner, *Hermes*, lxxii (1937), 106-7, Eisenberger, *Studien*, 166-7. For 52^b cf. iii 453, x 149. Schwartz, *Odyssee*, 318, regards 52 as a doublet of 53-4.

55. =87, 395.

56. =396.

57-8. 57 = 155. Odysseus' question as to how Elpenor on foot had reached Hades before them does not imply that Odysseus has failed to recognize that his companion is dead: the question is not so much an expression of surprise as an attempt to elicit information. **ζόφον** (usually the gloom of dusk: see E. Risch, *MH* xxv (1968), 213) **ἠερόεντα:** cf. Ἀΐδεω δόμον εὐρώεντα (x 512).

59. =ix 506.

60-5. 60 = x 504 etc. There are some (deliberate) differences between Elpenor's account and x 551-60. Elpenor attributes his drunkenness to a δαίμων (cf. J. Grüber, op. cit. (x 68 n.), 61 ff.); the claim is out of keeping with his character (cf. x 552-3), as is the diction (ἀθέσφατος οἶνος); ἐκλάθετο (x 557) is softened to οὐκ ἐνόησα (62). Already we are aware of a disproportion between Elpenor's personality and his self-estimation, which is developed later. 62 ∼ x 554-7. 63-5 = x 558-60. **ἐν μεγάρῳ** (62): as ἐν δώμασι (x 554).

66-78. Elpenor requests an honourable burial. The heroic language, which intentionally recalls the *Iliad*, highlights the incongruity of Elpenor's claim to status: his birth, station in life, achievements, as well as the manner of his death, are profoundly unheroic.

66-8. Elpenor's appeal in the name of (on πρὸς in this sense see Chantraine, *Grammaire*, ii 134) those left at home, ὄπιθεν, and not yet in Hades, οὐ παρεόντων, is modelled on the phraseology of the speech before battle (cf. Nestor rallying his comrades in the name of their far away kin, *Il.* xv 661-6; here 66 recalls, absurdly, *Il.* xv 665) or the beaten foe's appeal for clemency (cf. the pleas of Hector, *Il.* xxii 338-43, and Priam, *Il.* xxiv 466-7, 486-506). Elpenor does not include Odysseus' mother in his list because she is already in Hades (a detail which prepares for the scene with Anticleia).

69-73. Elpenor concludes his appeal with a warning; in the background stand the plea for a worthy burial addressed by Patroclus' ghost to Achilles (*Il.* xxiii 69-91), and the dying Hector's warning (*Il.* xxii 356-60, esp. *Il.* xxii 358 ∼ *Od.* xi 73). By thus warning Odysseus to beware of divine wrath this unheroic figure shows how he misconceives his position. 69-70 also give the first concrete indication that after visiting Hades Odysseus will return to Circe. **νοσφισθείς:** 'by cruelly abandoning me in my hour of need'.

74–8. Again Elpenor's choice of words and his wishes betray a lack of self-knowledge. Cremation with all his weapons and the raising of a σῆμα to proclaim the dead man's fame to succeeding generations are appropriate for the hero who has fallen honourably, e.g. Eëtion, *Il.* vi 417–20; the supreme example is, of course, Achilles, *Od.* xxiv 80–5; for σῆμα ... ἐπὶ θινὶ θαλάσσης (75) cf. xxiv 82–3; for 76[b] cf. ii 204 etc., *Il.* xxii 305. The τύμβος is to be surmounted by the oar which Elpenor wielded in life—a request which reveals the reality behind Elpenor's delusion of grandeur: his heroic deeds consist of his work as a rower. On the burial rites see M. Andronikos, *Archaeologia* W, 21–34. On the orthography of κακκῆαι (74) cf. Meister, *Kunstsprache*, 148 f., esp. 151, Chantraine, *Grammaire*, i 9, van der Valk, *Textual Criticism*, 164 ff., R. Werner, *H u. ει vor Vokal*, 26.

79. = iv 375 etc.

80. Cf. i 293. Odysseus promises to fulfil, and by the brevity of his reply distances himself from, Elpenor's request: τελευτήσω (cf. τελέσαι 77). It is significant that the epithet δύστηνος, which also belongs to Odysseus himself (93), is used again (cf. 76).

81–3. 81 = 465. Odysseus obeys Circe's instructions (x 535–7). **ἄνευθεν:** here used almost as opposite of ἐτέρωθεν, 'on my side (of the βόθρος)'; E.-M. Voigt, *LfgrE* s.v. **εἴδωλον:** here for the first time in the *Nekuia* as a synonym for ψυχή, 'ghost'.

84–6. Anticleia, daughter of Autolycus (cf. xix 394–7), wife of Laertes, and Odysseus' mother, has long since died (197–203); but Odysseus only now learns of her death.

87–9. 87 = 55. Anticleia, like the other spirits, is attracted by the blood before she recognizes her son; cf. 142–54. Odysseus at first keeps her back from the trench; we therefore have to wait for the expected exchange between mother and son (152–225). 89 = 50, x 537.

90–1. The anaphoric ἦλθε (cf. 84) introduces the second major encounter of the book, the one which is the purpose of Odysseus' journey to Hades. Tiresias also has no need to taste the blood before recognizing Odysseus; cf. x 494.

92. Evidence for the authenticity of this line (omitted by most MSS) lies in its similarity to 473 and 617, which likewise are followed by vocatives (σχέτλιε, ἆ δείλ'; here ὦ δύστηνε).

93–6. Tiresias' opening question is rhetorical (cf. x 281), as the prophet knows full well the reason for Odysseus' coming. αὖτε has almost the force of a sympathetic reproach (Ameis–Hentze on x 281). 94[b]: cf. vii 279[b]; Hades is the ἀτερπὴς χῶρος, the place where by definition there can be no τέρπεσθαι. ἴδη is to be preferred to ἴδης; cf. J. Bechert, op. cit. (ix 142–5 n.), 73. The draught of blood is here (cf. 90–1 n.) necessary before any prophecy can be given. 96[b]: cf. iii 19[b].

97–8. cf. *Il.* i 219–20. **κουλεῷ:** cf. κολεῷ (x 333); Bechtel, *Lexilogus*, 177.

100–37. The prophecy itself, particularly in relation to Circe's preceding announcement (x 539–40) and directions (xii 37–141), has given rise to a multiplicity of analytical theories. To name only a few of the more modern approaches, see Schwartz, *Odyssee*, 138–45, Focke, *Odyssee*, 199–207, J. Irmscher, op. cit. (x 249 n.), 57–9, W. Theiler, *MH* vii (1950), 104–7, *MH* xix (1962), 11, Merkelbach, *Untersuchungen*, 186 ff., Marzullo, op. cit. (ix 526–35 n.), 107, Kirk, *Songs*, 238 ff., and Lesky, *Homeros*, 121. The unitary approach is preferable: cf. van der Valk, *Beiträge zur Nekyia* (Kampen, 1935), 19–73, W. Büchner, *Hermes*, lxxii (1937), 119 ff., Reinhardt, 'Abenteuer', 126–32, F. Eichhorn, op. cit. (ix 228 n.), R. Spieker, op. cit. (x 551–60 n.), 77, G. Bona, op. cit. (ix 106–15 n.), 53–67, U. Hölscher, in *Festschr. f. R. Alewyn* (Cologne/Graz, 1967), 13, Rüter, *Odysseeinterpretationen*, 109, Erbse, *Beiträge*, 25, and (particularly useful) Besslich, *Schweigen*, 53–60. Admittedly Tiresias only partly fulfils the task for which he has been introduced (x 539–40); the remainder is completed by Circe, xii 37–141. But the seer passes over what Circe will later say and what he, as a divinely inspired seer, scarcely can say. It falls to him to reveal the background to events: hence his allusions to the anger of Poseidon, the decisive events on Thrinacia, and the necessity for an atoning sacrifice later; Circe is in a position to enlarge on this. It is not Tiresias' role to give details of itinerary and practical advice; these come more fittingly from Circe, once she, from Odysseus' detailed account of his journey to Hades (xii 34–5), has learned the most important point, notably the fact that Odysseus must proceed via Thrinacia. She may then advise on a detailed route (xii 25–6). This division of the narrative elements between the speeches of Tiresias and Circe results from well-considered poetic structuring, in a form particularly characteristic of the poet of the *Odyssey*.

100. The objective, taken from x 539–40, is emphatically stated at the outset: 'you are seeking a happy journey home'.

101–3. Odysseus now discovers what he could not have known at the time of his adventure with the Cyclops, that Poseidon has heard Polyphemus' prayer (ix 528–39), and is angry with Odysseus for blinding his son (τοι depends on κότον 102). The god will make Odysseus' νόστος ἀργαλέος (πολλὰ ἄλγεα i 4). In 119–37, however, Tiresias indicates how the god is to be appeased at the last. The construction of 101–2 is οὐ γὰρ ὀίω⟨σε⟩ (subj.) λήσειν ἐνοσσίγαιον (obj.).

104–15. In 101–3 Tiresias looked forward to the homecoming predestined for Odysseus. Polyphemus had been right to allow for such a possibility: ἀλλ' εἴ οἱ μοῖρ' ἐστὶ ... ἱκέσθαι ... ἐς πατρίδα γαῖαν (ix 532–3). In 104 ff. Tiresias resumes this line of thought and pursues it further: κακά περ πάσχοντες enlarges on ἀργαλέον (101). Only one of the hazards to come is specified: the episode at Thrinacia, which, within the framework of destiny, will decide the Greeks' fate. If the cattle are spared, ship and crew will return home safely (111 refers back to 104). But if the animals are slaughtered, the minimum demand of Polyphemus' curse will be fulfilled (114–15 = ix 534–5): through the anger of Helios Odysseus will lose the ship with all hands, and he will come home only after long delay and on a ship not his own. The anger of the two gods, Poseidon and Helios, is differentiated, and at the same time integrated into the story's concept of fate. The doubts expressed by Wilamowitz, *Untersuchungen*, 145, and Schwartz, *Odyssee*, 318–19, partly with reference to 104–13, are unfounded.

109. = xii 323, *Il.* iii 277.

110–14. = xii 137–41. The εἰ μέν clause (after the subordinate clause of 104–9) resumes and amplifies the αἴ κ᾽ phrase of 105. The parallelism (110 εἰ μέν κ᾽ : 111–12ᵃ εἰ δέ κε : 112ᵇ–15) is underlined by the diction (ἀσινέας 110 : σίνηαι 112). On τεκμαίρομαι (112) see Bechtel, *Lexilogus*, 310–11.

115–20. The prophecy of 114–15 leads to a description of what awaits the hero at home (πήματα) and how he is to deal with the situation. 116–20 have often been seen as interpolation (Wilamowitz, *Untersuchungen*, 145, Focke, *Odyssee*, 203. 1, Eisenberger, *Studien*, 171. 38); against this view, see Merkelbach, *Untersuchungen*, 187 (with bibliography). Three main arguments are put forward for regarding the passage as inauthentic: that the introduction of the suitors does not fit the present context; that it makes the form of Odysseus' question to his mother (174–9) inappropriate; and that the economy of the poem as a whole demands that the introduction of the problem of the suitors be left to Athena (xiii 374–81). However, the lines are necessary to avoid an otherwise abrupt transition: πήματα (115) requires some explanation; and ἔρχεσθαι δὴ ἔπειτα (121) makes sense only in the context of the preceding αὐτὰρ ἐπὴν … (119–20). Odysseus can not embark on his last journey (121) until he has not only found πήματα at home, but also overcome them. His later conversation with Athena (xiii 374 ff.; 117 = xiii 378) does not imply that Odysseus knew nothing of the suitors before.

116–17. These lines define the πήματα as the unlawful and violent actions of the suitors (cf. βίας ἀποτίσεαι 118); inexactly interpreted by Wilamowitz, *Untersuchungen*, 145. On the artificial form ἔδνα for ἔεδνα (i 277, ii 196) see Beekes, op. cit. (ix 42 n.), 58–9.

119–20. The slightly altered repetition of i 295 is thematically conditioned and deliberate: the advance indication of later events in Ithaca, where Odysseus will overcome the suitors both δόλῳ and ὀξέϊ χαλκῷ is best presented as the utterance of a seer.

˙121–37. = xxiii 268–84. As befits his role as a prophet Tiresias places human experience in the context of the divine order. After dealing with possible divine retribution for an outrage on Thrinacia, and Odysseus' revenge on the wicked suitors, Tiresias speaks of the atonement needed to propitiate Poseidon and assuage the divine anger still unappeased even after the killing of the suitors. The instructions of 121 ff. conclude this speech on the theme of ὕβρις/τίσις, outlining the hero's fate beyond the time-period covered by the poem after the manner of the *Iliad*; cf. e.g. the prophecy given by Hector, *Il.* xxii 356–60. Odysseus is to make a pilgrimage to a place far inland, whose inhabitants indeed know nothing of the sea and seafaring, and there sacrifice to Poseidon; on his return home he is to make another sacrifice, to all the gods; and finally he will die at a ripe old age, an easy death after a happy reign. The prophecy has led to a number of speculative analytical theories, in which an important part is played by a hypothetical earlier epic *Thesprotis*, knowledge of which is alleged to be presupposed in the *Odyssey's* necromancy: Schwartz, *Odyssee*, 140 ff., Wilamowitz, *Heimkehr*, 79 ff., von der Mühll, *Philologus*, xciii (1938), 3–11, Theiler, *MH* xix (1962), 11, and Merkelbach (who gives a useful survey), *Untersuchungen*, 220–30. It is certainly possible that Tiresias' instructions contain older, traditional material drawn from mythology or cult, and that already in pre-Homeric tradition Odysseus may have visited an oracle of the dead: we cannot say anything more precise. The significant point is that the lines have an important function in the context of the present poem; the poet must say something about the propitiation of the angry god, since without the god's goodwill the reign of peace in Ithaca, the τέλος of both action and poem, could not be established on a firm basis; hence the ceremonies of expiation outside the sea-god's own domain; cf. F. Jacoby, *Die Antike*, ix (1933), 190; van der Valk, op. cit. (100–37 n.), 19–20, F. Dornseiff, *Hermes*, lxxii (1937), 351–5, Reinhardt, 'Abenteuer', 126–32.

121. εὐῆρες: 'easy to handle'; formed like χαλκήρης (i 262, x 206); Risch, *Wortbildung*, 80–1; cf. the Mycenaean name *e-u-wa-re/E(h)u-(w)ārēs* PY Jn 693.

122. On the strange form ἴσᾱσι (also 124) cf. Chantraine, *Grammaire* i 179. 2, 470–1; Hoekstra, *Modifications*, 91. 2.

123. The inland people are ignorant even of the use of salt (here pl. ἅλες) to season food. The poet may be drawing here on tales of far-away peoples who were popularly supposed not to use salt.

124. φοινικοπαρῄους (*hapax*): 'purple-cheeked' (cf. μιλτοπάρῃος ix 125); on φοῖνιξ, 'purple, etc.', see D. Muhly, *Berytus*, xxix (1970), 19–64.

125. The oars are metaphorically described (kenning) as the ship's wings; cf. iv 708, where ships are seen as ἁλὸς ἵπποι; I. Waern, Γῆς ὀστέα: *The Kenning in Pre-Christian Greek Poetry* (Uppsala, 1951).

126–8. 126 = *Il.* xxiii 326. Tiresias gives Odysseus an 'unmistakable' sign (σῆμα ἀριφραδές) by which he may recognize the country indicated in 122–5: he will know he has arrived in the right place when someone mistakes his shouldered oar for a winnowing fan. **ἀθηρηλοιγόν** (*hapax*) is formed like βροτολοιγός, with ἀθήρ, 'awn, chaff' as the first element (cf. Risch, *Wortbildung*, 198, S. Laser, *LfgrE* s.v.): literally 'consumer of chaff', another kenning (see 125 n.).

129. καὶ τότε δή refers back to αὐτὰρ ἐπήν ... (119). The echo of 77 is deliberate: the gesture of planting his oar in the earth will represent an end to Odysseus' wanderings.

130–1. The threefold sacrifice prescribed (later τριττύα) is exceptional in Homer, corresponding as it does to the Roman *suovetaurilia*. **ἐπιβήτορα:** 'of the boar' (lit. 'mounting'); this is the only instance in which the word is used as an adj.; cf. ἐ. ἵππων, 'charioteer' (xviii 623).

132–4ᵃ. After the atoning sacrifice to Poseidon, Odysseus is to offer a thanksgiving sacrifice on his return home to all the gods; cf. Proteus' directions to

Menelaus (iv 478–9) and the Mycenaean offerings *pa-si-te-o-i/pansi thehoihi* KN Fp 1 etc., Ventris–Chadwick, *Documents*, 303–4.

134ᵇ–7. Odysseus will die a gentle death ἐξ ἁλός, in old age. The phrase ἐξ ἁλός is obscure, and the subject of some dispute: cf. the analytical discussions by Schwartz, *Odyssee*, 140–1 and Theiler, *MH* vii (1950), 120–1. We may, however, be sure that Tiresias foresees for Odysseus a death 'away from the sea', on dry land. Odysseus will then be at home, having finally been released from the perils of the sea; cf. Reinhardt, 'Abenteuer', 131, U. Hölscher, *Gnomon*, xxxix (1967), 443; for a similar use of ἐξ cf. xv 272, xvi 288 etc. Reinterpretation of the expression ἐξ ἁλός played an important part in the development of the Telegonus saga in the epic cycle; cf. A. Hartmann, *Untersuchungen über die Sagen vom Tod des Odysseus* (Munich, 1917), 73–5, 90 ff. On the co-existence of ἀβληχρός and βληχρός (since Alcaeus) see Leumann, *Wörter*, 55, Forssman, *Untersuchungen zur Sprache Pindars* (Wiesbaden, 1966), 117–18; Beekes, *Laryngeals*, 49. On ἀρημένος (cf. ix 403, vi 2, and esp. γήραϊ λυγρῷ ἀ. *Il.* xviii 434–5), here 'weakened', see B. Mader, *LfgrE* s.v. **λιπαρῷ**: 'sleek', as an epithet of γῆρας (as at xix 368; cf. λιπαρῶς γηρασκέμεν iv 210) almost with the meaning 'rich, wealthy'. Similarly ὄλβιος (137), 'possessed of ὄλβος, fortunate' (cf. J. Gruber, *Gnomon*, xliii (1971), 17) here means 'blessed with all worldly goods'. 135–7 present an ideal, corresponding to the inner τέλος of the *Odyssey*, which is consciously very different, indeed opposed to that of the *Iliad*. The one epic depicts the young hero, crowning a life of brave deeds with an early, glorious death on the battlefield; the sequel portrays the conquering hero as a ruler of men, returning from war to rule long and wisely over a happy country blessed with riches. 137ᵇ = 96ᵇ.

139. ἐπέκλωσαν: cf. i 17, iii 208.

140. = i 169 etc.

144–9. 'How might she recognize me for what I am?' Odysseus as yet knows neither the reason for the behaviour of his mother's ψυχή nor the means to change it. Tiresias' answer explains the reasons behind both the blood sacrifice and the behaviour of the ψυχαί (36–43): spirits which taste the blood will recall, for a little while, their previous existence (cf. 51–4 n.) and be able to give information. It is questionable whether the poet is here drawing on a genuine ancient belief, or whether he has not in fact invented this aspect of the life of ψυχαί, and hence introduced the blood motif with so much supporting detail, in order to make possible the various discourses which are in fact the main substance of the book; cf. Focke, *Odyssee*, 213 ff. *et passim*.

146. ἐπί (which is given in most MSS) is to be preferred to ἐνί; cf. v 427, *Il.* i 55, van der Valk, *Textual Criticism*, 44.

148ᵇ. Cf. iii 93, 101. As at 149, δέ is 'apodotic', introducing the main clause after the relative protasis.

152–225ᵃ. The meeting with Anticleia is particularly carefully prepared (84–9 and 140–9) in order to underline its importance (Reinhardt, 'Abenteuer', 135–6). At the same time it is closely linked with the encounter with Elpenor; both figures had been close to Odysseus, but how different their behaviour!

154. = x 324 etc.

155. ~ 57, but with an essential difference: the question Odysseus put to Elpenor is here asked of Odysseus by his mother.

156-9: 157-9 were rejected as spurious by Aristarchus, and after him, *inter alios*, by Wilamowitz (*Untersuchungen*, 158. 20), van Leeuwen, Schwartz (*Odyssee*, 318), and W. Schadewaldt (in his translation); cf. also von der Mühll, *Odyssee*, 727, Merkelbach, *Untersuchungen*, 190, and, for a different view, Focke, *Odyssee*, 214, who sees 156 (imitated *h.Cer.* 111) as a later interpolation. For an elucidation of the meaning see J. Bechert, op. cit. (ix 142-5 n.), 412: 156 does not mean that the scene is a hard, i.e. sad, sight for mortal eyes (Wilamowitz, loc. cit.), but that it is difficult, indeed impossible, for a living man to see it; the concepts of both coming and seeing are contained in the one word ὁρᾶσθαι. 157-9 give the explanation, concentrating on the difficulty for a living man in reaching Hades.

μέσσῳ: between the realm of the living and Hades.   **ποταμοί** is almost certainly not a reference to the rivers of the Underworld (x 513-15); cf. the explicit reference to the river (!) Oceanus, reinforced by μὲν: 'of all these, the Oceanus especially'.   **περῆσαι:** cf. 14-19 n.

161-2. Rejected as spurious by Aristophanes; similarly Wilamowitz, *Untersuchungen*, 158. 20, Schwartz, *Odyssee*, 319. It is, however, clear that in 166-7 Odysseus refers back to 160-2. πολὺν χρόνον: with ἀλώμενος.

164-5. 165 ~ x 492. Odysseus first answers the question πῶς ἦλθες (155-9).   **χρειώ:** cf. Circe's words (χρή x 490).

166-7. These lines answer the question posed in 160-2; οὐ ... πω ... ἦλθον (166) answers οὐδέ πω ἦλθες (161); ἀλάλημαι (167) answers ἀλώμενος (160). The keyword γυναῖκα (162) is left to the end of Odysseus' reply (177-9).

169. = xiv 71; modelled on *Il.* xvi 576.

170-9. After giving his answer Odysseus in turn asks three questions, each occupying three lines: about his mother's death; the fate of his father and son; and the position of his wife.

170. = 140.

171. = 398.   **κὴρ ... θανάτοιο** (cf. *Il.* ii 302): here almost 'type of death'.   **τανηλεγέος θανάτοιο:** cf. ii 100.

172-3. δολιχὴ (here temporal) **νοῦσος:** 'chronic disease', as opposed to a swift, painless death, attributed to the arrows of Apollo or Artemis (173 = iii 280, v 124).   **ἰοχέαιρα:** cf. vi 102.

174. The remarkable construction εἰπεῖν + gen. is perhaps derived from expressions such as i 10 τῶν (originally partitive) ... εἰπέ; cf. L. R. Palmer in *Companion*, 133. Father and son are mentioned proleptically: 'Do my father and son still enjoy princely status?' (γέρας); cf. *Il.* xx 182; H. Erbse, *RhM* cx (1967), 12-13.

177-9. Odysseus enquires about his wife's βουλή and νόος (cf. ii 281). His meaning becomes clear with his double question at 178-9. The parallels in construction between 171-3, 174-6, and 177-9 are quite clear and

COMMENTARY

deliberate; they also indicate that 178ab, which are modelled on xix 526–7 (cf. also xvi 75; 178 = xix 525; 179 ~ xix 528, xvi 76), are a late interpolation. The most important question is given last: whether Penelope is still faithful to Odysseus, or now married to another. The awkwardness of these lines following the information given by Tiresias (115–17) is less than is often supposed: knowledge of the outline of the situation at home impels Odysseus to seek to know more.

180. = 215.

181–203. Anticleia answers the questions in reverse order, 177–9 at 181–3; 174–6 at 184–96; and 171–3 at 197–203. The question as to whether Anticleia is describing the situation in Ithaca at the time of her death, or whether she is giving an up-to-date account, must be seen in perspective. Odysseus is doomed to spend seven years on the island of Calypso; and yet Tiresias speaks of the suitors, who according to ii 89 and xix 152 begin their wooing only three to four years before the hero returns home; and Anticleia (184–7) speaks of Telemachus as a young adult who has already won men's respect; cf. C. M. Bowra in *Companion*, 70. The poet almost imperceptibly alters the time-scale quite substantially, allowing the hero to report conversations the content of which really only fits the period immediately before he lands in Phaeacia, in order to prepare the reader for the events of xiii–xxiv. It is in this context that we must understand Anticleia's failure to mention the suitors: 181, referring back to 178, shows that she is aware of them, but Odysseus has already been warned by Tiresias; cf. Erbse, *Beiträge*, 27, (with bibliography).

182–3. = xiii 337–8. ὀϊζυραί (cf. iii 95): here predic., 'full of misery'.

184–7. These lines give the answer to 175–6. No one as yet has usurped the throne. This is of course as much of a warning as a reassurance; but it is a comfort to Odysseus to know that his son has the use of his father's possessions (Odysseus' τέμενος is mentioned again at xvii 299; cf. the τέμενος of Alcinous, vi 293) and gives banquets in keeping with his status as a δικασπόλος ἀνήρ. The implication is that Telemachus is carrying out the duties of his royal father, and that he is a welcome guest in the homes of others.

184. ἕκηλος: cf. ii 311.

185–6. δαῖτας ἐΐσας δαίνυται: cf. iii 6 and vii 98. δικασπόλον (only here and *Il.* i 238): 'law-giving' (cf. *Il.* i 238 and ii 205–6); cf. Bechtel, *Lexilogus*, 192, Chantraine, *Dictionnaire* s.v. δίκη. ἀλεγύνειν: cf. i 374.

187. καλέουσι: 'they invite him' (to meals and to councils); cf. viii 53–5.

187–96. Odysseus' enquiry after his father (174) must be answered; but the lines also prepare for the description in xxiv. For an analytical view see von der Mühll, *Odyssee*, 726; cf. Merkelbach, *Untersuchungen*, 187–8.

188–9. = xix 318, xxiii 180; cf. iii 349 n. εὐναί (predic.) sc. εἰσιν, 'serve as a bed'. On Homeric beds see S. Laser, *Archaeologia* P 1–15.

190. χεῖμα (acc.) μέν (cf. vii 118): contrast with 192.

191. On εἶται and the MS variants cf. Ameis–Hentze, *Anhang*, ii 109, Chantraine, *Grammaire*, i 297, van der Valk, *Textual Criticism*, 100; cf. εἶμαι in an identical hemistich, xix 72, xxiii 115.

88

192. ὀπώρη: cf. -ῖνός (v 328).

193. Cf. i 193 (also about Laertes).

194. His makeshift bed is improvised from fallen leaves on the ground (χθαμαλαί). **κεκλιμένων,** 'fallen, lying on the ground', is unusual (hence the attempts to 'correct': -μένῳ, κεκλαμένων, κακχυμένων; cf. Stanford, ad loc.), formed perhaps after expressions such as ἔντεα ... χθονὶ κέκλιτο (Il. x 471–2).

195. μέγα: predic., with πένθος.

196. The reading of the χαριέστεραι, σὸν νόστον ποθέων, is probably an attempt to 'improve' on the much better attested reading, σὸν πότμον γοόων (cf. Il. xvi 857); Ameis–Hentze, Anhang, ii 109, van der Valk, Textual Criticism, 162. **ἐπὶ:** with ἱκάνει (pf. in sense). **χαλεπὸν:** here predic.

197–203. Odysseus' second and third questions could be answered in terms of the alternatives given. His first question is not so easily answered, since Anticleia died neither a swift, painless death (198–9 refer to 172ᵇ–3) nor one brought about by a long, wasting disease (200–1 answer and amplify the question as given in 172ᵃ). Longing for Odysseus brought about her death; and this is the climax to which the conversation has been building from 170 onwards.

197. οὕτω: the same experience which drove Laertes to despair and resignation drove Odysseus' mother into a premature grave; 202–3 are anticipated here.

198. ἐΰσκοπος: used elsewhere only as an epithet of Hermes; this is not, however, sufficient reason to reject 198–9 as spurious (V. Bérard).

201. τηκεδόνι ('wasting away') **στυγερῇ** amplifies δολιχή (172). **ἐξείλετο:** gnomic aor.

202–3. σός ... πόθος, 'longing for you': this idea is then developed (and syntactically altered; cf. x 245 n.) as 'pining for your μήδεα and your ἀγανοφροσύνη' (elsewhere only at Il. xxiv 772, a characteristic of Hector's praised by Helen). **μελιηδέα θυμὸν:** as at Il. xvii 17. **ἀπηύρα** (cf. iii 192): cf. K. Strunk, Glotta, xxxvii (1958), 118–27.

204. μερμηρίξας: here, most unusually, used absolutely; ἔθελον μερμηρίξας means almost the same as μερμήριζον (cf. x 151–5, 438–42 nn.) or θυμὸς ἀνώγει (206; cf. μεμαῶτα 210).

206–7. The model for this scene is Il. xxiii 97 ff. (on Il. xxiii 65–101 as a model for the encounter with Elpenor cf. 69–73 n.); the structure is also reminiscent of Il. v 436–7, xvi 702–3, 784–5. Elements of heroic epic are here, however, combined with an intensely human drama (Reinhardt, 'Abenteuer', 135 ff.). For the comparison of the soul to καπνός cf. the images of σκιά (x 495) and ὄνειρος (xi 222).

208. γενέσκετο: iterat. because of the threefold repetition, τρὶς μὲν, τρὶς δέ (206–7).

210. τί ... μ' οὐ μίμνεις; 'why do you avoid me?'

212. Cf. Il. xxiii 97. On the interpretation cf. J. Latacz, op. cit. (ix 5–11), 189.

213–14. The intensity of the experience causes Odysseus to mistake the ψυχή

89

for the figure of his mother in life; he cannot understand her behaviour (206–8) and wonders if it is possible that Persephone has sent the form he sees standing before him (τόδ') as a phantom, a deceptive apparition (εἴδωλον, predic. with τόδ'). The answer is given in 216–24: the figure is an εἴδωλον, but in the sense of a ψυχή. Compare 214 with ix 13.

215. = 180.

216. κάμμορε: cf. ii 351.

217–20. Anticleia's answer neatly summarizes the main points of Homeric belief concerning the ψυχή; cf. J. Böhme, *Die Seele und das Ich im hom. Epos* (Leipzig, 1929), W. Marg, *Der Charakter in der Sprache der frühgriech. Dichtung* (1938; 2nd edn. Darmstadt, 1967), B. Snell, *Die Entdeckung des Geistes* (1946; 3rd edn. Hamburg, 1955), 43–64, O. Regenbogen, *Kleine Schriften* (Munich, 1961), 1–20 (1st. publ. 1948), L. Moulinier, *Universitas*, xxi (1966), 1077–92, A. Schnaufer, *Frühgriech. Totenglaube* (Hildesheim, 1970), J. Warden, *Phoenix*, xxv (1971), 95–103. The lines explain the nature of δίκη βροτῶν after death, the law to which mankind is subject. In life the ψυχή contained within the body is the *sine qua non* for bodily and mental activity. On death the ψυχή escapes from the body, now merely dead matter; the soul, which made life possible, lives on in Hades as an εἴδωλον, with the outward form of the human body which it had once imbued with life. Thus Odysseus had recognized the ψυχή of his mother, and indeed assumed that the ψυχή was his mother.

217. Anticleia's assurance that Persephone is not deceiving Odysseus answers his question of 213–14; what he sees really is the εἴδωλον of his mother.

218. Only ὅτε τίς κε θάνῃσιν is possible; Ruijgh, τε *épique*, 298; cf. Schwartz, *Odyssee*, 319.

219. ἔχουσιν: 'hold together'.

220–1. τὰ μέν: the parts of the body given at 219. The formulaic πυρὸς αἰθομένοιο and κρατερὸν μένος are most unusually combined. Cremation is assumed to be the normal method of disposal of corpses; cf. G. S. Kirk, *MH* xvii (1959), 193, M. Andronikos, *Archaeologia* W, 129–31. Like the ψυχή, the θυμός, source of the affections and emotions, leaves the body on death; it does not, however, live on after death.

222. The ψυχή is compared to a dream, because neither possesses any corporeal reality. On πεπότηται, 'flutters hither and thither', see Chantraine, *Grammaire*, i 436.

224. The line prepares for xxiii 310–41, esp. 325.

225ᵃ: cf. 81ᵃ.

225–332. 225–34 form the introduction to the so-called catalogue of heroines which relates the lineage and fate of a number of women from mythology. The catalogue has long since been regarded as a late interpolation, or the work of the last reviser of the *Odyssey* (cf., among others, Wilamowitz, *Untersuchungen*, 147–51, von der Mühll, *Odyssee*, 726 ff., Focke, *Odyssee*, 217–22, C. M. Bowra in *Companion*, 45). Certain similarities in form and content with post-Hesiodic catalogue poetry have led some to conjecture that it was based on the *Ehoiai*: R. Pfeiffer, *Philologus*, xcii (1937), 1–18, Merkelbach, *Untersuchungen*, 177, 188, Page, *Odyssey*, 35–8, M. Treu, *RhM* c (1957), 169–86, esp. 173 ff., Kirk, *Songs*, 237, W. Theiler, *MH* xix (1962), 22. 96, Lesky, *Homeros*, 126, A. Dihle, op. cit. (x 509–12 n.), 151. Not only is there no proof of such dependence; it is also highly improbable. A common source for both the post-Hesiodic catalogue poetry and the genealogical passage in xi seems more probable (Heubeck, *Dichter*, 19–22, 33–5, Webster, *Mycenae*, 178 ff.); indeed J. T. Kakridis (*Poetica*, v (1972), 152–63) has demonstrated the existence of a pre-Homeric oral tradition of catalogue poetry in Ionia, and shown its importance in the development of myth and epic. This, however, does not establish the authenticity of 225–332. The difficulties inherent in the introductory lines 225–34 and in the catalogue itself are most clearly defined by W. Kühlmann, op. cit. (ix 14–15 n.), 62–5: the catalogue seems hardly integrated in the narrative context; on the contrary, its introduction seems artificial and forced, and its relevance to the main thrust of the poem's action and the fate of Odysseus seems minimal. Odysseus as narrator here exchanges roles, from that of relating his own experiences to that of the genealogical poet. Without denying the validity of these arguments it is, however, possible to see the lines in question as fitting into an overall concept of the poem; cf. van der Valk, loc. cit. (100–37 n.), W. Büchner, *Hermes*, lxxv (1940), 107, Reinhardt, 'Abenteuer', 136 ff., Heubeck, *Dichter*, 33–5, F. Eichhorn, op. cit. (ix 228 n.), 76. 54 ff., Erbse, *Beiträge*, 27 ff. The catalogue is an essential part of the formal structure of the book (cf. introduction to xi above), and, as the analytical critics have also stressed (Focke, *Odyssee*, 217 ff., Lesky, *Homeros*, 126), closely connected in thought and composition with the so-called 'intermezzo', which has an undoubted place in the structure of the Phaeacian episode. The encounter with Anticleia prepares for the catalogue, which itself then prepares not only for the 'intermezzo', but also for the encounter with the three heroes from the Trojan War (385–565) (Erbse, *Beiträge*, 27 ff.). The lack of any direct connection between the stories related in this episode and the fate of Odysseus is a flaw in composition, but does not detract from the episode's function within the story as a whole, as demonstrated by Reinhardt (op. cit., 36): 'It is in the very nature of the encounters in the Νέκυια that they have to be wide-ranging to be meaningful. The overall plan of the *Odyssey* requires such a richness of experience: the hero comes face to face with the whole Greek heroic world, and beyond that, with the whole of departed humanity.'

225–8. While Odysseus was speaking the spirits of all the wives and daughters of outstanding men have gathered, and are now pressing forward towards the blood of the sacrifice. The transition to this scene from the preceding episode (νῶϊ μὲν ... αἱ δὲ) may seem a little forced, but is in keeping with normal epic technique. The scene is prepared by 36–43 (νύμφαι (38) is entirely possible as a description of the heroines); and the ὀτρύνειν of Persephone is not in fact as strange as often supposed, as the goddess encourages the women to approach (before all the others).

COMMENTARY

229–32: a typical deliberation scene of the same sort as *Il.* ii 3 ff., x 3 ff., xiv 159 ff., *Od.* ix 295 ff., 420 ff.; C. Voigt, op. cit. (ix 299–305 n.), 21 ff., 29. The hero has a clear aim, to speak with as many of the heroines as possible and learn their lineage and fate. He therefore decides to allow them to taste the blood, which will briefly restore memory and speech, (148 and 153), only one at a time. To this end he brandishes the sword with which he had previously prevented the other ghosts from tasting the blood before Tiresias (48–50; 280 ~ 48).

233. προμνηστῖναι (only here and xxi 230): 'stepping forward one after the other'; B. Forssman, *ZVS* lxxix (1964), 26–8, and *MSS* xx (1967), 9–16 (in opposition to earlier explanations, e.g. Bechtel, *Lexilogus*, 284).

234. ἐξαγόρευεν: the only example of a cpd. of ἀγορεύω (Wackernagel, *Untersuchungen*, 219, Shipp, *Studies*, 336): approx. 'give an extensive account of'.

235–59: the encounter with Tyro. The fiction of a conversation is briefly maintained (φάτο 236, φῆ 237) before Odysseus assumes his new role as narrating genealogical poet. The dry account of Tyro's genealogical situation is enlivened by elements of epic narrative (the heroine's meeting with Poseidon, and the introduction of direct speech, 248–52); here we may see the influence of pre-Homeric genealogical poetry. The scene is also linked with the meeting with Chloris (280–97: wife of Neleus, mentioned at 254 as one of Tyro's sons), and the picture is completed by the account of Theoclymenus' antecedents (xv 225–55); the manner in which these three sections are combined into a whole is a sure sign of the organizing hand of the master poet; cf. Heubeck, *Dichter* 19–22. We are here told how Tyro, daughter of Salmoneus (a son of Aeolus), falls in love with the river-god Enipeus; Poseidon assumes the appearance of Enipeus, and fathers two sons by Tyro, Pelias and Neleus, of whom the first remains in Iolcus, and the second founds a kingdom at Pylos. Tyro later marries Cretheus, another son of Aeolus, and bears him a further three sons. The same story is related in the *Ehoiai*, often with similar wording: 240 = fr. 30,35; 243–4 ~ fr. 32; 249–50 = fr. 31,2–3; 253 ~ fr. 31,6 M–W. The poet of the *Ehoiai*, like the poet of the *Odyssey*, drew his material from old epic tradition, but also had 235–59 before him. Sophocles uses the same material in his *Tyro* (frr. 648–669); cf. Apollodorus, *Bibl.* i 90–2. Some scholars, including Webster, *Mycenae*, 119, 178 ff., have suggested a historical basis for this legend. It is possible that events of Mycenaean history do indeed lie behind this legend (there is some supporting archaeological evidence: Iaolkos (Iolcus) like Pylos has been shown to have been an important centre in Mycenaean times), but if so, then only in a form mutated by distant memory.

238. ἠράσσατ' (ο): (ingress.) aor. of ἔραμαι: 'fell in love with' (+ gen.).

241. ἄρα εἰσάμενος is to be preferred to ἄρ' ἐεισάμενος; cf. Beekes, *Laryngeals*, 59 ff., who discusses the genesis of the old formula.

243. οὔρεϊ: the metrical lengthening is strange; cf. Meister, *Kunstsprache*, 128; Shipp, *Studies*, 336.

244. κυρτωθέν (*hapax*), from κυρτόω: 'arch above'.

245: perhaps interpolation: rejected by critics in antiquity, but defended by van der Valk, *Textual Criticism*, 260–1.

246. φιλοτήσια (*hapax*), from φιλότης; on -ήσιος forms see Risch, *Wortbildung*, 115; there is no reason to regard the form as Attic, as Shipp (*Studies*, 336) argues.

249. The choice between τέξεις and τέξεαι is a difficult one. τέξεαι may be cj. by Zenodotus; cf. van der Valk, *Textual Criticism*, 98. On ἀποφώλιος cf. Bechtel, *Lexilogus*, 52, Chantraine, *Dictionnaire* s.v., *LfgrE* s.v.

251. μηδ' ὀνομήνῃς: 'do not mention my name!'

255. θεράποντε Διός (dual), probably modelled on Ἄρεος θεράποντε (*Il.* xix 47); cf. G. Ramming, op. cit. (x 348–9 n.), 27, G. Stagakis, *Historia*, xv (1966), 408–19.

258–9. Three of the names given are attested in Myc.: *ke-re-te-u*/Krētheus, *a₃-so-ni-jo*/Aisŏnijos (an -ιος formation from Αἴσων), and *a-mu-ta-wo*/Amythāwōn. ἱπποχάρμην: the second element is χάρμη, 'joy of battle': J. Latacz, op. cit. (ix 5–11), 20–38. In the first half of the cpd. we have the word *i-qi-ja*/hiqquijā, 'battle-chariot', which later fell into disuse. ἱπποχάρμης thus means 'finding the joy of battle in the clash of chariots'; cf. H. Mühlestein, *MH* xii (1955), 123. On the orthography of Ἰαωλκός (256) see M. West, *Glotta*, xli (1963), 278–82.

260–5. Antiope's claim to fame is that she bore to Zeus the twins Amphion and Zethus, who built the walls of Thebes (κιθάρᾳ, with the lyre: Hes. fr. 182 M–W). For further details of the legend see Apollodorus *Bibl.* iii 42–4; cf. L. Preller–C. Robert, *Griech. Mythologie*⁴ (Berlin, 1894/1926), ii 1, 164 ff. Euripides' *Antiope* (fr. 231–78 Mette) is also based on the legend.

261. ἐν ἀγκοίνῃσιν ἰαῦσαι: modelled on *Il.* xiv 213; cf. 268.

264. ἀπύργωτον (*hapax*): 'unfortified'.

266–70. Alcmene, wife of Amphitryon, bore Heracles, again to Zeus; cf. *Il.* xix 95–113, Hes., fr. 195. 8 ff. (*Sc.* 1 ff.) M–W; the legend receives dramatic treatment in Plautus' *Amphitryon*. Megara is Heracles' Theban wife; cf. Apollodorus *Bibl.* ii 70.

267ᵇ. = *Il.* v 639ᵇ, where again Heracles is the subject; it is possible that this is a fragment from earlier poetry about Heracles.

270. ἀτειρής (etym. uncertain): metaphorically used as a description of people (as here), perhaps 'hard, unyielding'; originally an epithet of χαλκός; cf. Bechtel, *Lexilogus*, 72; Chantraine, *Dictionnaire* s.v.

271–80. The description of Epicaste, wife of Laius, and mother of Oedipus, is the oldest identifiable version of the Oedipus legend, and contains all the central elements of that story: Oedipus' murder of his father, marriage with his mother (generally called Jocasta in subsequent treatments of the story), the discovery of the crime, and his mother's curse and suicide. The account, which is probably based on, but does not enable us to reconstruct, a pre-Homeric epic, makes no mention of children born to Oedipus and Epicaste nor of any self-blinding or voluntary exile on the part of Oedipus.

COMMENTARY

Cf. C. Robert, *Oidipus* (Berlin, 1915), L. Deubner, *Oidipusprobleme* (Abh. Ak. Berlin, 1942), F. Dirlmeier, *Der Mythos von König Oidipus*² (Mainz–Berlin, 1964), F. Wehrli, *MH* xiv (1957), 108–17, W. Pötscher, *Eranos*, lxxi (1973), 12–44.

271. On gen. Οἰδιπόδαο see Schwyzer, *Grammatik*, i 582.

272–3. The μέγα ἔργον lies in marrying her own son, which she does unwittingly (ἀϊδρείῃσι): Epicaste is quite unaware that her new partner is her own son, and the murderer of her first husband.

274. ἀνάπυστα (*hapax*): 'open, public knowledge'; probably formed as contrary of ἄ-πυστος (both derived from πυνθάνομαι). The gods brought to light things previously unknown to any man.   ἄφαρ cannot mean 'at once', since this would preclude the possibility of children from the union in the pre-Homeric saga (*Il.* iv 377 and 386 give us two names: Eteocles and Polyneices). ἄφαρ must mean 'after a while, after a year or so, after the birth of their sons'; cf. Deubner's convincing account, op. cit., 34–7.

275–6. After the discovery of his crime Oedipus continued to rule (impf.) in Thebes, albeit ἄλγεα πάσχων. The sufferings are not defined, but are seen as stemming from the ὀλοαὶ βουλαί of the gods; cf. 279–80 n.   πολυηράτῳ: not found in the *Iliad*; in the *Odyssey* only here as an epithet for a city.

277. πυλάρταο (πυλ-άρτης; its only instance in the *Odyssey*; in the *Iliad* viii 367 and xiii 415): an epithet of Hades, 'guardian of the gates'; Bechtel, *Lexilogus*, 287. It can also be used as a personal name (as at *Il.* xi 491); cf. Myc. *pu-ra-ta*/*Pulartās* PY Jn 605; Risch, *Wortbildung*, 31–2.

278. βρόχον (only here and xxii 472): 'noose'. It is 'precipitous' (αἰπύς) because it brings about a sudden swift death. On the construction see *LfgrE*, 1122. 67.

279–80. σχομένη + dat. (as in viii 182): 'seized by'. Epicaste leaves Oedipus many ἄλγεα, 'as many as can be inflicted by a mother's Ἐρινύες'. This last concept is as much abstract (meaning 'curses', cf. *Il.* xxi 412 μητρὸς ἐρινύας ἐξαποτίνοις) as a concrete image of revenging spirits (cf. *Od.* ii 134–6 μήτηρ στυγερὰς ἀρήσετ' ἐρινῦς). For a better understanding of the passage we should look at ii 134–6: the gods will mete out suffering when, driven from her home, the mother 'implores the spirits of vengeance, pronounces curses in her prayer'. The poet explains the origins of the ἄλγεα mentioned in 275–6 and brought about by the βουλαὶ θεῶν. Epicaste curses Oedipus, the Erinyes prevail on the gods to fulfil her curse, and it is the gods themselves who send the suffering on the victim.

281–97. Chloris (281–6), daughter of Amphion, married Neleus; Pero (287–97) was their daughter. On the connection between these lines, 235–9, and xv 225–55 see above (235–59 n.).

282ᵇ. = *Il.* xvi 190ᵇ, xxii 472.   πόρε sc. πατρί.   ἕδνα: cf. 116–17 n.

283–4. ὁπλοτάτην: cf. iii 465. Amphion, son of Iasus, ruled in Orchomenus, principal city of the Minyae (*Il.* ii 511), who were neighbours of the Thebans.   ἴφι ἄνασσεν: as at *Il.* vi 478; ἴφι is an old instrumental form (pl.) of ἴς; cf. the Myc. name *wi-pi-no-o*/*Wīphinohos*.

94

286. Of Neleus' twelve sons (*Il.* xi 692; Hes. fr. 33 (a) 9–12 M–W; xi 286 = fr. 33 (a) 12 M–W) only three are named here, among them Nestor.   ἀγέρωχον: used only once in the *Odyssey*, ἀγέρωχος appears in the *Iliad* as an honorific epithet of various peoples. Its exact meaning and derivation are unclear.

287. On acc. *Πηρώ* see Hoekstra, *Modifications*, 132–3.

288–91. περικτίται (*hapax*): 'dwellers around'; cf. Myc. *me-ta-ki-ti-ta/metakti-tai* PY An 610; Risch, *Wortbildung*, 31–2. Neleus was willing to give his daughter in marriage (impf. ἐδίδου) only to the suitor (οὐδέ ... τῷ ..., ὅς μή; cf. Chantraine, *Grammaire*, ii 333) who succeeded in bringing the refractory cattle (ἀργαλέας sc. ἐλάσαι) of Iphicles (βίης Ἰφικληείης ~ Ἰφίκλου) from Thessalian Phylace. The reason for the condition is assumed to be well known: Iphicles had himself lifted the cattle from Neleus' mother, Tyro. For 289^b cf. i 92, iii 382.

291–7. The only volunteer for the task is a prophet, identifiable from xv 226–7 as Melampus (son of Amythaon; cf. 259), who wished to win the girl for his brother Bias (xv 233, 237–8, Hes. fr. 37. 1–7 M–W). The story behind the formulaic lines 292–3 is that a θεοῦ μοῖρα ensured that in Phylace Melampus fell into the hands of Iphicles' herdsmen, was put in chains (Hes. fr. 37 M–W), but released after a year (294–5; cf. xv 230–4) when he had told Iphicles θέσφατα πάντα (296–7). The story is continued at xv 235–8: Melampus brought the cattle to Pylos, and so won the hand of Pero for his brother. Nevertheless the story cannot be entirely recon-structed, even when both passages are taken in conjunction (on the θέσφατα (296) cf. the explanations offered in the MV-schol. on 287); in the background must lie a pre-Homeric epic version; see further Heubeck, *Dichter*, 19–22.   βουκόλοι ἀγροιῶται (293) is a combination of two phrases, βουκόλοι ἄνδρες (*Il.* xiii 571) and ἄνερες ἀγροιῶται (*Il.* xi 549). βουκόλος: cf. Myc. *qu-u-ko-ro/guou-kolos* PY An 18. 9 etc. ἀγροιώτης: 'living in the country', possibly a metrical alternative to ἀγρότης (xvi 218); Risch, *Wortbildung*, 35–6.

294–5. = xiv 293–4; cf. x 469–70. Cf. also 295^a with i 16^b.

297^b. = *Il.* i 5^b.

298–304. Leda is named as the wife of Tyndareus. Only the twins Castor and Polydeuces are named as their children, not Helen, whose father in Homer is Zeus (*Il.* iii 199, *Od.* iv 184). Hesiod (fr. 24 M–W), following a tradition which the name Διόσκουροι shows to be ancient, made Zeus the father of the twins too; for a third form of the story see Pi. *N* x 80 ff. Hes. (fr. 23,7 ff.) also names as the first three children of the marriage of Tyndareus and Leda, Timandra, Clytaemestra, and Phylonoe.

299. γείνατο παῖδε: as at *Il.* vi 26^b.

300–5. 300 is taken unchanged from *Il.* iii 237, while 301 quotes *Il.* iii 243. The formulaic κατέχει φυσίζοος αἶα, which in the *Iliad* refers always to men who rest in the earth after their death (*Il.* iii 243 etc., cf. *Od.* xiii 427, xv 31), is here transformed by the addition of the paradoxical ζωούς, which prepares for 302–4. After death the twins were given a singular honour

COMMENTARY

(τιμή): in the Underworld they alternate daily (ἐτερήμεροι; hapax) between life and death—an almost divine privilege (304). This differs considerably from the more usual version of the legend (cf. esp. Pi. *N*. x 55 ff.) in which the Dioscuri live alternately in Hades and on Olympus.

301. φυσίζοος: a so-called *terpsimbrotos* cpd.; the second element is based on ζειαί (triticum dicoccum): 'bringing forth grain' but very early misinterpreted as 'life-giving'.

302. καὶ νέρθεν γῆς: 'although they lie under the earth'.

304. ἴσα: on the unusual adv. use see Hoekstra, *Modifications*, 105.

305–20. Iphimedeia (on the name cf. 283–4 n.) is introduced as wife of Aloeus, and (by Poseidon) mother of Otus and Ephialtes. The legend is already assumed to be familiar at *Il*. v 385–91; it was also related in the *Ehoiai* (frr. 19–21 M–W).

307. μινυνθαδίω: adj. from μίνυνθα, 'living only a short while' (cf. 311), used in the *Iliad* e.g. of Achilles (i 352).

308. τηλεκλειτόν (< *-κλεϝετός): synonymous with, and used as a metrical alternative to, -κλυτός; Bechtel, *Lexilogus*, 315–16, Chantraine, *Dictionnaire* s.v. κλέος. It is difficult to decide between Ἐφ- and Ἐπιάλτης (acc. to the Suda s.v. the Homeric and Hesiodic forms respectively); cf. Leumann, *Wörter*, 80.

309. ζείδωρος: cf. iii 3.

310. Ὠρίωνα (cf. v 121 n.): cf. Meister, *Kunstsprache*, 250, Chantraine, *Grammaire*, i 16.

311–12. ἐννέωροι (cf. x 19 n.): here predic. **ἐννεαπήχεες** (only here and *Il*. xxiv 270) **εὖρος** (acc., as μῆκος), 'nine cubits in width'. **ἐννεόργυιοι** (*hapax*; for ὄργυια cf. ix 325, x 167): 'nine fathoms'.

313. ἀπειλήτην (dual): an Aeolic form ionicized; Palmer, in *Companion*, 119; cf. Hoekstra, *Modifications*, 134 (with bibl.).

314: formulaic; cf. φυλόπιδος ... πτολέμοιο, *Il*. xiii 635; 314ᵇ = *Il*. i 165ᵇ.

315–16. The Aloidae threaten to storm heaven, by piling on Olympus the other Thessalian mountains Pelion and Ossa. This seems to imply, in contrast to 313, that the seat of the gods is in heaven, not on Olympus. But the Homeric conception is always a little vague; cf. vi 41–6 on the one hand, and the formulaic i 67ᵇ etc. on the other. There are therefore no grounds for supposing the lines spurious, as have a host of critics after Aristarchus, incl. Bechtel and Duentzer; cf. van der Valk, *Textual Criticism*, 189. **εἰνοσίφυλλον:** cf. ix 22 n. Hes. seems to refer to 316 in fr. 21. 1 M–W (]αμβατο[).

317ᵇ: cf. iv 668ᵇ.

318ᵇ. = *Il*. i 36ᵇ (Apollo).

319. ἰούλους (*hapax*): '(hairs of a) beard'.

320. πυκάσαι (πύκα): 'cover thickly'. **εὐανθέϊ** (*hapax*): 'well sprouting'. **λάχνη** (only once in the *Odyssey*) ~ ἴουλοι.

321–5. Next follow three unhappy heroines of Attic legend: Phaedra (daughter of Minos, wife of Theseus, and stepmother of Hippolytus), Procris (daughter of Erechtheus and wife of Cephalus), and Ariadne

96

(another daughter of Minos). Ariadne is the only one whose story is given, with a reference to her role as helper of Theseus in Crete; cf. J. Hoog, *LfgrE* s.v. Wilamowitz, *Untersuchungen*, 149, considered the lines to be an Attic interpolation.

322. ὀλοόφρονος: cf. x 137.

323. γουνόν (cf. i 193): here 'acropolis'.

324–5. ἦγε (impf.!): 'he wanted to bring'.   **ἀπόνητο:** from ἀπ-ονίναμαι, 'to enjoy a profit from'. Artemis kills the girl on the island of Dia (north of Crete) 'on Dionysus' indictment'. The version of the legend here presupposed cannot be reconstructed, as it was later supplanted by another according to which she became the god's lover on the island of Naxos (cf. Plu. *Thes.* 20). 325 is one of the few Homeric passages which mention Dionysus (*Il.* vi 132, 135, xiv 325, *Od.* xxiv 74; explained analytically by Marzullo, *Problema*, 93–5), and the only one to give the god's name in its Attic form; Erbse, *Beiträge*, 173. Myc. di-wo-nu-so-jo/Diwon(n)usojo (gen.) is attested at Pylos.

326–7. The last trio consists of Maera (daughter of Proitus and Anteia), Clymene (wife of Phylacus and mother of Iphiclus; cf. 288–91 n.), and Eriphyle (wife of the prophet Amphiaraus). Here too only the third character receives any attention: 'she accepted precious gold for her husband' (on the construction cf. Palmer, in *Companion*, 135), i.e. she accepted Polynices' bribe (the famous necklace) to betray her husband's hiding place and thus forced him to take part in the expedition of the seven against Thebes, sending him to certain death (cf. xv 246–7). The episode is intentionally placed last in the catalogue of heroines, partly because it recalls Tyro, Epicaste, and Chloris (Amphiaraus was Melampus' great-grandson), but also as preparation for the meeting with Agamemnon, whose death was also brought about by a στυγερὴ ἄκοιτις (cf. iii 310).

328–84. The increasing brevity of the encounters with heroines prepares for the breaking off of this catalogue (328 ff.); and indeed the account continues only after a lengthy exchange with Odysseus' hosts (the so-called 'intermezzo'). This 'intermezzo', often dismissed (with or without the catalogue of heroines) by earlier critics as interpolation or the work of the last 'editor' (among others Focke, *Odyssee*, 140–4, Merkelbach, *Untersuchungen*, 190), has in recent times won the critical acceptance it deserves; cf. W. Büchner, *Hermes*, lxxii (1937), 107 ff., Mattes, *Odysseus*, 80–92, Besslich, *Schweigen*, 131–5, Erbse, *Beiträge*, 27 ff., Eisenberger, *Studien*, 178–81. Alcinous has already (vii 317–18) fixed the πομπή for the next day (αὔριον ἔς). If we understand this intermezzo as resulting in the postponement of the voyage, then we must also understand vii 317 ff. as preparing for xi 328 ff.

328–32. Odysseus tells his audience that a complete account of his encounter with the women of legend would last the whole night; it is therefore time to retire. He himself could either go on board his ship (and here the implication is that he would leave immediately, according to the original plan, vii 317–18, viii 444–5) and sleep on board or he could sleep in the palace (which would postpone departure until at least the next evening). The decision on the timing of the πομπή is left to the king (332). With this polite speech, which leaves it to the Phaeacians to decide, Odysseus also asks indirectly whether he is to continue his tale that evening or next day. The Phaeacians must express their views on all this.

328. Like iv 240 the line is based on *Il.* ii 488, although there the formula stands at the opening of a catalogue, and here it concludes a recital.

330. φθῖτ'(o): aor. opt.; Chantraine, *Grammaire*, i 381.

331. ἐταίρους: the Phaeacians detailed to accompany Odysseus home.

333-4. (333 = *Il.* iii 95, *Od.* viii 234) = xiii 1–2.   **κηληθμῷ** (*hapax*) is derived from κηλέω ('enchant'): 'the spellbound silence produced by a tale well told'.   **ἔσχοντο:** cf. 279 n.

335. = vii 233.

336–41. Arete breaks the silence. 'What do you think of this man with regard to … (εἶδος etc.: acc. of respect.)?' In other words: 'What a splendid man this is!' She continues: 'And this man, for his part, is my guest; so each has his τιμή' (W. Burkert, *Gymnasium*, lxviii (1961), 560. 4). Only in 339–40 does Arete address herself to 330–2: 'So do not be too hasty to send him on his way!' She also urges them to be generous in preparing the gifts he so badly needs. This prepares for the additional presents which Odysseus is to receive in addition to those already given to him (viii 387 ff., 438 ff.). Nothing is yet said of the relevance of these gifts to the decision for which Odysseus has asked.

337. = xviii 249.   **ἔῖσας:** here used metaphorically of the φρένες, as elsewhere of ships and shields, 'evenly balanced'.

340. κολούετε: cf. viii 211.   **ἰότητι:** cf. vii 214.

342–6. Echeneus, the most senior of the Phaeacian nobles, intervenes, as at vii 155 ff. He supports the queen's suggestion, while pointing out that the decision about carrying out the plan (ἔργον τε ἔπος τε) lies with the king (ἔχεται).

342. = vii 155.

343 (= vii 156) is missing in many MSS, and has been rejected, although without compelling reasons, by, among others, F. A. Wolf. Even the authenticity of 343a (= vii 157) is worth considering; van der Valk, *Textual Criticism*, 278.

344. The queen speaks 'in accord with my own intentions and opinion' (ἀπὸ δόξης ~ παρὰ δόξαν). The similarity to *Il.* x 324 can only be explained by assuming that the one is derived from the other, and the artificial formulation in the Doloneia must represent conflation of *Il.* xiii 10 and *Od.* xi 344; W. Theiler, *MH* xix (1962), 13, Heubeck, *Gymnasium*, lxxi (1964), 56; although S. Laser, *Hermes*, lxxxvi (1958), 408–9, disagrees.   **δόξης:** only here and *Il.* x 324; on the form see Leumann, *Wörter*, 173–8.

347–53. Alcinous will translate the suggestion made by Arete and supported by Echeneus (ἔπος) into action (347). He points to his position as king as assurance that his word may be relied on, with good reason: his decision involves altering the promise made the day before, and delays the sailing, which had then been firmly fixed (τεκμαίρομαι vii 317) for the following day (αὔριον ἔς), until the next day (ἐς αὔριον 351). Alcinous clearly answers the points made by Arete and Odysseus: he agrees to the suggestion of further gifts; he responds to Arete's call not to proceed too hastily with sending their guest on his way with the commitment ἐς αὔριον; and he reassures Odysseus, referring back to the concern expressed in 332, that he will take care of the voyage home. He leaves open for the time being the question as to when Odysseus should continue his story.

350–1. τλήτω: 'he must resign himself'; ἐπιμεῖναι is dependent on it. ἔμπης follows on from concessive μάλα περ νόστοιο χατίζων.

353–4. Modelled on *Il.* vi 492–3, but intentionally varied as at i 358–9 and xxiii 352–3.

356–61. Odysseus comes to the aid of the king, who is not in a position to honour his earlier pledge: Odysseus reassures him, with courteous exaggeration, that with the assurance of the πομπή and gifts to come he would gladly remain a year.

354–5. = 377–8 = ix 1–2.

368. = xx 316; both are taken from *Il.* iii 316.

360: cf. v 88 n.

362. = 317.

363–76. The question of the πομπή and δῶρα is already settled: Odysseus will depart the next evening with further gifts. The question raised in 328–32, of when Odysseus is to continue his tale, is still outstanding. Alcinous' approach is similar to that of Arete: he begins by praising Odysseus (363–9) and his art as a storyteller (367–9); he is then in a position to answer Odysseus' indirect question (330–2) by proposing that he continue his story that evening.

363. Arete expressed her admiration in the form of a question; Alcinous' comment is more direct, balancing a negative observation (363–6) with a positive remark (367–9). On the expression 'You do not give us the impression that ...' see W. Marg, op. cit. (217–22 n.), 67. **ἐΐσκομεν** corresponds to φαίνεται (336).

364–6. ἠπεροπῆα (*hapax*; *Il.* ἠπεροπευτής): 'deceiver', from which ἠπεροπεύω is derived (e.g. xiii 327), or vice versa (E. Bosshardt, *Die Nomina auf -εύς* (diss. Zurich, 1942), 26; etym. unknown. **ἐπίκλοπον** (κλέπτω): 'impostor, cheat'. On the constr. of the clause introduced by οἷά τε ... see Ruijgh, τε épique, 531. The meaning is that 'the earth provides nourishment for many impostors, deceitful and lying men', i.e. there are many deceivers among men. πολλά is an unnecessary attempt by Aristarchus to improve on πολλούς, the reading of the MSS and of Zenodotus; van der Valk, *Textual Criticism*, 100. **πολυσπερέας** (σπείρω): *hapax*. 365[b] is adapted from *Il.* ii 804; the consequent metrical difficulty should be accepted (*pace* von der Mühll (ad loc.)) and not removed by substituting the variant -σπερχέας (only in P³); cf. Bechert, op. cit. (ix 142–5 n.), 393. 366[b] (cf. viii 280[b]): such people devise (ἀρτύνοντας) such lies that no one is able to see through them; cf. Bechert, 133–5.

367. μέν–δέ: Odysseus' charm (μορφή; cf. viii 170) is matched by the φρένες ἐσθλαί (ii 117) already singled out by Arete (336).

368–9. Alcinous praises Odysseus the story-teller in much the same terms that Odysseus had praised Demodocus (viii 487–98); cf. also Eumaeus' appreciation of Odysseus' narrative gifts (xvii 513–21). 369 is in apposition to μῦθον.

370. = i 169 etc.

371–2. While Arete had been most interested in the catalogue of heroines, Alcinous requests an account of Odysseus' encounter with the ghosts of those who had been his comrades in war; and so the scene is set for the account of Odysseus' meeting with Agamemnon, Achilles, and Ajax.

373–6. Alcinous refers back to Odysseus' words of 330–1: 'the night is still long, and it is not yet time to retire to bed' (οὐδέ πω ὥρη | εὕδειν 373–4: ἀλλὰ καὶ ὥρη | εὕδειν 330–1). Now at last, with the invitation to continue (374), Odysseus' implicit question is answered. ἀθέσφατος: cf. vii 273. θέσκελα (only here, 610, and *Il.* iii 130): 'divinely inspired' (?); probably formed from θεός (< *thehos < *dhə₁so-; cf. H. Rix, *Kratylos*, xiv (1969), 179–80) and κέλομαι; morphologically puzzling; Risch, *Wortbildung*, 218.

377–8. = 354–5 = ix 1–2.

379–84. Odysseus replies first to 373–4 with the proverbial-sounding 379, which means something like: 'There is indeed time to tell much (373–4), but it might also be time for sleeping (as I have mentioned before, 330–1). But I yield to your wishes'; cf. the similar situation at xv 392–6. Odysseus does not wish to deny Alcinous (φθονέω + inf.) an account of events even (καὶ) more heart-rending than what he had asked to hear (τούτων (381) refers back to 371–2), the story of those who met death after their return home, by the will of a wicked woman. This prepares for the Agamemnon scene; the accounts of Achilles and Ajax meet Alcinous' wish of 372.

380. The MS-reading δέ τ' is impossible; Ruijgh, τε *épique*, 701.

385–6. The account broken off at 327 is resumed. The ghosts of the heroines originally summoned by Persephone (225–7) are now dispersed by the goddess. θηλυτεράων (cf. viii 324): 'female'; M. Wittwer, *Glotta*, xlvii (1970), 57–8.

387–9. = xxiv 20–2.

387. ἦλθε δ' (cf. 84, 90) begins the Agamemnon scene, which continues until 466. There is no mention here of drinking blood (the motif last appeared at 230–4). This inconsistency is probably determined by the need to prepare for the encounter with the suicide Ajax, who could not make for the blood as if thirsting for life; Reinhardt, 'Abenteuer', 140.

388–9. ἀγηγέραθ' (plpf.): 'they were gathered together' (subj. ἄλλαι, sc. ψυχαὶ πάντων, ὅσσοι ...). The murder takes place in Aegisthus' palace (cf. Proteus' account, iv 528, 536–7).

390. πίεν αἷμα κελαινόν: given by many MSS, but surely an ancient cj. (Aristarchus'?): we should read ἴδεν ὀφθαλμοῖσιν; cf. Wilamowitz, *Untersuchungen*, 151. 11, Schwartz, *Odysse*, 147. 1, Focke, *Odyssee*, 220. 2, van der

Valk, *Textual Criticism*, 177, Bona, op. cit. (ix 106–15 n.), 66. 33, Erbse, *Beiträge*, 28. 64; Merkelbach, *Untersuchungen*, 190. 2 defends πίεν αἷμα κελαινόν.

391–4. The scenes with Anticleia and Agamemnon are consciously contrasted. In the first the attempt to embrace ends the episode; here the scene opens with an attempted embrace. Whereas Odysseus attempted to touch his mother, here it is the ghost trying to embrace Odysseus; and while Anticleia began the conversation with Odysseus, here Odysseus speaks first. Anticleia's report of Penelope's faithfulness is a foil to Agamemnon's account of his murderous wife.

391: cf. x 201.

392. ὀρέξασθαι: here 'embrace'.

393–4: cf. 219–21.   ἀλλ᾽ οὐ γάρ (elliptical): 'but in vain, for ...'; cf. J. C. B. Lowe, *Glotta*, li (1973), 39.   κῖκυς: cf. ἄκικυς (ix 515). 394 is based on *Il.* xi 669.   γναμπτοῖσι μέλεσσι: cf. B. Snell, *Ges. Schriften* (Göttingen, 1966), 62–4.

395–6. = 55–6.

397. (= xxiv 121): taken from the *Iliad* (ii 434 etc.).

398. = 171.

399–403. The repetition of these lines at xxiv 109–13 has given rise to analytical speculation, which began in antiquity. Aristophanes, and possibly Aristarchus, judged 399–403 inauthentic; cf. Schwartz, *Odyssee*, 319, Merkelbach, *Untersuchungen*, 190. 2, Page, *Odyssey*, 103. But excision of the lines would leave Odysseus with only two lines, which could scarcely form the basis for such a long reply from Agamemnon. Van der Valk (*Textual Criticism*, 192), Besslich (*Schweigen*, 30), Erbse (*Beiträge*, 198–9), and B. Snell (in *Festschr. f. G. Storz* (Frankfurt-on-Main, 1973), 16. 15) have argued for the authenticity of the lines. Odysseus imagines a number of scenarios for Agamemnon's death—a storm at sea or an attempted raid that failed (cf. G. Micknat, *AAWM* (1954), 11)—but he cannot guess the true circumstances of the hero's death. However the poet allows him to let fall the keyword γυναικῶν at the end of his question. This unleashes an impassioned reply.

399. ἐν νήεσσι is in contrast to ἐπὶ χέρσου (401; chiasmus).

400. The first half of the line is based on *Il.* xiv 254ᵃ.   ἀμέγαρτον (elsewhere only at 407, xvii 219, xxi 362, *Il.* ii 420): 'unenviable, horrible'.   ἀϋτμήν: here 'storm, blast'.

401: cf. x 459.

402. περιταμνόμενον, from περιτάμνομαι (like τάμνομαι *Il.* xviii 528): 'carry off by force' (here conative).

403: cf. *Il.* xviii 265. Odysseus thinks Agamemnon may have fallen in battle, in an attempt to sack a town and take its women captive; cf. G. Micknat, loc. cit. (399–403 n.), esp. 22 ff.   μαχεούμενον here refers to σ᾽ (401), i.e. Agamemnon (in contrast to xxiv 113). The unusual form (for comment cf. Page, *Odyssey*, 103, Wyatt, *Lengthening*, 135–6, Shipp, *Studies*, 338) results from the adaptation of *Il.* xviii 265 to fit the syntax of the sentence; cf. K. Witte, *RE* viii (1913), 2224, Erbse, *Beiträge*, 199.

COMMENTARY

405–34. Agamemnon's own account of his murder complements iii 254–312, iv 512–37, and xxiv 192–202. The discrepancies between these various accounts, above all, as to the part played by Clytaemestra, are not due to a variety of sources; all are based on a unitary tradition; cf. Hölscher, op. cit. (130–6 n.), 1–16, P. Bergmann, *Der Atridenmythos in Epos, Lyrik und Drama* (diss. Erlangen, 1970), 5–41. The viewpoint and intention of each narrator influences his presentation of events. In xi and xxiv Agamemnon speaks from his own experience. In the context of the poem as a whole the most significant element of his story of home-coming is the contrast between the welcome extended by his own wife, and that which awaits Odysseus.

406–8. 407 is given only in K, and is perhaps a secondary insertion from 400. In true epic style Agamemnon repeats the questions posed: οὔτ'–οὔτε–ἀλλά; cf. *Il.* xvi 50–2.

409–11. The narration begins with a brief summary of the salient facts: Aegisthus conspired with Clytaemestra to invite the returning hero to the palace for a feast (δειπνίσσας), and there the murder took place (cf. iv 524–35; 411 (=iv 534) is surely authentic, despite the objections of Schwartz, *Odyssee*, 319). The story is then given again, in detail. (The motivation for the murder, and the details of the journey home, have already been presented in iii and iv.) 409ᵇ = ix 61ᵇ.

412. οἰκτίστῳ θανάτῳ: only here and xxiv 34.

413. νωλεμέως (cf. iv 288, ix 435): 'unceasingly', i.e. there was no pause until all the intended victims had been killed. On 413ᵇ cf. viii 60, 476.

414–15. The missing verb κτείνονται should be supplied from the main clause; cf. Ruijgh, *τε épique*, 440. ἐν sc. δόμῳ; for 414ᵇ cf. i 276ᵇ. 415 (cf. i 226) features three temp. dats.: 'on the occasion of a wedding or ...'.

416. = xxiv 87. ἀντεβόλησας: cf. iv 547; on the reading see van der Valk, *Textual Criticism*, 149–50. For the antithesis ἤδη μὲν–ἀλλά cf. iv 267–9.

417. μουνάξ (only here and viii 371): here 'in single combat' as opposed to ἐνὶ ... ὑσμίνῃ; cf. Risch, *Wortbildung*, 364.

418. = xxiv 90. κεῖνα looks ahead to 419–20.

420. The usage here of θύω is unique. The meaning is unclear ('steamed, flowed?'); cf. Chantraine, *Grammaire*, i 372. 420ᵇ = xxiv 185ᵇ.

421. οἰκτροτάτην: predic., with ὄπα.

422. Cassandra (*Il.* xiii 366, xxiv 699), daughter of Priam, was brought home as booty by Agamemnon. Homer makes no mention of her prophetic role (as used by A. *Ag.*); cf. K. Ledergerber, *Kassandra* (diss. Fribourg, 1950). On the form of the name Κλυταιμ(ν)ήστρη cf. iii 266 n.

422–6. The passage has been variously interpreted. Cf., among others, Ameis–Hentze, *Anhang*, ii 117–18, D. Mülder, *Bursians Jahresber.*, ccxxxix (1933), 33, E. Bornemann, op. cit. (ix 362–90 n.), 131–2, Chantraine, *Grammaire*, ii 171. 2, H. F. Bornitz, *LfgrE* s.v. ἀμφί (col. 667), Bergmann, op. cit. (405–34 n.), 229–31. Agamemnon relates that once all the returning Greeks had fallen, Clytaemestra killed Cassandra ἀμφ' ἐμοί. Since ἀμφί + dat. can only have a local meaning, this must mean that Cassandra, who had been standing beside Agamemnon, is stabbed (probably from behind) and falls on top of the hero's corpse (ἀμφ' ἐμοί sc. χυμένην as at *Il.* xix 284 ~ *Od.* viii 527). χεῖρας (423) belongs equally with ἀείρων and βάλλον: Agamemnon is run through (probably also from behind) by the sword of Aegisthus, and falls to the ground. There he lies, ἀποθνῄσκων περὶ φασγάνῳ 'with a sword in my chest' (for the expression cf. *Il.* viii 86, xiii 441, 570). He raises his hands, and immediately lets them fall (βάλλον) to the ground (ποτὶ γαίῃ; cf. ii 80). We have here a practice mentioned also at *Il.* ix 568 and *h.Ven.* 333: beating the ground with the hands is a form of supplication to the powers of the Underworld for vengeance. **κυνῶπις:** cf. iv 145. On κύων as a term of abuse (the dog lacks all αἰδώς) see M. Faust, *Glotta*, xlviii (1970), 8–31; cf. κύντερος (427). **νοσφίσατ'(ο):** 'she turned her back on me, she went away' (cf. 75, iv 263). She even refuses her husband the last service of closing his eyes (κατ' ... ἐλέειν) and mouth (σὺν ... ἐρεῖσαι).

427. ὥς (as at ix 34) draws together the material from 409–26. **κύντερον** is an intensification of subst. κύων; cf. 424 n.

428. This line was probably rejected as spurious by Aristarchus (cf.schol. H ἐν πολλοῖς οὐ φέρεται), and, after the universalized statement of 427 (cf. Hes. *Th.* 591), introduces a somewhat unexpected limitation. Nevertheless the syntactical progression of 427–8 conforms to the usual Homeric pattern (for examples see Ruijgh, *τε épique*, 449), and 429 follows on well from 428: τοιαῦτα μετὰ φρεσὶν ἔργα βάληται · | οἷον ... ἐμήσατο ἔργον (cf. also 433–4 n. and Besslich, *Schweigen*, 30. 28.

430. **κουριδίῳ** (derived from κούρη, κοῦρος < *korwā/-os*): here 'lawful'; on the development of the meaning see Bechtel, *Lexilogus*, 200–1. On dat. πόσει see Hoekstra, *Modifications*, 115. **ἔφην:** here 'I supposed'.

432. On the orthography of λυγρὰ ἰδυῖα cf. i 428 n., Leumann, *Kleine Schriften* (Zurich, 1959), 251–2.

433–4. (=xv 442, xxiv 202): 'Clytaemestra has brought shame (κατ' ... ἔχευε) on herself (reflex. οἷ) and future generations of women, even if (καὶ) one of these were to be honest'. This form of words is further evidence for the authenticity of 428 (εὐεργός–τοιαῦτα ἔργα). For an analytical discussion see Theiler, *MH* xix (1962), 19.

435–43. These lines were rejected by Aristophanes (and possibly also Aristarchus; cf. Schwartz, *Odyssee*, 319), and have also been questioned by modern scholars; cf. Ameis–Hentze, *Anhang*, ii 118–19, Merkelbach, *Untersuchungen*, 190. 1.

436–9. Agamemnon's speech culminated in a condemnation of women generally; the universality of his complaint is not compromised by 428, if this is retained (Besslich, *Schweigen*, 30. 38). Odysseus alters the line of argument by concentrating on the role of two women of the house of Atreus and setting their deeds in the context of Zeus' anger towards that house.

437. **γυναικείας ... βουλάς:** precisely the means (διὰ) used by Zeus to effect his will.

441–3. Odysseus' deflection of the argument away from an outright condemnation of all women provokes Agamemnon to give a most particular warning: 'Beware of your wife too!' His words indicate some of the action to come, for Odysseus will indeed be cautious on his arrival home, although for different reasons.

441. ἤπιος (cf. ii 47): the specialized meaning here ('blindly trustful') is determined by the context of 442–3.

442. μηδ' οἵ: the elision is unusual (Marzullo, *Problema*, 367, Shipp, *Studies*, 45), but is not a reason for emendation (μή οἵ, Bentley); cf. van der Valk, *Textual Criticism*, 69.

443. The construction changes: τὸ μὲν is object, τὸ δὲ subject.

444–53. Agamemnon corrects himself (ἀλλ' οὐ σοί γ') and admits that there really is no comparison between Penelope and the women of his family; Penelope is the very opposite of Clytaemestra. She will not murder Odysseus (cf. 409–10), for she is πινυτή (not δολόμητις, 422) and εὖ φρεσὶ μήδεα οἶδε (cf. λυγρὰ ἰδυῖα 429 and 432).

446–7. 446 = i 329 etc. Agamemnon recalls meeting Odysseus in Ithaca to secure his help for the war (xxiv 115–19), when Penelope was still a young woman (νύμφη; cf. 39 n.).

449. On the shift in time perspective cf. 181–203 n.   μετ' ἀνδρῶν ... ἀριθμῷ: i.e. ἐν ἀγορῇ.

450–1. ὄλβιος (see 134–7 n.): Telemachus' ὄλβος consists in what is described in 449–51, cf. Gruber, *Gnomon*, xliii (1971), 17: he has taken his place among men, and will welcome his father home, ἦ θέμις ἐστίν (449–51); cf. iii 45 n.

452–3. Thinking of Telemachus reminds Agamemnon again of his own fate. His murder deprived him of the satisfaction of seeing his own son (ἐμπίμπλαμαι + gen.).

454–6. The lines have been suspected because of the supposed contradiction of 444–6, both in antiquity (cf. schol. on 452) and by modern critics (Ameis–Hentze, *Anhang*, ii 118–19, Schwartz, *Odyssee*, 319); but they are indispensable. At the end of the first part of his account Agamemnon's thoughts return again to the advice given at 441–3 (456 ~ 441; κρύβδην 455 ~ κεκρυμμένον 443), and thus effectively round off this section. Agamemnon's fall was due to his lack of circumspection; so the qualification of 444–53 in no way invalidates his counsel of caution; cf. Hölscher, loc. cit. (100–36 n.), Besslich, loc. cit. (ix 16–18 n.), Bergmann, op. cit. (405–32 n.), 33–4, Erbse, *Beiträge*, 27. These lines (like 441–3) also foreshadow future events, for Odysseus will arrive home secretly, unrecognized—although not out of distrust towards his wife.

454. = xvi 281 etc.

455. ἀναφανδά: see iii 221–2 n.

457–61. ἀλλ' ἄγε signals clearly the beginning of the second part of the speech. Agamemnon exchanges the role of answering and offering advice for that of seeking information, specifically about Orestes, who was mentioned at 452–3.

457. = i 169 etc.

458. The emphasis is not so much on ἔτι (as at iv 833) as on που. Agamemnon knows that his son is still alive, for he has not seen his ghost in Hades, and so suggests a number of places where he might be living on earth.

459. Ὀρχομενῷ: cf. 284.

461: cf. i 196. The line was rejected by Aristarchus, but in fact there is no reason to doubt its authenticity.

463–4. = iv 837. Odysseus' reply is surprisingly brief. He simply deals with the question asked in 457–61: he does not know of the boy's whereabouts, and his answer, unlike the confident assertion of Agamemnon, leaves open the possibility that Orestes is dead. The lack of any response to 441–56 gives Agamemnon's contribution the feel of a monologue, which greatly enhances the pathos of the scene.

465. = 81, 225.

466. ~ x 570.

467–70. = xxiv 15–18. The encounter with Achilles is also introduced by ἦλθε δ' (cf. 84, 90, 387). The ghosts of the four heroes listed together by Nestor at iii 109–12, Achilles, Patroclus, Antilochus, and Ajax, appear as a group (cf. also xxiv 76–84). The *Odyssey* here clearly already presupposes the story related in the Cyclic *Aethiopis* (Memnon, son of Eos, kills Nestor's son, Antilochus, and is himself killed by Achilles; cf. Proclus' account (Bethe, *Odyssee*, 168) and also iv 188). On the pre-Homeric forms of the saga see W. Kullmann, *Die Quellen der Ilias* (Wiesbaden, 1960), 27–8, 314–16, *et passim*.

467ᵇ. = *Il.* i 1ᵇ.

469–70. Cf. *Il.* xvii 279–80 and *Od.* xxiv 17–18 (of Ajax); *Il.* ii 673–4 (Nireus); *Od.* viii 116–17 (Euryalus).

471. ἔγνω: cf. 390. 471ᵇ = *Il.* ii 860ᵇ etc. The -ίδης form is here a papponymic, Aeacus being Achilles' grandfather.

472. = 154.

474. τίπτ'(ε) (cf. i 225): here, most unusually, not simply 'Why then?' but an expression of uncomprehending amazement: 'What bolder act (sc. than the descent into Hades), stubborn as you are (σχέτλιε) could you have planned?'

475. πῶς: cf. 57, 155.

476. ἀφραδέες: here (in contrast to ii 282 'foolish'): 'without intelligence' (νόος, φρένες; cf. x 493–5). 476ᵇ = *Il.* xxiii 72ᵇ.   καμόντων: 'those worn out (in death)', almost τεθνηῶτες (cf. 37, 541).

478–82. Odysseus begins by answering Achilles' question, taking πῶς (475) to mean in the first instance 'why'.

478. = *Il.* xvi 21, xix 216.

479. χρέος + gen.: 'need for'; κατὰ χ. Τειρεσίαο almost means T. εἵνεκα; the diction is perhaps influenced by x 492 χρησομένους.

480. παιπαλόεσσαν: cf. iii 170.

481. = 166.

482ᵃ. ~ 167ᵃ.

482ᵇ–6. Once more addressing Achilles by name, Odysseus turns to another thought, reacting to Achilles' behaviour (ὀλοφυρομένη 472) and his words of 475–6: 'Do not grieve for your death' (486). Odysseus' reasoning is that Achilles is the most fortunate of men (μάκαρ: one enjoying in full measure the good fortune which makes a man happy and draws him near to the gods). This uniquely good fortune continues even in death: the honour paid to Achilles in his lifetime (ἶσα θεοῖσιν: cf. 304 n.) is paralleled by his position among the dead (Achilles' ghost is envisaged surrounded by a crowd of companions). The contrast between life and death (πρὶν μὲν: νῦν αὖτε) is central: ζωὸν: ἐνθάδ' ἐών; ἐτίομεν ἶσα θεοῖσιν: μέγα κρατέεις; Ἀργεῖοι: νεκύεσσιν (loc. dat.; 'among the dead').

488–503. Achilles' violently angry response, 'Do not try to reconcile me to death!' is all the more surprising since the expression of an unconditional preference for life appears not to be in keeping with the attitude expressed by Achilles when alive (*Il.* xviii 88–93; αὐτίκα τεθναίην 98; κῆρα ... δέξομαι 115). It is, however, quite in character, for in Hades the perspective has dreadfully changed. Now that Achilles is dead, his spirit yearns for life with the same vehemence with which it had once embraced death. In wild hatred of Agamemnon and wilful contradiction of his own character Achilles had once played briefly with the idea that life was dearer to him than anything else; now, in death, this has become his genuine conviction. Odysseus has entirely misjudged the situation (483–7), for in Hades there are no μάκαρες. Cf. Reinhardt, 'Abenteuer', 139, Hölscher, op. cit. (100–36 n.), 8; Rüter, *Odysseeinterpretationen*, 87–8. Achilles' words (like those of Odysseus, 484–6) are entirely centred on a contrast of life with death: 'Better θητευέμεν on earth than ἀνάσσειν in Hades'. θής is apparently a free man, who receives pay (xviii 356–7) for occasional work (θητεύει). This man, who must hire himself out to another, who owns no land (κλῆρος) himself (ἄκληρος), a tenant-farmer with scarcely enough to live on himself, is reckoned to be on the lowest rung of the social scale, rather than a slave who at least belongs to a household (cf. G. M. Calhoun, in *Companion*, 433 ff., 440; Finley, *World*, 54–6). ἐπάρουρος (ἐών) probably means simply 'one living on the earth' rather than 'serf', since it stands in apposition to νεκύεσσι (and ἐνθάδ' ἐών 486), and connects the passage with *Il.* xviii 104, where Achilles describes himself as ἐτώσιον ἄχθος ἀρούρης; cf. Stanford, ad loc. The final climax is reached in 491 with πᾶσιν νεκύεσσι (νεκύεσσιν 485). On the secondary variant κε πάρουρος see Leumann, *Wörter*, 53, F. Bader, *RP* xlvi (1972), 207. On Plato's citation of the passage (*R.* 386 c) see G. Lohse, *Helikon*, v (1965), 278–9.

492. The transition to the second part of the speech, in which Achilles is the one enquiring, is similar to that in the speeches of Odysseus (170) and Agamemnon (457). The similarity of form is paralleled by a similarity of content between the questions posed in 170–9, 457–61, and 492–7 on home and family.   ἔνισπες: cf. iii 101, iv 642 nn. Cf. van der Valk, *Textual Criticism*, 45, and Chantraine (who takes a different view) *Grammaire*, i 467.

493. πρόμος (*Il.*; *hapax* in the *Odyssey*): 'champion'.

494-7. As at 174–6 the enquiry after the hero's father is really also a question about the kingship; τιμή (495): γέρας (175). It is a particularly important one for Achilles, whose τιμή lies at the heart of the action of the *Iliad*. 495ᵇ = *Il.* xvi 240ᵇ, xxiii 60ᵇ; 496ᵇ = *Il.* ix 395ᵇ (ii 683). Cf. Simpson–Lazenby, *Catalogue*, 128–31.   κατὰ γῆρας ἔχει: (γῆρας) κατ' ... ἔχει, 'age restricts'.

498-503. The third part of the speech evolves from 493–7, but the mood is that of 488–91. Achilles passionately wishes himself back on earth to support his father. The diction echoes the words in which the aged Nestor recalls his youth (*Il.* vii 132–57, xi 671–782, xxiii 629–43; cf. also *Od.* iii 218–23, iv 341–5); this deliberate allusion favours Zenodotus' reading εἰ γὰρ; but cf. van der Valk, *Textual Criticism*, 94. 2.

498. ἐπαρωγός (*hapax*) from ἀρήγω: 'helper (in war)', and here specifically 'living helper', ὑπ' αὐγὰς ἠελίοιο being contrasted with the darkness of Hades. 498ᵇ = ii 181ᵇ.

500. λαὸν ἄριστον: 'the boldest fighters', sc. among the enemy.

502. στύξαιμι: στυγέω is used here in an unusual form (aor. is usually ἔστυγον) with an unusual meaning ('to make something dreadful for someone'). 502ᵇ is modelled on *Il.* vii 309ᵇ etc.   ἀάπτους: ἄαπτος, used only in conjunction with χείρ, means something like 'terrible, difficult to overcome, mighty'. The derivation is uncertain; either from ἄπτομαι or from *ἄ(ϝ)επτος (Zenodotus and Aristophanes), 'unspeakable'. Cf. H. Erbse and S. Laser, *LfgrE* s.v. and Chantraine, *Dictionnaire* s.v.

503. οἵ belongs with (sg.!) τεῳ, which was wrongly altered by Aristarchus to τεων.   βιόωνται: βιάομαι is equivalent to βιάζομαι. 503ᵇ: 'they attempt to depose him by violence'. Achilles imagines the very situation which will confront Odysseus.

505-37. Odysseus answers Achilles' questions precisely: he has no information concerning Peleus (οὔ τι πέπυσμαι 506: εἴ τι πέπυσσαι 494), and so speaks of Neoptolemus in all the more detail. The poet takes the opportunity, here as in the speeches of Nestor, Menelaus, and Helen in iii–iv, and the songs of Demodocus (viii), to present material not treated by the *Iliad*. These passages are a valuable source of information on the pre-Homeric Troy saga later embodied in the cyclic epics.

507. ἀληθείην: cf. vii 297 n.

508-9. After Achilles' death Odysseus brought Neoptolemus from Scyros, where he had grown up (cf. also *Il.* xix 326–33). The *Little Iliad* relates that Achilles had fathered his son there after the Telephus episode (cf. 519–22 n.); cf. fr. 5 Allen, Bethe, *Odyssee*, 173–4, 252–3.

511-16. Neoptolemus distinguished himself as much by his counsel (in which he was second only to Nestor and Odysseus: νικάσκομεν) as by his performance in action. He was truly a πρόμος (cf. 493) who surpassed all (515). 513–15 describe the bravery in battle of this πρόμαχος, who is the embodiment of the ideal prescribed for his father's own education (*Il.* ix 443).

511. Neoptolemus, like Menelaus (*Il.* iii 215; cf. also 343–4), was οὐδ' ἀφαμαρτοεπής: he always found just the right words to convey sound advice.

513. μαρναίμεθ': the thematic form is surprising; Chantraine, *Grammaire*, ii 464.

514–15. The model here is *Il.* xxii 458–9 (which refers to Hector).   πληθυῖ: πληθύς in conjunction with ὅμιλος means the ranks close-packed in battle.   τὸ ὃν μένος: acc. of respect.   εἴκων: here 'standing behind, second to'.

516. The second half of the line is formulaic; cf. *Il.* iii 20 etc. On δηϊοτής, 'strife, warfare', see Leumann, *Wörter*, 129.

518. ὅσσον λαὸν: the antecedent is πάντας (517); anacoluthic for ὅσσους. The words refer back to 500: the son is the worthy successor of his father. 517–18 are intended to round off the section 510–16 and to lead into the next: of many heroic deeds Odysseus will describe just two, his defeat of Eurypylus (519–22) and his conduct in the Wooden Horse (523–32).

519–22. Eurypylus was son of King Telephus of Teuthrania in Mysia, who had previously been wounded by Achilles (the story was told in the *Cypria*; cf. Wilamowitz, *Untersuchungen*, 152–3, Bethe, *Odyssee*, 153, 237–40). After Achilles' death Priam bribed Eurypylus' mother, Astyoche, with the golden vine made by Hephaestus (γυναίων εἵνεκα δώρων 521), to persuade her son to fight in support of the Trojans; Eurypylus' fate was to fall at the hands of Achilles' son. The pre-Homeric version of the legend, to which the poet refers, was worked into epic form in the *Little Iliad*: fr. 6 Allen; Bethe, *Odyssee*, 23, 26, 171, 174, 252–3.

519. ἀλλ' οἷον (predic.) continues the thought of 517: 'but I shall tell only of his killing Eurypylus'.   κατενήρατο (*hapax*) = ἐνήρατο (*Il.* v 53 etc., *Od.* xxiv 424) from (κατ-)ἐναίρομαι.

521. Κήτειοι (*hapax*): Eurypylus' subjects—misunderstood by Aristarchus as κήτειοι derived from κῆτος and meaning the same as μεγάλοι; cf. Wilamowitz, *Untersuchungen*, 152. 12. Κήτειοι is a genuine ethnic, used also by Alcaeus of the Mysians (fr. 177 Lobel). P. Kretschmer (*Kleinasiat. Forschungen*, i (1927–30), 8 ff.) has attractively suggested (following W. E. Gladstone) that the name of the people is derived from the name of the Hittite kingdom, Ḫatti; cf. also G. L. Huxley, *PP*, xiv (1959), 281 ff.

522. Μέμνονα: cf. 467–70 n. δῖον is significant: Memnon is son of Tithonus and Eos.

523–32. The story of the Wooden Horse, the background here and at iv 271–88 and viii 492–520, was a subject of pre-Homeric epic and later was handled in the *Iliou Persis*, cf. Bethe, *Odyssee*, 169–70.

523. κάμ' (κάμνω): here 'construct (with much toil)'.   Ἐπειός: cf. viii 493 n.

525. Aristarchus omitted this line from his edition, but referred to it in his Hypomnemata. It is in fact the same as *Il.* v 751 (= xv 395), apart from λόχον for νέφος (πυκινὸν λόχον as at *Il.* xxiv 779). It serves to define πάντ' of the preceding line. Odysseus' particular responsibility lies in the timely ἀνακλῖναι/ἐπιθεῖναι. Cf. C. M. Bowra in *Companion*, 31–2, van der Valk, *Textual Criticism*, 260.

526ᵇ: as at vii 186.

527. The first half of the line is modelled on *Il.* xviii 124, the second is formulaic (cf. viii 88, *Il.* x 95, 390, xviii 31).

528. For the first hemistich cf. iv 693, for the second cf. iv 269.

529. ὠχρήσαντα (*hapax*; here ingress. aor.): 'turn pale'; χρόα κάλλιμον (iv 130): acc. of respect.

530: cf. 527.

531. MS-reading ἐξίμεναι (only Eust. gives ἐξέμεναι) makes sense if we compare ix 224–5. Neoptolemus begs Odysseus for permission to make a sortie from the Wooden Horse; cf. Ameis–Hentze, *Anhang*, ii 121–2.   ἐ-πεμαίετο (conative): 'wished to seize'; cf. ix 302.

532. χαλκοβαρές (cf. *Il.* xxii 328 etc.): 'heavy with bronze' (on account of the bronze head); Risch, *Wortbildung*, 81, 86, 186.   μενοίνα: 'he was passionately eager' to fall on the Trojans.

533–7. After the fall of Troy Neoptolemus could leave in great honour, and unwounded. Odysseus knows nothing of what became of him after the war. It is not clear to what extent the details related in the *Iliou Persis* (cf. Bethe, *Odyssee*, 179–83, 256–61) belong to pre-Homeric saga, in this case whether γέρας ἐσθλόν is a reference to Andromache.

533. = iii 130.

534. μοῖραν: here '(just) share of the booty'—a reminder of Achilles' bitter recriminations against Agamemnon (*Il.* i 163–8).

535–6. ἀσκηθής (v 26) is explained by οὖτ' ... οὐτασμένος. Neoptolemus remained unscathed by missiles (spear or arrow) and in the cut and thrust of fighting at close quarters. 535ᵇ = *Il.* xiii 212ᵇ. For 536ᵃ cf. *Il.* xii 192ᵃ.

537. The account finishes with a gnomic observation: Ares rages ἐπιμίξ (μείγνυμι), 'blindly', without respect for individuals; cf. ξυνὸς Ἐνυάλιος (*Il.* xviii 309).

538–40. Achilles departs without a word, his earlier passion driven out by joy over his son's achievements.

539. μακρὰ βιβᾶσα (cf. ix 450 n.). The ghost strides out as the living heroes had done in the pride of their strength (539ᵃ = *Il.* xv 686ᵃ, of Ajax). The MS-tradition supports βιβῶσα; but the deliberate reminiscence of *Il.* xv 686 etc. makes βιβᾶσα the more probable reading. The fields of asphodel belong to ancient tradition; asphodel featured in the cult of Persephone.

540. γηθοσύνη (adj.) is linguistically the only possible reading; Latacz, op. cit. (ix 5–11 n.), 152–3.   ἀριδείκετον: cf. ix 2.

541–67. The meeting with Ajax has already been prepared by 469–70. His ghost stands aloof, and will not respond to Odysseus' advances: his anger, over losing the arms of Achilles to Odysseus, lies too deep. The story of the ὅπλων κρίσις and Ajax's suicide (cf. 548–50) is thus evidently pre-Homeric (W. Kullmann, op. cit. (467–70 n.), 79–84); the first written version was in the Epic Cycle (schol. xi 547; cf. Bethe, *Odyssee*, 168–73). The most

COMMENTARY

famous treatment of the subject is of course the play by Sophocles, who was probably the first to portray the hero as mad.

541ᵇ. = x 530ᵇ.

542. For the first half of the line cf. 466ᵃ. Each ghost asks after his κήδεα, whatever is most important to him (as did Agamemnon (457–61) and Achilles (492–7)); cf. ix 402 εἴροντο ... ὅττι ἑ κήδοι.

545. The contest was thus settled by arbitration.   δικαζόμενος: Odysseus pleads his case, and agrees to be bound by the decision of the tribunal.   νίκησα is ingressive.

546. ἔθηκε sc. τεύχεα. Thetis had decided to award the arms to the man who had contributed most to the task of securing the body.

547. The line was rejected by Aristarchus. Its content is too general to allow reconstruction of the form of the legend here alluded to. It remains unclear whether the Cyclic version is pre-Homeric; cf. Wilamowitz, *Untersuchungen*, 153–4, Bethe, *Odyssee*, 249.

548–51. Odysseus curses the victory which won such a prize. The ἄεθλον is the death of Ajax, as 549–51 (γὰρ) explain: 'for such a man (τοίην prepares for ὃς περὶ ... Πηλείωνα; on κεφαλή as meaning the man himself cf. x 239 n.) was brought to his grave on account of the arms of Achilles (ἕνεκ' αὐτῶν)'—a clear reference to the hero's suicide.

550–1. Cf. 469–70 n. For the construction cf. i 66.

552: cf. ix 363.

553–62. Odysseus attempts to make his peace with the still angry Ajax with persuasive words (note the extensive enjambment).

553. οὐκ ἄρ' ἔμελλες: cf. ix 363.

554–5. ἐμοὶ with χόλου: 'anger against me'.   εἵνεκα τευχέων | οὐλομένων: 'fatal, unlucky' (cf. iv 92, *Il.* i 1), like ἕνεκ' αὐτῶν, 549. τὰ δὲ (τεύχεα) is the obj., πῆμα the predic.

556–60. τοῖος γάρ (constr. as at 549: τοίην γὰρ) justifies πῆμα: 'your death meant the loss of such a bastion'. He had proved himself a πύργος most of all in the fight for the ships (*Il.* xv, xvi).   σεῖο ... φθιμένοιο depends on ἀχνύμεθα.   ἶσον Ἀχιλλῆος κεφαλῇ: 'in the same way as over Achilles'. In 558–9 Odysseus places the death in a theological context: οὐδέ τις ἄλλος | αἴτιος (cf. viii 311) ⟨ἐστιν⟩, ἀλλὰ Ζεὺς ⟨αἴτιός ἐστιν, ὃς⟩ ... (560ᵃ = 437ᵃ). Zeus allowed the quarrel to arise on account of his own anger against the Achaeans, and so laid his μοῖρα on Ajax. On τεΐν = σοί cf. Chantraine, *Grammaire*, i 265, G. Giangrande, *Hermes*, xcviii (1970), 262.

561. ἔπος καὶ μῦθον: cf. iv 597.

562. μένος: 'vehemence', here almost: 'anger'.   ἀγήνορα (i 106): here 'obstinate'.

563–4. Odysseus took an emotional leave of Agamemnon (465–6); Achilles left without a word, but with pride and joy (538–40); Ajax, on the other hand, departs in stony silence, unmoved by the generous and heartfelt words of his rival.

565–7. These lines, which introduce the final major scene with great figures from the past, have often been criticized and ascribed to an interpolator who inserted 568–635 in an earlier context; cf. Ameis–Hentze, *Anhang*, ii 122–3, Wilamowitz, *Untersuchungen*, 141–2, Schwartz, *Odyssee*, 319. They are indeed somewhat harsh, but in keeping with the context: 'He might yet, in spite of his anger (κεχολωμένος), have spoken to me, or I to him', i.e. 'a conversation might still have developed, had not ... (ἀλλά μοι ...)' Any chance of further contact is hindered by Odysseus' θυμός, as he is distracted by the figures which present themselves to his gaze and an overpowering wish to speak to the many other ghosts around him; cf. Focke, *Odyssee*, 222–4.

568–627. Aristarchus' assessment of this passage as interpolation has been followed by many modern scholars: Wilamowitz, *Untersuchungen*, 199–226, Schwartz, *Odyssee*, 319, von der Mühll, *Philologus*, xciii (1938), 3–4, *Odyssee*, 727, Merkelbach, *Untersuchungen*, 177, 189–90, Page, *Odyssey*, 26–7, Bowra in *Companion*, 45, Kirk, *Songs*, 236–7, Lesky, *Homeros*, 126, W. Kühlmann, op. cit. (ix 14–15 n.), 65–9, and the critical review in Eisenberger, *Studien*, 83–91. Wilamowitz himself later withdrew his hypothesis of an 'Orphic' interpolation, *Glaube*, ii (Berlin, 1932), 200. The overall structure of the book guarantees the place of these disputed lines. The two main sections, divided by the 'intermezzo', correspond to each other; the first three meetings with heroines are followed by a catalogue of heroines (each section being introduced by ἴδον, 235 etc.); similarly the encounters with the three heroes of the Trojan War are followed by a catalogue of six heroes, whom Odysseus sees without any words being spoken except in the last case (ἴδον (568), cf. 572, 576, 582, 592, 601). The first, second, and sixth figures are 'positive'; the third, fourth, and fifth characters 'negative'. A major difference from the catalogue of heroines is the omission (as in the meeting with the three heroes of Troy) of any tasting of blood—with good reason, since Odysseus is now looking at figures deep within Erebus, rather than at those which had drawn close to his sacrifice (cf. 539). It is wrong to say (as does e.g. Kirk, *Songs*, 236–7) that Odysseus is now walking around within Hades: he observes from his standpoint by the trench.

568–71. Minos, son of Zeus and Europa, and in life king of Crete. His ghost is seen, in keeping with the εἴδωλον concept, continuing in Hades the activity characteristic of him in life (Nilsson, *Geschichte*, 454, on the concept of 'iteration'). The outward attributes and circumstances correspond to the man's activity on earth. It was only in later tradition that Minos became judge of the dead (Pl. *Grg.* 523 e 6–7).

569. This line is quoted in Pl. *Grg.* 526 d 2. On θεμιστεύω cf. ix 114.

570. δίκας εἴροντο: 'they asked him for δίκαι', i.e. they allowed him to decide on cases brought to him, δικάζοντο (cf. 545).

571ᵇ. = *Il.* xxiii 74ᵇ. The doors of Hades stand wide open.

572–5. Orion, the great hunter, beloved of Eos, and victim of Artemis (see v 121–4; cf. F. Wehrli, *RE* xviii (1936), 1065–82), is also portrayed as pursuing the same occupation as in life. The correspondence between the outward appearance of the ghost in death and the activity of the man in life is here emphasized by the idea that Orion in Hades hunts the very same prey that he once pursued on earth.

573. εἰλεῦντα: εἰλέω (ὁμῶς), 'drive together, round up'. For the second half of the line cf. 539.

574ᵇ: cf. *Il.* xxiv 614ᵇ.   **οἰοπόλοισιν:** οἰοπόλος (*hapax* in the *Odyssey*) is an epithet of ὄρος: 'mountains on which only the solitary dwell (πέλομαι); lonely mountains'.

575. ῥόπαλον: cf. ix 319.   **ἀαγές** (*hapax*): from ἄγνυμι, i.e. 'unbreakable'. The surprising lengthening of the second syllable corresponds to the lengthening of ἐάγη in the line on which this is modelled, *Il.* xi 559ᵇ ῥόπαλ' ἀμφὶς ἐάγη ...; cf. Chantraine, *Grammaire*, i 18, M. Bertheau, *LfgrE* s.v. ἄγνυμι, Shipp, *Studies*, 16, Wyatt, *Lengthening*, 78–9.

576–81. Tityus is one of the trio of great sinners (the other two being Tantalus and Sisyphus) who undergo punishment in Hades (576–600). Although the scene supports to a certain extent the concept of Hades mirroring life (e.g. 592), the overriding impression here is of a group of exceptions to the general epic conception of the world of the dead. Here Hades is the place of eternal punishment; for the 'sinners' death is not the end of everything; by their sufferings in Hades they make an atonement which they could not achieve in life. Similar concepts are also found at *Il.* iii 278–9; as a counterpart there is the picture of Elysium, to which chosen heroes come after death, thus escaping Hades (iv 561–9); similarly Hes. *Op.* 166–73, on the Isles of the Blessed. The inconsistency is no doubt to be explained thus: by contrast with the diversity of current views of the soul, the underworld, and life after death, the poet in general presents a conception in which very various elements are unified into a single coherent picture; but, from time to time (as here and at iv 561–9) we catch a glimpse of popular beliefs which he has otherwise excluded. Tityus, son of Gaea, attempted to violate Leto and suffers in death a fate similar to that of the living Prometheus; cf. Hes. *Th.* 521–5.

576. ἐρικυδέος: cf. iii 66.

577. πέλεθρα (only here and in the passage on which this line is modelled, *Il.* xxi 407; Ion.-Att. πλέθρον): a measure of length later defined as 100 feet; etym. uncertain (cf. Frisk, *GEW* s.v. πλέθρον).

578. On the surprising dual γῦπε (for γῦπε δύω) cf. Chantraine, *Grammaire*, ii 25, Shipp, *Studies*, 128.

579. δέρτρον (*hapax*): 'peritoneum (or part of it)'; cf. Chantraine, *Dictionnaire* s.v. δέρω.   **δύνοντες:** 'penetrating (violently)'.

580. ἕλκησε (*hapax* in the *Odyssey*): 'dragged about, did violence to' (*sens. obsc.*).

581. Πυθώδ': cf. viii 80.   **Πανοπῆος** (Πανοπεύς): city of the Phocians, listed in the *Iliad* (ii 520) with Pytho; cf. Simpson–Lazenby, *Catalogue*, 42–3.

582–92. No reason is given here for the punishment of Tantalus, a mythical king of Phrygia from the neighbourhood of Mt. Sipylus and father of Pelops. The poet takes for granted his audience's knowledge of the cause of these sufferings (582); later authors (beginning with Pi. *O.* i) give very different accounts, but common to all is an offence against the gods. Cf. Preller–Robert, op. cit. (260–5 n.), i. 1, 285–6.

582. Quoted by Pl. *Prt.* 315 c 8, to introduce Prodicus.

583. προσέπλαζε (cf. i 2; κῦμα προσπλάζον *Il.* xii 285): the wave strikes Tantalus' chin.

584. στεῦτο: originally (as in the *Iliad*) with the infin.; here there is a change in the meaning and constr. (with ptcp.) of the isolated epic form. It may mean 'he wanted (to drink)', or 'he was constantly thirsty', or 'he behaved like a man suffering from thirst'. Cf. Leumann, *Wörter*, 211, Erbse, *Beiträge*, 228. On διψάων cf. Meister, *Kunstsprache*, 88, Shipp, *Studies*, 17. **ἐλέσθαι:** with οὐκ εἶχεν, 'he could not reach (the water) to drink it (πιέειν)'.

585. κύψει' (κύπτω; hapax in the *Odyssey*): 'stoop'.

586. ἀναβροχέν: partic. (intrans.) of the strong aor. pass. of -βρόξαι, 'swallow': cf. iv 222, xii 240; Bechtel, *Lexilogus*, 84–5, Frisk, *GEW* s.v. βρόξαι.

587. καταζήνασκε (hapax): frequentative form (like ἀπολέσκετ' and φάνεσκε) from aor. of ἀζάνω (cf. ἄζομαι), 'make to dry up'. On these forms see P. Wathelet, *AC* xlii (1973), 379–405.

588–90. ὑψιπέτηλα: cf. iv 458. **κατὰ κρῆθεν:** fruit hangs down in plenty from the tops of the trees. On the expression cf. Leumann, *Wörter*, 56–8, Chantraine, *Grammaire*, ii 113. On the similarity between this passage and the description of Alcinous' orchard (583 ~ vii 114, 589–90 = vii 115–16) cf. F. M. Combellack, *TAPhA* xcvi (1965), 53.

591. ἰθύσει' (ἰθύω) + gen. (τῶν): 'stretch out towards'; the infin. (expressing purpose) ἐπὶ ... μάσασθαι (μαίομαι ix 302) is dependent on it.

593–600. Sisyphus, son of Aeolus, erstwhile king of Corinth, was the wiliest of all mortals; the non-Homeric tradition also makes him father of Odysseus. Again no reason for the punishment is given, but very likely, as with Tantalus and Tityus, the cause was ὕβρις which encroached on the privilege of the gods. Later authors again give a variety of reasons for the punishment; cf. Bethe, *RE* iiia (1927), 371–6.

593. The parallel with 582 is intentional.

594. βαστάζοντα: βαστάζω (elsewhere only at xxi 405; here conative) is a technical term, originally perhaps 'weigh', later 'lift, carry'; cf. Chantraine, *Dictionnaire* s.v. **ἀμφοτέρῃσι** sc. χερσί.

595. σκηριπτόμενος: σκηρίπτομαι (only here and xvii 196), 'support oneself'; cf. Bechtel, *Lexilogus*, 300–1. 595ᵇ = *Il.* xx 360ᵇ.

597. ἀποστρέψασκε: 'constantly turned back again'. **κραταιῗς** as an adv. (as Aristarchus supposed) is linguistically impossible, as is κραται' ἴς offered by Ptol. Ascal. But even a fem. abstract from κραταιός ('force, weight'), as Bérard and Stanford suggest, would be morphologically (Risch, *Wortbildung*, 144) and syntactically strange. We would expect to find a personal subject for ἀποστρέψασκε, e.g. a mythical figure Κραταιῗς, homonymous with the mother of Scylla (xii 124). Cf. van der Valk, *Textual Criticism*, 112.

598. λᾶας ἀναιδής: modelled on *Il.* iv 521 (cf. also *Il.* xiii 139); the stone, anthropomorphically, has no pity.

COMMENTARY

599. This line repeats, and gives a variation on, the situation at 596–7 (τιταινόμενος: σκηριπτόμενος). **κατὰ … μελέων:** as at *Il.* xvi 109.

600. ἐκ κρατὸς is scarcely intelligible. The usual explanation (that Sisyphus hangs his head, so that the rising cloud of dust appears to be coming from it) is hardly convincing; nor is the cj. ἔκπαγλος (v. Herwerden).

601–27. The encounter with Heracles is deliberately placed last: Heracles had pioneered the descent to Hades (for quite different reasons from Odysseus'), successfully venturing to transcend the normal limits of human endeavour. The legend was surely told in epic form before Homer, but hardly in the form of an independent *catabasis* (cf. von der Mühll, *Philologus* xciii (1938), 8–9, *Odyssee*, 727, Merkelbach, *Untersuchungen*, 190); much more probably it was related within the framework of a Heracles epic, which may have influenced the content, perhaps also the form, of 601–27 (and likewise of *Il.* viii 366–9, v 395–7 etc., Hes. *Th.* 287–332). It is tempting to suppose (cf. Erbse, *Beiträge*, 31–3) that the *catabasis* of Heracles inspired the poet to make Odysseus undertake a journey to the Underworld; thus, at the end of the *Nekuia*, he may be supposed to cite his 'source'. The difficulties of the passage have been the object of scholarly discussion from antiquity onwards; cf. G. Petzl, *Antike Diskussionen über die beiden Nekyiai* (Meisenheim, 1969), 28–41, and latterly E. Heitsch, op. cit. (ix 364–7 n.), 8–10. 602–4, regarded by ancient scholars as the work of an interpolator (Onomacritus, in the sixth century) cause particular difficulty: how is the presence of an εἴδωλον of Heracles in Hades to be reconciled with the continued existence of Heracles in heroic divinity on Olympus? This runs counter to the principle, elsewhere strictly maintained by the poet, that physical death is the precondition for the presence of an εἴδωλον in the Underworld. Moreover, 616–17 seem incongruous after 602–4. Excision of 602–4 (as Focke suggests, *Odyssee*, 228–9) would indeed remove many difficulties. It is, however, possible that the poet did not wish to suppress the idea of Heracles' divine status, which had gained widespread currency (in this differing from the poet of the *Iliad* (xviii 117–19)) but was unwilling to forgo the scene planned for 601–27, and so attempted a (strictly speaking, illogical) compromise between the popular belief about the hero and the εἴδωλον concept fundamental to the rest of the book. For further reading cf. Heitsch, loc. cit., and W. Pötscher, *Kairos*, iii (1965), 208–10.

601. βίην Ἡρακληείην (as at *Il.* v 638, xix 98, Hes. *Th.* 289 etc.) = 'Ηρακλέεα; possibly derived from pre-Homeric poetry.

602. On 602–4 see above. **εἴδωλον:** amplification (or rather correction) of βίην Ἡ., to which it is in apposition. The antithesis εἴδωλον: αὐτὸς δὲ is similar to that at *Il.* i 3–5, although there αὐτούς means bodies bereft of ψυχαί, i.e. dead.

603. ἐν θαλίῃς (*hapax* in the *Odyssey*; θαλίη ἐνὶ *Il.* ix 143 = 285; imit. in Hes. *Op.* 115, cf. also *Th.* 65): 'in the fullness of joy and happiness, which lacks nothing'; cf. Latacz, op. cit. (ix 5–11 n.), 217. **ἔχει:** 'has to wife' (as at 270).

604 (= Hes. *Th.* 952): athetized early; cf. Ameis–Hentze, *Anhang*, ii 124–5. **χρυσοπεδίλου** (*hapax*): 'with golden sandals'.

605. κλαγγή: similar to ἰαχή (43); cf. the comparison with the νυκτερίδες (τετριγυῖαι) xxiv 6–9.

606. ἀτυζομένων: ἀτύζομαι (common in the *Iliad*; in the *Odyssey* only here and xxiii 42), 'be terrified, run in terror'. **νυκτὶ ἐοικώς:** as at *Il.* i 47, which refers to Apollo as he comes with his plague-arrows.

607. γυμνὸν τόξον: the bow is out of its quiver.

608. παπταίνων: from παπταίνω, 'look round'; in the *Iliad* used of warriors observing enemy positions. **αἰεὶ βαλέοντι** (fut.): Heracles is like a man ready to fire an arrow at any moment.

609–14. The lines describe the τελαμών ('broad strap, belt') which Heracles wears as an ἀορτήρ (predic., 'baldric'; on ἀείρω cf. Frisk, *GEW*, i 24) 'across his chest', i.e. over the shoulder; the quiver is evidently secured on his back. The broad leather strap is decorated with gold chasing, depicting a number of different scenes. The poet is clearly inspired by contemporary works of art imitating Oriental models or actually coming from the east; cf. Focke, *Odyssee*, 229–33. The description is comparable to those of the aegis at *Il.* v 738–42, and that of Achilles' shield in *Il.* xviii (on which see K. Flittschen, *Archaeologia* N, 1–17).

609. σμερδαλέος: vi 137.

610. ἵνα: here used locatively, 'where'. **θέσκελα:** cf. 374.

611. ἀγρότεροι: cf. vi 133 (M. Wittwer, *Glotta*, xlvii (1970), 59–60). **χαροποί** (*hapax*) has not been satisfactorily explained; Risch (*Wortbildung*, 172) suggests 'with a look full of the joy of battle (?)'; Latacz (op. cit. (ix 5–11 n.), 38–43) suggests 'looking round greedily'. Or perhaps it means 'with shaggy mane'?

612. The line is modelled on *Il.* vii 237, xxiv 548, and was in turn used by Hes. *Th.* 228; cf. Focke, *Odyssee*, 229–31, Krafft, op. cit. (x 239–43 n.), 67–8, G. P. Edwards, *The Language of Hesiod in its Traditional Context* (Oxford, 1971), 169–70. **ὑσμῖναι:** xi 417. **ἀνδροκτασίαι** (*hapax* in the *Odyssey*): 'slaughter of men'.

613–14. The lines may be corrupt (Schwartz, *Odyssee*, 320), and are not easily explained even by reference to iv 684–5 (Ameis–Hentze, *Anhang*, ii 126). The meaning may be, following Chantraine (*Grammaire*, ii 213), 'I would wish that the artist did not make a second masterpiece like it'. Even ἐγκατατίθεσθαι, otherwise connected with κόλπῳ, θυμῷ (xxiii 223), or οἴκῳ (Hes.), is here difficult to interpret: 'he set down the belt in his τέχνη', i.e. he entrusted production of the belt to his skill.

615–16. The deliberate repetition (615 = 390; 616 ~ 472) is intended to link this meeting and the encounter with the three heroes of Troy. The same end is achieved by giving Heracles' words in direct speech.

618–19. ἡγηλάζεις: in the *Odyssey* only here and xvii 217, explained by ὀχέω and ἄγω respectively: 'drag about with one'; cf. Bechtel, *Lexilogus*, 150–1, Chantraine, *Dictionnaire* s.v. Heracles means that Odysseus surely has to bear a burden of fate not unlike the one he endured in his mortal life. (619[b]: cf. 498.)

620. Heracles is a son of Zeus; cf. *Il.* v 637–9, xiv 323–4, xix 105.

621. ἀπειρεσίην: cf. ix 118 n.

622. δεδμήμην (with μάλα 621): 'I was subject to'; the labours (ἄεθλοι) which Heracles performed in the service of another, much weaker man (621), Eurystheus, son of Sthenelus (*Il.* xv 639–40, xix 122), belong to an ancient tradition; cf. *Il.* viii 363.

623–4. The greatest of Heracles' deeds was the capture of the hound of Hades (κύων; cf. Hes. *Th.* 311–12 on Κέρβερος); cf. *Il.* v 395–6, viii 367–8 (the model for these lines, and for the guidance of Athena (626); cf. *Il.* viii 362–9). The descent into Hades is deliberately mentioned as an example of the ἄεθλοι; it is a deed which both heroes have in common and the most dangerous enterprise undertaken by either.

627: cf. 150. That Heracles had come up to Odysseus is implied, but not directly stated, at 615.

628: cf. 152.

629ᵃ. = iv 268ᵇ. 629ᵇ: cf. 382ᵇ.

630–1. According to ancient tradition 631 was added by Pisistratus, and should thus be classed with such passages as *Il.* i 263. The mention of Theseus and Pirithous, after the encounter with Heracles, clearly intended as the concluding climax to the episode, is indeed somewhat surprising. It is not, however, necessary to agree with Focke (*Odyssee*, 236–7) that 630 is dubious: Odysseus waits in hope that other heroes might appear, 'and indeed I might have seen yet more (ἔτι) heroes of the past (προτέρους; cf. πρόσθεν 629), whom I longed to see, but then …'. Cf. Wilamowitz, *Untersuchungen*, 140, J. A. Davison in *Companion*, 219–20, Eisenberger, *Studien*, 189. 97.

632–3. These lines recall the situation at the beginning of the episode. 632: cf. 36–42; 633 ~ 43.

634–5. Odysseus' fear (δέος 633), which earlier had been quite general (43), is now concentrated on a particular terror, that Persephone might send towards him out of the depths of Hades (to the βόθρος) 'the head of the Gorgon, that terrible monster'. The legend was that Perseus cut off the head of Medusa, the only one of the three Gorgons who was mortal (Hes. *Th.* 274–80); anyone looking at the head was instantly turned to stone. Athena's aegis was decorated with a representation of the head (*Il.* v 741–2). The theme became popular in art in the seventh century.

636–8. 636 ~ ix 177; 637–8 = ix 178–9.

639. τὴν sc. νῆα.   κῦμα ῥόοιο: 'the current of the stream'; Oceanus is thought of as a river.

640. εἰρεσίη: cf. x 78.   κάλλιμος οὖρος (sc. φέρει): cf. ἴκμενος οὖρος (7). On the geographical conceptions cf. 14–19 n.

1–4. The ship, having arrived in the mythical east, leaves the encircling river for the sea (εὐρύπορος by contrast with the river Oceanus), and makes for Aeaea. 1^b = xi 21^b; 2^b = iv 432^b; 3^a = xi 70^a. 3–4 indicate the mythical topography exactly (cf. x 135–9): the island of Aeaea lies where Eos has her palace and dancing-grounds and where Helios rises each day (ἀντολαί).

5. = ix 546; 6–8 = ix 150–2. The journey from Circe to Hades had lasted from dawn to dusk (x 541, xi 11–12); the return journey (after the period spent by the entrance to Hades) takes until dawn (the same length of time). Cf. xi 14–19 n.

9^a. = ix 88^a, x 100^a; 9^b = x 287^b.

10–15. Odysseus fulfils his promise of xi 80 to bury Elpenor (x 551–60). **οἰσέμεναι:** on the genesis of the artificial form see Chantraine, *Grammaire*, i 417–18, Leumann, *Kleine Schriften* (Zurich, 1959), 234–41, C. L. Prince, *Glotta*, clviii (1970), 155–63.

11. φιτρούς (*hapax* in the *Odyssey*; *Il.* xxiii 123 in a similar context): 'trunk, log'.

12: cf. x 570.

13–18. The details of the burial follow Elpenor's wishes (13: cf. xi 24; 14–15 ∼ 75–8). The barrow (τύμβος 14 ∼ σῆμα xi 75) is constructed over the ashes of the pyre, and surmounted (ἐπὶ ... ἐρύσαντες) by a στήλη. The monument would normally be a stake held in place by two stones (cf. *Il.* xxiii 326–31; M. Andronikos, *Archaeologia* W, 32–4); here it takes the form requested by the dead man: an oar.

16. 'We carried out all the details of our task in sequence (δι-)'. 16^b = *Il.* xi 706^b.

18. ἐντυναμένη (cf. ἐντύνασαν ἕ αὐτήν *Il.* xiv 162) expresses briefly the actions described at x 542–5. **ἅμα ... αὐτῇ:** 'accompanying her'. 18^b ∼ *Il.* xxii 461.

21–2. The daring behind the journey to Hades (σχέτλιοι) is underlined by striking phraseology: 'as living men you descended to Hades (to the dead), so you are men who will die twice (δισθανέες: an artificial *ad hoc* neologism; criticized by Bechtel, *Lexilogus*, 103), whereas (on contrasting ὅτε see Ruijgh, τε *épique*, 494) other men die only once'.

23. = x 460.

24. πανημέριοι: cf. xi 11. 24^b is formulaic (*Il.* ix 618, xxiv 600, *Od.* xv 396): 'at the break of day'.

25–7. The words in which Circe (x 539–40) had adumbrated Tiresias' instructions (xi 100–37) are deliberately echoed. Circe explains her intention, δείξω ὁδόν, and adds ἕκαστα σημανέω. Unlike Tiresias, who in his role as prophet had concentrated largely on Thrinacia as an unavoidable and fateful stopping-point, Circe, as a divine helper, gives precise instructions and in particular reveals how Odysseus will reach Thrinacia. On the connection between x 539–40, xi 100–37, and xii 37–141 see also Besslich, *Schweigen*, 53–60.   **κακορραφίη** (cf. ii 236; 26ᵇ is modelled on *Il.* xv 16ᵇ): Odysseus must be on his guard against 'wicked designs', whether on the part of the strange beings whom he will encounter or of his own crew.

27. ἁλός (gen. of place) is also dependent on ἐπί.

28–32. 28 = x 466 etc.; 29–31 = x 183–5, 476–8; 32 = *Il.* i 476 (cf. *Od.* x 186, 479).

33. As at x 480–540 the conversation between Circe and Odysseus takes place at night, out of hearing of the crew, who are not briefed until the following day (on 154–64 cf. x 562–5). Again the parallel is quite intentional.

34. εἷσε: as at x 233.   **προσέλεκτο:** cf. λέκτο (iv 453). They talk by the shore, so Odysseus does not enter Circe's palace again (cf. 143).

35. = x 16.

36. = xi 99.

37–141: Circe's speech.

37. πεπείρανται: attested elsewhere only at xxiii 175 and 192, where it means 'tie on'; hence Meuli's interpretation (*Odyssee*, 47. 1), 'These things then are thus (οὕτω: as you have reported) bound by fate (you are fated to travel via Thrinacia)'. But ταῦτα πάντα suggests rather 'All that (the descent to Hades) is now completed'.

38. μνήσει δὲ … αὐτός: likewise governed by ὥς (with change of subject), it may prepare for 169 (θεός: δαίμων).

39–54. The first landmark of the journey named is the home of the Sirens. Circe describes the threat they pose, and suggests a stratagem for avoiding it. There are two main difficulties with the passage, and these have led to differing explanations. First, Circe's warning and the description of the adventure itself (158–200) are both rather short, and concentrate on the recommended stratagem at the expense of any detail of the Sirens' appearance or descent, the nature of the danger of their singing, how their victims meet their end, or the Sirens' fate after the encounter with Odysseus. The second difficulty is of reconciling the poet's account with the treatment of the subject in the visual arts; see E. Buschor, *Die Musen des Jenseits* (Munich, 1944). No satisfactory theory of the genesis of the Homeric account or of the true nature of the Sirens has yet emerged. The episode belongs to folktale, to the common stock of sea adventure material. Many such stories feature supernatural female beings who by their enchanting songs lure sailors to their deaths; cf. Radermacher, *Erzählungen*, 21–3, G. K. Gresseth, 'The Homeric Sirens', *TAPhA* ci (1970), 203–18, esp. 212–13, Page, *Folktales*, 85–90, esp. 87–8. Even the motif of the seaman stopping his ears with wax appears in the folklore tradition of other countries. Eisenberger (*Studien*, 193–8), however, quite rightly questions Meuli's hypothesis (*Odyssee*, 91–4, cf. Merkelbach, *Untersuchungen*, 204) that in the pre-Homeric Argonaut epic Orpheus countered the Sirens with his own singing, and so broke the spell (echoed by AR iv 891-2) and that this was a direct model for the *Odyssey*.

The attempts to determine what exactly the ancient Greeks understood by the concept 'Siren' have concentrated on the evidence of the visual arts; there are many depictions of the Sirens, apart from what may be described as simply illustrations of scenes of the *Odyssey*. The conclusions reached are varied: vampire-like souls of the dead or spirits embodied in birds (G. Weicker, *Der Seelenvogel* (Leipzig, 1902), opposed by Nilsson, *Geschichte*, 228-9, Gresseth, op. cit., 203-4); beings from the world of spirits, who delight the souls of the dead with their song in the after-life (Buschor, op. cit.; countered by J. Pollard, 'Muses and Sirens', *CR* lxvi (1952), 60-3); or even 'daemones meridiani', demons of the midday heat, who paralyse seamen, and so endanger their lives (K. Latte, 'Die Sirenen', *Kleine Schriften* (Munich, 1968), 106-11, criticized by Gresseth, op. cit., 209-10). One thing is certain: that both the conception and the portrayal of man-beast hybrids—besides the Sirens (birds with human faces) there are sphinxes and griffins—are influenced by oriental models (Nilsson, loc. cit.). This influence can be traced back to Mycenaean times. Cf. the fresco from Pylos, K. Blegen, *AJA* lxvi (1962), plate 40, 12. H. Mühlestein, ('Sirenen in Pylos', *Glotta* xxxvi (1957), 152-66) has plausibly suggested that the word *Seirēmes* (> -*ēnes*) is to be read in the Pylos Ta tablets; the heads of Sirens appear to be mentioned there also as ornamentation on thrones (Ta 708.2 *se-re-mo-ka-ra-a-pi/Seirēmōn krahapphi*, instr. pl.; the sg. appears at Ta 707.2, 714.2; cf. also E. Risch, *SMEA* i (1966), 53-69).

It is quite possible that the nameless enchantresses of folktale, who lure sailors to their doom by a fatally bewitching song, were at first quite unconnected with the fabulous, half-human, half-animal creatures which may from an early date have been known as Sirens. It is conceivable that the poet of the *Odyssey* was the first to give the name 'Sirens' to the enchantresses who endangered Odysseus (like others before him) by their singing, without, however, intending that these characters are to be understood as having the half-animal form of true Sirens. In the pseudo-Hesiodic *Catalogue* (fr. 27 M–W) the number of Sirens is increased from two to three, and they are given individual names and a genealogy; their home is given as Ἀνθεμόεσσα (cf. xii 159); and they are credited with the power to calm winds (θέλγειν; cf. fr. 28 M–W). Artistic representations show that in later times the Homeric characters were given the half-human, half-animal features of the traditional Sirens. The story, depicted on vases from the sixth century onwards, that the Sirens threw themselves to their deaths in the sea out of despair at their defeat by Odysseus will be a later invention; Eisenberger, *Studien*, 195. The attempt to place the home of the Sirens on the map dates back at least as far as Timaeus; they were localized on the Σειρηνοῦσσαι, the rocky isles between Sorrento and Capri; cf. Strabo i 22-3, Steph. Byz. s.v. Among modern critics see esp. J. Bérard and A.-C. Blane, *Mélanges d'archéologie et d'histoire* (1954), 7-13. On the various allegorical interpretations (from the Sirens representing the temptations of lust, to the Sirens as the embodiment of knowledge pursued at the expense of faith), which began with Euripides and Plato, spread during the Hellenistic period, and continued in Christian authors, see Rahner, op. cit. (x 302–6), 281–328 (Engl. edn. 328–86).

39. Σειρῆνας: pl., but the dual in 52 indicates a pair.

40: cf. xvi 228 (= xx 188). The θέλγειν, the consequences of which are described at 41–3, is brought about by λιγυρὴ ἀοιδή whereas Circe bewitches through φάρμακα. In both cases the normal mental processes are altered; cf. x 213 n. What exactly happens to a man entranced by the Sirens is a matter for conjecture. He is probably distracted from steering his course, and shipwrecked; the bodies are later washed up on shore (45–6). θέλγειν ἀοιδῇ later gave rise to the Sirens' other names, Θελξιόπη (or -νόη), Μολπή, Ἀγλαόφωνος (Hes. fr. 27 M–W); cf. also Pindar's designation Κηληδόνες (Pae. 8b 9 Snell; κηλέω ∼ θέλγω).

41. ἀϊδρείη: here 'ignorance (of danger)'.

43. The combination of παρίσταται and γάνυνται is surprising. It is not, however, necessary to resort to conjecture (παρίσταντ', Kayser, Ameis) or the strained explanation of Stanford (ad loc.); cf. Chantraine, Grammaire, ii 17.

44. ἀλλά τε: Bentley's cj. ἀλλά ἑ is rightly rejected by Ruijgh (τε épique, 787–8). **θέλγουσιν** (refers back to 40): here used in the absolute sense, 'they exercise their enchantments'.

45. ἐν λειμῶνι: the Sirens are portrayed on vases as sitting on a rock. 45ᵇ can only be understood as a (somewhat strained) adaptation of an expression such as φθινύθει δ' ἀμφ' ὀστεόφι χρώς (xvi 145); ἀμφ' has become an adv., and ὀστεόφιν almost the same as gen. ὀστέων. **θίς** 'heap' (elsewhere 'beach, shore') is also odd; perhaps we have here the original meaning, from which developed the sense 'heap of sand, dune, beach'.

46. For the first half of the line cf. i 161. **μινύθουσι:** here 'shrink, shrivel up'.

47. After the description of the danger follow (ἀλλά onwards) the instructions on counter-measures (with infin. for imper.). **ἐπὶ ... ἀλεῖψαι:** from ἐπαλείφω, 'plug, seal'.

48. κηρόν: 'wax'. **δεψήσας** (hapax): 'knead, soften'.

51. ὀρθὸν: with σ' (50). **ἱστοπέδη:** 'hole for fixing the mast'; the mast is held in place by two wooden supports: cf. ii 424–5 n. **ἐκ δ' αὐτοῦ:** 'on to it, i.e. the ἱστός'. **πείρατ'** (πεῖραρ): here in its secondary meaning, 'rope, cable' (∼ δεσμός 54); cf. Heubeck, Glotta, l (1972), 140–1. **ἀνήφθω** (from ἀνάπτω): 'you should remain bound'.

52. τερπόμενος: 'with enjoyment'; cf. Latacz, op. cit. (ix 5–11 n.), 209–10. Odysseus will achieve a double victory over the Sirens: he will escape death, and still hear the singing; the old story is enlivened by this new twist. **Σειρήνοϊν:** gen. dual; cf. Schwyzer, Grammatik, i 557.

54. οἱ δέ: δέ is apodotic, introducing the main clause. The MS-reading δεόντων is to be preferred to διδέντων (Aristarchus' conjecture?); cf. van der Valk, Textual Criticism, 138. The Alexandrian athetesis of 53–4 is approved by Schwartz (*Odyssee*, 320), who also rejects 51–2. There is in fact no reason to reject these lines: they prepare for what happens at 192 ff., in a manner entirely characteristic of the poet, and 52 is indispensable for its content.

55–72. After dealing with the Sirens Circe describes alternative routes to Thrinacia (which Odysseus has learned from Tiresias he must visit). The first route would take Odysseus past the Planctae (ἔνθεν μὲν ... 59 ff.); the second leads past Scylla and Charybdis (οἱ δὲ ... 73 ff.). The difficulties of 55–72, which cannot be removed by excision of individual lines (Schwartz, *Odyssee*, 267. 2), arise mainly because the poet conflates two concepts from mythological geography: the Wandering Rocks, which the ship would have to travel between (62–5: the doves of Zeus); and cliffs with dangerous surf (67–8), which the ship would have to travel past (παρέρχεται 62, παρέπλω 69, παρέπεμψεν 72). The source of the first motif is apparent from 69–71, which recall Jason's famous journey in the Argo, and in fact cite a widely known Argo-epos as 'source' (Ἀργὼ πασιμέλουσα 70). The passage is the most important evidence for a pre-Homeric Argonautica as a source and model for Odysseus' adventures in ix–xii (Meuli, *Odyssee*, whose view is developed by, among others, Schwartz, *Odyssee*, 263 ff., Merkelbach, *Untersuchungen*, 203 ff.). Although the extent and nature of the influence on the *Odyssey* is disputed, it seems probable that in the pre-Homeric Argonautica Jason had to negotiate moving rocks (Συμπληγάδες), set in a distant, mythical sea; and that he did so with the aid of Hera, but only at the cost of some damage to his ship, the Argo. It is also possible that the source also included the idea that the rocks were brought to a standstill by Jason's successful passage breaking the spell. At all events, the author of the *Odyssey* borrowed the motif of a dangerous passage between hazards, and attempted to outdo the older version with the option Odysseus chooses, steering between Scylla and Charybdis. The new element in the story, the alternative route via the straits between Scylla and Charybdis, also influences the depiction of the Planctae; cf. the obscurity of the word πλαγκταί, which can suggest both Wandering and Clashing Rocks; Lesky, *WS* lxiii (1948), 36–9, von der Mühll, *Odyssee*, 728, R. Carpenter, *AJA* lii (1948), 1 ff., van der Valk, *Textual Criticism*, 245–6, Heubeck, *WJA* iv (1949/50), 215 ff., F. Gisinger, *RE* xx (1950), 2187 ff., J. Lindsay, *The Clashing Rocks* (London, 1965), Eisenberger, *Studien*, 198–9. The name Πλαγκταί is attributed to the language of the gods (61); cf. μῶλυ (x 305, and x 302–6 n.). In both instances the poet omits any name from human language; here perhaps we are meant to think of the name Symplegades (from the Argonautic source?). The process of trying to place the rocks of the *Odyssey* and Argonautica on the map (Hes. fr. 241 M–W) began in the seventh century; the Symplegades were early localized at the Bosphorus. AR in his Argonautic epic (cf. Apollod. *Bibl.* i 9, 22, 25) systematized the various localizations: on the outward journey the Argonauts negotiate the Κυάνεαι (ii 318), the dangerous cliffs at the Bosphorus (ii 317–45, 551–608); they encounter the Planctae (iv 922–61) in the Tyrrhenian Sea on the return journey.

COMMENTARY

56. διηνεκέως: cf. iv 836.

58. Circe wishes to tell Odysseus the way ἀμφοτέρωθεν ('from both sides'); i.e. she will brief him on both routes (59 ff., 73 ff.).

59. ἐπηρεφέες: cf. x 131.   προτὶ may be Aristarchus' cj.: van der Valk, *Textual Criticism*, 138; ποτί is well attested here, and given by almost all MSS at 71.

60. κυανώπιδος (κυανῶπις): modelled on γλαυκῶπις; Leumann, *Wörter*, 152.   **Ἀμφιτρίτης:** cf. iii 91.

61–5. Nothing else is known of the legend here mentioned. The loss of birds (which may be more easily understood if the birds flew between rather than alongside the rocks) is made good by Zeus.   ἐναρίθμιον ('the full complement') belongs with ἄλλην: 'to make up the full number'.

62. ποτητά (*hapax*): possibly formed by analogy with ἑρπετόν; Shipp, *Studies*, 339.

66. τῇ δ': anaphora, picking up τῇ μὲν (62), after parenthetic 62–5.
φύγεν: 'escaped intact'.

67. πίνακας: here, unusually, 'planks'; elsewhere (i 141 etc.) πίναξ retains its more usual meaning.

68. φορέουσι: 'toss hither and thither'. The second half of the line is obscure, suggesting volcanic activity.

70. Here the Argo is depicted as undergoing this danger on the return journey from Aeetes. On later versions of the legend see 55–72 n.

71. 'Vix integer': von der Mühll; Schwartz (*Odyssee*, 320) diagnoses ἔνθ' ὦκα as corrupt. The subject of βάλεν is κύμαθ' ἁλὸς (68).

73–126. Circe turns to the alternative route: between Scylla and Charybdis. The introductory words οἱ δὲ δύω σκόπελοι prepare for a twofold division of the account: first (ὁ μὲν 73) the rock of Scylla; then (τὸν δ' ἕτερον σκόπελον 101) the rock of Charybdis. The gap between them, which Odysseus must negotiate to reach Thrinacia, is narrow (102). The author's intention is to confront his hero with all three dangers in turn: Scylla, Thrinacia, and Charybdis. His originality lies in combining two very different elements from the mythology of seafaring, the monster and the whirlpool, to form a twin danger which exceeds the perils faced by Jason at his passage through the Symplegades; cf. von der Mühll, *Odyssee*, 729, Merkelbach, *Untersuchungen*, 205. In antiquity the passage between Scylla and Charybdis was at an early date localized at the Straits of Messina (Hecataeus, *FgrH* 1 F 82, Th. iv 24). In modern times many have followed suit (latterly H.-H. and A. Wolf, op. cit. (ix 105 ff. n.), 57–9), but others have suggested the Bosphorus (W. Kranz *et al.*) or the Straits of Gibraltar (R. Hennig, op. cit. (ix 21–7 n.), 29–32, A. Klotz, *Gymnasium*, lix (1952), 299)—although Scylla and Charybdis have obviously no real geographical counterpart.

73–4. Scylla's rock reaches far into the sky. ὁ μὲν is picked up not at νεφέλη δέ ... (74) but at 101 τὸν δ' ... (cf. Ruijgh, τε épique, 682), where we find the contrast to 73 (the rock of Charybdis is much lower).   ἀμφιβέβηκε: cf. viii 541.

75. τὸ μὲν refers to the whole of νεφέλη ... κυανέη; the natural phenomenon described here 'never ceases'.   **αἴθρη** (cf. vi 44): 'the summit is never surrounded by clear skies'.

77. Most MSS give οὐ καταβαίη, which leaves the verbs connected, abnormally, by οὐδὲ ... οὐ. The reading given by Aristarchus (and a minority of the MSS), οὐδ᾽ ἐπιβαίη, removes the syntactical difficulty, but gives an unsatisfactory meaning; we would not expect to see here two verbs of roughly similar sense coupled.

79: cf. ix 241.

80. ἠεροειδές: cf. ii 263.

81–2. ᾗ περ ἄν ... παρὰ ... ἰθύνετε (subj.): 'where you will probably steer your ship past' (cf. Chantraine, *Grammaire*, ii 211–12). Circe is indirectly advising Odysseus to choose this second route, and emphasizes the point by addressing him by name (cf. 101).

83–4. Scylla's cave is so far above the level of the sea that it is out of bowshot from a ship.   **αἰζήιος** (∼ αἰζηός 440; used only once in the *Odyssey*, but often in the *Iliad* as adj. (with ἀνήρ) and noun): the exact meaning is unclear, but it is obviously meant to suggest the youthful strength of a warrior, hunter, or herdsman; etym. unknown (cf. V. Pisani, *LfgrE*, Chantraine, *Dictionnaire* s.v.).

85–100. The appearance and behaviour of Scylla are described in detail here in order to economize on description at 223–59. The fabulous creature with twelve legs and six heads belongs with the monsters described by Hes. (*Th.* 270–336), among others. It seems unlikely that the account is influenced by descriptions of the giant octopus found beyond the Straits of Gibraltar; cf. Hennig, op. cit., 32–5, J. Schmidt, *RE* iiia (1927), 647–53.

85–8. The description begins with an indication of the monster's cry (85), which we are later told belies its ferocity (86–8). Scylla may yelp like a pup (the comparison is due to an etymologizing interpretation of the name: Σκύλλα: σκύλαξ), but is in fact 'a terrible monster' (how terrible we learn from the more detailed description of 89–92), 'whom no one could look on with delight' (cf. Latacz, op. cit. (ix 5–11 n.), 145), 'not even a god, if he met and glimpsed the monster' (83ᵇ = xiii 292ᵇ). There is no essential contradiction between δεινὸν λελακυῖα (85) and φωνὴ ... σκύλακος νεογιλῆς (86), which would support the Alexandrians' view that 86–8 are spurious. Schwartz (*Odyssee*, 320) takes 86–8 as a summary intended to replace 89–100.   **λελακυῖα** (*hapax* in the *Odyssey*; cf. in the *Iliad* λάκε (xiii 616), λεληκώς (xxii 141)): 'barking'.   **νεογιλῆς:** *hapax*, with second element from *γιλ(λ)ος, which must be colloquial, and is found also in names such as Γίλλος and Γίλλις (Bechtel, *Lexilogus*, 233), and possibly also in Myc. *ki-ra-/gil(l)a-* ('girl'?) MY V 659.7 (J. Chadwick).

89. ἄωροι: meaning and etym. unknown; on the ancient explanations cf. Ameis–Hentze, *Anhang*, ii 132–3, Bechtel, *Lexilogus*, 80, Chantraine, *Dictionnaire* s.v.

91. τρίστοιχοι (*hapax*): 'in three rows'.

92. πυκνοὶ καὶ θαμέες (v 252): 'set close together in great numbers'. πλεῖοι μέλανος θανάτοιο: a daring expression (cf. xvii 326, xv 446) to describe mortal danger.

93. μέσση ... δέδυκεν: 'up to the middle she hides in ...'.

94. βερέθρου (only here and *Il.* viii 14): βέρεθρον = βάραθρον, here synon. with σπέος.

95. περιμαιμώωσα (*hapax* in the *Odyssey*): from -μαιμάω, a redupl. intensive form of μαίομαι, 'greedily seeking round'; Bechtel, *Lexilogus*, 219–20, Chantraine, *Grammaire*, i 361, Risch, *Wortbildung*, 341.

96. δελφῖνας (elsewhere only at *Il.* xxi 22): on the derivation see Heubeck, *Kadmos*, xi (1972), 90–1. κύνας: here 'seals'.

97. κῆτος: cf. iv 443. ἀγάστονος (*hapax*): 'loud groaning'. 97ᵇ is imitated at *h.Ap.* 94; cf. ἀγαστόνωι ἐμ[πεσε] (?) (Hes. fr. 31. 6 M–W).

98–100. No sailor can boast of having passed the spot without loss among his shipmates (ἀκήριος, 'unscathed', is attested elsewhere only at xxiii 328; on the homonym ἀ., 'lifeless', see Chantraine, *Dictionnaire* s.v. κήρ, Risch, *Wortbildung*, 113). φέρει: 'carries off'. Together with 90–1 these lines prepare for 245–6.

101–10. Circe now describes Charybdis. The σκόπελοι of Scylla and Charybdis are a bow-shot apart (102); Odysseus must negotiate the channel between them. πλησίον ἀλλήλων (= *Il.* iii 15, *Od.* xiv 14): the expression is abbreviated; there is no need to alter the punctuation following Schwartz (*Odyssee*, 320) to πλησίον, ἀλλήλων καί ...); cf. van der Valk, *Textual Criticism*, 104–5. The description of the twin dangers depends on contrast: Scylla's lair is a high rock, Charybdis' rock is lower; Scylla's cave is matched by Charybdis' fig tree; Scylla has her cave high on the side of the mountain, while Charybdis, the spirit of a whirlpool, lives in the deep. The outward appearance of Scylla is described in detail; Charybdis is portrayed solely in terms of the damage she causes. Both descriptions (85–100, 103–10) are designed to correspond precisely in form and content with the account of what happens later (235–59, 428–46). One detail illustrates perfectly the author's technique here: the significance of ἐρινεός (103) becomes apparent only at 432–44.

103–4. τῷ δ' ἐν sc. σκοπέλῳ; τῷ δ' ὑπό sc. ἐρινεῷ. τεθηλώς: cf. v 69, vi 293. Χάρυβδις: etym. unknown (although certainly not Greek); the verb which follows immediately after is intended to explain the derivation of the name—hence the less well attested reading ἀναρρυβδεῖ 'she swallows' should be preferred, as Blass saw. Charybdis is 'the swallower'. The reading -ροιβδεῖ (cf. ῥοῖβδος, 'noise') probably emerged at a time when the pronunciation of οι and υ was identical (as 'ü'); cf. Frisk, *GEW* s.v. ῥυβδέω (with bibliography), van der Valk, *Textual Criticism*, 73, Scheibner, op. cit. (ix 445 n.), 252–3.

105. ἐπ' ἤματι belongs with both verbs; the waters are sucked down, and regurgitated, three times a day. Polybius' reading δίς–δίς (following Crates?) is pure conjecture. Verg. (*A.* iii 421) and Ovid (*Pont.* iv 10, 28) presuppose Homeric τρίς. Callistratus took exception to the line (referring to 235 ff., 439–41), so too Schwartz (*Odyssee*, 320), who also rejects

439–41. But it is indispensable and only trivial pedantry can see discrepancies in the description here.

106. τύχοις sc. ἐών.

108. μάλα belongs with πεπλημένος (cf. πίλναμαι vi 44, ἐπέλασα iii 291, from which derives the secondary form πελάζω): 'steering close to' + dat. 108–9ᵃ resume and elaborate the instructions of 81–2.

110. Circe means it is better to lose six of the crew to Scylla (ποθήμεναι: cf. ix 453) than to lose all to Charybdis. In the event Odysseus will experience both horrors.

111. ἀμειβόμενος: there is a well supported variant ἀτυζόμενος; cf. xi 606.

112. ἐνίσπες: cf. xi 492 n.   τοῦτο for τόδε is strange: see Palmer, in *Companion*, 139.

113–14. μὲν–δέ: here almost 'not only–but also'. Odysseus asks if it is possible both to avoid Charybdis (as at 108–9) and to prevent the loss of six of his men by resisting Scylla with force (τὴν ... ἀμυναίμην). He recalls the apparently hopeless situations he has faced before. These lines, and Circe's reply, anticipate the action of 225 ff.   **σίνοιτο**: cf. vi 6, xi 112.

116. καὶ δὴ αὖ ...: 'Again!' Circe knows Odysseus' bellicose nature; cf. x 321 ff. 116ᵇ: cf. *Il.* ii 338ᵇ.

117. πόνος: here, as in the *Iliad*, 'the toil of war'.   **θεοῖσιν ... ἀθανάτοισιν**: refers forward, still in general terms, to 118.

119ᵃ. = v 175ᵃ.

120. ἀλκή: 'the possibility of successful defence'.   **κάρτιστον** sc. ἐστίν: 'it is best'; φυγέειν (ingress.), 'to take to flight'.

121. δηθύνησθα (for δηθύνῃς, like τίθησθα (ix 404); elsewhere in the *Odyssey* only at xvii 278 δηθύνειν): 'if you linger'.

122–3: 'I fear that she may sally forth a second time (ἐξαῦτις) with as many (i.e. six) heads, and attack you again.'   **ἐκ ... ἕληται** sc. νηός. 123 is rejected by Schwartz (*Odyssee*, 320).

124–6: 'Therefore row past with all your strength' (σφοδρῶς, hapax); contrasted with δηθύνησθα 121, cf. 109.   **βωστρεῖν** (hapax): intensified form of βοάω (> βω-), cf. ἐλαστρέω and ἐλα(ύν)ω; Bechtel, *Lexilogus*, 86.   **Κράταιϊν**: cf. xi 597 n.   **πῆμα βροτοῖσιν** (imitated, with variation, by Hes. *Th.* 329): predicative, with μιν.   **ἐς ὕστερον ὁρμηθῆναι**: cf. ἐξαῦτις ἐφορμηθεῖσα 122. F. Blass has rightly defended these lines against Aristarchus' athetesis (*Die Interpolation in der Odyssee* (Halle, 1904), 136); Merkelbach, on the other hand, sees 125–6 as possibly late additions (*Untersuchungen*, 194. 2).

127–41. Circe concludes her speech. The passage between Scylla and Charybdis will bring Odysseus to his next goal, Thrinacia. She adds a number of details which are lacking in Tiresias' account and would there be out of place, but which agree with the purpose behind her own speech and are entirely in keeping with what she has already said; cf. Besslich, *Schweigen*, 55.

128. This is still modelled closely on xi 108; the incorporation of detail missing from Tiresias' account begins at 129–36.

129ᵇ. = xi 402ᵇ.

130. ἕκαστα belongs with πώεα.   **γόνος**: here 'descendants'.

131. οὐδέ ποτε: 'and yet never'.   **ἐπιποιμένες** (*hapax*) ~ ποιμένες; on the formation (by secondary concretion of elements) see Risch, *Wortbildung*, 214.

132. The poet gives the nymphs 'significant' names of similar meaning appropriate to their father's nature: 'Shining', 'Radiant'.

133. Ὑπερίονι: cf. i 8. After this a few MSS have the line αὐτοκασιγνήτη Θέτιδος λιπαροκρηδέμνου (133a); it is probably an interpolation, to make Neaera a Nereid, and to give her a genealogy.

134. θρέψασα τεκοῦσά τε: *hysteron proteron*. On 133–4 see Stanford, *CR* lix (1945), 38–9.

135–6: 'Their mother brought them to a different dwelling-place (Thrinacia)'; ναίειν (final) depends on ἀπώκισε (*hapax*), and φυλασσέμεναι (again final) in turn depends on ναίειν.   **πατρώϊα**: cf. i 175.

137–41. Circe repeats once more the fateful directions of Tiresias (xi 110–14) to conclude what she has to say. 140–1 are missing in some MSS, and have been rejected by Kirchhoff (*Odyssee*, 235) and Schwartz (*Odyssee*, 319); they are not however dispensable.

142. = x 541. The repetition is deliberate: Circe's advice has taken all night, as did her instructions before Odysseus' descent into Hades.

143. Circe leaves the shore and returns to her palace. There is no mention of any formal leave-taking.

144–7: 144–5 = xi 636–7. 146 = xi 638, ix 103. 147 is probably an interpolation (influenced by ix 103–4; 147 = ix 104), and contradicts the lines which follow: the ship can sail with a favourable wind; so εἰρεσίη is superfluous.

148–52. = xi 6–10.

153–200. The encounter with the Sirens; cf. 39–54. Only now, shortly before they arrive at the island of the Sirens, does Odysseus tell his companions of what he had learnt from Circe. At this point he tells them only of the immediate threat (the Sirens), and restricts his account to the bare minimum required: he describes the threat in general terms, and issues detailed instructions on counter-measures which at this point could not make sense to the crew.

153. = 270; cf. x 67.

153a. The extra line given in some MSS, κέκλυτέ μευ μύθων, κακά περ πάσχοντες ἑταῖροι, is surely not authentic (although van der Valk, *Textual Criticism*, 274–5, disagrees); cf. x 174–7, 190–7 nn. The οὐ γάρ clause of 154–5 provides the reason for an order equivalent to κέκλυτε, which may be easily supplied from ὦ φίλοι.

156–7. ἀλλ' ἐρέω: 'so I will tell you'. Forewarned of the danger, they may either continue in the full knowledge that they are risking their lives, or they may flee. Indirectly this prepares for the episode on Thrinacia. On the unusual constr. (ἵνα κεν; θάνωμεν subj. alongside φύγοιμεν opt.) cf. Palmer, in *Companion*, 161, Chantraine, *Grammaire*, ii 272.

158ª. = 39ª.   **θεσπεσιάων:** here in its original meaning: the Sirens proclaim divine things (their singing is heavenly).

159. **λειμῶν' ἀνθεμόεντα:** the phrase prompted later writers to name the Sirens' island (201) Ἀνθεμόεσσα (Hes. fr. 27 M–W).

161. **αὐτόθι:** 'there, on the spot'.

162. = 51.

163-4. The lines rejected by Aristarchus are a deliberate repetition of 53–4; they are necessary in the context (cf. 193 ff.).

165: cf. xi 442.

167-9. The ἵκμενος οὖρος (145; here οὖρος ἀπήμων) sent by Circe brings the ship (ἔπειγε) to within a short distance from the Sirens' island. (The alternation of gen. forms Σειρήνοιιν (167) and Σειρήνων (158) is for metrical reasons only.) Then suddenly there follows a lull (168 ~ v 391; 169ª = v 392ª) which may equally be attributed to divine influence. Unable to identify the god concerned, Odysseus refers only to a δαίμων, and makes the connection with Circe's advice that divine intervention would remind him of her words (38). The calm is neither meant to indicate midday (O. Crusius, *Philologus*, l (1891), 93, K. Latte, loc. cit. (39–54 n.)) nor intended to allow the Sirens' song to be heard more clearly (Ameis–Hentze, *Anhang*, ad loc.): it is a warning to Odysseus of imminent danger (cf. Gresseth, op. cit. (xii 39–54 n.), 210). Odysseus appreciates the warning, and takes the precautions advised by Circe. Cf. Meuli, *Odyssee*, 93–4, Focke, *Odyssee*, 263–5.

170-4. The calm forces the crew, who had been sitting idle (ἥμεθα 152), to stand up, furl the sail (μηρύσαντο, *hapax*) and lay it in the ship (leaving in place the mast, unlike at xi 3; it will soon have a part to play), and take to the oars.   **λεύκαινον** (only here and *Il.* v 502: ὑπο-λ.): 'they made the water white'; for the white foam produced by the action of the blades cf. 180.   **ἐλάτῃσιν:** lit. 'pines', i.e. the oars made from pine wood.

173-4. Following Circe's advice (47–8) Odysseus cuts a large round of wax (τροχόν, 'wheel') into small pieces, which he then kneads (πίεζον; δεψήσας 48); τροχὸν is the direct object, and τυτθὰ a proleptic predicate.

175-6. **αἶψα δ' ἰαίνετο κηρός:** 'at once the wax became soft' (cf. Latacz, op. cit. (ix 5–11 n.), 225) due to the great strength (μεγάλη ἲς) sc. of the hands working it, and the warmth of the sun ('Ηελίου τ' αὐγή).   **Ὑπεριονίδαο** (*hapax*) is a metrical alternative to Ὑπερίονος.

177: cf. 47–8.

178-9. ~ 50–1.

180. (~ ix 104): the line recalls 172.

181. = ix 473 (= v 400). The repetition of this line is significant: the threat is as great as that of the Cyclops.

182. **ῥίμφα:** cf. viii 193.   **διώκοντες** sc. νῆα: 'travelling'.   **ὠκύαλος** (only here and xv 473; cf. the name Ὠ. viii 111): the second element is from ἅλλομαι; Risch, *Wortbildung*, 207.

183. **ὀρνυμένη:** with οὐ λάθεν: the Sirens noticed the ship appear and swiftly approach.   **ἔντυνον** (cf. 18): they broke into clear song (cf. 44).

184–91. Here the effect of the song is determined by its content whereas traditionally the enchantment of the Sirens lay in the compelling quality of their voices (θέλγειν 40, 44). The Sirens know that their way to Odysseus' heart is to praise the heroic deeds of the Trojan War (and hence praise Odysseus himself); cf. the effect of Demodocus' performance on Odysseus at the Phaeacian court. In the far-away world of folktale Odysseus is reminded of his identity as a hero, as he himself had reminded Polyphemus. In 184–91 the Sirens announce their theme, and kindle in Odysseus, in spite of Circe's warning, the desire to hear more. We do not, however, learn more of the Sirens' song; the important point is how Odysseus escaped the danger.

184. The fact that the introduction 'quotes' the *Iliad* (ix 673) tells us a great deal about the song the Sirens have in mind.　πολύαιν'(ος) is ambiguous: it can mean one about whom many αἶνοι are told, or it could mean one who knows many αἶνοι (as Odysseus does: cf. xiv 508); the meaning probably oscillates between the two. Cf. Bechtel, *Lexilogus*, 280. 184^b = iii 79^b.

185. νῆα κατάστησον: 'draw up your ship here (with us)'.

187. μελίγηρυν ... ὄπ'(α): 'the voice from our lips, which has a tone (γῆρυς) as sweet as honey'.

188–91. One who listens to the song will enjoy the experience, and find it instructive. 189–91 emphasize above all the idea of returning home a wiser man. The Sirens not only know all that happened at Troy, but also everything else that had been happening in the world; their knowledge is comparable to that of the Muses (cf. ἴστέ τε πάντα *Il.* ii 485). Hes. was probably thinking of these lines with their impressive anaphora when he composed the words which he puts in the mouth of the Muses themselves (*Th.* 27–8). 191^b = viii 378^b.

192–3. ἱεῖσαι: 'sending forth, letting sound'. 192^b = iv 259^b. As Circe had foreseen, Odysseus cannot resist the magical singing, and longs to stay to hear more (which would mean beaching the ship; cf. 185). He orders his men to free him, and signals his wish with a gesture (ὀφρύσι νευστάζων) since they cannot hear him; cf. ix 468; κρατὶ κατανεύων ix 490 (∼ 193). On νευστάζω (only here and xviii 154, 240, *Il.* xx 162), an intensive form of νεύω, cf. Bechtel, *Lexilogus*, 234.

195–6. While the rest of the crew continue rowing, Perimedes (cf. xi 23) and Eurylochus (x 205 etc.) carry out the orders Odysseus had given in advance (196 ∼ 164), disregarding the counter-order of 193–4, as bidden. The variant πιέζευν is difficult to assess.

198. The author distinguishes here between φθόγγος, 'quality of tone, sound' (comparison with 159 shows that φθόγγον is preferable to -ὴν or -ῆς), and ἀοιδή (44), which refers more to the content than the presentation.　οὐδέ τ' ἀοιδήν: the only possible reading here is οὐδ' ἔτ' ἀοιδήν; cf. Ruijgh, τε épique, 705–6.

199^b. = ix 172^b.

200. The poet does not recount the subsequent fate of the Sirens: it is not known to Odysseus, nor is it of any consequence for his νόστος. It has often been assumed that in earlier legend, as on sixth-century vases, the Sirens drowned themselves in the sea after Odysseus had passed by; see for example Reinhardt, 'Abenteuer', 72. But this is dubious; Eisenberger, *Studien*, 193-8, is sceptical.

201-59: cf. the advance warning of the danger of Scylla, 73-126.

201-2. 201 = 402, xiv 310. In contrast with the Sirens here the danger is unmistakably apparent—to both sight and hearing—well in advance. καπνός, κῦμα, and δοῦπος best fit Circe's description of the Planctae (60, 68). The two routes, past the Planctae and through the straits of Scylla and Charybdis, are thought of as lying close together. Cf. 219-21 n.

203. cf. xxiv 534.   τῶν ... δεισάντων (ingress.): the ptcp. is here either used absolutely ('they were afraid and ...') or dependent on ἐκ χειρῶν.

204. βόμβησαν (viii 191) ... κατὰ ῥόον: all the blades fell from the oarsmen's hands, fell in the water with a splash (ingress. aor.), and hung from the rowlocks, still disturbing the water, and still angled in the direction in which the ship had been travelling. The ship remained in the same place (αὐτοῦ).

205. ἐπεὶ ... ἔπειγον (sc. ἑταῖροι): 'since my companions were not moving the oars that had propelled us'.   προήκεα (*hapax*): 'pointed in front'.

206-7. = x 546-7 (cf. x 173).

208-21. Odysseus' words of comfort to his men parallels his words to them before the Sirens. Again he gives them the absolute minimum of advance warning: just before they meet the danger he describes the threat in vague terms (here he does not even give the names Scylla and Charybdis), and concentrates on detailing the action to be taken. Again the crew is not in a position to understand (nor do they need to understand) the purpose behind Odysseus' plan. The structure of Odysseus' speech follows that of x 174-7 (see n. ad loc.). He begins (οὐ γάρ πώ τι) with words of encouragement (209-12 ~ x 174-5) and then proceeds (νῦν δ' ἄγεθ' 213; cf. ἀλλ' ἄγετ' x 176) to assign tasks (213-21 ~ x 176-7). 209-12 give the reason (γάρ 208) for the crew to give the trust (πειθώμεθα) which Odysseus demands: 'You have much experience in (overcoming) κακά' (208); this is illustrated by one example, the escape from the Cyclops. There they overcome one κακόν, albeit with casualties; and now they should have confidence that they will also overcome this κακόν. All this points to the authenticity of 209-12, (suspected by Kirchhoff (*Odyssee*, 235), Schwartz (*Odyssee*, 320), and Focke (*Odyssee*, 255), but defended by Merkelbach (*Untersuchungen*, 183. 1) and Eisenberger (*Studien*, 193. 2)). Odysseus' choice of supporting example for his argument at 208 is justified by events: the crew escapes Scylla with the loss of six men, exactly the same number that were lost to Polyphemus. The only difficulty is posed by 209, which has the unusual scansion ἔπῑ, which should, however, be accepted. Zenodotus' reading ἔχει is probably a conjecture (suggested by xx 83?) based on the MS-variants ἔπει/ἔπει/ἐπεὶ (which are in fact impossible); cf. Ameis–Hentze, *Anhang*, ii 136, van der Valk, *Textual Criticism*, 49, 99.

Odysseus means that the κακόν before them (τόδε) is in fact (δή) no more formidable (μεῖζον ἔπι = ἔπεστιν) than that before.

210: cf. x 476. **εἶλει** (sc. ἡμᾶς): 'he held us captive'.

211–12. **καὶ ... καὶ** is used here almost in a comparative sense: 'as we escaped then, so ...'. Odysseus imagines his crew in the future looking back on this adventure, and judging their leader to have saved them with the ability he has so often shown before. There is a famous imitation in Verg. (*A.* i 203).

213. = xiii 179; *Il. passim*. Odysseus prepares to give his orders.

214–15: cf. 180. **κώπῃσιν** = ἐρετμοῖς; cf. ix 489. ῥηγμῖνα βαθεῖαν | τύπτετε, with its unusual variation of formulaic ἐπὶ (παρὰ) ῥηγμῖνι θαλάσσης (ῥηγμῖν- means the breakers, the broken sea near the σκόπελοι): cf. H. Erbse, *RhM* cx (1967), 14–15. 215ᵃ means 'remain at your places, at the rowlocks (cf. ii 419), and row on'.

217–18. Odysseus addresses the helmsman to give him particular directions (ὧδε, 'as follows'; 219–21). **ἀλλ' ... νωμᾷς** is parenthetic: 'take them to heart, since you control (νωμᾷς) the helm': cf. ix 483.

219–21. The helmsman must steer clear of the καπνός and κῦμα which had (at 202) so alarmed the crew (τούτου). To avoid losing control of the ship (λάθῃσι ... ἐξορμήσασα sc. ναῦς) he should set his course (ἐπιμαίεο) for the σκοπέλου/-ων. The MSS give pl. σκοπέλων, Aristarchus read the sg. σκοπέλου, which would refer to Scylla's lair (108), while transferring the dangers named at 219 (and κεῖσ' 221) to Charybdis; cf. Merkelbach, *Untersuchungen*, 193. This is, however, impossible for semantic reasons: καπνός cannot mean 'foam'. Van der Valk (*Textual Criticism*, 136–7) relates σκοπέλων to Scylla and Charybdis as at 73, 101, and 239, whereas καπνοῦ καὶ κύματος (219), and 221, refer to the Planctae (68). His explanation is preferable (also in connection with 202 and 239: see nn.).

222. = x 178, 428.

223. **οὐκέτ'**: besides the mention at 222 (σκοπέλων). **ἄπρηκτον**: cf. ii 79. **ἀνίην**: cf. vii 192.

225. If the crew had known more about Scylla, they would have sought shelter below deck (ἐντός), huddled together (πυκάζω, cf. xi 320) and abandoned the oars (εἰρεσίη, cf. x 78) that were their only hope of survival (as Circe had said (124): σφοδρῶς ἐλάαν).

226–35. In his orders to the crew Odysseus had followed the advice of Circe. He himself, however, prepared to put into action the idea which had then immediately occurred to him (112–14), though Circe had dismissed it as sheer folly (116–23): he prepares to do battle with Scylla. His heroic stature is no more diminished by this ignoring of a warning (ἐφημοσύνη 226; elsewhere only at xvi 340) than by his clever tactics towards his own men. Ignoring all that he knows of his opponent, Odysseus attempts the impossible and foolish because it is also the heroic. He must be true to his own nature, and, faced with a hopeless situation, nevertheless risk his own life for the sake of his men. The heroic gesture of arming against an ἄπρηκτος ἀνίη (223) in a world where there is no place for the heroic, is here almost grotesque, but it also vividly illustrates the tragedy of the hero with his limited outlook, and the incommensurability of this fabulous world and that of the *Iliad*; cf. Reinhardt, 'Abenteuer', 70, Eisenberger, *Studien*, 200. The critic who would excise 226–33 and 116–26 has misunderstood the poet's purpose. On 226–7 cf. L. J. D. Richardson, *Hermathena*, lxxxiii (1954), 66–74, Stanford, ibid., 75–8.

228–9. The arming is deliberately described in the phraseology of the *Iliad* (cf. e.g. vi 504, xiii 241 etc.).

230–1. πρῴρης (*hapax*; but cf. xiii 84 n.) here probably adjectival with νηός. Odysseus takes up position on the forecastle, believing (ἐδέγμην) that there Scylla (μιν), from her cave (πετραίην), ready (as he knows from 110) to attack his crew (φέρε, impf.), will come face to face with him first (φανεῖσθαι).

232–3. ἀθρῆσαι (in the *Odyssey* only here and xix 478): 'glimpse' (trans.), in contrast to παπταίνω (233), which means the continuous activity of gazing which precedes ἀθρεῖν (here aor. ἀθρῆσαι); cf. οὐδέ πη: πάντη. 233[b] is analogous to the usual ἠ. πόντον (ii 263 etc.).

234. The ship enters the channel as prescribed by Circe (102).   στεινωπόν (here used as a noun; only once in the *Odyssey*; used as an adj. in the *Iliad*, qualifying ὁδός): lit. 'having a narrow exit'; Risch, *Wortbildung*, 171.

235–6. ἔνθεν sc. ἦν. 236: cf. 104; the minor change (ἀνερροίβδησε for -εῖ 104) matches the situation here, where Odysseus arrives just as the waters are sucked down.

237–43. An arresting description follows of the natural phenomenon of which Odysseus has been forewarned (by Circe), and which he now sees with his own eyes. With the information given to him at 105 Odysseus can recognize what he observes as a regular occurrence (hence the iterative forms). The description is clearly divided into sections on the alternating draining and regurgitation, ἦ τοι ὅτ' (237) and ἀλλ' ὅτ' (240); the parallels are emphasized, particularly at 238: 241.

237–9. On refilling, the whirlpool foamed (always) right to the top (ἀναμορμύρεσκε, *hapax*; in the *Iliad* μορμύρω), seething (κυκωμένη: cf. x 235) like the water in a cauldron over fierce heat. The spray flies high (238[b] = *Il.* xi 307[b]) and falls on the rocks (cf. 101–2). The description supports the reading σκοπέλων at 220; here we also have the proper word for 'foam, sea-spray', ἄχνη; cf. 219–21 n.

240–3. On draining (ἀναβρόχω, here synonymous with ἀναρυβδέω; cf. xi 582 n.) the interior of the whirlpool is clearly visible. The rock (πέτρη, meaning the σκόπελος of Charybdis, 101) roars (βεβρύχει; cf. v 412) and the sea-bed can be seen, κυανέη (following Aristarchus and the majority of MSS) ψάμμῳ (*hapax*), 'dark with sand'. On the constr. cf. Palmer, in *Companion*, 135, Chantraine, *Grammaire*, ii 75. κυανέη, qualifying ψάμμῳ, is also conceivable. 243[b] cf. xi 43[b].

244–6. While everyone's gaze is on the natural phenomenon (τὴν sc. Χάρυβδιν; no contradiction to 232–4 is implied), just as all are distracted (τόφρα), Scylla seizes six of the crew, as Circe had predicted (110). For οἵ ... ἦσαν (246), cf. xxi 315, 373, vi 6, xxi 371.

COMMENTARY

247–50. σκεψάμενος (ingress.): Odysseus looks back to the ship to see above him (ὕπερθεν) the limbs of his six comrades as they are carried away. 248[b] is formulaic; cf. xxii 173, 406, *Il.* v 122 etc. (with a different function for ὕπερθεν). 249[b] = x 229[b]. **ἐξονομακλήδην:** 'calling by name'; modelled on *Il.* xxii 415, although used rather differently. **ἀχνύμενοι κῆρ:** cf. x 67.

251–5. The grisly scene prompts Odysseus to a comparison with a scene from peaceful everyday life, an angler reeling in a writhing fish from the sea. Cf. the similes of *Il.* xvi 406–9, xxiv 80–2. **ἐπὶ προβόλῳ:** cf. πέτρῃ ἔπι προβλῆτι (*Il.* xvi 407). **περιμήκεϊ ῥάβδῳ** (cf. x 293) belongs with κατὰ ... βάλλων (252): the fisherman is angling for the smaller fish with his long rod (larger fish are harpooned; cf. x 124), and throws in morsels of food (εἴδατα, probably small pieces of meat) as bait (δόλον); he casts into the water an ox-horn (ἀγραύλοιο: cf. x 411; 235[b]: cf. *Il.* xxiv 81), using a tube of horn set above the hook to protect the line from being bitten. When the angler has caught a fish he hauls it, struggling, from the water (θύραζε): cf. ἰχθὺν ἐκ πόντοιο θύραζε (sc. ἕλκει) *Il.* xvi 407–8. The similarity between the two scenes lies particularly in ἀσπαίρειν (254:255). On the technical details see H.-G. Buchholz, *Archaeologia* J, 169. ἀείροντο προτὶ πέτρας resumes the scene before the simile: ὑψόσ' ἀειρομένων.

256. αὐτοῦ δ' εἰνὶ θύρῃσι is explained from 93–7.

257. The account concludes with an attempt to convey the sense of outrage at a scene so devoid of human values that it is almost inconceivable and inexpressible. The poet deliberately introduces a quotation from the *Iliad* (257[b] = xi 516[b]; *Il.* iii 20[b] etc.), whose language is here out of place. Odysseus' plan to resist the monster by force, criticized as unworkable at 116–26, but entertained nevertheless at 226–33, here proves in fact to be impossible. Circe was right not only to dismiss the suggestion that Odysseus might defend his crew, but also to recommend that they travel through the straits as speedily as possible (124). This they now do (213–21) to avoid a second attack from Scylla (122). There is no mention here of the other device recommended by Circe, prayer to Crataiis (124–6), either because it no longer seems needed, or because the poet deliberately allows Odysseus to forget this.

258. οἴκτιστον: predic. of κεῖνο, which summarizes the content of the preceding lines.

259. πόρους ἁλὸς: like ὑγρὰ κέλευθα (iii 71 etc.).

260–402. The episode on Thrinacia is vital to the development of the story, and may well be the poet's own invention; cf. Reinhardt, 'Abenteuer', 111–15. It may have been suggested by the old epic Argonautica, which could have given him the motif of the anger of Helios (Merkelbach, *Untersuchungen*, 206), but not the whole story (Meuli, *Odyssee*, 94–7). The episode as a whole is more closely related to religious beliefs. Divine commandments against use of that which belongs properly to the gods, and fearful punishments for men who transgress divine taboos are rooted in ancient belief; and stories of sinners who infringed the privileges of the gods, and were punished for their sacrilege, must at an early date have been attached to various figures; cf. Radermacher, *Erzählungen*, 23–6, Reinhardt, 'Abenteuer', 111–15, Page, *Folktales*, 79–83. Moreover the conception of cattle sacred to Helios is found elsewhere in Greek tradition: cf. *h.Ap.* 410–11 and Hdt. ix 93. 1, who speaks of such herds in NW Greece. Reinhardt, loc. cit., has also shown that this tale differs substantially from the other adventures in that it requires absolutely the element of divine guidance and forewarning, and represents a πεῖρα rather than a conventional type of folk-tale, though it is set in the folk-tale world. Thucydides' statement (vi 2) that Sicily was once known as Τρινακρία indicates that already before his time the Sun god's herds were localized there. The Homeric name for the island, Θρινακίη, seems to have played an important role in the various attempts to identify its location. The name (certainly non-Greek) was thought to mean 'three-cornered' (which would describe Sicily). Alteration of the mythical name to a form which seemed linguistically more correct, Τρινακρία, was arbitrary but consistent.

260. πέτρας is not an element in a list of three: acc. δεινήν τε X. and Σκύλλην τ' amplify πέτρας, which means here the same as σκόπελοι (73, 101; cf. πέτρας 255). These lines do not, then, refer to the Planctae, as some have supposed (Ameis–Hentze, *Anhang*, ad loc., Merkelbach, *Untersuchungen*, 193. 1).

261–3. The poet assumes familiarity in his audience with the name of the island (cf. ix 107, xii 127), but reminds us nevertheless of the sacred cattle mentioned by Tiresias and Circe. 262ᵇ: cf. xi 289ᵇ; 263: cf. xi 108 ∼ xii 128. 263ᵇ = i 8ᵇ.

264–6. While still far out at sea, Odysseus hears the lowing (μηκυθμός, only here and *Il.* xviii 575) of the cows being penned in the αὐλή (αὐλιζομενάων: only here and xiv 412) for the night (cf. 284), and the bleating (βληχή, *hapax*) of the sheep. The juxtaposition of gen. and acc. to express the object of ἤκουσα is unobjectionable; cf. Chantraine, *Grammaire*, ii 54. 264–6 have a function similar to that of 202.

267–8. Odysseus remembers the various warnings (ἔπος 266) he has been given (xi 104–11 and xii 127–41). 267ᵃ = x 493ᵃ; 267ᵇ = x 492ᵇ (cf. nn. ad loc.).   μάλα πόλλ': 'most insistently'. Schwartz (*Odyssee*, 318) deletes 267 (and 272), following W. C. Kayser; cf. von der Mühll's comment ad loc.: 'vix recte'.

269. Odysseus has extracted from Circe's warning words which she did not in fact use: νῆσον ἀλεύασθαι. His idea is to escape temptation by avoiding the island altogether.   τερψιμβρότου (only here and 274): 'giving joy (τέρψις) to man'.

270. = 153.

271–4. Odysseus' speech corresponds closely to the pattern established at 154–64 and 208–21. Again he warns his crew of the danger only just before they approach it; he describes the nature of the peril in general terms only (that an αἰνότατον κακόν (275) awaits them, and that they are approaching the island of Helios); and concentrates on the measures he considers necessary to avoid disaster.

271. = [x 189], [xii 153a], xii 340. Cf. x 190–7, xii 153a nn.

272. μαντήϊα (*hapax*): 'prophecies'.

273–4. = 268–9 (see 267–9 n.).

276. The generalized warning leads to an exhortation to pass by the island (τὴν) that lies before them.

277. = x 198, 566. The reason behind the crew's reaction, which takes Odysseus by surprise, is not given until Eurylochus (279) gives vent to their feelings.

278. The behaviour of Eurylochus is foreshadowed by x 244 ff. and 429 ff. His destiny is to challenge Odysseus, and his speech here (μῦθος) is described as στυγερός—Odysseus as narrator knows the terrible consequences.

279–93. Eurylochus expresses the views of the crew (279–90) and makes a counter-proposal, that they spend at least the night on shore (291–3).

279. The meaning Eurylochus gives to σχέτλιος (somewhat different from its usage at e.g. xi 474) becomes clear at 279–85: Odysseus, with his own iron constitution, has no understanding of the needs of the men, and has misjudged what he may reasonably expect of them. περί ('in excess, above others') τοι μένος sc. ἐστίν.

280. 'One would suppose you were entirely made of iron.' Cf. expressions such as κραδίη σιδηρέη (iv 293), θυμὸς σιδήρεος (v 191), which can assume negative connotations.

281. ἀδηκότας (only here and, in a similar context, *Il.* x 98, 312, 399, 471): meaning and derivation uncertain. The context suggests 'overworked; worn out (by their labours and by lack of sleep)'; according to Bechtel, *Lexilogus*, 12–13 from *ἀϝαδέω (similarly H.-J. Mette, *LfgrE* s.v.); Chantraine, on the other hand, *Dictionnaire* s.v., sees a connection with ἄδην. Cf. also i 134 n. on ἀδήσειεν. The similarity between 281 and *Il.* x 98 is surely to be explained by the dependency of the Dolonia on the *Odyssey*; S. Laser, *Hermes*, lxxxvi (1958), 293–4, but cf. F. Dornseiff, *Mélanges H. Grégoire*, ii (Brussels, 1950), 248.

282. αὖτε: here 'again'.

283ª. = i 50ª; 283ᵇ = xiv 408ᵇ; cf. also *Il.* xix 316. λαρόν: 'pleasant to eat, tasty'; on the derivation see Frisk, *GEW* s.v.

284. αὔτως: 'so without further ado'. νύκτα θοήν is formulaic (cf. *Il.* xii 463 etc.). θοός: 'quickly falling' (?).

286. ἐκ νυκτῶν: 'after nightfall' (originally local: 'from out of …'); Chantraine, *Grammaire*, ii 99, R. Renehan, *Glotta*, l (1972), 173, R. Dyer, *Glotta*, lii (1974), 31–6. δηλήματα (*hapax*) from δηλέομαι: 'causes of destruction'.

287ᵇ: cf. ix 286ᵇ.

288. ἀνέμοιο θύελλα: cf. v 317.

289: cf. v 295.

290. θεῶν ἀέκητι (here concessive): cf. iii 28. On ἀνάκτων see Leumann, *Wörter*, 42–3.

291–2ª. = *Il.* viii 502–3ª, ix 65–6ª. ἦ τοι νῦν μὲν introduces ἠῶθεν δ':

they want to give the night its due, i.e. land, make themselves something to eat, and sleep on shore, before continuing in the morning. 293ᵇ: cf. ii 295ь.

294ᵇ: cf. *Il.* iii 461ᵇ. ἐπὶ ... ἤνεον: cf. viii 226. The crew sides with Eurylochus, continuing the process begun at ix 44 and continued at x 34 ff.

295. 295ᵃ = viii 299ᵃ; 295ᵇ = iii 116ᵇ. As at 169, Odysseus suspects the influence of an unknown δαίμων; this is the only explanation he has for the reaction of the crew. He is alert to the warning and attempts to make the best of a bad situation. Here, as at 169, there is a link with 38.

297–302. As a single individual (μοῦνον ἐόντα) Odysseus cannot resist the majority. He must withdraw his original proposal, to avoid the island altogether, and asks in exchange, in the altered circumstances (νῦν, 298), for an oath from the crew that they will not kill any of the cattle on the island, but restrict themselves to the rations they have brought with them. He conceals the fact that the cattle belong to Helios, and that theft would incur divine vengeance (loss of the ship and all her crew). The only hint of the potential dire consequences is in the word ἀτασθαλίῃσι which implies that it would be a serious offence to kill any of the animals; cf. Odysseus' similar procedure at 271–6. The oath restores the situation: Odysseus has the agreement he needs. It is also a vital element in the plot. Against Schadewaldt (*Hellas und Hesperien*², i (Zurich, 1970), 93–104) who considers 296–304 the work of the B poet see G. Bona, op. cit. (ix 106–15 n.), 11–34, Eichhorn, op. cit. (ix 228 n.), 154 ff., Eisenberger, *Studien*, 201–10; Ø. Andersen, *SO* xlix (1973), 7–27, esp. 19–20.

297: cf. *Il.* xxii 229. The majority reading βιάζετε μοῦνον is defended by van der Valk, *Textual Criticism*, 97–8.

298. = xviii 55.

299: cf. *Il.* xv 323.

301. ἔκηλοι (cf. ii 311, xi 184): here 'limiting your desires, being content'.

302: cf. 18–19.

303–4. ∼ x 345–6 (cf. also ii 377–8). Theiler gives an analytical discussion, *MH* xix (1963), 16–17, 60.

305. στήσαμεν ...: 'we anchored ...'.   γλαφυρῷ, elsewhere used as an epithet of σπέος and νηῦς, here exceptionally qualifies λιμήν, in this case evidently a harbour with a narrow entrance, like a cave, and sheltered.

306. The crew find fresh water near their anchorage, as on the island of the goats, ix 140 (ἀγλαὸν ὕδωρ): ὕδωρ γλυκερόν.

308. = i 150 etc.

311ᵇ. = iv 793ᵇ, where ἐπήλυθε takes the acc.

312. ∼ xiv 483.   τρίχα (adv.; cf. viii 506) νυκτὸς: 'in the last third of the night'. 312ᵇ (cf. ix 58 ἠέλιος μετενίσσετο βουλυτόνδε): 'as the stars had passed to the other side of the sky'; cf. *Il.* x 251–3.

313. ∼ ix 67; 314–15 = ix 68–9.   ζαῆν: cf. v 368. The repetition of the lines is significant: the story of Odysseus' wanderings began with a storm from Zeus which kept the fleet from sailing for two days. Here again a storm, sent by Zeus, prevents Odysseus from leaving, this time for a month, with fatal consequences. The second half of 315, which is very effective in the context of ix 69, is less effective here, since it is still night. The meaning is probably that clouds cover the stars, so that there is total darkness. Focke, *Odyssee*, 262–3, refutes Wilamowitz's objections (*Untersuchungen*, 117–18). The reading ὦρσε δ' (δέ introducing the main clause) is defended by van der Valk, *Textual Criticism*, 148.

316. = ii 1 etc.

317–18. The crew drag the ship from the harbour, where it had been anchored (305), to a cave on the edge of the bay and make it fast there. Again (cf. 306 n.) the scene is reminiscent of the island of the goats (ix 140–1), also an area where Nymphs live (ix 154–5). Cf. also the descriptions of the harbour of Phorcys on Ithaca (xiii 96–112). **θόωκοι:** cf. ii 14.

319. = i 171, x 188.

320–3. Odysseus' third speech reflects the change in the situation: they had hoped to leave in the morning, but the storm has not abated and they cannot tell how long it will last. Since their stay on the island will be longer than he had hoped, Odysseus tells his men of his reason for exacting the oath (298–302): now he explains that the cattle belong to Helios, and therefore any injury to them would be κακαὶ ἀτασθαλίαι (300) for which they would be terribly punished by the god who sees and hears everything. Now at last the crew know their danger, and that their fate lies in their own hands. 320 (∼ x 176) recalls 301–2. **τῶν** (!) **βοῶν:** 'the cattle here on the island'. 322ᵇ = x 128ᵇ. 323 = xi 109.

324. = x 550 etc.

325. ἄλληκτος (*hapax* in the *Odyssey*), from λήγω: 'incessantly'.

326: cf. v 295. 326ᵇ amplifies the reference to the Νότος (325): the winds are only south-easterly.

328. Comparison of 328ᵇ with xxiv 536ᵇ suggests that βίοτος is to be understood here too in its (rarer) meaning, 'life' (cf. i 287): to save their lives the crew heed the warning.

329: cf. iv 363 and ix 163.

330–1. ἄγρην ἐφέπεσκον: the following ἰχθῦς ὄρνιθάς τε shows that ἄγρη should not be understood as 'hunting' (so B. Hansen, *LfgrE* s.v.), but as 'prey'; ἰχθῦς ὅ. τε is in explanatory apposition to ἄγρη. ἀλητεύοντες: ἀλητεύω (cf. Risch, *Wortbildung*, 333) ∼ ἀλάομαι. The fact that the men are catching fish and birds illustrates the gravity of their plight; epic heroes (unlike the men of the poet's own time) usually eat only beef, mutton, and pork.

332. = iv 369.

333. δὴ τότ' refers back to ἀλλ' ὅτε δὴ (329).

334. εἰ introduces a wish. ὁδόν: used in its transferred meaning, 'possibility'. The captain's piety and good intentions in fact begin the process that leads the companions to disaster.

335. ἤλυξα: aor. from ἀλύσκω; the verb often implies difficulty, danger or impossibility in escaping; Odysseus thus had trouble in slipping away unnoticed.

336ᵃ. = ii 261ᵃ, x 182ᵃ; 336ᵇ: cf. v 443, vi 210, vii 282.

338. The gods pour sleep over Odysseus' eyelids (cf. ii 398) and so further the plot, continuing the fateful intervention begun with Zeus' storm. The crew is forced into a situation where they are bound to incur guilt and then are justly punished. We are reminded of the situation at x 31 ff.; there too, as Odysseus sleeps, his companions are tempted to decisions and actions which prove fatal.

339. Med. ἐξάρχομαι (+ gen.) is used only here; cf. βουλὰς (!) ἐξάρχων (Il. ii 273). Eurylochus begins the speech which will lead to a κακὴ βουλή; the phraseology indicates both his evil intention and the fearful consequences.

340–51. In form and argumentation Eurylochus' second address clearly resembles his first speech (352 = 294). What he has to say there about the hazards of sailing on (286–90) has a counterpart here in his observations on the imminent prospect of death by starvation (in both cases he makes use of sententious generalizations (286–7, 341–2)). Both speeches conclude with an exhortation to ignore the warnings (291–3, 343–50), but the second contains a new idea: the sacrilege of slaughtering the cattle is justified and recommended not as a necessity to still the pangs of hunger, but as a pious act, a sacrifice to the gods; the distortion is characteristic of a demagogue. The possible consequences are described in terms of clear alternatives (εἰ δέ κεν ... 345–7; εἰ δέ ... 348–51): the first implies the possibility of their escaping immediate punishment and then atoning for the misdeed later; the second covers the danger of divine vengeance. Since sparing the cattle will lead to a death that is both certain and painfully lingering, Eurylochus argues the case for slaughtering the animals, which has the merit of offering at least some hope, while the risk involved is acceptable, as a quick death is preferable to a lingering one. Eurylochus articulates the feelings and intentions of the men (352). Despite the pressure of circumstances the crew make their decision to do wrong in full knowledge of what is involved. They fail the πεῖρα, and so must pay the penalty.

340. = 271, x 189.

341. θάνατοι (used as a pl. only here): 'ways of dying'.

342ᵇ. = iv 562ᵇ etc.

344. ῥέξομεν: (aor. subj.) expressing exhortation.

346. The vow to dedicate a νηός is all the more remarkable because, with one exception (the νηός of Athena at Athens, Il. ii 549), there are no references to Greek temples in Homer. (However, there is a temple of Athena in Troy (Il. vi 88 etc.), and Apollo has temples in Troy and at Chryse (Il. vii 83, i 39); there are νηοί among the Phaeacians (Od. vii 10).) The poem mirrors historical developments: the 'Dark Age' Greeks began only relatively late to build temples to the gods, possibly under foreign influence. The νηός is πίων on account of the ἀγάλματα (iii 274) which will be brought to it; cf. h.Ap. 52.

348. ὀρθοκραιράων (hapax in the Odyssey; 348ᵇ = Il. viii 231ᵇ, xviii 3ᵇ): 'with straight horns'; cf. Risch, Wortbildung, 138–9.

137

COMMENTARY

350–1. (modelled on *Il.* xv 511–12). **βούλομ'(αι):** here 'I would rather' (Lat. *malo*). **ἅπαξ:** 'at once, instantly' (cf. *Il.* xv 511 ἕνα χρόνον), as opposed to δηθά (351). **χανών:** 'gaping, with mouth opened' (and swallowing water). **ἀπὸ θυμὸν ὀλέσσαι** (tmesis): 'to lose one's life'. **στρεύγεσθαι** (only here and *Il.* xv 512): 'to waste away'; cf. Frisk, *GEW* s.v.

352. = 294.

353: cf. 343.

355ᵇ. = 262ᵇ.

356. After the parenthesis the narrative is continued with τὰς δέ. **περι-στήσαντο** (for -έστηραν, -έσταν) is attested without variant both here and in the passage on which this is modelled, *Il.* ii 410; cf. also ix 54. Bekker's conjecture περίστησάν τε is difficult to justify.

357–9. **τέρενα** (as at ix 443): 'delicate'; on 357ᵇ cf. ix 186ᵇ. The men's strange activity is explained at 358: for want of barley (κρῖ: cf. iv 41) they substitute leaves for the barley ritually strewn over the victim (οὐλοχυταί; cf. iii 447) after prayer. In what follows, too, the peculiar circumstances impose certain departures from the normal ceremonial—obliging the author to adapt the formulaic description. On the atypical elements in the scene see Reinhardt, *Der Dichter der Ilias* (Göttingen, 1961), 88–95.

359–61. 359 = *Il.* i 458ᵃ + 459ᵇ (the οὐλοχυταί mentioned at *Il.* i 458ᵇ have no place here; cf. 357–9 n.). 360–1 = *Il.* i 460–1 (furthermore 360 ∼ iii 456–7; 361 = iii 458).

362–3. What we would expect here, ἐπὶ δ' αἴθοπα οἶνον|λεῖβε (*Il.* i 462–3 = *Od.* iii 459–60) is replaced by another formulaic expression owing something to *Il.* xi 775. **ἐπώπτων** both retains and varies the formulaic καῖε δ' ἐπὶ σχίζῃς (*Il.* i. 462ᵃ etc.). **ἔγκατα** (∼ σπλαγχνά): cf. ix 293.

364–5. = *Il.* i 464–5, *Od.* iii 461–2.

366. After 365 the scene is rudely interrupted by the return of Odysseus. The actual cooking and eating of the meat (cf. *Il.* i 466–8) are delayed. The cattle are roasted later, with terrible omens (395–6), and the men eat the food over the following week (397–8). **τότε:** 'at that moment'. **ἐξέσσυτο ... ὕπνος:** 'sleep fled'. **νήδυμος ὕπνος:** as at 311ᵇ (= iv 793ᵇ; cf. n. ad loc.).

367. = x 407 (iv 779).

368. = x 156.

369. The echo of vi 122 με ... ἀμφήλυθε θῆλυς ἀϋτή, should not lead to analytical conclusions (Marzullo, *Problema*, 313–14). On fem. form ἡδύς (cf. ἡδεῖα ix 210) see Chantraine, *Grammaire*, i 252.

370. **μετ'** is unusual (cf. e.g. 270, 319), for Odysseus is not in the company of the gods. Bekker suggests μέγ', Schwartz ἐπ' (*Odyssee*, 321, citing similar passages). Von der Mühll (ad loc.) rightly compares 385, where μετά has a similar extended meaning. Odysseus makes himself heard among the gods by his prayer. **γεγώνευν:** see ix 47 n.

371. = 377, v 7, viii 306.

372. **εἰς ἄτην:** 'to my ruin'; cf. G. Müller, op. cit. (x 68 n.), 6, Gruber, op. cit.

(x 63 n.), 60. The line refers back to 338, with a significant variation from γλυκὺς ὕπνος (cf. νήδυμος ὕ. 366) to νηλὴς ὕπνος (cf. ix 17). The pitiless cruelty of the gods is seen in their sending sleep.

373. μέγα ἔργον: here depreciatory, 'great wickedness'.   **μένοντες:** i.e. 'during my absence'. The paratactic structure of 372-3 clearly expresses how divine decree and human responsibility combine to bring disaster.

374-90. Odysseus recounts the scene on Olympus as Helios seeks permission from Zeus to avenge the outrage. Odysseus himself answers the unvoiced criticism from the audience, that he cannot know what happened on Olympus: he claims to have heard the tale from Calypso, who heard it from Hermes (389-90). There is, however, no reference to this in the conversation between Calypso and Hermes in v, and Calypso does not tell Odysseus about Hermes' visit. Such observations have prompted many critics, from the Alexandrians onwards, to reject the whole of 374-90 as interpolation. Kirchhoff in particular won much critical acclaim for his theory: he saw these lines as most important evidence for a wholesale transfer of much of the material in ix-xii from an older version of the story, in the third person, to the *Odyssey*, with a simple change of narrative perspective to the first person; cf. Schwartz, *Odyssee*, 45-7, Marzullo, *Problema*, 88, 112-13. The lines are, however, essential. The poet must explain the divine forces at work in the background in order to show the ethical and theological significance of the train of events culminating in the destruction of the companions. It is no 'ordinary' storm at sea which sinks Odysseus' ship, but natural elements used as the instrument of the will of Zeus, who has undertaken to champion Helios' cause. Cf. W. Suerbaum, *Poetica*, ii (1968), 157-61, Erbse, *Beiträge*, 12-16.

375. Λαμπετίη: cf. 132.   **τανύπεπλος:** cf. iv 305. It is not easy to decide between ἔκταμεν ἡμεῖς (favoured by Aristarchus, and after him Marzullo, op. cit., 114, von der Mühll, ad loc.) and ἔκταν ἑταῖροι (preferred by van der Valk, *Textual Criticism*, 136); cf. Bona, op. cit. (ix 106-15 n.), 26, n. 44. It is possible that the Vulgate attempted to 'correct' an expression which strangely implies an element of guilt in Odysseus.

377. = 371.

379. ὑπέρβιον (cf. i 368), here used as an adv., 'wantonly, in their sinful arrogance'.

380-1: cf. xi 17-18.

382-3. Helios supports his initial demand, τῖσαι, 'let them pay for it', with a threat. The punishment must fit the enormity of the crime (ἀμοιβὴν τίνειν like ποινὴν τίνειν; on ἀμοιβή cf. i 318 and iii 58, where the idea is expressed in a positive form: may Poseidon reward the Pylians for the sacrifice, δίδου ἀμοιβὴν ἑκατόμβης). The threat is that Helios may descend (fut.) to Hades, and shine (φαείνω subj.) on the dead rather than the living. On the combined use of fut. and subj. to refer to the future cf. Palmer, in *Companion*, 163, and particularly A. Scherer, in *Indogerm. u. all-gem. Sprachwissenschaft* (Wiesbaden, 1973), 101.

384. = i 63 etc.

385–8. Zeus agrees to Helios' request, pointedly contrasting ἦ τοι μὲν σύ ... against τῶν δέ κ' ἐγώ ... The passage is closely related to ix 550–5 (see n. ad loc.). After the Cyclops incident both Zeus and Poseidon have been pursuing the same goal, of allowing Odysseus to reach his home, but alone, and only after much delay (ix 532–6). Zeus' plan now is to accomplish the fate prescribed for Odysseus; and the anger of Poseidon and Helios accord with his own will. Helios' justified demand enables him to destroy the crew, who are fated to die, but who could not be held responsible for the violation of Poseidon's τιμή by Odysseus (blinding of Polyphemus): they will die for the violation of the τιμή of Helios. Their crime was provoked by Zeus, but they themselves were wholly responsible for its perpetration; the punishment is both justified and part of Zeus' plan.

385ᵇ: cf. iii 2ᵇ.

386. = iii 3.

387–8. 387ᵇ = v 131ᵇ, vii 249ᵇ. 388: cf. v 132, vii 250.   τῶν δέ sc. ἑταίρων; cf. 378.   ἀργῆτι κεραυνῷ: with βαλών, τυτθά: ('in small pieces') with κεάσαιμι.

389–90. The lines are indispensable, as the narrator must justify his account of events which clearly lie outside his province; cf. 374–90 n., and Reinhardt, 'Abenteuer', 113.

391: cf. viii 50.

392–3. Odysseus rebukes his men, confronting each one in turn (cf. 207).   οὐδέ ... δυνάμεσθα is modelled on *Il*. ii 342–3.   τι μῆχος: any possibility of making good the damage. There is little to favour the hypothesis that we have here an abbreviated form of an originally longer text (Merkelbach, *Untersuchungen*, 194).

394. τοῖσιν: 'my companions and myself'.

395–6. Odysseus describes the τέραα: the hides crawl on the ground; the meat, both the cooked (ὀπταλέος only here and xvi 50, *Il*. iv 345) and the uncooked flesh on the spit, lows (cf. x 227, 413). The description broken off at 365 is resumed in a most unusual form (cf. 357–8 n.), with dreadful portents (discussed by H. Stockinger, *Die Vorzeichen im hom. Epos* (diss. Munich, 1959), 135) which demonstrate the gods' attitude towards the crime, and foreshadow the doom which the perceptive will recognize as inevitable. The unusual form of these uncanny τέραα (cf. Stockinger, op. cit., 60–3, 134 ff.) is paralleled in the mysterious occurrences of xx 345–8. There too, in the confusion of the suitors' wits and the 'second sight' of Theoclymenus, the guilty receive a supernatural warning of the doom that awaits them from the gods; cf. Reinhardt, 'Abenteuer', 115.

397–8. Here too atypical development of the scene is observable: in place of the expected description of the feast we have the time taken over cooking and eating the meat, despite the portents (398 ~ 353!): six days.

399. (= xv 477) is formulaic.   ἐπὶ ... θῆκε: as at xi 560.

400: cf. 168 (= v 391; Focke, *Odyssee*, 265). The storm which has kept the ship from sailing for a month (325–6) now abates.   λαίλαπι θύων: only here and 408, 426; cf. λ. τύπτων (*Il*. xi 306). θύω: as at xi 420 (see n. ad loc.), but with a change of meaning; the wind drops with the storm (cf. σὺν λ. 408).

401: cf. 293; Odysseus' advice is at last followed, but too late.

403. = ix 77.

403-6. = xiv 301-4; cf. Reinhardt's discussion, 'Abenteuer', 59-60. The threatened storm from Zeus begins.   ἤχλυσε (ἀχλύω, *hapax*), from ἀχλύς: 'darkened'.

407. The ship could not proceed for long (cf. ἐπὶ χρόνον *Il.* ii 299).

408: cf. 400 n.

409. προτόνους: the cables from the mast-head to the bow deck; cf. ii 424-5 n. On the technical details of 409-25 cf. D. Gray, *Archaeologia* G, 92-109.

410: ὅπλα: the sail and rigging.

411. ἄντλον (elsewhere only at xv 479): the hold (which is open to the sky) and the bilge-water; cf. D. Motzkus, *LfgrE* s.v.   πρυμνῇ (adj.) ἐνὶ νηΐ: as at ii 417, 'on the poop'; cf. B. Forssman, ZVS lxxix (1964), 11-31.

412-14. As it falls aft, the mast strikes the helmsman, standing aft, and breaks all his bones (ἄμυδις).   ἀρνευτῆρι: 'diver'.   ἀπ' ἰκριόφιν: cf. ἐπ' ἰ. (iii 353).   λίπε δ' ὀστέα θυμὸς: cf. xi 221. The scene is described in the same terms as the slaughter of men in battle in the *Iliad*: compare 412-14 with *Il.* xiii 384-6, xvi 742-3.

415-19. = xiv 305-9. Cf. 403-6 (= xiv 301-4).

415. ἄμυδις: cf. 412. The thunder peals just as the lightning strikes.

416. ἐλελίχθη: cf. v 314.

417. θεείου: 'sulphur, the smell of sulphur'.

418. κορώνῃσιν: cf. v 66-7. W. K. Kraak, *Hermeneus*, xxvi (1955), 129-32: *Phalacrocorax pygmaeus*.

420. τοίχους: here 'the side of the ship', spars and planks.

421. κλύδων: 'wave'; cf. κλύζω (ix 484, 541).   τρόπιος: v 130. The keel is 'bare' (ψιλή), because the τοῖχοι have been removed.

422. The wave tears the mast, which had been lying astern (410-12), out of its socket, and smashes it against the keel (after the ἴκρια have been torn away with the τοῖχοι).   ἄραξε (Aristarchus and Vulgate) is preferable to ἔαξε (Zenodotus).

423. ἐπίτονος (tetrabrachys): with metrical lengthening of the first syllable (so-called *versus acephalus*); cf. Wyatt, *Lengthening*, 221-2. The backstay (ἐπίτονος), made of leather, still hangs from the mast.   τετευχώς is an unusual participial form (with pass. meaning) from τεύχω; from *tetu-khwόs*; cf. Myc. *te-tu-ko-wo-a₂*/*tetukhwoha* (neut. pl. and also pass.); cf. Chantraine, *SMEA* iii (1967), 19-20.

424. Odysseus improvises a raft by lashing together the mast and keel with the ἐπίτονος (τῷ).

425. ἐπὶ τοῖς: on the mast and keel. 425ᵇ = ix 82ᵇ. R. Hampe, *Die Gleichnisse Homers und die Bildkunst seiner Zeit* (Tübingen, 1952), has suggested that Odysseus' shipwreck is depicted on an eighth-cent. Munich vase; but the identification of the scene is unconvincing; cf. Kirk, *Songs*, 402, K.

Fittechen, *Untersuchungen zum Beginn der Sagendarstellungen bei den Griechen* (diss. Tübingen, 1969), 59–61.

426–46. Odysseus now faces the danger of Charybdis, which on the first passage through the straits he had avoided (on the advice of Circe) by steering closer to Scylla. The wind (Νότος) drives him back towards the channel, which he must now face alone; cf. Reinhardt, 'Abenteuer', 116–18. The nature of the danger is already familiar to the audience, so Odysseus does not need to describe it in detail but assumes that enough was said at 103–7 and 235–43. On the treatment of the subject in art cf. P. Zancani Montuoro, 'Odisseo a Carridi', *La parola del passato*, xiv (1959), 221–9.

426. The line repeats and varies material from 408 (cf. also 400) to conclude the description of the storm at sea.

427. ἄλγεα is amplified at 428.

428. ἀναμετρήσαιμι: the exact meaning is difficult to determine; comparison with iii 179 (πέλαγος ... μετρήσαντες) and xii 444 (διήρεσα) suggests 'travel past'.

431. = 236 (see n. ad loc.).

432–3. Just as (i.e. just before) Charybdis begins to gulp down water, Odysseus swings himself up from his raft (ὑψόσ' ἀερθείς; cf. viii 375) on to a large fig tree, which, as Circe had told him (103), grows on the lower section of the rock, above the whirlpool. Odysseus clings on (προσφύς) like a bat; on the constr. cf. Ruijgh, τε épique, 571.

433–6. The description suggests that Odysseus embraces the trunk—at least this is the only explanation which accounts for all the details given. He has no chance (οὐδέ πη εἶχον) of securing a foothold (cf. Il. xxi 242) because the roots are far below him (ἑκάς); and he cannot clamber up (ἐπιβῆναι) because the long and broad branches, which hang over the whirlpool (and which he might otherwise have sat on), are ἀπήωροι (hapax, from παρήορος etc., with unusual lengthening o > ω; cf. E.-M. Voigt, *LfgrE* s.v.).

437ᵃ. = ix 435ᵃ.

438. Odysseus waits, longing (ἐελδομένῳ) for Charybdis to throw the planks to the surface. At last (ὄψ' with significant enjambment) they reappear.

439–41. The time at which the timber reappears from the whirlpool (441), and the length of Odysseus' ordeal, are illustrated by a picture drawn from everyday life. He was released just at the time of day when the man who hears cases brought by those seeking justice (on δικαζομένων cf. xi 545; on αἰζηῶν xii 83–4) in the market-place (ἀγορή usually 'assembly' in Homer, but here and at Il. xvi 387 and xviii 497 in its later meaning; cf. Webster, in *Companion*, 454) rises having finished his work (ἀνέστη) and returns home (δόρπος), i.e. in the evening. So Odysseus clings to the tree all day (cf. 429–30). We should not quibble over the inconsistency with the details given earlier (esp. 105; cf. also 237–43). There is no reason to delete these lines, which have been suspected since ancient times (Schwartz, *Odyssee*, 320–1); cf. van der Valk, *Textual Criticism*, 227–8.

442. Odysseus lets go with both arms and legs (ἧκα), so that he falls (φέρεσθαι) from above (καθύπερθε).

443. With a thud (δουπέω is used in the *Iliad* of falling soldiers) he drops into the middle of the water (μέσσῳ with strange ellipsis of the subst.; ὕδατι/πόντῳ?), near the δοῦρα.

444. διήρεσα: aor. from δι-ερέσσω. Sitting astride the beams Odysseus paddles with his hands, and so makes his way through the straits between Scylla and Charybdis.

445–6. Σκύλλην δ'(ἐ) continues from ἡ μὲν (Χάρυβδις) 431. με needs to be supplied as a subject for ἐσιδέειν (almost in the sense of 'meet, encounter'; cf. Bechert, op. cit. (ix 142–5 n.), 167–8, with reference to xi 161). 446ᵇ = ix 286ᵇ. There is nothing to support Aristarchus' athetesis of these lines (cf. also Schwartz, *Odyssee*, 321).

447–53. Odysseus returns to what he had already related on the first day, hence the deliberate repetition: 447–50ᵃ = vii 253–6ᵃ (cf. also 387–8 and vii 249–50).

450: cf. vi 207. **μυθολογεύω** (dubit. subj.) appears only here and at 453, and means almost the same as μυθέομαι (451).

451. Odysseus refers directly to his account at vii 241–97. **χθιζός:** in fact it is gone midnight (cf. xi 330 ff.), but the expression makes sense if a day is reckoned from dawn to the end of the following night.

453. αὖτις belongs with μυθολογεύειν; ἀριζήλως (used only this once in the *Odyssey*; in the *Iliad* as an adj., and with a somewhat different meaning), 'clearly, in full' (cf. E.-M. Voigt, *LfgrE* s.v.), with εἰρημένα.

BOOKS XIII–XVI

Arie Hoekstra

INTRODUCTION

1. *The composition*

When xiii opens, Odysseus, as one of the most famous heroes of the Trojan War,[1] is still the honoured guest of the Phaeacians.[2] But he is not to remain so for long. Soon afterwards, ignorant of the fact that he has arrived in his native land, he finds himself in a state of helplessness on a lonely shore. It is at this moment that Athena comes to the rescue and her intervention is the key to the question of the composition of xiv–xvi, both in a wider and in a narrower sense. For one thing, as Erbse has pointed out,[3] the hero of the Wanderings cannot be abruptly replaced by the 'Heimkehrer': this can only be done by the goddess disguising him as an old beggar and by her instructions on how to proceed and to behave. For another, Athena's intervention marks the starting-point of a new development of the action. From now on, as against the hero's retrospective recital of his adventures in ix–xii, the narrative moves straight ahead, and it does so on different lines. The main plot results from Athena's instructions (303–10, 375–81, 404–11), and a secondary one has its starting-point in the passage 412–15, where the goddess announces that she is going to recall Telemachus from Sparta. These lines gradually approach one another and meet in the recognition scene (xvi 172–219). After attention has been shifted towards the suitors by Odysseus' and Telemachus' plotting to kill them, there begins, in connection with them, a short third episode (xvi 322–451) which takes up the narrative broken off in iv 847 and points forward to the development of the action in xvii–xxiv. Thus the three threads appear to have been skilfully interwoven. In spite of the objections made by analytic critics, and whatever the genesis of the *Odyssey* may be, xiii–xvi show a well-considered composition.

---

[1] There is much to be said for the view that Odysseus was originally a folk-tale hero and was later drawn into the heroic poetry about the Trojan War, cf. e.g. W. Schmid in Schmid–Stählin, *Geschichte der griechischen Literatur*, i (Munich, 1929, repr. 1959), 1, 78. On the complex nature of Homer's Odysseus see Kirk, *Myths*, 167–9.

[2] The division of the story between xii and xiii is due to the Alexandrian scholars and is misleading to the reader who is unacquainted with this fact, cf. also Erbse, *Beiträge*, 145.

[3] *Beiträge*, 153; on the 'homecoming' motif S. West, introduction i–iv, 56.

2. The 'atmosphere' of the narrative

In the beginning of xiii Odysseus has finished the tale of his adventures. The atmosphere of the old folk-tales surrounding the hero's encounters with exotic peoples such as the Lotus-eaters and the Laestrygonians, with dangerous monsters and with beings divine and semi-divine, now dissipates. Instead we see Odysseus as a distinguished 'Achaean' guest of the Phaeacians,[4] and though the latter have some traits of a *Märchen*-people, their individual representatives (for instance Nausicaa, Alcinous, Arete, Demodocus) are already much more human than those of the strange world Odysseus has left. Yet the scene and the atmosphere of his actions are about to develop still more towards that of everyday life, for when he arrives in Ithaca he associates with herdsmen and slaves, meets a son who is far from 'heroic', and is confronted with the vulgar behaviour of an insolent *jeunesse dorée*. We are given 'character sketches of the daily life in Odysseus' household',[5] 'as it were some comedy of manners'.[6] The action, as Stanford puts it, is domesticated.[7] This change of atmosphere is even perceptible in the digressions, which are conspicuous in this part of the poem (xiii 256–86, xiv 199–359, 468–517, xv 223–55, 403–83). Odysseus' false tales, the final part of the digression about Theoclymenus,[8] and Eumaeus' story are devoid of mythical and fabulous elements, and, though they have the heroic world as a background, the persons and events described appear in reduced dimensions as compared with those found elsewhere in the epics.[9] Unfortunately we do not know anything about Ionian story-telling in the archaic period, but the tales in question look like the ancestors of certain stories by Herodotus.[9a]

3. The tempo of the narrative

Attention has rightly been drawn to the fact that in the latter part of the *Odyssey* (and in some passages of the Telemachy as well) the pace

---

[4] According to Rüter, *Odysseeinterpretationen*, 242 ff., Odysseus' stay with the Phaeacians, besides serving as a transition phase in the hero's return to the world of human beings, has another compositional function: it is meant to contrast the conditions prevailing in two otherwise similar island communities, Scheria and Ithaca.

[5] Eumaeus' hut and pigsty included; the quotation is from Ps.-Longinus *De Sublimitate* ix 15 (the translation is Hamilton Fyfe's).

[6] Ps.-Longinus, ibid.   [7] *Odyssey*, li.

[8] On its former part see xv 223–81, 231–6 nn.

[9] In this respect they resemble the stories told by Phoenix (*Il.* ix 447–95), and by Patroclus' ghost (*Il.* xxiii 85–90).   [9a] Cf. e.g. xv 456 n

of the narrative is strikingly unhurried.[10] This phenomenon is particularly noticeable in the treatment of Odysseus' stay in Eumaeus' hut (incidentally, this contains three 'tales', two by Odysseus and one by Eumaeus). Whether this is a disadvantage from a poetical point of view is largely a matter of taste, but the phenomenon itself seems to be typical of a later stage of epic narrative when the treatment of the traditional material had become at once more matter-of-fact and more detailed. It is likely to be due to the same modernizing tendency shown by several linguistic peculiarities discussed in the commentary and by the less 'heroic' character of the digressions mentioned above.

4. The diction

To employ terms such as 'modernizing tendencies' and 'a later stage of epic narrative' may seem out of place in the introduction to a commentary on a particular part of the *Odyssey*. It would indeed be if the poem, and especially its second part, did not, time and again, raise questions of tradition and innovation which have a direct bearing on the interpretation of the poem as a work of art. To take a few examples from passages which have little in common: does the discussion of Athena and Odysseus in xiii 291–328 show a personal conception on the part of the poet? What kind of head-dress is meant in the metaphor used in xiii 388? Are Telemachus' words in xv 88 in any way remarkable? Why does Odysseus shed a tear 'to the ground' in xvi 191? In such cases the relation to (or departure from) the tradition cannot be disregarded if we want to get some insight into the nature of this kind of poetry. In this connection it may be recalled that one of the first books which, after decennia of quarrels between unitarians and separatists, and of the latter among themselves, proceeded to examine Homer's other poem as a work of art, was given the title *Tradition and Design in the Iliad* by its author.[11]

What, then, do we know about this poetical tradition? Right from the start we must make an important restriction: about the pre-Homeric poems we know next to nothing. It would be very strange if the c.27,000 lines of Homer's epics did not reflect a single poem by his predecessors, yet these poems cannot be identified with certainty, and even if they could, the passages in question would be of very little use for our purpose. Agamemnon's reminder of Tydeus' behaviour

---

[10] Cf. Kirk, *Songs*, 357 ff.; on the other hand, it must be added, some passages show a conspicuous quickening of tempo: see xv 222 n.

[11] C. M. Bowra (Oxford, 1930).

addressed to Diomedes in *Il.* iv, Glaucus' tale about Bellerophon in vi, Phoenix's story about Meleager in ix, the songs sung by Demodocus in *Od.* viii, and the fragments of the Melampus myth in xi and xv, supposing they were inspired to the poet by older poems, are abbreviated versions[12] which do not allow for any comparison to be made with his own epics in so far as the relation tradition–innovation is concerned.

However, there is a field in the poetic tradition in which such a comparison is not wholly impossible: that of diction. Here too, of course, little is certain, but at least we have some help from historical grammar, from our knowledge—however limited—of the Greek dialects in the pre-Homeric period (mainly thanks to the Linear B tablets), from some features of prosody, and even, indirectly, from archaeology. What, then, can be said in this respect about Homer's diction?

The nature of the diction

The first thing that strikes the eye is its very close resemblance to the diction of the Hesiodic poems, the exiguous fragments of the Cycle, and the oldest Hymns. Apart from differences in quality and those determined by the subject-matter the diction is so similar to Homer's that only trained observation and a philological schooling can detect the deviations. And yet these deviations exist and they grow more numerous in the course of time.[13] They have various origins, but an important cause is to be found in the fact that the poets, though composing in Homeric *language*, changed the *diction* by breaking up the formulae one way or another, and by removing them from their traditional positions.[14] However, there is incontrovertible proof that Homer and his predecessors did the same in a number of cases.[15] That means that we need not despair of tracing the previous history of some elements at least of that diction, however few these may be, nor of acquiring some idea of Homer's poetic intentions by identifying innovations and by viewing them against 'the dense background of the inherited tradition'.[16]

[12] Cf. Kirk, *Songs*, 326–8.

[13] Cf. e.g. G. P. Edwards, *The Language of Hesiod in its Traditional Context* (Oxford, 1971); Hoekstra, 'Hésiode, *Travaux* 391–2', *AC* 1979, 98–111; C. Brillante, M. Cantilena, C. O. Pavese (eds.), *I poemi epici rapsodici non omerici e la tradizione orale* (Padua, 1981); R. Janko, *Homer, Hesiod and the Hymns* (Cambridge, 1982).

[14] Here the term 'diction' is to be understood as 'language moulded into form by choice, use, and arrangement of words'. On this point the lexica, though differing in detail, are generally agreed.

[15] See e.g. Severyns, *Homère*, ii 59–60.   [16] Kirk, *Homer*, 203.

The above may seem unduly optimistic because the language of the diction, as has been generally recognized, is a *Kunstsprache*, a language that was never spoken by anyone in whatever part of Greece. In this respect it is certainly not unique (the same applies to choral lyric and even to the iambics of Attic tragedy), but this character is most striking in a genre which is narrative *par excellence*, and the more so because this narrative idiom not only contains many words which had long before gone out of fashion (this is still true of the dialogue of Euripides), but because it swarms with morphologically different elements, has many 'artificial' creations, and, moreover, numerous *groups* of words which were already highly archaic, either wholly or partly, by the time the poems were composed. And—what is its most striking characteristic—all these different linguistic elements (often combined with certain prosodical phenomena)[17] are found in what has been called an 'inextricable confusion'.[18]

Now if this characterization were literally true, any attempt at tracing the history of the diction would be futile, nor would it be possible to discover any cases of innovation in Homer. But fortunately this is not so. Although Chadwick's characterization is certainly adequate in a general sense, some old nuclei at least can be isolated and some lines of development traced back. Since, however, our purpose is to detect how the individual poet called Homer operated, it seems advisable to proceed in the reverse order and to ask: where and when did this amalgam of elements varying in provenance and date come into being? The divergent theories on this subject cannot be dealt with here, however briefly, nor can the opinion of the present writer and the arguments on which it is based be expounded in detail. A few things, however, seem clear.

Origin

The diction cannot have originated in Ionia.[19] That possibility is definitely ruled out by the linguistic evidence, which comprises

---

[17] Cf. e.g. ὥς τε (λ)λίς/ὥς τε λέων; see F. Solmsen, *Untersuchungen zur griechischen Laut- und Verslehre* (Strasburg, 1901), 164–6, and Leumann, *Wörter*, 50–3, where more literature is given.

[18] J. Chadwick, 'Mycenaean Elements in the Homeric Dialect', in G. S. Kirk (ed.), *The Language and Background of Homer* (Cambridge, 1964), 119.

[19] *Contra* W. F. Wyatt, 'Homer's Linguistic Ancestors', Ἐπιστημονικὴ Ἐπετηρὶς Θεσσαλονίκης xiv (Thessalonica, 1975), 133–47; Heubeck, 'Zum Problem der Homerischen Kunstsprache', *MH* xxxviii (1981), 65–80; D. G. Miller, *Homer and the Ionic epic tradition* (Innsbruck, 1982). M. L. West now defends an origin in Greece proper, 'The Rise of the Greek Epic', *JHS* cviii (1988), 151–72.

singular genitives in -οιο, infinitives in -μεν and -μεναι, not to mention other features which play as essential part in the old formulae.[20] The same is true of the hypothesis advanced by Wilamowitz that the language of the poems should be that of a region of mixed Ionic and Aeolic speech stretching from Chios to Smyrna.[21] That supposition has been conclusively refuted and need no longer be gone into. But what about the area of 'colonial' Aeolic speech, Lesbos, Tenedos, Pordoselene ('Nesos'), and the opposite coast of Asia Minor? In a different connection it has been argued that, since our earliest testimonies for this branch of Aeolic appear in Sappho and Alcaeus, the dialect of the earliest Aeolian settlements (which were founded at least some four centuries earlier) may have closely resembled the later speech of east Thessaly.[22] That is certainly a possibility, and it may be added that the dialect of these early foundations might have preserved words which in historical times only appear in Arcadian and Cypriot,[23] and are also found in Homer. To be sure, this could have happened. But did it? Although the influence of Ionic on the dialect of Lesbos cannot be discounted and thus might be held responsible for some old features becoming extinct on the island, it would be very strange if elements as widely differing as ποτί, singular genitives in -οιο, and the distribution of -σ(σ)- and -ξ- in the future and aorist of certain verbs in -ζω had disappeared without leaving a single trace. Moreover, there is an argument of a quite different nature which militates against the supposition: the cultural conditions prevailing in such early Aeolian settlements as have revealed any relevant remains (mainly Smyrna) might have been compatible with the genesis of a diction that stylistically resembled that of Yugoslav and other oral poetry or of some kind of balladry. However, they can hardly have given rise to the *amplitudo* that we find in βοῶπις πότνια Ἥρη, θεὰ γλαυκῶπις Ἀθήνη, Ποσειδάων Ἐνοσίχθων, etc., in Ἑρμείας ἐριούνιος, Ἥλιος φαεσίμβροτος, etc., in θεόφι [μ]μήστωρ ἀτάλαντος, πολέεσσ' ἄνδρεσσι (ϝ)άνακτα, etc., in ἐΰ κτίμενον πτολίεθρον, πολυάϊκος πολέμοιο, ἐϋσσέλμων ἐπὶ νηῶν, etc., and in θηλυτέρῃσι γυναιξί, βοῶν ὀρθοκραιράων, ἵπποι ἀερσίποδες, etc. Such formulae presuppose the hexameter and take up a large part of it. In a phase in which epic composition was

---

[20] Of course not all formulae are of the same age: some few were probably created by Homer, others by his recent predecessors, but several are highly archaic. See further n. 18 and Hoekstra, 'Metrical Lengthening and Epic Diction', *Mnemosyne*, xxx (1978), 1–26.

[21] *Die Ilias und Homer* (Berlin, 1916), 357.   [22] Kirk, *Songs*, 145–6.

[23] The tradition that Orestes (or his son Penthilus) should have led the Aeolians to Lesbos might reflect some 'Achaean' participation in the migration (details in Bérard, see n. 24).

still oral, expressions of this type were useful, and indeed indispensable, to the singers, as Milman Parry has proved,[24] but that is only one aspect of their existence: no less important is the fact that at a comparatively early period singers did actually compose in such a style and in a verse form which left room for this kind of *amplitudo*.[25] And it is difficult to see how this style could have originated in the overseas Aeolian settlements around 1100–900 BC.

If this is correct, the diction must have been created on the mainland of Greece. However, it is self-evident that what is true of the early post-migration settlements in Aeolis applies *a fortiori* to the situation in Greece proper in the eleventh century;[26] and for different reasons neither the period of Mycenaean IIIC (*c.*1190–1100) nor the final phase of the palace-state civilization are likely to have seen the creation (as distinct from the continued existence) of this type of diction. How much earlier it came into being we cannot tell, but in any case it must be of Mycenaean origin. In its oldest elements it has preserved—to vary L. H. Jeffery's characterization of the Mycenaean plastic arts—the stylized conceptions of a settled people.[27]

But what was its linguistic form? The predominantly Ionic character we find in Homer is the result of a much later evolution, and the same is likely to be true of certain scattered Aeolisms. Nevertheless the diction contains other Aeolic elements which are too deeply embedded in old formulae to be ascribed to a secondary development,[28] so this leaves us with a phase of the diction in which Achaean and Aeolic were so closely connected as often to be inseparable.[29]

---

[24] To be precise, it is only the epithet which Parry called 'useful'. For *amplitudo* see Hoekstra, *Epic Verse before Homer* (xiii 62 n.), 52–3, 81 ff.; on conditions in early Aeolian foundations see J. Bérard, 'La Migration éolienne', *RA* (1959), 1–28; J. Boardman, *The Greeks Overseas* (London, 1980), 29–33.

[25] In this respect a comparison with the simple epithets and the simple verse of Yugoslav oral poetry is instructive: it brings out the striking *differences*. See now also F. Dirlmeier, *Das serbokroatische Heldenlied und Homer* (Heidelberg, 1971), *passim*.

[26] See e.g. A. M. Snodgrass, *The Dark Age of Greece* (Edinburgh, 1971), 29–30.

[27] 'The secure ornaments of a settled people', *Archaic Greece: The City-States c.700–500 B.C.* (London, 1976), 29. In Ἐνναλίῳ ἀνδρεϊφόντῃ (*Il.* ii 651 etc.), the epithet perhaps goes back to *ἀνϝg^whóντᾳ (as is assumed by Mühlestein, Wathelet, Durante, Heubeck, Pavese), so here we may have a formula which was created at a stage preceding that of the Pylos tablets (ἀνδρ- Ta 707, 708, Ventris–Chadwick, *Documents*, nos. 242, 243). But unfortunately this is not beyond all doubt: was a later epic poet really so much influenced by Ἀργεϊφόντης (Wilamowitz, *Untersuchungen*, 299 n. 1) that he created a linguistic and metrical monstrosity out of a 'Mycenaean' form? See also n. 36.

[28] Cf. e.g. Ὀρσίλοχον, πολέεσσ' ἄνδρεσσιν ἄνακτα (*Il.* v 546) < Ὀρτίλοχον πολέεσσ' ἄνδρεσσι ϝάνακτα (see xiii 260, xv 177 nn., and below) ∼ πόλεσσ' ἄνδρεσσιν ἄνακτα/ἀνάσσων (*Il.* xiii 452/xvii 308), where πόλεσσ' is a late modification of πολέεσσ', see also below, p. 155 and n. 33.   [29] Cf. however Wathelet, *Traits*, 369 (but also 366).

That conclusion may be drawn from Homer—and it accords with the scanty historical data we have at our disposal.

The distribution of the Greek dialects in classical times makes it inevitable to posit a mainland Aeolic existing before the beginnings of the migrations. However, our idea of this dialect is the result of reconstruction, and for that reason it is far from precise. Moreover, though we may assume that this old form of Aeolic was mainly spoken in northern Greece, its borders cannot be fixed (see below), nor are its regional differentiations known. And since the idiom of the Linear B tablets is a chancellery language, the same applies to 'Achaean'. This much, however, may be said, that the geographical extension of Aeolic may have been rather wide and that there were probably areas of mixed speech: Thucydides mentions Aeolians in Aetolia[30] and in Corinth;[31] according to Bechtel[32] Strabo's statement about Aeolic in Elis[33] contains a germ of truth; and in Pylos Aeolians are likely to have penetrated as a result of southward-moving migrations.[34] Moreover, the two dialects had much more in common than their respective historical descendants (Arcado-Cypriot and East Thessalian etc.) had in the earliest known period, for instance the vocalization of the sonants λ and ρ,[35] the suffix -φι, the genitives in -αο, -οιο, and -άων, forms such as πτόλις and πτόλεμος. In short, although Achaean and Aeolic differed on certain important points, it would be wrong to separate them rigorously *in concreto* in the historical context of the Late Bronze Age. And since, in spite of the amalgam, we can indeed isolate some Ionic formulae but are not able to distinguish between Aeolic and Achaean formulae, there is every reason to assume that in epic diction the Aeolic-Achaean phase was a historical reality around 1200 BC.[36]

[30] iii 102. 5.   [31] iv 42. 2.   [32] *Die griechischen Dialekte*, ii (Berlin, 1923), 828.
[33] viii 2 (= 333). According to Bechtel his source was an Alexandrian grammarian.
[34] See e.g. xv 233 n.
[35] On ολ/λο and ορ/ρο in Lin. B (θόρνος etc./kʷetro- etc.), Arcado-Cypriot, and Aeolic see e.g. Lejeune, *Phonétique*, 142–3, 196–7, Ruijgh, *Études*, 69-71. The athematic infins. in -μεναι (ἔμμεναι etc.) need not have been created in Lesbos (under Ionic influence) but may be survivals from the pre-migration period which continued to exist in 'colonial' language, L. R. Palmer, *The Greek Language* (London, 1980), 72–3.
[36] See, however, xiii 182 n. Of the *-h- formulae to which Ruijgh, *Études*, 53–4, is inclined to ascribe an Achaean ('Mycenaean') origin, one, πότνια Ἥρη, might also have come from contemporary Aeolic (Hera is still 'the Aeolian goddess' to Alcaeus, 129 Voigt, cf. Sapph. 17 Voigt). The hyperbolical nature of the other expression, Διὶ μῆτιν ἀτάλαντος, (the only parallel for which (ἴκελος Διὶ τερπικεραύνῳ) is found in *Il*. ii 478, certainly very late, cf. also 479) is to my mind hardly compatible with a highly archaic origin. Another formula, θεόφι ⟨μ⟩μήστωρ ἀτάλαντος (also acc., *Il*. vii 366 etc.), which is likely to be older (cf. Schwyzer, *Grammatik*, i 530 n. 4) may have served as its model; this would explain the prosodical irregularities. For the reasons outlined above the term 'Achaean-Aeolic' has also been employed in the commentary in

And yet in its Homeric form the diction is far from being a mixture of Aeolic and Achaean. How is this to be explained? In one of his later studies Milman Parry has argued that the diction was a closed, self-contained affair,[37] which, from the 'Arcado-Cypriot singers' onwards, underwent only slight changes, largely confined to pronunciation. That supposition was a consequence of his dogmatic view on the nature of a formulaic diction, and it is of course untenable: it is refuted time and again by Homer's language, not to mention the fact that the undoubtedly Mycenaean practices and objects described or referred to are few and sometimes misunderstood. What really happened was something quite different. As a result of the destruction of the palace societies around 1200 BC, the subsequent invasions by Dorians and north-western Greeks, and the disturbances they caused, opportunities for singing the old lays became fewer and fewer and thus little remained of the old oral poetry—and of its formulae (it is significant that very old formulae such as θεὰ δασπλῆτις Ἐρινύς and εἰαροπῶτις Ἐρινύς[38] only just managed to survive and that neither was understood afterwards, with the result that the latter was changed).[39] Still, this poetry had not yet disappeared completely on the eve of the migrations and some of it survived them: after all Homer still has formulae such as ἱερὸν μένος −∪∪οιο.[40] Thus the ancient *amplitudo* remained a characteristic of epic poetry at a time when, after the scattered remnants of the old population had gained a stable foothold on the foreign coasts, the memories of a splendid and distant past[41] led to a revival of the old songs. What remained of them was expanded and adapted to contemporary idioms, attracting 'colonial' Aeolisms in the process,[42] and finally becoming so much Ionicized that to us it appears as an inextricable amalgam.

cases where the evidence from ancient myth (as preserved by Homer) together with the presence of certain linguistic features seems to justify that designation and in any case would make the use of either 'Mycenaean' or 'Aeolic' much more questionable. This applies for instance to the case of Ὀρτίλοχος, at home in the west Peloponnese (see n. 28): although assibilation is normal in the Lin. B dialect, a tablet from Pylos has O-ti-na-wo, presumably to be transcribed as Ὀρτιναῥος, PY Cn 285. Cf. *Od.* xv 187, and xiii 260 n. See also Thumb–Scherer, *Handbuch*, 105, 210 ff.

[37] *Homeric Verse*, 358, 360.

[38] 'The blood-drinking Erinys', cf. Ruijgh, *Élément*, 166–7. On θεὰ δασπλῆτις Ἐρινύς see xv 234 n.

[39] Viz. into ἠεροφοῖτις Ἐ. (*Il.* ix 571, xix 87), probably by association with bird *daimones*: Ate, too, runs through the air in xix 92–3.

[40] See xiii 20 n. L. A. Stella, *Tradizione micenea e poesia dell'Iliade* (Rome, 1978), goes much further.

[41] Cf. C. M. Bowra, *Homer and his Forerunners* (Edinburgh, 1955), 28.

[42] E.g. ζάκοτος, Webster, *Mycenae*, 162; πίσυρες, ibid. 161 (?); see xvi 249 n.

Homer and the Tradition

It is of course impossible to find out how this evolution pursued its course in Asia Minor before it entered the phase which emerges in the *Odyssey*. Still, it is not wholly unfeasible to relate some innovations at least to older types, and that—as has been said—is the object we have in view. And in this connection it is necessary to stress a point which is so obvious that it is generally overlooked by Homeric scholars and especially by philologists. Thanks to the progress made by linguistic studies and archaeology since the beginning of the nineteenth century we have some knowledge of historical grammar and of Mycenaean conditions. We indeed have it, but Homer had not. To him the past he depicted was a 'heroic' past in which the prominent figures were on familiar terms with the gods, and all of them (even Penelope's suitors) were 'godlike'. Similarly, the language in which he composed was 'epic', an idiom completely different from his own vernacular.

We know, for instance, that the long initial vowel of the word which our manuscripts transmit as εἶδαρ is due to compensatory lengthening,[43] but that the lengthening which causes ἐρεσίη to appear as εἰρεσίη is 'metrical' (whatever the explanation of that phenomenon in this case may be). However, if one could have reminded the poet of the fact that he said ἐρέσσω and ἔδομαι (future) in his own vernacular and had asked him why he used those particular forms of the nouns in his poetry, he would have given the same answer in both cases, probably that it was necessary in his craft. If this is borne in mind[44] it is easy to see that the Ionian singers believed that the 'epic' accusative corresponding to εὐρέϊ πόντῳ could be εὐρέα πόντον, that they took (Aeolic) πέλωρα for the plural of πέλωρον,[45] that they declined οἷο δόμοιο into ὅνδε δόμονδε,[46] and that they created αἰενάοντα (or ἀενάοντα) on the model of αἰὲν ἐόντας,[47] etc. It was the same in matters of prosody: since they no longer pronounced the initial digamma, e.g. in οἶνος, this brought about hiatus in the old formula αἴθοπα ϝοῖνον, and since such cases occurred regularly, the Ionian bards also came to say τε αἴθοπα οἶνον,[48] whereas much earlier singers had created ϝοῖνον ἐρυθρόν for just such occasions: to the Ionians of Homer's time and a few preceding generations the use of the latter formula would also have caused hiatus. Since, moreover, in spoken Ionic compounds in

[43] From *ἔδ-ϝαρ.   [44] See now Hainsworth on *Od.* v 59.
[45] See xv 161 n. Similarly they created (ἔπεα >) ἐπέεσσι (e.g. *Od.* xiii 323, xv 440) alongside (ϝ)έπεσσι, and conversely πόλεσσι as a substitute for πολέ(ϝ)εσσι, so as to be able to use the same formula (see n. 28) after the *trochaic* caesura.
[46] See xiv 424 n.   [47] See xiii 109 n.   [48] See xv 500 n.

-εἴη and -ίη already tended to be confused, the poets came to feel that in 'epic' one could say ἀτιμείῃσιν or ἀτιμίῃσιν.[49] Similarly the remoteness of 'epic' from ordinary language brought about the reinterpretation of several forms and words, hence, for instance, the appearance of ὄχα πάντες.[50] That old words, the exact meaning of which was no longer understood, came to be used in a different sense also happened in spoken language,[51] but the verbs μερμηρίζω and ὀπάζω were both ancient and poetical in Homer's time, so in this case their employment in a slightly different sense in a few lines of the *Odyssey* is probably due to the poet.[52]

We have already examined some examples of the influence of spoken Ionic. As it has long since been recognized that this was the most potent factor in the changes which epic diction underwent, and since, accordingly, the relevant phonological and morphological phenomena are dealt with in all Homeric grammars, it may here suffice to call attention to a few lexicological elements. The difference between early and late is manifest in the two nouns denoting footwear. They are πέδιλα and ὑποδήματα. The former was already used in the Mycenaean period[53] and is not likely to have survived into the Ionic vernacular of the eighth century. Anyhow, this noun, apart from a few unrevealing instances,[54] is used in two closely related ancient formulae,[55] but ὑποδήματα, the contemporary word, is found combined with an Ionic form and only appears in the second half of the *Odyssey*.[56] Much less striking is the pair τέκος/τέκνον, but all the same the relative proportions of its use in the *Iliad* and the *Odyssey*,[57] parallel as they are with those found in other fields of the diction, clearly show the direction of the evolution. Furthermore the use of the present stem of εἴρω, 'say', is clearly a relic of the past,[58] a fact which reveals its true significance when compared with the employment of λέγω as a synonym, which is only just beginning.[59] These comparisons, be it understood, only apply to epic diction. It is very possible that by the end of the eighth century spoken Ionic had already dropped the old equivalents, some of them in a recent, some in a distant past, and that the 'new' forms had already been in use for a considerable time. That, at all events, is true of the noun ἀριθμός[60] (as is proved by the frequent occurrence of the derivation ἀριθμέω in

---

[49] See Wyatt, *Lengthening*, 160–4; xiii 142 n.
[50] See Leumann, *Wörter*, 133–6, and xiii 365 n.
[51] e.g. with Mycenaean *di-pa*, see xiii 388 n.   [52] See xiv 62, xvi 256 nn.
[53] See e.g. Ruijgh, *Élément*, 151–2; Ventris–Chadwick, *Documents*, 490 ff.
[54] *Od.* xiv 23, xvi 154.   [55] *Od.* i 96 etc., ii 4 etc.; xvi 80, xxi 341.
[56] xv 369; conjugated xviii 361.   [57] See xv 125 n.   [58] See xiii 7 n.
[59] See xiii 296 n.   [60] Only *Od.* iv 451, xi 449, xvi 246.

Homer), so we may assume that ἀνάριθμος (and ἀναρίθμητος) already existed in spoken Ionic. Nevertheless, the poet confines himself to μυρίος(-οι) and the significance of ancient νήριτος is no longer clear to 'him.[61]

The above also applies to words denoting conceptions of various kinds. The later employments of ὅσιος do not yet occur, but we do find (οὐδ', οὐχ) ὁσίη, though only twice[62] and in two different positions. This suggests three things: first, that the word is a late newcomer to epic diction, secondly that it was already current in Homeric times in spoken Ionic, and thirdly that earlier singers were less 'specific' in expressing such ideas: they still employed the old formula (οὐ) θέμις (ἐστί).[63]

The pressure of spoken language can also be seen in the tendency to loosen the old paratactic structure of the diction and thus to 'produce much subtler and more complex effects both for rhythm and for meaning'.[64] The old paratactic enjambment, as seen for instance in Il. iii 334–5: ... ξίφος ἀργυρόηλον | χάλκεον, αὐτὰρ ἔπειτα σάκος μέγα τε στιβαρόν τε[65] is still frequent in Homer, but the poet also has a much more developed type, found e.g. in Od. xiv 40–1: ... ὀδυρόμενος καὶ ἀχεύων | ἧμαι, ἄλλοισιν δὲ ... That this way of joining two lines is much more recent appears from the bold hiatus which separates the run-over word[66] from the new sentence beginning with an element marked by nu-movable making 'position'. But its nature is also quite different. Here the run-over word does not constitute a mere paratactic extension of the preceding clause by adding a new detail to a sentence which is complete in itself. On the contrary, being a finite verb and hence a semantic element of the first order, it transfers a great deal of the meaning of the sentence to the next line, and thus weakens the verse as a unit of thought and expression. However, the old formulaic technique was based on this very unit[67] and its

---

[61] See below, p. 159. The absence of ἀνάριθμος, ἀναρίθμητος has a significant parallel in the sporadic employment (as against the frequent (formulaic) use of ἀπείρων, ἀπειρέσιος), of ἄμετρος (only in ἀμετροεπής, Il. ii 212), and ἀμέτρητος (only πένθος ἀμέτρητον (Od. xix 512), ἀμέτρητος πόνος (xxiii 249)).

[62] Od. xvi 423 (see n.), xxii 412.   [63] See xiv 56, 59 nn., xiii 2, 3.

[64] Kirk, Homer, 147; see also M. W. Edwards, 'Some Stylistic Notes on Iliad xviii', AJPh lxxxix (1968), 279–80.

[65] Here we find several archaic elements: the silver-studded sword (see Kirk, Songs, 111), the combination αὐτὰρ ἔπειτα (see Ruijgh, Élément, 29–55), the ancient adjective στιβαρός (Risch, Wortbildung, 69), σάκος (Ruijgh, Élément, 94–5); it is to be noted, however, that the position in which this word is used here already presupposes a single σ and excludes (σ)σάκος; contrast φερε-σσακέας Καδμείους, Hes. Sc. 13.

[66] A run-over word is a single word in enjambment at the head of the verse.

[67] Cf. the examples given by Parry, Homeric Verse, 253 ff.

disruption provided much more room for innovations and for the effects the individual poets wished to produce (see also below). In this respect it should be noticed that, whereas in the old technique hiatus was a concession the oral poets had to make to their impromptu versification,[68] in our line the phenomenon has a stylistic function: it creates a perceptible pause between the two sentences and this, in its turn, helps to stress the next word.

If epic diction originated in the Mycenaean period, it must have suffered heavy losses on the mainland in the twelfth and eleventh centuries, especially in the period of the migrations. Even what was left of it by that time can hardly have been integrally preserved by the Aeolian and Ionian singers of the 'colonial' areas. Probably the longer formulae stood the best chance of surviving, but we have already seen that θεὰ δασπλῆτις Ἐρινύς[69] had a narrow escape; so had ancient ἐν ὦπα ϝιδών,[70] and of some other formulae only a single element remained.[71] The dative singular ἀλκί owed its survival to its being part of a verse-end formula;[72] the other grammatical cases of this noun got lost, with the exception of the accusative singular, yet this was only preserved in the proper name Ἀλκά-θοος.[73] Similarly, *ἀριτός, 'countable', 'counted', only continued to exist in the name of a fictional figure in the Odyssey[74] and in a curious compound;[75] νήριτος, 'countless', had a similar fate: it became the name of a mountain[76] and afterwards that of its eponymous hero.[77] And so one might go on; what matters is that such relics allow us to get some idea of the changes undergone by epic diction in the course of its evolution, and of the causes. The survival of its old elements was determined by what has been called 'le jeu des formules'. Under the pressure of contemporary speech new formulae were created in the post-migration period and at least partly amalgamated with the older ones. But that tended to loosen 'the interplay of formulae' and the increasing flexibility which ensued afforded new opportunities for innovations to enter the diction. Thus it came about that Homer could call his hero πολύτλας δῖος Ὀδυσσεύς with an age-old formula,[78]

---

[68] Parry, *Homeric Verse*, 191 ff. [69] Above, n. 38.
[70] Transmitted as κατ' ἐνῶπα ἰδών and κατένωπα ἰδών (*Il.* xv 320). Note ἐν with acc.
[71] e.g. ἰῶκα (*Il.* xi 601), cf. ἰωκή (*Il.* v 740), ἰωκάς (*Il.* v 521), and ἀλκ-ί/ἀλκή.
[72] ἀλκὶ πεποιθώς (*Od.* vi 130 etc.). [73] *Il.* xii 93 etc.; cf. βοὴν ἀγαθός, sim.
[74] Ἐπήριτος (xxiv 306), cf. Ruijgh, *Élément*, 161.
[75] εἰκοσινήριτ'(a), *Il.* xxii 349, Ruijgh, *Élément*, 161.
[76] See *Od.* xiii 351 n. [77] *Od.* xvii 207.
[78] It is significant that this formula is already used in the *Iliad* although Odysseus must still commence his *nostos*. On the form πολύτλας see Chantraine, *Grammaire*, i 21–2, *Dictionnaire* s.v. ταλάσσαι.

that he could also give him the archaic epithet πτολίπορθος (probably borrowed from other heroes),[79] and that he could simply say Ὀδυσσεύς and use the very recent forms Ὀδυσσέος, Ὀδυσέος as its genitive.[80]

Examining the prehistory of epic diction cannot tell us, for instance, whether or not the singers from whom Homer learnt his technique still employed any grammatical cases other than ἀλκί, but, besides shedding some light on the relation of archaisms and innovations, it does permit us to see how this age-old diction became such a magnificent instrument in the hands of a great poet.[81]

---

[79] See xiv 182 n.

[80] *Il.* iv 491, *Od.* xxiv 398; in the latter case the MS-tradition even has Ὀδυσεῦς ('Ὀδυσεύς).

[81] Cf. also M. W. Edwards (see n. 64), 282–3.   Since the above largely deals with the history of a diction, the use of the name 'Homer' for the *c.* 27800 verses seems justifiable for the sake of brevity. The question whether the – undoubtedly later – *Odyssey* was created by the same poet as the *Iliad* I do not feel competent to answer (cf. e.g. xiv 158, 207, 317; xvi 421, 438–44 nn.). For a definite 'chorizontic' view see Heubeck, general introduction, 7.

BOOK XIII: COMMENTARY

1. **Ὣς ἔφαθ'**: subject: Odysseus (who has just finished the story of his wanderings). **οἱ δ'**: Alcinous, Arete, and the guests. **ἄρα**: serves to draw the audience's attention, and here means something like 'as you will understand'. **ἀκὴν ἐγένοντο σιωπῇ**: in this formula (cf. vii 154 etc.) the old adverb ἀκήν (cognate with ἧκα, 'softly' (?), cf. xiv 195 n.) has been joined as a predicate to ἐγένοντο (cf. Schwyzer, *Grammatik*, ii 414, Chantraine, *Grammaire*, ii 9) and the expression thus created (cf. ἀκὴν ἔσαν, ii 82 etc.) has been reinforced by σιωπῇ, a clear instance of epic copiousness.

2. = xi 334 (read κηληθμῷ). The Greeks were as sensitive to a well-told story as they were to song and music, cf. also the use of θέλγω, xiv 387, xvii 514, and Plato's ironical use of κηλέω, *Prt*. 315 a κηλῶν τῇ φωνῇ ὥσπερ Ὀρφεύς, and ibid. 328 d. The verb κηλέω itself, though it must have been known to the poet of the *Odyssey* (cf. also ἀκήλητος, x 329), is not employed either in this poem or in the *Iliad*: they always have θέλγω—a verb later replaced by κηλέω in spoken Greek. This is a symptom (among many others) of the power of the tradition in epic language, cf. words such as σοφίη, προθυμίη, ἐπιχειρέω, which are isolated and rare phenomena in the Homeric epics, not because they were recent creations of spoken Ionic (which is impossible), but because in epic diction the same *or similar* ideas had for a long time been expressed in a different way. See Hoekstra, 'Aèdes anciens et poètes ioniens', in J. Bingen, G. Cambier and G. Nachtergaal (eds.), *Le Monde grec*, hommages à Claire Préaux (Brussels, 1975), 25 ff., and id., 'Metrical Lengthening in Epic Diction', *Mnemosyne*, xxxi (1978), 10 ff. **ἔσχοντο**: 'were seized', middle aor. in a pass. sense, cf. e.g. ᾧ ἄχεϊ σχομένη (xi 279). **σκιόεντα**: an *epitheton ornans*: it does not distinguish Alcinous' 'great hall' from those of the other rulers, but it denotes an (appreciated!) quality that was common to all the μέγαρα. (On this part of the Mycenaean house see e.g. A. J. B. Wace, 'Houses and Palaces', in *Companion*, 494, and on the corresponding room in houses of the Geometric period H. Drerup, *Archaeologia* ii O, 128–30). On the question of Homer's indications in this matter see now Hainsworth on *Od*. vi 304; on confusion in the tradition resulting from adaptation and modernization see xvi 336–7, 411, 413 nn. The use of the pl. (virtually 'complex of rooms') is less harsh than it looks because the epic poets, probably already long before Homer, often employed pls. analogically as sgs. on behalf of their versification (e.g. δώματα, στήθεα, στήθεσσι, κλισίῃσι, cf. ἀεσιφροσύνῃσι, xv 470), see e.g. K. Witte, *Singular and Plural* (Leipzig, 1907), *passim*, Schwyzer, *Grammatik*, ii 39, 43–5, Chantraine, *Grammaire*, ii 29 ff. For the sg. Homer never employs a metrically equivalent formula (cf. xv 533 n. and Hainsworth's observations cited there) and even ἐνὶ μεγάρῳ εὐπήκτῳ,

which would have met the *metrical* requirements in i 365 etc., occurs only once (*Il.* ix 144 = 286). It looks as though the development mentioned above, which contributed much to the genesis of the 'poetical plural', is *stylistically* gathering momentum in Homer, cf. ἀνὰ μέγαρα (σκιόεντα) 4 times (the suitors are in the hall) and xx 167, xxiii 299 (but in x 479 the house may be meant, cf. 554).

3. ἀπαμείβετο φώνησέν τε: the act of 'answering' is envisaged as a combination of two elements (on the original sense of ἀμείβομαι in formulae see xv 434 n.) and these component parts are distinguished by their verbal aspect; see also xvi 154 with n. In the sense of 'answering' ὑποκρίνομαι is only just beginning to enter the diction (xv 170 n.; see also 2 n. and introduction, pp. 157–8.

4. χαλκοβατὲς: originally said of the palaces of the gods (*Il.* i 426 etc., see below). Its second element is cognate with βαίνω, but the exact meaning of the adj. is unknown. For 'standing on bronze' (i.e. 'with bronze floor'? schol.) there is no evidence in the poems (bronze walls *Od.* vii 86). For the alternative given by the schol., 'with bronze threshold', we may adduce *Od.* vii 83 (*Il.* viii 15 refers to Tartarus) and (later) βα-θμός, βα-τήρ. At any rate the epithet is likely to be due to the fantasy of the poets: it has no counterpart in reality, Mycenaean or other; cf. xvi 41 n.   **δῶ**: sometimes explained as an archaic ō-grade of δέ 'towards' (cf. the formula ἡμέτερον δῶ, *Od.* i 176 etc. ~ ἡμέτερόνδε, *Od.* xv 513 etc.), which was later felt to be a noun (cf. esp. αἶψά τέ οἱ δῶ/ἀφνειὸν πέλεται, *Od.* i 392). However, a connection with δέμω, δόμος, δῶμα, though uncertain in detail (literature in Frisk, *GEW* s.v.) looks more plausible. At any rate the poet understood the word as 'house', cf. S. West on i 176.

5–6. On the analogy of *Il.* i. 59–60, where παλιμπλαγχθέντας and ἀπονοστήσειν go closely together, οὐ has sometimes been taken to refer to the whole phrase, so that ἀπονοστήσειν would come to mean 'to Scheria', cf. *Od.* x 54, where Odysseus is driven back to Aeolus' island. Since, however, the formula ἂψ ἀπονοστήσειν always means 'to return home', it is preferable to take the negation with the participle only. Alcinous feels justified in making his statement because of the excellent seamanship of his men. (Grammatically of course the negation goes with οἴω, cf. e.g. οὐ γὰρ ὀΐω (iii 27 etc.), οὐδέ σ' ὀΐω (*Il.* i 170 etc.), cf. Kühner–Gerth, ii 2, 180).

5. τῷ: rather τώ or τῶ, see Chantraine, *Grammaire*, i 248–9, Risch, *Wortbildung*, 362.

7. ἐφιέμενος: on the metrical lengthening see Wyatt, *Lengthening*, 155–6.   **εἴρω**: pres. tense only here, ii 162, and xi 137 (always with 'observed' digamma, cf. Chantraine, *Grammaire*, i 136); its use is already dying out in Homer and λέγω hesitantly begins to take its place, cf. 296 n. The behest is not expressed until 13: 10–12 are 'introductory', see xiv 292 and 299–301 nn.

8. γερούσιον: the 'elders' to whom the adjective refers have already become 'the chieftains assembled in the royal council', cf. *Il.* iv 259, where the formula is used with Ἀργείων οἱ ἄριστοι. A Lin. B tablet, PY An 261, has ke-

ro-si-ja, but even if this is to be interpreted as γερουσία, the reference to 'elders' is questionable; cf. Palmer, *Interpretation*, 228-9. On the position of the chief nobles at Alcinous' court see Finley, *World*, 94.

9. ἀκουάζεσθε: the -άζω suffix often describes the action as a usual one, cf. e.g. A. Debrunner, *Griechische Wortbildungslehre* (Heidelberg, 1917), 125-6.

12. These presents are those given by the twelve 'kings' of Scheria, viii 389 ff. In 13-14 the assembled guests (only the 'twelve'?—their number is not specified; cf. van Leeuwen ad loc., who refers to schol. viii 59) are invited to offer additional gifts. These are of less value than those already given, though tripods and cauldrons were treasures. On the sociological aspect of gift-giving see Finley, *World*, 69 ff. and *passim*. (It is to be noted that Alcinous does not remind the Phaeacians of what has been said at xi 339-46, 351-2). On the gifts, the escort (16-22, 47-9, 70-92), and the banquet (24-8) treated as a repeated 'theme' see Hainsworth on viii 385-468.

14. ἀνδρακάς: in antiquity no longer understood by some scholars (see schol. and app. crit.), obviously because of its archaic formation (cf. the parallels from Sanskrit in Schwyzer, *Grammatik*, i 630), but the schol. rightly refers to ἑκάς (< *ϝε-κάς, originally 'by himself'). **ἀγειρόμενοι**: 'gathering (for ourselves) among the people'. The middle has its full strength, cf. 15 n.

15. τισόμεθ': 'we shall have ourselves requited'. The nobles are asked to provide gifts to a guest who is socially their equal; afterwards they will in their turn (αὖτε, 14) indemnify themselves by 'gathering things for themselves among the people', cf. ἀρεσσάμενοι κατὰ δῆμον, xxii 55, where the middle also has its full strength. Finley, *World* (see 8 n.), 113, rightly observes that it would not have been 'fitting for the common people to provide the gifts ... In a society so status-bound, in which gift-giving had a quality of ceremonialism about it, no one could just give a gift to anyone else'. In this connection it deserves notice that in Odysseus' false tale in xix 172 ff. the *meals* which Aethon is said to have given to Odysseus' *comrades* came directly from the people (δήμοθεν) and that in this case the host uses the active (ἀγείρας, 197). The poet may still have pronounced τεισόμεθ' (and φθείσεσθαι, xiii 384) etc. (thus Wackernagel, *Untersuchungen*, 74 ff., followed e.g. by Risch and Chantraine), but in view of a possibly early influence of analogy (τίνω, φθίνω) the question is difficult to decide. (Attic scribes, at any rate, would not have changed τείσω, ἔτεισα if these forms had still been employed in the rhapsodical tradition). **χαρίσασθαι**: originally 'to show (and acquire) favour', cf. xv 139 n. **προικὸς**: an archaism, the original meaning of which ('for a gift', gen. of price) is already passing into 'gratis', 'at one's own cost', cf. Attic προῖκα.

16-18. These lines abound in formulae, some of them presumably very old (e.g. ἔβαν *ϝοῖκόνδε ϝέκαστος). **κακκείοντες** is generally explained as a future or as a desiderative of κεῖ-μαι, but the details are not clear; cf. Chantraine, *Grammaire*, i 453.

17. Since dawn (viii 1) a great many things have happened and all of them have been described in considerable detail. In other words, from a compositional point of view this has not only been a long, but also an extremely full day. It is different with the next one: now preparations for sailing (19–22, 70–7), dinner, and leave-taking are the only events, and it is significant that in this passage not even the subject of Demodocus' song (26–7) is mentioned (contrast viii 73–82, 265–366, 500–20). It has been argued that the function of this part (18–77) is to fill the additional day of Odysseus' stay in Scheria (announced xi 350–61) and that this day was inserted in order to adapt later expansions (the *Nekyia* or parts of it, see Page, *Odyssey*, 32 ff., 49 n. 16) to the original poem. Whatever may be the truth of those separatist views (cf. Heubeck on xi 225–332), it is at least certain that the account of Odysseus' last day with the Phaeacians does not essentially differ from the description of Telemachus' last day in Pylos (iii 404–85) in so far as its length and events are concerned. What is more, in xiii–xvi the poet, as we shall see (xv 222 n.), varies the proportions of both narrative sections and speeches to a remarkably high degree and he does so with great skill. Here we have an instance of this technique.

19. εὐήνορα: a pre-Homeric compound (< ἐυ-άνορα), originally meaning 'having good (i.e. 'strong', 'valiant') men', cf. e.g. Pi. *O.* i 24 and Leumann, *Wörter*, 110 n. 73. Subsequently—but still before Homer (cf. Leumann, ibid.)—it was applied to weapons, i.e. to bronze, and accordingly came to be used in the sense 'making men strong, making men display their prowess' (cf. Bowra, *HP*, 149–54), a meaning no longer understood afterwards (τὸν κοσμοῦντα τὸν ἄνδρα, schol.); cf. also εὐήνορα οἶνον (iv 622) and the development of ἐύφρων (when used with οἶνος), xiv 464 n.

20. ἱερὸν μένος Ἀλκινόοιο: such periphrases (cf. 'His Royal Highness' etc.) have their factual basis in the conventions of court style: analogies from Egypt and the Near East in Stella, *Ulisse*, 16 ff., 65 ff., 107 ff., 163–4. Since in Greece comparable conditions are only found in Mycenaean times, some of these formulae may well reflect Mycenaean titles, cf. Webster, *Mycenae*, 70 and *passim*. On their stylistic value see F. Dornseiff, *Pindars Stil* (Berlin, 1921), 28 ff. For ἱερός see Hainsworth on vii 167; on its meaning in this formula (∼ Vedic iṣiréṇa mánasā, instrumental of iṣirá-, mánas-) most recently J. T. Hooker in *Innsbrucker Beiträge zur Sprachwissenschaft* (Innsbruck, 1980), 7–30.

25. κελαινεφέϊ: probably from *κελαινονεφής, cf. e.g. ἀμφορεύς < ἀμφιφορεύς (on the cause of its application to blood see Leumann, *Wörter*, 202–6); cf. 147 n.

27–8. Demodocus made his first appearance at viii 43–4 and has already sung several songs. The singers share the epithet θεῖος with heroes such as Odysseus, Achilles, and Heracles. The fact that in 28 Demodocus is said to be 'honoured among men' after being called 'divine' in the preceding line proves that in this and similar cases Milman Parry's contention about the ornamental value of the epithet is correct, cf. also νηυσὶ θοῇσιν ... ὠκείῃσι (vii 34). Probably Demodocus and Phemius (i 154 etc.) already had predecessors at the Mycenaean courts (but the lyre-player on the fresco from Pylos is sitting on a rock and has been supposed to be a god). Whether the *name* Demodocus (see Hainsworth on viii 44) was inherited we cannot tell, nor can the age of λαοῖσι τετιμένος (also viii 472, ~ θεοῖσι τετιμένος *Il.* xxiv 533) be assessed; cf. also xiv 205 n. and Ruijgh, *Études*, 376, on Lin. B *qe-ja-me-no*. In any case the part played by this singer in the *Odyssey* is largely, if not wholly, due to its poet. In this connection see Hainsworth on v 11, and Ruijgh, *Études*, 198-202 on θεῖος.

30. δῦναι ἐπειγόμενος: 'infinitivus finalis praeter morem nunc additus designat rem quae festinando mutari nequit; cf. νόστον ὀδυρόμενος', van Leeuwen, ad loc.   **δὴ γὰρ** is not to be considered (with Denniston, *Particles*, 228) as an equivalent of γὰρ δή, where δή merely serves to stress γάρ; see also 1 n.

31. πανῆμαρ: has replaced *πὰν ἦμαρ, cf. e.g. *Il.* i 592 πᾶν δ' ἦμαρ φερόμην, Leumann, *Wörter*, 98.

32. The resemblance to ἀλλ' ὥς τ' ἐν νειῷ βόε οἴνοπε πηκτὸν ἄροτρον ... (τιταίνετον) (*Il.* xiii 703) is all the more remarkable since βόε οἴνοπε is confined to these lines and πηκτὸν ἄροτρον only once occurs elsewhere in Homer (*Il.* x 353, where it is also associated with νειός). As direct imitation is very unlikely (cf. xv 293 n.), the most plausible explanation of the phenomenon is that the combination of the single elements had already occurred before Homer (in similes?), the more so because βόε οἴνοπε (with dual and 'observed' digamma) must be pre-Homeric, and since two Lin. B tablets recording yokes of oxen (KN Ch 897, 1015) seem to show an older form of ϝοινοπ-. The epithet πηκτόν might be generic (cf. τυκτός, ποιητός), but in view of αὐτόγυον καὶ πηκτόν Hes. *Op.* 433 (see T. A. Sinclair, *Hesiod, Works and Days* (London, 1932) and M. L. West, *Hesiod, Works and Days* (Oxford, 1978), ad loc.) it is likely to be distinctive and to denote a plough of which the beam and the share are not all of one piece (thus also the schol.); representations of both types in W. von Schiering, *Archaeologia* ii H, 48 and pls. i, ii.

34. βλάβεται δέ τε γούνατ' ἰόντι: also *Il.* xix 166; βλάβεται also *Il.* xix 82. According to Shipp, *Studies*, 84, βλάβεται is more recent than the forms based on βλαπτ- (from *βλαπ-?; epigraphical evidence in Chantraine, *Dictionnaire* s.v. βλάβη, cf. also Lejeune, *Phonétique*, 79 n. 6). Still, whatever the original form of the root may be, βλάβεται is likely to have entered the diction at an early stage (cf. also Chantraine, ibid.; there is no trace of it in Ionic prose) and our phrase may well be an 'inadequately represented formula' (cf. 32 and 306 nn.) and an ancient one at that, see xv 293 n.

35. ὣς Ὀδυσῆ' ἀσπαστὸν: also v 398. For Ὀδυσῆ'(ι) see xv 364 n.

37. πιφαυσκόμενος: lit. 'showing' (cf. *φάϝ-ος), a sense still preserved in πιφαυσκόμενος τὰ ἃ κῆλα (*Il.* xii 280) and even remembered by Aeschylus, cf. e.g. ἡμερήσιον φάος πιφαύσκων (*Ag.* 22-3).

38. = viii 382 etc. On ἀριδείκετε see Hainsworth ad loc.

39. πέμπετέ: in 66 the verb means 'to send', but here the sense of 'escorting'

COMMENTARY

is still dominant, cf. πομπῆες (71); πομπή (e.g. in 41) has kept its old meaning longer because it became a ritual term.

41. θεοὶ Οὐρανίωνες: see Hainsworth on vii 242 and Ruijgh in *Minos*, ix (1968), 140, who points out that names in -ίων are derivatives from adjectives in -ιος and not by themselves patronymics, although they often serve as such. Hence οὐρανίωνες is nearly always an epic synonym of οὐράνιοι (found *h.Cer.* 55), created for use at the verse-end (cf. Δαρδανίωνες etc., Risch, *Wortbildung*, 57) and like Ὀλύμπιος (except when that word refers to Zeus, the god of the mountain peak(s), see Nilsson, *Homer und Mycenae*, 266–9), always used in the plural. See also West on Hes. *Th.* 127.

42–3. In spite of A. A. Parry, *Blameless Aegisthus*, 71–93, there is no valid reason to question Kretschmer's derivation of ἀμύμων from μῦμαρ, which according to Hesychius is Aeolic (cf. πεῖραρ/ἀπείρων); and actually the Greek and Byzantine grammarians explain the word with ἀμώμητος, ἄμεμπτος, *sim.* This makes it unlikely, moreover, that its true meaning had got lost in Homeric times. That its original sense has been doubted is due to the fact that, like so many old epithets (see 79, xiv 3 nn.), it had become largely 'ornamental', in particular because in only 9 of their *c.*90 occurrences are the oblique cases separated from their noun (all of them between the trochaic caesura and the diaeresis; cf. Parry, *Homeric Verse*, 162 ff.). Given this state of affairs it is also quite natural that the adj. is regularly used as an attribute, even in most of the cases which show separation, e.g. Ἕκτωρ δ' ὡς οὐκ ἔνδον ἀμύμονα τέτμεν ἄκοιτιν (*Il.* vi 347). This employment might seem doubtful in xv 14–15, where Athena urges Telemachus to make haste, adding ὄφρ' ἔτι οἴκοι ἀμύμονα μητέρα τέτμῃς, but here, as xv 19 shows, the important word is οἴκοι (cf. also xvi 76), so that in this case too the adj. appears to be an attribute; cf. also *Il.* vi 347. Thus the only really dubious instance is found in our lines, where Ameis–Hentze–Cauer, agreeing with the schol., take it predicatively. As *Il.* vi 347 shows, 'separation' is inconclusive, yet the position of the adj. at the beginning of the sentence and widely separated from the *finite verb*, in addition to the fact that σὺν ἀρτεμέεσσι φίλοισιν can only mean 'with my loved ones safe and sound', seems to tip the scales in favour of the predicative employment. Perhaps Aeschylus was influenced by these lines when he wrote γυναῖκα πιστὴν δ' ἔν δόμοις εὕροι μολών (*Ag.* 606), 'But for his wife—may he come and find her to be faithful' (Eduard Fraenkel). Cf. also xvi 216–18 with n.

45. κουριδίας: lit. 'who were κοῦραι, "virgins", when they were taken to wife', as against the παλλακίδες, Bechtel, *Lexilogus*, 200–1.   **ἀρετὴν:** 'well-being', cf. Hes. *Op.* 289, and *Od.* xiv 402 n.; a schol. refers to ἀρετῶσι δὲ λαοί (*Od.* xix 114); cf. also οὐκ ἀρετᾷ κακὰ ἔργα (viii 329). The blessings Aeschylus' choirs implore on Argos (*Supp.* 625–709) and Athens (*Eu.* 916–25) may well serve as a commentary on 44–6.

47. ἐπήνεον: The original sense of αἰνέω, 'tell', 'say' (cf. xiv 508 n.) developed into 'say yes' (cf. φημί), the opposite of ἀναίνομαι: in the sense 'agree' the word occurs not only in Homer (*Od.* xvi 380 etc.) but as late as Euripides. Hence ἐπ-αινέω originally meant 'to say yes to something', 'agree', 'approve' and this is still its normal sense in Homer, cf. e.g. ἐπὶ δ' αἰνεῖτον βασιλῆες (*Od.* xviii 64 etc.); it is found only once with an obj. (*Il.* ii 335).

48. κατὰ μοῖραν: on the scansion see xiii 385 n.

49–50. Similarly in the Middle Ages the task of the herald was not limited to making proclamations, though it was less diversified than that of his Homeric counterparts. In Old Indian 'kārú-' meant 'singer'.

50. κρητῆρα κερασσάμενος: Though Homer's similes, notably in the *Iliad*, are numerous and often very elaborate and refined, his metaphors are unemphatic (cf. W. B. Stanford, *Greek Metaphor* (Oxford, 1936), 118–19) as compared with those used by choral lyric and Attic tragedy (ποιμένα λαῶν, κακὰ ῥάπτειν, *et sim.*). Still simpler are his metonymies. The custom of mixing wine with water is proved for Mycenaean times by *ka-ra-te-ra* on a vessel tablet, MY Ue 611, Ventris–Chadwick, *Documents*, no. 234. The expressions κρητῆρα κέρασσε(ν) (*Od.* iii 390), κρητῆρα κεράσσατο (iii 393) are probably old formulae, cf. δώματα ναῖε, οἰκία ναίων, εἵματα ἕσσεν (<*ϝέσματα ϝέσσε), and xiv 326 n.

51. εὐξάμενοι: see xiv 199 n.

53. ἐκίρνα: Forms of this present-stem also occur in Herodotus, Hippocrates, and Ionic inscriptions. Both ἐκίρνᾱ and κίρνη (e.g. xiv 78, cf. Wackernagel, *Untersuchungen*, 1 n. 3) might be Ionic (if so the former is a contracted form), but they may as well represent κίρνᾱμι (Chantraine, *Grammaire*, i 21, 300–1) and be ancient elements of the formulaic diction, conserved in the second half-line after the trochaic and penthemimeral caesuras in the complementary formulae μελίφρονα οἶνον (*ϝοῖνον) ἐκίρνᾱ (*Od.* vii 182 etc.) and κίρνη μελιηδέα οἶνον (<*κίρνᾱ μελιϝᾱδέα ϝοῖνον, *Od.* xiv 78, xvi 52).

57. ἀμφικύπελλον: only in this formula (divided *Od.* xv 102, *Il.* xxiii 663, 667) and in δέπα᾽(α) ἀμφικύπελλα. Of the word δέπας as used in Homer we know no more than that it normally means 'drinking-vessel' (contrast Lin. B *di-pa*, which is illustrated by ideograms PY Ta 641, Ventris–Chadwick, *Documents*, pl. iii) nor can the meaning of the epithet be established with certainty. See further S. West on iii 63, Hainsworth on viii 89.

60. τά τ᾽: a typical case of τε used in a 'digressive' clause in order to express a 'permanent truth', see Ruijgh, τε *épique*, 358 and *passim*.　　**ἐπ᾽ ἀνθρώποισι πέλονται:** 'who rove about among men'; in such phrases πέλομαι has kept its original meaning 'to turn', cf. e.g. *Il.* iii 287 ἥ τε καὶ ἐσσομένοισι μετ᾽ ἀνθρώποισι πέληται (which has faded at *Od.* viii 160, xv 408).

62. παισί: with an irresolvable contraction. The contracted forms of παῖς entered the diction in great numbers at its Ionic stage. Before that, epic language only had *πάϝις (alongside *κόρϝος and υἱύς, which were used much more frequently, cf. A. Hoekstra, *Epic Verse before Homer* (Amsterdam, 1981), 75–81).

63. ἐβήσετο: see S. West on i 330, Hainsworth on vi 321.

67. Do the clothes mentioned here represent an additional gift? Or has the poet forgotten that in viii 441 Arete put the very same articles in the chest? The latter seems more probable, since he is likely to introduce a traditional motif (because of χιτῶνα the words ῥῆγός τε λίνον τε in 73 cannot refer to

67). **φᾶρος**: here serving as a cloak (without sleeves!). The term appears to have been felt to be more archaic and dignified than χλαῖνα (cf. the formulae χλαῖνάν τε χιτῶνά τε et sim.), but in origin it denoted no more than a rectangular piece of textile which could be used for different purposes, for instance as a shroud, cf. *Od.* ii 97 etc. In the forms *pa-we-a, pa-we-a₂* (i.e. φάρϝεα, φάρϝεά, cf. Ruijgh, *Études*, 54) the word is found on the Lin. B tablets (KN Ld 571 = Ventris–Chadwick, *Documents*, no. 214 etc.) combined with the ideogram for CLOTH and sometimes with the one for WOOL. Here the epithet ἐϋπλυνές may point to linen (Lorimer, *Monuments*, 373) and this was certainly the material Odysseus used for making sails, v 258–9.

71–2. Since τά γ' refers to the whole of the gifts, the use of 'all the drink and food' as an apposition is, strictly speaking, illogical. It might be due to the poet having as stock-in-trade (ἐν νηΐ θοῇ) βρῶσίς τε πόσις τε (x 176, xii 320) and βρῶσίν τε πόσιν τε (i 191 etc.), see 185 n.

71. πομπῆες ἀγαυοί: for πομπῆες see 39 n; for the use of the epithet, xiv 3 n. It is mostly regarded as cognate with ἄγαμαι (hence in origin 'admirable'), but the details are not clear (from *ἀγα-ϝϝος with Aeolic doubling of the digamma, i.e. ultimately < *ἀγα-σ-ϝος, Pisani in *LfgrE*?).

73. στόρεσαν ῥῆγός τε λίνον τε: owing to the situation this is much more concise than iv 297 ff. (= vii 336 ff., *Il.* xxiv 643 ff.) and even than x 352–3 (note that this has the same prothysteron), on which see Heubeck. That Odysseus is going to cover himself with his χλαῖνα (viii 455; cf. also xiv 460, 504, 520 ff.) is taken for granted. See further Frisk, *GEW* s.v. 2 ῥέζω. Leaf's suggestion of a hendiadys (*Iliad*, ix 661) is mistaken.

74. ἐπ' ἰκριόφιν: (ἰκριόφι I. Bekker) also iii 353, xv 283; ἀπ' ἰκριόφιν xii 414, xv 552 (not in *Il.*). For the use of -φι see xv 148 n. and Hainsworth on v 59 (but in Lin. B. already *e-re-pa-te-jo-pi o-mo-pi*, Ventris–Chadwick, *Documents*, no. 276 and p. 369; on its possible locative function, 403). **γλαφ-υρῆς**: see F. Càssola, *Inni Omerici* (Fondazione Lorenzo Valla, 1975), on *h.Ap.* 405.

75. πρύμνης: the accentuation is uncertain because the word may have been used as an adj. in a paratactical enjambment, cf. ii 417, xv 206, etc. Although ἐπ' ἴκρια νηὸς ἔβαινον | πρῴρης (xii 299–30) is inconclusive in this respect (cf. e.g. Risch, *Wortbildung*, 139), this expression shows why in our line the poet thought it necessary to add πρύμνης (πρυμνῆς?). Odysseus was to sleep in the stern since here he would keep comparatively dry when the bow plunged into the waves.

76. ἐπὶ κληῖσιν: for the origin of the mistranslation 'on the benches' see Leumann, *Wörter*, 33, 209.

78–9. The *lectio facilior* ἔνθ' seems to have originated from a misunder-standing of καί in 79 (cf. καὶ τότε (δή) introducing the main clause (*Od.* v 459 etc.), and Denniston, *Particles*, 308). On ἀνερρίπτουν see Chantraine, *Grammaire*, i 62.

79. νήδυμος: see Bechtel, *Lexilogus*, 150; an artificial form, which originated from ἔχε *ϝήδυμος ὕπνος > ἔχεν ἤδυμος ὕπνος. In spite of ἥδιστος (80), the poet may have understood it in this sense (cf. xiii 27–8 with n., and ὠκέϊ ... ὅς τ᾿ ὤκιστος πετεηνῶν (*Il.* xv 238)), but that is of course far from certain (schol. on iv 793: ὁ μὴ δύνων, from Aristarchus on *Il.* ii 2; see further Ebeling, *Lexicon* s.v.).

81. **ἡ δ᾿:** with a slight anacoluthon resumed by τῆς (84). The four-horse chariot does not appear on the monuments until the late Geometric period. In the epics it is still extremely rare (*Il.* viii 185 (spurious?), where its presence has to be presumed because of the four horses addressed: the following lines, however, have the dual; xi 699, cf. ἐλατῆρ᾿(α), 702), but not necessarily a post-Homeric addition; see e.g. J. Wiesner, *Archaeologia* i F, 22–3, 66 ff. **τετράοροι:** the ᾱ (cf. e.g. συν-ήορος (viii 99), originally 'linked together', < συν-άορος) is probably due to influence of unelided τετρᾰ- in cpds. (cf. Chantraine, *Grammaire*, i 21) with a poet who no longer associated the word with 'to harness' (see *Il.* x 499, xv 680), cf. the misinterpretation of παρήορος in *Il.* vii 156 (xxiii 603?), Leumann, *Wörter*, 222–30.

83. **ὑψόσ᾿ ἀειρόμενοι:** 'As Hayman notes, a horse's gallop is really a series of leaps', Stanford.

84–8. Note that the verb-forms are all in the impf., except the 'timeless' ὁμαρτήσειεν (87).

84. **πρύμνῃ:** one would expect πρῴρῃ (proposed by Rochefort and adopted by Ameis–Hentze–Cauer ad loc.); perhaps the stern is mentioned because Odysseus is sleeping there.

85. **πορφύρεον:** see 108 n.

86–7. On ἴρηξ see Thompson, *Birds*, 114 ('the generic term for the smaller hawks and falcons'); on κίρκος, ibid. and 145 ('not identifiable as a separate species'). Appositions of this kind are a typical feature of epic style (cf. e.g. βοῦς ... ταῦρος (*Il.* ii 480–1), ὄρνισιν ... αἰγυπιοῖσι (vii 59), συὸς κάπροιο (xvii 21), see also 57 n.) and no doubt had their origin in oral poetry.

89. **θεοῖς ἐναλίγκια μήδε᾿:** a *comparatio compendiaria*, cf. e.g. κόμαι Χαρίτεσσιν ὁμοῖαι (*Il.* xvii 51).

90. The end of Odysseus' wanderings is marked by a resumption of the phrase πολλὰ ... πάθεν ἄλγεα ὃν κατὰ θυμόν (i 4), just as the passage describing his arrival in Scheria ὣς ὁ μὲν ἔνθα καθεῦδε κτλ. (vi 1) has an echo in the repetition at vii 344, where the line is followed by the significant addition τρητοῖς ἐν λεχέεσσι.

91. = viii 183 (see Hainsworth), xiii 264, *Il.* xxiv 8.

93. **ὑπερέσχε:** above the earth, cf. *Il.* xi 735 εὖτε γὰρ ἠέλιος φαέθων ὑπερέσχεθε γαίης, the only other place in Homer where the verb is used in this sense; elsewhere it denotes the stretching out of arms to afford protection (*Il.* ix 420 etc). The star is probably Venus.

96. 'Topographical' introductions to a new development are rather frequent in Homer, cf. e.g. *Od.* iv 354, xv 403, xix 172, *Il.* xi 711, xiii 32. Vividly interrupting the normal flow of epic narrative, they focused the attention of the hearers on what was coming. They are still employed by Thucydides. In Hdt. their form is sometimes very striking, e.g. ii 75. 1.

The line has been taken to contain precise topographical knowledge and the harbour is believed by some scholars to be the Gulf of Molo with its arm Dexia Bay, cf. e.g. F. H. Stubbings, 'Ithaka', in *Companion*, 398–421. On the other hand Φόρκυνος λιμήν may well have been a floating traditional expression which could be applied to many bays: according to a schol. the historian Herodorus (*c*.400 BC) taught that before migrating to Ithaca Phorcys had his dwellings on the coast of Achaea. Probably he was a pre-Greek divine being who was called 'the old man of the sea' by the Greeks, just like Nereus, Proteus, Porkos (Alcman, *Partheneion*, fr. i 19 Page), and other deities of the sea who were important in popular imagination (Nilsson, *Geschichte*, i 240 ff., cf. also Wilamowitz, *Glaube*, i 215–16). At *Od.* i 72 he is mentioned as the grandfather of Polyphemus and bears the resounding title ἁλὸς ἀτρυγέτοιο μέδοντος, though he never became a true god with the Greeks. His name is shared by an ally of the Trojans (*Il.* ii 862, xvii 218, etc.). (Non-Greek, as e.g. Πάλμυς, *Il.* xiii 792 (see Risch, *Wortbildung*, 76)? If so, Hesychius' φορκόν· λευκόν, πολιόν, ῥυσόν (!) is an attempt at interpretation; see, however, Chantraine, *Dictionnaire* s.v.).

98. ποτιπεπτηυῖαι: πότι πεπτηυῖαι (Cauer) is preferable; the ptcp. (still without -κ-) belongs to an old pf. of πίπτω or πτήσσω, cf. Chantraine, *Grammaire*, i 428. From a poetical point of view the latter is more probable: the rock 'crouches' into the sea.

99. ἀνέμων … κῦμα: cf. κύματα … παντοίων ἀνέμων, *Il.* ii 396–7. κῦμα often appears as a *collectivum* (cf. Hainsworth on v 438), as is only natural in view of its origin (κυέω lit. 'to swell').

100. ἄνευ δεσμοῖο μένουσι: in 113–15 we are told that in this very harbour the ship of the Phaeacians is run ashore. In our line, however, the poet is less specific: here he speaks of ships in general, and these are imagined as being not tied up in any way, whether by πείσματα, 'hawsers', or by a combination of πρυμνήσια, 'stern-cables', and εὐναί, 'anchor-stones', cf. e.g. xiii 77, x 96, 127, and xv 498. Hence in 100 the poet does not employ any of these terms but uses the general word δεσμός instead. What he means is well illustrated by the description of another quiet harbour, ix 136 ff.: … λιμὴν εὔορμος, ἵν' οὐ χρεὼ πείσματός ἐστιν, | οὔτ' εὐνὰς βαλέειν οὔτε πρυμνήσι' ἀνάψαι, | ἀλλ' ἐπικέλσαντας μεῖναι χρόνον … In such a bay the obvious method would be to beach the ships (ix 138, 148–9), but this is considered irrelevant by the poet in 100.

101. ἐΰσσελμοι: some scholars translate, rightly perhaps, 'with good upper planking' or 'well-timbered', and no doubt σέλμα (not in Homer) originally meant 'plank' or 'cross-beam', cf. Frisk, *GEW* s.v. σελίς, A. *Sept.* 32 (Hesych. s.v. ἔλματα?). But did Homer still understand it thus (cf. ζυγόν, *Od.* ix 99, xiii 21)? See further the scholars cited on xiv 350, Càssola, op. cit. (74 n.), on *h. vii* 6 and D. Gray, *Archaeologia* i G, 94. **ὅρμου μέτρον**: probably 'the measure (of their voyage) that consists in the anchorage' just as ἥβης μέτρον, appositely quoted by van Leeuwen and Stanford, signifies a measure of life that consists in ἥβη, cf. also τέλος θανάτοιο (κιχείη), *Od.* xvii 476 etc.

102. τανύφυλλος: see xv 171 n.

103–7. The cave of Marmarospilia, though not in the immediate neighbourhood of Dexia Bay, would answer to this description, cf. e.g. Lorimer, *Monuments*, 501; Stubbings, op. cit. (96 n.), 416. If the poet drew on local knowledge, the question arises how he got this detailed and precise information. It has been argued that he did so by autopsy, a view which might entail important consequences about the genesis and (for unitarians) even about the birthplace of a poem which is generally supposed to have been created in Ionia. Miss Lorimer assumes that the poet visited Ithaca on a journey which carried him as far as Thesprotia. However, the fact that some topographical details fit the local situation exactly, while others are far from clear—to say the least—may be typical of a poetic tradition (cf. xiv 257–8, 335, xv 117–18, 403, xvi 247–53 nn.; the 'identifications' that have been proposed for Homeric Ithaca range from Corfu to Cephalenia; for particulars see S. West, introduction to i–iv, and Heubeck on ix 21–7).

103. ἄντρον ... ἠεροειδές: also σπέος ἠεροειδές (366). The cpd. ἠεροειδές (the second part of which denotes the outward appearance of a person or thing, cf. e.g. ἐπ' ἠεροειδέα πόντον etc.) is properly employed at *Od.* xii 80, where it is used of a cave which is situated half way up in a sky-high peak shrouded in fog, cf. 74–6, 231–3. In our line, however, the interior of the cave must be meant, so ἠερόεις, 'where vapours linger', would have been more suitable (cf. ἄντρον ἐς ἠερόεν *h.Merc.* 234), but the neut. gender of this word was metrically impossible at the verse-end. The phenomenon of the second part of a compound losing its proper meaning is well known in Attic tragedy, but there it has nothing to do with reuse and occasionally improper employment of formulae, see also 185 n.

104–12. On the island of Helios there is a cave where the Nymphs have their 'seats and dancing-floors' (xii 317–18). Here they have mixing-bowls, jars, and looms at their disposal, but the main difference is that in this part of the world, where mortals live, they also have a cult (104, 349–50), just as they may safely be supposed to have had in the real world of the poet (cf. H. Herter in *Der Kleine Pauly* s.v. Nymphai, col. 314). Hence probably the separate entrance for men.

105. ἀμφιφορῆες: since the short form ἀμφορεύς, which is the current term in the historical period, is already found on the Lin. B tablets alongside the original ἀμφιφορεύς (MY Ue 611, see 50 n.), we may have to do with a Mycenaean survival that owed its preservation to a poetical tradition going back to that time: Kirk, *Songs*, 115.

106. ἔπειτα: here serves to introduce a new element in a *description*, cf. e.g. *Od.* i 106, and xiii 96 n. **τιθαιβώσσουσι:** exact sense and etym. unknown.

108. ἁλιπόρφυρα: elsewhere only *Od.* vi 53 ~ 306, where it is said of wool on the distaff. Often explained as 'of sea-purple', but probably a poetical formation (like the other ἁλι-cpds. of this type) referring to the bright variety of colour shown by the (Aegean) sea under certain circumstances

COMMENTARY

(in particular to foam?), cf. Armenian *p'r-p'ur-k*: A. Meillet, 'Sur le représentant arménien *ur,ul* d'anciennes sonantes voyelles', *BSL* xxxvi. 2 (1935), 121–2; V. Pisani, 'Armenische Miszellen', *Sprache*, xii. 2 (1966), 227, cf. e.g. *Od.* ii 427–8 and πορφύρω. 'Quel pur travail de fins éclairs consume maint diamant d'imperceptible écume', Paul Valéry, *Le Cimetière marin* (Bibliothèque de la Pléiade, Paris, 1957), i 148 (2nd stanza). See also Hainsworth on vi 53.

109. ἀενάοντα: a remarkable form, because there is no evidence for the existence of ἀέ in spoken Greek (of the two instances from poetry given by *LfgrE* s.v., the one attributed to Pisander rests upon lexicographical authority, while the other is a (necessary) emendation by Hermann to Pi. *P.* iv 88). The difficulty is aggravated by the fact that ἀέναος appears in prose. However, since the verb νάω itself had become an archaism at an early time, the cpd. must be a poeticism (Hdt.!), and since it is already found in Hes. *Op.* 595 it is likely to have been created by epic poets, probably on the model of τηλεδαπός, τηλέπυλος, ἀγχέμαχος, etc. In our line ἀενάοντα (or αἰενάοντα, as in Hes. *Op.* 550) has been influenced by this adj. and/or by the current epic formula [θεοὶ(-οὺς, -ῶν)] αἰὲν ἐόντες (-ας, -ων).

111. θεώτεραι: 'belonging to gods', not to mortals, cf. 110. The suffix -τερος originally denoted a contrast, an opposition, cf. e.g. Chantraine, *Grammaire*, i 257, and xv 422 n.

113. πρὶν εἰδότες: A schol. vainly tries to reconcile this phrase with viii 556–60, where the Phaeacian ships themselves know their destination. Here we have left the *Märchen* atmosphere (see introduction to xiii–xvi, and xiii 125–87 n.).

114–15. Normally the Greeks ran (or drew) their ships ashore stern first, yet here the phrase ἡ μὲν (contrast οἱ δ', 116) ... ἠπείρῳ ἐπέκελσεν followed by σπερχομένη· τοίων [*potius* τοῖον] γὰρ ἐπείγετο χέρσ' suggests that in this case we have an exception to that rule (as also in Hdt. vi 16. 1 and vii 182. 1 where ships are pursued and subsequently abandoned), cf. also D. Gray, *Archaeologia* i G, 103. The obvious explanation is that the crew only intended to make a very short stay (thus also D. Gray; given the context it would be far-fetched to refer to the magical qualities of the Phaeacian ships, see 113 n.). The point deserves notice because some scholars have based their interpretation of the term ἐφόλκαιον (*Od.* xiv 350) on the implicit assumption that Homer *never* makes his sailors depart from the 'stern first' custom, although there the situation is similar, see n. ad loc.

114. ὅσον τ' ἐπὶ ἥμισυ πάσης: it is doubtful whether here ἐπί still governs ⟨τόσον⟩ ὅσον, as it does at *Il.* x 351, xxi 251. Probably the use of ὅσον τε as an independent phrase was a feature of the poet's vernacular: in Hdt. it is current and does not look like an epic borrowing, e.g. τὸ δὲ κάτω λελειμμένον [of the papyrus] ὅσον τε ἐπὶ πῆχυν τρώγουσι (ii 92. 5). On the origin and meaning of τε in this expression see Ruijgh, *τε épique*, 556 ff.

119. δεδμημένον ὕπνῳ: the story, as conceived by the poet, requires that Odysseus shall not wake up until he is alone in his native land.

120. κτήματ': some MSS have χρήματ', a word which is not found in the

Iliad but is frequent in the *Odyssey*, cf. e.g. 215, where it is used (without a variant being attested) of the same 'goods'. In the sense of 'money' (not coined) it is for the first time found in Hes. *Op.* 686.

125–87. It has been argued that the function of this passage is to stress that Odysseus has finally left the world of wonder (see now Erbse, *Beiträge*, 145–8). If this is so, the result is rather mediocre. The junction with the preceding lines would lead us to expect additional measures of Poseidon against Odysseus, but it turns out that only the Phaeacians are the victims. His dialogue with Zeus is a flat copy of similar Olympic scenes in the *Iliad* and his main action is merely touched upon, in a subordinate clause (163–4). The intermezzo (deleted by F. Meister) might have been created after the island of the Phaeacians had been 'identified' with Corcyra (see 157–8 n.; if so, we should adopt Aristophanes' correction μή in 158). The question cannot be decided.

128. Ζεῦ πάτερ: the usual title, though Poseidon is Zeus' brother, cf. *Il.* xix 121.

130. See *Od.* vii 61–3.

132. ἀπηύρων: a late form, created by singers who mistook the archaic athematic aor. ἀπ-ηύρᾱ (probably from Aeolic, cf. the accent of ἀπούρας, Chantraine, *Grammaire*, i 191) for a contracted impf. of the type ἐτίμα (cf. e.g. Chantraine, ibid., 380).

135. εἰν Ἰθάκῃ: probably on analogy of εἰς Ἰθάκην (Wyatt, *Lengthening*, 91, whose examples make it improbable that the lengthening is due to any *direct* influence of a possible *ἐν-ἅλιος or ἐν ἁλί, cf. xv 479 n.). See also introduction to xiii–xvi.

136. This line (=xvi 231) and v 38 (=xxiii 341, with δόντες instead of ὑφαντήν) are formulaic variants, no doubt of pre-Homeric origin: they have no late characteristics and their digammas are 'observed' (ϝάλις, ϝεσθῆτα); xiv 324 (see n.) looks like another variant.

137. ἐξήρατ': from ἄρνυμαι; probably an artificial form substituted for ἐξήρετο and created under the influence of the aor. of αἴρω, cf. Chantraine, *Grammaire*, i 387–8; conversely νηῦς ... ἄχθος ἄροιτο (*Il.* xx 247), cf. νέες ἄχθος ἄειραν (*Od.* iii 312).

138. λαχὼν ἀπὸ ληΐδος αἶσαν: see xiv 232–3 n.

142. πρεσβύτατον: at *Il.* xiii 355, as a schol. points out, Zeus is said to be the older, whereas in Hes. *Th.* 453 ff. he is the youngest of Cronus' children. The etym. of the word is not certain (see Frisk, *GEW* s.v.) nor is its exact original sense. In Homer it means both 'venerable' and 'old', cf. γέροντες, γερούσιος (8 n.). How far the superlative corresponded to any historical reality in pre-Homeric times we cannot tell, but on the tablets Poseidon appears at Cnossos and Pylos (PY Es 646 = Ventris–Chadwick, *Documents*, no. 169 etc.) and in the latter place, at any rate, he seems to have been an important god. We do not know whether in Mycenaean times he still kept some characteristics of the 'Lord of the Earth' (πόσις Δᾶς), which according to the most probable etymology (cf. also ἐνοσίχθων, e.g. 125, ἐννοσίγαιος, e.g. 140) he must originally have been. See Hainsworth on viii

173

322–3 (cf., however, A. Heubeck, 'Poseidon', *IF* lxiv (1959), 225–40). **ἀτιμίῃσιν ἰάλλειν:** 'to smite with insults'. The strange form of the expression (cf. scholl.; 'elsewhere ἰάλλειν is only found with an acc. of the thing thrown', Monro) is due to the fact that it was created by combining the old epic verb with an abstract and non-traditional substantive (used only here in Homer). The innovation involved metrical lengthening, cf. e.g. ᾗσι προθυμίῃσι πεποιθώς (*Il.* ii 588).

144. σοὶ δ': a clear instance of δέ *apodoticum*, cf. Denniston, *Particles*, 177, and xiv 178 n. **καὶ ἐξοπίσω:** in such contexts the particle tends to express mere emphasis, see xv 435 n.

147. αἶψά κ' ἐγὼν ἔρξαιμι: the potential opt. can express politeness, cf. e.g. xv 506. Since the aor. is timeless the alternative past–present does not exist (in Homeric Greek, that is to say; Attic is different): 'I would have liked (and would still like) to do so, but ...' (ἀλλά, 148). **κελαινεφές:** see 25 n. Usually the adj. is found in formulae such as κελαινεφέϊ Κρονίωνι (e.g. *Il.* i 397) or when Zeus is addressed in his full majesty of (Indo-European) Sky-god, cf. e.g. Ζεῦ, κύδιστε, μέγιστε, κελαινεφές, αἰθέρι ναίων (*Il.* ii 412). Here and at *Il.* xv 46, however, the word is denuded of its solemn associations and has become as familiar as γλαυκῶπις (389, *Il.* viii 406) and *Il.* viii 373 ὅτ' ἂν αὖτε "φίλην γλαυκώπιδα" εἴπῃ. It looks as though the spirit of such lines and of the conversations in which they occur, though not unhomeric, is typical of a late stage of epic composition.

148. ὀπίζομαι: see xiv 82 n.

151. σχῶνται: the general word is specified by ἀπολλήξωσι δὲ πομπῆς, cf. *Il.* xxii 416.

154. ὡς: thus most good MSS, but ὥς is preferable, since μέν (on its affirmative sense see Denniston, *Particles*, 359 ff.) is much better accounted for, and ὁππότε κεν (155) is more natural if in 154 the sentence ends with the line.

157–8. The wording of νηΐ ... ἅπαντες ἄνθρωποι makes the impression of giving an αἴτιον for the fact that the rock which rises from the sea just outside the harbour of Corfu was taken to be 'Odysseus' ship'. This 'identification' is mentioned by Pomponius Mela 110–11 and Plin. *HN* liii, but is no doubt much older. Judging from the tone of Th. i 25, it was common opinion by his time that Corcyra was the island of the Phaeacians. A possible *terminus post quem* is the third quarter of the eighth century when Eretrians, soon followed by Corinthians, settled there.

158. See 125–87 n. The schol. on 152 referring to Aristophanes' reading μή belongs here, as was already seen by Cobet and others, see e.g. Ameis-Hentze, *Anhang* on xiii 152–8.

160. ὅθι Φαίηκες γεγάασιν: after all we have been told, a flat stop-gap.

163. ὅς μιν λᾶαν θῆκε: because of its form the phrase is an anticlimax.

164. νόσφι βεβήκει: the plpf., in accordance with its original function of expressing the state of the subject in the past, here denotes the result of the action of βῆναι: 'he was (already) far away', as e.g. in *Il.* i 221 ἡ δ' Οὔλυμπόνδε βεβήκει, 'but she was (already) on her way to Olympus'.

Normally this use is most graphic (as in βοὴ δ' ἄσβεστος ὀρώρει etc.), but here it is mechanical.

165. ἔπεα πτερόεντ': according to several scholars 'feathered words', flying to their mark like arrows, πτερόεντες ὀιστοί (*Il.* v 171 etc.). See, however, Ameis–Hentze, *Anhang*, on *Od.* xvii 57 and E. Fraenkel *ad* A. *A.* 276 (ii, 152 n. 1), who argues that the phrase τῇ δ' ἄπτερος ἔπλετο μῦθος (*Od.* xvii 57 etc.), means 'she did not reply (but acted as she was told). This the poet expresses by saying "to her the thought was without wings, i.e. remained unuttered"'. This explanation, it is true, ignores the original difference between πτερόν, 'feather' and πτέρυξ, 'wing', but since the two words are already associated in Homer (*Od.* ii 149–51 etc.) the interpretation appears to be substantially correct, cf. also the scholia, which have οὐκ ἀπέπτη ὁ λόγος, ἀλλ' ἐπέμεινε μὴ ἔχων πτερόν among several other explanations. This implies that the poet of xvii 57 etc. took the formula ἔπεα πτερόεντα as referring to young birds that have already got feathers (or wings), which makes it possible for them to fly (in this phrase, from the nest of the mouth). Hence the translation 'winged words' seems best, at any rate in the *Odyssey*.

172–8. ~ viii 564–70; see now Erbse, *Beiträge*, 145–8, and Hainsworth ad loc.

173. ἀγάσεσθαι: presumably an emendation by Aristarchus (cf. viii 565) for the much better attested ἀγάσασθαι (thus here MSS and schol.; not mentioned by Allen), which, besides, is at the same time the *lectio difficilior* (cf. e.g. *Il.* iii 28) and unobjectionable, since the prophecy is not mentioned until 175.

182. ἱερεύσομεν αἴ κ': cf. *Il.* vi 309. A type of formula which is certainly pre-Homeric and probably Aeolic (αἴ κ'(ε); the short-vowelled subj. can alternate with an infin. in -έ-μεν, cf. xii 49; *Il.* vi 275, xxiv 301, 592).

183. We are not told whether this happened or not. Erbse, *Beiträge*, regards the fulfilment of the prophecy as a matter of course.

185. ὣς οἱ μέν ῥ' εὔχοντο: a formula of the traditional type, (cf. ὣς οἱ μὲν δαίνυντο, *Od.* iv 15 etc., ὣς οἱ μὲν μάρναντο, *Il.* xi 596 etc.) here loosely employed: it does not summarize what precedes; cf. 71–2, 164, 296, 320–3, 374, 395, xiv 52, xv 134, 354, xvi 366 nn.   Ποσειδάωνι ἄνακτι: also a traditional formula. On Poseidon see 142 n.; ϝάναξ and derivatives are well attested on the Lin. B tablets (e.g. PY Ta 711 (=Ventris–Chadwick, *Documents*, no. 235); see moreover Ruijgh, *Élément*, 113–17), *Études*, 335.

187–8. ἔγρετο ... εὔδων: van Leeuwen quotes e.g. ἀναπνεύσωσι ... τειρόμενοι (*Il.* xi 800–1).

189. ἤδη δὴν ἀπεών: 'after he had been absent so long'; the ptcp. refers to the past (Erbse appositely quotes παρών γε ... φράσαιμ' ἄν, A. *Pers.* 266–7); because of περὶ γὰρ κτλ., and since it is not apparent why his long absence should have prevented Odysseus from recognizing his own land, its meaning cannot be causal. But one may wonder why the phrase is there at all (for the sake of pathos? thus Stanford; but it will not do to take the expression as an addition to εὔδων, since this would reduce οὐδέ μιν ἔγνω, the most important element of the sentence, to a casual, parenthetical remark).

190–1. The poet does not employ the mist in the normal epic way: elsewhere the gods use it to conceal either themselves or mortals and they do not act in such a roundabout way in order to advise and change their protégés. At 190 Aristophanes read αὐτῷ, but if μιν refers to Ithaca, μή ... γνοίη (192) makes no sense (ἄγνωστον (191) means 'unrecognizable'). Some scholars have rejected 192–3; see also 333–8 n.

192. ἀστοί: elsewhere in Homer only at *Il.* xi 242, where it may (but need not) mean 'townsfolk'. Here 'fellow-countrymen', 'people', a sense still common in Hdt. (cf. Sanskrit vā̆stu, 'dwelling-place'), is equally possible; cf. F. Gschnitzer, 'Vocabulaire et institutions: La Continuité historique du deuxième au premier millénaire', in E. Risch and H. Mühlestein (eds.), *Colloquium Mycenaeum* (1975, Neuchâtel–Geneva 1979), 126.

194. ἀλλοειδέα φαινέσκετο: Porson's ἀλλοειδέ' ἐφαίνετο is the least unsatisfactory correction of the MS–tradition.

195. διηνεκέες: 'running through (the country without a break)'; cognate with ἐνεγκεῖν and preserving an old, intrans., sense of that verb, 'to reach'; cf. ποδηνεκής and the parallels quoted from other Indo-European languages by Frisk, *GEW*, and by Chantraine, *Dictionnaire* s.v.

196. ἠλίβατοι: etymology and exact meaning unknown.

197. ἔσιδε: read εἴσιδε (MSS).

198. καὶ ὣ πεπλήγετο μηρώ: probably an old, pre-Ionic, formula (note the duals and the reduplicated thematic aor.) originally designed to serve after the penthemimeris (the neglect of the digamma of the possessive pronoun is due to the phrase being used after the trochaic caesura, cf. Hoekstra, *Modifications*, 63). It denotes a gesture of sorrow, despair, or anger, cf. *Il.* xii 162, xv 113, 397.

200–2. Odysseus used the same words when arriving in Scheria, vi 119–21; a piece of irony on the part of the poet? Cf. 219–21. See also Hainsworth on vi 119, 121 and Heubeck on ix 172–6.

203. φέρω: taken as an indicative by Monro and van Leeuwen because of πλάζομαι (204), but the two questions are not parallel.

204. ὄφελον: in view of 207–8 it is probably preferable to take this as a 3rd pl. (subject: χρήματα; see Erbse, *Beiträge*, 152). Odysseus feels handicapped by his treasures.

210. ἦσαν: the so-called 'imperfect of discovery' with ἄρα, cf. *Od.* xvi 420.

212. εὐδείελον: probably not a poetical and artificial form (from δέελος (*Il.* x 466), with metrical lengthening), but one of those words which were originally part of spoken Greek (cf. Ruijgh, *Élément, passim*) and were not transmitted in what is left of Greek literature: see G. Klaffenbach, *Glotta*, xlviii (1970), 204–5, who quotes a Locrian inscription where the context appears to exclude borrowing from a poetical source. But the translation 'clear', 'distinct' is not necessarily affected.

213–14. ἄλλους | ἀνθρώπους: i.e. 'all other people', so that here καὶ ἄλλους has become a near synonym of πάντας, cf. e.g. Ζεὺς ... καὶ Ἐρινύες, αἵ θ' ὑπὸ γαῖαν | ἀνθρώπους τίνυνται, ὅτις ... (*Il.* xix 258 ff.), and, on the other hand Φαίηκές μ' ἄγαγον ναυσίκλυτοι, οἵ τε καὶ ἄλλους | ἀνθρώπους πέμπουσιν (*Od.* xvi 227), i.e. 'not only me, Odysseus, but all other people as well'; see also iv 826-7, xx 187-8, xxi 293-4, *Il.* ix 513-14, 553-4. In these cases τε is used because we have to do with fixed elements in the universe of the poet's heroes (in the last-mentioned case the Phaeacians had ceased escorting people, but of course Odysseus could not know that), cf. also Ruijgh, τε *épique*, 391.

213. τίσαιτο ἱκετήσιος: with both hiatus and lengthening of a short syllable *in arsi.* These phenomena cannot be satisfactorily explained by the poet applying any 'law' which should have distinguished between 'legitimate' and 'illegitimate' cases: see Parry, *Homeric Verse*, 192-6. Generally speaking they are a normal consequence of the fact that the epic poets had to combine and change existing formulae (Parry, *passim*). Here, however, the 'formulaic' explanation will not do since τίσαιτο has an unusual position and metrical value and because ἱκετήσιος is a bold coinage (cf. Chantraine, *Formation*, 41-2: 'un arrangement de ἱκέσιος'). Here, therefore, the prosodical irregularities are not due to adaptation of formulae, but to drastic innovation in verse-making; cf. 142, 243, xiv 41, 459, 473, xv 88, xvi 191 nn. Zeus is mentioned as the protector of suppliants in *Il.* xxiv 570, *Od.* xvi 422, etc.

216. οἴχωνται: the right reading (not even mentioned by Allen) is of course οἴχονται (cf. Kühner–Gerth, *Grammatik* ii 395), the more so as the verb means 'they *have* left', cf. e.g. *Od.* v 300 and ὅρα ... μὴ κατθανών σε σύγγονος λέληθ' ὅδε (Eur. *Or.* 208-9). The scholl. remark that Odysseus has forgotten Circe's magic knot (viii 448).

217-18. Thirteen tripod-cauldrons, dating from the ninth to eighth centuries, were found in the cave of the Nymphs at Polis Bay (not at Marmarospilia! cf. 103-7 n.): see Stubbings in *Companion*, 418-19, who again assumes local knowledge and remarks that even their number fits that of Alcinous and the twelve 'kings' mentioned at viii 390. If these kings are identical with the assembled guests addressed at 8 ff. (see n.) and if the real objects are the 'originals' of those received by Odysseus, the question arises whether the number of the 'kings' was equally determined by what the poet—on a voyage? Cf. 103-7 n.—is supposed to have seen. If it was, a large part of the *Odyssey* would begin to look more like a historical novel than an epic poem. However this may be, the whole complex of problems regarding possible autopsy is most important for the genesis of the poem.

218. ἠρίθμει: one of Odysseus' first acts. The poet no doubt intended it as a tiny piece of character-drawing (cf. xiv 212-13 n.) and it is characteristic of his individualizing the old folk-tale hero. The non-traditional wording is significant: the verb ἀριθμέω (cf. introduction to xiii-xvi n. 61) has been used with an irresolvable contraction as a run-over word in a 'violent' enjambment (cf. introduction, and xv 78-9 n.).

219-21. Cf. 200-2 n.

219. πατρίδα γαῖαν: a similar acc. is found with ὀδύρομαι (379, v 153 (νόστον)), cf. also (intermediate?) ὀδύρονται οἶκόνδε νέεσθαι (Il. ii 290) and Od. xiii 30 n. The intrans. use of the verb (cf. e.g. Od. xiv 40) might be older.

221–5. Athena's intervention here and elsewhere in the epics is a reminiscence of Mycenaean and Minoan times when, as Nilsson has explained, she was the patron of the princes and their household goddess, cf. e.g. Od. vii 80 ff. (a tablet from Cnossos probably shows her name and title in the form Ἀθάναι Ποτνίαι (?), KN V 52); cf., however, 313 n. For Pallas Athena see Hainsworth on vi 328. The lines have a traditional ring (cf. e.g. the formulae based upon *ϝεϝικυῖα), which contrasts sharply with other features observed above, cf. 142, 213 nn. Unfortunately the context in which e-pi-ro-pa-ja occurs on a tablet (KN Od 696) is too uncertain to make sure a connection with λώπη (224; after Homer only in poetry, but cognates in Ionic and Attic). On πέδιλα, see xv 369 n.

222. ἐπιβώτορι: an expressive and probably poetic creation, cf. βοῶν ἐπιβουκόλος ἀνήρ (Od. iii 422, etc.), ὑῶν ἐπίουρος (Od. xiii 405 = xv 39), alongside βώτορες (ἄνδρες), βουκόλος, οὖρος. There is no reason to suppose (with Leumann, Wörter, 92–3) that these cpds. came into being because of Umdeutung of Κρήτῃ ἔπι οὖρον as Κρήτῃ ἐπίουρον (Il. xiii 450). A schol. reminds us that in Homer sons of kings and nobles guard the flocks, quoting Il. vi 423 and xx 91, to which other examples might be added. The trait does not seem to fit in with Mycenaean conditions as we know them from the tablets.

224. λώπην: What kind of 'cloak' or 'mantle' is meant is wholly unknown, cf. also 221–5 n. and Marinatos, Archaeologia i A, 10. It is likewise called δίπτυχα by AR ii 32, and δίπλακα by Theoc. xxv 254, but with these poetae docti these may be Homeric reminiscences.

229. νόῳ: 'disposition towards somebody' according to E. Fraenkel on A. A. 1228, but not yet distinct from 'intention', as in the formula βουλῇ τε νόῳ τε (e.g. 305). See also B. Snell, Die Entdeckung des Geistes⁴, (Göttingen, 1975), 19 ff.

230. σάω: probably an athematic form, cf. Il. xvi 363 etc.

231. φίλα γούναθ': see xvi 92 n.

232. = i 174.

234. εὐδείελος: see 212 n.

235. κεκλιμένη: cf. νήσων … αἵ θ' ἁλὶ κεκλίαται (iv 607–8), λίμνη κεκλιμένος Κηφισίδι (said of a Boeotian whose grounds lie sloping down to lake Copaïs, Il. v 709), κλει-τύς, 'sloping hillside', Lat. clī-vus.

237. νήπιός: see xiv 264 n.

238. τήνδε τε γαῖαν: Ruijgh, τε épique, suggests that, since here and at xv 484 the first consonant following is a γ, rhapsodes who no longer knew the true function of τε introduced it for reasons of euphony.

241. ποτὶ ζόφον: see Heubeck on xi 57; ζόφος is cognate with Ζέφυρος.

243. οὐδὲ: = οὐ δέ, 'but, on the other hand, not …', see xv 246, xvi 475 with nn.   **λυπρή:** only here; no cognate forms either in Od. or Il.; see 2 (ἀκήλητος), 213 (hiatus) nn.   **ἀτὰρ οὐκ** (οὐδ'; Aristarchus?) **εὐρεῖα τέτυκται** seems to be meant as a sort of parenthesis.

244. σῖτος ἀθέσφατος: the adj. (cf. Chantraine, *Dictionnaire* s.v. θέσφατος; Hainsworth on vii 273) must have been used *in bonam partem* (it refers to abundance). Hence the expression is somewhat exaggerated if the historical Ithaca is meant, and it is at variance with τρηχεῖα (242), τρηχεῖ'(α) (ix 27), κραναή (e.g. xv 510).

245. ἔχει: cf. 269 and xiv 239 with n.

246. βούβοτος: this does not support the supposition of local knowledge either (see 244 n.). In iv 605, on the other hand, Telemachus stresses the absence of meadows in Ithaca.

247. ἐπηετανοί: see S. West on iv 89 (but the η has not been satisfactorily explained).

248. The use of ξεῖν'(ε) and the coupling of Ithaca with Troy shows a kind of light-hearted humour which is seldom found with Homeric gods.

252. αἰγιόχοιο: πελεμαίγιδος Ἀθάνας (Bacchylides xxii 7, cf. Snell, ad loc.), unless inspired by σείειν (cf. *Il.* iv 167, xv 321), suggests *αἰγίροχος (from ϝέχω 'to carry', in this compound perhaps 'to wield'), see further Bechtel, *Lexilogus*, and Chantraine, *Dictionnaire* s.v. The etym. and original meaning of αἰγίς are still uncertain.

254. πάλιν δ' ὅ γε λάζετο μῦθον: also *Il.* iv 357, but here used in a different sense: 'he took back the word (he was about to say) before it could cross the fence of his teeth', as Ameis–Hentze–Cauer rightly explain.

255. νωμῶν: for the meaning cf. e.g. *Il.* v 594 (ἔγχος, 'spear'), vii 238 (βῶν, 'shield'), *Od.* x 218 (οἰήια, 'rudder-oars').

256–86. In his made-up tales Odysseus always pretends to be a Cretan. This has been put down to people in Homer's time being fascinated by the great Minoan island (Ameis–Hentze–Cauer) or to the fact that its inhabitants were renowned as adventurous sailors and raiders (Stanford). Of course the two reasons are not mutually exclusive, and one may add that as Odysseus always affirms that he belonged to the nobility, it was safer for him to choose a country which, besides being mysterious (xix 172 ff.), was far away, cf. also *h.Cer.* 123–4 and F. Càssola, op. cit. (74 n.), ad loc.: 'Creta ha grande parte in tutti i falsi racconti, perché in età homerica era una terra nello stesso tempo famosa e poco frequentata'. The details of the speech are rightly explained by Erbse, *Beiträge*, 154–5, as accounting for the situation the way Odysseus imagines it must appear to the 'young shepherd': a well-dressed stranger carrying with him many treasures on a lonely beach he cannot identify.

259. A frequent theme in Homer: the same happened to an anonymous Aetolian (*Od.* xiv 380), to Theoclymenus (*Od.* xv 272–3), to Medon (*Il.* xiii 695–6), to Lycophron (*Il.* xv 431–2), and to Patroclus (*Il.* xxiii 85 ff.).

260. Ὀρσίλοχον: other contexts in which the name occurs (*Od.* iii 489 = xv 187, cf. *Il.* v 542 ff., *Od.* xxi 16), and the fact that it is sometimes given as Ὀρτίλοχος, suggest that it goes back to the Aeolian-Achaean nobility. The latter form is likely to have been preserved by aristocratic family pride, so that we need not assume a 'restored' τ. See also introduction to xiii–xvi n. 36 (*O-ti-na-wo* on a tablet from Pylos).

261. ἀλφηστὰς: an archaism, probably from ἄλφι and ἐδ- (ἔδω), and created as a counterpart of ὠμηστής, cf. Chantraine, *Dictionnaire* s.v.

265. χαριζόμενος: see 15 n.   **θεράπευον:** only here; see xv 95 n.

267. χαλκήρεϊ δουρί: probably a very old formula (also found in the form χαλκήρεα δοῦρα), cf. Myc. [e]-*ke-a ka-ka-re-a*, KN R 1815 (according to the numeration of Chadwick–Killen–Olivier, *The Knossos Tablets*[4] = Ventris–Chadwick, *Documents*, no. 263 and p. 515) = ἔγχεα χαλκᾱρέα; see also xv 282 n.

267-8. κατιόντα ... | ἀγρόθεν: cf. μίμνει | ἀγρῷ, οὐδὲ πόλινδε κατέρχεται (xi 187-8).

270. θυμὸν ἀπούρας: also a pre-Ionic formula, mostly occurring in the form θυμὸν ἀπηύρα; see 132 n.

272. Φοίνικας ἀγαυοὺς: Their activity in western Greek waters in Mycenaean times—as distinguished from contacts of Mycenaeans with the Syrian coast, cf. 285 n.—cannot be proved or disproved, but as they only appear in the *Odyssey* and at *Il.* xxiii 744, it would not be surprising if, as has been supposed, they are an anachronism introduced by an eighth-century Greek poet; see J. D. Muhly, 'Homer and the Phoenicians', *Berytus*, xlx (1970), 19–64, whose archaeological arguments, apart from some generalizations, look convincing (43–63) and are usefully supplemented and corroborated by P. Wathelet, 'Les Phéniciens dans la composition formulaire de l'épopée grecque', *RBPh* lii (1974), 5–14. See also S. West on iv 618. On the treatment of history by heroic poets see Bowra, *Heroic Poetry*, 519–36.

274. καταστῆσαι καὶ ἐφέσσαι: 'to put me ashore—and take me on board—'. For ἐφέσσαι in this sense cf. ἀλλά με νηὸς ἔφεσσαι (*Od.* xv 277, middle). The 'prothysteron' is a common phenomenon in Homer, cf. 434 n.

275. Though the verse may well have been created by an Ionian poet (its formulaic variants (*Od.* xv 298, xxiv 431, *h.Ap.* 426), at any rate, are shown to be comparatively recent by the 'neglect' of the digamma of Ἤλις), it describes a state of affairs which is likely to have existed in a very distant past: the Epeans vanished without a trace and the same is true of their neighbours, the equally mysterious Caucones (*Od.* iii 366, cf. Strabo 321 ff., esp. 345; according to Hdt. iv 148 they were expelled from their country by 'Minyans'). The case of the Taphians is similar, cf. xiv 452 n. Probably we have to do with peoples that disappeared in the 'dispersals and shiftings of population which mark the end of the Bronze Age in the eastern half of the Mediterranean region' (Lorimer, *Monuments*, 121). The line also suggests that the Epeans were not confined to Elis; this is consistent with *Il.* xiii 691–2, where they are implicitly mentioned as inhabitants of Doulichion (cf. xiv 335 n.) and the Echinades.

276. ἲς ἀνέμοιο: a typical instance of a pre-Ionic formula that was originally designed to be used (in the form ϝὶς ἀνέμοιο) after the 3rd sg. of impfs. and aors. in ∪∪ preceding the bucolic diaeresis (many examples in Parry, *Homeric Verse*, 41–9; cf. also Hoekstra, *Modifications*, 49–53). It is still employed in this way here and at *Od.* ix 71, xix 186, but is already being made to serve under different conditions in Homer: after a pres. tense (ἐπιβρέμει; without hiatus, *Il.* xvii 739), and in enjambment (with a gen. in -ου, *Il.* xv 383).

277. Contrast xiv 288-97, xv 419-82. Here Odysseus stresses the honesty of the Phoenicians in question because the stranger has seen his treasures, cf. 258.

281. αὔτως: 'just like that'. A similar situation is described by the advb. in *Od.* xii 284, where Odysseus' comrades have to wander across the sea without an evening meal.

285. Σιδονίην: country, town, and inhabitants are mentioned repeatedly in the epics (cf. e.g. *Od.* xv 118, 425), Tyre never, though from the tenth century onwards it was far more important. This has been taken to mean that in this respect Homer reflects a tradition going back to the Bronze Age (on this question see Lorimer, *Monuments*, 67, 80), but cf. Dunbabin, *The Greeks and their Eastern Neighbours* (London, 1957), 35. However this may be, Mycenaean contact with the Syrian coast (Ugarit!) is an established fact: see the literature listed by Stubbings in *Companion*, 544 and W. F. Albright, 'Some Oriental Glosses on the Homeric Problem', *AJA* liv (1950), 165.

286. ἀκαχήμενος ἦτορ: 'sorrowful in (my) heart', also xv 481 etc.; ἀκαχήμενοι ἦτορ ix 62 etc. Always used after the hepthemimeris caesura, as is its 'complementary' formula τετιημένος (-οι) ἦτορ. In antiquity the accentuation of the ptcp. was considered Aeolic, and some modern scholars attribute the noun itself (because of -ορ instead of -αρ) to this dialect. Yet it might at the same time have existed at an early stage in Achaean, i.e. in the dialect represented in a standardized form by the Lin. B tablets (Ruijgh, *Études*, 71), see also introduction to xiii-xvi. At any rate we probably have to do with two highly archaic, non-Ionic formulae. See also xvi 92 n.

288. δέμας δ' ἤϊκτο γυναικί: on the expressive use of the plpf. see 164 n. Here, however, the tense does not serve to conclude a series of events: the change itself is not even hinted at and the poet abruptly uses what is probably a very old formula (cf. *Od.* iv 796, xvi 157, xx 31) that described the manifestation of a goddess (ἤϊκτο from *ἤϝικτο, or a substitute for *ἐϝέϝικτο (Chantraine, *Grammaire*, i 479, *Morphologie*, 190)? Rather δ' ἤϊκτο < *δὲ ϝέϝικτο).

289. ἔργα ἰδυίη: read ἔργ' εἰδυίη: 417 n.

291. παρέλθοι: νικήσει, μεταφορικῶς (schol., with reference to ἐπεὶ οὐ παρελεύσεαι οὐδέ με πείσεις, *Il.* i 132), lit.: 'run past', 'outstrip'.

293. σχέτλιε: probably originally 'tenacious', 'obstinate', 'relentless' (if from *σχέ-θλιος, E. Hermann, *Sprachwissenschaftlicher Kommentar zu ausgewählten Stücken aus Homer* (Heidelberg, 1914), 157; Chantraine, *Dictionnaire* s.v.) and here used, like the other adjs., in a tone of mock-reproach.   ἆτ' from ἄατ'(ε) by contraction.

295. πεδόθεν: only here in Homer; variously explained by the scholl. (as a metaphor), but found in its original meaning in πεδόθεν δὲ τινάσσετο μακρὸς Ὄλυμπος Hes. *Th.* 680 (*funditus*, West ad loc.). In our line it has the same sense ('from the bottom', sc. of thy heart; thus rightly LSJ), cf. also E. *Tr.* 98, Pi. *O.* vii 62. H. Fränkel, *Wege und Formen frühgriechischen Denkens* (Munich, 1955), 47 n. 2, considers it a synonym of ἔμπεδον, 'unablässig', but, whatever the word may mean in Pi. *I.* v 38 and in Ibyc. fr. v 12 P. (where the context is uncertain because φυλάσσει is corrupt), neither the parallels quoted nor the arguments for such an evolution are convincing (πέδον does not mean 'Stelle', 'place', but 'ce sur quoi on pose le pied', Chantraine, *Dictionnaire* s.v., 'ground', 'bottom'). In our line πεδόθεν was corrupted into unmetrical παιδόθεν in many MSS, even in some of the oldest, and this reading in its turn was 'corrected' to the nonsensical παῖδες in some copies.

296. ἀλλ' ... λεγώμεθα: in this formula (*Il.* xiii 292 etc.) the verb already has the sense of 'telling', 'saying', though still with the connotation of 'recounting'. The formula may have been created to serve after lists (of ancestors, warriors, etc.), which are common in heroic poetry, cf. e.g. C. M. Bowra, *Tradition and Design in the Iliad* (Oxford, 1930), 71–2. At *Il.* xx 244 it is preceded by a genealogy; see 185 n.

297. ὄχ' ἄριστος: see 365 n.

299. μήτι: i.e. μήτιι, cf. *Il.* xxiii 315, 316, 318, and Chantraine, *Grammaire*, i 217.

305. ὤπασαν: see xiv 62 n.

306. ὅσσα τοι αἶσα: also *Od.* v 206 (at the verse-end; cf. ἄσσα οἱ αἶσα, *Od.* vii 197); probably an 'inadequately represented formula' (on this subject see Hainsworth, *Flexibility*, 40) of pre-Ionic origin, cf. also the formula ἐπεί νύ τοι αἶσα and its variants (Ruijgh, *Élément*, 58–9). **δόμοις ἔνι ποιητοῖσι:** Stanford, following J. Berlage, *Mnemosyne*, NS liii (1925), 289–98, argues that in such expressions ποιητός, τυκτός, τετυγμένος have preserved their proper meaning (not *bene factus*, but simply *factus*) and that they are 'simple-minded and metrically useful epithets derived from the time when any such construction was still wonderful' (on *Od.* iv 627). This is a tempting view, but since it seems to be at variance with Mycenaean conditions in art and architecture, we would have to suppose that these phrases were introduced after the fall of that civilization (by people who shortly before had been nomads? Cf. xiii 222, xiv 62 nn.). Perhaps it is safer to assume a pregnant (technical?) use of the words at the time the phrases were created; curiously enough Myc. *te-tu-ko-wo-a(a₂)* (KN Ld 871, PY Sa 682 = Ventris–Chadwick, *Documents*, nos. 216, 289), neut. pl. of the pf. ptcp. active in a passive sense, found with ideograms of CLOTH and WHEEL, is not specified either, cf. Palmer, *Interpretation*, 326. However this may be, in Homer we also find expressions and formulae such as (βοῶν) εὐποιητάων (ἐϋ π.; *Il.* xvi 636), πύλης εὐποιήτῃσι (*Il.* v 466), τέγεος πύκα ποιητοῖο (*Od.* xvi 415 etc.), κυνέην (κλισίην) ἐϋτυκτον (*Od.* xiv 276 etc.), and none of them has any late characteristics.

310. ὑποδέγμενος: perhaps an athematic pres., cf. δέχαται (*Il.* xii 147) and Chantraine, *Grammaire*, i 296; however, cf. *Od.* xiv 52, 54.

313. In the preceding part of the *Odyssey*, up to 221, Athena, when in direct contact with Odysseus, has disguised herself only twice, viz. when she changed herself into a girl (vii 20) and when she appeared as a herald (viii 194). Therefore, even if we ignore—as I think we should—the fact that in neither case is she said to have been recognized by Odysseus (so that Aristarchus came to reject 322-3), there is little reason to press the use of παντί. Admittedly, it is not impossible that by using this word the poet made Odysseus remember similar cases in the Trojan War (at *Il.* ii 280, iv 87, vii 59, xvii 555, xxii 227 Athena appears as a herald, as Laodocus, as a vulture, as Phoenix, as Deïphobus respectively), but it is highly doubtful whether the poet intended any such recollections to enter the mind of the hero or of his hearers (who were no classical scholars!) at this moment. The context in which παντί is used rather suggests that it is due to Odysseus' amazement at seeing the young prince change into a woman and at the same time hearing the goddess speak.

This scene, however, raises a more important question: how far does it show any influence of the Mycenaean tradition (221-5 n.) on the poet's conception of the relation Odysseus–Athena? In this connection it is first of all worth noting that although Homer believed in the previous existence of the heroic world he depicted—no less than Hes. (cf. *Op.* 156-65)—he did not have any knowledge of what *we* call 'Mycenaean conditions' (cf. e.g. the chapter entitled 'Homer the Pseudo-historian' in J. Chadwick, *The Mycenaean World* (Cambridge, 1976), 180-7, Kirk, *Homer*, 40 ff., and esp. P. A. L. Greenhalgh, *Early Greek Warfare* (Cambridge, 1973), 156-72). Thus it is far from surprising that the old beliefs which have left traces in his poetry appear to have been transformed in his mind (and probably in the conceptions of his Ionian predecessors too), cf. e.g. his treatment of Enyalius and Paeaon. Secondly it is to be realized that, whereas the old patronage-motif seems to be original in the Perseus and Heracles myths, this is not necessarily true of its presence in certain versions of the old sagas about Bellerophon, Cadmus, and Jason, as has long been recognized: there, in actual fact, it is likely to have been borrowed from the first group and may even have been introduced by poets. Whether it is also derivative in the *Odyssey* is uncertain, nor can it be established where the influence of the tradition ends and poetical elaboration begins (a difficulty not fully realized by M. Müller, *Athene als göttliche Helferin in der Odyssee* (Heidelberg, 1966), *passim*, who makes her two concepts neatly coincide with the *Iliad* (x excepted) and the *Odyssey*). It is certain, however, that in the *Odyssey* the latter factor plays a dominating part, cf. also Nilsson, *Geschichte*, i 369 and 371. This is well illustrated by our passage, which shows the goddess in her old role of patroness of the princes, but at the same time elaborates this role and transforms it to a very high degree: it presents a unique scene of 'unusual subtlety' by depicting 'the ambivalent relationship' (Kirk, *Myths*, 124) between Athena and her protégé.

315. ἦος: Synizesis resulting from quantitative metathesis is common in Homer and due to the poet himself (e.g. τέως μέν xv 231). However, here and at xv 109, 153 'disyllabic' ἕως (MSS)—contrast ii 78 etc.—would necessitate an impossible scansion (*pace* M. L. West, 'Epica', *Glotta*, xliv (1967), 135–9), and as the same applies to εἵως, we are faced with the vexed question whether to adopt εἶος or ἦος, the latter of which is conjectural, while εἶος appears to have little if any MS-support, thereby contrasting sharply with βείομεν, στείομεν, τεθνειότος, ῥεῖα, etc. On the other hand the poet never replaced κεκμηότας, κεκαφηότα, τετληότι, etc., by 'compromise-forms', presumably because these were already felt to be archaisms. And since by Homer's time the metathesis probably was a comparatively recent phenomenon (see E. Crespo, 'La chronología relativa de la metátesis de cantidad en Iónico-Ático', *CFC* vii, Madrid, 1977), he may have employed ἦος/τῆος alongside the new forms ἕως/τέως (xv 231, xvi 370), i.e. as archaisms, and 'protected' as such by another couple of archaisms, ἦμος/τῆμος. **υἷες Ἀχαιῶν:** we do not know whether in this formula a difference of generations was originally implied and, if so, whether this had any connection with historical events. For Homer, however, the phrase was synonymous with Ἀχαιοί (as such it was imitated by Hdt., Λυδῶν παῖδας (i 27. 3), Αἰθιόπων παισί (iii 21. 3); examples from other authors in West, *Theogony*, on 240). When the preceding word ends in a vowel we find κοῦροι Ἀχαιῶν or δῖοι Ἀχαιοί (a complete survey of all the formulae for 'Greeks' in D. L. Page, *History and the Homeric Iliad* (Berkeley, 1959), 280 ff.).

317. ἐκέδασσεν: alternates with σκέδασεν, etc.; it did not survive in spoken Greek.

318. The fact that Athena did not come to the rescue of Odysseus in the dangers described in ix–xii may be due, in origin, to the influence of the old folk-tales. That is a plausible conjecture, but no more. It is clear, however, that the poet had no use for the presence of the goddess in that part of the *nostos*, otherwise he would doubtless have introduced her, as he introduced her in our passage: see xiii 313 n.

320–3. Aristarchus condemned 320 because of ἧσιν being used for the first person, 321 on the ground that it shows little politeness towards Athena and 322–3 because the goddess was not recognized by Odysseus in vii 20 ff. His method of regarding violations of τὸ πρέπον (as he conceived it) as symptoms of interpolation is inadmissible, but his objection to 322–3 is worth considering: the presence of these lines may be due to an inaccurate attempt to reconcile 318–19 with vii 14–77. As for ἧσιν: if the 'general' sense of the possessive pronoun ὅς were original in Greek (because of the meaning of *sva-* in Vedic, Chantraine, *Grammaire*, i 273), the Homeric uses in question (discussed by Chantraine, ibid.) would be archaisms. The actual cases, however, do not support this far-reaching supposition. In ix 28 the 1st pers. meaning is at least partly due to formulaic causes (ἧς γαίης (i 59, vii 196), 'his own' > 'one's own' in this context); 320 looks like a normal epic verse that was created for the 3rd pers. (cf. Hoekstra, *Modifications*, 92 and 96–9) and was either inserted, together with 321, by a rhapsode who no longer understood the meaning of the pronoun or was carelessly adopted by the poet who had used it himself in a different context or heard it recited in another epic poem, cf. 185 n. For φρένες see S. West on iv 661–2 and esp. the article of Ireland–Steel cited ad loc.

321. ἠός: read εἵως (MSS).

324. πρὸς πατρὸς: sc. Διός; a rather familiar addition, but the whole of the scene has an air of familiarity, cf. esp. 248, 291 ff., 327, 364, 389.

326. ἀναστρέφομαι: only here in Homer; probably a comparatively late compound. Actually Odysseus has not yet done any 'roaming about the country'; he uses the word for the sake of pathos, instead of mentioning his ἑρπύζειν (220).

327. ἠπεροπεύσῃς: a typically epic word, no doubt already an archaism at the poet's time; etym. uncertain.

332. ἐπητής: etym. and exact meaning are unknown ('decent', 'friendly'?); cf. ἐπητύς (xxi 306), where the context excludes the meaning 'eloquence'. **ἀγχίνοος:** 'quick-witted', 'observant', cf. Arist. *HA* 587 a. **ἐχέφρων:** cf. ἐχέφρων Πηνελόπεια, Ἔχενος (vii 155, etc.), Ἐχέπωλος (*Il.* iv 458, xxiii 296), Ἐχεκλῆς (*Il.* xvi 189 = *Ἐχεκλέης, 'having fame').

333–8. Rejected by Aristarchus, according to the scholl., on the ground that Odysseus has shown no sign of not wishing to rush off to Penelope and that 335–8 are at variance with his own words in 383–5. The lines are defended by Erbse, *Beiträge*, 158–60, but πειρήσεαι (336) remains offending. Do we have to suppose that Athena is already suggesting a line of conduct to her protégé? At all events little would be lost if the lines did not exist.

336. αὔτως: see 281 n.

339. ἀπίστεον: only here; probably a symptom of the influence of contemporary Ionic.

343. υἱὸν φίλον: Polyphemus, the Cyclops.

345. ~ 96.

346. ~ 102.

347–8. = 103–4. The lines are omitted by a number of MSS and two papyri. 349 does not favour their authenticity.

350. τελήεσσας: from *τελεσ-ϝεντ', see Lejeune, *Phonétique*, 136; lit.: 'having τέλος', but the exact sense is uncertain; often regarded as a synonym of τέλειος, 'perfect', 'without blemish', but τεληέντων οἰωνῶν (*h.Merc.* 544) suggests 'bringing fulfilment'; neither meaning is appropriate in Hes. *Th.* 242 = 959.

351. In the *Odyssey* the mountain Νήριτον is also mentioned (ix 21–2) ἐν δ' ὄρος αὐτῇ | Νήριτον εἰνοσίφυλλον, ἀριπρεπές and in the *Iliad* (ii 632) οἵ ῥ' Ἰθάκην εἶχον καὶ Νήριτον εἰνοσίφυλλον. As an adjective νήριτος is almost certainly an 'Achaean' survival, see Ruijgh, *Élément*, 161. Its meaning 'countless' exactly fits the collective noun ὕλη (Hes. *Op.* 511; cf. also μεγήριτα (*Th.* 240), 'numerous', said of the Nereids), but hardly a mountain, nor does a development to 'immense' (Ruijgh, ibid.) look very probable in spoken language. Leumann, *Wörter*, 243–7, argues that here and at *Il.* ii 632 the mountain got its name by a reinterpretation of ὄρος ... νήριτον (*Od.* ix 21–2). Though this is still more questionable, Leumann may be right in so far as that the proper name is likely to be a poetic creation; see now E. Meyer in *Der kleine Pauly* s.v. 'Ithake', Lorimer, *Monuments*, 495 ('Thiaki has no outstanding peak'), above 103–7 n.; and in connection with the eponymous Νήριτος, introduction to xiii–xvi, p. 159. It may have come from an epithet, e.g. νηριτόφυλλος (Hesych.), which in lost epic poetry probably served as a complementary epithet to ἀκριτόφυλλος (ὄρος ἀκριτόφυλλον, *Il.* ii 868), cf. 315 n., but in view of the technique of transposition (Hoekstra, *Modifications*, Index s.v.) the explanation appears to be that it was derived from *ὕλην|νήριτον εἰνοσίφυλλον. Hence a pre-Homeric poem appears to have had ὄρος καταειμένον ὕλην [xix 431 ὕλη *lectio facilior*]|νήριτον, εἰνοσίφυλλον.

354. κύσε: as he did at v 463 (which has the same formula) and Agamemnon did on his return (*Od.* iv 522). Both ζείδωρος (probably from *ζεϝέδωρος) ἄρουρα and its complementary formula φυσίζοος αἶα (cf. Bechtel, *Lexilogus*, 148) are probably highly archaic. For ζειαί, *Triticum monococcum* (and/or *bicoccum*?), see S. West on iv 41; on the problem of ζ (as compared with y in Sanskrit yáva- 'barley') see M. Leroy in *Mélanges Chantraine*, op. cit. (xiv 199 n.), 106–17. ἄρουρα, lit. 'arable land', already in Mycenaean, PY Eq 213 (Ventris–Chadwick, *Documents*, no. 154), cf. also Ruijgh, *Élément*, 111 and 122–3.

358. διδώσομεν: here and at xxiv 314 the fut. is formed from a stem that is actually a pres.-stem (δι-). The phenomenon is exceptional but appears also in Homeric διζήσομαι, κιχήσομαι, and in διδάξω, βιβάσω. Chantraine, *Grammaire*, i 442, holds that διδώσομεν differs in meaning from δώσομεν ('we shall offer'–'we shall give'), but cf. Shipp, *Studies*, 139.

359. ἀγελείη: since Bechtel, *Lexilogus*, 6, mostly rendered as 'driver of spoil', 'forager' (=ἀγελτηίη, from ληίη 'spoil'), but, on the strength of Ἀθηνᾶι Ἀγελάαι in a fourth-century Attic inscription, explained again by W. S. Ferguson, *Hesperia*, vii (1938), 29, as 'leader of the host' with reference to ἀγέστρατον Ἀτρυτώνην (Hes. *Th.* 925, cf. West on 318). However, the explanation of the Attic form is not beyond doubt. On Athena as a wargoddess see e.g. Nilsson, *Geschichte*, i 347–8; cf. 221–5, xiv 216 nn.

360. αὐτόν τε ζώειν ... ἀέξῃ: a slight anacoluthon, cf. e.g. xvi 6, *Il.* iii 80. After αὐτόν τε ζώειν the regular continuation of the sentence would have been καί μοι φίλον υἱὸν ἀέξεσθαι, but instead of ἀέξεσθαι the poet says ἀέξῃ, co-ordinating this form (subjunctive) with the subjunctive ἐᾷ in 359.

363. θεσπεσίοιο: from *θεσ-σπέτιος, 'spoken by a god', (cf. θέσφατος), but already in Homer's time its meaning had got blurred; here it means no more than θεῖος, cf. 103–4.

364. θείομεν: see 324 n. At *Od.* xix 33–4 Athena performs a similar service.

365. ὄχ' ἄριστα: this combination is already much more frequent in Homer than ἔξοχ' ἄριστα (-οι etc., 5 times), from which it was derived at a time when ἐξ in ἔξοχα was felt as an intensive element of the type found in ἔκδηλος etc. More in Leumann, *Wörter*, 133 ff.

374. τοῖσι δὲ μύθων ἄρχε: (*potius* ἦρχε, cf. xv 2, xvi 142) a case of the application of a formula to a situation for which it was not created, since it means 'among them began to speak' (thus e.g. at *Od.* i 28), cf. 185 n.

377. τρίετες: the scholl. quote *Od.* ii 89 ἤδη γὰρ τρίτον ἐστὶν ἔτος, τάχα δ᾽ εἶσι τέταρτον. **κοιρανέουσι** 'have been lording it', see xvi 124 n.

378. = *Od.* xi 117. **ἕδνα διδόντες,** 'offering bride-prices', describes the older custom, which is often referred to in Homer, e.g. *Od.* xv 18. Probably it was out of date or falling into disuse in the poet's own time, for the more recent practice which requires the father of the bride to provide a dowry is already mentioned, cf. Cauer, *Homerkritik*, 333–40, Hainsworth on viii 318. The form ἕδνα comes from ἔεδνα (e.g. xvi 391) < *ἔϝεδνα with a 'prothetic vowel', cf. Beekes, *Laryngeals*, 58–9, who is inclined to think that ἕδνα is artificial.

379. νόστον ὀδυρομένη: see 219 n.

380. πάντας μὲν ἔλπει: cf. ii 91, where a few MSS omit ῥ᾽. As the active (only in these lines) looks like an archaism, μὲν ἔλπει, with 'observance' of the digamma, may be genuine; cf. e.g. *Il.* iv 467.

384. ἔμελλον: the oldest contexts where the verb occurs show that basically it expresses likelihood, not futurity (thus rightly Stanford) cf. e.g. the formula μέλλει φίλον εἶναι, *Il.* i 564 etc., and *Od.* xiv 133; here: 'it was to be expected that ...'. The expectation concords with the threats uttered by one of the suitors at ii 246–50.

385. κατὰ μοῖραν: a more recent scansion (∪∪–∪) for older ∪––∪ (becoming ∪––– in the hexameter, e.g. in κατὰ μοῖραν κατέλεξα, *Od.* x 16) based upon *smer-, cf. e.g. Lejeune, *Phonétique*, 119–20.

388. λύομεν λιπαρὰ κρήδεμνα: cf. e.g. ὄφρ᾽ οἷοι Τροίης ἱερὰ κρήδεμνα λύωμεν (*Il.* xvi 100). The word κρήδεμνον is also used in connection with a city in ὃς Θήβης κρήδεμνον ἔχει ῥύεταί τε πόληα (said of Poseidon, Hes. *Sc.* 105), and in ἰδὲ κρήδεμνα πόληος | εἰρύαται (said of the rulers, *h.Cer.* 151–2). In Homer it is usually explained as a metaphor for the wall(s) of a city, an interpretation which is already found in the scholia on our line: μεταφορικῶς τὸ τεῖχος. But to what kind of headgear does κρήδεμνον refer in these phrases? Richardson, *The Homeric Hymn to Demeter* (Oxford, 1974), ad loc., holds that the expression Τροίης ἱερὰ κρήδεμνα λύωμεν 'may have been suggested by the idea of a captive woman whose veil is torn off' and refers to Lorimer, *Monuments*, 386, who, adducing *Od.* v 346, vi 100, and the lines mentioning Penelope's κρήδεμνα, i 334 etc., argues that this head-dress was a kind of veil or shawl, a view already put forward by Helbig and by Leaf (see his fig. 3, *Iliad*, ii 596), adopted by H. P. and A. J. B. Wace in *Companion*, 501–2 and by Marinatos, *Archaeologia* i A, 13, 46. This opinion is based upon vase-paintings from the sixth century BC which actually show women wearing some kind of veil or shawl that hangs down their back. It is indisputable that, generally speaking, Homer took κρήδεμνον to be a dress of this kind.

However, in some passages this explanation is not as satisfactory as it looks at first sight. First, what resemblance has the circular wall of a city to a veil or shawl? Secondly, expressions such as ἐυστεφάνῳ ἐνὶ Θήβῃ (*Il.* xix

99, Hes. *Th.* 978), στεφάναν πύργων (E. *Hec.* 910; more examples in West on *Th.* ad loc. and Richardson ad *h.Cer.* 151) refer to a στεφάνη, i.e. a ribbon or diadem (cf. *Il.* xviii 597), and here the likeness is clear. Is it to be assumed, then, that this is a different and more apposite metaphor? Yet Russo on *Sc.* 105 seems to be right in referring to ἐυστέφανον ... Θήβην (*Sc.* 80), and in fact Richardson does the same. Moreover, why the *pl.* in the case of Penelope's κρήδεμνα? The answer is to be found in the original meaning of κρήδεμνον, which is not 'veil' or 'shawl' (καλύπτρη, e.g. *Od.* v 232, *h.Cer.* 197; κάλυμμα, *Il.* xxiv 93, *h.Cer.* 42, cf. e.g. A. *A.* 1178, with Fraenkel's n., and E. *IT* 377), but 'head-binding'. It looks as though Homer had inherited a formula λιπαρὰ κρήδεμνα from the tradition, in which it still meant 'shiny head-bindings' and that he employed this figuratively in *Od.* xiii 388 ~ *Il.* xvi 100 (there replacing λιπαρὰ by ἱερὰ, a substitution which was impossible in *Od.* xiii 388, i 334, etc.), but applied it to denote the contemporary head-dress in *Od.* i 334 etc., just as he did with the mere noun in other cases. In this connection it is to be noted that λιπαρός is a very old adj. (cf. βριαρός, στιβαρός, etc., see also Chantraine, *Formation*, 226–7) and that the noun is a highly archaic cpd., as is proved by the suffix -μν- (Chantraine, op. cit., 214 ff.) and by the form κρη- (< κρᾱ-) of its first part (Chantraine, *Dictionnaire* s.v. κάρᾱ, Ruijgh, *Études*, 85 n. 56). Besides, 'ribbons' are clearly depicted on frescoes from Mycenae and Tiryns (see e.g. Marinatos–Hirmer, *Kreta, Thera und das Mykenische Hellas* (Munich, 1973), 20 and liv–lvii) and on the Warrior Vase (ibid., 256). The only remaining question is: was the word also preserved outside epic language? If it was, we have simply to do with an example of a term which in the course of time came to be applied to a different type of garment. However, outside poetry the word is only found in the inventory of the sanctuary of Hera in Samos, and Leumann, *Wörter*, 296, suspects that in this inscription it owes its existence to the description of Hera's dress in *Il.* xiv 170–86. However that may be, reinterpretation of archaic words and forms is, as the use of βοῶπις and φάλος proves, a well-established phenomenon in Homer, cf. also 351, 365, xiv 317, 453–6, xv 171, xvi 256 nn.

The metaphor κάρηνα, 'heads' (*Il.* ii 117 = ix 24) is much simpler and would easily suggest itself, cf. the formula ὀρέων αἰπεινὰ κάρηνα, *sim.*

389. γλαυκῶπι: see 147, 324 nn. It is uncertain how the poet understood the epithet ('with light-blue eyes'? 'with gleaming eyes'?), but in view of βοῶπις and βλοσυρῶπις and their reinterpretations it may well originally have had the 'ritual' sense of 'owl-eyed' (Chantraine, *Dictionnaire* s.v. γλαύξ); see also E. Townsend-Vermeule, *Archaeologia* iii V, 85.

390. Cf. *Il.* viii 233–4.

391. πότνα: only here and v 215, xx 61 (only in this voc. formula), a by-form of the much more frequent πότνια. The latter form is already attested in Mycenaean (in various combinations, see A. Morpurgo, *Mycenaeae Graecitatis Lexicon* (Rome, 1963), s.v.), the former is not. Beekes, *Laryngeals*, 156, regards it as artificial.   **πρόφρασσ':** fem. of πρόφρων, after the model of the old participles in -nt-ya (> Greek -ασσα), see e.g. Thumb–Hauschild, *Handbuch des Sanskrit*, ii² (Heidelberg, 1959), 98–9, Chantraine, *Morphologie*, 281.

394. τιν': the usual litotes, cf. 427 πρὶν καί τινα γαῖα καθέξει.

395. ἄσπετον οὖδας: elsewhere this combination only occurs in the complex formula ὅδαξ ἕλον ἄσπετον οὖδας, where it refers to the surface of the earth, so that 'unspeakable' is appropriate (xxii 269 (?), *Il.* xix 61, xxiv 738). If here it is meant to denote the floor of Odysseus' palace (thus Ameis–Hentze–Cauer, cf., moreover, xxii 269 and κραταίπεδον οὖδας ἔχοντες xxiii 46), we have again to do with a loosely employed formula, cf. 185 n.

398. κάρψω ... χρόα καλὸν: well illustrated by Archilochus fr. 113 Diehl (= 188 West = 209 Tarditi) οὐκέθ' ὁμῶς θάλλεις ἁπαλὸν χρόα· κάρφεται γὰρ ἤδη. The adj. καρφαλέος, 'dry', is used (*Od.* v 369) of chaff. On χρώς see xvi 145 n.

399. ξανθὰς ... τρίχας: conflicts with xvi 176 κυάνεαι ... γενειάδες (the exact meaning of ὑακίνθινος (*Od.* vi 231) is uncertain), but the inconsistency is a minor one and such as might be expected in poetry that was still oral or had only recently developed from the oral stage (the phenomenon, moreover, is not unknown in modern literature). ξανθός—which seems to denote all shades between yellow and auburn—is not only the epithet of Menelaus, Meleager, Agamede, but also of the definitely pre-Greek Rhadamanthys (*Od.* vii 323). Achilles' hair is called ξανθή (*Il.* i 197, xxiii 141). With regard to the later development of the story it is to be noted that the transformation is only a superficial one, see now Erbse, *Beiträge*, 62–3 and xvi 454–7 n.

400. Though van Leeuwen's references to *Il.* iv 194, v 649, xvi 263 for ἄνθρωπος used as τις are not convincing, this is not sufficient to adopt ἄνθρωπον. If we do, however, we should at the same time read στυγέη τις (see app. crit.), for ὅσ(σ)ον τε γέγωνε βοήσας (*Od.* v 400 etc.) cannot be adduced in support of ἰδών without a subject: it is a generic—and probably very old—formula. For the word order in the text of the MSS cf. εὐνὴ ... κάκ' ἀράχνια κεῖται ἔχουσα (xvi 34–5).

401. κνυζώσω: probably 'I shall make dim', cf. Hesych. s.v. κνυζόν, but the exact meaning of the verb is uncertain.

404. συβώτην: the noun is already attested in Mycenaean, PY Eq 59 (Ventris–Chadwick, *Documents*, no. 140), etc. See further xiv 55 n.

405. ὑῶν ἐπίουρος: cf. οὖρος Ἀχαιῶν (*Od.* iii 411 etc.) and 222 and xiv 104 nn. ὁμῶς: the advb. has been explained in strange ways (e.g. as going with τοι: 'in the same way as you to yourself'! thus a schol.; see moreover Stanford ad loc.), but its meaning is easily understood if 'as before' is tacitly implied (as proposed by the same schol.), cf. *Il.* ix 605 οὐκέθ' ὁμῶς τιμῆς ἔσεαι and the fragment of Archilochus quoted in 398 n.

407. δήεις: a pres. tense regularly used as a fut., cf. εἶμι, νέομαι (Schwyzer, *Grammatik*, ii 265).

408. Here local knowledge has again been assumed, see Stubbings, in *Companion*, 414 ff., and 96 and 217–18 nn. In any case, the fact that at the beginning of the nineteenth century a certain cliff was called Koraka can be disregarded in view of the fact that already in Hdt.'s time local antiquarian interest had resulted in falsifications (v 59 ff.), not to speak of the Hellenistic age and of the virtual depopulation of Ithaca in the Middle Ages, cf. Lorimer, *Monuments*, 498 n. Moreover, Raven's Rock may have been a widespread name in Greece, and Arethusa certainly was: according to Steph. Byz., Didymus knew eight springs of that name (scholl. mention four). That the Κόρακος πέτρη is the same as the rock mentioned at xiv 533 (and 399?) can hardly be inferred from the text.

410. τρέφει: 'causes to grow (thick)', cf. e.g. ἥμισυ ... θρέψας λευκοῖο γάλακτος (*Od.* ix 246), μάλα δ' ὦκα περιτρέφεται κυκόωντι (*Il.* v 903, likewise said of milk), πολλὴ δὲ περὶ χροῒ τέτροφεν ἅλμη (*Od.* xxiii 237, and xiv 476–7 with n.). This meaning is clearly very old, cf. τραφερήν (not 'dry', LSJ, but 'solid', xv 474 n.), ταρφύς, 'thick', 'close' (viii 379 etc.).

414. εὐρύχορον: the sense 'spacious' is not demonstrable until Pindar, with whom it is a case *abusio* (cf. *O.* vii 18, *P.* iv 43 and scholl.). One gets the impression that 'with broad dancing-place' was originally said of towns and small communities and was later somewhat loosely applied to districts, cf. *Od.* iv 635 and xiv 3 n. Anyway the epithet is graphic and typical of early Greek life and civilization. See also Hainsworth on vi 4.

415. μετὰ σὸν κλέος: this means at the same time 'in quest of news of you' and 'following the track of your fame': μετά with acc. has preserved its original sense (expressing both pursuit and sequence, cf. English 'after') and κλέος still denotes the result of 'hearing', cf. ἔκλυον and κλέομαι (299).

417. τ' ἄρ': the v.l. γάρ often occurs with τίς, πῶς, etc. (e.g. *Il.* ii 76), and is to be explained (with Ruijgh, τε *épique*, 806–7) as due to the influence of post-Homeric Greek.   **πάντα ἰδυῖα:** it is tempting to read this instead of MSS πάντ' εἰδυῖα (with 'observed' digamma), and if the phrase represents an old formula this was certainly its original form, cf. e.g. ἀγλαὰ ἔργ' εἰδυίῃ (289, xv 418, xvi 158), which comes from ἀγλαὰ ϝέργα ϝιδυίᾳ. But Homer himself already used the more recent (analogical) form of the ptcp., as is proved by οὐ πρὶν εἰδυῖα τόκοιο (*Il.* xvii 5).

419. ἀτρύγετον: etymology unknown; meaning uncertain; see S. West on i 71–3, Hainsworth on viii 49.

421. ἐνθύμιος: cf. ἐννύχιος, *sim.* Only here in Homer, but frequent in later Greek.

422. αὐτή μιν πόμπευον: 'I myself was his guide' (as described in ii 416–iii 370). The use of the emphatic πόμπευον (only here; instead of the regular ἔπεμπον, see 39 n.) stresses the element of reassurance.   **ἵνα κλέος ἐσθλὸν ἄροιτο:** cf. i 95 ἠδ' ἵνα μιν κλέος ἐσθλὸν ἐν ἀνθρώποισιν ἔχῃσιν. The formulae κλέος ἐσθλὸν ἀρέσθαι (ἄροιτο, etc.) and κῦδος ἀρέσθαι look very old and are typical of the Homeric epics, see also Bowra, *Heroic Poetry*, 100–3.

425–6. See iv 669–72 and 842–7.

427. καί τινα: see 394 with n.

429. ῥάβδῳ ἐπεμάσσατ' Ἀθήνη: the same expression, extended by χρυσείη, in xvi 172. The magic wand, so well known in Germanic fairy-tales, is largely a survival in Greek myths. In Homer Hermes still has one, but it soon becomes a herald's wand (Nilsson, *Geschichte*, i 509–10). In *Od.* x 238 the magic effect seems primarily to lie in Circe's potion, see 326, 392–4. In *Il.* xiii 59–60 Poseidon, in order to make the Ajaces fit for the impending battle with Hector, beats them with his staff, but he does not change them. The magic effect of the action of touching has already receded into the background.

434. ῥάκος ἄλλο: presumably replacing his χλαῖνα (cf. viii 455) or his φᾶρος. Compare and contrast xiv 341–2 (stripping Odysseus of his Phaeacian clothes would of course be beneath the dignity of the goddess). On the prothysteron see 274, xiv 49, 201, 279, xv 146 = 191, 188, xvi 173, 341 nn.

435. ῥωγαλέα: see 438 and xiv 343 nn. **μεμορυγμένα:** the form μεμορυχμένα, given by a papyrus and as a v.l. by Eustathius, is preferable; it has preserved an archaic remnant (again adopted by Hellenistic poets) of the root that characteristically survived in Μόρυχος, the cult-name of the 'besmeared' Dionysus, see Frisk, *GEW* s.v. μορύττω.

438. = xvii 198, xviii 109. **πυκνὰ ῥωγαλέην:** the lengthening of the final syllable of πυκνά is either due to the nature of the liquid (cf. e.g. ποσσὶ δ' ὑπὸ λιπαροῖσιν and Leumann, *Wörter*, 51) or to the fact that ῥωγαλέος still had its initial digamma when the expression was created. As this adj. (not found after Homer) is an archaism, and since its connection with the neut. pl. πυκνά recalls ἔξοχ' ἄριστος, the latter alternative seems preferable; cf. also ἀνὰ ῥῶγας μεγάροιο (*Od.* xxii 143, see 306, xiv 40, 64, 170, xv 234, 293 nn.), which is also likely to be an inadequately represented pre-Homeric formula.

BOOK XIV: COMMENTARY

1–7. These lines are cited by DH *Comp.* 217 as an example of rhythmical variety and suppleness.

1. ἐκ λιμένος: the bay of Phorcys, see xiii 96, 345.

2. δι᾽ ἄκριας: though originally the acc. with διά, 'through' (in a local sense), must have differed from the (partitive) gen. in denoting mere 'extent' ('the ground traversed'), only the slightest traces of this distinction remain in Homer. The construction itself has already disappeared in the earliest Ionic prose, but is still found in a Pamphylian inscription of the fourth century, see Schwyzer, *Grammatik*, ii 453.

3. δῖον ὑφορβόν: just as in δῖ᾽ Εὔμαιε (xvi 461 etc.) and συβώτης, ὄρχαμος ἀνδρῶν (cf. 22 with n.), the choice of the epithet is strange. It has been thought to express parody or to refer to Eumaeus' noble birth, but according to Parry, *Homeric Verse*, 151–2, it was simply used to denote a person of the heroic age. This explanation is no doubt the right one, but needs the qualification that here we have to do with a late adaptation of an old prototype (δῖος ᾽Οδυσσεύς etc.) that was created for kings and noblemen, cf. also ἱερὴ ἲς Τηλεμάχοιο (xvi 476 etc.), which does not seem particularly suitable for the young man we meet in the *Odyssey*.

4. οἰκήων: 'those who are part of the *oikos*'; the word is employed to denote inmates of the house in general, exclusive of the master (*Il.* v 413, vi 366, *Od.* xvii 533?), slaves (*Od.* iv 245), and in particular those slaves who occupy a favourite position (here and xiv 63), a use that seems to have a parallel in the Gortyn Law Code (see xv 21 n.), which makes a distinction between a ϝοικεύς and a δῶλος. On the vagueness of the term in Homer cf. Finley, *World*, 61: 'Below the main line there were various other divisions, but, unlike the primary distinction between aristocrat and commoner, they seem blurred and they are often undefinable'; see also xv 95, xvi 248, 326 nn. Just as in matters of geography (see xiii 103–7, xiv 335, xv 33, 36, 403 nn.) and in the use of formulae and epithets (see 3 n. and *passim*) this lack of precision may be due to the nature of the epic tradition in which various stages had become confused when the Homeric poems were composed, cf. D. H. F. Gray, 'Homeric Epithets for Things', *CQ* lxi (1947), 109–21 (=G. S. Kirk (ed.), *The Language and Background of Homer* (Cambridge, 1964), 55–67).

5–6. αὐλὴ | ὑψηλὴ δέδμητο: the same phrase as at ix 184–5, where the noun, as here, means a wall surrounding a courtyard (περίδρομος, 7). The sense 'courtyard' predominates in Homer (cf. also the formulae ἐϋρκέος αὐλῆς and ἑρκίον (τειχίον) αὐλῆς, used in both *Iliad* and *Odyssey*) and is found combined with the sense 'wall' in *Il.* v 138–42. The oldest meaning, 'night's lodging', hence 'steading (for cattle) in the fields' (cognate with ἰ-αύ-ω, see Frisk, *GEW*, and Chantraine, *Dictionnaire* s.v.) is still visible in ἄγραυλοι πόριες, ποιμένες ἄγραυλοι, and αὐλίζομαι. **περισκέπτῳ**: probably (and at any rate in the mind of the poet) from σκέπω, 'to shelter', because of 532-3 (as compared with σκέπας ... ἀνέμοιο (v 443 etc.) and ἀνεμοσκεπής (*Il.* xvi 224)), though the verb itself is found for the first time in Hippocrates (see, however, xiii 212 n., S. West on i 426, Heubeck on x 211, and the denominative σκεπάω, xiii 99). Alexandrian poets took it as 'seen from all sides', 'conspicuous'.

10. ῥυτοῖσιν: probably cognate with ἐρύω. The long initial syllable has led some scholars to propose other derivations, but cf. Ruijgh, *Études*, 358 n. 32. Alternatively metrical lengthening might be supposed; see also Hainsworth on vi 267. **ἐθρίγκωσεν**: this word too has been considered an element of parody (see 3 n.), but the shade of meaning it had in Homer's time is unknown.

11. Cf. *Il.* xxiv 452-3 ἀμφὶ δέ οἱ μεγάλην αὐλὴν ποίησαν ἄνακτι | σταυροῖσιν πυκινοῖσι. The Cyclops, however, had enclosed his cave with trees (ix 186).

12. πυκνοὺς καὶ θαμέας: cf. πυκνοὶ καὶ θαμέες (xii 92). Although in early Greek these two adjs. seem to have been near synonyms (cf. θάμ-νος), the latter (which disappeared from spoken language) sometimes has the connotation 'numerous' in Homer; θαμά, 'often', and θαμίζω, 'to do often' suggest that this development set in a considerable time before the epics were composed; see also 85 n. **τὸ μέλαν**: τὸν φλοῦν, 'the bark', according to Aristarchus. Or 'the core'? For the presence of the article see Kühner-Gerth, *Grammatik*, i 579, who cites this case as an example of expressions in which the old pronoun has come to substantivize adjs., ptcps., etc.; cf. also τοῖς ἀγαθοῖσι (xv 324), ὡς αἰεὶ τὸν ὁμοῖον ἄγει θεὸς ὡς τὸν ὁμοῖον (xvii 218), and xiv 414 with n. In such cases 'the original demonstrative force has been so whittled away that we have no alternative but to classify them under the heading of "article"' (Palmer, in *Companion*, 138). Characteristically the phenomenon appears to be more frequent in the *Odyssey* than in the *Iliad* (Chantraine, *Grammaire*, ii 165; see also introduction to xiii–xvi p. 159 and xiii 7, 213, 243, 272, xiv 62, 221, 392, 469, 473, xv 22, 88, 98, 125, 236-7, 310, 322, 329, 369, xvi 42, 184-5, 191, 216, 234, 256, 290, 336-7). **δρυὸς**: the meaning 'tree' goes back to Indo-European and is still found in Homer (e.g. in δρυτόμος (*Il.* xi 86), cf. also the scholl. and Myc. *du-ru-to-mo*, PY Vn 10 (Ventris–Chadwick, *Documents*, no. 252) and in several cpds. But the word soon came to mean 'oak' (e.g. 328) and oak-wood must have served Eumaeus' purpose best.

13. ποίει: the change from the plpf. (6) to aors. (8 etc.) which merely state the facts, and then to the durative-descriptive impf. is noteworthy.

15. χαμαιευνάδες: see Heubeck on x 242-3. **ἐρχατόωντο**: a typical instance of an artificial form (from ἔρχατο, 'they were enclosed', cf. Meister, *Kunstsprache*, 72, Risch, *Wortbildung*, 321), Leumann, *Wörter*, 178 ff.; see 73 n.

16. ἐκτὸς ἴαυον: cf. 532-3 and 5-6 n.

18. ἀντίθεοι μνηστῆρες: νῦν οἱ ἐναντίοι τοῖς θεοῖς (!) schol. According to Eustathius 'because of their beauty, race, riches, courage' (of which

Ameis–Hentze–Cauer and Stanford only leave physical perfection), whereas for Parry, *Homeric Verse*, 122–3, the epithet was no more than ornamental and its idea had nothing to do with the idea of the sentence. This last explanation comes nearest to the truth, but it does not follow that this particular combination was a 'traditional formula' (it occurs only here). The epithet was probably borrowed from formulae such as ἀντίθεον θεράποντα, ἀντιθέοις ἑτάροισι, etc. and the expression is no doubt a late adaptation, cf. 3, 22, 438, 453–6 nn. The formulae normally used for the nom., μνηστῆρες ἀγήνορες and μνηστῆρες ἀγαυοί, though typically 'epic', are less honorific.

19. ζατρεφέων: see xiii 410 n.   **σιάλων:** already attested in Mycenaean, PY Cn 608 (Ventris–Chadwick, *Documents*, no. 75).

21. θήρεσσιν: 'wild beasts', 'beasts of prey', as often; never said of domestic animals. Even nowadays the comparison applies to Greek dogs on isolated farms.

22. ὄρχαμος ἀνδρῶν: a schol. refers to Eumaeus' noble birth (mentioned at xv 413 ff.), which will not do, since at xx 185, 254 the expression is used of the obscure Philoitios; see 3 n.

23. Imitated by Theoc. xxv 102–3. On πέδιλα see xv 369 n.

24. εὔχροές: an unusual form, but cf. μελαγχροιής (*Od.* xvi 175). Later εὔχροος is the current word (Hippocrates, Xenophon), so the variant εὔχροον is clearly due to modernization of the text. It is doubtful whether here the mere colour is meant; cf. also πέδιλα βοὸς ἶφι κταμένοιο (Hes. *Op.* 541 and West ad loc.).

27. ὑπερφιάλοισιν: see xvi 346–7 n.

28. ἱερεύσαντες: the meaning of 'sacrificing' is as good as lost here.

29. ὑλακόμωροι: etym. and meaning of -μωρος are unknown.

30. κεκλήγοντες: a semi-Ionicized form (Aeolic κεκλάγοντες), cf. Wathelet, *Traits*, 324–9; as a survival of course to be retained here and elsewhere (*Il.* xii 125 etc.; Aristarchus preferred κεκληγῶτες (schol. *Il.* xvi 430), but why should a 'metrically lengthened' κεκληγότες have been changed to κεκλήγοντες?); see also Chantraine, *Grammaire*, i 430–1, Russo on ἐρρίγοντι, ps.-Hes. *Sc.* 228.

30–2. On the effectiveness of Odysseus' behaviour and the inconsistency between 31 and 32 see Hainsworth, 'Odysseus and the Dogs', *G&R*[2] viii (1961), 122–5, who rightly adds that an archaic epic is tolerant of incongruence in the combination of different topics; see also 86–8 n.

33. μετασπών: probably an archaism transmitted in the body of a formula, not, with Shipp, *Studies*, 340, to be regarded as a wrong active form (what about μεθέπεις (*Od.* i 175), μέθεπε (*Il.* v 329), etc.?). Although the semasiological development is obscure, certain compounds of the old verb ἕπω (< *sep- 'to be busy about', 'to tend') would seem to have acquired the connotation of 'movement' rather early (cf. also πότμον ἐπέσπον etc., ἐπὶ ἔργον ἔποιεν, *Od.* xiv 195) under the influence of ἕπομαι (< *seqʷ-).

37. ὀλίγου: 'nearly', with a mere indicative (only here), has sometimes been taken as an Atticism, but Ionic (not to speak of Lesbian and Arcado-

Cyprian) is too little known in this respect to justify that conclusion; Stanford supplies χρόνου.

38. κέν ... κατέχευας: lit.: 'you would have poured over me', cf. *Il.* xxiii 408 μὴ σφῶϊν ἐλεγχείην καταχεύῃ. In its proper sense the word is used with 'water', 'mist', 'snowflakes', etc.; as a metaphor esp. with χάριν (*Od.* ii 12 etc.) and once with πλοῦτον (*Il.* ii 670). On the nature of such metaphors cf. xiii 50 n.

40. ἀντιθέου γὰρ ἄνακτος: the 'neglect' of the digamma of ϝάναξ may have resulted from the insertion of γάρ, the original formula being ἀντιθέοιο ϝάνακτος, cf. 20, xiii 185 nn.; more examples in Hoekstra, *Modifications*, 54 ff. On the gen. see xiii 219 n.

41. ἧμαι, ἄλλοισιν δὲ: Stanford regards this as a 'legitimate' hiatus, a term which since Milman Parry (see *Homeric Verse*, 191–221) has lost much of its force. In this case the phenomenon, esp. striking between two spondees, is due to ἧμαι being used as an isolated run-over word, as against ἧσται ὀδυρόμενος (*Il.* xix 345, *Od.* xvi 145), ἧσται ἐνὶ μεγάροισιν (*Od.* xiii 337 etc.). Its relatively late character is, moreover, shown by ἄλλοισιν δέ (with numovable making 'position'); cf. xiii 213 n. and introduction to xiii–xvi, pp. 158–9.

43. For ἐπί, 'through' (not 'to'), cf. iii 252 πλάζετ' ἐπ' ἀνθρώπους, but in πολλὰ βροτῶν ἐπὶ ἄστε' ἀλώμενος (ἐπὶ ἄστεα διηνθῆναι) (xv 492, xix 170, xvi 63) this meaning is less certain. The formula δῆμόν τε πόλιν τε (vi 3 etc.) is used here in a collective sense.

46–7. As usual, eating and drinking takes precedence over making a closer acquaintance.

49. εἶσεν δ': because of the seemingly illogical sequence Ameis–Hentze–Cauer translate 'offered him a seat'. This is unnecessary: what is most important is mentioned first, see xiii 434 n.

50–1. Cf. xvi 47 with n.   **ἰονθάδος:** 'shaggy'; only here in Greek, but cognates are found in prose, see Chantraine, *Dictionnaire* s.v.   **αὐτοῦ ἐνεύναιον:** 'on which he himself used to sleep', cf. also xvi 35.

52. ἔκ τ' ὀνόμαζε: in view of the unambiguous meaning of ὄνομα this formula must originally have meant 'and called his (her) name', an expression added to ἔπος τ' ἔφατ' because of the importance of the act not only in prayer and cult, but also with regard to mortals (cf. e.g. 145–6 and R. Harder, *Eigenart der Griechen* (Freiburg, 1962), 14). In Homer, however, it is used without a name following in the large majority of cases. This means that in those lines we have again to do with a loosely employed formula, cf. xiii 185 n. (In our case the possibility that, although this is not mentioned in his actual speech, the speaker does address the other person by his name is obviously ruled out by the situation). A satisfactory translation of the phrase is of course out of the question. See further S. West on ii 302 and Hainsworth on v 181.

55. προσέφης, Εὔμαιε συβῶτα: in the *Iliad* several persons are addressed by the poet himself, esp. Patroclus, and sometimes this apostrophe serves to heighten the pathos of the scene (as was already observed by the schol. on

Il. xvi 787). In the case of Eumaeus, however, it is difficult to see why this should be the case in the 15 places where the phrase occurs (merely to avoid the hiatus?). Probably we have to do with a late adaptation of older formulae (such as προσέφη πόδας ὠκὺς Ἀχιλλεύς (24 times) etc.) to a character that largely owes his prominence in the *Odyssey* to the poet—as Patroclus probably does in the *Iliad*. On the other hand the fact that Patroclus, when mentioned for the first time in the *Iliad* (i 307), is simply called 'the son of Menoetius' shows that he was already known to the audience, and the absence—here or e.g. iv 640 ff.—of a formal introduction may suggest the same for the name of Eumaeus and *a fortiori* for the motif of 'the faithful swineherd' (on the latter see V. Zhirmunsky, 'The Epic of "Alpamysh" and the Return of Odysseus', in *Proceedings of the British Academy*, lii (1966), 270, 278, 284). The name itself (whose connection with μαίομαι 'is not obvious', Chantraine, *Dictionnaire* s.v.) might be a shortened form of εὐμενής (not in Homer, but implied by εὐμενέτῃσι (vi 185); Lin. B *e-u-me-ne* is a man's name) and may have been made by folklore on the model of Ἀνταῖος etc. (Πτολεμαῖος in Homer).

56. θέμις: originally 'what has been laid down' (on its difficult etymology see Frisk, *GEW*, and Chantraine, *Dictionnaire* s.v. The word, very frequent in Homer (e.g. in ἦ (ἧ, οὐ) θέμις ἐστί (ἦεν) 17 times), is sometimes associated with Zeus and royal power (e.g. in Διὸς μεγάλοιο θέμιστες *Od.* xvi 403) and may in Mycenaean have been the term for 'due', cf. Webster, *Mycenae*, 25–6, 106, 121. It tends to become 'custom' and to be used as a synonym of δίκη, see 59 n.

58–9. ~ vi 207–8, see below.　　**δόσις … ἡμετέρη:** again an adaptation of a standing expression. Here the adj. φίλη is used in an 'active' sense, 'friendly', a meaning comparatively rare in Homer and due to a later development of φίλος (originally 'own'?, cf. Chantraine, *Études*, 15 and M. Landfester, *Das griechische Nomen φίλος und seine Ableitungen* (Hildesheim, 1966), 1 ff., but also E. Benveniste, *Le Vocabulaire des institutions indo-européennes* (Paris, 1969), i 338–53). *Od.* vi 208 δόσις δ' ὀλίγη τε φίλη τε and *Il.* i 167 ὀλίγον τε φίλον τε (ἔρχομ' ἔχων) have preserved the older meaning.

59. δίκη: here 'way', 'manner', the oldest traceable meaning in Greek (from an old Indo-European root found e.g. in Sanskrit diś- = Greek δείκνυμι). Coupled with θέμις in οὔτε δίκας εὖ εἰδότα οὔτε θέμιστας (*Od.* ix 215), but in Hes. *Op.* 9 we already find δίκη δ' ἴθυνε θέμιστας (in a prayer addressed to Zeus; cf. also *Op.* 221, *Th.* 85–6, 235–6). On this much-discussed subject see now H. Lloyd Jones, *The Justice of Zeus* (Berkeley, 1971), esp. 166.

61. κατὰ νόστον ἔδησαν: the same metaphor as in κατέδησε κελεύθους (κέλευθα) (v 383, x 20), but we also find ἔδησε κελεύθου (iv 380 = 469), cf. βλάπτουσι κελεύθου (i 195).

62. ἐνδυκέως: here 'carefully', but see 109 with n.　　**κτῆσιν ὄπασσεν:** here and at xxi 214 (see below) the verb has become an 'epic' synonym for mere 'giving'. Often, however, the original sense of this verb (used as causative of ἕπομαι), 'to send along with', (cf. ὀπάων, ὀπηδός, 'companion'), is still observable in Homer, e.g. in ἅμα λαὸν ὄπασσε (*Il.* xviii 452, cf. also *Od.* xv

119). In *Il.* xiv 491 the formula denotes a gift of Hermes, god of the shepherds, to Phorbas ('Grazier'), who was 'rich in flocks', πολύμηλος. Characteristically it has been given the form κτήματ' ὀπάσσω at *Od.* xxi 214 so as to suit changed conditions.

63. οἰκῆϊ: see 4 n.   **ἄναξ:** see xiii 185 n.

64. The line summarizes a theme well known in *Märchen* and heroic poetry, cf. *Il.* vi 192 ff., *Od.* vii 312 ff., Hes. fr. 37, 11 ff. M–W, where the king of Lycia, Alcinous, and Proitos act (or consider to act) in the same way towards Bellerophon, Odysseus, and Bias. This origin accounts for the presence of πολυμνήστην, which seems to be on a par with δῖος (ὑφορβός) and ὄρχαμος (ἀνδρῶν), cf. 3 n. Here 'parody' is out of the question, and using the term 'much-wooed' because of his princely origin would seem rather unrealistic and presumptuous on the part of Eumaeus. Probably the phrase οἶκον ... γυναῖκα was traditional in several forms (οἶκος καὶ κλῆρος also at *Il.* xv 498) and Hesiod's οἶκον μὲν πρώτιστα γυναῖκά τε βοῦν τ' ἀροτῆρα (*Op.* 405) is an adaptation of one of them, cf. Hoekstra, *Mnemosyne*[4] iii (1950), 91 ff. The order of 64 and 65 has been rightly explained by van der Valk, *Textual Criticism*, 60, with reference to *Od.* xviii 357–8, as due to Eumaeus mentioning first what is for him the most important point; see also xiii 434 n.

65. ἔργον ἀέξῃ: Hes. has ἔργον ὀφέλλει (*Op.* 412), cf. 223 n.

67. αὐτόθι γήρᾳ: this reading, though weakly attested, (*i.a.* by the Monacensis 519 B, Ludwich's U, app. crit.) deserves serious consideration because an unaugmented form may well go with an archaism (cf. γήρας (*Il.* xvii 197), ptcp. of an athematic aor., Chantraine, *Grammaire*, i 380). However, we also find ἐνὶ μεγάροισιν ἐγήρα (*Il.* vii 148). In our line ἐγήρα may have been understood as an impf. of γηράω (=γηράσκω), cf. ἀπηύρα (xiii 132 n.).

68. ὤφελλ': a non-Ionic form, see Chantraine, *Grammaire*, i 314.
Ἑλένης: the testimonies from antiquity (e.g. DH i 20. 3, schol. Dionysius Thrax, *Grammatici Graeci*, 187 Hilgard) which mention an initial digamma are late and of a literary nature, and, accordingly, have been generally disregarded in the recent past. However, confirmation has now been provided by the discovery of a sixth-century inscription, see H. W. Catling–C. Cavanagh, 'Two Inscribed Bronzes from the Menelaion, Sparta', *Kadmos*, xv (1976), 146–77. For epic poetry this means that if the abduction of Helen was among its older subjects, the digammated form of the name must have been part of early formulae. However, only a few traces of this state of affairs remain in Homer, the most notable being Ἀλέξανδρος Ἑλένης πόσις ἠυκόμοιο.

68–9. ὀλέσθαι | πρόχνυ: cf. ἀπόλωνται | πρόχνυ (*Il.* xxi 459–60). Though the aspiration is difficult to explain, the archaic advb. (after Homer only in a few imitations) must mean 'with the knees forward', 'going down to the knees', cf. also *Il.* ix 570 πρόχνυ καθεζομένη. It suits ὀλέσθαι as a graphic description of a dying soldier, cf. γνὺξ δ' ἔριπ' οἰμώξας (*Il.* v 68 etc.), and the current formulae λύτο γούνατα, (ὑπὸ) γούνατ' ἔλυσε, γούνατ' ἐδάμνα.

70. τιμῆς: oscillates between 'satisfaction' and 'honour', cf. e.g. *Il.* i 159 τιμὴν ἀρνύμενοι Μενελάῳ σοί τε.

72. Eumaeus girds himself for the work just as in Hes. *Op.* 345 people gird themselves for a journey.

73. ἔρχατο: a curious but certainly Homeric form, not to be read (with van Leeuwen) as εἴρχατο (ἐρχατόωντο was derived from it, see 15 with n.); sometimes regarded as a cognate of ἔρχατος, 'enclosure' (Hesych.), and Lithuanian *sergmi*, 'to guard' (see Bechtel, *Lexilogus*, 141). However, the poet seems to have taken it as a plpf. of ϝέργνυμι, (ἐ)ϝέργω, cf. Leumann, *Wörter*, 178 ff. If he was right in doing so, the absence of reduplication is hard to explain. Are we dealing with a case of drastic modification (influence of ἔρκος? Cf. *Il.* xvi 481, 'are a fence')? *Il.* xvii 354 ἔρχατο is preceded by γάρ (cf. 40 n.: < *σάκεσσι ϝεϝέρχατο?); in *Od.* ix 221, x 283 the form occurs as a run-over word. None of these cases looks traditional; cf., on the other hand, ἐέρχατο (*Od.* x 241), where the 'neglect' of the digamma might be due to the 'exposed' position of the verb after the trochaic caesura.

74. ἱέρευσεν: see 28 n.

75. ἀμφ' ὀβελοῖσιν ἔπειρεν: lit.: 'he pierced them so as to make them stick round the spits'.

77. αὐτοῖς ὀβελοῖσιν: 'spits and all', *dativus sociativus*, cf. e.g. αὐτῷ φάρει (viii 186), αὐτῇσι βόεσσιν (xx 219). In such expressions the preposition ξύν (σύν) is sometimes added, but the mere dat. remains current in classical Greek.

78. κισσυβίῳ: ἀγροικικῷ ἐκπώματι, 'a rustic drinking vessel', schol.; in Homer also at *Od.* ix 346 and xvi 52 (= xiv 78). On its size and shape already the Alexandrian poets and scholars disagreed, cf. Athen. xi 476 f–477 e as compared with Theoc. i 38, and Gow, *Theocritus*² (Cambridge, 1952), ad loc. In antiquity its name was sometimes derived from κισσός, 'ivy(-wood)' (see e.g. Athen. 477 a and schol. ix 346), but that is probably due to popular etymology. That the same vessel is called a δέπας in l. 149 of Theocritus' poem is not surprising, because there its proud owner is speaking.

82. ὄπιδα: the meaning here and in 88 oscillates between older '(divine) regard', 'watch (kept by the gods)' (cf. θεῶν ὄπιν xxi 28 etc., and Hes. *Op.* 187 etc.) and 'vengeance' (ἀπὸ τῷ δώωσι κακὴν ὄπιν Hes. *Th.* 222). Hdt. uses it in the sense 'respect for the gods'.

83. σχέτλια ἔργα: also ix 295, xxii 413. On the original meaning of the adj. see xiii 293 n. In this formula it has already come to mean 'reckless' or even 'cruel' (ix 295). Its use in xi 474, where it is followed by πῶς ἔτλης ... shows an intermediate stage in this development.

84. δίκην: here already 'justice', or coming quite close to it.

85. δυσμενέες καὶ ἀνάρσιοι: according to H. Trümpy, *Fachausdrücke*, 181 ff., these words are synonyms and both mean *hostes*. Although this is doubtless the connotation which has come to predominate in a number of cases in the *Iliad* (e.g. xvi 521) and the *Odyssey* (e.g. x 459), it deserves attention that in those lines the words are used separately. In our line, however, they are found combined. As this expression recurs at *Il.* xxiv 365 (in apposition to οἵ), it is probably a formula, and since most formulae are of pre-Homeric origin, it is not surprising that this particular phrase has preserved the older meaning of either word in these two places, viz. 'evil-disposed (people)' and '(men) not conforming to the rules (of society; of decent warfare)' respectively; ἀνάρσιοι (cf. ἀρ-αρ-ίσκω) means 'ill-adapted', cf. also ἄρτια βάζειν and ἄρθμιος, xvi 427 n.

86-8. The mention of Zeus as the god who gives booty to wicked people and privateers (and clearly *not* as the guardian of justice) alongside ὄπιδος (88) is typical of the amalgam of the conceptions of the gods in the epics. Hesiod's view of Zeus is much more consistent, cf. e.g. *Op.* 267 ff. πάντα ἰδὼν Διὸς ὀφθαλμὸς καὶ πάντα νοήσας | καί νυ τάδ', αἴ κ' ἐθέλησ', ἐπιδέρκεται, οὐδέ ἑ λήθει, | οἵην δὴ καὶ τήνδε δίκην πόλις ἐντὸς ἐέργει, though αἴ κ' ἐθέλησ' contains a qualification. After 86 punctuate with a comma: καί (85) is taken up by καί, 'even' (88), with a slight anacoluthon. See also Ruijgh, τε épique, 748 ff.

86. βῶσιν: the contracted form of this subjunctive (confined to the *Odyssey*: ἀναβῇ ii 358, ἐπιβῆτον xxiii 52) and its use in a 'violent' enjambment with nu-movable making 'position' (see xiv 41, xv 78-9 nn.) are characteristic of a comparatively recent and free type of composition, contrast e.g. ἐπιβείομεν (ἐπιβήομεν) (vi 262, x 334) closing the 4th foot, cf. xiii 182 n. Criticism of a certain aspect of the heroic way of life (see 262 n., where Odysseus is the narrator, and S. West on i 398) involves innovation in form.

89. θεοῦ ... αὐδήν: cf. θεοῦ ὀμφῇ (iii 215 = xvi 96 and *Il.* xx 129).

90. ὅ τ': called a *conjonction chimérique* by Ruijgh, τε épique, 810 ff., who argues that we have to do with a causal connotation of ὅτε, 'when', 'now that', but see 221, 366 nn. With its use here compare e.g. χωόμενος ὅ τ' ἄριστον Ἀχαιῶν οὐδὲν ἔτισας (*Il.* i 244). **δικαίως:** 'according to the custom'. Negatively this involves the absence of wanton violence ὕβρις τε βίη τε (xv 329 = xvii 565, cf. also iii 216, xvi 255), positively it involves a behaviour such as is implied in Telemachus' reproach to the suitors in ii 52-3, cf. also *Il.* xxii 471-2, where it is said of Andromache ὅτε μιν κορυθαίολος ἠγάγεθ' Ἕκτωρ | ἐκ δόμου Ἠετίωνος, ἐπεὶ πόρε μυρία ἕδνα, passages which show that in our line the meaning 'justly' is still difficult to distinguish from 'according to custom'; see also 59 with n.

93. Cf. Διὸς ὧραι (*Od.* xxiv 344), Διὸς μεγάλου ἐνιαυτοί (*Il.* ii 134), and xv 297 with n.

94. ἱρεύουσ' (I. Bekker, ἱερεύουσ' MSS, but cf. xix 198, *sim.*) **ἱερήϊον:** a clear instance of the amalgam of forms in epic diction, see Thumb-Scherer, *Handbuch*, ii 88, 250.

97-8. ἠπείροιο ... Ἰθάκης: not 'local', but partitive gens. (meaning 'within the range of', cf. e.g. Schwyzer, *Grammatik*, ii 111-12), of which only a few survivals remained after Homer outside poetry.

100-1. 'This custom of grazing flocks belonging to the islands on the mainland is still practised in NW Greece' (Stanford). In the parallel

COMMENTARY

passage *Il.* xi 678–9 one MS, the Vindobon. 5, reads μήλων; here this MS also reads οἰῶν, but Strabo 453 has μήλων. Since goats are mentioned separately in the next line, οἰῶν is genuine. The hiatus is likely to have resulted from a modification of an older formula, *πώεα μήλων (πώεσι μήλων iv 413; the contracted form οἰῶν, though certainly Homeric, cf. e.g. οἰῶν πώεα καλά xii 129, is relatively late). Alternatively we might have a case of misapplication of a formula (cf. xiii 185 n.) that was 'corrected' after Strabo's time (and perhaps earlier in some branches of the tradition).

101. = *Il.* xi 679.   **αἰπόλια πλατέ' αἰγῶν:** also 103, *Il.* ii 474. πλατέ'(α), here 'wide-ranging' (Leaf), as against μῆλ' ἀδινά (i 92 = iv 320), see xvi 216 n.

104. ἐσχατιῇ: i.e. on the land beyond the cultivated area: the goats fed on lean herbs and shrubs. On the original meaning of ἔσχατος (simply 'he who is outside') see Leumann, *Wörter*, 158 n. 1.   **ἐπὶ ... ὄρονται:** this expression has often been quoted in connection with the Mycenaean tablet PY Ae 134 (Ventris–Chadwick, *Documents*, no. 31) which mentions a 'shepherd ... keeping watch over (*o-pi* = ἐπί) the four-footed (animals)'; ὄρομαι (*o-ro-me-no* (= ὀρόμενος) on the tablet) probably from *ser-, Lat. servare.

105. ἐπ' ἤματι: Monro's 'for the day' is not supported by the lines he quotes nor indeed by any Homeric case. It generally means 'in a single day' (also Hes. *Op.* 43), and a phrase such as τρὶς ἐπ' ἤματι might easily come to mean 'three times a day' (*Od.* xii 105).

109. ἐνδυκέως: here no longer 'carefully', as e.g. 62, but 'eagerly', 'di buona voglia', see C. F. Russo on ps.-Hes. *Sc.* 427. For κρέα see xv 140 n.

110. It seems questionable whether Wackernagel's ἁρπαλέως ('with relish', cf. Risch, *Wortbildung*, 104) goes better with the context than MSS ἁρπαλέως ('greedily'); see also Hainsworth on vi 250.

112–13. The interpretation is open to doubt. Who is the grammatical subject of δῶκε? According to Athen. xi 498, Asclepiades of Myrlea (*c.*100 BC) already took it to be Eumaeus (followed by Monro, van Leeuwen, ed. 1897, and Ameis–Hentze–Cauer), but van Leeuwen, ed. 1917 and Stanford thought it was Odysseus, and if it is, ὁ δ' ... θυμῷ is a parenthesis. The objection to the former explanation is that the change of subject— Odysseus of δείπνησε and ἤραρε, but Eumaeus of δῶκε—has not been expressed and that this feature is contrary to normal epic practice. The other interpretation has been considered impossible because one would not expect a guest (Odysseus) to fill his own cup and offer it to his host (Eumaeus). However, in *Il.* ix 224 Odysseus, though a guest in Achilles' tent, also fills his cup himself (πλησάμενος δ' οἴνοιο δέπας -) and, more important, Stanford has pointed out that he himself offers wine (a meal) to his hostess (a servant of his host, Demodocus) in xiii 57 and viii 475–8 respectively. This may be meant as a tiny piece of character-drawing, and that consideration applies *a fortiori* to Odysseus' gesture in our line: instinctively he is acting as the master, cf. xvi 100, where Odysseus comes much nearer to forgetting the role he is playing (101 n.), and also

Eumaeus' words δαιμόνιε ξείνων (xiv 443 with n.). For these reasons I adopt Stanford's explanation, though with all proper reservations. At any rate καί (112) is apodotic (cf. also xiii 79 and Denniston, *Particles*, 308), a phenomenon which Aristophanes Byzantinus and Aristarchus tried to get rid of, see app. crit.   **σκύφος**: generally taken to denote a cup without a stem and with short, semicircular horizontal handles at the level of the rim or a little lower. For a specimen from classical times see the photography in Stanford xliii–xlix; a rare one from the Geometric period in G. Bruns, *Archaeologia* ii Q, pl. v e, f.

120. **εἴ**: 'if not'. In such cases 'the words imply a slight disposition to accept the affirmative', Leaf on *Il.* v 183, cf. also *Il.* xi 792, xv 403, *Od.* iii 216.

124. **ἄλλως**: with ψεύδοντ'(αι) in the next line (it already tends to acquire the meaning 'merely', which it has attained in the Ionic of Hdt., cf. iv 77. 2 οὗτος ὁ λόγος ἄλλως πέπαισται (v.l. πέπλασται), iii 16. 7 ἄλλως σεμνοῦν, v 41. 2 κομπέειν ἄλλως). Such cases of *Sperrung* do not favour the supposition of Milman Parry that the Homeric poems were created by oral composition in a wholly formulaic language. See also xvi 42 with n.

128. **ἕκαστα μεταλλᾷ**: notwithstanding 122–3, 130. A schol. points to the psychological verisimilitude of this. Stanford, moreover, draws attention to Penelope's loneliness.

130. **θέμις**: see 56 n.; here the sense has developed into 'custom', 'habit'.

131. **παρατεκτήναιο**: cf. *Il.* xiv 54, μῆτιν ἀμύμονα τεκτήναιτο (*Il.* x 19), and παρὰ μοῖραν (*Od.* xiv 509). The cpd. looks comparatively recent.

132. **χλαῖνάν**: not a φᾶρος, as in the parallel formula φᾶρός τε χιτῶνά τε εἵματ' (ἔθηκαν, ἰδοῦσα, vi 214, vii 234), though here the word would have suited the metre equally well; see xiii 67 n. On the other hand the use of the more 'modern' word χλαῖνα is determined by its metrical value, not by the circumstances and the social rank of the person(s) in question, e.g. *Od.* x 542 ἀμφὶ δέ με χλαῖνάν τε χιτῶνά τε εἵματα ἕσσεν (of Odysseus; cf. also iv 50, used in the case of Telemachus and Pisistratus). It appears that for the poet of the *Odyssey* the choice between the antiquated garment and the one still in use depended on the formulaic context, with the restriction that a φᾶρος could not be worn by ordinary persons. In the latter respect Homer's view is not different from that of Hdt., who reserves φᾶρος for foreign priests (ii 122) and kings (ix 109). Its replacement by χλαῖνα may have started before Homer, ἀμφὶ δέ μιν becoming ἀμφὶ δ' ἄρα in the formulae in question.

133. **μέλλουσι**: see xiii 383 n.

134. **ἀπ' ὀστεόφιν**: on the question whether the suffix originally had the force of an ablative and on the problem of the syncretism of case-endings see e.g. Ruijgh, *Études*, 93 and Wathelet, *Traits*, 248–9 and 278 ff.

136. **ψαμάθῳ εἰλυμένα**: cf. ὄρος ψάμμῳ κατειλυμένον (Hdt. ii 8. 2). εἰλυμένος probably from *ϝε-ϝλῡ-μένος, but the original form of the verb is hard to establish (see Chantraine, *Grammaire*, i 131); cf. e.g. εἰλύω (ψαμάθοισιν, *Il.* xxi 319), εἴλῡμα (*Od.* vi 179), ἔλυμα (Hes. *Op.* 430, 436, without digamma), γέλουτρον (Hesych.).

137–8. ἀπόλωλε ... τετεύχαται: the use of the pf. stem serves to stress Eumaeus' convinction that the situation is beyond remedy.

139. ὁππόσ' ἐπέλθω: cf. 43 n.; ὁππόσ' = ὁππόσα.

140. μητέρος: this artificial form is especially striking since it is used alongside πατρός in this formula, cf. Meister, *Kunstsprache*, 18. Eumaeus' father was a *wanax*, but in a different sense, cf. xv 413–14.

142. ἱέμενός περ: see app. crit. From a grammatical point of view there is no objection to ἀχνύμενός περ, since ἰδέσθαι in 143 can depend on ὀδύρομαι: see xiii 219 n.

145. οὐ παρεόντ': note the irony here and in 147 νόσφιν ἐόντα; see also 321–33 with n.

147. ἠθεῖον: according to the scholl. this was the term to address an elder brother, but there is no evidence for this in the few cases in which the word (limited to poetry) occurs. Here it is certainly not used in a traditional context, since the digamma (cf. εἴωθα from *σέ-σϝω-θα, Latin *suēsco*, etc.) is neglected.

149–51. Cf. xxiii 71–3, but there we have ἀλλ' ἄγε and this is preceded by a separate clause, so that the construction is 'regular'. Here, however, we have an ἐπεί-clause, and its adaptation (ἐπεὶ ... ἄπιστος) is not yet complete, a phenomenon which is frequent in Homer (many examples in Denniston, *Particles*, 11), though it is nearly always found with *conditional* clauses; with our line compare e.g. Hdt. ix 48. 3 and esp. ix 42. 2 Ἐπεὶ τοίνυν ὑμεῖς ἢ ἴστε οὐδὲν ἢ οὐ τολμᾶτε λέγειν, ἀλλ' ἐγὼ ἐρέω. So after 150 we should punctuate with a comma.

149. ἀναίνεαι: probably 'you won't hear of it', not 'you deny' so as to be a mere synonym of οὐ φῇσθα, cf. e.g. iii 265, iv 651, xiv 239. Odysseus means that Eumaeus' attitude is negative and that he even rejects the possibility that his guest could bring him any good news about his master.

151. αὔτως: see xiii 281 n.

154. This formulaic line (~ 396, xvi 79, etc.) is omitted in many of our sources (see app. crit.). It probably does not belong here.

156. = ix 312. The phrase 'the gates (or, rather, 'gate', for the word is a *plurale tantum* in Homer) of Hades' is also found at *Il.* v 646, xxiii 71 (πύλας Ἀΐδαο περήσειν/-ήσω), cf. moreover ἀν' (κατ') εὐρυπυλὲς Ἄϊδος δῶ (*Il.* xxiii 74, *Od.* xi 571) and Ἀΐδαο (Ἄϊδος [– – –]), πυλάρταο (κρατεροῖο; *Il.* viii 367, *Od.* xi 277, *Il.* xiii 415). Heaven, too, has a gate (*Il.* v 749 = viii 393) and so have Olympus (*Il.* viii 411), the Sun (*Od.* xxiv 12), the 'Land of Dreams' (δῆμος ὀνείρων, *ibid.*; ἐν ὀνειρείῃσι πύλῃσι *Od.* iv 809, πύλαι ἀμενηνῶν ... ὀνείρων *Od.* xix 562), Tartarus (σιδήρειαί τε πύλαι καὶ χάλκεος οὐδός *Il.* viii 15). Are all these gates a product of poetical fantasy, that of Hades included? And how did the poet imagine the relation of this particular gate to its surroundings in view of the fact that he never calls Hades' realm a πόλις nor describes it as surrounded by a wall?

In order to answer the second question we have first of all to realize that, as has often been pointed out, Homer is far from consistent when speaking of Hades' dwelling-place: often he calls it a 'house' (cf. εἰς Ἀΐδαο δόμους etc.), often he regards it as an area in the depths of the earth or on the other side of Ὠκεανός (*Od.* x 508 ff. etc.), twice he mentions a 'field of asphodel' (*Od.* xi 539, xxiv 13), and once he speaks of ἐν Πύλῳ, ἐν νεκύεσσι in connection with Hades (*Il.* v 395-7), cf. e.g. D. Wachsmuth in *Der kleine Pauly* v s.v. *Unterwelt*, 3, 1055, and H. J. Rose, *A Handbook of Greek Mythology*[3] (London, 1945), 79, who also observes that 'consistency in such matters ... is not to be looked for in the traditions of any people'. Hence it is not surprising that there is no clearly marked relation between the 'gate' and any surroundings whatever. But is this all there is to say? We find that in historical times local traditions of places having 'entrances to the underworld' still survived in many parts of Greece (see e.g. E. Rohde, *Psyche*[5] (Tübingen, 1925), i 213); and since the formula Ἀΐδαο πυλάρταο (see below and Heubeck on xi 277) and the tale about Heracles wounding the god ἐν Πύλῳ, ἐν νεκύεσσι (*Il.* v 395-7, on which passage most recently Kirk, *Myths*, 191) are also highly archaic, it follows that the conception of 'the gate of Hades' is very old and in the past had no connection (or had lost any connection long before Homer) with any other ideas about the god's kingdom. It was simply a piece of genuine popular belief which became part of epic diction at an early date and was ultimately inherited, as such, by Homer (Ἀΐδαο πύλῃσι in our line makes a slightly worn-out impression). And this makes it possible to answer the first question in so far that Homer (and perhaps already some of his recent predecessors) elaborated this conception (e.g. in *Il.* xxiii 74, *Od.* xi 571), by adding εὐρυπυλές (δῶ), which is proved more recent than πυλάρταο by its suffix, and extended it to the Tartarus and to the 'Land of Dreams' by association.

158-9. = xvii 155-6 etc.; see also app. crit. 159, at any rate, is less appropriate here than in xvii, because of ἱστίη τ᾽ Ὀδυσῆος. Telemachus' σταθμῷ ἐν ἡμετέρῳ (xvi 45), quoted by Ameis–Hentze–Cauer, does not provide a parallel.

158. The absence of compensatory lengthening in ξενίη is difficult to explain, cf. Chantraine, *Grammaire*, i 161-2. According to Meister, *Kunstsprache*, 208, contemporary Ionic already had ξένος etc., and ξεῖνος (i.e. ξῆνος) is merely an adaptation of pre-Homeric and traditional ξένϝος, even adopted by Ionian authors such as Heraclitus and Hdt. However, since the latter assertion is highly questionable (on the spurious diphthong ει in prose inscriptions of the sixth century see Thumb–Scherer, *Handbuch*, ii 252), it is perhaps preferable to adopt Wathelet's explanation, *AC* i (1981), 819-33, who ascribes the phenomenon to influence of singers from Euboea on Homer. As to ἱστίη, Wyatt, *Lengthening*, 162-4, holds that its second syllable was 'metrically' lengthened on the analogy of -ίη in compounds which originally had -είη.

160-4. In antiquity some or all of these lines were for several reasons suspected of having been interpolated, partly from xix 303-7 (see app. crit.). Some modern scholars have argued that the oath is at variance with Eumaeus' words in 171, but cf. 392.

COMMENTARY

160. τελείεται: a *praesens profeticum*, here not so much used to denote an instant fut. (thus Chantraine, *Grammaire*, ii 190)—although this idea too may play a part (cf. 161)—as to stress the firmness of the beggar's conviction in the face of Eumaeus' incredulity, see Kühner–Gerth, i 138, Schwyzer, *Grammatik*, ii 273.

161. λυκάβαντος: of unknown etymology: scholl. explain it as 'year' (with absurd derivations); sometimes connected with *λυκ- and βαίνω—see Stanford and Ameis–Hentze, *Anhang*, ad loc.—and according to H. Koller, *Glotta*, li (1973), 29–33, from *λυκα βάντα; probably a pre-Greek word which survived in Arcadian (cf. Ruijgh, *Élément*, 147, *Studia Mediterranea Piero Meriggi dicata* (ed. O. Carruba, Pavia, 1979), 559–60) and cognate with Λυκαβηττός, the pre-Greek name of the Attic mountain. At any rate the word can hardly be taken to mean 'the day of the new moon' (Leumann, *Wörter*, 212 n. 4) in the *Odyssey*, for in that case τοῦδ' αὐτοῦ would be incomprehensible not only here (where interpolation might be assumed), but also in xix 306: there the next day would be meant, so that, humanly speaking, Penelope would hardly have reacted the way she actually does. In sum, the next line is rather a specification than an explanation, and the poet of the *Odyssey* understood the noun either as 'year' or '(period of a) month' (Ruijgh); see also 162 n.

162. φθίνοντος μηνός: the old meaning of μείς, 'moon', is still felt in this expression, cf. Leumann, *Wörter*, 213, and Stanford ad loc. The view that Penelope was originally a moon-goddess and Odysseus a sun-god returning at the first new moon of the year was widely held in the nineteenth century (cf. e.g. O. Seeck, *Quellen der Odysse* (Berlin, 1887), 267 ff.) but later abandoned as mere speculation; see also 457 n. In this connection a more recent derivation of the name of Penelope (from πήνη, 'the woof', and *elop, cf. ὀλόπτω, 'to tear out') proposed by Kretschmer (see Frisk, *GEW* s.v.) deserves notice. Whatever this may imply, certain independent indications (cf. xv 526 n. and, in general, Austin, *Archery*, 244–53) suggest that the return of the hero on the day of the new moon was an element of the pre-Homeric saga.

170. κεδνοῖο: etym. and original meaning uncertain; after Homer confined to poetry and in the epics always found in phrases which have no late characteristics (e.g. ἄλοχον(-ους) κεδνήν(-άς), *κεδνὰ ϝιδυῖα(ν), 5 times), so the expression κεδνοῖο ἄνακτος may well be an inadequately represented pre-Homeric formula see xiii 438 n.

174–84. These lines too were suspected by an ancient grammarian (probably Aristarchus, cf. van der Valk, *Textual Criticism*, 190), but here the scholl. abstain from criticism.

174. ἄλαστον: 'without the grief leaving my thoughts'; from λαθ-, cf. Homeric λήθομαι, 'forget'.

175. θρέψαν ... ἔρνεϊ ἶσον: the comparison and its poetic form are likely to be much older than Homer (note the conspicuous hiatus resulting from the dropping of the initial digamma of ἶσος), cf. *Il.* xviii 56 = 437 ὁ δ' ἀνέδραμεν ἔρνεϊ ἶσος and the next line: τὸν μὲν ἐγὼ θρέψασα φυτὸν ὣς γουνῷ ἀλωῆς. The

204

image was elaborated by the poet(s) of the *Iliad* and the *Odyssey* into refined similes: *Il.* xvii 53–8, *Od.* vi 163–7; see also xiii 388 n.

176. χέρεια: (*potius χέρηα?*) the origin of this comparative form is uncertain; see Risch, *Wortbildung*, 90 with n.

177. ἀγητόν: probably masc. as in δέμας καὶ εἶδος ἀγητός *Il.* xxiv 376, εἶδος ἀγητοί *Il.* v 787 = viii 228 (but φυὴν καὶ εἶδος ἀγητὸν | "Εκτορος *Il.* xxii 370–1). εἶδος ἀγητός comes within the category of those formulae that were liable to expansion, a usage 'especially common among the −∪∪−∪ formulae. The effect is to bring back the whole phrase to the main caesura', Hainsworth, *Flexibility*, 82–3, who cites e.g. ⟨μένος καὶ⟩ χεῖρες (-ας) ἄαπτοι(-ους), 6 times, ⟨θάνατος καὶ⟩ μοῖρα κραταιή (6 times). The adj. comes from ἀγάομαι, a thematic form appearing alongside ἄγαμαι.

178. τὸν δέ: a slight anacoluthon. Since ἐπεί (175) has a temporal sense, the use of the particle is not to be explained (with Ameis–Hentze–Cauer) on the assumption that the clause was still felt to be independent, the less so as δέ 'apodoticum' immediately following the protasis is common in Homer, see Denniston, *Particles*, 178 ff. **βλάψε φρένας:** cf. φρενοβλαβής, found e.g. in Hdt. **ἐΐσας:** The use of this adj. in connection with φρένες is confined to this formula, which occurs only here and in εἶδός τε μέγεθός τε ἰδὲ φρένας ἔνδον ἐΐσας (xi 337 = xviii 249; note the correspondence of the former hemistich with δέμας καὶ εἶδος in 177). Just how the expression is to be understood is hard to say. Probably the epithet still had a semi-concrete meaning, cf. πυκινὰς φρένας (*Il.* xiv 294 ~ πυκινὰς στίχας etc.), πυκινὸν νόον (*Il.* xv 461 ~ πυκινὸν δόμον etc.). It may even have been borrowed from the primitive ship- and shield-formulae (νῆας ἐΐσας, ἀσπίδα πάντοσ' ἐΐσην) at a rather late stage. If so, it may have meant something like 'well-balanced' (if the modern associations are subtracted from the translation); cf. xvi 310 n.

179. μετὰ πατρὸς ἀκουήν: see xiii 415 n.

182. Ἀρκεισίου: the father of Laertes. In iv 755 one MS has Ἀρκεσσιάδαο, from which Fick concluded that the man belonged to the 'Aeolic' *Odyssey*. His original name, however, may have been Ἀρκέσιος (from ἄρκος (neut.), 'defence', cf. Myc. *We-we-si-jo*, presumably *ϝερϝέσιος, from *ϝέρϝος 'wool') with normal metrical lengthening. As far as we know he has no history—which does not necessarily mean that he is a creation of the poet. The form of his name as well as the incidental way in which he is referred to might point in the opposite direction. Like so many figures who are mentioned by the way in Homer, he may have been important in earlier tales and later have faded from Greek legend; cf. G. Murray, *The Rise of the Greek Epic*⁴ (Oxford, 1934), 220, and xv 231–6 n. Kirk's view (*Myths*, 168, see introduction n. 1) that, with the exception of Odysseus' Trojan connections, neither the hero himself nor his ancestors are 'integrated into the general heroic pattern' and 'involved in the elaborate network of mythical events' is subject to two qualifications (even apart from *Od.* xxi 13–33, which may or may not be a Homeric elaboration): (1) several Homeric passages (e.g. *Od.* xv 186–7) presuppose the existence of pre-migration stories on the mainland which have got irretrievably lost (I deliberately use the vague term 'story', see below); (2) as to those mainland stories which have left slight traces it is always difficult and often impossible to make out whether they come from myths, heroic sagas, or folk-tales (or a mixture of two of these types). The passage about Odysseus' maternal grandfather Autolycus (*Il.* x 266–8) is a case in point.

184. Cf. ὄφρα ἴδητ' αἴ κ' ὔμμιν ὑπέρσχῃ χεῖρα Κρονίων (*Il.* iv 249).

186. ὄφρ' ἐὖ εἰδῶ: cf. xvi 236 n.

187. The usual question in the usual form; see S. West on i 170.

188–90. These verses are repeated four times with slight variations in the first line (i 171 ff., xvi 57 ff., 222 ff.). 190 has been considered a joke that was attributed by the poet to the Ithacans. The partisans of the Ithaca = Leucas theory, on the other hand, have argued that it must have referred to an island that could be reached on foot under certain circumstances (cf. e.g. Cauer, *Homerkritik*, 214–15, who, however, translates πεζὸν as 'by land' because of the ferry mentioned at *Od.* xx 187–8).

195. δαίνυσθαι ἀκέοντ': cf. δαίνυσθαί τ' ἀκέοντα καὶ εὐφραίνεσθαι ἔκηλον (ii 311). According to Stanford, 'in silence' is inappropriate here, but Odysseus may use the word as it were provisionally (so that there is no real contrast with 197) and qualify his meaning in the latter part of the line, cf. 299–301 n. If this interpretation is rejected, we have to translate 'in quiet' (thus Stanford) and to suppose that here the older meaning of the ptcp. (or advb.? Cf. xxi 89 ἀκέων δαίνυσθε καθήμενοι and *Il.* iv 22 = viii 459) has been preserved, cf. xiii 1 n., schol. Pi. *P.* iv 156 on ἀκᾷ, and Leumann, *Wörter*, 167 n.: 'der Kernbegriff des Schweigens liegt in den Iliasstellen noch gar nicht im Wort ἀκήν selbst, sondern in dem dabeistehenden σιγῇ, σιωπῇ'. However, neither 195 (with hiatus) nor ii 311 (with contraction in εὐφραίνεσθαι and 'neglect' of the digamma of ἔκηλον) looks highly archaic, and the poet understood the word as 'in silence' in 110. **ἔποιεν:** see 33 n.

196. ἐνιαυτὸν: originally 'turning-point of the year', 'the day on which the year-cycle is completed' (Bechtel, *Lexilogus*, 125, Frisk, *GEW* s.v.), see now Beekes, *Glotta*, xlvii (1969), 138–42, who shows how the word came to be used for 'year', as in our line (ἅπαντα; yet the preposition still points to the original meaning; properly speaking εἰς ἐνιαυτόν is a remnant of a formula—cf. e.g. 292—which kept its form but changed its meaning, cf. 52 n.). It is better to punctuate with a dash at the end of this line, as Ameis–Hentze–Cauer do, who observe: 'the speaker has λέγοιμι in mind; then he corrects himself before he has completed his sentence and expresses himself even more forcefully'. The transition is facilitated by the fact that εἰς ἐνιαυτόν (see above) can mean 'for a year' and 'within a year', cf. e.g. iv 526, 86 and LSJ s.v. εἰς ii 2.

197. λέγων: see xiii 296 n.

199. ἐκ μὲν Κρητάων: on Crete as the scene of Odysseus' false tales see xiii 256–86 n. The pl. alternates with Κρήτη, just as, conversely, Θήβη with Θῆβαι, etc.: see Ameis–Hentze, *Anhang*, ad loc., van Leeuwen on *Od.* iii 278. Applied to Crete (only here and in the parallel line xvi 62) it is artificial: the tradition had ἀπὸ Κρήτης εὐρείης, Κρήτῃ ἐν εὐρείῃ, etc., and the modification is bound up with the untraditional beginning of the line (on the introduction of μέν see Hoekstra, *Modifications*, 56 ff.), which brought about another innovation (see below). **γένος εὔχομαι:** the normal formula is (γένος) εὔχομαι (-εται etc.) εἶναι, which is no doubt one of the oldest elements of the diction: εὔχετοι in the sense of 'declaring', 'claiming' (see now J.-L. Perpillou, 'La Signification du verbe εὔχομαι dans l'épopée', in *Mélanges de linguistique et de philologie grecques offerts à Pierre Chantraine* (Paris, 1972), 170–1) is Mycenaean (PY Ep 704, Ventris–Chadwick, *Documents*, no. 135, etc.); εἶναι < *ἐσ-ναι (the form ἦναι is found in Arcadian). The traditional position of the shorter form of the formula is after the diaeresis (32 times), of the longer one after the hephthemimeral caesura (3 times); variations in xxi 335, xxiv 269. Thus the absence of the infin. is due to the phrase being shifted into a position for which it was not created and this, in its turn, is closely bound up with the untraditional beginning of the line.

201. τράφεν ἠδ' ἐγένοντο: again a formula (iv 723, x 417, *Il.* i 251) the ancient nature of which is shown by τράφεν (= ἐτράφησαν, cf. e.g. Chantraine, *Grammaire*, i 472, but maybe we should read τράφον, Chantraine, ibid., 390), 'they were brought up', or perhaps rather 'they grew up' (Chantraine, *Morphologie*, 169, 172). The word-order, a prothysteron (cf. e.g. θρέψασα τεκοῦσά τε xii 134, γαμέοντί τε γεινομένῳ τε iv 208), shows the normal epic preference for naming first what is most in evidence, cf. xiii 434 n. It must have been a traditional feature of epic verse-making, cf. xiii 434 n.

203. ἰθαγενέεσσιν: ἰθαιγενέεσιν (see below)? Perhaps from *ἰθα, Prakrit *idha*, 'here' (Risch, *Wortbildung*, 217: *ă > Gr. αι (cf. παραί etc.) > ā). Used in the sense of 'legitimate' (only here) but neither the original meaning of this archaism nor its form (see app. crit. and Ἰθαιμένης *Il.* xvi 586) are certain, see Frisk, *GEW*, and Chantraine, *Dictionnaire* s.v.

204. Κάστωρ Ὑλακίδης: the patronymic is baffling ('Son of the Barking One'?); it might reproduce a pre-Greek Cretan name. Or are we to suppose that κάστωρ, though as a class-noun it means 'beaver', could originally denote a certain race of dogs (cf. καστόριαι (κύνες), X. *Cyn.* iii 1) and that Odysseus is punning?

205. θεὸς ὣς τίετο δήμῳ: the lengthening of the syllable preceding 'postpositive' ὥς is mostly regarded as a survival from the time when the latter still had the form *ϝώς, cf. Frisk, *GEW* s.v., Ruijgh, τε épique, 856. This is consistent with the content of the formula since such a position of a ruler is out of the question in the eighth century and highly doubtful in the Dark Ages: it is most probably a reminiscence of Mycenaean times, cf. Webster, *Mycenae*, 108 and *passim*. Here—the only time it occurs in the *Odyssey*—its significance is no longer understood, for the poet thinks it necessary to add ὄλβῳ τε κτλ. (206) by way of explanation.

207. κῆρες ἔβαν θανάτοιο φέρουσαι: for the etymology of κήρ (uncertain) Chantraine, *Dictionnaire* s.v. Whatever the original conception or mental picture may have been, it is at least certain that in spite of *Il.* xviii 535–40 (exaggerated in ps.-Hes. *Sc.* 249–57), the 'meaning' of this old fem. root noun had already become so abstract to Homer that he could even say θάνατον καὶ κῆρα φυτεύει(-σω) (ii 165, xvii 82) and θάνατον καὶ κῆρ' ἀραρόντε (xvi 169).

209. ἐπὶ κλήρους ἐβάλοντο: certainly not 'they took possession of', but 'they cast lots for (the parcels)'.

211. πολυκλήρων ἀνθρώπων: here 'possessing much land' (cf. 64 with n.), whereas shortly before (209) κλῆρος is still used in the sense of 'lot'. The pl. denotes the tribe of the wife (Monro ad loc.).

212. ἀρετῆς: see xiii 45 and xiv 402 nn.; the translation 'valour' does no justice to the fact that originally the word had a much more general and elementary meaning (cf. the use of ἔργον in the *Iliad* and 222 n.), which is still faintly visible in 214 (see n.)). ἀποφώλιος is probably not cognate with the archaic aor. ἀπαφεῖν (cf. 379), 'to deceive', nor does it mean 'deceptive' (cf. v 182, viii 177), but rather 'unsound', 'sans valeur', 'untauglich', probably from ἀπό (cf. ἀπ-ηλεγέως) and ὀφελ- (W. Schulze, *Quaestiones Epicae* (Gütersloh, 1892), 242–3), cf. e.g. οἶκον ὀφέλλειν, 223 n.

214. καλάμην: of course this is not simply a metaphor for 'old age', as Arist. (who comments 'for both have lost their bloom', *Rh.* iii 1410 b) would have it. It primarily refers to Odysseus' appearance, which is part of his ἀρετή (see 212 n.).

215. δύη ἔχει: see 239 n.

216. Ares and Athena are occasionally associated in Homer (also *Il.* xvii 398, xviii 516), but whereas Athena is primarily the protector of the citadel (cf. xiii 221–5 n.) and partly owes her warlike aspect to the conditions of the society depicted by the poet (see e.g. Guthrie, *Gods*, 106), Ares, as is shown by his epithets (and probably by his name, cf. ἀρή 'harm', 'ruin'), is the fierce god of onslaught and destruction: he is ἆτος πολέμοιο, βροτολοιγός, μιαιφόνος, cf. also Wilamowitz, *Glaube*, i 316, Nilsson, *Geschichte*, i 518–19.

217–18. Cf. λόχονδ' ἰέναι σὺν ἀριστήεσσιν Ἀχαιῶν (*Il.* i 227). In *Il.* xiii 277 Idomeneus explains that the valour of a man is best discerned in an ambush. It is perhaps for this reason that in three of his false tales Odysseus mentions it in connection with himself. In 469, however, the word is already in the act of acquiring its later 'technical' meaning 'troop of soldiers'; in xx 49 it is used in this sense.

218. δυσμενέεσσι: here refers to a war, cf. ἐν πολέμῳ (222 and 225); but see 85 n.

220. ἐπάλμενος: although the athematic asigmatic aor. of ἅλλομαι (< *sal-, cf. Latin *salio*) must be highly archaic (the 'modern' form ἐσήλατο is found at *Il.* xii 438 ∼ xvi 558), in nearly all cases the cpds. show elision of the preposition (ἐπ-, κατεπ-, μετ-). The phenomenon is characteristic of the development of epic diction, in particular if ἐπιάλμενος (*Il.* vii 15, *Od.* xxiv 320) is an archaism—which is uncertain—and if o-pi-a₂-ra, PY An 657 (= Ventris–Chadwick, *Documents*, no. 56), is a cpd. meaning 'the coastal regions'; cf. also Ruijgh, *Études*, 53, and xv 479 n. ἔγχεϊ ἔλεσκον: may go back to ἔγχε' ἔλεσκον, but contraction (with shortening of the final syllable before a vowel) seems more probable. On the other hand uncontracted forms such as ἔγχεϊ (< *-εσ-ι) are remarkably well preserved, cf. ἔγχεϊ μακρῷ etc., cf. Chantraine, *Grammaire*, i 48–50. This is of course due to the influence of the formulaic diction.

221. ὅ τέ μοι: ὅτε μή Bothe (the MS-authority in such cases is slight). Ruijgh, τε *épique*, 464–5 argues that the unusual ἀνδρῶν δυσμενέων = ἀνδρῶν τινα δυσμενέων may have led some grammarians to take ὅτε as ὅ τε, 'any man who', cf. *Il*. xiv 121 Ἀδρήστοιο δ' ἔγημε θυγατρῶν. Yet there the use of the gen. results from an abbreviation of the formula θυγατρῶν εἶδος ἀρίστην (*Il*. xiii 365 etc.), whereas a similar explanation of ἀνδρῶν δυσμενέων is hard to find. On the other hand there are certainly cases in Homer, as Ruijgh himself admits, where τε, though artificial, is genuine (e.g. xvi 216, see n.). εἴξειε πόδεσσι: for an abstract meaning of the verb ('was inferior to me in speed of foot' Stanford) see *Od*. xi 515; for a semi-abstract use, *Od*. xiv 262. Here the phrase makes a concrete impression, and 'shrinking back' (thus also Ameis–Hentze–Cauer) is perhaps to be explained by the poet having in mind some kind of contemporary phalanx (of hoplites? On this hotly debated subject see Snodgrass, *Armour*, esp. 197–9): a withdrawing man would no longer be covered by the shield of his right-hand comrade.

222. ἔα ἐν: to be scanned ἔ' ἐν or ἔα ἰν, but see app. crit. ἔργον: its meaning is specified by the context as e.g. in ἔργον ἐποίχεσθαι, πόλεμος δ' ἄνδρεσσι μελήσει (*Il*. vi 492), and, on the other hand, in those cases where the word is said to mean 'battle' (of course it does not).

223. οἰκωφελίη: from ϝοῖκος (note the 'neglected' digamma) and ὀφέλλω (cf. οἶκος ὀφέλλετο 233, οἶκον ὀφέλλειν xv 21, οἶκον ὀφέλλοι Hes. *Op*. 495), a verb which died out later and was replaced by αὔξω, αὐξάνω (ἀέξω in Homer, cf. e.g. ἔργον ἀέξῃ (65) and *Il*. xv 383 κύματ' ὀφέλλει, *Od*. x 93 ἀέξετο κῦμά γ'). The derivatives ὠφελίη and ὠφελέω are not yet found in the epics—which does not mean that they did not yet exist in Ionic, cf. xiii 2 n.; on their relation with ὀφέλλω see Wyatt, *Lengthening*, 76–7.

224. ἐπήρετμοι: an old type of a cpd. with ἐπι-, little developed after Homer. The prefix is still an advb. (but cf. εἴατ' ἐπήρετμοι (*Od*. ii 403), which is non-formulaic), so the second part does not depend on it; lit.: (ships) 'with oars to them', cf. also ἐπηρεφής (*Od*. x 131), ἔφυδρος (xiv 458), and Debrunner, *Griechische Wortbildungslehre*, op. cit. (xiii 9 n.), 24–5, Risch, *Wortbildung*, 187.

228. Gnomic, hence τε, cf. xv 54, 400 (see Ruijgh, τε *épique*, 721 ff.), and Archil. fr. 25. 2 West, quoted by the schol.

229. Τροίης ἐπιβήμεναι: see 356–7, 469 n.

230–1. The same theme as in 85–7, 245 ff., and in several passages of the *Iliad*, e.g. i 365–8.

230. ὠκυπόροισι νέεσσιν: the form of the noun (with Ionic νε- and Aeolic -εσσι) is artificial and the formula is comparatively late (probably derived from νηυσὶ ... ὠκυπόροισι or νηῶν ὠκυπόρων).

231. τύγχανε πολλά: in Homer this construction only recurs in οὕνεκά μοι τύχε πολλὰ νέῳ πόλεμόνδε κιόντι (*Il.* xi 684). In prose the simplex is replaced by ἐπιτυγχάνω.

232–3. ὀπίσσω|λάγχανον: after the leader of the expedition had set apart a certain amount of booty for himself (ἐξαιρεύμην), the rest of the spoils were distributed by lot and now he received a share like every one of his men, cf. the formula λαχὼν ἀπὸ (λαχόντα τε) ληΐδος αἶσαν (*Od.* xiii 138 etc.). **καί ῥα ἔπειτα:** this phrase is a modification of the pre-Homeric formula αὐτὰρ ἔπειτα, hence the hiatus.

235. εὐρύοπα: the nom. is artificial; it was created, on the analogy of μητίετα Ζεύς, sim., by 'declension' of the age-old formula εὐρύοπα Ζῆν (acc.) < *εὐρύ-ϝοπα Ζ. (this kind of 'declining' was not unusual in a period when epic poetry was still composed by oral improvisation, nor were the resulting forms (cf. also εὐρέα πόντον < εὐρέϊ πόντῳ etc., and Meister, *Kunstsprache*, 18–19; below, 424 n.) felt to be artificial or ungrammatical by the singers, see introduction to xiii–xvi, p. 156). As the god of sky and weather Zeus manifests himself most impressively in the thunder, his 'far-sounding voice', cf. τοῦ καὶ ὑπὸ βροντῆς πελεμίζεται εὐρεῖα χθών (Hes. *Th.* 458).

239. δήμου φῆμις: cf. xv 468 with n., xvi 75. After Homer φῆμις occurs only in poetry. **ἔχε:** lit.: 'held me in its power', as in ἔχε ... ὕπνος etc., cf. also 215; in this way it is still used by Hdt., cf. e.g. i 69. 3: the Lacedaemonians made a treaty with Croesus, 'an act they were morally obliged to' καὶ γάρ τινες αὐτοὺς εὐεργεσίαι εἶχον ἐκ Κροίσου πρότερον ἔτι γεγονυῖαι.

242. ~ iii 131 = xiii 317. Here θεὸς δ' ἐκέδασσεν Ἀχαιούς is a superfluous addition, but that does not mean that the line is spurious. On ἐκέδασσεν see xiii 317 n.

245. κουριδίη: see xv 22 n.

246–72. The raid has been thought to recall the attacks on the Nile delta known from Egyptian records from the times of Merneptah and Rameses III. But even if Mycenaean Greeks took part in these enterprises (which is far from certain, see Page, *History and the Homeric* Iliad (cit. xiii 315 n.), 21–3) and if the tradition preserved some memory of these events, the picture changed considerably in the course of time (as is only natural): here Odysseus does not take part in a large-scale attack by several peoples, but acts as an individual soldier of fortune; see also Kirk, *Songs*, 41–3 and D. Gray, *Archaeologia* i G, 129.

246. Αἴγυπτόνδε: see 257–8 n.

249. ἐρίηρες: see xvi 375 n. and Chantraine, *Dictionnaire* s.v. ἦρα.

251. θεοῖσίν τε: synizesis in θεός only here and *Il.* i 18, doubtless an innovation; cf. 255, 287 nn. and Richardson on *h.Cer.* 55. **δαῖτα πένεσθαι:** cf. δαῖτα πένοντο (*Il.* xviii 558). In the *Odyssey* the formula is current in both forms.

253. ἀκραέϊ: the long ᾱ is etymological and due to a prehistoric contraction, cf. οἰκωφελίη (223). The second element of the compound (-αη-) is also found in the verb ἀῆναι (from *ἄ-ϝη-μι, cognate with Lat. *ventus*, Germanic *wind*), cf. e.g. ἄλληκτος ἄει Νότος (xii 325), ἀνέμων διάει μένος ὑγρὸν ἀέντων (v 478 ~ xix 440, in which ἄει and διάει are ionicized forms of ἄη, διάη), τῷ τε Θρήκηθεν ἄητον (*Il.* ix 5), ἄησιν (Hes. *Op.* 552), διάησιν (ibid. 517). This verb too is a pre-Ionic element in the Homeric language, surviving only in Cypriot, see Ruijgh, *Élément*, 68. It was replaced by πνέω which is already much more frequent in the epics, cf. θέλγω—κηλέω, ὀφέλλω—ἀέξω (αὔξω), *sim.*; see xiii 2, xiv 223 nn.

255. ἀσκηθέες: the v.l. ἀσκεθέες is to be rejected: elsewhere only ἀσκηθής (v 26 etc., *Il.* x 212, xvi 247, post-Homeric poetry, and inscriptions). The variant is likely to have been introduced by a grammarian to whom the word was a γλῶττα (see below) and who took exception to the synizesis (-έες) in the arsis of the fifth foot. Here synizesis is most unusual indeed, and suggests that the poet had a compelling reason to admit it. The reason may well be that here he declined (or adopted in a declined form) an old, pre-Ionic formula *ἀσκηθὴς καὶ ἄνουσος (neither ἀσκηθής nor the form ἄνουσος are Ionic, see Ruijgh, *Élément*, 128 and Chantraine, *Dictionnaire* s.v. νόσος). In the same way the formula Τυδείδην (-η) Διομήδεα (-εϊ) became Τυδεΐδεω Διομήδεος (*Il.* xvi 185 etc.), the formula μάκαρες θεοὶ αἰὲν ἐόντες became μάκαρας θεοὺς αἰὲν ἐόντας (*h.Cer.* 325), and the formula ἵπποι ἀερσίποδες (*Il.* iii 327, xxiii 475) became ἵππους ἀρσίποδας (with contraction, *h.Ven.* 211).

256. = ix 78 etc.   **ἤμεθα**: see Heubeck on x 507-8.

257-8. Αἴγυπτον: the Hellenized form of the name which Memphis bore at the time of the New Empire, see A. H. Gardiner, *Ancient Egyptian Onomastica*, ii (Oxford, 1947), 211, with bibliography. Here and iv 477 ~ 581 Homer uses it for the river (Νεῖλος is first found in Hes. *Th.* 338). The indication πεμπταῖοι, 'on the fifth day', sharply contrasts with Nestor's words in iii 318 ff., where the phrase 'whence not even the birds return in the same year' (321-2) refers to the sea they have to cross. Nestor may be 'making the most of his story' (Thomas-Stubbings in *Companion*, 310), but this can hardly account for such a dissimilarity: his words reflect a different idea of the geographical situation, which is likely to have originated in the Dark Ages, whereas our line might express the knowledge of the early historical period or of Mycenaean times.

258-72. = xvii 427-41.

258. ἀμφιελίσσας: see Hainsworth on vi 264.

261. νέεσθαι: the meaning 'to go' is secondary, cf. van Leeuwen on *Il.* xxi 48, Chantraine, *Dictionnaire* s.v.

262. οἱ δ': the ἑταῖροι mentioned in 259, for ὕβρει εἴξαντες does not refer to the act of piracy ('which was quite a gentleman's profession in the Heroic Age', Stanford, cf. also *Od.* ix 40-1) mentioned in 264. It refers to the fact that the men who had been left to guard the ships neglected their duty and threw precaution to the winds, see also van Leeuwen, ad loc.

263-84. In the *Iliad* the battles mostly consist of a series of duels, and in both poems expeditions of this kind are generally merely alluded to, but here, as in *Od.* ix 39 ff. and *Il.* xi 670 ff., we get a picture of the whole of the raid, a panoramic view, in which some details stand out clearly.

264. νήπια: convincingly connected with νηπύτιος and Myc. *na-pu-ti-jo* (KN Db 1232, PY Jn 845, man's name) and derived from *ν-* and *ἀπύω* (Homeric ἠπύω, cf. ἠπύτα *Il.* vii 384, Ἠπυτίδης *Il.* xvii 324: βρι-ήπυ-ος *Il.* xiii 521) by Heubeck, *Studi micenei ed egeo-anatolici*, xi (1970), 70–2. Cf. also νηπύτιον· νήπιον, ἄφωνον (Hesych.). Further details op. cit., 72.

267–8. Cf. *Il.* xx 156–7 τῶν δ' ἅπαν ἐπλήσθη πεδίον καὶ λάμπετο χαλκῷ | ἀνδρῶν ἠδ' ἵππων. The alliteration is striking.

272. ἄναγον: though there are no mountains in the Delta; for a Greek, however, 'to carry off inland' automatically involves 'to lead up from a lower place to a higher one'.

279. γούναθ' ἑλών: this gesture is typically epic (cf. formulae such as λάβε γούνων), but κύσα looks like an attempt to introduce some *couleur locale* or an exotic feature; in *Il.* viii 371 γούνατ' ἔκυσσε, the only parallel, expresses Athena's scorn. How the kissing is done—the 'king' is presumably in his chariot—is left to the hearer's imagination. **ἐρύσατο καί μ' ἐλέησεν:** again a prothysteron, cf. xiii 434 n.

281. μελίησιν: in the sense of 'spear' the word is already a survival in the *Iliad*, found only in a few formulae and denoting in particular Achilles' famous weapon.

282. δὴ γὰρ κεχολώατο λίην: also xvi 425; on δὴ γὰρ see xiii 30 n.

283. ὡπίζετο: cf. 82 n.

284. Cf. ix 271 and xiv 406 with n.

285–6. According to Merkelbach, *Untersuchungen*, 65–6, these lines were interpolated by the poet who introduced 'the Thesprotian passage' (299–338): following Bethe he argues that in the original version the king gave his slave to a Cypriot guest-friend, as is told in xvii 442–4. However, that the defeated invader was well treated and was able to 'collect many gifts' (as Menelaus did, iv 90, 125 ff., 615 ff.) may be an exotic touch and certainly serves to enhance the stranger's prestige, cf. 212–21.

285. ἐπτάετες: see S. West on iii 305.

287. = vii 261.   **δὴ ὀγδοόν:** the hiatus and the synizesis (ὀγδοόν) are again due to the modification of a formula (see 251 n.), cf. ἀλλ' ὅτε δὴ δεκάτη (μοι) (*Il.* vi 175, xxiv 785, ix 474). The tradition may well have had a whole formulaic line *ἀλλ' ὅτε δὴ δέκατόν ϝοι (σφι) ἐπιπλόμενον ϝέτος ἦλθε. Vaguer indications of time are expressed by the well-known ἀλλ' ὅτε δὴ ἔτος ἦλθε (περιπλομένων ἐνιαυτῶν).

289. τρώκτης: the scholl. propose several meanings, of which φιλοκερδής, κλέπτης are most apposite. The noun comes from τρώγω, 'nibble', which could still be used in the sense of 'tricking a person out of something' in fifth-century Attic, cf. περιτρώγω, 'purloin', Ar. *Ach.* 258 etc.   **ἀνθρώποισιν ἐώργει:** this may go back to *ἀνθρώπους ἐϝεόργει (Chantraine, *Grammaire*, i 517, cf. app. crit.), but is more likely to be due to a declension of *μετ' (ἐν) ἀνθρώποισι ϝεϝόργει, cf. xiii 288 n.

290. παρπεπιθών: here an isolated archaism.   **ᾗσι φρεσίν:** one of the not very numerous cases in which the noun has lost all corporal and local associations, but in post-Homeric hexameter poetry even νόου φρενί, 'with the mental faculty of thinking' (Xenophanes 25 B Diels–Kranz); ἐνὶ φρεσί and μετὰ φρεσί are old (complementary) formulae.

292. The sentence is 'introductory' (see 299–301 n.), with an aor. (μεῖνα) denoting the 'total event' as against the descriptive impfs. ἐξετελεῦντο and περιτελλομένου (293, 294); hence the—seemingly illogical—use of ἀλλ' ὅτε δὴ ... ἐξετελεῦντο (293) after τελεσφόρον εἰς ἐνιαυτόν (on which see 196 n.).

294. ὧραι: 'the (new) seasons', i.e. the seasons of the new year. It is neither a 'poetic' pl. for 'spring' nor a synonym of ἔτος—which is a more abstract term—, but denotes the whole of the changing vegetation cycle, the sequence of changes in the 'terrestrial' year, cf. e.g. Hdt. ii 4. 1 and ἐς ὥρας h. Hom. xxvi 12, see also LSJ s.v. ὥρα AI3 (ossified).

295. ἐέσσατο: from *sed-, cf. e.g. ἔσας (280); either a very old form or an artificial one, cf. Meister, Kunstsprache, 179. In view of ἐφέσσαι (xiii 274), ἔφεσσαι (xv 277), we might be inclined to follow Rhianus in reading ἐφέσσατο, but it is difficult to see how this form came to be corrupted to ἐέσσατο, cf. also van der Valk, Textual Criticism, 45.

297. δέ: 'but (in reality) ...'. The original digamma of ὦνος (cf. Latin vēnum) is neglected in all the (8) Homeric cases. Recently its existence has been denied by J. Chadwick, 'Deux notes sur le digamma', in Mélanges de linguistique et de philologie grecques offerts à Pierre Chantraine (Paris, 1972), 29; see, however, Frisk, GEW s.v.

299–301. The geographical indications are confused. Does ὑπὲρ Κρήτης (300) mean north-west, north, or north-east of the island (Monro, Stanford, Ameis–Hentze–Cauer), or south of it (Lorimer, Monuments, 79)? And does it really refer to a course along the shore, as is assumed by these scholars? There is no doubt that in the mind of the poet the Phoenician and his companions actually hugged the coast as long as possible, since this was the normal practice of Greek seamen (cf. also Κρήτην μὲν ἐλείπομεν 301). It is impossible, however, that this is expressed by ἔθεεν ... μέσσον ὑπὲρ Κρήτης (a phrase conspicuous for its brevity; πέλαγος μέσον εἰς Εὔβοιαν | τέμνειν (iii 174–5), besides giving a clear geographical picture, is much more explicit): μέσσον is obviously incompatible with such a course. The expression, therefore, should be regarded as 'introductory', see 292, 337–8, 375, 474, xv 161–5, 228, xvi 422–3 nn. It means 'through the open sea, beyond Crete' (cf. e.g. ὑπὲρ πόντου xiii 257), i.e. through the sea between Crete and Libya (thus a schol.). Of course ἀλλ' (301) does not refer to what immediately precedes.

301–2. Verg. adds to the suggestive force of οὐδέ ... θάλασσα by introducing a graphic chiasmus: caelum undique et undique pontus (A. iii 193), maria undique et undique caelum (A. v 9).

301. ~ xii 403.

302–4. = xii 404–6.

303. κυανέην: for κύανος and its colour see Hainsworth on vii 87 and R. Halleux in Studi micenei ed egeo-anatolici, ix (1969), 47–66.

305–6. = xii 415–16.   ἐλελίχθη: here instead of original *ἐϝελίχθη (from ἐλίσσω, 'turn round' (< *(σ)ϝελ-), see Chantraine, *Dictionnaire* s.v. ἕλιξ), cf. v 314. But the reading is not due to scribes but to epic poets who no longer pronounced the digamma and thus confused the old forms of ἐλίσσω with those of ἐλελίζω, cf. Chantraine, *Grammaire*, i 312, and *introduction* to xiii–xvi, pp. 156–7.

307. ~ xii 417.

308–9. = xii 418–19.   κορώνῃσιν: according to Thompson, *Birds*, 173, the bird is a shearwater (= αἴθυια, cf. v 66 and scholl.).

311. ἀμαιμάκετον: elsewhere (only *Il.* vi 179, xvi 329) used as an epithet of the Chimaera. Its etymology and exact meaning are unknown, but it is certainly an age-old archaism.

314–15. As Monro points out, the wind must have shifted to the S. or SE, a change brought about by the thunderstorm. The ship which carried St Paul likewise drifted from Crete to the Adriatic Sea (Acts 27: 14 ff.). In both cases the current may have played an important part, see xv 482 n.

315. γαίῃ Θεσπρωτῶν: the name Thesprotia does not always cover the same geographical reality in historical times (cf. e.g. E. Meyer, *Der kleine Pauly*, v s.v., 756) nor is it clear how Homer intended our phrase to be understood. In any case he thus designated a coastal area (see also 334–5 = xix 291–2) not very far from Ithaca (cf. 335 = xix 292; xvi 427). But did he regard Dodona as being part of it? It looks as though he did not, but Hdt. certainly did (ii 56. 2). Th. (i 46. 4, 50. 3) described the country as lying opposite Corcyra and on both sides of the Acheron river (see also below), but does not voice an opinion on its extension eastwards. On its southern frontiers Hdt. (viii 47) and Th. (ii 50. 3) seem to agree in that they call the Ambracians a separate people. Against this N. G. L. Hammond, though without quoting evidence in support, states that in Homeric times 'the name appears also to have comprised the Ambraciote plain' (in *Companion*, 271). Since Ambracia was a Corinthian colony this is not impossible. However, even supposing it were true, this hypothesis does not shed any light on the question of how much the poet 'knew' about this part of Greece (see also xiii 103–7, xv 296 nn.) nor on the possible influence in this matter of the epic tradition. In this connection an archaeological discovery should be mentioned. At Xylokastra, about two and a half miles inland from the mouth of the Acheron, impressive remains of the 'nekromanteion' mentioned by Hdt. (v 92. η 2) were discovered by S. J. Dakaris, 'The Dark Palace of Hades', *Archaeology*, xv (1962), 85–93, who identifies the site with Homeric Ephyra and finds strong evidence for the view that the burial customs connected with this 'entrance to Hades' go back to 'the very early Mycenaean Age'. More traces of the age-old belief that it was here that the souls entered the nether regions have been found in Homer by E. Janssens, 'Leucade et le Pays des Morts', *AC* xxx (1961), 381–94. On the other hand there is no evidence that either the Thesprotians or the king mentioned in 316 played a prominent part in the epic tradition. This people has no epithet nor, as Miss Lorimer, *Monuments*, 465, observes, does Pheidon have a patronymic. Even his epithet has been added as an afterthought, in enjambment (contrast ἥρως Ἀτρεΐδης, ἥρως Ἰδομενεύς, etc.). Just as some suitors and Phaeacians (e.g. Ἀναβησίνεως) he is likely to be a creation of the poet of the *Odyssey*. Probably his name is significant, from φείδομαι (Stanford, Chantraine).

316. ἐκομίσσατο: cf. ἥ τινά που πλαγχθέντα κομίσσατο ἧς ἀπὸ νηός (vi 278). In our line, however, (and in κομίσσατο ᾧ ἐνὶ οἴκῳ *Il.* viii 384, as compared with e.g. εἰ δ᾽ ἐθέλεις, σὺ κόμισσον *Od.* xvi 82) the middle is more difficult to explain than when ironically used by the people with regard to Nausicaa. Had the middle become idiomatic in such cases (as it did in Sanskrit, cf. B. Delbrück, *Altindische Syntax* (Halle, 1888, repr. Darmstadt, 1968), 228-31, 233-4) or is its employment a feature typical of epic verse-making? See e.g. Meister, *Kunstsprache*, 19-20, Chantraine, *Grammaire*, ii 173 ff., Hoekstra, *Epic Verse before Homer* (Amsterdam, 1981), 66 ff., and *Od.* xiv 488, xvi 446 with nn.

317. ἀπριάτην: both its use (as an advb.) and its meaning ('without payment') show that we are dealing with a case of reinterpretation: at *Il.* i 99 it is said of Chryses' daughter and used in its proper sense 'not bought off', cf. Leumann, *Wörter*, 167. We cannot be sure, however, that it is this particular passage which was misunderstood by our poet: the word may have been employed (as a component part of a formula?) in pre-Homeric epic poetry, either for Chryseis or for another woman, cf. xvi 438-44 n.

318. αἴθρῳ: the adj. αἴθριος still denotes a clear sky in Hdt. (ii 25. 1, cf. αἰθήρ, αἴθρη; see further LSJ s.v. αἰθρία). However, this condition of the atmosphere must of old have been associated with cold, cf. ἀλεξαίθριον, 'screening from cold air' (S. *fr.* 117 Radt, *TGF* iv (Göttingen, 1977)), and the examples quoted by Pearson, *The Fragments of Sophocles* (Cambridge, 1917, repr. Amsterdam, 1963, i 75), ad loc. **ἤγεν ἐς οἶκον:** also xvii 84; one of the rare formulae that are based upon the loss of digamma. The fact that such a simple and useful phrase occurs only twice in the whole of the Homeric epics is typical of the conservative character of their diction.

320. ~ x 542 etc., cf. 132 and xiii 434 nn.

321-33. Given the development of the plot in xiii 404-xiv 48, Eumaeus was bound to ask Odysseus 'Who are you?' The poet could have made him reply briefly and could have made him spend the two days (virtually three; xv 1-3 n.) preceding the arrival of Telemachus in several ways. Why did he choose to fill up this time with conversations? In the preceding part of the poem much had already happened in the way of adventures and tribulations and more was soon to come: apparently the poet preferred to create some intermezzo of pleasant story-telling in Eumaeus' hut. At the same time this story-telling—in this atmosphere—made it also possible to characterize Eumaeus and, especially, to contrast the πολύμητις with his guileless servant who 'believes all the false parts of the story, but refuses to accept the one sure fact it contains' (Fenik, *Studies*, 170). This kind of humour ('irony' according to Fenik) is particularly noticed in 321-33 (the real but disguised Odysseus talking about the false Odysseus and thus

215

trying to convince his pessimistic servant by means of a fantastic yarn) and reminds one of xiii 253–95, the difference being that there Odysseus' interlocutrix is not deceived. In both passages folk-tale and heroic saga have come to function as a mere background; see also xiii 313 n.

322. φιλῆσαι: here rendered with 'to entertain' by Ameis–Hentze–Cauer, but in view of ξεινίσαι better translated as 'to befriend', 'to show kindness', cf. e.g. *Od.* xv 370. However, in a case like this the alternative may have been vacuous to the poet and his hearers. On φίλος see 58–9 n.

323. = xix 293. **ξυναγείρατ':** see 285–6 with n. The motif of acquiring wealth in foreign countries is certainly a frequently recurring epic 'theme' (Fenik, *Studies*, 168–9), but it has its basis in reality: carrying treasures when coming home from overseas voyages looms large in the mentality of all seafaring peoples.

324. πολύκμητόν τε σίδηρον: the phrase may date from the eighth century when good products of iron were made throughout Greece, but the epithet 'wrought with much toil' rather suggests that this formula (and probably the whole of the formulaic line) was created in the Dark Ages or perhaps even in late Mycenaean times, when the metal begins to appear, cf. Kirk, *Songs*, 130, Heubeck on ix 391–4, and xvi 294 with n.

325–8. = xix 294–7.

325. ἕτερόν γ': i.e. the next owner again and again; subject: the treasures, hence comma after 325. The next sentence begins with an emphatic τὸν δ' (327).

326. κειμήλια κεῖτο: the formula (cf. iv 613 etc.) is likely to represent a highly archaic idiom; κειμήλιον comes from κεῖσθαι, see Frisk, *GEW*, and Chantraine, *Dictionnaire* s.v. It denotes the movables as against livestock, cf. κειμήλιά τε πρόβασίν τε (ii 75).

327–8. The historic Dodona was near the eastern foothills of Mt. Tomaros, 18 km. SW of the modern town of Joannina. In Homer the name only recurs at xix 296, *Il.* xvi 234, and in the 'Catalogue of Ships' (*Il.* ii 750), a passage which shows some puzzling geographical features, see e.g. W. H. Parke, *The Oracles of Zeus* (Oxford, 1967), 5 ff. In our line the geographical situation of the place as suggested by the context presents no problems, although it is not clear whether the poet mentions it as part of Thesprotia, see 315 n. and Parke, op. cit., 11–12. Roughly speaking the same region is indicated by ps.-Hes. (see below), which also mentions the oracle and the oak of Zeus (for 'Hellopia', cf. Σελλοί or Ἑλλοί (*Il.* xvi 234), possibly cognate with Ἕλληνες, cf. also Pi. fr. 57–9 Snell–Maehler). Whether the god (together, as has often been asserted, with his consort Dione) had replaced the ancient Earth-Mother is uncertain (cf. Parke, op. cit., 115–16), but Hdt. ii 52. 2 says his was the oldest oracle of Greece, according to his compatriots, and this well accords with the primitive customs referred to in *Il.* xvi 234–5. The sacred oak, as Parke observes (op. cit., 22 ff., 26), may have been introduced from the northern plains of Europe and in this connection it is to be noted that, as archaeology seems to show, Dodona, as distinct from the coastal area (see 315 n.), remained outside the ambit of the Mycenaean civilization. Originally the god may have been believed to dwell in the oak, but of such a belief no trace is preserved in Homer (a different question is whether any pigeons (whose name survived in that of the priestesses called Πελειάδες Πέλειαι) once roosting in the oak (cf. ps.-Hes. fr. 240 M–W) were regarded by him as (Διὸς) προφήτιδες). However this may be, there is a marked difference between *Il.* xvi 233–5 and our lines: there the terms employed give expression to age-old Aeolian memories, here the wording is much more matter of fact.

331. ~ xix 288.   **ὤμοσε δὲ πρὸς ἔμ' αὐτόν:** subject: Pheidon. The emphatic character of the expression is far more strongly motivated by Odysseus' desire to impress Eumaeus than by the actual circumstances as described in his tale. According to a schol. the so-called Aeolian edition had ἐπισπένδων, a reading also given by a papyrus. ἀποσπένδων recurs only at iii 394, where it is justified by the context, and in the parallel line xix 288 (with the same variant). It is hard to see why ἐπισπένδων should have been changed into ἀποσπένδων; it is no doubt due to an attempt at modernization (thus rightly van der Valk, *Textual Criticism*, 18).

332–5. ~ xix 289–92.

332. ~ viii 151.   **κατειρύσθαι:** a perfect of ϝερύω, but its development is difficult to retrace (cf. Chantraine, *Grammaire*, i 136, 422). Expressions of the same kind, not looking like Homeric *flosculi*, are still found in Hdt., e.g. ἀνειρύσαι τὰς νέας (ix 96. 3).

335. **Δουλίχιον:** not identified with certainty. The island is often supposed to be Leucas (cf. Stubbings in *Companion*, 400 ff., Simpson–Lazenby, *Catalogue*, 101), but the name 'Long Island' and the fact that Leucas was not an island until the sixth century BC (Strabo 452) are obstacles (Strabo himself (458) favours Δολίχα, one of the Echinades, but these are very small). If the name could be taken to refer to the coastline, it would be somewhat more appropriate for Cephallenia, the only plausible alternative (favoured by Dörpfeld and Leaf), since we are given to understand that Doulichion is comparatively large and fertile: it provides by far the largest number of suitors (fifty-two, xvi 247–8) and is called 'rich in wheat' and 'grassy', e.g. xvi 396. This supposition, however, raises difficulties with regard to the identification of Same (see xv 29 n.). In *Il.* ii 625, moreover, Doulichion is mentioned together with the Echinades, which lie off the coast of the mainland. Its ruler is Meges, son of Phyleus, not Acastus as in 336 (but see n.). All this suggests that we have to do with a tradition which became confused in the course of time, cf. xiii 103–7, 275 nn. If this is correct, the problem is best solved by the old hypothesis (cf. Pherecydes and Andron *ap.* Strabo 456, Paus. vi 15. 7, Hesych. s.v. Δουλίχιον; see Stanford xxxix n. 2, S. West on i 246–7) that imagining two islands instead of a single one, the poet (or some predecessor) gave the name Doulichion to what is, roughly speaking, the western part of Cephallenia and called its eastern part Same (Samos).

336. **Ἀκάστῳ:** see 335 n. This man is not mentioned with a patronymic any more than is *Φείδων* (xiv 315 n.). Is he, as a king of Doulichion, a creation of the poet? As far as we know his only namesake in Greek myth is a son of Pelias who is likely to have played a rather important part in ancient (Thessalian) saga, cf. e.g. ps.-Hes. fr. 208–9 M–W, and Paus. v 17. 10. Clearly there is no connection between the two of them, and a comparison with *Ἀκάστη* (used in Catalogues, cf. Hes. *Th.* 356, *h.Cer.* 421, and N. J. Richardson, *The Homeric Hymn to Demeter* (Oxford, 1974), ad loc.) shows that the epic poets sometimes gave such mythical names to creations of their own fantasy (cf. also the examples of Phorbas, *Il.* ix 665, xiv 490, and Hippocoon, *Il.* x 518) whereas in other inconspicuous vignettes they incidentally preserved names which had come from very old traditions in their ancient heroic-mythical context, cf. *Od.* xv 186–7 and xiii 260, xiv 182 nn.

337–8. 'Introductory' lines, hence *ἀλλ'* in 339, see 292 and 299–301 with nn.

338. **δύης ἐπὶ πῆμα γενοίμην:** the eds. refer to *πῆμα κακοῖο* (iii 152); *γίγνομαι* can of course mean 'to arrive', but it is surprising to find it combined with *ἐπί* with an 'acc. of the place whither' (already the grammarian Aristophanes objected to the construction, see app. crit.), an employment which seems to have been brought about by a conflation of *ἔτι πῆμα φύγοιμι* (312) and the Ionicism *γίνομαι* = 'to come' (still rare in Homer (*Il.* ii 397, viii 117, 180), but *c.*60 instances in Hdt., e.g. i 70. 2).

339. **ἀπέπλω:** the athematic asigmatic aor. has been preserved in a few cases, e.g. *παρέπλω ποντοπόρος νηῦς* (xii 69), said of the Argo. The formula is probably very old.

342. ~ xiii 434, see n.

343. **ῥωγαλέα:** the lengthening of the final syllable is perhaps to be explained as resulting from 'abbreviation' of a traditional phrase, since *ῥωγαλέα ῥυπόωντα* (xiii 435) may be an inadequately represented formula (see xiii 438 n.). The form *ὅρηαι* could be a remnant of older Ionic (Wackernagel, *Untersuchungen*, 71) or an Aeolism (athematic *ὅρημ(μ)ι* in Sappho 31. 11 L–P), cf. Chantraine, *Grammaire*, i 305. There is a little reason to regard it, with Meister, *Kunstsprache*, 176, as an artificial form.

344. **εὐδειέλου:** see xiii 212 n.

346. **ὅπλῳ ἐϋστρεφέϊ:** cf. e.g. *ὅπλον ... βύβλινον* (xxi 390–1). In the sense of 'rope' *ὅπλον* is still found in Hdt. and Hippocrates.

348–9. Cf. e.g. *Il.* iii 381 *ῥεῖα μάλ', ὥς τε θεός* and 357–8 with n.

349. **κεφαλῇ ... ἀμφικαλύψας:** so as not to be hampered by it when swimming and to keep it dry.

350. **ἐφόλκαιον:** only here in Greek. It would be most plausible to connect the word with *ἐφολκίς*, 'little rowing boat towed behind a ship' (cf. e.g. E. *Andr.* 200, *HF* 631, 1424, schol. Ar. *V.* 268), were it not for *ξεστόν*, 'planed'. The same objection applies to the other explanation proposed by the schol., viz. 'rudder'. Monro took the word to denote a kind of 'lading-plank', which, in view of the circumstances and the descriptive touch added by the adj., looks the most satisfactory solution (cf. *ἐφέλκεται Od.* xvi 294, *ἐπέλκεται* Hdt. iv 50. 4, *ἐφολκὰ λέγειν* Th. iv 108. 5). J. L. Myres still saw such devices mounted on Mediterranean vessels in the nineteenth century, see Monro ad loc. and his fig. on 44. Sp. Marinatos, *Archaeologia* i G, 146 ff., compares the objects represented under the sterns of the 'Mycenaean war-ships' on the Theran wall-paintings ('landing-bridges'). According to Morrison in J. S. Morrison–R. T. Williams, *Greek Oared Ships, 900–322 BC* (Cambridge, 1968), 49, 54, 198, followed by L. Casson, *Ships and Seamanship in the Ancient World* (Princeton, 1971), 46, and by Kurt, *Fachausdrücke*, 115–16, the word was the term for a cross-beam projecting on each side of the bow, in classical times denoted by the plural ἐπωτίδες. These authors, however, argue from the assumption that in Homer ships are invariably run ashore stern first, yet this is highly questionable in the case of a crew intending to interrupt their voyage only for a short time (see xiii 114–15 n.), and that this was the very purpose of the Thesprotians in our passage appears from ἐσσυμένως (347). Moreover, the interpretation breaks down on 'I brought my *breast* to the sea' (ἐπέλασσα θαλάσσῃ στῆθος), for it can neither describe a dive (even apart from the fact that on this very assumption the water would have been too shallow and that, if it was not, a plunge would have alarmed the crew) nor can it depict a man 'lowering himself' (from a cross-beam!) into the water (thus both Morrison and Casson, as if our poet had said something like καθῆκ' ἐμαυτὸν εἰς ἅλ', E. *Hel.* 1614), see also next n.

350–1. ἐπέλασσα θαλάσσῃ | στῆθος: 'I brought my breast to the water' (-σσ-, -σσ-, στ-): the expression denotes the avoidance of sound.   **διήρεσσ'**: the reading διήρεσα (cf. διήρεσα χερσὶν ἐμῇσι xii 444) is preferable, not so much because it is given by the great majority of the MSS as because the variant adopted by Allen looks like a correction in order to remove the hiatus (which might be due to a modification of the formula *ἀμφοτέρῃσι δὲ χερσὶ διήρεσε(ν), cf. e.g. v 428). The passage shows, if this is at all necessary, that χείρ also means 'arm'.

352. θύρηθ': only here in Homer; for its sense cf. θύραζε, e.g. v 410.

353. δρίος: only here in Homer; later confined to poetry. The gen. ὕλης and Hesiod's ἀνὰ δρία βησσήεντα (*Op.* 530), might suggest that it means not so much 'copse' as 'land covered with copse' (cf. schol.).

356–7. πάλιν ... ἐπί: = πάλιν κιόντες (cf. xvi 177 etc.) αὖτις ἔβαινον ἐπὶ νηός (cf. xi 435, *Il.* viii 512, xiii 665, etc.; here πάλιν may, however, already have become a synonym of αὖτις (xvi 456), cf. *Il.* ii 276). In Homer βαίνω often has the meaning 'to step', 'to set down one's feet', see Ruijgh, τε *épique*, 574, and cf. βεβαώς as a synonym of ἑσταώς, Hoekstra, *AC* xl (1979), 108.

357–8. ἔκρυψαν: this is best rendered with 'had concealed', because a modern language requires a plpf. in this context. Actually we have here a clear instance of an aor. expressing the 'total event', the event *in abstracto*, regardless of time, contrasting as such with the 'autoptic' impfs. φοίτων, ἐφαίνετο (355), ἔβαινον (356); cf. also Chantraine, *Grammaire*, ii 184.   **θεοὶ αὐτοί**: here and at 348 the expression might seem to betray the hero (see e.g. *Il.* xxi 215), as compared with Eumaeus' words in 386 ἐπεί σέ μοι ἤγαγε δαίμων. In xvi, however, Antinous attributes

Telemachus' escape to the θεοί (364) and to a δαίμων (370) in the same speech.

359. ἐπισταμένου: used without either an attempt to specify (for instance by ἄρτια βάζειν, cf. e.g. viii 240) or a direct reference to the context, as in xiii 313; probably an innovation. The closest parallel is *Il.* xix 80.

361. δειλὲ ξείνων: cf. δαιμόνιε ξείνων (443) and the traditional formulae δῖα θεάων, δῖα γυναικῶν.

363–4. Punctuate: , ἀλλὰ τά γ' οὐ κατὰ κόσμον, ὀΐομαι,—οὐδέ με πείσεις— εἰπὼν ἀμφ' Ὀδυσῆϊ. This involves a double 'parenthesis', but avoids the harshness of τά γ' οὐ κατὰ κόσμον ὀΐομαι (Allen). Moreover οὐ κατὰ κόσμον goes with εἰπών, cf. εἰπὼν οὐ κατὰ κόσμον (viii 179) and the formula κατὰ μοῖραν ἔειπες(-ε).

366. ὅ τ': Ruijgh, τε *épique*, 816, would read ὅτε, 'now that', but this is strained. We have to do with a construction of the well-known type οἶδα Πρωταγόραν ὅτι σοφός ἐστιν. In such cases τε had lost its meaning and could be used more or less mechanically, for instance in order to obviate hiatus, cf. e.g. 90 and xvi 216 n. ἤχθετο: 'got himself hated'.

368–71. = i 238–41, but 369 and 370 are omitted in many MSS, see S. West on i 238. On the various spellings of ἀνηρείψαντο see West, *Hesiod*, Theogony, on 990. There is some doubt whether it comes from ἐρέπτω (-ομαι) or from an old stem *ἀρεπ-, cf. Bechtel, *Lexilogus*, 64. On the latter supposition the original epic formula was probably Ἅρπυιαι ἀνᾱρέψαντο (Fick; the form Ἀρέπυια is found on a vase from Aegina, cf. P. Kretschmer, *Die griechischen Vaseninschriften* (Gütersloh, 1894), 208, and in the *Etymologicum Magnum* 138, 21). It would be tempting indeed to assume an old *figura etymologica* (cf. 326 with n.), but the independent evidence for *ἀρεπ- is extremely weak (a *varia lectio* in Hes. *Th.* 990). Since, moreover, ἐρέπτομαι does not seem to mean 'to eat', 'to feed on'—as is often supposed, e.g. by Chantraine, *Dictionnaire* s.v. and by O. Szemerényi, *Syncope in Indo-European and the Nature of Indo-European Accent* (Naples, 1964), 204—but 'to tear off', 'to snatch' ('wohl eig. abrupfen' Frisk, *GEW* s.v.; see below) there is little reason to introduce *ἀρεπ-, and therefore it seems preferable not to go beyond reading ἀνηρέψαντο and admitting an alliteration with Ἅρπυιαι or Ἀρέπυιαι. These are *daimones* of storms, cf. ἀνηρέψαντο θύελλαι (iv 727) and its formulaic declension ἀναρπάξασα θύελλα (iv 515 etc.). In this connection it deserves notice that the med. of the verb ἐρέπτω is used of animals (xix 553, *Il.* ii 776, etc., 5 times) and of hungry men (*Od.* ix 97), but the act. of the angry river Scamander tearing away the sand from under Achilles' feet (ὑπέρεπτε *Il.* xxi 271).

370. ἤρατ': see xiii 137 n.

375. ἀλλ': marks a transition rather than an opposition, see Denniston, *Particles*, 7 and 299–301 n., though the introductory function of 375–7 is less conspicuous than in other cases.   ἐξερέουσιν: with some exaggeration one could render this word here as 'they turn him inside out with questions'; on the probable origin of ἐρέω, εἴρομαι, etc., see Risch, *Wortbildung*, 286, 300.

378-85. The same motif as in 124-5, but now elaborated with personal and graphic detail.

379. ἐξήπαφε: see 212 n.

380. A constantly recurring theme, cf. xiii 259 with n.

381. ἦλθεν ἐμὰ πρὸς δώματ': it is difficult to choose between this reading and ἤλυθ' ἐμοὶ πρὸς σταθμόν (found without a variant at xvi 66, but there Eumaeus is speaking to Telemachus); here the latter phrase might be a correction made by someone for whom δώματα had too solemn a ring to fit Eumaeus' hut, but cf. e.g. v 6, xvi 78.

382. In his made-up tale the Aetolian mentions Crete and Idomeneus, just as Odysseus himself does in xiii 256 ff., xix 172 ff., cf. also xiv 199 ff.; see xiii 256-86 n.

383. ἀκειόμενον: here, in spite of ἕλκε' ἀκειόμενοι (*Il.* xvi 29), not necessarily 'healing' used metaphorically: in the sense of 'repairing', 'mending', especially of clothes, the verb ἀκέομαι and its derivatives are found in inscriptions and prose. Its long syllable is etymological (< *ἀκέσ-yo-μαι), cf. τελείω < *τελέσ-yω; see e.g. Wyatt, *Lengthening*, 133.

386. δαίμων: all that cannot be explained otherwise is attributed to this agency, cf. Nilsson, *Geschichte*, i 216, παρά μ' ἤπαφε δαίμων (xiv 488), and 358-8 and xv 261 nn.

387. θέλγε: see xiii 2 n.; in 379, when speaking of the Aetolian, Eumaeus used ἐξήπαφε, 'he deceived'.

389. ξένιον: see 158 n.

391. Cf. 150.

392. οἷόν: lit. '(judging from the fact) how' (thus rightly Ameis–Hentze–Cauer, cf. e.g. iv 611), cf. xv 212. Originally such clauses were independent. **ἐπήγαγον:** in this sense the word occurs only here in Homer, and without any formulaic connections. Since, moreover, in post-Homeric Greek the adj. ἐπαγωγός is used to characterize *arguments* (e.g. in Hdt.), the employment of the verb in this sense seems to come from the poet's Ionic vernacular; see also xiii 2 n.

393. ῥήτρην: only here in Homer; later frequently used in various senses and in several dialects, see Frisk, *GEW* s.v. εἴρω. **ὄπισθε:** 'hereafter'; for this meaning cf. e.g. xxii 55. The variant ὕπερθε(ν) looks like a *lectio facilior*.

395. νοστήσῃ ἄναξ τεός: after the initial digamma had been dropped in Ionic, the old pre-Ionic formulae such as *ϝάναξ ἐμός (τε(ϝ)ός), ϝάναχθ' ἐ(ϝ)όν could be preceded by a long vowel, since then the rule *vocalis ante vocalem corripitur* applied. Previously they required a subjunctive in -ῃσι, cf. 398 ἔλθῃσιν ἄναξ τεός (< *ἔλθῃσι ϝάναξ τεϝός) an expression which represents the old type, see Chantraine, *Grammaire*, i 461 ff.

397. Δουλίχιόνδ': see 335 n.

399. βαλέειν: *infinitivus pro imperativo*, cf. e.g. σὺ δὲ τετλάμεναι (xiii 307); more examples in Chantraine, *Grammaire*, ii 316 ff., who notes that the employment found here and in 396 (i.e. without either a voc. or a personal pron. added, but with a mere predicative adjunct in the nom. (ἔσσας, ἐπισσεύσας here) is much more frequent in the *Odyssey* than in the *Iliad*, cf. also

COMMENTARY

introduction to xiii–xvi. Here ἐπισσεύας ... βαλέειν means 'setting the
slaves on me fling me down ...'. ἐπισσεύας: in this compound the
double σ is etymological (< *ky-, cf. Skrt. cyávate (middle), 'he moves',
Thumb–Hauschild, *Handbuch des Sanskrit* (Heidelberg, 1958), i 1, 290) and
was preserved in a number of formulae because it was bound up with the
metre.

402. ἐϋκλείη τ᾽ ἀρετή τε: in this phrase ἀρετή τε is not parenthetical: in ἀρετή
recognition by the people is implied. The element of 'people's opinion' is
still more noticeable in τὴν δυσσέβειαν εὐσεβοῦσ᾽ ἐκτησάμην (S. *Ant.* 924)
and many similar expressions, cf. Jebb ad loc.; see further xiii 45, xvi
76–7 nn.

405. αὖτις δὲ: see 178 with n. The fact that in Ionic this expression used to be
employed paratactically at the beginning of a clause (cf. xxii 272, *Il.* xv
696, many examples in Hdt.) may also have influenced the structure of the
sentence.

406. Δία Κρονίωνα λιτοίμην: read Δία Κρονίων᾽ ἀλιτοίμην᾽ with two good
MSS and part of the scholl.; Κρονίωνα λιτοίμην, though better attested, is
to be rejected: πρόφρων could not mean 'with good heart' (Stanford), and
the interpretation 'I should be fain to entreat Zeus' (Monro) is strained.
On the other hand πρόφρων ... ἀλιτοίμην has a parallel in πρόφρονι
θυμῷ|δασσάμενος προύθηκε Διὸς νόον ἐξαπαφίσκων (Hes. *Th.* 536–7, said of
Prometheus, who is deliberately deceiving Zeus) and is illustrated by μή ...
Διὸς δ᾽ ἀλίτωμαι ἐφετμάς (*Il.* xxiv 569–70, said by Achilles with regard to a
possible violation of a suppliant's (Priam's) rights; cf. also ἀθανάτους
ἀλιτέσθαι (iv 378), Ἀθηναίην ἀλίτοντο (v 108), etc. Here Eumaeus refers to
his own words in 389.

408. λαρὸν τετυκοίμεθα δόρπον: also xii 283; λᾱρός (< *λαϝ-ερός or *λαϝ-
αρός, cf. ἀπο-λαύω) and τετυκοίμεθα are archaic elements. The latter word
occurs in 'typical scenes' and τετυκοίμεθα δόρπον is a formulaic conjugation
of ὁπλίσσατο δόρπον (δεῖπνον), in which the verb has preserved its old
meaning. The phraseology is clearly traditional.

411. ἔρξαν κατὰ ἤθεα: from pre-Homeric *ϝέρξαν κατὰ ϝήθεα. In its concrete
sense, 'accustomed place', 'abode', ἤθεα (always in the pl.) is still used by
Hdt. The abstract meaning is not found in Homer, but occurs already in
Hes., once—significantly—with a 'neglected' digamma (ἐπίκλοπον ἦθος *Op.*
67, 78).

412. ἄσπετος: given the number of the swine the description is hardly
exaggerated.   **αὐλιζομενάων:** see 5–6 n. and Heubeck on xii 264–6.

414. ἄξεθ᾽: if this form is a 'mixed' aor., it is artificial (Chantraine,
Grammaire, i 417–18). However, it is more likely to be a fut. used as an
imperat., see Schwyzer, *Grammatik*, i 788, Risch, *Wortbildung*, 250; most
recently J. Th. Hooker, *MSS* xxxviii (1979), 87–92.   **τόν:** has already
become an article, as in 19, see 12 n.

417. Cf. ἀλλότριον κάματον σφετέρην ἐς γαστέρ᾽ ἀμῶνται (Hes. *Th.* 599), said
of the drones, and *Op.* 305.

418. νηλέϊ χαλκῷ: a loosely applied formula, cf. xiii 185 n.

222

419. πενταέτηρον: it has been pointed out that 'five years old' is not proper for pork, cf. Monro ad loc., who suggests 'imitation (or parody?) of *Il.* ii 402'.

420. ἐπ' ἐσχάρῃ: see Hainsworth on vii 153.

421. φρεσὶ γὰρ κέχρητ' ἀγαθῇσιν: also iii 266 (see S. West ad loc.), xvi 398, and cf. 290 n.

422. ἀπαρχόμενος: see S. West on iii 446.

423. πᾶσι θεοῖσι: see Heubeck on xi 132-4.

424. ὅνδε δόμονδε: after the possessive adj. the directional particle -δε is only found in this phrase coupled with nouns plus -δε (never *ὅνδε ... οἰκόνδε, *sim.*). Since, as far as we know, it is neither an element of spoken Ionic nor an archaism, it is likely to result from a declension of the old formula *ϝοῖο δόμοιο (οἷο δόμοιο i 330 etc.). But this is not 'poetic licence' in the modern sense of the term. To the poet (and probably also to his Ionic predecessors) epic language, being vastly different from the Ionic spoken around 700 BC, was a traditional idiom which had its own 'laws' (cf. e.g. εὐρέα πόντον *Il.* vi 291 etc.), hence he treated this directional particle syntactically in the same way as the demonstrative one in τόνδε.

425. ἀνασχόμενος: 'drawing himself up', not just 'raising his hand aloft' (Monro), which would be insufficient; cf. *Il.* iii 362 etc.   **κείων:** from *κεσ-, Skrt. śas-, 'to cut', cf. κεάζω (418).

427-8. Cf. iii 456-8, xii 360-1, *Il.* i 460-1, ii 423-4. Here the untypical description involves a middle, an impf., and irresolvable contraction (ὠμοθετεῖτο).

428. ἀρχόμενος: used in a ritual sense, lit.: 'making a beginning (i.e. taking the first offering) from ...', cf. ἀπαρχόμενος (422) and W. Burkert, *Homo Necans* (Berlin–New York, 1972), 13.

429. παλύνας ... ἀκτῇ: (ἀκτήν?) see app. crit. and cf. 77, x 520, xi 28. For ἀλφίτου ἀκτή see S. West on ii 355.

430-1. These lines are regular units in sacrificing scenes, *Il.* i 465-6 etc.

431. περιφραδέως: the adj. περιφραδής does not occur in Homer. It is rare in post-Homeric Greek and is found for the first time in *h.Merc.* (464, said of Hermes); cf. xiii 2, xiv 446, xv 456, xvi 427 nn.

432. βάλλον δ' εἰν ἐλεοῖσιν: as against the actions mentioned in 430-1 this detail is rare in descriptions of a sacrifice: it recurs only at *Il.* ix 215, in a different wording. ἐλεός is explained by Athen. iv 173 a as 'the cook's table'; it is certainly not a typically 'epic' word, cf. Ar. *Eq.* 152 etc.

433. περὶ ... ἤδη: this probably refers to the cutting up and dividing of the meat being normally done by a person subordinate to the master of the house (a δαιτρός in the palaces). Together with ἂν (=ἀνὰ) ... ἵστατο δαιτρεύσων it marks the occasion as a special one (cf. also 414), but it would have more relevance if it were immediately followed by 437. The lines 434-6 have been suspected for other reasons, most recently by Shipp, *Studies*, 340 (but see 435 n.).

434. διεμοιρᾶτο: only here in Homer; on the scansion of μοῖρα see xiii 385 n.

435. It is true that the gods have already received their share (Shipp, ibid.), but that is not a sufficient reason to reject a special sacrifice to Hermes and the Nymphs. Nor are the contracted form Ἑρμῇ and the mentioning of Μαιάς (sic) proof of spuriousness (Ἑρμῆς, Ἑρμῆν are found (Il. xx 72 etc., 5 times), and probably come from the poet's vernacular, whereas Ἑρμείας was inherited from the tradition, see xv 319 n.). At any rate the line seems already to have been known to Semonides, who imitated it in a passage which mentions the Nymphs and the son of Maias in connection with herdsmen, (fr. 18 Diehl, fr. 20 West; attributed to Simonides by a schol.). On the monuments and in inscriptions the god and the Nymphs are often found together (see Nilsson, *Geschichte*, i 274, with his explanation) and also in a prayer in Ar. *Th.* 997, where Pan is added. The use of non-Ionic ἵαν (Aeolic? Cf. Wathelet, *Traits*, 296 ff.) together with the Ionic form Ἑρμῇ is typical of the inextricable linguistic amalgam into which the epic diction had developed at the time of the composition of the *Odyssey*, see also 94 n.

437. ~ *Il.* vii 321; the chine was considered the portion of honour (cf. e.g. iv 65); it was still given to the Spartan kings in the fifth century BC, see Hdt. vi 56.   διηνεκέεσσι: cf. xiii 195 n.

438. κύδαινε δὲ θυμὸν ἄνακτος: the verb κυδαίνω means 'to give honour to', 'to glorify', so one would expect something like κύδαινεν ἄνακτα (< κύδαινε ϝάνακτα) or ἴαινε (εὔφραινε) δὲ θυμόν. That we have to do with a comparatively late conflation is confirmed by θυμὸν ἄνακτος: before its initial digamma had been dropped the latter word could not be immediately preceded by the parisyllabic forms θυμός, -όν, -ῷ; this excludes simple declension of an old formula following the bucolic diaeresis as a cause of the 'neglect'. Hence the modification is of a more drastic type (similar instances of conflation at xv 61–2, *h.Ap.* 506, *h.Cer.* 302, and probably *Od.* xiv 18).

440. Εὔμαιε: Eumaeus did not mention his name at any time in the preceding part of the story—so far as we have been told! The 'inconsistency'—if such it is—should warn us against taking similar cases as symptoms of interpolation or divided authorship. Many more examples are given by S. E. Bassett in his chapter 'The Poet and his Audience' in *The Poetry of Homer* (Berkeley, 1938), 114–40. The author refers in particular to G. Fraccaroli, *L'irrazionale nella letteratura* (Turin, 1903), 397 ff.

441. τοῖον ἐόντ': according to Stanford, Odysseus intentionally and ironically repeats Eumaeus' own words (see 364). Since, however, the poem was composed—whether orally or not—for listeners, this is not very probable. Such a little touch would be lost on an audience.

443. δαιμόνιε ξείνων: see 361 with n.; δαιμόνιος means 'someone who is under the influence of a δαίμων'. Stanford rightly observes, 'Eumaeus has sensed something "queer" about his guest'.

446. ἄργματα: see 428 n.; presumably the share mentioned in 435 is meant, though the praying had already been done in 436.   αἰειγενέτῃσι: cf. θεῶν αἰειγενετάων (xxii 81 etc.). Several interpretations were proposed in antiquity and in the Byzantine period, among which ὧν τὸ γένος ἀεὶ διαρκεῖ

(Eust. 245. 25 v.d.V. (*Il.* ii 400)) is both clear and correct (see also schol. T and B on *Il.* iii 296). A derivation from γενετή, 'birth' or 'time of birth' (suggested by Risch, *Wortbildung*, 32) is incompatible with αἰει-, and the same applies to the supposition that the meaning of the word is passive ('ever-begotten' is nonsense; 'begotten for ever' would presuppose a meaning (= εἰς ἀεί) that is not found in Homer). Nor can the epic poet who created the epithet have meant it to be active (as was assumed by a philosophizing school of interpreters in antiquity). However, as this and similar poetical cpds. cannot be *nomina agentis*, they must have been created on the model of certain other nouns in -της, some of which were in origin 'possessive' cpds. (e.g. ἀκοίτης; thus rightly Risch), while many others (e.g. αἰχμητής, 'a man with a spear', see xvi 242 n.) were felt to have a similar sense, whatever their origin. This meaning was preserved by the epic poets in their 'derivatives', cf. ἐυρρεέταο alongside ἐυρρέεος ('having a good stream'), εὐμενέτῃσι (*Od.* vi 185) alongside δυσμενέεσσι in the same line, etc. Thus the poet who created our epithet understood it in the same way, namely as '(beings) whose race (γένος, cf. e.g. θεῶν γένος Hes. *Th.* 44) is everlasting', i.e. as ἀειγενέσι/-έων (see above). This adj., ἀειγενής, though not used in the epics, is actually found in Hippocrates, Plato, and Xenophon, who even has τοῖς ἀειγενέσι θεοῖς (*Smp.* 8. 1). On Homer's 'latent vocabulary' see xiii 2, xiv 392, xv 456, xvi 427 nn.

449. Μεσαύλιος: 'Yardman', Stanford. The name is probably a creation of the poet, cf. the names of the Phaeacians in viii 111-14 (Ποντεύς τε Πρωρεύς τε etc.).

450-2. Is there any connection between Eumaeus being called an οἰκεύς and the fact that he has been able to purchase a slave for himself? Cf. 4 n.

452. Ταφίων: this mysterious but doubtless historical people has already been mentioned in connection with Athena-Mentes, i 105 etc. Here the hearers are tacitly assumed to know that it made its living by piracy, a fact explicitly stated at xv 427, xvi 426. The contexts in which it appears suggest that it inhabited NW Greece, cf. Lorimer, *Monuments*, 52, 121, Thomas-Stubbings in *Companion*, 308, Russo on ps.-Hes. *Sc.* 19, and xiii 275 n.

453-6. After having dwelt in much detail on the sacrifice the poet rapidly dispatches the description of the actual dinner. In doing so he keeps to the old tradition (453-4 are frequently used formulaic verses), yet in the closing line (456) he imparts a new meaning ('they longed to go') to an ancient traditional element of the diction (cf. 399 n. and xiii 296, xiv 58-9, 62, xv 22): elsewhere ἐσσεύοντο always means 'they hurried, they ran', but here this meaning is impossible, as the herdsmen do not 'go to bed' until 523-4. Of course the Greek verbal aspect enabled him to use the form in this sense, but under the given conditions the employment of the word itself is somewhat exaggerated. The verbs traditionally used to denote 'longing' are ἵεμαι, λιλαίομαι, ἐπείγομαι. These, however, were confined to different formulae. Here, as in 438, the language is traditional, the diction is not. Influence of the old (Aeolic?) perfect participle ἐσσύμενος as used e.g. in iv 416, xv 73? Cf. also x 484, *Il.* i 173 etc.

453-4. Two much-repeated formulaic lines which look very old, esp. the latter, as compared with its late variant αὐτὰρ ἐπεὶ τάρπησαν ἐδητύος ἠδὲ ποτῆτος (v 201); for ἔρος (probably Aeolic) Ionic has ἔρως, cf. also M. Durante, *Sulla preistoria della tradizione poetica greca*, i (Rome, 1971), 55.

457. σκοτομήνιος: probably this does not mean that the moon was hidden by clouds, but that the month was drawing to its close, cf. 161. The 'Return of the Hero at New Moon' must have been a theme of the old saga, cf.: Wilamowitz, *Untersuchungen*, 114, and 162 n.

458. ἔφυδρος: lit.: 'attended with rain', see 224 n. With good reason Ameis–Hentze–Cauer connect the rainstorm with autumn, and Austin, *Archery*, 242, rightly points to the setting of the Pleiades (in the first days of November) as described by Hes. *Op.* 619-22.

459. συβώτεω πειρητίζων: a comparatively late innovation, see 251 n. and cf. Hoekstra, *Modifications*, 39.

463. εὐξάμενός: on the original sense of this old word see 199 n. Since it is unlikely that here it has come to denote a simple request (for a cloak), the interpretation 'wishing' (Monro, Ameis–Hentze–Cauer; 'I have formed a wish' Stanford) must refer to εἴθ' ... εἴη (468). In that case, however, it is difficult to see why the elaborate excuse made in 463-6 is required, and these lines stress the lack of self-restraint. Hence the beggar probably employs the word in the sense of 'boasting', and in this way apologizes in advance for a story in which he will appear to rank among the chieftains of the Achaeans (469 ff.). The aor. is no objection, see 357-8 n.

464. ἠλεός: cognate with ἠλίθιος, 'foolish', 'silly'; lit. 'distraught', 'crazy', cf. οἶνος ἐύφρων, 'the merry (i.e. merry-making) wine', cf. xiii 19 n. The 'distracting' wine brings about 'boasting' (463).

467. ἀνέκραγον: said in a tone of jocular exaggeration and self-deprecation, cf. 463 n.

469. ὑπὸ Τροίην: also iv 146, instead of (the probably older) ὑπὸ Ἴλιον (*Il.* ii 216 etc.), cf. the frequent formula προτὶ Ἴλιον; probably modelled on ἐνὶ Τροίῃ, which always denotes the country, and on ἐς Τροίην, ἐκ Τροίης, which usually do the same, but already have a less special signification in *Od.* x 40, xiii 248. **λόχον ἤγομεν:** see 217–18 n.

473-7. The atmosphere of the description is of course largely due to the subject (Odysseus asking for a cloak), but all the same our passage contrasts sharply in this respect with the *Iliad*, where hardships suffered by the soldiers because of the weather are never mentioned: from this point of view the *Iliad* is a more typical specimen of heroic poetry. It is characteristic that our passage comes closest to the picture of the besieged town on Achilles' shield, *Il.* xviii 509 ff. (Leaf, *Iliad*, i p. 425, points to some affinities with the 'Doloneia'). In A. *Ag.* 559–66 the messenger describes the experiences of the soldiers with a similar insistence on the weather.

473. περὶ ἄστυ: elsewhere this pre-Homeric formula (< *περὶ ϝάστυ) as well as the equally traditional περὶ πτόλιν (with the Achaean-Aeolic form of the noun), if used locally, means 'round the city'. Moreover there are no reliable parallels for περί meaning 'near' in Homer (at *Il.* ii 757 the preposition is likely to be used in the sense of ἀμφί). Yet an ambush of sufficient size to surround the town is out of the question, even if we should suppose that the poet had at the back of his mind not 'Troy with the wide streets', which it took the Achaeans ten years to conquer, but a small Ionian town of his own time. So should we read προτὶ, ποτὶ, or παρὰ with other MSS? These readings are likely to owe their existence to the above-mentioned considerations (for π(ρ)οτὶ, moreover, cf. 472). Therefore it is most probable that the poet employs the old formula without giving it much thought (cf. xiii 185 n.), perhaps interpreting it, in accordance with his own vernacular, as 'in the neighbourhood of', 'somewhere near': in the Ionic of Hdt. this meaning is current, cf. e.g. περὶ τὸ ἱρόν (viii 39. 1), see further Powell, Lexicon s.v., 3b, 4. Cf. also ἂν δόνακας καὶ ἕλος (474, only here) and xiii 142, 243 nn.

474. ὑπὸ τεύχεσι πεπτηῶτες: used by way of introduction (see 299-301 n.): not until 476 are we told the reason for it. For πεπτηῶτες cf. 354 and xiii 98 n.

475. πεσόντος: this has been taken (here and at Hes. Op. 547) as ἐπιπεσόντος because of νὺξ ... ἔφυδρος (457-8; thus most recently by G. P. Edwards, The Language of Hesiod in its Traditional Context (Oxford, 1971), 182, who follows I. Sellschopp, Stilistische Untersuchungen zu Hesiod (Hamburg, 1934), 74). Yet the fact that νὺξ δ᾽ ἄρ᾽ ἐπῆλθε κακή has already been used to describe the weather in Ithaca does not imply that in Odysseus' tale so many years earlier a wind must also have been blowing at Troy. On the strength of this argument one might even argue that it was not freezing and snowing but raining there (the Hesiodic passage would deserve a special discussion). Moreover, as many editors have pointed out, ἄνεμος πέσε (Od. xix 202) is in favour of 'subsiding', and we may also compare Il. xii 281, where Zeus makes it snow κοιμήσας ἀνέμους. In the similes Il. xv 170-1 and xix 357-8, used to describe movement, we have to do with driving snow; here the stress is on the frost, see also 476-7 n.

476-7. χιών ... πάχνη ... κρύσταλλος: a climax, as was already seen by Eust. ad loc., cf. also Athen. iii 104 c (fr. i 4-5 of the comic poet Theognetus, CAF iii 364): the snow was not sleet, but thick and hard, resembling hoar-frost. Against the fierce cold the shields were useless. On περιτρέφετο see xiii 410 n.

479. σάκεσιν εἰλυμένοι ὤμους: it is difficult to say whether or not the poet has 'body-shields' in mind (cf. Lorimer, Monuments, 188, Stanford ad loc.), though σάκος was no doubt the original term for such a piece of armour, see Trümpy, Fachausdrücke, 25 ff. At Il. xvii 492 we find βοέης εἰλυμένω ὤμους. On εἰλύω see 136 n.

482. ζῶμα: probably some kind of metal belt, but its precise nature and function are unknown, cf. Snodgrass, Armour, 183. **φαεινόν:** already an archaism at the time of the composition of the Odyssey, see xv 322 n.

483. τρίχα νυκτὸς ἔην: also in the parallel line xii 312. Advbs. sometimes occur as predicates of verbs (cf. xiii 1 with n.), but the development from 'in three parts' into 'in the third part' is difficult to explain.

485. ἐμμαπέως: an archaic word, elsewhere only at *Il.* v 836, ps.-Hes. *Sc.* 442, and *h.Ven.* 180 (whose author may have adopted ἐμμαπέως ὑπάκουσεν from our line); μαπέειν, 'to take hold of', only in ps.-Hes. *Sc.* 231, 252, 304.

488. δάμναται: the middle has completely lost its meaning (cf. xvi 446) and has been used in enjambment on the analogy of ἔρχεται, *sim.*   οὐ γὰρ ἔχω χλαῖναν: a remarkably short colloquial phrase in ancient surroundings (δάμναται, ἤπαφε).

489. φυκτὰ πέλονται: cf. viii 299 (πέλοντο), *Il.* xvi 128 (πέλωνται), οὐκέτ' ἀνεκτὰ πέλονται (*Od.* xx 223).

490. νόον σχέθε τόνδ': in view of βουλευέμεν (491), τόνδε must refer to the trick described in 495–8. The verb is no obstacle to this interpretation, for, though it mostly means 'to hold back', 'to keep off' in Homer, it is sometimes simply used in the sense of 'holding' (e.g. *Il.* iv 113 σάκεα σχέθον, vii 277 σκῆπτρα σχέθον, the only difference being that here the ingressive function of the aor. is more in evidence): although we may translate 'he conceived', Homer's terminology goes no further than 'he began to hold', cf. 494 and Alcaeus fr. G i 10, L–P θῦμον σκέθοντες ('to get' first in Pi. and A.).

494. ἐπ' ἀγκῶνος: a brachylogy: '(leaning) on his elbow', cf. ὀρθωθεὶς δ' ἄρ' ἐπ' ἀγκῶνος, κεφαλὴν ἐπαείρας (*Il.* x 80).

495. Rejected by Aristarchus (see app. crit.) because of Odysseus' 'ridiculous' confession that he has been sleeping—an argument typical of the grammarian's 'prosaic mentality and too punctual matter-of-factness' (van der Valk, *Textual Criticism*, 189). Moreover, Odysseus' speech could hardly begin with λίην γάρ. Admittedly the device of the dream seems to be mechanically applied, but that impression is due to its content (fear because of the exposed position) being no more than hinted at, cf. xvi 442–3 with n.   ἐνύπνιον: the v.l. ἐνύπνιος is not inferior idiomatically, but poorly attested, and the advb. is supported by e.g. ἦλθον ἐναίσιμον (*Il.* vi 519).

498. νέεσθαι: whether this simply means 'to come' (261 n.) or is used as a brachylogy for 'to accompany you on your return' (van Leeuwen), the influence of formulae such as ἐν (σὺν) νηυσὶ νέωμεθα no doubt played a part in the change of meaning, cf. 469 with n.   ναῦφι(ν) (note the accent) is probably an Achaean-Aeolic survival, cf. Wathelet, *Traits*, 228, 343 and 134 n.

499. Θόας, Ἀνδραίμονος υἱός: an Aetolian, mentioned several times in the *Iliad* (ii 638 etc.).

500. χλαῖναν: 'what a χλαῖνα was we do not know', H. P. and A. J. B. Wace in *Companion*, 499. However, since in Homer the word is used as a variant of φᾶρος (see xiii 67, xiv 132 nn.), it cannot have differed very much from that garment (in the mind of the poet, that is) and seems to denote a cloak without sleeves (also used as a blanket, cf. 460, 520, etc.). It could be simple or double, cf. n. on λώπη, xiii 224; a possible specimen from the Geometric period in Sp. Marinatos, *Archaeologia* i A, 39, fig. 8a. Normally it was made of wool, cf. iv 299.   φοινικόεσσαν: the shade of φοῖνιξ varies between 'bay' (of a horse, *Il.* xxiii 454) and 'red', perhaps 'purpur', cf.

228

φοινικόεσσαι *Il.* xxiii 717 (said of blood-blisters) and *Il.* iv 140. Probably its original meaning was 'reddish-brown' (cf. also Chantraine, *Dictionnaire* s.v. 1. φοῖνιξ) and in our line this may be the sense of the adj. At any rate the false quantity of the form results from the adaptation of *φοινῑκ-ϝεσσαν to the hexameter, Palmer in *Companion*, 105.

501–2. The tempo of the narrative abruptly quickens. The use of the aor. φάε (from *φάϝε, an archaism) after κείμην is characteristic: it marks the end of the night as a reveille would do; contrast e.g. Ἠὼς μὲν κροκόπεπλος ἐκίδνατο πᾶσαν ἐπ' αἶαν (*Il.* viii 1).   **χρυσόθρονος**: in the case of Eos originally 'with golden flowers', see Càssola on *h.Ven.* 218 (with literature).

503–6. Because of αἶνος (508), and perhaps owing to their notion of ἀπρεπές? see xv 19 n., some Alexandrian critics held that Odysseus' story contained no more than an αἴνιγμα and accordingly rejected these lines. The argument seems a bit far-fetched, cf. 508 n. and Nestor's αἶνος (*Il.* xxiii 626–50). Moreover, Odysseus may be feigning to be unaware of the presence of the herdsmen (thus van Leeuwen, referring to *Od.* xi 355–68).

503. ~ 468: an instance of ring-composition, not to be destroyed by athetesis, cf. xv 333, 402.

505. ἀμφότερον: used as an advb., cf. *Il.* iii 179, iv 60, etc.   **ἑῆος**: read ἑῆος, gen. sg. of ἑΰς; the long vowel has been variously explained; it is not necessarily to be ascribed (with Wyatt, *Lengthening*, 158 ff.) to metrical lengthening: the question is far too complicated to justify this conclusion (see e.g. Beekes, *Glotta*, li (1973), 233).

508. αἶνος: originally simply a 'tale', but here already a 'tale containing an ulterior purpose', Verdenius, *Mnemosyne*, xv (1962), 389; cf. also xiii 47 n. The term is used for Nestor's story in *Il.* xxiii 652 and Hes. gives the same name to his parable of the hawk and the nightingale (*Op.* 202).

510–11. ~ vi 192–3.

511. ὧν ἐπέοιχ': sc. μὴ δεύεσθαι.

512. δνοπαλίξεις: 'you will shake' (?), only here and at *Il.* iv 472. Its etym. and exact meaning are unknown.

513. ἐπημοιβοί: εἵματα ἐξημοιβά are mentioned in viii 249 as a symptom of the luxurious way of life of the Phaeacians.

514. μία ... ἑκάστῳ: yet Eumaeus appears to have an extra cloak in 521.

515–17. These lines are essential in xv (337–9), but it is doubtful whether they are genuine here. They are left out by most good MSS.

519. ὀΐων: rather οἰῶν, MSS, but here still replaceable by trisyllabic ὀΐων (cf. e.g. ix 443), which was inherited from the tradition, cf. 100 with n.

527. οἵ ... ἐόντος: for the change from dat. to gen. cf. vi 155–6, *Il.* iii 300–1; cf. also xv 240, xvi 466 with nn.

529. χλαῖναν ... ἀλεξάνεμον: cf. χλαινάων ... ἀνεμοσκεπέων (*Il.* xvi 224).

530. Cf. Hes. *Op.* 543 ff.

532. κείων: see xiii 16–18 n.

533. πέτρῃ ὕπο γλαφυρῇ: in 16–17 we heard that the boars used to sleep outside the courtyard.   **ἰωγῇ**: only here (ἐπιωγαί, 'sheltered places', *Od.* v 404); plausibly connected with ἄγνυμι, 'break', see Frisk *GEW* s.v.

(presumably < *ϝιϝωγή, but then ἐπἴωγή would have to come from *ἐπιϝιϝωγή). The 'neglect' of the digamma is surprising with such archaic words, which are often preserved in the body of formulae; hence Wackernagel's Βορέαο ἰωγῇ and οὐδε ἰωγαί (in v) deserve serious consideration; at all events they are likely to restore the pre-Homeric prototypes.

BOOK XV: COMMENTARY

1–3. These lines provide a twofold instance of the treatment of 'chronology' in the epics (literature e.g. in Page, *Odyssey*, 77 n. 11; see also Erbse, *Beiträge*, 39–40). Scholars have calculated that about a month must have elapsed since the poet left Telemachus at Sparta (iv 624), and some have argued that this is what we are intended to understand, the more so because that town 'with beautiful women' would offer many attractions to the young man (see e.g. Delebecque, *Télémaque*, 25). Yet this reasoning only holds good if we assume that v 1 ff. is meant to follow iv 624 *in time*, whereas in fact the events which happen to Odysseus from that point onwards are to be viewed without any chronological relation to the Telemachy (cf. e.g. Page, *Odyssey*, 67), though in the narrative the story is presented as a continuous one. Something similar applies to the relation between the end of xiii and the beginning of xv. In the former passage (439–40) we are told that Athena leaves Odysseus and sets out for Sparta. The time must still be early morning (cf. xiii 93–5) and the goddess, given the travelling speed of the gods in the epics (cf. e.g. v 50–4), should have arrived soon afterwards. Actually she does so in xv only at the end of the night, and this must be the very same night that was mentioned at the end of xiv. Again there is a blank space of time, and here we cannot even argue that the events represented as successive (Odysseus' first day with Eumaeus and Athena's arrival at Sparta) are simultaneous. 'Chronology' clearly means nothing to the poet. Whether he intentionally 'improves upon the simple methods of the past by delicately weaving the old scene and the new one together' (Page, *Odyssey*, 66), or whether his leaving Odysseus when asleep at night suggested to him a picture of Telemachus in bed at night is difficult to tell.

1. εὐρύχορον: see xiii 414 n. and Hainsworth on vi 4.

2. οἴχετ': ᾤχετ' MSS, *nil mutandum* (cf. xiii 374); of course we may translate 'she had gone', but this does not save the 'chronology', see 1–3 n.

5. εὗδοντ': the meaning of this verb is not confined to 'sleeping': it can also denote 'lying at night', cf. e.g. ἐγὼ δὲ μόνα καθεύδω in the anonymous little poem sometimes ascribed to Sappho, fr. 976 *PMG*, and Ar. *Lys.* 282. ἐν προδόμῳ: cf. iv 297, 302.

7. ἔχε: see xiv 239 n.

8. νύκτα δι' ἀμβροσίην: also ix 404 etc. It is not clear what religious notion, if any, underlies the epithet (cf. ἱερὸν ἦμαρ ix 56 etc.). We also find νύκτα διὰ δνοφερήν (50) and νύκτα δι' ὀρφναίην (ix 143 etc.), which, on Milman Parry's supposition of the 'ornamental' character of such epithets, should be considered 'equivalents' and thus would be remarkable exceptions to the rule of 'thrift' which he regards as typical of the formulaic diction; see 50 n. On διά with acc. see xiv 2 n. ἔγειρεν: impf., 'kept him awake'.

231

9. In contrast with i 105, vii 20, xiii 222, xvi 157–8, Athena appears undisguised. It looks all the more curious at first sight that Telemachus does not show any sign of being impressed and does not even take the trouble to answer her. This has been taken as a symptom of the passage being late, cf. e.g. Cauer, *Homerkritik*, 397–8; yet a comparison with similar scenes in the *Iliad* shows that this conception of the encounter god–hero is not exceptional, though here the theme has been treated in a somewhat mechanical way; see xvi 184–5 n.

10. οὐκέτι καλὰ ... ἀλάλησαι: cf. e.g. οὐκέτι καλὰ μεθίετε (*Il.* xiii 116); the pf. means 'you are roving', cf. e.g. Chantraine, *Grammaire*, ii 197–8.

11. = iii 314.

12. ~ iii 315. ὑπερφιάλους: see xvi 346–7 n.   'The independent subjunctive with μή expresses apprehension, coupled with a desire to avert the object of fear, both ideas being inherent in the construction', Goodwin, *Syntax*, 90, with many examples from Homer.

13. = iii 316. τηϋσίην, 'futile' (only here in Homer), is an archaic survival, which originally may have meant 'thievish', 'deceitful', see Frisk, *GEW*, Chantraine, *Dictionnaire* s.v.

15. τέτμης: another survival; etymology unknown.   ἀμύμονα: see xiii 41–2 n.

16–17. The fact that this attitude of Icarius and Penelope's brothers is mentioned nowhere else need not be considered an indication of the passage being an interpolation or the result of reworking; the statement is likely to be a white lie on the part of Athena ('the ancient gods were not essentially truthful', Stanford).

18. ἔεδνα: see xiii 378 n.

19. The rejection of this line by Aristophanes of Byzantium because of its 'meanness' (ἐπὶ σμικρολογίᾳ schol.) provides a good example of the criteria of the Alexandrian scholars, whose notion of ἀπρεπές was as foreign to the Homeric one as the Ptolemaic court was to the world of the heroes.   μή: see 12 n.   φέρηται: again the middle has its full strength, cf. φέρεσθαι ἄεθλον (*Il.* xxiii 413 etc.).

21. οἶκον ὀφέλλειν: see xiv 223 n.; here with 'neglected' digamma; from *ϝοῖκον ὀφελλέμεν? ὅς κεν ὀπυίη: this phrase too may go back to a very old formula (*ὅς κέ ϝ᾽ ὀπυίη?). The verb still survives in the famous Cretan law-code of Gortyn, dating from the fifth century BC, iii 20 etc., see e.g. C. D. Buck, *The Greek Dialects* (Chicago, 1955), 316.

22. κουριδίοιο: elsewhere an epithet of ἀνήρ, πόσις, ἄλοχος, see xiii 45 n.; its use as a noun is a symptom of the decomposition of the old formulaic diction, cf. xiv 453–6 n.

26. φήνωσι θεοὶ ... παράκοιτιν: cf. θεοὶ γόνον ... ἔφαινον (iv 12).

27. See app. crit. The regular formulae are ἄλλο δέ τοι ἐρέω, σὺ δ᾽ ἐνὶ φρεσὶ βάλλεο σῇσι(ν) xvi 281 etc., and ἐκ γάρ τοι (τοὔνεκά τοι, etc.) ἐρέω, σύ δὲ σύνθεο (καί μευ ἄκουσον) (μοι ὄμοσσον) xv 318, *Il.* i 76 etc.

28. Cf. xiii 425, xiv 180–1.

29. Σάμοιό τε παιπαλοέσσης: the form Σάμος is found only in this line (= iv

671), in its variant iv 845 (which has μεσσηγύς instead of ἐν πορθμῷ), and at *Il.* ii 634; elsewhere we find Σάμη. In Strabo's time there still existed a town of that name in Cephallenia (καὶ Σάμος καὶ Σάμη καλουμένη), and the author (453) accordingly regarded this island as the Homeric one. This is indeed the most plausible identification, but unfortunately it does not provide a satisfactory solution for the problems raised by the course of Telemachus' ship (see 33 and xiv 335 nn.; cf. Lorimer, *Monuments*, 499 ff.). On Mycenaean settlements in Cephallenia see Desborough, *The Last Mycenaeans and their Successors* (Oxford, 1964), 103 ff., 126. The epithet παιπαλόεις, of uncertain meaning and etymology, is used for mountains, rocks, roads, and islands, cf. Frisk, *GEW* s.v. παιπάλη and Leumann, *Wörter*, 236 ff., Càssola on *h.Ap.* 39.

30–2. = xiii 426–8.

33. ἑκὰς νήσων: what islands? 'Samos' and Ithaca? If, contrary to common sense and in spite of any grammatical reference to 29, this should be the meaning of the expression, Telemachus would be still in the dark about the course to steer. Must he keep close to the mainland, as is often assumed, thus heading for other islands (299)? For the partisans of the Ithaca = Leucas theory there is no problem here: according to them Telemachus, when arriving off Elis, must steer a westward course leaving *all* the islands to starboard in order to avoid the ambush of the suitors at Asteris (iv 846, see S. West ad loc. and 36 n.; according to Dörpfeld identical with Arkoudi, some 8 km. from the SE coast of Leucas) when making for the SW point of his island. But those 'Ithacists' who find precise geographical indications everywhere should explain the extreme vagueness of the expression. As it stands, it seems to favour the view defended above (xiii 103–7, xiv 335 nn.) that this part of Homer's geography is a mixture of truth and fiction.

36. πρώτην ἀκτὴν Ἰθάκης: this has often been taken to denote Cape Hagios Andreas (Andri) on the south coast of Ithaca (see e.g. Stubbings in *Companion*, 414) on the supposition that Asteris, the island where the suitors lie in ambush (iv 844–7), is Daskalio, lying towards the northern end of the channel between Ithaca and Cephallenia—a view to which there are grave objections (see e.g. Cauer, *Homerkritik*, 215, Lorimer, *Monuments*, 499–500). Miss Lorimer assumes a conflation of a Leucas version (implying Arkoudi) and a Thiaki version (implying an imaginary island near Same), in which Telemachus landed at Cape Hagios Joannis, on the SE coast of Ithaca.

37. ὀτρῦναι: see xvi 355 n.

38–9. See xiii 404–5 n.

40. ἀέσαι: see xvi 367 n.

44. See 9 n.

45. λὰξ ποδὶ κινήσας: the same expression is used at *Il.* x 158. There Nestor and Odysseus find Diomedes sleeping and Nestor wakes him up in exactly the same way. A schol. on xv 45 tells us that in this case the 'kicking' was done προσηκόντως, 'fitly', 'suitably', because Nestor, owing to his old age, did not wish to stoop. Our line, however, (thus the same schol.) was considered spurious (presumably by Aristarchus), the implication obviously being that Telemachus did *not* have the excuse of old age. Another schol. (followed by M. Müller, *Athene* (see xiii 313 n.), 106) thinks it necessary to exonerate Telemachus from not observing τὸ πρέπον by alleging his 'excitement'. Of course such considerations are without value: Nestor does not even abstain from fighting (he takes part in the battle three times) nor does Telemachus show any trace of excitement in the whole of the passage. Clearly the Alexandrians had no feeling for such a sign of rough camaraderie, see also 19 n. and Stanford ad loc., who observes, 'Both incidents bear the authentic mark of H.'s flair for introducing vivid unconventionalities.'

46. μώνυχας: a highly archaic survival; on its etymology see Beekes, *Orbis*, xx (1971), 138–42.

47. ~ iii 476.   **ἅρματ':** see 145 n.   **ὁδοῖο:** a partitive gen., cf. e.g. ἔρχονται πεδίοιο (*Il.* ii 801) and Schwyzer, *Grammatik*, ii 111–12 with many examples. In the phrase ἐπειγομένους περ ὁδοῖο (49), however, the partitive origin of the gen. is no longer felt, cf. ἐπειγόμενός περ Ἄρηος (*Il.* xix 142).

50. νύκτα διὰ δνοφερὴν: the epithet is not 'ornamental' (see 8 n.): without good visibility a journey through the Peloponnese must have been a risky affair. Because of ὡς ἔφατ', αὐτίκα δέ in 56 the words have been regarded as an exaggeration due to Pisistratus' sleepiness, but the use of the formula αὐτίκα ... Ἠώς appears to be no more than a conventional device to wind up a scene after the important things have been said and done, cf. x 541, xii 142, xx 91, and esp. xiv 502 with n.

51. ἐπιδίφρια: predic. and proleptic use of the adj., as in ἐφέστιον᾽ ἤγαγε δαίμων (vii 248 *et sim.*).

52. δουρικλειτὸς: a good instance of an epithet being used without any special connection with the context, cf. also βοὴν ἀγαθὸν (-ὸς) Μενέλαον (-ος) in 14, 57, etc.

54–5. On guest-friendship as a practical relationship and social institution see Finley, *World*, 115–18.

56. αὐτίκα δὲ: see 50 n.

61. δῦνεν: its use as a run-over word is a symptom of modification of an older type of formula, see xiv 41 n.; the same applies to ἐπί instead of περί, cf. Shipp, *Studies*, 341, Hoekstra, *Modifications*, 104.

65–6. Stanford rightly points to the 'abrupt boyish candour' shown by these words; see also 88 n.

68. οὔ τί σ᾽ ἐγώ γε ... ἐρύξω: cf. οὐδ᾽ ἐγώ σ᾽ ἐρύξω, Stesichorus (fr. 32. i 10 *PMG*), who gives the words to Helen, see 160–78 n.

70. The form in which this line is found in ps.-Plu. *Vit. Hom.* 151 is due to an adaptation by the author and provides an instructive instance of the way Homer used to be quoted in antiquity; see van der Valk, *Textual Criticism*, 278–82.

71. ἔξοχα δ᾽ ἐχθαίρησιν: taken by itself this phrase can only mean that a host whose hate towards his guest does not exceed the average is not to blame. Since such a sense is out of the question, the expression is to be understood

234

as 'and (in doing so behaves in the same way as a man) who shows hate to an excessive degree'. As this is not the natural interpretation of the relative clause, we probably have to do with a proverbial expression ('in love as well as in hate one should be moderate, for "nothing in excess" is always better'), which came to mean something different by being brought into relation with a ξεινοδόκος (on similar phenomena in Hes. cf. Hoekstra, *Mnemosyne* iii (1950), 89 ff.). φιλέῃ (φιλοίη) and ἐχθαίρῃ(σι) are also found combined in gnomic-looking phrases in *Od.* iv 692 and Hes. *Op.* 300.

72. ἰσόν τοι κακόν ἐσθ' ὅς τ': again gnomic; cf. Hes. *Op.* 327 ff. ἴσον δ' ὅς θ' ἱκέτην ὅς τε ξεῖνον κακὸν ἔρξῃ κτλ.

74. See app. crit. A schol. rightly observes that the line has a 'Hesiodic character'. So have many other Homeric lines, however, (see the preceding nn. and van der Valk, *Textual Criticism*, 202–3, who cites several cases from the *Odyssey*) and διδαχή was no doubt an organic and traditional element of epic poetry (cf. e.g. Verdenius, *Homer, the Educator of the Greeks* (Amsterdam–London, 1970), 21–7). On the other hand the contracted form φιλεῖν (only here) shows that in its actual form the maxim cannot be very old.

77. δεῖπνον: Homer employs the term ἄριστον, 'breakfast', only at *Il.* xxiv 124 and *Od.* xvi 2 (see n.). With regard to the names of meals the epic tradition does not seem to have been very specific, cf. the use of δαίς, which is by far the most frequent term. Cf. also δεῖπνον ἐπηρτύνοντο παρὰ πρυμνήσια νηός· ἀλλ' ἐμοὶ οὐ δόρποιο μελίφρονος ἤρατο θυμός (*h.Cer.* 128–9, and Richardson, op. cit. (xiv 336 n.), ad loc.). **ἅλις:** in view of δότω ἔνδον ἐόντων (vii 166), it might seem preferable to take the advb. with τετυκεῖν, but the caesura and such phrases as ἅλις ἦσαν (*Il.* iii 384 etc.) probably point the other way.

78–9. ἀμφότερον: sc. ἐστί, explained by what follows. **κῦδός τε καὶ ἀγλαΐη καὶ ὄνειαρ:** these words have been taken as referring (*a*) to the guests (van Leeuwen, Stanford), (*b*) to the host (κῦδός τε καὶ ἀγλαΐη) and the guests (καὶ ὄνειαρ) respectively (Ameis–Hentze–Cauer). The objection to (*b*) is that δειπνήσαντας can only refer to the guests, so that any mention of a relation to the host is wanting in the text. As to (*a*): Stanford thinks (with van Leeuwen) that the emphasis is strongly on the ptcp.—a well-known phenomenon in Greek—and accordingly translates: 'for it is both honour and glory (cf. ἐρικυδέα δαῖτα 13, 26), as well as an advantage, to have lunch before going on a very long journey'. Now ὄνειαρ, as usual, refers to eating (cf. e.g. 316 and xiv 453–4 with n.), but κῦδός τε καὶ ἀγλαΐη (!) is a bit exaggerated in this connection. It seems rather to be the predicate of 'travelling far and wide', and to announce the attitude of a new age which broke down the barriers of cantonal seclusion existing in the preceding centuries and enjoyed 'seeing the world', Hdt.'s (γῆς) θεωρίη, cf. e.g. i 30. 2 γῆν πολλὴν θεωρίης εἵνεκεν ἐπελήλυθας, iv 76. 2 γῆν πολλὴν θεωρήσας. A similar spirit is shown by one of the most 'modern' similes of the Homeric epics, *Il.* xv 80–2: ὡς δ' ὅτ' ἂν ἀΐξῃ νόος ἀνέρος, ὅς τ' ἐπὶ πολλὴν | γαῖαν ἐληλουθὼς φρεσὶ πευκαλίμῃσι νοήσῃ | "ἔνθ' εἴην ἢ ἔνθα,"

μενοινήῃσί τε πολλά—, where ἐπὶ πολλὴν|γαῖαν, with its 'violent' enjamb-
ment (see Kirk, *Homer*, 150) as compared with πολλὴν ἐπὶ γαῖαν (*Od.* ii 364
etc., 3 times) is an innovation. In our line πολλὴν is a pointless (and
unique) addition to the formula ἐπ' (κατ') ἀπείρονα γαῖαν (*Od.* i 98 etc., 7
times, see also Kirk, *Songs*, 206). These phenomena confirm the impression
that 79 as well as *Il.* xv 80–2 are among the most recent elements of
Homeric poetry.

80–2. The difficulties of the syntax have been ascribed to the omission of the
apodosis after 80 (thus Monro) or after ἡγήσομαι 82 (thus van Leeuwen;
the closest parallel to such a construction is *Il.* xxi 487–8). I would suggest
the following explanation: the helpful Menelaus considers it his duty
himself to accompany Telemachus on a longer journey and hastens to
announce his readiness; hence after the conditional clause he continues
with ὄφρα τοι αὐτὸς ἕπωμαι, and thus the order, which grammatically had
to be ὑποξεύξω ... ὄφρα ..., becomes inverted; for δέ following an ὄφρα
clause, cf. *Il.* xvi 653–6.

80. τραφθῆναι: the only instance of τρέπομαι having an aor. of this type in
Homer. In spite of the fact that the development of the -θη- aor. (though
uncertain in detail, see e.g. H. Jankuhn, *Die passive Bedeutung medialer
Formen untersucht an der Sprache Homers* (Göttingen, 1969), 40 n. 15) must
largely antedate the composition of the Homeric poems, and although this
aor. started its career as an intrans. formation, the use of τραφθῆναι instead
of τραπέσθαι (e.g. *Od.* v 350, cf. also (ἐ)τράπετο etc.) is likely to be very
recent. Probably this particular form was modelled upon intrans. aors. of
denominative verbs such as δινηθῆναι (xvi 63), θωρηχθῆναι (xxii 139 etc.),
ὁρμηθῆναι (xii 126 etc.), cf. Meister, *Kunstsprache*, 110 ff. This does not
necessarily mean that the form is of epic origin, although, curiously
enough, the state of affairs in Hdt. is similar: here τραφθέντες is the only -
θη- form of the verb used in an intrans.-reflexive sense, and it is employed
twice (iv 12. 3, ix 36. 2). **ἀν' Ἑλλάδα καὶ μέσον Ἄργος:** Ἑλλάς
originally denoted a district in southern Thessaly (and may or may not
have included other territory as well, cf. *Il.* ii 500, 683–4, ix 395, 447–8,
478, x 266), whereas ἄργος was a common noun (meaning 'plain';
testimonia given by Denniston on E. *El.* 1), that in epic poetry came to be
extended from the region of Argos to a great part or the whole of the
Peloponnese, cf. *Od.* iv 174 ff. The phrase, therefore, may in a certain
period have been used to denote 'northern and southern Greece', but it is
doubtful whether the poet of the *Odyssey* (who employs it also at i 344, iv
726 = 816) meant anything so specific, cf. xiv 205 n.

83. αὔτως: 'just like that', i.e. 'empty-handed', cf. xiii 281 n.

84. Cf. xiii 13 with 12 n.

85. δύ' ἡμιόνους: in iv 590 Menelaus offered horses, but now he does not
mention them: he appears to remember iv 601–7. **χρύσειον ἄλεισον:**
also iii 50, 53, *Il.* xi 774, always at the end of the line; cf. ἄλεισον
...|χρύσεον (viii 430–1), q.v. Hainsworth, whose observations fit in with
the presence of *a-re-se-si* (dat. pl. of a neut.) in Lin. B (PY Ub 1318,

Ventris–Chadwick, *Documents*, no. 317), if the article in question (here of leather) is a bag or a pouch; see further Ruijgh, *Études*, 356 with nn.

86. πεπνυμένος: whether or not its connection with πνέω is rightly questioned (see e.g. Hainsworth on viii 388), it is associated in the *Iliad* and *Odyssey* with φρένες and νόος (see Heubeck on x 493–5 and cf. *Il.* xxiv 377). For its meaning see *Il.* xxiii 440, where οὐ ... πεπνῦσθαι reflects ἀφραδέως (426) and alludes to Ἀντίλοχος πεπνυμένος.

88. βούλομαι ἤδη νεῖσθαι ἐφ' ἡμέτερ': again Telemachus uses a terse and matter-of-fact expression, cf. 65–6 n. The departure from the traditional style has involved the extremely rare contraction of νέεσθαι.

90. μὴ ... ὄλωμαι: see 12 n.

94. = 77 (see n.).

95. Βοηθοΐδης Ἐτεωνεύς: a θεράπων of Menelaus (see iv 22–3), a person, that is, of noble birth (hence patronymic added), to be distinguished from the obscure δρηστῆρες (e.g. xvi 248) and of course from the δμῶες, 'slaves'. Yet θεράποντες is already used as a general denomination of servants, xvi 326 etc.

98. κρεῶν: the only case of an irresolvable contraction of the gen. pl. (in the nom.–acc. -ε- hyphaeresis is normal, see 140 n.): elsewhere κρειῶν, ultimately from κρεάων (epigraphical material in Thumb–Scherer, *Handbuch*, ii 275). The gen. is partitive.

99. = *Il.* xxiv 191 ~ *Il.* vi 288.   **κηώεντα:** only found in these lines; with the dat. in ἐν θαλάμῳ εὐώδεϊ, κηώεντι (*Il.* iii 382). The word is a synonym of κηώδης, 'flagrant' (*Il.* vi 483), according to Risch, *Wortbildung*, 155, created on the analogy of θυήεις: θυώδης. However, it may as well be a cross between *κηϝ-ώδεα (which could not be used at the verse-end) and *κηϝᾱ-ϝεντα (cf. Chantraine, *Dictionnaire* s.v. κηύα), or even a survival from the older epic, *κηϝᾱ-ϝεντα (cf. τιμήεντα (*Od.* xi 327) < *τιμᾱ-ϝεντα etc.) having received a thematic vowel with consequent shortening of the α (> *κηϝᾱ-ο-εντα > κηώεντα), cf. e.g. *φοινίκ-ϝεντα > φοινικόεντα, xiv 500 n.

100. Μεγαπένθης: see iv 11–12.

101. ὅθι κειμήλια κεῖτο: the lengthening of the final syllable of ὅθι results from formulaic adaptation, cf. ἀλλ' ὅτε δή ῥ' (αἶψα δ' ἔπειθ' etc.) ἵκανον ὅθι (ξανθὸς Μενέλαος etc.) (*Il.* iv 210 etc.), 6 times) and κειμήλια κεῖτο (-ται) (8 times, see xiv 326 n.); see also A. G. Tsopanakis, *Problems in the Homeric Hexameter* (Thessaloniki, 1966), 359 ff.

102. δέπας ... ἀμφικύπελλον: see xiii 57 n.

104. ἀργύρεον· Ἑλένη: see xiv 68 n.; also for ἀειραμένη Ἑλένη (106).

105–8. ~ *Il.* vi 289, 293–5. The reading ἔργα γυναικῶν (105; see app. crit.) shows to what extent, how, and why the MS-tradition might be corrupted under certain conditions. It is obviously wrong (cf. 125–6) but is given even by some good MSS. It was introduced from *Il.* vi 289. The reason is apparent from the scholl.: some critics asserted that Helen could not have had sufficient time to manufacture these garments (the subsequent 'refutation' is as pedantic as the objection itself).

105. πέπλοι: It cannot be taken for granted that the poet used πέπλος (of uncertain etymology, see Chantraine, *Dictionnaire* s.v.) as the name of a garment identical with the garb which is seen on the statues and painted figures of the archaic period, nor can we be sure that he had in mind the attire shown by the representations of women on Geometric vases (which, besides, are too formalized to permit any detailed conclusions). All that can be said is that none of these presents any features which are irreconcilable with πέπλον μὲν κατέχευεν at *Il.* v 734 = viii 385 and with ἑλκεσιπέπλους *Il.* vi 442 etc. (this epithet is confined to Trojan women, but, given the methods of epic technique, it need not be distinctive). At all events Homer employs the term to denote a woman's garment, probably a long robe that could be fastened at the shoulder (on the last point, however, cf. *Il.* xiv 180 and Lorimer, *Monuments*, 378). Marinatos, *Archaeologia* i A, 11, 42, wrongly assumes that the Homeric πέπλος was a veil, a view presumably due to his conviction that two different words (πέπλος and ἑανός) must of necessity denote two different articles of dress (on this point, cf. introduction to xiii–xvi, p. 157). Further details are lacking, but it is noteworthy that the epics do not show a single trace of the elaborate flounced skirt of Mycenaean times, cf. introduction, p. 155. **παμποίκιλοι**: cf. also ποικίλμασιν (107). In post-Homeric Greek ποικίλος and its derivatives regularly refer to embroidery and inwoven decoration alike, and passages which by themselves, without the aid of external evidence, enable us to infer which of the two is meant are exceedingly rare. If only for this reason, the fact that Homer never mentions embroidery (rightly observed by H. P. and A. J. B. Wace, in *Companion*, 501) is inconclusive (for adornment sewn on the surface of the cloth—later called ἐπίβλημα—there is not the slightest evidence in Homer). However, Helen and Andromache are said to *weave* designs into the fabric of clothes at *Il.* iii 125 and xxii 441 respectively, so the words used in 105 and 107 of our passage probably indicate the results of the same procedure.

108. νείατος ἄλλων: see Hainsworth on v 105.

109. διὰ δώματος: elsewhere always διὰ δώματα, δώμαθ', δῶμα (11 times), cf. xiv 2 n. Yet this fact does not carry much weight, as the gen. and acc. are often found with διά, 'through', without any discernible difference of meaning and since the part of the line which follows the diaeresis begins (or once began) more often with a consonant than with a vowel. Alternatively, one might see in διὰ δώματος a symptom of the gradual replacement of the acc. by the gen., a process which is already complete in the earliest Ionic prose, cf. xiv 2 n.

113–19. = iv 613–19 (see app. crit.). The fact that the goblet (see 102, 120) is not mentioned in this passage is not a sufficient reason to reject the lines, and Homeric composition is such that repetitions should in principle be considered genuine unless they are either contradicted by the context or are completely vacuous. But of course we cannot be sure that in this case the lines were not added by a rhapsode; on the pros and cons see Heubeck, *Dichter*, 62–3. And in the present case it must be realized that a poet composing for listeners may have repeated the verses deliberately, after an interval of some five thousand lines, when he came to describe Telemachus' actual departure (on word-for-word repetitions of longer passages, cf. Hoekstra, *Modifications*, 18 ff.). And would he have thought it necessary to eliminate those verses from the final version of the poem? See also xvi 281–98 n. In any case 115–16 were probably known to Stesichorus, see 160–78 n.

115. τετυγμένον: see xiii 306 n.

115–16. ἀργύρεος δὲ|ἐστὶν ἅπας: a most unusual form of enjambment, showing a degree of suppleness in epic verse-making which is remarkable even in the highly developed technique of Homer. An older type is to be found in the 'progressive' enjambment in ἀργύρεον, χρυσῷ δ' ἐπὶ χείλεα κεκράαντο *Od.* iv 132 (the term is Kirk's, see 78–9 n.); see also 121–3.

117–18. A good instance of how the threads of (1) poetical phantasy, (2) a vaguely remembered tradition, and (3) contemporary ideas are closely interwoven in epic narrative: (1) neither the name nor the epithet of Φαίδιμος make a traditional origin likely (cf. Lorimer, *Monuments*, 80); (2) yet the mention of Sidonians—who are always associated with craftmanship, whereas the Phoenicians appear as traders—is suggestive of the Bronze Age (Lorimer, *Monuments*, 67, Stella, *Ulisse*, 38–9, Stubbings in *Companion*, 542–3, *Od.* xiii 285 n.); (3) their ruler, however, is called a βασιλεύς, not a (ϝ)άναξ (see xiii 185 n.); (1) though he possessed a piece of metalwork wrought by a god. See also S. West on iv 126 ff. and Hainsworth on viii 373.

119. τεῖν: a survival (= τοι, σοι) only recurring in the parallel line iv 619, in τεῖν τάδε μυθήσασθαι (*Il.* xi 201, *Od.* iv 829), and in τεῖν δ' ἐπὶ μοῖραν ἔθηκε (*Od.* xi 560).   **ὀπάσσαι:** see xiv 62 n.

120. χειρὶ: χερσὶ, besides being much better attested, is also preferable because 'non de pleno nunc poculo altera manu tenendo et ad os adducendo fit sermo' (van Leeuwen).

123. ἀργύρεον: see 115–16 n.   **καλλιπάρῃος:** this reading, in this case very weakly attested, is to be rejected in favour of καλλιπάρῃος (here not mentioned in Allen's app. crit.): it is probably due to the influence of παρειά, cf. Ruijgh, *Études*, 57 n. 53.

124. ἔκ τ' ὀνόμαζε: see xiv 52 n.

125. τέκνον φίλε: only here; τέκνον φίλον (*Od.* xxiii 26); φίλε τέκνον 3 times in the *Odyssey*, but only once in the *Iliad*: cf. the figures for τέκος and τέκνον used as vocs.: *Il.* 27:17, *Od.* 9:21. These simple variations show that the process of discarding older idioms (φίλον τέκος in this case) has progressed in our poem.

126. μνῆμ' Ἑλένης χειρῶν: see xiv 68 n.

127. τῆος: read τείως (MSS).

128. κεῖσθαι: see app. crit. As a *lectio difficilior* depending on δίδωμι (125) it is perhaps preferable to κείσθω, but it may equally well have been written under the influence of the preceding φορέειν.   **ἐνὶ μεγάρῳ:** probably 'in the palace', = ἐνὶ μεγάροισι, cf. the use of the phrase at *Il.* vi 91 as compared with ἐς θάλαμον κατεβήσετο κτλ. (288). Admittedly Helen has not been told by Telemachus that Penelope avoids the 'great hall' because of the suitors, but this does not prove that she is using the expression in its literal sense, cf. xiv 440, xv 354 nn., and also xi 62 as compared with x 554–9. But it is also possible that the expression refers to Penelope's own room, as it certainly does in xviii 316, see also Stanford ad loc.

129. ἐϋκτίμενον: from ἐϋ κτίμενον (cf. xiii 306 n.); the (athematic) verb originally meant both 'to cultivate' (cf. Myc. *ki-ti-me-na*, PY Eo 211 (= Ventris–Chadwick, *Documents*, no. 118), Palmer, *Interpretation*, 186–8) and 'to build' (cf. κτίζω, Chantraine, *Dictionnaire* s.v.); its use with οἶκος is normal, since this word denoted not only the house and its inmates (see xiv 4 n.) but also the land, cf. also ἐϋκτιμένη ἐν ἀλωῆ (*Od.* xxiv 226), the pres. ptcp. describing the state of affairs (but did the old meaning of the expression fully survive into Homeric times? Cf. e.g. xiv 205 n.).

131. πείρινθα: only here and at *Il.* xxiv 190, a survival, probably from a pre-Greek language (as many other words in -νθ(ο)-, cf. ἀσάμινθος, λαβύρινθος, etc.).

133. κάρη ξανθὸς Μενέλαος: an occasional extension of the formula ξανθὸς Μενέλαος (e.g. 110, 147) replacing the normal βοὴν ἀγαθὸς Μενέλαος. The addition κάρη was probably introduced on the model of κάρη κομόωντες Ἀχαιοί, 'a phrase of extreme antiquity' (Page, *History and the Homeric Iliad* (cit. xiii 315 n.), 243, see also 282 n. 67). It is a typical instance of archaizing.

134. κατὰ κλισμούς τε θρόνους τε: a formula confined to the *Odyssey* (i 145 etc.), but ἐπὶ κλισμοῖσι is found at *Il.* viii 436, xi 623. It might come from κατὰ κλισμούς *θόρνους τε: the form θόρνος is Mycenaean, PY Ta 707 (= Ventris–Chadwick, *Documents*, no. 242), cf. also εἰνὶ θρόνῳ (< ἐν θόρνῳ *Il.* viii 199, xv 150; D. J. N. Lee, 'Some Vestigial Mycenaean Words in the *Iliad*', *BICS* vi (1959), 7) and the parallel treatment of *φοινῖκϝεσσαν, xiv 500 n. This would explain the fact that τε remains short before θρ- in what looks like an old formula. Here the use of the expression with a dual subject is another instance of the poet employing a formula that was created for a different situation, cf. xiii 185 n.

135–9. A typical description, but only found in the *Odyssey* (i 136–40 etc.). On 139 see app. crit. and S. West on i 140, but also Monro on xvii 95, who concludes, 'It does not seem at all likely that a stately formula ... should have been framed for such a case' (i.e. of serving leftovers from a former meal, xvi 50).

135. ἐπέχευε: sc. over their hands, but in Greek such an addition would be superfluous after χέρ-νιψ.　**ἀμφίπολος**: see Fernández-Galiano on xxii 483.

137. ἐτάνυσσε: see 283 n.

139. χαριζομένη παρεόντων: the central meaning of χάρις (cognate with χαίρω) is best rendered with German 'Wohlgefallen'; it is reciprocal, cf. e.g. S. *Aj.* 522 χάρις χάριν γάρ ἐστιν ἡ τίκτουσ' ἀεί and E. Fraenkel on A. *A.* 354. Hence the sense of χαρίζεσθαι (med.) is 'sich gefällig machen', i.e. commending favour by doing favour, see also xiii 15 with n. The gen. is partitive, cf. 77.

140. κρέα δαίετο: the fact that in nearly all the Homeric cases κρέα is followed by a consonant—which makes κρέα'(α) impossible—is characteristic of the degree to which Ionic innovations (κρέα < *κρέεα < *κρέαα, cf. 98 n.) had already become established in epic language in Homer's time. An exception is probably to be found in κρέα ἔδμεναι (*Il.* iv 345, xxii 347), in which the hiatus may not be original and the non-Ionic form of the infin. is noteworthy (< *κρέα' ἔδμεναι).

142-3. See xiv 453-4 n.

145. ἅρματα: here, as often, said of a single chariot; perhaps not so much a poetic pl. as the result of a semantic development of Myc. *a-mo-ta*, 'wheels', PY Sa 790 (Ventris-Chadwick, *Documents*, no. 288) etc.; see in particular C. J. Ruijgh, 'Faits linguistiques et données externes relatifs aux chars et aux roues', in *Colloquium Mycenaeum* (cit. xiii 192 n.), 208 ff. and the observation by Risch, 220.

146. = 191 = iii 493 ~ *Il.* xxiv 323. Any attempt to reconcile the content of this line with what we know of Mycenaean palaces would be futile. Moreover the presence of a gen. in irresolvable -ου (alongside a parallel one in -οιο) proves that the verse must be a post-Mycenaean creation (καὶ αἰθούσης ἐριδούπου from older ὑπ' αἰθούσῃ ἐριδούπῳ iii 399 etc.?). Judging from Homer's description of the palaces the line seems to contain a prothysteron; see xiii 434 n.

148-50. ~ *Il.* xxiv 284-6; cf. 150 and 160-5 nn.

148. ἐν χειρὶ ... δεξιτερῆφι: in Mycenaean the ending -φι (= -φι) is attested for the pl. of the instrumental, though its use in the dual and sg. cannot be excluded, cf. M. Lejeune, *Mémoires de philologie mycénéenne*, i (Paris, 1958), 159-84. In Homer it is most often found in the sg., and has spread to several other grammatical cases: see e.g. Chantraine, *Grammaire*, i 234 ff., 499-500. A comparison of our line with χείρ' (364 n.) ἐπιμασσάμενος φάρυγος λάβε δεξιτερῆφι (xix 480) shows how the latter development might have taken place.

149. δέπαϊ: see xiii 57 n.

150. δεδισκόμενος: normally δειδισκόμενος etc. If the initial syllable was originally long (*δη-; thus Frisk, *GEW* s.v. δηδέχαται, and Chantraine, *Grammaire*, i 433-4, following Bechtel), the shortening is due to the formula δειδισκόμενος δὲ προσηύδα (iii 41) being used after the trochaic caesura instead of ἔπος τ' ἔφατ' ἔκ τ' ὀνόμαζε (cf. *Il.* xxiv 286). If it was short, we would have to do with a case of metrical lengthening in iii 41 (as is suggested by Wyatt, *Lengthening*, 105 n. 1), which resulted from the use of the formula after the penthemimeris (more examples of this phenomenon in Hoekstra, *Modifications*, 116 ff. and *passim*).

152. εἰπεῖν: sc. χαίρειν: 'give him my greetings'.

155. καὶ λίην: see xvi 37 with n.

156. πάντα τάδ': to wit, 'all your hospitality': cf. φιλότητος ἁπάσης, (158), hence καταλέξομεν; cf. xiii 296 n.

156-9. The meaning of this passage and especially of ὥς (156) and ὡς (158) is disputed. The parallel construction found in *Il.* viii 538-41 would suggest *tam certo* ... *ut*, but Ameis–Hentze–Cauer are probably right in explaining ὥς as (*eben*) *so*, sc. as we shall tell *Nestor*. In 157 the emphasis is on κιχὼν Ὀδυσῆ', and the general sense of the lines seems to be: 'Ah, if only I could also tell Odysseus, finding him in the house on my returning to Ithaca, how I come from you' etc.

160–78. The basic elements of this passage, together with some details of the preceding leave-taking (68, 113–19 nn.), have been adopted and remodelled by Stesichorus in his lyrical version of Telemachus' departure, fr. 209 *PMG*.

160–5. In the comparable scene in *Il.* xxiv (283–321, equally concluded with οἱ δὲ ... ἰάνθη) there also appears an eagle, this time, however, at Priam's special entreaty. The formulaic line 160 (=525 = *Il.* xiii 821) is again 'introductory', cf. 164 δεξιὸς ἤιξε; see xiv 299–301 n.

161. Cf. φοινήεντα δράκοντα φέρων ὀνύχεσσι πέλωρον (*Il.* xii 202 = 220). **πέλωρον:** originally there existed an Aeolic substantive πέλωρ (= τέρας (168), cf. Frisk, *GEW*, Chantraine, *Dictionnaire* s.v.) and an adjective πελώριος. Here πέλωρον may be either a substantive or an adj., but in any case it is a secondary formation (derived from the pl. of πέλωρ, cf. αἰνὰ πέλωρα (*Od.* x 219) and Bechtel, *Lexilogus*, 274). For the gradual fading of the original meaning in this development (final phase: Γαῖα πελώρη Hes. *Th.* 159 etc.) see H. Troxler, *Sprache und Wortschatz Hesiods* (Zurich, 1964), 174 ff.

162. ἰύζοντες: a good parallel in ἀμφὶ δὲ τόν γε κύνες τ' ἄνδρες τε νομ-ῆες|πολλὰ μάλ' ἰύζουσιν (*Il.* xvii 65–6), which is part of a lion-simile. Onomatopoeic ἰού (thus spelt owing to the change in pronunciation in Attic) also in Ar. and elsewhere. Here the verb denotes inarticulate shouting, but in μολπῇ τ' ἰυγμῷ τε (*Il.* xviii 572) the noun expresses a rhythmical yell.

170. ὑποκρίναιτο: in Homer its meaning oscillates between 'interpreting' and 'answering' (cf. e.g. *Od.* xix 535, 555 and, on the other hand, ii 111), but 'il valore fondamentale del verbo è quello di "pronunciarsi su una questione o su una proposta" esprimendo in forma definitiva un intimo convincimento ... Con ciò si accorda l'uso mediale del verbo e la composizione con ὑπο-' (B. Zucchelli, ΥΠΟΚΡΙΤΗΣ: *Origine e storia del termine* (Genoa, 1962), 21, with literature).

171. τανύπεπλος: must originally have meant 'with thin robe', cf. Frisk, *GEW* s.v. ταννυ-, but was perhaps taken as 'with flowing robe' by the poet and his listeners, because in such compounds ταννυ- became associated with τανύω, cf. e.g. ὄρνιθες τανυσίπτεροι (*Od.* v 65), οἰωνοῖσι τανυπτερύγεσσι (*Il.* xii 237), and Risch, *Wortbildung*, 190.

172. κλῦτέ μευ: Helen is not only quicker to take the initiative, as Stanford observes, but she does so with a self-assurance that remarkably contrasts with the position of women in classical Greece. See S. West on iv 120 ff.

175. ὅθι ... τόκος τε: a graphic addition by means of a formula (cf. *Il.* vii 128, xv 141), not relevant to the interpretation given in the next lines.

181. καὶ κεῖθι: in the parallel line *Od.* viii 467, καί may refer to Nausicaa's words καί ποτ' ἐὼν ἐν πατρίδι γαίη (461). Here it has no counterpart. This may be due to adaptation, or the particle may simply serve to stress the following word, see 435 n.

184–92. ~ iii 486–94. The simple lines 184–6 evoke with great suggestive power the atmosphere of an arrival at dusk in a Greek town after a day-long journey.

184. Literally, 'they rocked the yoke, supporting it on either side'. πανη-μέριοι: in flat country a distance of some forty miles could of course be covered in this way, but the poet takes no account of the barrier presented by Mt. Taygetos. On his knowledge about such geographical matters see 209–14 n.

185. δύσετό τ' ἠέλιος: see xiii 63 n. Because of the mountains surrounding this stretch of road an original secondary fut. ('the sun was about to set') would be particularly apt here. It may well be that the verse was created for such a situation, but if it was, it spread far beyond its original context, for we also find it in the description of voyages (xi 12, xv 296).

186. Φηρὰς: probably the classical Pharai (Kalamata); stretches of a Mycenaean-built road, presumably connecting the town with Pylos, have been found by W. A. McDonald, 'Overland Communications in Greece during LH III', in *Mycenaean Studies* (Madison, 1964), 224–34.

187. 'Ορτιλόχοιο: see xiii 260 n.

188. As ξείνια does not include breakfast (tacitly assumed in 189–90) we have again to do with a prothysteron, see xiii 434 n.

190. ἅρματα: see 145 n.

191. See 146 n.

193. αἶψα: see 184 n.   Πύλου αἰπὺ πτολίεθρον: the Mycenaean palace was built on the top of a high ridge (see e.g. Blegen in *Companion*, 423), and the town appears to have been on its slopes (ibid., 428; details in C. W. Blegen *et al.*, *The Palace of Nestor at Pylos in Western Messenia* (Princeton, 1966–73), i 33, iii 47–68, 219–37). Since the proper name can also denote the country, the gen. may be either possessive or explicative.

195–201. A tactful and elaborate address in order to escape being delayed by Nestor's hospitality. In this way the poet himself avoids a second stay of Telemachus at Pylos, cf. Page, *Odyssey*, 79.

195. πῶς: with a potential opt. used courteously to introduce an exhortation (in fifth-century Attic, notably in tragedy, it expresses a wish).   ὑποσ-χόμενος: here the verb does not mean 'to promise', but still has the sense of 'taking upon oneself'.

201. ἱκέσθαι: the omission of οἴκαδε is unusual and suggests haste on the part of Telemachus (see also 206 n.).

202–4. An elaborate and typically epic description of what was in fact a most natural reaction.

206. νηΐ ... ἐξαίνυτο: the condensed expression as well as the form of 207 (οἱ for Telemachus, omission of Helen) call up the image of a hurried proceeding (see also 218 n.).

209–14. It is often stated that the Mycenaean capital at Ano Englianos 'is'

Homer's Pylos. This is acceptable if it means no more than that it is this city, rather than Pylos-Kakovatos or Pylos-Koryphasion, from which the Homeric reminiscences are ultimately derived. Sometimes, however, the statement implies more than that, for instance that the *Odyssey* shows accurate knowledge of the topographical position of the Mycenaean settlement. Is that defensible? One might point to the opinion recorded by Strabo viii 359 that ancient Messenian Pylos had stood under Mt. Aigaleon, but this belief can neither have been deduced from Homer nor is it likely to have come from other epic poetry: the fact that Strabo disregards it when amply discussing the problem of *Homer*'s Pylos (336 etc.) suggests that it was based upon an old local tradition (the existence of which is intrinsically likely in view of the probability that the site continued to show at least some material remains for several centuries). Moreover, it would seem that such precise geographical information as was preserved by post-migration epic poetry must have survived in— necessarily short—formulae and incidentally. Even in the case of Mycenae itself the only characteristic of this kind is 'in the corner of horse-feeding Argos', and even this is not as specific as it looks, for the same formula is used for the mysterious Ephyra. Nor does Homer present any specific data concerning Pylos unless they are of a formulaic nature (such as e.g. αἰπὺ πτολίεθρον, though it is to be noted that this could be said of many cities and that the epithet is actually added to two other names). Blegen in *Companion*, 429, referring to *Od.* iii 386 ff., envisages the Homeric palace as 'remote enough from the seashore for refreshment and libations to be in order when the *megaron* was reached', but unfortunately the text itself presents no evidence whatever for any preparations having been made, let alone for any connection between the opening of the wine-jar and the length of the walk (or drive?). What is more, a comparison of iii 5 ff., 329–68 with 386–94 clearly shows that the poet imagined the palace somewhere near the beach, and the same is true of our passage. The phrase σπουδῇ νῦν ἀνάβαινε (209) does not suggest a palace lying some four miles from the nearest point of the shore as the crow flies, and πρὶν ἐμὲ οἴκαδ' ἱκέσθαι (210, i.e. 'if you wait till I have arrived at the palace you will not be able to escape my father') makes it clear that the distance (which both Pisistratus and Nestor would have to cover) was very short indeed.

A different problem is whether behind our passage there is some notion of Pylos-Koryphasion, which lay on a nearby peninsula that still shows Mycenaean remains, cf. also Strabo viii 339, 359, etc., Paus. iv 36. 1–2. That point is more difficult, but at all events a hypothesis of autopsy would be far-fetched, see xiii 96, 103–7, 217–18, 246, 351, 408, xv 33 nn.

212. οἶος: see xiv 392 n.

213. εἴσεται: see xvi 313 n.

214. ἔμπης: variously interpreted (a schol. calls it 'superfluous'); here too probably 'all the same': 'for in spite of my explaining (that it was your own decision not to return to his house) he will surely be angry (and as a result his overbearing spirit will cause him to come and fetch you if you are still there)'. Pisistratus is apprehensive of his reception by his father.

215. καλλίτριχας: rather 'with beautiful coat' (Fr. *pelage*) than 'with beautiful manes', as it is usually translated, cf. J. C. Opstelten, *Hermeneus*, xxxii (1960), 77 ff. Cf. also ὅτριχας (*Il.* ii 765), and Chantraine, *Dictionnaire* s.v. ὄ-.

216. θοῶς ... ἵκανε: a parenthetical addition. From another point of view 215-17 are a miniature instance of the Homeric treatment of 'simultaneous events' (see 1-3 n.), for of course Telemachus does not wait to give his order until the moment of Pisistratus' arrival at the palace.

218. Again the tempo of the narrative becomes hurried and the style matter-of-fact, see also 201, 206 and 222 nn. The poet varies the leisurely epic style with condensed expressions that look like his own creations: note the irresolvable contraction in ἐγκοσμεῖτε (only here) as against ἐκόσμεε, ἐκόσμεον, etc., comparable with νεῖσθαι (88). At any rate the line shows a considerable difference from the exhortations in the *Iliad* and in the first half of the *Odyssey*, which abound in elaborate vocatives and motivations. **τεύχε':** here probably not 'weapons' (Monro), but either 'vessels for victuals' (van Leeuwen, with reference to iv 784; cf. also ἀπεκόσμεον ἔντεα δαιτός vii 232) or 'the oars and rigging' (schol.); see however xvi 360 n.

222. θῦε: 'simplex aliquod dicitur sacrificium; urget enim tempus' (van Leeuwen). It may be added that in this respect the wording is in accordance with the action; see 201, 206, 218, xvi 322, 336-7, 355, 358-9, 422-3, 454-7 nn. The metrical lengthening in θῦε (as against regular θύοντα 260) has not been satisfactorily explained.

223-81. From Kirchhoff onwards the figure of Theoclymenus has been unanimously regarded by analytic critics as an intrusive figure—a secondary question being, on this supposition, whether or not he played a more important part in a pre-Homeric version of Odysseus' home-coming (as Odysseus himself in disguise? Cf. Page, *Odyssey*, 87-8). Even Kirk denies that the passages in which he makes his appearance are the work of the main composer and considers him 'the only character in the *Iliad* or *Odyssey*—with the possible exception of Phoinix—whom one feels to have arrived there almost by mistake' (*Songs*, 240). The main objections of the analysts may be summarized in Page's words: 'The poet now introduces, with quite extraordinary elaboration, a new character in his story, for whom he will hereafter find (to his manifest embarrassment) no useful employment' (*Odyssey*, 83). In his defence Erbse, *Beiträge*, 53-4, argues that 225-56 serve to legitimate Theoclymenus to listeners as a prophet: later on they will feel his predictions will come true because they have been told by the poet that he must be a master of his trade, belonging, as he does, to an ancient and renowned family of seers. That may be so, but the length of the digression is out of proportion to such a purpose (in a poem addressed to an audience the passage 223-56 can hardly be regarded as an instance of 'stückweise Komplementierung' (Heubeck, *Dichter*, 22) and still less (together with xi 281-96! See 231-6 n.) as 'a highly wrought introduction of almost gorgeous splendour [*sic*] to the appearance of the fugitive suppliant Theoclymenus' (Thornton, *People*, 62). The poet dwells upon genealogy for its own sake, and the compositional value of the details is much less than that of the vignettes giving short biographies and genealogies of warriors in the *Iliad*.

225. Μελάμποδος: a prophet who belonged to the famous Aeolid line (full pedigrees in Stanford, on xi 235 and xv 225). After Homer his story was told by 'Hes.' in the Μεγάλαι 'Ηοῖαι, the *Melampodia*, and (in outline) in the *Catalogus*, frr. 261, 270(?) ff., and 37 M–W; see further 231–6 n.

226. μητέρι μήλων: elsewhere said of Iton (in Thessaly, *Il.* ii 696), Phthia (*Il.* ix 479), and Thrace (*Il.* xi 222). The Linear B tablets show that it was appropriate to Pylos in the Mycenaean period, but it must have suited most Greek districts at any time, so we cannot tell whether the combination Πύλῳ ἔνι, μητέρι μήλων goes back to an Achaean stage of the epic diction or whether the poet merely availed himself of an epithet that would not be at variance with the real facts in the majority of cases.

228. ἄλλων δῆμον ἀφίκετο: an 'introductory' anticipation of ὁ δ' ἄλλων ἵκετο δῆμον, Ἄργος ἐς ἱππόβοτον (238–9); cf. xiv 299–301 n.

230. τελεσφόρον εἰς ἐνιαυτὸν: see xiv 196 n.

231–6. A piece of 'Minyan' and Aeolian mythology, which is all the more interesting since from Thessaly, a district which appears to have been important in the Bronze Age and to have had historical relations with Pylos, comparatively few myths have reached us, the most important being of course the sagas of Achilles and the Argo. In all probability the story to which the poet alludes never was a consistent whole, but was told, as far as we can see (cf. Heubeck, *Dichter*, 21) with several variants. If, with this proviso, we try to piece the oldest fragments together (see 225 n.), we get something like this: Melampus' brother Bias wooed Pero, a daughter of the Pylian ruler Neleus, but her father demanded as a bride-price a number of cows which were the property of the Thessalian Iphiclus (or of his father Phylacus, see 231 n.). The task of acquiring these cattle was undertaken by Melampus, a seer who understood the speech of beasts and birds. Melampus tried to steal the cattle, but was captured by the herdsmen and put in gaol. When in prison (cf. ἐνὶ μεγάροις Φυλάκοιο 231) he heard the woodworms tell one another that the building was about to collapse because its ceiling was nearly eaten through. Hence Melampus made a servant warn Phylacus (Iphiclus?, see fr. 261 M–W and schol. *Od.* xi 287, where the slightly different version given by Pherecydes is quoted). As a result, when the house indeed came tumbling down, Phylacus was so thankful and so much impressed by the prophecy that he promised him the cattle if he could cure his son Iphiclus of his sterility. This Melampus was able to do and accordingly he acquired the cattle and drove them to Pylos.

The same part of the Melampus story is told with more details in xi 281–97, but without the name of the principal character being mentioned. Here the poet confines himself still more to allusions. These phenomena show that the myth was still to a large extent known to the audience (see also Heubeck, *Dichter*, 20–1; later it was treated in more detail by 'Hes.', see 225 n.; Heubeck, 21–2, rightly rejects the supposition that the two Homeric passages depend on 'Hes.'). Even a secondary character such as Iphiclus (see 231 n.) is likely to have been much more important in earlier myth (cf. Merkelbach–West, 62–4), and accordingly more familiar to the people and its singers than we might be inclined to suppose. This, however, has nothing to do with the compositional function of our passage, cf. 223–81 n.

231. Φυλάκοιο: also mentioned in passing (*Il.* ii 705) as the father of Iphiclus and the grandfather of Podarkes, who led the men from the part of southern Thessaly that borders on the western coast of the Gulf of Pagasae (cf. e.g. Simpson–Lazenby, *Catalogue*, 132). In *Od.* xi the cows that Melampus had to acquire are the property of Iphiclus, cf. 231–6 n. On the question of a twofold version see Heubeck, *Dichter*, 21. The details of these stories suggest that we have to do with age-old myth and folklore rather than with poetic invention. **τῆος**: τέως μὲν MSS; *nil mutandum.*

233. Νηλῆος κούρης: see 231–6 n. The mythological connections of the Neleids with Thessaly doubtless have a historical background, cf. e.g. Nilsson, *The Mycenaean Origin of Greek Mythology* (Berkeley, 1931), 142 ff., F. Kiechle, 'Pylos und der pylische Raum in der antiken Tradition', *Historia*, ix (1960), i 38 ff., and S. Hiller–O. Panagl, *Die frühgriechischen Texte aus Mykenischer Zeit* (Darmstadt, 1976), 252–5, with literature.

234. δασπλῆτις: only here; its etym. and meaning are unknown. Nor is it clear what part the Erinys played in this myth, but it is likely to have been known to listeners (see 231–6 n.), and the allusion probably had its origin in a full-sized version. The phrase θεὰ δασπλῆτις Ἐρινύς may be an inadequately represented archaic formula, cf. xiii 438 n. (in Mycenaean times the Erinys had a cult in Crete, KN Fp 1 (Ventris–Chadwick, *Documents*, no. 200, cf. 208, pp. 411, 476).

236–7. Originally τίνυμαι meant 'to make someone pay to oneself' (xiii 15 n.) and so could only have the 'guilty' person and the penalty as grammatical objects, but its evolution to 'punishing' brought about the use of the acc. of the deed (already in Homer, e.g. *Il.* xv 116). The combination of this acc. (instead of the gen.) with the personal obj. is unique in Homer; it was facilitated by epic verse-making being largely paratactic and formulaic (ἔργον ἀεικές 6 times at the verse-end, ἀντίθεον Νηλῆα ∼ ἀντίθεον θεράποντα, etc.).

237. κασιγνήτῳ: his name, Bias, is found for the first time in ps.-Hes. in the *Catalogus*, fr. 37 M–W. The *dativus commodi* (indicating the prospective bridegroom) is used here combined with the med. of the person who obtains a wife for someone else, whereas in the usual idiom the bridegroom himself is the grammatical subject of that voice (so that a dat. would be redundant). In itself this abnormal feature is far from surprising because the development of 'carrying away for oneself' to 'taking with one' is already completed in Homer, cf. vi 28. However, since the construction also occurs in iv 10 and xxi 214, but does not show any trace of formulaic employment, it probably comes from the poet's Ionic vernacular in which the middle had already lost much of its force in cases like this. This inference is supported by Hdt.'s use of ἄγεσθαι (Powell, *Lexicon* s.v., vii 2) and in particular by his employing the very same construction in i 34. 3, ix 108. 2, 111. 3.

238. ὁ δ' ἄλλων ἵκετο δῆμον: see 228 n. ὁ δ' refers to the subject of the preceding sentence (here: Melampus), as in *Il.* i 191, iv 491, etc.

240. ἀνάσσοντ': according to Hdt. (ix 34. 1) and Pherecydes (schol. on 225) he received a part of Proitos' kingdom (as a reward for healing the king's frenzied daughters); ps.-Hes. (see 237 n.) only mentions a κλῆρος, a 'plot of land', but the line is incomplete. For the acc. see xvi 466 with n.; cf. also xiv 527.

241. A half-line noteworthy for its three trochaic word-ends, cf. G. S. Kirk in *YClS* (1966), 94–102.

243. Ὀϊκλῆα: for *Ὀϊκλέεα. The lengthening of the third syllable of Ὀϊκλῆης and its variant Ὀϊκλείης (244) is artificial, cf. Chantraine, *Grammaire*, i 10–11.

244. λαοσσόον Ἀμφιάραον: the epithet (λαο-σσόος, from *σσοϝ-, ο-grade of *σσεύ-ω, see xiv 399 n.) refers to Amphiaraus as a military commander in the war of the 'Seven against Thebes'. His prophetic gifts are hinted at in φίλει ... φιλότητα (245–6). His name was read as Ἀμφιάρηος by Zenodotus (schol.) and this form (on whose origin see Risch, *Wortbildung*, 178 n. 156) has been found on a Corinthian vase, see P. Kretschmer, *Die griechischen Vaseninschriften* (Gütersloh, 1894), 32. The form with ā is clearly a false archaism or (van der Valk, *Textual Criticism*, 95) an Atticism introduced by Aristarchus.

246. οὐδ': *non tamen*, cf. e.g. iii 143 and Denniston, *Particles*, 191. As van Leeuwen remarks, the idea ὃν οἱ θεοὶ φιλοῦσιν ἀποθνῄσκει νέος (Menander, quoted by the schol.) is foreign to the heroic world.   γήραος οὐδόν: here, in view of 247, 'the threshold leading up to old age', though elsewhere (e.g. *Il.* xxii 60) the phrase denotes the extreme end of old age; see, however, Wyatt, *Lengthening*, 227–8.

247. γυναίων εἵνεκα δώρων: the formula (also used xi 521, but in a different context) here refers to the necklace given by Polyneices to Eriphyle, who persuaded her husband to join the former's army. As an adj. γύναιος (= γυναικεῖος) disappeared after Homer, but is found in Mycenaean, PY Ta 711 (Ventris–Chadwick, *Documents*, no. 235).

249. τέκετο: the middle of the aor., originally only used of the father (cf. e.g. τέκετο Κρόνος ἀγκυλομήτης *Il.* iv 59), is an old formulaic survival, hence the metrical irregularity here, cf. xvi 118–20 n.

250. Stanford notes that Tithonus and Orion 'also had this interesting experience'. See further Hainsworth on v 121.

253. ὄχ' ἄριστον: see xiii 365 n.

254. Ὑπερησίηνδ': mentioned *Il.* ii 573 together with some towns of the northern Peloponnese. According to Paus. vii 26. 2 it lay near the coast and was called Aigeira at a time when it was still inhabited by Ionians, i.e.

before the coming of the Dorians. Mycenaean remains were found on what is presumably its acropolis by Simpson and Lazenby (*Catalogue*, 68); for later finds see e.g. *AR* xix (1972–3), 19. Our line might reflect the withdrawal of Achaeans from Argolis to the district later called Achaea, a migration for which there is archaeological evidence, see Desborough, *The Last Mycenaeans and their Successors* (cit. 29 n.), 100, 226.

256. Θεοκλύμενος: the name is announced by the poet, not by the suppliant himself, who according to epic custom should have introduced himself instead of asking Telemachus who he is and where he lives. This is one of the objections raised to the passage, cf. Page, *Odyssey*, 84. Erbse, *Beiträge*, 44, following Ameis–Hentze–Cauer, argues that it is the suppliant's purpose to ascertain whether the stranger can help him to escape his pursuers, and that in fact the two parts of his speech, 260–4 and 272–8, are closely connected. And if, in actual fact, the introduction (261–3) refers to 277–8 rather than to the simple question 'Who are you? Where do you live?', its emphatic nature is easily accounted for. Meanwhile the suppliant's incognito is (intentionally) preserved (*Beiträge*, 45).

261. ὑπὲρ θυέων καὶ δαίμονος: cf. e.g. *Il.* xxii 338 λίσσομ' ὑπὲρ ψυχῆς καὶ γούνων σῶν τε τοκήων. **θυέων:** *tu-we-a* seems to indicate 'aromatic substances' (Ventris–Chadwick, *Documents*, no. 103) on a tablet from Pylos (Un 167), but here Theoclymenus employs the term because he has just said θύοντα, so its meaning remains unspecified—as was no doubt the poet's intention, see 222 n. Cf. also *Il.* vi 270 with Leaf's n., ix 499, and West on Hes. *Op.* 338. Though a δαίμων ('who deals out', 'who gives share of') is a much vaguer divine being than a θεός (Wilamowitz, *Glaube*, i 356 ff., Nilsson, *Geschichte*, i 216 ff.; see also xiv 386 n.), δαίμονες are mentioned as recipients of offerings at *Il.* vi 115; the word is even used for a specific god, e.g. *Il.* iii 420.

268. εἴ ποτ' ἔην: implies a change so radical that the previous existence of a certain person (*Il.* xxiv 426, *Od.* xix 315, etc.) or of a certain state of affairs (*Il.* iii 180, xi 762) seems almost beyond belief.

272–6. See xiii 259 n.

272. ἐκ πατρίδος: according to 254 this must be Hyperesia (see n.), but that seems to be at variance with ἔμφυλον (273, cf. ἀπενάσσατο 254) and with Ἄργος ἀν' ἱππόβοτον (274, cf. 239). In 273–4 we probably have a traditional motif (see 273 and 272–6 nn.) which the poet incorporated in his tale about Theoclymenus without minding any slight discrepancies; see also 80 n.

273. κασίγνητοί τε ἔται τε: usually translated as 'brothers and clansmen', and this was doubtless what the poet meant here. Originally, however, this old formula (also *Il.* xvi 456 = 674; note Achaean-Aeolic κασίγνητος, Ruijgh, *Élément*, 137–8, and the 'observed' digamma of ἔται) probably denoted something like *cognati et socii*, see Chantraine, *Dictionnaire* s.vv. (with literature), Risch, *Wortbildung*, 20 n. 18, and Càssola on *h.Cer.* 80.

275. τῶν: governed by θάνατον καὶ κῆρα μέλαιναν (Ameis–Hentze–Cauer and likewise van Leeuwen, who refers to κύματα ... παντοίων ἀνέμων *Il.* ii

396–7) rather than by ὑπό in ὑπαλευάμενος (Monro, Stanford); cf. also τεύχειν θάνατον (*Od.* xi 409 etc.); θάνατον καὶ κῆρας ἀλύξαι (-ξει etc.) is a current formula.

277. ἔφεσσαι: cf. xiii 274 n.

280. νηὸς ἐΐσης: on the translation 'well-balanced' see D. Gray, *Archaeologia* i G, 95; on the difficult problems concerning the original form and meaning of the epithet and their interrelation see Kurt, *Fachausdrücke*, 42.

281. φιλήσεαι: on the med. used in a pass. sense see xiii 2 n. The pass. fut. in -θήσομαι is not yet found in Homer, cf. 80 n.

282. οἱ: a so-called *dativus ethicus*, cf. δέξατό οἱ σκῆπτρον (*Il.* ii 186).   χάλκεον ἔγχος: of course only the point of the spear was made of bronze. It is characteristic of the evolution of epic diction that in the *Odyssey* μείλινον ἔγχος and δόρυ μείλινον have disappeared (the latter in favour of δόρυ χάλκεον; δόρυ originally meant 'tree' or even 'wood'), all the more remarkable as the μείλινον and χάλκεον formulae are metrically equivalent (see 8 and 50 nn.): obviously the formulaic diction was not as conservative as Milman Parry would have it; see also 125, xiv 281 nn.

283. τάνυσεν: lit. 'stretched', i.e. put down horizontally; van Leeuwen aptly compares the use of the verb with 'spits' (*Il.* ix 213), and with 'tables' (i.e. table-tops, e.g. *Od.* xv 137).

284. ἂν ... νηὸς ἐβήσετο: see Heubeck on ix 177.

286–92. In 221 the comrades 'sat down at the tholes'. Now they cast off the stern-cables, which is perfectly natural if you are going to row, but preposterous if you are going to raise the mast and hoist the sails. The problem cannot be solved by assuming that the Theoclymenus episode, including the latter half-line of 286, is an interpolation, for the discrepancy between 221 and 287 ff. remains in any case. Are we to understand that the stage of rowing is passed over in silence and that Telemachus does not give the order until they have left the coast (cf. 495–7)? Such a procedure, however, is not so much as hinted at, and the order of 291–2 seems to contradict it. Or is 285–92 simply an awkward imitation of ii 417–26 (ii 417–18 ~ xv 285–6) where the change results from the intervention of the goddess, who sends a fair wind *before* the preparations for sailing have been made, ii 420 (= xv 292)?

291. ἐϋστρέπτοισι βοεῦσι: lit.: 'with well-twisted ropes of ox-hide'. Unlike hemp and similar materials, leather does not look particularly suited to being twisted into ropes, but cf. *Il.* xv 463, where ἐϋστρεφής is said of a bow-string (which was certainly made of leather, *Il.* iv 122). On βοεύς see Kurt, *Fachausdrücke*, 165. But in view of the formation of the word, the meaning 'halyard', 'rope for raising (or lowering) the yard', is too specific.

292. ἵκμενον: formally of the same type as ἄρμενος, ἄσμενος (Schwyzer, *Grammatik*, i 524; athematic aor. ptcp. of ἵκω, supported by Hes. *Th.* 481?). In sense, however, it seems rather comparable with οὐλόμενος, ὀνήμενος, hence probably = ὅς ἵκοιτο, i.e. 'welcome' (Boisacq, *Dictionnaire étymologique de la langue grecque* (Heidelberg–Paris, 1938) s.v.). Willcock on *Il.* i 2 aptly compares English 'perishing'.

293. λάβρον ἐπαιγίζοντα: the expression recurs only once, and in a passage that has no connection with ours (λάβρος ἐπαιγίζων, said of the Ζέφυρος *Il.* ii 148), which suggests that it is an 'inadequately represented' formula, cf. xiii 438 n. On the verb (cf. αἰγίς, 'hurricane', καταιγίζω, etc.) see *LfgrE* s.v. (ἐπ)αιγίζω.

294. ἀνύσειε: this verb (< *ἄνυμι, cf. Attic ἀνύσας; thematic form ἄνω < *ἄνϝω) means 'to effect', 'to accomplish', and is often used of journeys, cf. ὅσσον τε ... νηῦς ἤνυσεν (iv 356–7), ἦνον ὁδόν (iii 496). Here the grammatical object may have been omitted (Monro), θέουσα going with ὕδωρ (on the analogy of πλεῖθ᾽ ὑγρὰ κέλευθα ix 252 etc.?). But the verb is more likely to have been used slightly metaphorically with the formula ἁλμυρὸν ὕδωρ.

295–8. Quoted by Strabo (350, cf. also 447), see app. crit.; also found, 296 excepted, in a different order in *h.Ap.* 425–7, with minor variations and καὶ παρὰ Δύμην instead of καλλιρέεθρον in 425. Line 295 is omitted by all our MSS, but it is hard to see how Strabo could have known it, if not from a text of the *Odyssey* (the Hymn seems to be excluded as his source, cf. Allen–Halliday–Sikes ad loc.). Van der Valk, *Textual Criticism*, 89–90, may be right in explaining its omission and the reading καλλιρέεθρον (Strabo) as due to the fact that, as against the poet of the Hymn, 'Homer ... was in antiquity considered the father of history (cf. *i.a.* Lehrs Ar. 234), in whom no geographical error would be tolerated'. However, Càssola on *h.Ap.* 425, referring to the poet Antimachus fr. 27, 28 Wyss, plausibly argues that the 'Dyme' meant by the Hymn was a town of the same name in the country of the Epeians (i.e. in Triphylia) which was afterwards sacked by the Caucones. This also applies to our case (provided the line is genuine), so if Antimachus' statement is true, Homer made no geographical error at all in saying καὶ παρὰ Δύμην. 296–7 are a parenthesis.

295. Κρουνοὺς καὶ Χαλκίδα: small streams according to Strabo (343, 351).

296. σκιόωντό ... ἀγυιαί: a good example of the use of a formula without direct reference to the context: here we are no longer between the high mountains, as in 185 and iii 497. Whatever place the poet may have had in mind in 297 (see n.), he made Telemachus drive from Pherae to Pylos, embark there, and reach some point off the coast of the NW corner of the Peloponnese in a single day; see 184, 193, and 209–14 nn.

297. Φεάς: thus Strabo 350; all the MSS have Φερὰς, which already the Alexandrian scholars found difficult to explain. But they also read Φεάς, Φεαῖς, and identified that place with Φειά, a town described as Ἰαρδάνου ἀμφὶ ῥέεθρα *Il.* vii 135 (where, on this supposition, the appearance of Arcadians raises yet another problem). On its location see Simpson–Lazenby, *Catalogue*, 94.   **Διὸς οὔρῳ:** though it was Athena who sent the 'fair wind' in 292, in this phrase (probably a traditional formula, cf. v 176) the phenomenon is envisaged under the wider and more elementary aspect of the Sky-god causing the winds to blow, cf. *Il.* xiv 19 πρίν ... καταβήμεναι ἐκ Διὸς οὖρον.

298. ∼ xiii 275, see n.

299. νήσοισιν ... θοῇσιν: rightly called enigmatic by Monro. The schol. explain the adj. as a metaphor for ὀξείαις (ἐκ τοῦ κατὰ κίνησιν ὀξέος ἐπὶ τὸ κατὰ σχῆμα). Though there is some evidence for the existence of a word θοός, 'sharp', a homonym of θοός, 'swift' (cf. ix 327, Bechtel, *Lexilogus*, 166, Frisk, *GEW*, and Chantraine, *Dictionnaire* s.v.), this does not solve the problem of which islands are meant. Strabo, 351, 458 identified them with the southern Echinades, αἱ Ὀξεῖαι καλούμεναι (cf. 'the᾽ Needles', van Leeuwen ad loc.), but there is little to support this; cf. also 29 and 33 nn. It may be added that the use of ἐπιπροέηκε without an obj. is strange (cf. *Il.* ix 520, xviii 58) and that the line shows a suspicious resemblance to κεῖνον μὲν δὴ νηυσὶν ἐπιπροέηκα θοῇσιν (*Il.* xvii 708), whatever that may imply.

301–2. The poet resumes the narrative he broke off at xiv 533. About the way Odysseus passed the day we are told nothing—nor is this necessary.

303. See xiv 453–4 n.

304–6. Cf. xiii 411–13.

304. συβώτεω πειρητίζων: see xiv 459 n.

305. ἐνδυκέως: see xiv 62 n.

308. ἀπονέεσθαι: this form and similar ones (ἀπονέοντο etc.) occur 20 times, always at the verse-end. They are a puzzling feature of the diction because the poet, having the traditional νέεσθαι at his disposal, might easily have avoided a cpd. which could only be used with an unusual metrical lengthening; cf. Hoekstra, *Mnemosyne*, xxx (1978), 15–23.

309. κατατρύχω: in the same way the simplex is used of the parasitical drones by Hes. *Op.* 305.

310. εὖ ... ὑπόθευ: marked by its colloquial ring and the irresolvable contraction in ὑπόθευ as a phrase coming from the poet's Ionic vernacular, cf. 98 and xiv 435 nn. Formulaic expressions such as εἰπέμεναι (οἱ φάσθαι) πυκινὸν ἔπος (*Il.* vii 375, xi 788, cf. εἴπω (εἶπες) πυκινὸν ἔπος) represent the older, traditional type.

311. αὐτός: already in the act of coming to mean 'alone', cf. *Il.* viii 99 etc.

312. κοτύλην καὶ πύρνον: cf. πύρνον καὶ κοτύλην xvii 12, further 362, *Il.* xxii 494.

314. ἀγγελίην: cf. xiv 321–33. On δαΐφρονι, Eust., 356 n., Richardson *ad L. Cer.* 359.

317. δρώοιμι: in Homer verbs and nouns coming directly from the root δρā- are confined to the *Odyssey*, and all of them are used in the specific sense of 'performing service'. These facts can hardly be explained as a linguistic innovation peculiar to this poem because the verbs show diektasis (instead of contraction) and because the derivatives δραίνω and ὀλιγοδρανέων (< δραίνω) are already found in *Il.* x 96, xv 246, etc. Probably the reason is that the words and forms in question (in our passage δρώοιμι, δρηστοσύνη 321, παραδρώωσι 324, ὑποδρηστῆρες 330, ὑποδρώωσι 333) were already employed in older and traditional 'themes'. In this connection it deserves notice that this specific meaning of the root independently survived in religious contexts (see Chantraine, *Dictionnaire* s.v. δράω and R. J. Richardson on *h.Cer.* 476), which suggests that it is much older than the *Odyssey*.

319. Ἑρμείαο ... διακτόρου: if *E-ma-a₂* on the Linear B tablet PY Tn 316 (Ventris-Chadwick, *Documents*, no. 172) denotes the god, Ἑρμείας must be regarded as a metrically necessary compromise between *ʽΕρμάᾱς (< *ʽΕρμάᾱς) and Ionic Ἑρμέης (later Ἑρμῆς), see Ruijgh, *Études*, 226 n. 154. Under the given circumstances the invocation of the god is natural: 'he was essentially the god of the simple people', Guthrie, *Gods*, 91. The epithet has been variously explained ('guide', 'conductor'?, cf. J. Chittenden, *AJA* lii (1948), 24 ff.; if this is correct, the form must be a pre-Homeric reinterpretation of the gen. of διάκτωρ, used in e.g. *ʽΕρμείαο διάκτορος, cf. χρυσαόρου (*Il.* v 509, *h.Cer.* 4), χρυσάορον (*Il.* xv 506, likewise before the diaeresis), as if from *χρυσάορος, but χρυσάορα (Hes. *Op.* 771, *h.Cer.* 123), from χρυσάωρ (Hes. *Th.* 281 (X.) etc.); see also Troxler, *Sprache und Wortschatz Hesiods* (cit. xv 161 n.), 121-2). The noun διάκτωρ is not found in archaic and classical times in what is left of Greek literature, but διάκτορσι (Hesych.) does not necessarily come from a late source; more details in R. Janko, *Glotta*, lvi (1978), 192-6. The explanation of the phrase by the schol. is typical of the method which consisted in Ὅμηρον ἐξ Ὁμήρου σαφηνίζειν and of its drawbacks: ὅτι κῆρυξ. καὶ γὰρ παρ' Ὁμήρῳ τὰ πολλὰ οὗτοι ποιοῦσι (follows a quotation of *Od.* i 109), cf. xiii 49-50 n. As an explanation this statement, although literally correct, is far from adequate, nor do the god's cult-epithets point to his being a patron of servants attending to household duties such as cleaning the tables. On the other hand, however, it deserves notice that the god is not only called Zeus' servant (διάκονος) by Prometheus (A. *Pr.* 941-2, cf. also E. *Io* 4), but is also represented as the keeper of the crockery of the absent gods in Ar. *Pax* 201-2. This, it is true, merely gives us a hint of the ideas of an Athenian public in the fifth century BC on the status of the god among his fellow Olympians, but earlier Sappho and Alcaeus (frr. 141, 447 L-P respectively) had already attributed to him the function of cupbearer of the gods. Hence it is not surprising that the Ionians of Homer's time regarded the god as a patron of those servants who performed household work, cf. also Nilsson, *Geschichte*, i 508, Càssola, *Inni Omerici* (Rome, 1975), 156 (Hephaestus provides an obvious parallel).

321. δρηστοσύνη: see 343 n.

322. δανά: only here in Homer, but the word is certainly not one of those ἅπαξ λεγόμενα that survived only in poetry, cf. Ar. *Pax* 1133, where it is used without any poetical association. This is confirmed by its contracted form (< *δαϝ-εσ-νός, cf. δαϝ-γω > δαίω; lit.: 'combustible'), which shows, on the other hand, that φαεινός (*Od.* xiv 482 etc., < *φαϝ-εσ-νός, cf. Chantraine, *Grammaire*, i 32) was already an archaism at the time of the composition of the *Odyssey*.

324. τοῖς ἀγαθοῖσι: denotes the aristocrats, as it still does, when the archaic age is already coming to a close, in the poetry of the conservative nobleman Theognis. The article marks them off as a separate class, see xiv 12 n.

329. σιδήρεον οὐρανὸν: only here and in the parallel line xvii 565. Miss

COMMENTARY

Lorimer's suggestion, *Monuments*, 118, that the idea may be due to the fall of some conspicuous meteorite in the Aegean area is far-fetched. In the Dark Ages, when the use of iron was spreading (cf. xiv 324 n.), it naturally developed from the older one (χάλκεον οὐρανόν *Il.* xvii 425, οὐρανὸν ἐς πολύχαλκον *Od.* iii 2, etc.).

330. ὑποδρηστῆρες: cf. ὑποδμώς (iv 386), ὑφηνίοχος (*Il.* vi 19), ἐπιβώτορι (*Od.* xiii 222 (see n.)), etc.; see Risch, *Wortbildung*, 214–15 (δρηστῆρες *Od.* xvi 248 etc., δρήστειραι x 349, xix 345).

333. οἵ σφιν ὑποδρώωσιν: the relative clause probably does not go with 332, which is itself a continuation of 331, but, recalling ὑποδρηστῆρες ἐκείνων (330), rounds off the whole of the passage (ring-composition, cf. xiv 503).

334. The spondees may have been used, according to Stanford, 'to express the notion of heaviness in βεβρίθασι'. Cf., however, xxi 15, xxii 175 = 192, *Il.* ii 544, xi 130, xxiii 221 (Ameis–Hentze, *Anhang*, ad loc.).

338. See xiii 434, xiv 132 nn.

343. πλαγκτοσύνης: As Cauer, *Homerkritik*, 438, has shown, the total number of abstract terms is greater in the *Odyssey* than in the *Iliad* and this also applies to the nouns in -οσύνη and -φροσύνη (439). In this case the noun is likely to have been derived from the verbal adj. (πλαγκτέ occurs at *Od.* xxi 363, although there it means 'distracted') and to mean 'the (social) position of a man driven from home', cf. δουλοσύνη (xxii 423).

344. οὐλομένης: cf. *Il.* i 2 and *Od.* xv 292 n.

345. This line is omitted by one good MS and has been added in the margin in two others. It does not belong here and was probably interpolated by someone who thought that ἔχουσιν in 344 required a subject (see 373 n.). Not only is it exceedingly flat in this context, but it is also inappropriate to the preceding line. That line clearly marks the end of the statement by explaining why people take to wandering in spite of the inevitable sufferings, 'because of their belly'; 345 ignores this explanation and represents the roaming as something befalling them through outside influences (*pace* Stanford, ὅν τιν' ἵκηται cannot mean 'involving themselves in'). Moreover, after the wanderers have explicitly been said to have κακὰ κήδεα, the addition πῆμα καὶ ἄλγος is a truism.

348. ἐπὶ γήραος οὐδῷ: see 246 n.

349. ζώουσιν ὑπ' αὐγὰς ἠελίοιο: a 'conjugation' of the formulaic ζώει καὶ ὁρᾷ φάος ἠελίοιο, e.g. xiv 44; ὑπ' αὐγὰς ἠελίοιο also ii 181 etc. Unless his encounter with his mother's ghost in xi 152 ff. is part of a later addition— which I consider unlikely—Odysseus already knows the answers. That is probably the reason why he does not ask his questions until now. He might of course have omitted to ask them altogether, but given the situation— and the natural curiosity of the Greeks—the stranger was expected by his host (and by the poet's hearers) to inquire after the weal and woe of the reigning family. Not so many years ago a Greek peasant asked a visiting archaeologist from western Europe, 'How are the kings?'.

354. οἷς ἐν μεγάροισιν: as Laertes lives in a hut in a far-off orchard (cf. i 189 ff., xi 187 ff., etc.), this phrase might emphasize that he wishes to die in his palace. This would be only natural in itself, but in view of 355 (γάρ) and of iv 557, xvii 521, it seems more likely that the poet here uses a traditional formula without giving it much thought, cf. 408 and xiii 185 nn.

356. δαΐφρονος: derived by Bechtel, *Lexilogus*, 92 from the old dat. δαΐ and explained as 'the man whose mind is turned towards battle', a sense no longer understood by the 'Flickpoet' who composed this part of the *Odyssey*. Earlier, Curtius had connected the word with Skrt. *das-rá-*, 'wonder-working', hence 'skilful' (on this supposition the meaning 'warlike' is obviously secondary; see also Frisk, *GEW* s.v. δαῆναι). This would accord with the etymology of Πηνελόπεια proposed by Kretschmer, see xiv 162 n. Penelope's usual epithet is περίφρων, a metrical equivalent in all the grammatical cases. If δαΐφρων originally meant 'skilful' it may have been replaced by περίφρων at a time when it was generally taken as 'warlike'. But it is equally possible that in Homer's time the word no longer suggested a definite quality to the poets anyway. On Anticleia see xi 84-6 n.

357. ὠμῷ: the translation 'premature' (cf. ὠμοτόκος?) is uncertain, but the word does not mean 'savage' elsewhere in Homer (its occurrences, though, are few). The statement that Laertes was already ἐπὶ γήραος οὐδῷ when Odysseus left Ithaca cannot decide the question one way or another, see 246 n. However, Hesiod's variant καὶ ὠμῷ γήραϊ δῶκεν (*Op.* 705), where the meaning is certain, supports 'untimely', 'premature' in our line, in particular because in his grief Eumaeus is likely to express himself forcibly; cf. xvi 143 with n.

361-79. In 361 Eumaeus actually starts a digression, but he does so almost imperceptibly, develops it quite smoothly and concludes it very much in character by complaining about the changed conditions (374-5 : 361-2) of himself and his fellow-servants (374-9). Meanwhile, however, he has provoked Odysseus' curiosity (363-5), in other words the poet has unobtrusively managed to prepare the way for making Eumaeus tell a colourful tale before the scene is to shift again to Telemachus.

363-4. This is the only place where a sister of Odysseus is mentioned (ὁπλοτάτην παίδων might even imply that there were several, but may be a loosely applied epic phrase, cf. e.g. ὁπλότατον τέκε παῖδα (Hes. *Th.* 821) and *Od.* xiii 185 n.). Odysseus was the only son, see xvi 119.

363. τανυπέπλῳ: see 171 n.

364. ἰφθίμη: etym. and exact meaning unknown; probably not derived from *ϝίς. The expression θυγατέρ' ἰφθίμη itself is 'artificial' and comparatively recent. On the analogical form θυγατέρ', which only recurs at *Od.* x 106 (in the same phrase), see xiv 140 n.; in the gen. sg. we only find θυγατέρος ἧς *Il.* xxi 504, *Od.* xix 400 (on the model of *θυγατέρα ϝήν *Il.* v 371 etc.). Moreover, elision of final ι is rare in Homer (see Chantraine, *Grammaire*, i 86), and no doubt secondary (cf. e.g. ἰφθίμη ἀλόχῳ (*Od.* xii 452), ἰφθίμην ἄλοχον (*Il.* xix 116 etc.), etc.): the expression was created by declining *ἰφθίμη θυγάτηρ.

367. Σάμηνδ' ἔδοσαν: on Same see xv 29 n. With the construction compare Σκάνδειαν δ' ἄρα δῶκε (*Il.* x 268).   **μυρί' ἕλοντο:** see xiii 378 n.

369. ὑποδήματα: only here and, in a similar context, xviii 361. It seems to be a newcomer to epic diction, the traditional word for 'footwear' being 'Achaean' πέδιλα (cf. e.g. xiii 225, xiv 23), already attested in Mycenaean, PY Ub 1318, see Ruijgh, *Élément*, 151–2.

370. φίλει ... μᾶλλον: in similar combinations μᾶλλον usually means 'more than before', 'still more', cf. e.g. ἐχώσατο κηρόθι μᾶλλον (v 284), so we may have to supply 'from the day her beloved daughter had been far away' (thus Ameis–Hentze–Cauer) or 'from the day she had sent me away', cf. the elliptical use of ὁμῶς, xiii 405 n. However, on the analogy of ἀπήχθετο κηρόθι μᾶλλον (*Il.* ix 300), which requires *quam cui ignoscas* (van Leeuwen), 'than can be balanced by his apology' (Leaf), it is possible to supply 'than her action of sending me away would suggest'. At any rate there is nothing to show that the advb. has lost its comparative force (as was the case with θᾶσσον) and come to mean 'right well' (Monro, Stanford).

373. αἰδοίοισιν: probably suppliants are meant (cf. v 447, vii 165, etc.) and after the word a line beginning with e.g. *ξείνοις ἠδ' ἱκέτῃσι (cf. e.g. ἱκετάων τε ξείνων τε ix 270) has been omitted. Or 345 (see n.) may originally have belonged here in the form *ἀνδράσιν ὅν τιν' κτλ., cf. v 448 ἀνδρῶν ὅς τις ἵκηται ἀλώμενος. To paraphrase the line with *hinc edi bibi amavi* is a desperate expedient.

375. οὔτε τι ἔργον: balancing 'word' with 'deed' was already an ingrained habit of the Greeks before Homer, as is shown by the pre-Homeric formula *ϝέργον τε ϝέπος τε (*Od.* ii 272 etc.). Here this custom involves a slight zeugma.

379. ἀεὶ δμώεσσιν: some MSS have ἐνὶ στήθεσσιν. This gives a satisfactory sense and eliminates the difficulty presented by ἀεί scanned with a short initial vowel. That phenomenon, however, also occurs at *Il.* xii 211, xxiii 648 (elsewhere αἰεί or Atticized ἀεί), so it seems preferable to keep to the reading which has the best MS-authority. The copyist to whom the variant is due may have remembered the ubiquitous formula θυμὸν (-ὸς) ἐνὶ στήθεσσι(ν) (often followed by a verbal form (ἔπειθεν, ὄρινεν, etc., κελεύει, etc.) at the verse-end). But so has the poet, and this may explain θυμὸν ἀεὶ δμώεσσιν ἰαίνει: it seems to be a conflation of that remodelled formula with *θυμὸν ἰαίνει, cf. τά κε θυμὸν ἰήνῃ (*Il.* xxiv 119 etc.). In this connection it is to be noted that in the two lines of the *Iliad* ἀεί also appears in incidental combinations.

384. διεπράθετο: the sense is unambiguously passive.

386. οἴεσιν: though its creation may have been influenced by genuine Aeolic dats. (see Wathelet, *Traits*, 264), the fact that the ending -εσιν has been combined with the contracted stem makes it likely that the form is artificial.

388. The construction is again paratactic; on ὦνον see xiv 297 n. The existence of 429 is not a sufficient reason to consider our line an interpolation, and this also applies to τοῦδ' ἀνδρός. So far Laertes has only been mentioned incidentally by Eumaeus (xiv 173, xv 353), hence it is only natural that Odysseus, continuing to play his role, speaks vaguely of 'this man'.

391. πῖνέ: the verbal aspect is essential (as in πίνοντε 398).

395-6. As Stanford observes, Eumaeus shows himself to be well aware of the fact that his men know the story, and gives them an opportunity to withdraw.

397. δειπνήσας: see 77 n.   **ἀνακτορίησιν:** derived from ἀνάκτωρ. Older ϝανάκ-τερος is already found in Mycenaean, e.g. PY En 74 (Ventris–Chadwick, *Documents*, no. 115), cf. Ruijgh, *Études*, 381-2.

398. νῶϊ: νώ only 475, *Il.* v 219; see Chantraine, *Morphologie*, 136.

400-1. Cf. *Od.* xii 212; the most famous form of this τόπος is Verg.'s 'forsan et haec olim meminisse iuvabit' (*A.* i 203).

402. A case of ring-composition, cf. 390; see xiv 503 with n. The following story shows the poet indulging in his 'Lust zu Fabulieren', just as he did, in a different way, in 225-55.

403. Νῆσός τις Συρίη: on such 'topographical' introductions to a new development of the narrative see xiii 96 n. Attempts to identify the island were already made by Aristarchus, Herodian (see schol.), and Strabo. In modern times they have been continued, but it is questionable whether the 'geographical' data of this phrase and of the next line tally with any real place. The name Ortygia has been taken to denote either Delos or the islet in the bay of Syracuse, but for this there is no Homeric evidence. Nor are the corresponding candidates, Σῦρος and Συράκουσαι, supported by the forms of their names. On the other hand, Ortygia is mentioned in v 123 as the country of Eos (cf. Lorimer, *Monuments*, 81-2), and the setting of Eumaeus' story is decidedly oriental (cf. 415, 425, and 482 n.). These facts, while conflicting with the identifications mentioned above, perfectly accord with the normal meaning of Συρίη. Hence Miss Lorimer was no doubt right in thinking that the story contains a vague reminiscence of Mycenaean settlements at the mouth of the Orontes (Al Mina, Sabouni), a view which, contrary to her opinion, derives some support from Hesiod's use of τροπὰς ἠελίοιο (*Op.* 564, 663) for the summer and winter solstice. This phrase is clearly the declined form of an epic formula, and in our passage must signify the place on the horizon where the sun was seen to rise either on midsummer or midwinter day (Hoekstra, *Mnemosyne*, x (1957), 118, G. P. Edwards, *The Language of Hesiod in its Traditional Context* (cit. xiv 475 n.), 176). On the former supposition it makes no sense—it would point to a place somewhere in the interior of Asia Minor—but in the latter meaning it points to Syria. The remembrance is necessarily vague (νῆσος) and intermixed with mythical elements (408-11), cf. xiv 257-8, 315, xv 117-18 nn.

404. Ὀρτυγίης: lit. 'Quail Island'.

405. ἀγαθὴ μέν: for other examples of this use of the particle, which stresses a contrast with what precedes, see Denniston, *Particles*, 378.

406. εὔβοτος: as βόσκω simply means 'to graze', 'to feed', and since alongside εὔμηλος one would expect 'with good oxen', Wackernagel, *Untersuchungen*, 245-6, referring to οὔτ᾽ εὔβων (v.l. εὔβουν) σε ἔσεσθαι ὀίομαι οὔτ᾽ εὔμηλον

257

(*h.Ap.* 54), would read εὔβοος. With regard to βόσκω he is obviously right (cf. moreover πάντεσσι βοτοῖσιν *Il.* xviii 521, etc.), but since the contemporary existence of e.g. βο-τόν/βο-ηλασίη, πολύ-βο-τος (πουλυ-βό-τειρα)/πολυ-βοῦ-ται, βο-τήρ/βού-της is partly certain, partly most probable, the poet may have associated an original εὔβοτος, 'well-feeding', (cf. πάμβοτος etc.) with 'oxen'.

408. δειλοῖσι: this adj. might seem to be in flat contradiction with the description of the fortunate conditions enjoyed by the inhabitants of 'Syria'. These, however, are only 'wretched' in so far as they are 'mortals', in other words we have again to do with a general formula (6 times) being used without any specific reference to the context, cf. 52, 296 and xiii 185 nn. **πέλεται:** see xiii 60 with n.

411. κατέπεφνεν: a so-called gnomic aor. Artemis brings a painless death to the women, but cf. v 123–4. Elsewhere the formulaic line is used—with the variation ἐποιχόμενος, -μένη—for either the god or the goddess. The origin of this belief is not known, nor are Apollo and Artemis by themselves gods of death, see e.g. Nilsson, *Geschichte*, i 541. The arrows, however, seem to be a characteristic feature in this conception, so the Artemis who sends a *sudden* death (this seems to be essential, cf. also xv 478–9) was probably derived from the 'Huntress-Goddess', who in her turn developed from the 'Mistress of Animals', see Nilsson, *Geschichte*, i 484, Guthrie, *Gods*, 100; on her special connection with women, Guthrie, 101–4. As regards Apollo, it is uncertain whether his habit of killing men in the way described goes back to a very old belief, because the character of the god is contradictory and his origin highly controversial (Guthrie, 183 and 73–87). Yet even if in his case too the belief should be ancient (Nilsson, 541, compares him to Rudra in Vedic mythology), the exact parallelism expressed by the lines in question must be due to a secondary (poetic?) development, for, as Nilsson, 500, observes, there is no evidence whatever for Artemis and Apollo having originally been twins; see moreover W. Burkert, *Griechische Religion der archaischen und klassischen Epoche* (Stuttgart, 1977), 228. Therefore it seems probable that the relation 'sudden death of women'—'arrows of Artemis' is original and that Apollo (cf. *Il.* xxiv 759, *Od.* iii 280) is a newcomer in this respect. In our line, however, he has already taken precedence over the ancient goddess who had become his sister.

412. δύω πόλιες: see Lorimer, *Monuments*, 83; with the use of πάντα, 'the whole of it', compare *Il.* xv 189 τριχθὰ δὲ πάντα δέδασται.

414. Κτήσιος Ὀρμενίδης: the name is significant (cf. 406), the patronymic is obviously not: it is one of those floating genealogical elements that are numerous in the Homeric epics (cf. e.g. Αἱμονίδης, Ἱππασίδης, etc.), although at an earlier stage it is likely to have designated a particular figure (or particular figures) of old mainland saga, cf. *Il.* ix 448, x 266, and the mysterious Ὦψ (*Od.* i 429 etc.), see Paus. viii 28. 5; cf. xiv 182, 336 nn. and on the type Ὄρμενος Risch, *Wortbildung*, 54.

415. On the Phoenicians see xiii 272, xv 117–18 nn.

416. τρῶκται: see xiv 289 n.

419. πολυπαίπαλοι: cognate with παιπαλόεις, see 29 with n.   **ἠπερό-πευον:** see xiii 327 n.

420. πλυνούσῃ: cf. vi 85 ff., where Nausicaa meets Odysseus when waiting for her linen to dry. We are probably dealing with a traditional motif, which was elaborated in a refined manner in that part of the poem.

422. θηλυτέρῃσι γυναιξί: the expression is probably very old and pre-Ionic (an Epidaurian inscription of the fourth century BC (Schwyzer, *Delectus*, 109, 84) still has ἄρσενα ἢ θηλυτέραν, so the translation 'gentle' is certainly wrong); originally the phrase must have meant 'the women that give suck'; on the suffix -τερος see xiii 111 n.

424. Does this line, by way of introduction (cf. τὸν δ' αὖτε προσέειπε etc.), announce the contents of 425-6? If so, πατρὸς must mean 'of her father'. However the normal meaning of ἐπέφραδε and especially τοῦδ' ἀνδρός (429) seem to require the interpretation 'of my father', although on this supposition the transition 424-5 is unusually abrupt.

425. πολυχάλκου: this knowledge is likely to go back to the Bronze Age (Lorimer, *Monuments*, 80, and xv 117-18 with n.). See however S. West on iv 618.

426. ῥυδὸν: only here and in the imitation by Callimachus ῥυδὸν ἀφνύνονται, fr. 366 Pf.; derived from the zero grade of the root found in ῥέω (< *ῥέϝ-ω).

427. Τάφιοι: if we adopt the explanation of 403-4 given above, their appearance here is at first sight surprising, since they are at home in the western region of Greece (see xiv 452 n.). Still, as Miss Lorimer observes, 'the Phoenician woman could not have been kidnapped by her compatriots; another set of recognized slave-traders had to be found'.

428. ἀγρόθεν ἐρχομένην: cf. τὸν ... κατιόντα ... ἀγρόθεν, xiii 267-8.

433. ἀφνειοὶ καλέονται: this statement does not question the wealth of the parents but stresses its recognition, cf. e.g. *Il.* xiv 268 ὀπυιέμεναι καὶ σὴν κεκλῆσθαι ἄκοιτιν, A. *Ch.* 320-1 χάριτες δ' ὁμοίως κέκληνται γόος εὐκλεής, and *Od.* xiv 402 n.

434. ἀμείβετο: not exactly 'she answered', but used in its more general (and earlier) sense: 'she acted (i.e. spoke) in her turn', 'she reacted', as often.

435. εἴη κεν καὶ τοῦτ', εἰ: it might be assumed that καὶ ('also') refers to 420-1, but cf. *Il.* xxiv 56-7 εἴη κεν καὶ τοῦτο τεὸν ἔπος ... εἰ δὴ κτλ. Probably καὶ τοῦτο means 'that very thing' and is equivalent to an emphatic τοῦτο, cf. καὶ ἄλλο τόσον (*Il.* xxii 322) and other examples given by Denniston, *Particles*, 319-20; cf. also 181 and 513 with nn.

442. ἐπὶ κρήνῃ: cf. x 105 ff., where Odysseus' comrades meet a Laestrygonian girl at a well. The style is simple, transparent, and graceful throughout the passage.

446. βιότοιο: cf. 406 (βίοτον πολὺν 456).

450. ἑῆος: potius ἐῆος, see xiv 505 n.

451. κερδαλέον δὴ τοῖον: cf. ἀβληχρὸς μάλα τοῖος (xi 135 = xxiii 282), σαρδάνιον μάλα τοῖον (xx 302). These lines show that ἅμα τροχόωντα θύραζε need not be taken (with Ameis-Hentze-Cauer who translate: 'who is

COMMENTARY

already so clever that—') as an epexegetic addition. iii 321 is different because here ἐς πέλαγος μέγα τοῖον is followed by ὅθεν.

456. ἐμπολόωντο: 'acquired by traffic' (i.e. barter), only here in Homer; a diektasis-form of ἐμπολάομαι, itself a denominative from ἐμπολή (etymology uncertain), 'merchandise', sim. The latter word is wanting altogether in the epics, though afterwards both of them are current (see xiv 446 n., and on the subject in general J. Stark, *Der latente Sprachschatz Homers* (Munich–Berlin, 1908, repr. Hildesheim, 1973)). Is ἐμπολάομαι a newcomer to the epic vocabulary (cf. xiii 2 n.), and are kidnapping-tales such as this one and 425–9 (the daughter/son of a rich man/king carried off by Taphian/Phoenician pirates/traders) a motif coming from early Ionian story-telling (cf. xiv 257–8 n.)? At any rate Hdt.'s account (i 1. 3, with its equally unique use—in a cpd.—of the same verb) of the 'Persian' information about Io's abduction by Phoenicians is likely to be an offshoot of our passage or a similar tale.

457. ἤχθετο: the impf. seems strange because, as the final-consecutive use of νέεσθαι shows, the ship was ready to sail. The explanation is to be found in the verb itself, its θ-stem denoting 'the state arrived at', cf. βρίθομαι; see Chantraine, *Grammaire*, i 326–7, *Dictionnaire* s.v. In its literal meaning the verb is used only here in Homer and only very rarely afterwards.

460. μετὰ δ' ἠλέκτροισιν ἔερτο: cf. xviii 295–6 ὅρμον ... χρύσεον, ἠλέκτροισιν ἐερμένον. The noun and the verbal forms are closely related (cf. Lat. *sero*) and the fact that they are twice found combined in a single expression does not favour the supposition of Meister, *Kunstsprache*, 178, that ἔερτο and ἐερμένος are pseudo-archaisms, cf. xiv 326 n., as well as ἐέλμεθα, ἐελμένος (*Il.* xxiv 662 etc.), ἐέρχατο (x 241, see xiv 73 n.). That the pl. ἠλέκτροισιν points to the material being amber (and not an alloy of gold and silver) was already observed by Monro. Amber necklaces were found in Mycenaean tombs, cf. e.g. H. P. and A. J. B. Wace in *Companion*, 503, and E. Bielefeld, *Archaeologia* i C, 16 ff., 54, 56. The necklace from Cyprus on pl. ii b is Late Geometric, but cf. Bielefeld, 66. See also S. West on iv 73, with literature.

462. ὀφθαλμοῖσιν ὁρῶντο: here virtually = θηεῦντο, 'they were gazing on it' (A. T. Murray), cf. xix 36.

463. ὑπισχόμεναι: 'offering', cf. 195 with n.

464. βεβήκει: see xiii 164 n.; again the poet mentions only the final phase of the action, omitting the preceding details.

466. δέπα: read δέπα'(α); the transmitted forms throw some light on the state of the MS-tradition, and on its history. With one exception the MSS read δέπας or δέπατ', but the scholl. only know δέπα (which they explain as ποτήρια). Of course the pl. is required (τρί' ἄλεισα 469).

467. ἀμφεπένοντο: as subordinate 'kings' or γέροντες, see xiii 8 with n.: the situation is similar to that in Scheria and Ithaca (cf. i 394–5, vi 54, etc.).

468. θῶκον: here, as in v 3 and ii 26 (θόωκος), with the connotation of 'session'. In our line the contracted form (< *θόακος, cf. Hainsworth on v 3) is resolvable, so that the phrase might reflect an older employment (see also ii 14) than is found in ii 26, xii 318 (θόωκοι with diektasis), and *Il.* viii 439 (θώκους at the end of the line).   **δήμοιό τε φῆμιν:** here used in a local sense to denote the ἀγορή, cf. xiv 239 n. Ameis–Hentze–Cauer aptly refer to οὔτε ποθ' ἡμετέρη ἀγορὴ γένετ' οὔτε θόωκος (*Od.* ii 26). Curiously enough, φήμη shows a similar development in classical times, see R. Renehan, *Greek Lexographical Notes* (Göttingen, 1975) s.v.

469. ὑπὸ κόλπῳ: cf. S. West on iii 154, who appositely quotes Hdt. vi 125. 3.

470. ἀεσιφροσύνῃσι: probably a coinage, cf. e.g. φρένας ἄασεν (xxi 297) and 343 n. On the origin of the form (as if from ἄεσα) see Bechtel, *Lexilogus*, 14 and Chantraine, *Dictionnaire* s.v. ἀάω.

473. ὠκύαλος: the second part of the cpd. might come from ἅλλομαι (thus Bechtel, *Lexilogus*, 343), but was probably understood as 'sea' by Homer and his audience, since 'Ωκύαλος appears as a proper name in the catalogue of Phaeacians (viii 111).

474. ὑγρὰ κέλευθα: probably not 'the wet paths' but 'the flowing paths', a meaning which is more satisfactory from a factual and graphic point of view. The sense 'fluid' is certainly old, cf. ὑγρὸν ἔλαιον and the formula ἐπὶ τραφερήν τε καὶ ὑγρήν (xx 98, *Il.* xiv 308, with *Od.* xiii 410 n.).

475. Ζεὺς οὖρον ἴαλλεν: see 297 with n.

476. νύκτας τε καὶ ἦμαρ: the use of the sg. ἦμαρ alongside the pl. has been differently explained, see Leumann, *Wörter*, 100, with literature. Probably we have to do with a highly archaic formula, cf. also Ruijgh, *Élément*, 121. If this is correct, it also explains the short-distance repetition ἐξῆμαρ ... ἦμαρ ... ἔβδομον ἦμαρ. The combination νύκτες τε καὶ ἤματα (xvi 39 etc.), though probably of a later origin, may still be very old, cf. Ruijgh, ibid.

477. δὴ ἔβδομον: cf. ἀλλ' ὅτε δὴ τρίτον ἦμαρ ἐυπλόκαμος τέλεσ' Ἡώς (v 390), and xiv 287 n.

478. ἰοχέαιρα: cf. Hainsworth on vi 102; Heubeck's explanation ('having arrows in her hand', from *χεσαρ, Hittite keššar, 'hand') is attractive because of Sanskrit iṣu-hasta-, see also Frisk, *GEW* s.v.

479. ἐνδούπησε πεσοῦσ': cf. the formula δούπησεν δὲ πεσών, 21 times.
εἰναλίη: the lengthening (ε̄) is generally regarded as 'metrical' (Wyatt, *Lengthening*, 92, derives the adj. from εἰν ἁλί). However, Ruijgh, *Études*, 53–4, may well be right in explaining it as etymological (< *ἐν-άλιος < *ἐν-σάλιος cf. ἅλ-ς, Lat. *sal*, etc.).   **κήξ:** the bird may have been some kind of tern, Thompson, *Birds*, 133. Its name is an onomatopoeic formation, an imitation of its cry, cf. Frisk, *GEW* s.v. καύαξ. Other forms are καύηξ, κῆυξ.

482. ὕδωρ: this is likely to have been the same current as the one mentioned in xiv 315. According to J. L. Myres, *Who Were the Greeks?* (Berkeley, 1930), 220, it is a geographical reality (direction: coast of the Lebanon– south coast of Asia Minor–south side of Crete–west coast of Greece).

484. τήνδε τε γαῖαν: if τε is sound, it is a mere metrical stop-gap, cf. xiii 238 with n.

486–7. A comparison with xiv 361–2 shows how a poet could adapt the formulaic diction to different situations.

487. λέγων: see xiii 7, 296 nn.

488. παρὰ καὶ κακῷ: the unusual position of καί may have been brought about by its having replaced a gnomic τοι, for παρά τοι κακῷ ἐσθλὸν ἔθηκε (sc. Ζεύς or θεός) may very well have been a proverb, cf. e.g. 72 and, for the idea, vi 188–9, *Il.* xxiv 527 ff.

492. ἀλώμενος: the emphasis is on the ptcp. By using this in the pres. tense (cf. ἀλήθης xiv 362) Odysseus acts in character.

494–5. After the leisurely descriptive (and formulaic) expression ὣς οἱ μὲν τοιαῦτα πρὸς ἀλλήλους ἀγόρευον, the bare statement of fact καδδραθέτην ... ἐΰθρονος and the abrupt transition are striking; cf. xiv 502 with n. Partly imitated in his *Hecale* by Callimachus, fr. 260. 63–4 Pf., who, characteristically, replaces Ἠὼς ... ἐΰθρονος by στιβήεις ἄγχαυρος.

495. οἱ δ': here too the change is remarkable, all the more so as 496–502 are again in the unhurried epic style. With ἐπί one would expect the dat., since Telemachus and his men are not yet on the shore, cf. 497; the phenomenon is rare (ἐπ' αὐτάων ... ἐγγύς, *Il.* xxii 153), cf. Chantraine, *Grammaire*, ii 107.

499. ~ ix 150 etc. For ῥηγμίς see Heubeck on xii 214–15.

500. δεῖπνόν τ' ἐντύνοντο: cf. xvi 2 and xv 77 n.   **τε αἴθοπα:** the hiatus is all the more curious since in pre-Homeric times the 'complementary' formula ϝοῖνον ἐρυθρόν (cf. δῖος Ὀδυσσεύς ~ ἐσθλὸς Ὀδυσσεύς etc., Parry, *Homeric Verse*, 39 and *passim*) had been created for such cases, cf. e.g. ἐπέσχε τε οἶνον ἐρυθρόν xvi 444 (but πίνουσί τε αἴθοπα οἶνον ii 57 = xvii 536; perhaps we should rather be surprised that the mixing up of formulae which had become 'equivalents' after the disappearance of the digamma did not take place on a larger scale, cf. Hoekstra, *Modifications*, 22–3).

504. ἀγροὺς ἐπιείσομαι: see xvi 313 n.

506–7. That the meal promised by Telemachus to his comrades is not mentioned in xvii is as natural as the fact that eventually he himself does not return to the town in the evening (cf. xvi 476–81).

507. καὶ οἴνου ἡδυπότοιο: τε καὶ οἴ. ἡ. MSS, *nil mutandum*; the 'neglect' and 'observance' of the digamma in the same expression has led some scholars, from Bentley onwards, to delete τε, but in view of cases that do not admit such a restoration this is an arbitrary proceeding; nor does this way of archaizing rid us of the two different gens. in the same phrase. Probably the expression is a modification of *ϝοίνοιό τε ϝαδυπότοιο, cf. xx 312 οἴνοιό τε πινομένοιο.

509. φίλε τέκνον: see 125 n. Though we have been told nothing about Theoclymenus' age, it follows from the genealogy given in 241–56 that he belongs to the generation of Amphiaraus and therefore must be very old. But just as in the case of Homeric chronology (1–3 n.), it is doubtful whether the point should be pressed.

510. ~ xvi 124, see n.

513–22. Page's censure of what he calls 'the absurdity of committing the suppliant, for whose protection you are responsible, to the hospitality of your most dangerous enemy', *Odyssey*, 98 n. 5, is beside the point. Under the given circumstances Odysseus' house is certainly not the most obvious place to go to for a stranger in search of hospitality. This Telemachus realizes very well, and in the case of Odysseus he acts accordingly: before he has recognized him he flatly refuses to take him in (xvi 70 ff., esp. 85–6). Still, Theoclymenus has to go somewhere, so Telemachus recommends Eurymachus' house to him. Why not? With a stranger whose only relation with the young man is that he has been his passenger, Eurymachus has no quarrel at all, and of course he is bound by the normal laws of hospitality. Moreover, Theoclymenus is of most noble descent and Eurymachus is socially πολλὸν ἄριστος among the inhabitants of Ithaca (521).

513. καὶ ἡμέτερόνδε: the particle may imply 'as well as taking you this far on the ship' (Stanford), but, since it seems to be closely linked with ἡμέτερόνδε, it may simply serve to stress this word, cf. 435 n.

514. ξενίων: see xiv 158 n.

517. See xvi 449 n.

519. δαΐφρονος: see 356 n.

520. ἶσα θεῷ ... εἰσορόωσι: said with bitterness. The form of the expression (note the neut. pl.) probably results from a combination of the formulae *τίε ϝῖσα θεοῖσι (cf. *Il.* xiii 176 etc. and *Od.* xi 304 etc.) and *θεὸν (θεοὺς) ὡς εἰσοράουσι (-άοντες etc., cf. vii 71 etc.), the latter being the pres. tense counterpart of θεὸς ὡς τίετο δήμῳ, see xiv 205 n.

521–2. Cf. 16–18.

521. ἄριστος: denotes no more than social standing, cf. 324 n.

524. τελευτήσει: this form (given by all the MSS) has been considered a short-vowel subj.; it is certain, however, that in a number of cases κε is found with forms that cannot be anything but futs., cf. e.g. καί κέ τις ὧδ' ἐρέει (*Il.* iv 176); see Chantraine, *Grammaire*, i 154, 156, ii 225–6.　**σφι:** the suitors.

526. κίρκος: see xiii 86–7 n.　'Απόλλωνος ταχὺς ἄγγελος: in spite of τά γε Ζεὺς οἶδεν (523); at *Il.* xxiv 315 ff. it is Zeus himself who sends an eagle as a ταχὺν ἄγγελον (292). The (unique) attribution of the bird to Apollo has been ascribed to the fact that Odysseus is going to kill the suitors on the day that was sacred to the god, cf. *Od.* xx 276–8, xxi 258–9, and van Leeuwen ad loc. If this is correct, we may have to do with an old element of the saga, cf. xiv 162 n. Yet in our poem Apollo's festival is mentioned only incidentally and the phrase may simply refer to Apollo as the god of the birds of omen, a function he must already have had before Homeric times (that he made Calchas an augur is told at *Il.* i 72 as a normal fact).

531–4. Against the remark by Page that Theoclymenus 'might, without excessive intellectual effort, have interpreted the killing of a dove by a hawk as symbolizing the killing of the Suitors by Odysseus' (*Odyssey*, 85), Erbse, *Beiträge*, 46, rightly argues that the prophet is now only concerned with taking away the fear expressed in 522.

533. γένεος: γένευς *fere omnes*, see app. crit. If the gen. is sound, we have the choice between admitting a very late contraction and a case of synizesis. Either form is likely to be due to the fact that the poet did not have many γένεος-formulae at his disposal: contrary to what one would expect, the gen. of this frequently used noun occurs only here—one more example of the formalized nature of epic diction, see also Hainsworth, *Flexibility*, 72, and in particular 117: 'all formula-systems have gaps'. βασιλεύτερον has already become a comparative, cf. xiii 111 n.; on the situation in Ithaca cf. e.g. 510, i 394 ff. and 467 n.

534. καρτεροί: usually said of physical strength (originally even in καρτερὸν ὅρκον), but the transition to 'having sovereign power' was of course an easy one (cf. κρατέω); in this sense the word survives in inscriptions, e.g. in the Gortyn Law Code iv 25 etc.

536–8. = xvii 163–5, xix 309–11.   **ὡς:** 'in such a way that', cf. xxiii 133–5.

540–3. Since Theoclymenus' conviction (531–4) would not make him an ideal guest of the most ambitious suitor, Telemachus' change of mind is perfectly natural.

542. καὶ νῦν: 'and so now', cf. E. Fraenkel on A. *A*. 8.   **δώμασι σοῖσιν:** actually the house of Piraeus' father Clytius, see xvi 327.

544. δουρικλυτός: see 52, xiv 3, 18 nn.

545. εἰ γάρ: here this combination introduces a conditional clause, not a wish, so that κεν is normal, cf. Chantraine, *Grammaire*, ii 277 ff. (but perhaps we should read καὶ for κεν with G. Hermann); γάρ is to be regarded (with Monro) as a kind of interjection ('why, if—').

546. ξενίων ... ποθή: cf. 514 and n.

548. Not to be taken (with Monro) as a prothysteron: why should the whole of the crew have been needed to unfasten a few cables? See also 549, 552.

551. This formulaic line (3 times *Il.*, 3 times *Od.*), which is of course much older than the poet's description of Telemachus' arrival, contributes to conferring a heroic status on the young squire.

552. ἀπ' ἰκριόφιν: see xiii 74 n.

553. οἱ μὲν ἀνώσαντες πλέον: here the departure is treated as an incidental fact, without any formulaic and typical details: ἀνώσαντες (sc. νῆα) only here.

555. προβιβάντα: προβιβῶντα MSS, Eust., although elsewhere βιβάς, βιβάντα, etc., are still transmitted, e.g. ix 450, *Il.* vii 213, xiii 18 (under the influence of Aristarchus? Cf. e.g. Heubeck on xi 539), see Chantraine, *Grammaire*, i 300. The poet may have used both the original and the new forms.

557. ἐνίαυεν: the impf. denotes Eumaeus' custom: actually he is preparing breakfast, xvi 1–2.   **ἀνάκτεσιν:** perhaps an Aeolic form of the dat., cf. 386 n.

BOOK XVI: COMMENTARY

1. αὖτ': one of those words which a translation would make far too emphatic, but of course the particle ('on the other hand', 'on their part') has an essential function in the Greek context: it draws attention to the picture that corresponds with the one describing Telemachus coming up to the hut.

2. ἐντύνοντ' ἄριστον: recurs only at *Il.* xxiv 124 in the form ἐντύνοντο ἄριστον at the verse-end, with a suspicious hiatus and a short initial syllable of the noun; from ἐντύνοντ' *ἄεριστον (cf. Leaf ad loc., Frisk, *GEW* s.v. ἄριστον, Lejeune, *Phonétique*, 169; Ger. *Frühstück*) which had a truly epic rhythm; see also δεῖπνόν τ' ἐντύνοντο, xv 500 with n.

3. ἔκπεμψάν: as against the impf. ἐντύνοντο, the aor. denotes the simple occurrence. The temporal relation of the 'sending away' to the preparation of breakfast is not considered worth mentioning, though we may take it that before leaving the herdsmen had already had their meal, cf. xv 396–7.

4. περίσσαινον: here given by only two good MSS, but in 10 read by many more. The indirect tradition unanimously has a single σ. As the etymology of the simplex is uncertain (see Chantraine, *Dictionnaire* s.v.), it is impossible to make out whether we should read περίσαινον with metrical lengthening or περίσσαινον < *(περί-)σσαινον, cf. ὑπο-σσείουσι ix 385 (σσ < *tw), ἐπι-σσεύας xiv 399 n. **ὑλακόμωροι:** immediately followed by οὐδ' ὕλαον: a typical example of the use of an 'ornamental' epithet; the formula recurs at xiv 29 (see n.).

5. ὕλαον: in post-Homeric Greek replaced by ὑλακτέω. As this verb is used with an acc. in the sense of 'barking at (a person)', the same may apply to ὕλαον. But it is of course possible to regard οὐδ' ὕλαον as a parenthesis.

6. τε ... τε: a slight anacoluthon, cf. *Il.* iii 80. With περί ... ἦλθε compare περὶ δέ σφεας ἤλυθ' ἰωή (*Od.* xvii 261) and ἀμφήλυθε θῆλυς ἀυτή (vi 122).

9. γνώριμος: only here in Homer; probably a comparatively late element in epic diction, see xv 456 n. (γνωρίζω Hdt. ii 121).

10. ὑπό: 'faintly' is improbable because of δοῦπον and περί τε κτύπος ἦλθε in 6; perhaps 'from under (the feet)', but most probably freely used to denote the attendant circumstances, cf. *Il.* viii 4 θεοὶ δ' ὑπὸ πάντες ἄκουον, *Il.* xi 417–18 ἀμφὶ δέ τ' ἀΐσσονται (the dogs), ὑπαὶ δέ τε κόμπος ὀδόντων | γίγνεται (of the wild boar) (= 'threat').

11. Οὔ πω πᾶν εἴρητο ἔπος, ὅτε: the same colloquial-sounding phrase at *Il.* x 540, cf. also οὔ πω πᾶν εἴρηθ', ὅτ'(ε) (*Od.* xvi 351). It is typical of the formalized nature of the Homeric diction that the form εἴρητο is only used in these expressions, cf. xv 533 n. on γένευς. The 'observance' of the initial digamma and the lengthening of the final syllable of ἔπος are probably due to its frequent employment in the same position in old formulae such as ἔπος τ' ἔφατ', ἔπος φάτο, *sim.*

15. κύσσε δέ μιν κεφαλήν: probably the accs. κεφαλήν and φάεα are still on a par with μιν, both words being external objects of the verb, as is the pronoun, cf. Wilamowitz on E. *HF* 162. **φάεα:** Wyatt, *Lengthening*, 100–1, suggests a connection with Vedic bhāsaḥ, 'light', so that the long a may not be due to metrical lengthening.

17–19. Cf. ἀμφαγαπαζόμενος ὡς εἴ θ' ἐὸν υἱὸν ἐόντα (*Il.* xvi 192) and ὡς εἴ τε πατὴρ ὃν παῖδα φιλήσῃ μοῦνον τηλύγετον (*Il.* ix 481–2). The etym. of ἀγαπάω, ἀγαπάζω is unknown, but their original sense seems to have been 'to welcome with affection', conserved here and in xxiii 214. Of τηλύγετος both the meaning and the etymology are uncertain; see further S. West on iv 11.

18. ἀπίης: probably from ἀπό (on the model of ἀντί-ος) and certainly thus understood by the poet, cf. τηλόθεν ἐξ ἀπίης γαίης (vii 25).

21. πάντα: an exaggeration, as πάντα ἄνακτ' ἐμὸν ἀμφαφάασθαι (xix 475); probably a masc. sg. depending on περιφύς, cf. κύσσαι καὶ περιφῦναι ἑὸν πατέρ'(α) (xxiv 236). **ὡς ἐκ θανάτοιο φυγόντα:** cf. xiv 180–2.

23–4. = xvii 41–2.

24. ἐπεὶ ... Πύλονδε: see 142 n. (read ᾤχεο).

25. φίλον τέκος: cf. xv 125 with n.

27. ἀγρὸν: 'the fields', cf. 330 with n.

28. ἐπιδημεύεις: only here; the opposition between the 'people' (of the town) and the isolated country-dwellers is lacking in the post-Homeric ἐπιδημέω and in ἐπιδήμιος (*Od.* i 194 etc.).

29. ἀΐδηλον: probably used in an active sense ('destructive'), cf. the formula πῦρ ἀΐδηλον (*Il.* ii 455 etc.); but see also *LfgrE* s.v. ('detested', 'abominable').

31. ἄττα: an old Indo-European word, implying some familiarity, which in Greek survived only as an address of Phoenix (*Il.* ix 607, xvii 561) and of Eumaeus (in the latter part of the *Odyssey*) and in a few inscriptions, see Chantraine, *Dictionnaire* s.v.

35. ἐνευναίων: because of xiv 51, the only place where the word recurs in classical Greek, the interpretation 'spider-webs have taken the place of bedclothes' (τῶν περιβολαίων, schol.) looks obvious. But can χήτει ἐνευναίων mean 'whereas there are no blankets'? The dat. can hardly be anything else than causal (cf. χήτει τοιοῦδ' ἀνδρός (*Il.* vi 463), τοιοῦδ' υἱὸς (xix 324), and *h.Ap.* quoted below), and as Stanford observes, 'the spiders would not be interested in the presence or absence of such amenities'. The alternative explanation, 'for want of people who sleep in it', has a parallel in πουλύποδες δ' ἐν ἐμοὶ θαλάμας φῶκαί τε μέλαιναι | οἰκία ποιήσονται ἀκηδέα χήτεϊ λαῶν (*h.Ap.* 77–8). The objection that Penelope, as we are repeatedly told (i 362 ff. etc.), was sleeping in the upstairs room, so that the absence of occupants must have been a fact for a long time, is not valid (a schol. tries to meet it by relating ἐνευναίων to the future: τῶν εὐνηθησομένων). Telemachus is not concerned with this state of affairs (nor would an audience be), but voices his fear that his mother may have married in a graphic expression.

37–9. = xi 181–3.

37. καὶ λίην: in Homer this always introduces an emphatic and affirmative reaction to a preceding question, statement, or adhortation. Neither here nor in xvii 312 (where Ameis–Hentze–Cauer rightly take it with the principal clause and punctuate accordingly) is it to be taken as implying a note of regret.

38–9. Cf. xiii 337–8.

39. νύκτες τε καὶ ἤματα: see xv 476 with n.

40. = xv 282, see n.

41. Erbse, *Beiträge*, 15, explains xv 520–2, and implicitly xvi 33–5, as Telemachus' reaction to Athena's warning in xv 16–18. This is plausible, but if Telemachus was in a state of continuous suspense up to the moment of his arrival at the hut, it is all the more remarkable that he does not react in any way to Eumaeus' reassuring words. **λάϊνον οὐδόν:** Though there is no reason why the swineherd, who built a stone αὐλή (xiv 5–10) should not have furnished his hut with a stone threshold, it seems that here this detail primarily owes its appearance to (ὑπέρβη) λάϊνον οὐδόν being a formula (probably of Achaean origin, cf. Ruijgh, *Élément*, 124 ff.). The coexistence of stone and wooden thresholds in Mycenaean times (see Wace in *Companion*, 496) has a parallel in Homer: μελίνου οὐδοῦ (*Od.* xvii 339), οὐδόν ... δρύϊνον (xxi 43). But of course it is not confined to that period: H. Drerup, *Archaeologia* ii O, 11, 49.

42. In Homer the nom. sg. of πατήρ is used some 90 times (*c.*50 *Il.*, *c.*40 *Od.*) after the trochaic caesura, but in the vast majority of cases as a constituent of formulae such as πατὴρ ἀνδρῶν τε θεῶν τε, πατὴρ Ζεύς, πατὴρ καὶ πότνια μήτηρ, πατὴρ φίλος, πατὴρ ἐμός (τεός), etc. It is rarely followed by a verbal form and, apart from our line, by no more than two verbs ending in nu-movable: ἀποδῶσιν *Od.* viii 318 (proved late by the contraction, v.l. ἀποδώσει), τέκεν xvi 119 (in this context certainly late, cf. Hoekstra, *Epic Verse before Homer*, op. cit. (xiii 62 n.), 73–4). Its use in our line has only two (closely related) parallels: (σοί γε) πατὴρ ἐπετέλλετο (ἠρήσατο) Πηλεύς (*Il.* ix 252, xxiii 144). All this suggests that the second hemistich of our line is a piece of late epic verse-making and was probably created by the poet himself (who made the old form *ὑπόϝειξε end in nu-movable). But this striking innovation is closely bound up with the even more striking and highly unusual hyperbaton τῷ δ᾽ ἕδρης ἐπιόντι πατὴρ ὑπόειξεν (contrast τὸν δ᾽ ἀπαμειβόμενος προσέφη, τὸν δὲ μέγ᾽ ὀχθήσας προσέφη, etc.), so it may reasonably be inferred that the verse as a whole is non-formulaic and largely untraditional. But this also reflects on the hotly debated question whether the Homeric poems were orally composed (on this subject most recently A. Heubeck, *Archaeologia* iii X, 127–84). For could an improvising poet compose a line with so little aid from the tradition and at the same time create such an involved word-order? Cf. also xiv 124 with n.

44. ἡμεῖς: cf. ἡμετέρῳ, 45, 442, xix 344.

46. κατ᾽ ἄρ᾽ ἕζετο: introductory, cf. 47–8 and xiv 299–301 n. Here the connection between this stylistic feature and the formulaic diction is clear:

κατ' ἄρ' ἕζετο, always before the diaeresis, *Od.* 7 times, *Il.* 6 times, variations not counted.

47. Cf. xiv 49–51, but in contrast with the descriptions of offerings, meals, arrivals, etc., neither passage is 'typical'; cf. also 50 with n.

48. Adduced by Parry, *Homeric Verse*, 203, as an example of hiatus being brought about by interchanging of formulae.

49. κρειῶν πίνακας: the same formula in i 141, [iv 57]. For the gen. cf. e.g. κρητῆρα ... οἴνου (iii 390–1); for κρειῶν see xv 98, 140 nn.

50. ἅ ... ὑπέλειπον: a domestic trait, and as such exceptional in the epics. The verbal aspect contributes to the graphic nature of the phrase.

51. This line is an incidental variation of a traditional verse (cf. i 147), ἐσσυμένως taking the place of δμωαί, cf. also σῖτον δ' αἰδοίη ταμίη παρέθηκε φέρουσα (i 139 etc.). **παρενήνεεν:** cf. παρενήνεον (i 147) and ἐπενήνεον (*Il.* vii 428). That these forms are due to a copyist is unlikely in view of the consensus of the MSS and their distribution. And since Homer still has νήεον (e.g. *Il.* xxiii 139) etc., they were probably created by rhapsodes who, not knowing any impfs. in -ήεον and having only words such as ἐπινέω (Hdt.) in their own Ionic dialect, introduced an artificially 'reduplicated' formation (the short form already existed in Homer's time: νητός ii 338). The etym. of the verb is unknown.

52. = xiv 78, see xiii 53 n.

54–5. = xv 142–3 etc., see n.

57–9. See xiv 188–90 n.

62–6. This is a summary of the relevant details of Odysseus' false tale (xiv 199–359).

62. See xiv 199 n.

63. πολλὰ βροτῶν ἐπὶ ἄστεα: the phrase recurs at *Od.* xv 492, xix 170, xxiii 267; it has three different positions in the line, an unusual phenomenon for formulae of this size, cf. Hainsworth, *Flexibility*, 56.

64. ἐπέκλωσεν: the function of deities who were part of a 'very ancient stratum' of popular religion (H. J. Rose, *A Handbook of Greek Mythology*[3] (London, 1945), 24). Here it has already been taken over by the much more abstract δαίμων (xv 261 n.), see also Hainsworth on vii 197, 198.

66. ἐγγυαλίξω: an old, probably Achaean word (see Ruijgh, *Élément*, 84), frequent in the *Iliad*, but occurring only three times in the *Odyssey*, and after Homer limited to poetry. Even in the *Iliad* few traces of its original, concrete meaning ('to put into the hollow of one's hand') remain (but cf. Hes. *Th.* 485–7, *h.Merc.* 497).

67. εὔχεται εἶναι: see xiv 199 n.

70. ὑποδέξομαι: a short-vowel subj., cf. e.g. πῶς τ' ἄρ' ἴω (iii 22).

75. δήμοιό τε φῆμιν: cf. xiv 239 and xv 468 with nn.

76–7. ἄριστος ... πόρῃσιν: ἄριστος is most probably cognate with ἀρετή (on the meaning of which see xiii 45 and xiv 402 nn.) and is said at any rate of the man who has this quality to a surpassing degree; πλεῖστα πορεῖν is one of its manifestations, cf. W. J. Verdenius, *Hermeneus*, xxix (1957), 6.

80. ξίφος ἄμφηκες: recurs at *Od.* xxi 341, *Il.* xxi 118 (φάσγανον ἄμφηκες *Il.* x

256); perhaps an archaic formula. An older (metrically equivalent) form of the noun is possibly attested in Mycenaean, PY Ta 716 (Ventris–Chadwick, *Documents*, no. 247, cf. Heubeck, *Minos*, v (1958), 149 ff.). The epithet is an archaism (after Homer only used in poetry) and could even fit the Mycenaean rapiers from the shaft-graves, which originally must have been 'sharp along both edges' (*contra* Lorimer, *Monuments*, 275). Cf. S. Foltiny, *Archaeologia* i E 2, 248, 255, fig. 49.

84. ~ xv 309, see n.

86. λίην ... ἀτάσθαλον: also *h.Ap.* 67; for ἀτάσθαλος (etym. unknown) see Hainsworth on vii 60.

91. ἀμείψασθαι: see xv 434 n.

92. φίλον ἦτορ: one of the usual formulae (*c.*20 times *Il.*, *c.*20 times *Od.*); also (as acc.) for 'in my (your, etc.) heart', a metrical variant of ἐνὶ θυμῷ and κατὰ φρένα/μετὰ φρεσί/ἐνὶ φρεσί. For the old 'possessive' meaning of the adj. cf. e.g. φίλα γούναθ' xiii 231, *Il.* ix 610, etc., xiv 58 n., and Hainsworth on v 28, 297 (the formula λύτο γούνατα καὶ φίλον ἦτορ is used at iv 703 etc.). The noun is cognate with Ger. *Ader* (see further Frisk and Chantraine s.v.), but except for a sporadic ἤτορι (Simonides, Pindar) it always occurs in the nom./acc. and was clearly so obsolete in Homeric times that very few cases (*Il.* ii 490? xvi 660? xvii 535? xxii 452) still suggest a physical organ at all (ἦτορ ἐνὶ κραδίῃ xx 169!). It was Aeolic (or originally common to Aeolic and Achaean, see xiii 286 n.). All this shows that φίλον ἦτορ is one of the most archaic Homeric formulae. In the sense 'in my heart' it got an 'equivalent'—κατὰ θυμόν—by 'declension' of ἐνὶ θυμῷ.

93. οἷά: see xiv 392 n.

94–6. ~ iii 213–15.

95. ὑποδάμνασαι: as ἑκών shows, Med. ('you let yourself be overpowered'), cf. xiii 15 with n. and Monro, *Homeric Dialect*, 10.

96. ἐπισπόμενοι θεοῦ ὀμφῇ: it is improbable that this alludes to something specific (for instance an oracle): an event which is felt to be inexplicable is often ascribed to the agency of a god (parallels given by Merry–Riddell on iii 215). Nor are such vague phrases necessarily to be regarded (with Kirk, *Songs*, 165, who cites e.g. θεῶν ὕπ' ἀμύμονι πομπῇ and θεῶν τεράεσσι πιθήσας) as belonging to a relatively late stage of composition. At any rate the element θεοῦ ὀμφή closely resembles θεῶν ὄπις (see xiv 82 n.), which is no doubt pre-Homeric.

97. οἷσί περ: 'those very persons on whom (a man relies)', see Denniston, *Particles*, 484.

98. μαρναμένοισι: must mean 'as helpers in battle' (Ameis–Hentze–Cauer), but the construction is harsh and cannot be put on a par with σφῶϊν ἐελδομένοισιν (ἱκάνω) xxi 209, *sim.* A comparison with ὕμμιν ἔγωγε | μαρναμ-ένοισι πέποιθα σαωσέμεναι νέας ἁμάς (*Il.* xiii 95–6) suggests that the poet omitted the infin. of a type of phrase he knew (not necessarily from the line quoted) in order to adapt the expression to the formula (μέγα) νεῖκος ὄρηται (ὀρεῖται, ὄρωρε, ὀρώρει) *Il.* xv 400 etc., 13 times; cf. the treatment of the formula εὔχεται εἶναι in xiv 199 = xvi 62.

101. Already condemned in antiquity on the ground that 'it is superfluous and weakens the whole of the thought' (schol.). Cauer adopted Eust.'s defence of it, arguing that Odysseus has come near to revealing himself and hastily changes his tack (*Homerkritik*, 525).

102. = *Il.* v 214, where Leaf rightly observes: 'a foreigner is of course an inferior, and therefore defeat from such is the deepest degradation'; cf. also ἀτίμητον μετανάστην (*Il.* ix 648, xvi 59) and, by contrast, *Od.* xv 272 ff. **ἀλλότριος φώς:** 'a foreigner', also xviii 219; in post-Homeric Greek the adj. is sometimes used in the same sense.

105. δαμασαίατο: the Med. may still have preserved some of its force, but cf. ἀλλά με χεῖμα | δάμναται (xiv 487–8).

108–10. Monro and Stanford rightly call attention to the three successive hephthemimeral caesuras expressing the speaker's indignation. One might add that perhaps the change of voice in 109 (and again in 110), and certainly the use of ἀνηνύστῳ ἐπὶ ἔργῳ after ἀτέλεστον (see 111 n.), are symptoms of Odysseus' passion. About the treatment of the women servants (described by the iterative ῥυστάζω) Odysseus has not previously been informed, but it required little imagination to conjecture this.

111. αὔτως: strengthens μάψ, see xiii 281 n. **ἀνηνύστῳ ἐπὶ ἔργῳ:** 'on a business that will never be done' (Stanford), not, *pace* Monro, an explanation of the easily understandable term ἀτέλεστον, but emphatically added as a climax: cf. ἀτελευτήτῳ ἐπὶ ἔργῳ (*Il.* iv 175) and further *Od.* xv 294, xvi 373.

114. ἀπεχθόμενος: probably 'applies to both sides of the supposed quarrel' (Monro, who translates 'having become your enemy'), cf. ἐχθαίρουσι (96); see also Ameis–Hentze, *Anhang*, ad loc., Leumann, *Wörter*, 158 n. 1, and Chantraine, *Dictionnaire* s.v. ἔχθος.

118–20. The emphatic anaphora of μοῦνον has a parallel in *Il.* ii 671–3, where Νιρεύς is repeated three times at the beginning of the line. **ἔτικτε ... τέκεν ... τεκών:** though the use of the impf. in such cases has long since been explained (as dwelling on a continuous state of affairs, see e.g. Goodwin, *Syntax*, 10, W. S. Barrett on E. *Hipp.* 419–21), here the reason for the variation is difficult to establish, cf. Chantraine, *Grammaire*, ii 193–4 (the case of τέκε/τέκετο is similar, Chantraine, ibid., 173). Probably the different tenses, appropriate in earlier contexts, were amalgamated in the course of the development, the structure of the hexameter being an important factor: thus before the hephthemimeral caesura we find ἐν χερσὶ τίθει (*Il.* i 441 etc.), but at the verse-end we have ἐν χερσὶν ἔθηκε (*Il.* vi 482 etc.). Cf. also xv 249 n., iv 252–3.

118. Ἀρκείσιος: see xiv 182 n.

122–8. = i 245–51.

123. Δουλιχίῳ: see xiv 335 n. **Σάμη:** see xv 29 n. **ὑλήεντι:** the masc. form is due to declension, cf. ὑλήεσσα Ζάκυνθος in the parallel line ix 24, *h.Ap.* 429. The fact that its final syllable is not lengthened before Ζακύνθῳ (-ος) is commonly explained as due to metrical necessity, because otherwise the name could not be used in the hexameter, cf. Ζέλεια *Il.* ii 824 etc.,

Σκάμανδρος *Il.* v 36 etc. (which are also non-Greek names, see below). This seems obvious, but on the other hand it is possible that the classical form of this loan-word (see below) is the result of a later generalization (Linear B has *za-ku-si-jo*, but origin and phonetical value of the phoneme rendered as *z* are disputed). However this may be, it is certain that the island was already inhabited in Mycenaean times, see Simpson–Lazenby, *Catalogue*, 104 (according to Paus. viii 27. 3, Zakynthos, its οἰκιστής, was a son of Dardanus (from Psophis) who is also associated with 'Arcadians' by Arctinus, see Allen, *Homeri Opera* v, 137). Its name is pre-Hellenic (cf. e.g. Ἀμάρυνθος, Τρικόρυνθος, etc., Schwyzer, *Grammatik*, i 61 and xv 131 n.) and was also used for the Aegean island of Paros, see St. Byz. p. 507 M. It is likely to have been a compound of Κύνθος, the name of the famous hill on Delos.

124. κραναὴν Ἰθάκην: see xiii 244, 246 nn. **κοιρανέουσι:** an archaic word (later replaced by βασιλεύω and ἄρχω), somewhat pompous-sounding when denoting the princelings of a little island, and probably used in the sense of 'lording it', to wit in Odysseus' absence; see also 247–53 n.

125. τρύχουσι: see xv 309 n.

130–1. ἔρχεο ... εἴφ': an uncommon form of asyndeton, expressing haste on the part of the speaker, cf. 154–5 n.

136. = xvii 193, 281.

138. αὐτὴν ὁδόν: already less local than in viii 107, x 263 (see Heubeck ad loc.), and in τὴν αὐτὴν ὁδόν, 'along that same road' (*Il.* vi 391). Fifth-century Attic has τῆς αὐτῆς ὁδοῦ 'in passing'.

139. τῆος: read τείως (cf. xv 127).

142. σύ γε οἴχεο: (read ᾤχεο with the MSS, cf. xv 2). The hiatus, which one MS 'corrects' (see app. crit.), is to be explained as resulting from modification, cf. ἐπεὶ ᾤχεο νηὶ Πύλονδε (24 = xvii 42). A formula *(ἐπεὶ) (ὁ δ') οἴχετο νηὶ Πύλονδε may well have been one of the narrative elements of the older saga.

143. αὔτως: interpreted as 'in the same way as before' by Ameis–Hentze–Cauer and Stanford, apparently because Laertes cannot have fasted during the whole of Telemachus' absence and still be alive; see, however, xiii 281 n. The exaggeration that he has 'not so much as barely eaten and drunk' (Monro) would perfectly fit the people's talk (φασίν).

145. ἀμφ' ἀστεόφι: on the use of -φι in such cases see xiii 74, xv 148 nn. **χρώς:** lit., as appears from ἀμφ' ὀστεόφι, 'the outer part of the body', implying both 'skin' and 'flesh'.

147. ἐάσομεν: a short-vowelled subj. of the aor.

148. αὐτάγρετα: the verbal part of this cpd. has often been considered an Aeolism. Forms of ἄγρημι are indeed found in Lesbian and Thessalian inscriptions, but elements of vocabulary are notoriously difficult to assign to definite dialects. The verbal adj. is found in Cos, the verb itself perhaps in Myc. *a-ke-re-se* (= ἀγρήσει?), PY Sn 64 (Ventris–Chadwick, *Documents*, no. 43).

154–5. These lines suggest a rapid movement not only—as has often been pointed out—by the absence of spondees, but also because epithets are wanting; cf. ἄψ δ' ὅ γ' ἐπ' οὐδὸν ἰὼν κατ' ἄρ' ἕζετο· τοὶ δ' ἴσαν εἴσω (xviii 110).

154. Ἦ ῥα καὶ ὦρσε: the preceding address is referred to by means of the impf. (cf. ὡς φάτο); its effect is expressed by the aor.

157. δέμας δ' ἤϊκτο γυναικί: see xiii 288 n.

159. ἀντίθυρον: only here in Homer; 165 shows that it may have been part of (or identical with) the πρόθυρον (cf. also S. *El.* 1433), mentioned at xiv 34, xvi 12 in similar scenes.

160. ἴδεν ἀντίον: not 'looked straight ahead' (thus Ameis–Hentze–Cauer, referring to ἄντα ἰδών *Il.* xiii 184 etc.), but 'did *see* her (before him)', cf. ἀλλ' Ὀδυσεύς τε κύνες τε ἴδον (162).

161. On the way gods appear to mortals see xv 9, xvi 184–5 nn. That animals sense the presence of a god (or of a ghost) that men do not see is a well-known phenomenon in Germanic folk-tales, see e.g. Jacob Grimm, *Deutsche Mythologie*, ii (Berlin, 1876⁴), 555–6, iii (Berlin, 1878⁴), 476. The way it is mentioned here suggests that it was not considered abnormal by the audience, but in actual fact it is rarely mentioned in the part of Greek literature which has come down to us. Perhaps another example is found in Theoc. ii 12, and, according to Nilsson, *Geschichte*, i 724, in Sophron fr. 6 Kaibel, but in these cases the interpretation is uncertain.

162. ὑλάοντο: the middle is clearly not different from ὕλαον (5), cf. ὑλάουσιν (9); see 118–20 n. and xiv 488.

163. κνυζηθμῷ: onomatopoeia.

164. ἐπ' ὀφρύσι νεῦσε: one is reminded of the famous line ἦ, καὶ κυανέῃσιν ἐπ' ὀφρύσι νεῦσε Κρονίων (*Il.* i 528), but here and at *Od.* xxi 431 the expression does not imply the emphatic assent it denotes in that context.

165. τειχίον: cf. xiv 5–12 and Chantraine, *Formation*, 64–5, on the chronology of the development, which explains why any diminutive force of the suffix -ίον was no more felt (μέγα!) than in μάλα μέγα θηρίον (x 171) and in the formula οἰκία ναίων. Words having a diminutive *meaning* are avoided in the epics as being at variance with the heroic style.

168. ἔπος φάο: cf. the ubiquitous form (ϝ)έπος φάτο of the formula. With φάο (also xviii 171, in the same formula) and μάρναο (*Il.* xv 475, xvi 497) compare ἵστασο (*Il.* xi 314 etc.), κεῖσο (*Il.* xviii 178 etc.) and similar forms (Chantraine, *Grammaire*, i 474–5), which have a 'restored' intervocalic σ (but sometimes the MS-tradition is divided, so that not all the forms with σ need be authentic, see Chantraine, ibid.). The fact that *φάμαι and μάρναμαι are archaisms is likely to have counteracted the restoration.

169. κῆρ' ἀραρόντε: see xiv 207 n.

170. προτὶ ἄστυ περικλυτόν: also iv 9, xxiv 154; cf. περικλυτὸς Ἀμφιγυήεις etc.; the adj. is clearly a 'generic' and 'ornamental' epithet (Parry, *Homeric Verse*, 83 ff., 145 ff.).

171. μεμαυῖα μάχεσθαι: Athena does not take part in the actual fighting in xxii, though she encourages Odysseus in the shape of Mentor; see also xxii 256, 297 ff.

172–6. Erbse, *Beiträge*, 106, rightly points out that this is not a recognition scene: Telemachus has never seen his father. In order to convince him that the stranger is Odysseus, something spectacular has to happen.

172. See xiii 429 n.

173. See xiii 67, 434, xiv 132 nn.

174. δέμας δ' ὤφελλε: cf. τὸν μὲν Ἀθηναίη θῆκεν ...|μείζονά τ' εἰσιδέειν καὶ πάσσονα (vi 229–30). On ὀφέλλω see xiv 223 n.

175. μελαγχροιής: the only case in Homer, with the possible exception of xix 246, where a person is said to have a sunburnt complexion.   τάνυσθεν: this must mean 'were pulled tight' (so that they lost their lines), but is peculiar, especially with γναθμοί, which rather means 'jaws' than 'cheeks'. Does the poet have in mind a 'stretched' sail (AR i 606) or a 'stretched' bow (cf. κυκλοτερὲς μέγα τόξον ἔτεινε *Il.* iv 124)?

176. κυάνεαι: already the scholl. wondered how this could tally with the ξανθὰς τρίχας Odysseus is said to have had before his change in xiii 399, see n. The inconsistency can hardly be adduced in support of the view that the two passages were created by different poets. See also Stanford.   γενει-άδες: according to a schol. on Theoc. i 34 this reading was introduced by Aristotle (? Aristarchus, Lehrs) because ἔθειρα meant 'hair of the head'. Van der Valk, going back on his view set forth in *Textual Criticism*, 51, now rejects Lehrs's cj. and argues that Aristotle, interested as he was in biological facts, somewhere explained ἐθειράδες, which he interpreted as 'hairs of the head'—cf. his conduct (method?) in the case of *Il.* x 457 (adduced in *PA* iii, 10)—and added that Homer presented γενειάδες, *not* ἐθειράδες. The source of our schol. on Theoc. wrongly thought that γενειάδες was a reading of Arist. Thus van der Valk *per litteras*.

179. ἑτέρωσε βάλ' ὄμματα: cf. κατ' ὄμματα καλὰ βαλοῦσα (*h.Cer.* 194, *h.Ven.* 156). Elsewhere in Homer τρέπεν (τρέψεν ...) ὄσσε (*Il.* xiii 3 etc.). In this connection it is noteworthy that βλέπω is never used by the poet.

184–5. For us Telemachus' emotion is perfectly natural, yet it not only contrasts sharply with his own behaviour in xv 9–44 (see n.), but also with the absence of any consternation or mere surprise when the heroes meet a god (who is undisguised), e.g. Athena (*Il.* i 201 ff., ii 172 ff.), Apollo (*Il.* xv 243), not to speak of Iris; similarly Odysseus is far from being impressed when Athena reveals herself at *Od.* xiii 300. In these encounters the gods intervene with exhortations, counsels, or messages, and since Athena's role in xv was similar, the poet made Telemachus behave in the usual way, focusing the attention of listeners not on the goddess herself, but on her words. Our scene is of course wholly different: it is the climax of Telemachus' search for his father, its background is Eumaeus' hut, which is not exactly 'heroic', and here Telemachus is not the typical prince belonging to the heroic world; the last point is also borne out by his first words (181–2): they are not in the traditional style, but much more direct and could have been used by a character of Hdt. Compare also Odysseus' reply in 187–9 and 191.

184. ἵληθ': also iii 380, see S. West ad loc. and Lejeune, *Phonétique*,

122.   **κεχαρισμένα**: xv 39 n.   **ἱρά**: cf. 94 with n.

185. τετυγμένα: xiii 306 with n.

189. ὑποδέγμενος: see xiii 310 n.

191. Taken by itself crying was not considered to be beneath the dignity of a man at any time in Greece (Stanford on xxiii 232 quotes the proverb ἀριδάκρυες ἀνέρες ἐσθλοί and E. *Hel.* 950–1, where Menelaus says that it is πρὸς ἀνδρὸς εὐγενοῦς, 'natural to a noble man'). Yet in this respect, too, the Homeric heroes outdid the Greeks of historical times: they were 'quite easily moved to tears', as is noted by a schol. on *Il.* i 349, where his wounded pride makes Achilles weep (see S. West on ii 81), cf. also schol. on *Il.* xix 5. Of course they do not cry from fear, and tears brought on by physical pain are only mentioned in the case of the contemptible Thersites (*Il.* ii 263), but otherwise the emotions which make them weep are extremely varied (see Hainsworth on viii 522) and differ in strength. Accordingly the expressions for 'crying' range from a simple δακρύσας or δάκρυ χέων, δάκρυα λείβων to τὸ κλαῖον ... λιγέως (xvi 216), κλαίοντα λιγέως (*Il.* xix 5). However, the expression used in our line is rather peculiar: whereas elsewhere in 187–92 the poet employs several formulaic expressions (πατὴρ τεός, ἄλγεα πολλά, ὣς ἄρα φωνήσας, νωλεμὲς αἰεί, ὃν πατέρ'(a)) in a simple, direct way, here he tries to create more pathos by putting into use an old formula which was not created for his purpose (see below). The result ('he shed tears to the ground') is an odd exaggeration (a similar phenomenon in 216–18, see n., and at xvii 490 δάκρυ χαμαὶ βάλεν). Working in the traditional manner he might have concluded 190 with δάκρυα λείβων (8 times; δάκρυα λεῖβον *Il.* xiii 88; cf. also (θαλερὸν) (τέρεν) (κατὰ)/(ὑπ' ὀφρύσι)/δάκρυον εἴβων (εἶβεν, etc.), 10 times), but he clearly preferred a description that was more detailed and impressive. Perhaps the new phrase was modelled on ἐκ δ' ἄρα χειρὸς/φάσγανον ἧκε χαμᾶζε, which, though only found at *Od.* xxii 83–4, may have been used in earlier epic poetry. At any rate the old formula (ἀπὸ '(ϝ)έο, '(ϝ)έθεν) ἧκε χαμᾶζε (always at the verse-end) is quite properly employed (with lightning, a snake, Patroclus' foot as grammatical objects) at *Il.* viii 134, xii 205, xvii 299, cf. also *Od.* xxi 136.

194–5. δαίμων | θέλγει: see xiii 2 and xiv 386, 387 nn. and cf. ἀσέ με δαίμονος αἶσα κακή (xi 61).

198. ἠὲ: the well attested v.l. ἠδὲ (not mentioned by Allen) has been rightly adopted by Monro (and von der Mühll), who cites e.g. ἀποπεμπέμεν ἠδὲ δέχεσθαι (*Od.* xix 316).

200. After Athena has changed Odysseus in vi 229 ff., Nausicaa voices her amazement in the same words (243).

206. = xix 484 etc. The hiatus and lengthening in the hephthemimeral caesura could have resulted from modification of a line of an old *nostos*. On possible prototypes see Beekes, *Laryngeals*, 60–1, Hoekstra, *Modifications*, 51.

207. ἀγελείης: see xiii 359 n. Like other gods, Athena herself takes the form of a mortal rather often in Homer (see xiii 313 n.). In the *Odyssey*, moreover, she assists her protégés by transforming them on several occasions: here, in vii 229 ff., viii 18 ff., xiii 429 ff., xxiii 156 ff., xviii 190 ff., and xxiv 367 ff. It is to be noted, however, that in these cases the changes only affect the outward appearance of the persons in question: they always remain the human beings Odysseus, Penelope, Laertes. In this connection it has to be pointed out that the ancient motif of folk-tale and *Märchen* which makes men and women be turned into (or, by some divine agency, turn themselves into) animals, trees, plants, stars (revived by the learned poets of Hellenistic and Roman times), plays an insignificant part in Homer (for the 'Cyclic' poems see J. Griffin, 'The Epic Cycle and the Uniqueness of Homer', *JHS* xcvii (1977), 39–53). The only instance of a tale of this kind being set out in full is the description of Circe turning Odysseus' comrades into pigs in *Od.* x 233 ff., and even here the metamorphosis is not complete, cf. 240. Was Homer not acquainted with other folk-tales of this type? Of course we cannot prove that he knew of the metamorphoses of Periclymenus and Mestra (ps.-Hes. frr. 33 a, 43a–b–c M–W respectively), but the brief allusion to the story of Pandareos' daughter Aëdon (*Od.* xix 518 ff.), the incidental character of his reference to Niobe (*Il.* xxiv 614 ff.), and his suppression of Thetis' metamorphoses (Griffin, op. cit., 41) show that he purposely reduced such elements to a minimum or eliminated them altogether, see also D. Page, *Folktales in Homer's* Odyssey (Cambridge, Mass., 1972), 56–69.

211–12. Hes. speaks in a strikingly different tone when, in twelve hammering half-lines, he attributes this power to Zeus (*Op.* 3–8): not only is that passage much more elaborate, but above all it is intensely passionate in its insisting on Zeus' omnipotence and in its implicit appeal that he may use this power to bring down the arrogant evildoers. The comparison shows how free from personal involvement the conception of the epic poet really is in religious matters.

213. ἄρα ... ἄρ': the double particle is due to the 'juxtaposition' of the formulae ὡς ἄρα φωνήσας and κατ' ἄρ' ἕζετο. The combination is found only here: elsewhere (*Il.* i 68 etc.) the latter formula is preceded by ἤτοι ὅ γ' ὡς εἰπών.

214. ἀμφιχυθείς: assigned by a schol. to Aristarchus without a variant being mentioned.

216–18. These lines have been regarded by analytic critics as an indication that the recognition of Odysseus as we have it is the work of a *Bearbeiter*, cf. e.g. von der Mühll in *RE Suppl.* vii, 740–1. The emphasis on the noise made by weeping men and the simile of the bereaved birds would rather suit a dirge (the clause οἷσί τε ... γενέσθαι is of course not an instance of the well-known epic elaboration of similes, so the defence that Homer's images are often unilateral does not hold good). Yet there is nothing wrong with the simile itself and ἁδινώτερον, with its odd ἤ τ' (see next n.), suggests *ἁδινὰ στενάχοντε(ς) (cf. ἁδινὰ στενάχοντα vii 274, *Il.* xxiv 123, ἁδινὰ στεναχίζων *Od.* xxiv 317, *Il.* xxiii 225), i.e. an adaptation of an existing description of a lament; see also 191 n.

216. ἁδινώτερον ἤ τ': the comparative only here in Homer, see the preceding

n. The adj. never means 'loud' (a sense wrongly assumed in LSJ and in *LfgrE*), but always refers to the shortness of intervals of time and space, cf. e.g. μῆλ' ἀδινά (*Od.* i 92 = iv 320), μελισσάων (μυιάων) ἀδινάων (*Il.* ii 87, 469), Σειρήνων ἀδινάων φθόγγον (*Od.* xxiii 326), and Erbse, *Beiträge*, 189–91 (*be-dichte* in Middle Dutch). After ἤ, 'than', the particle τε is out of place; Ruijgh, τε *épique*, 828, convincingly suggests that it may have been introduced under the influence of ὥς τε, see also the preceding n.

217. φῆναι: esp. 'bearded vultures', Thompson, *Birds*, 303–4.   **αἰγυπιοί:** according to the same scholar (25), an old name for various vultures.

218. ἀγρόται: 'countrymen' (from ἀγρός, see 330 n.). A similar image in A. *A.* 49 ff., Verg. *G.* iv 511 ff.

221. αἶψα: here 'suddenly' seems to be a psychological and realistic trait (note the unusual position of the word).

222–4. See xiv 188–90 n.

226. = xx 420 ~ *sim.* For καταλέξω see xiii 296 n.

227–8. See xiii 213–14 n.

229–31. ~ xiii 134–6.

232. θεῶν ἰότητι κέονται: the thematic form of the indic. recurs only in the identical half-line *Od.* xi 341 (preceded by ἐνὶ μεγάροισι) and *Il.* xxii 510 (ἐνὶ μεγάροισι κέονται). The origin of ἰότης is uncertain. Leumann, *Wörter*, 127 ff. regards it as an artificial form, derived from δηιοτῆτος (*Il.* xii 248, xiv 129), by misinterpretation (!).

233. ὑποθημοσύνῃσιν Ἀθήνης: also *Il.* xv 412; see xv 310, 343 nn.

234. φόνου πέρι βουλεύσωμεν: looks like an adaptation, under the influence of contemporary Ionic (note irresolvable -ου), of (Τρώεσσι etc.) φόνον καὶ κῆρα φέροντες (φυτεύσω etc.) (*Il.* ii 352 etc., 6 times); see also 191 and 216–18 nn.

236. ὄφρα ἰδέω: see app. crit. Read ὄφρ' εἰδέω. The presence of ἰδησῶ, 'I shall see', in Theoc. iii 37 (probably a dialect-form according to Gow) can hardly be adduced in support of the supposition that ἰδέω (cf. *Il.* xiv 235) is a genuine (and presumably archaic) subj. of οἶδα. Most likely the form is a conflation of ἴδω and (Ionic) εἰδέω. The combination ὄφρ' εἰδῇς, -ῇ is also found in the MSS at *Od.* ix 348, *Il.* viii 406, 420, and *Od.* xxii 234 (here with a v.l. ὄφρα ἴδῃς), always at the head of the line. Though the vast majority of the Homeric formulae originated before the digamma was dropped in spoken Ionic (cf., in this case, [ὅς κεν ...] πεπνυμένα εἰδῇ *Od.* viii 586, *sim.*), the creation of the combination (and of ὄφρ' εἴπω) was so easy that we should actually be surprised that such expressions are not used more often in Homer. The existence of ὄφρα ἴδης (found as a variant of ὄφρα ἴδη, 2nd pers. middle, in the MSS) and of the frequently used verse-end formula ὄφρ' ἐῢ εἰδῇς, -ῇ must have contributed to the creation of ὄφρ' εἰδῇς, ὄφρ' εἰδῇ (which eventually brought about ἵν' εἰδῇς *Od.* ii 111). On Ionic εἰδέω and the accentuation εἰδῶ for older εἴδω see Chantraine, *Grammaire*, i 420–1.

238–9. On δυνησόμεθ' and διζησόμεθ' see xv 524 n.

242. αἰχμητὴν: perhaps already felt to be an adj. (meaning 'warlike'; thus

Stanford). At any rate the Homeric use of the word clearly shows the evolution from an objective, businesslike sense ('a man with a spear', cf. e.g. ἀσπιστής, κορυστής, θωρηκτής, κορυνήτης, τοξότης) towards a laudatory (and vaguer) meaning, culminating in Pi.'s θυμὸν αἰχματάν (N. ix 37). **ἐπίφρονα:** best taken as a masc. (with a chiastic word-order), but cf. ἐπίφρονι βουλῇ (iii 128).

243. ἄγη μ' ἔχει: see xiv 239 n.

245. ἀτρεκὲς: this form recurs only at Il. v 208, where the meaning 'truly', 'surely' (Leaf, Ameis–Hentze) is far from certain: 'precisely', 'exactly' (with βαλών, LSJ) seems preferable. This may have developed into 'simply' (cf. Hippocrates Περὶ ἄρθρων ἐμβολῆς 14: ἢν ἀτρεκέως ἀποκαυλισθῇ) and that may have been meant here (μόνον schol.); contrast πολὺ πλέονες (246).

246. τάχα δ' εἴσεαι: also Od. ii 40, but still σάφα εἴσεαι (Il. vii 226), based upon initial digamma, cf. σάφα οἶδα, σάφα εἰδώς (Od. xvii 307 and passim). Here the 'neglect' of the digamma is due to an increasing flexibility in syntax, cf. xiv 68 n.

247-53. Of course the fact that the house of the king of a little island cannot have held so many suitors is no valid reason to condemn the passage. Yet the poem may have conserved traces of a different (older) form of the saga in which the suitors, all from Ithaca, were only twelve, cf. van Leeuwen on i 245-8 and, on the contradictions, Monro, ad loc.

248. δρηστῆρες: see xv 95 n. Though they are socially lower than the θεράποντες (as was still felt by Pi.: θεράπων δέ οἱ, οὐ δράστας ὀπαδεῖ P. iv 287) and the κήρυκες (cf. e.g. Od. xviii 423-4, where the κῆρυξ Moulios is called a ἥρως), the distinction made here has no special significance for the context, cf. e.g. 253 and, on the other hand, xv 321-3.

249. πίσυρες: see Hainsworth on v 70, to whose observations it may be added that, although the form has often been cited as evidence for the importance of Lesbian Aeolic in the development (or even the genesis) of epic language, none of the six Homeric cases (Il. 3, Od. 3) show marked formulaic connections.

252. Μέδων: see 412 n.   **ἀοιδός:** Φήμιος—see i 154.

253. δαιτροσυνάων: see xiv 433, xv 343 nn.

255. πολύπικρα: only here, but cf. Od. xvii 448.   **μὴ ... ἀποτίσεαι:** see xv 12 and 236-7 nn.

256. μερμηρίξαι: the use of this old verb (cf. Ruijgh, Élément, 87) in the sense of 'discovering' with a personal obj. does not seem traditional, but to be due to a reinterpretation on the part of the poet.

261. ἀρκέσει: see xv 524 n.

263-5. If Telemachus' reply should be ironical (thus Monro, followed by Stanford), his concluding words ὥ τε ... θεοῖσι would be hard to explain and his reaction would be a bit strange after his experience in xv 9 ff., not to speak of i 113-323 (cf. 420 φρεσὶ δ' ἀθανάτην θεὸν ἔγνω and his prayer ii 261 ff.), ii 267 ff., 399 ff. (cf. 432 λεῖβον ... Διὸς γλαυκώπιδι κούρῃ).

265. As Ameis–Hentze–Cauer rightly observe, ἀνδράσι ... καὶ ἀθανάτοισι

277

θεοῖσι is an apposition specifying ἄλλοις in 264. See also 227–8 n. The dat. with κρατέω only here and at xi 485; contrast the old formulaic type *ἄνδρεσσι (πάντεσσι, Ἀργείοισι, etc.) ϝάνασσε.

269. μένος κρίνηται Ἄρηος: probably the phrase was coined by the poet (in order to give an epic colour to an expression like ἡ μάχη κρίνεται, which belonged to the vernacular) on the model of στυγερῷ κρινώμεθ' (κρίνονται) Ἄρηϊ (*Il.* ii 285 ∼ xviii 209), cf. Kirk, *Songs*, 206 on ἔριδα ῥήγνυντο βαρεῖαν (*Il.* xx 55) and other 'attempts at innovation and improvement'.

273. = *Od.* xvii 202, xxiv 157 ∼ xvii 337. The line is likely to embody an old element of the saga; it has no late characteristics and λευγαλέος and ἐναλίγκιος are archaisms.

278. ἀφροσυνάων: see xv 343 n.

281–98. Already Zenodotus and Aristarchus held that these lines were spurious in this place and had been partly copied from xix 5–13 (see the scholl. on the two passages and Eust. 1803. 4, 1853. 10). To their arguments others have been added by modern scholars (cf. e.g. Page, *Odyssey*, 92–100, Shipp, *Studies*, 342–3), some of whom would atheticize the lines in question in xix or ascribe both passages to a *Bearbeiter*. The main difficulty is that 295–8 are ignored both in xix and xxii 101 ff. Erbse, *Beiträge*, 35 ff. argues that leaving the two sets of arms in the 'great hall' would only have served to arouse the suspicion of the suitors, that in xvi Odysseus' only purpose is to encourage Telemachus, and that the change in xix has the compositional function of preparing us for the bow-fight. Regardless of the value of the last two arguments, one may wonder what might have decided someone who knew the xix and xxii passages to insert 295–8. Hence we cannot exclude the possibility that the whole of the passage was created at (or for: see 42 n.) a partial performance (of, say, xvi–xviii), at a time, that is, when the poet had not yet composed xix, and that the passage 295–8 was preserved by accident in the final version of the complete poem; see also xv 217–18 n.

281. Cf. 299. Several scholars have taken exception to the line being used twice in the same speech.

283. The situation at the beginning of xix would make such a signal preposterous.

290. κατήκισται: a very late contraction, according to Shipp, *Studies*, 342, probably Attic; van Herwerden proposed κατη(ϝ)είκισται ὅσον, but cf. τιμῆς (*Il.* ix 605), χρυσὸν τιμῆντα (*Il.* xviii 475), alongside τιμήεις (*Od.* xiii 129), χρυσὸν τιμήεντα (*Od.* xi 327), etc.

294. αὐτὸς ... σίδηρος: the proverb must have come into being at a time when iron weapons—and especially swords—were in common use, so after the beginning of the Dark Ages at earliest; see xiv 324 n. On its origin see Russo on xix 13.

297. ἐπιθύσαντες: from ἐπ-ἰθύω, cf. Shipp, *Studies*, 342. The cpd. recurs only at *Il.* xviii 175, but the simplex is frequent; see also 304 n.

298. This line connects the passage on the removal of the arms with 260 ff.   **θέλξει:** see xiii 2 n.

301. μή τις ... ἀκουσάτω: for the explanation of the fact that this construction is still rare in Homer (elsewhere only found in μή τις ... λελαθέσθω *Il.* xvi 200) see Chantraine, *Grammaire,* ii 231.

304. ἰθύν: 'right direction', 'way', cf. Risch *Wortbildung,* 41; as a noun found only in Homer (and perhaps once in *h.Ap.* 539), in whose time it may have been an archaism: its use is confined to the acc. sg., e.g. in πᾶσαν ἐπ᾽ ἰθύν (*Il.* vi 79, *Od.* iv 434).

305. τεο: cf. xiii 394 and n.

306. ὅπου τις: see app. crit. Its interpretation (by Thiersch) as ὅ πού τις has rightly been adopted by Ameis–Hentze–Cauer, with reference to ὅ κέν τις (257).

307. τοῖον ἐόντα: refers to Telemachus' youth and isolated position.

310. χαλιφροσύναι: on the type of abstract cpd. see xv 343 n.; χαλίφρων (iv 371, from *χαλος, cf. χαλάω, 'slacken') may still have had corporal associations, cf. πυκινὰς φρένας (*Il.* xiv 294, *h.Ven.* 38, etc.): πυκινόφρων (ps.-Hes. fr. 253 M–W, *h.Merc.* 538). **ἔχουσιν:** see xiv 239 n.

312. φράζεσθαι: oscillates, as often, between 'to ponder' and 'to be one's guard'.

313. εἴσῃ: to the poet this probably was an 'epic' fut. of εἶμι, cf. ἔργα μετερχόμενος (314), ἀγροὺς ἐπιείσομαι (xv 504), but in actual fact it is likely to be a fut. of ἵεμαι (*Ϝίεμαι), see Chantraine, *Dictionnaire* s.v. 3. εἴσομαι. I. Bekker proposed to 'restore' the initial digamma of ἑκάστου by reading εἶσθα (from εἶμι, cf. xix 69 etc.), but in view of Homer's treatment of the older diction this is wrong, see xiv 68 n.

314. ἔργα μετερχόμενος: opera rustica perlustrans (van Leeuwen), cf. μετέρχεο ἔργα γάμοιο (*Il.* v 429).

316–19. Stanford remarks on Telemachus' 'special loathing for the immorality of some of the palace serving-women'. It must be added that it was their behaviour of which he had had a daily and first-hand experience and that, moreover, an inquiry into the loyalty of the men would have been impossible from a compositional point of view.

316. δεδάασθαι: a diektasis-form for δεδαέσθαι, a reduplicated aor., cf. e.g. λελαβέσθαι (iv 388), λελαθέσθ᾽(αι) (*Il.* xix 136), see Chantraine, *Grammaire,* i 395–6, Risch, *Wortbildung,* 243.

317. νηλίτιδες: see app. crit. The full grade νηλείτιδες (I. Bekker) is to be preferred (cf. νημερτής), see Beekes, *Laryngeals,* 108–9.

320. A surmise based upon 267 and 298. Telemachus does not mention his own experiences (described at xv 160–78, 525–34).

322. The absence of any indication that here the town is meant (cf. xv 503) is remarkable in a style which is generally detailed in such matters.

323. φέρε: cf. e.g. 50 and xiv 13 with nn.

326. τεύχεα: the ship's equipment may be meant (cf. ὅπλα (*Od.* ii 390) and Hes. *Op.* 627–9), but see on the other hand *Od.* iv 784 and xv 218, xvi 360 with nn. It deserves notice that Telemachus' comrades have never been said to have θεράποντες; in ii 415 they themselves put 'all things' on board after the ship's owner had supplied the ὅπλα, i.e. the rigging and oars. Is

326 (= 360 ~ iv 784) an interpolation? Or does the poet use a formulaic line without giving it much thought? Cf. xiii 185 n.

330. ἐπ' ἀγροῦ: not 'at the farm' (A. T. Murray), but 'in the fields', 'in the country'. The stress is on the fact that, although Telemachus is not in town (cf. ἄστυδ' 331), he has safely returned. Cf. also ἐπ' ἀγροῦ νόσφι πόληος (383).

333. συναντήτην: since in Ionic αε contracts to ᾱ, the form does not come from Ionic συναντάω, but is probably to be explained as an old athematic dual (*συναντᾱ́τᾱν) that was superficially ionicized at a later stage, cf. e.g. Chantraine, *Grammaire*, i 306. The athematic verb could be Mycenaean (in the form *ξυνάντᾱμι, but in that case the actual form cannot go back to 'Achaean' epic poetry, as *ξυναντᾱ́τᾱν was metrically impossible in the hexameter) and Aeolic, see Wathelet, *Traits*, 332–3.

335. θείου βασιλῆος: also iv 621; θείων βασιλήων (iv 691), cf. also θεῖος ἀοιδός (xiii 27 with 27–8 n.).

336–7. The brevity of the announcement made in 337 is unique in Homer. Even its introduction (336) is condensed: Penelope's presence among the serving-women is left to be understood. Elsewhere, moreover, the formulaic phrases μετὰ δμῳῆσιν (μετὰ μνηστῆρσιν, μετὰ δ' Ἀργείοισιν) ἔειπε serve to indicate the persons actually addressed. Together with the redundant μέσῃσι (cf. πολλήν *Od.* xv 79) this suggests adaptation (336) and innovation (337).

340. ἐφημοσύνην: see xv 343 n.

341. ἕρκεά τε μέγαρόν τε: the usual prothysteron, cf. xiii 434 n. Does μέγαρόν τε mean that Penelope and the serving-women are in the great hall? Or are they supposed to be in the women's apartment (thus Ameis–Hentze–Cauer)? See also 336–7, 413 nn.

342. ἀκάχοντο: ἄχνυμαι, ἄχομαι, etc. often have the connotation of 'feeling vexed'. **κατήφησάν:** cf. στῆ δὲ κατηφήσας (*Il.* xxii 293) and κατηφής, κατηφών, κατηφείη. Etym. and original meaning are uncertain, but the idea of ineffectualness combined with shame is present everywhere.

343. ~ 165, see n.

344. προπάροιθε θυράων: 343 and 351 show that here, as against i 107, the outer door must be meant, that of the πρόθυρον.

346–7. ~ iv 663–4, but in our lines, as Ameis–Hentze–Cauer rightly observe, the situation requires τετέλεσται and τελέεσθαι to be taken in a slightly different sense: here the verb means 'to be completed', 'to be brought to a successful close', as against 'to be realized' (cf. ἦμαρ εὐπλόκαμος τέλεσ' Ἠώς v 390, Ζεὺς ἀγαθὸν τελέσειεν ii 34, etc.) in the parallel passage, cf. also 111 n. **ὑπερφίαλως:** etym. uncertain. Here, as nearly always in Homer, it implies 'arrogance', 'insolence' (ὑπερηφάνως schol.), but cf. e.g. xvii 481, where it simply means 'exceedingly'.

349. ἁλιῆας: perhaps 'seamen' (thus Ameis–Hentze–Cauer, cf. also Monro and Stanford on *Od.* xxiv 419), but at *Od.* xii 251, xxii 384 ἁλιεύς already means 'fisherman'.

350. κείνοις: again the utterance is remarkably brief: the pronoun refers to

Antinous and his companions, who are believed to be still lying in ambush (cf. iv 842 ff., xv 28–30).

351. Οὔ πω πᾶν εἴρηθ᾽, ὅτ᾽: cf. 11 n.; the tempo of the narrative remains rapid.

354. ἡδὺ δ᾽ ἄρ᾽ ἐκγελάσας: Amphinomus is the most easy-going of the suitors, cf. e.g. xviii 412–21, xx 244–6.

355. ὀτρύνομεν: cf. the use of this verb (in various shades of meaning) with νῆα (xv 37), ὁδόν (ii 253), πομπήν (vii 151 etc.). Hence it is unnecessary to take ἀγγελίην (with Leumann, *Wörter*, 173) as the acc. of ἀγγελίης, 'messenger', i.e. as an artificial creation due to the misinterpretation of lines such as xv 41.   **οἴδε γὰρ ἔνδον:** once again a phrase conspicuous for its briefness, cf. xv 222 n.

358–9. Again the style is abrupt and hurried: οἱ δ᾽ in 358 must refer to Amphinomus and his companions, ἔρυσσαν (359) to the suitors who have just arrived (cf. σφ᾽(ι) 360), yet contrary to epic usage the change of subject is not expressed. Next, αὐτοὶ (361) abruptly refers to both groups (cf. ἀθρόοι).

360. τεύχεα: here either 'weapons' or, less probably, 'vessels for victuals', cf. iv 784.

366. ἐπασσύτεροι: 'one after another', here sometimes interpreted as 'one close upon another' (Monro, Ameis–Hentze–Cauer), but ἐπ᾽ ἄκριας, 'along the heights', and αἰὲν rather suggest 'relieving one another continuously' (etym. uncertain; the ending is not necessarily comparative, cf. θεώτεραι (xiii 111), θηλυτέρῃσι (xv 422), with nn.).   **ἅμα δ᾽ ἠελίῳ καταδύντι:** strictly speaking this is at variance with νύκτ᾽ ἄσαμεν (367); it provides another instance of the poet using a formula (ἅμα δ᾽ ἠελίῳ καταδύντι 4 times, ἐς ἠέλιον καταδύντα 12 times) that was created for other contexts, cf. xiii 185 n. Syntactically the result is a slight anacoluthon.

367. νύκτ᾽ ἄσαμεν: van Leeuwen suggested ἐπ᾽ ἠπείροιο ἀέσσαμεν, see app. crit. The aor., an archaism already in the act of disappearing, recurs as ἄεσαν (iii 490 = xv 188), ἀέσαι (xv 40), ἀέσαμεν (iii 151), ἄεσα (xix 342). Its original form must have been *ἄϝεσ-σα, cf. Anglo-Saxon *wesan*; the corresponding pres. tense is found in ἰαύω (xiv 16 with n. and Beekes, *Laryngeals*, 57) and this gives the analogical aor. ἰαῦσαι instead of (metrically possible) ἀέσσαι (xi 261). The Homeric cases show to what extent such archaic elements might become independent and be altered in the course of the evolution of epic diction; see also 387 n.

370. αὐτόν: thus the MSS, but αὐτοῦ (I. Bekker) has much more point; cf. also ἐνθάδε (371); read τέως μὲν with some MSS (cf. xv 231; others τέως metro invito).

372. ἡμας: only here (instead of Ionic ἡμέας), but σφᾶς *Il.* v 567 (for σφεας) provides an analogy. The two forms are probably artificial, introduced to replace Aeolic ἄμμε and σφε before vowels, cf. Chantraine, *Grammaire*, i 267, 269–70.

375. ἦρα: only found with φέρουσι, φέρων, etc., but the old root *ϝηρ- appears also in another archaism, ἐρίηρες (ἑταῖροι).

281

376. ὁμηγυρίσασθαι: if Myc. *a-ko-ra*, PY Cn 655 (Ventris–Chadwick, *Documents*, no. 62) is to be interpreted as ἀγορά, the noun ὁμήγυρις must be of Aeolic origin since the form with -υ- cannot come from elsewhere, cf. Wathelet, *Traits*, 166.

378. ἀπομηνίσει: elsewhere only said of Achilles, *Il.* ii 772 = vii 230, ix 426, xix 62; probably 'he will give rein to his wrath altogether', cf. 379 and ἀποσκυδμαίνω (*Il.* xxiv 65), ἀποθαυμάζω (*Od.* vi 49, q.v. Hainsworth). The verb denotes a climax.

379. φόνον αἰπὺν: cf. φόνον αἰπὺν ... ὁρμαίνοντες (iv 843), ἀλεξέμεναι φόνον (v.l. πόνον) αἰπύν (*Il.* xvii 365). The adj. is also used as an epithet of δόλος and χόλος in hexameter poetry, see Verdenius, *Mnemosyne*, vi (1953), 115, and in these cases must mean 'hard to overcome', 'irresistible', cf. also West on Hes. *Th.* 589. However, the phrase φόνον αἰπὺν (with ἐράπτομεν) is strained. Probably we have to do with a piece of late formula-making on the model of αἰπὺς (-ὺν) ὄλεθρος (-ον), where the metaphor, although its exact nature is disputed, was no doubt a fairly simple one (originally used to visualize the death of a warrior thrown back from an αἰπὺ τεῖχος? Cf. the fragment of the Mycenaean fresco reproduced in Emily Vermeule, *Greece in the Bronze Age* (Chicago, 1964), pl. xxxi).

380. αἰνήσουσιν: cf. 403 and xiii 47 n.

381. μή: see xv 12 n.

385. ἐφ' ἡμέας: instead of μεθ' ἡμῖν (δάσσαντο μετὰ σφίσιν *Il.* i 368), which was metrically impossible after μοῖραν; cf. μεθ' ὁμήλικας (419) instead of the impossible *μεθ' ὁμήλιξι.

387-92. Antinous is characterized as a *Realpolitiker* by his ruthless proposal in the preceding passage and by his readiness to steer a different course, if necessary; cf. Stanford on 375 ff.

387. βόλεσθε: cf. ἐβόλοντο (i 234), βόλεται (*Il.* xi 319); the form is also found in Arcadian and in the dialect of Eretria (see further Chantraine, *Dictionnaire* s.v. βούλομαι). The fact that it occurs here in the immediate neighbourhood of ἀφανδάνει—one of the rare cpds. based upon the loss of initial digamma—deserves to be mentioned in connection with Wathelet's hypothesis referred to in xiv 158–9 n.

389. χρήματ': see xiii 120 n.

393. = xiii 1, see n. ad loc.

395-7. Amphinomus, who already appeared in 351, is not given the traditional introduction until here—another symptom of the structure of epic narrative being sometimes much looser than its usual formalism would lead us to expect.

396. Δουλιχίου: see xiv 335 n.

399. ἐϋφρονέων: (rather ἐῢ φρονέων) at the same time 'meaning well' and 'wise'. Both meanings are still found in fifth-century poetry (cf. e.g. A. *Pr.* 387, *A.* 1436), but in the Ionic prose of Hdt. the former is wanting; see E. Fraenkel on A. *A.* 176 and 806, who rightly observes that in Homer φρονεῖν in the sense of 'having understanding' is very much in the background.

401. γένος: the word-order points to a personal construction, cf. also ἀργαλέος γὰρ Ὀλύμπιος ἀντιφέρεσθαι (*Il.* i 589, *sim.*).

403. αἰνήσωσι: see xiii 47 n.   **θέμιστες:** see xiv 56 n.

406. τοῖσιν δ' ἐπιήνδανε μῦθος: the poet does not trouble to give even the slightest hint as to how the plan is to be carried out; on the contrary he makes the suitors enter the palace, which they can hardly regard as a suitable place for continuing the discussion. In this way he brings the scene to an abrupt end in order to treat the same subject—the planned murder—from a different angle (409–48).

411. ἐνὶ μεγάροισιν: see 413 n.   **ὄλεθρον:** cf. ἀποκτείνεις (432) with n.

412. In the parallel passage iv 673 ff. this line is followed by αὐλῆς ἐκτὸς ἐών· οἱ δ' ἔνδοθι μῆτιν ὕφαινον, a verse which is rightly omitted here by most MSS (see 361–2). Medon's loyalty to Penelope is also mentioned at iv 697 ff.

413. The lines 414–16 are used several times to describe how Penelope makes her appearance among the suitors (i 332 ff., xviii 208 ff., xxi 63 ff.), but neither here nor in xxi is it said that she comes down from her private room upstairs (i 330, xviii 206). This is in accordance with the situation in xxi 8 ff. and also with that in our passage, provided ἐνὶ μεγάροισιν (411) is here taken as 'in her own (or the women's) apartment'. This loose employment (certainly late) appears to be confirmed by xvii 569 (and by xix 16?), cf. διὲκ μεγάροιο xviii 185 (as against its normal use at xvii 61 etc.) and xiii 185 n. But see also Russo on xvii 492–506

415. = i 333, viii 458, xviii 209, xxi 64.   **σταθμὸν τέγεος:** the natural interpretation seems to be 'a pillar of the roof' and Stanford appositely quotes A. *A.* 897–8 ὑψηλῆς στέγης στῦλον ποδήρη, but the description of the Mycenaean 'House of the Columns' given by Wace, in *Companion*, 491 ff., might favour 'the door-post of the hall' (σταθμός certainly means 'door-post': *Od.* vi 19, *Il.* xiv 167) and this interpretation fits into Homer's picture of Penelope; see also S. West on i 333 and Hainsworth on viii 458. We do not know, however, how far Homer reflects Mycenaean conditions in such matters (cf. xiii 2, 4, xv 146, xvi 41, 449 nn.), and the use of the phrase in *h.Cer.* 186 as well as παρὰ σταθμὸν μεγάροιο at *Od.* xvii 96 seem to point the other way.

418. καὶ δέ ... φασιν: = καὶ φασὶ δή, cf. Th. i 39 and Denniston, *Particles*, 200.

419. μεθ' ὁμήλικας: see 385 n.

420. ἄρα ... ἦσθα: see xiii 210 n.

421. θάνατόν τε μόρον τε: also ix 61, xi 409, xx 241. In the *Iliad* μόρος is found a few times as a near synonym of 'death' (e.g. xxi 133), but there it is never combined with θάνατος. In the *Odyssey*, moreover, this 'new' formula is not only employed with φύγομεν (ix 61), but also with τεύξας, ῥάπτεις, ἤρτυον, a phenomenon which marks a generalizing development, concomitant with a further fading of the original meaning of μόρος, and foreshadows the solemn use of the noun by Hdt. to indicate *violent death*. Cf. also φόνον καὶ κῆρα φυτεύει (-σω) ii 165, xvii 82, θάνατον καὶ κῆρ' ἀραρόντε xvi 169, and xiv 207 n.

422–3. The much discussed ἱκέτας can neither be taken to refer to Telemachus nor (with the scholl.) to both the suppliant and the one who is supplicated. Since, however, ἀλλήλοισιν must mean the two of them, it follows that Penelope's words are an elliptical introduction to 424 ff. (see xiv 299–301 n.): 'And don't you think of ⟨the state of⟩ suppliants, for whom Zeus is a witness? ⟨But so he is for those supplicated⟩ and ⟨thus⟩ it is not lawful …'. The second partner in a reciprocal relationship is likewise omitted in οὐδὲ πατὴρ παίδεσσιν ὁμοίϊος οὐδέ τι παῖδες κτλ. (Hes. Op. 182, 184). The fact, moreover, that Zeus surveys the behaviour of both partners is similarly implied in E. Stheneboea Ζῆνά θ' ἱκέσιον σέβων, fr. 1. 15 Page, Greek Literary Papyri, i (London, 1942) (said by Bellerophon), and in Hdt.'s well-known tale about Adrastus, where it is said of Croesus (i 44. 2) ἐκάλεε μὲν Δία καθάρσιον μαρτυρόμενος [sc. αὐτὸν] τὰ ὑπὸ τοῦ ξείνου πεπονθὼς εἴη κτλ., see also Stein's n. See also West on Hes. Op. 183, who rightly adds, 'The most outrageous aspect of Paris' seduction of Helen was that it was a crime against his ξεινοδόκος', and refers to Il. iii 354–5.

423. ὁσίη: in Homer only here and at Od. xxii 412, see xiii 142, xv 343 nn. In the abstract it denotes 'what may be (or is) done (according to divine regulation)' (Richardson on h.Cer. 211), so 'nec fas est' would not inadequately render οὐδ' ὁσίη in this context, cf. also οἷσιν ἄρα Ζεὺς | μάρτυρος and Hdt. ii 45. 2; 171. 2.

424. ἦ οὐκ οἶσθ' ὅτε: cf. ἦ οὐ μέμνῃ ὅτε (Il. xv 18). **πατὴρ τεός:** according to xxiv 422–4, at this moment still living in Ithaca.

425. δὴ γὰρ κεχολώατο λίην: also xiv 282. **δὴ γάρ:** see xiii 30 n.

426. Ταφίοισιν: see xiv 452 n.

427. ἄρθμιοι: only here in Homer; like ἀρθμέω (Il. vii 302), a derivative of ἀρ-θμός, 'bond', 'league', cf. ἀραρίσκω. In this case the older formation was not preserved in the Homeric epics, but is found for the first time in h.Merc. 524; cf. κηληθμός < κηλέω, in which case it is the verb that is still absent from the Iliad and the Odyssey; see xiii 2, xiv 446, xv 456 nn.

431. ἄτιμον: 'without paying for it', cf. τιμὴν … ἐεικοσάβοιον (Od. xxii 57), and xiv 70 n.

432. ἀποκτείνεις: not so much conative as emphatic (and as such related to the so-called praesens propheticum: (in so far as it depends on you) you kill …, cf. 411 n.

438–44. Several phrases in this passage suggest that the poet is familiar with the details of the story of Achilles' μῆνις as told in the Iliad: 438 χεῖρας ἐποίσει, i 89; 439 ~ i 88; 441 ~ i 303; 443–4, cf. ix 455, 488–9. ἡμετέρῳ (442), especially, looks like a symptom of adaptation. Still, as van Leeuwen already observed, Il. i 88 has two contractions (ἐμεῦ ζῶντος), whereas 439 has none (cf. Il. xxiii 70 μέν μευ ζώοντος < ἐμέθεν ζώοντος, owing to the introduction of the particle, see Hoekstra, Modifications, 56 ff.). It thus appears that the poet, though probably familiar with the elaborate story of Achilles' wrath and possibly identical with its creator, was not bound by its versification but handled the epic diction in an independent way.

445–7. This insolent conclusion of a hypocritical speech characterizes the brazen-faced liar Eurymachus as effectively as the ruthlessness of 371-2 pictured the *Draufgänger* Antinous.

446. τρομέεσθαι: the middle is also used at *Il.* x 492 (τρομέοιατο) and *Od.* xviii 77 (περιτρομέοντο). Here at any rate we have to do with a typically poetical usage, cf. xiv 316 n.

449. ὑπερώϊα σιγαλόεντα: Mycenaean palaces had a second floor (cf. e.g. Wace, in *Companion*, 490, E. Vermeule, *Greece in the Bronze Age* (cit. 379 n.), 172), and the women looking out of the windows on a Mycenaean sarcophagus recently found by Spyropoulos at Tanagra (see e.g. *BCH* xciv (1970), fig. 322) are most probably in the upper story of the house. Hence it is possible that the expression is of Mycenaean origin, but upper floors have also been found with buildings dating from proto-Geometric times, see Drerup, *Archaeologia* ii O, 130 ff.; moreover we do not know what exactly is meant by the epithet, when it is applied to ὑπερώϊα—if to the poet it meant anything specific at all, cf. ἐνώπια παμφανόωντα (*Od.* iv 42 etc.), where the adj. is a metrical equivalent of σιγαλόεντα. Probably this means that σιγαλόεντα is the older of the two. See further Hainsworth on vi 26.

453. ἐπισταδὸν: cf. xiii 54. Here the word is explained as ἐπιστημόνως, ἐπισταμένως by the scholl., but its sense remains obscure; 'standing close to it, i.e. attentively' (Stanford) seems best. On the other hand δόρπον ἐπισταδὸν ὁπλίζοντο shows a curious resemblance to δόρπον ἐπισταμένως τετύκοντο (xii 307), and if, as δόρπον ∪–∪∪– τετύκοντο/τετυκέσθαι (with its archaic aor.) suggests, the latter phrase was a pre-Homeric formula (*Od.* xx 390, xxi 428), the poet, when 'conjugating' this formula, may have used the old advb. (cf. ἀνασταδόν etc.) as though it could mean ἐπισταμένως, cf. πανθυμαδόν, 'most heartily' (*Od.* xviii 33).

454-7. The plot asks for a second transformation and it is natural that now the poet makes short work of it, cf. xv 494-5 with n. Analysts have argued that in the sequel to the story the poet proceeds as if the hero's transformation had never taken place and Odysseus is simply altered by the passage of time, cf. e.g. Page, *Odyssey*, 88 ff.—a supposition which is not sufficiently supported by the text, see now Erbse, *Beiträge*, 55 ff.

454. σῦν ... ἐνιαύσιον: see xiv 80-1, xiv 419 nn. Eumaeus gives Telemachus the best pork he has at his disposal.

458. ἐσάντα ἰδών: this probably represents a highly archaic formula (< *ἐν ἄντα ϝιδών, 'looking in the face'), cf. ἔναντα (*Il.* xx 67) and ἐνῶπα ἰδών (*Il.* xv 320, < *ἐν ὦπα ϝιδών), which likewise contains two archaic survivals: ἐν—for Ionic ἐς—and ὤψ (with the exception of late imitations only in the acc. sg. and confined to formulae). See further Risch, *Wortbildung*, 355.

459. εἰρύσσαιτο: here 'to guard' as a secret; in 463 the same verb means 'to watch', cf. Lat. *servare–observare*.

460. καὶ: in this type of line the particle precedes a proper name of the metrical value –∪∪– at *Il.* v 632 (where Leaf rightly calls it 'awkward'), xiii 306, *Od.* xvii 74. It may be emphatic (cf. xv 181, 435, 513 nn.), but at the same time its presence may be due to the poet (or his predecessors)

making the answering formula τὸν δ' αὖ Τηλέμαχος (Εὐρύμαχος, etc.)
πεπνυμένος ἀντίον ηὔδα fit a context where no speech precedes (πρότερος)
by introducing the well-known formula πρὸς μῦθον ἔειπεν, see xiv 52 and
55 nn.

463. αὖτ': more convincing is αὖθ'(ι) (some MSS) as opposed to ἔνδον (462).

466. καταβλώσκοντα (κάτα βλώσκοντα Herodian): in such cases the use of
the acc. instead of the dat. (cf. μοι 465 and xv 240) is still frequent in Hdt.;
cf. also xiv 527 with n.

468. ὠμήρησε: probably a denominative from ὅμηρος, originally 'companion' (later 'hostage'), cf. ὀμ-αρτέω (Od. xiii 87, etc.).

471. Ἕρμαιος λόφος (ἕρμαιος Herodian, ἑρμαῖος MSS, see below): 'the hill
of Hermes', i.e. a hill (or rather hill-top, see e.g. Od. xi 596) where Hermes
was worshipped, is the interpretation which naturally comes to mind.
That meaning is also mentioned by the scholia, but, curiously enough, as a
last resort possibility: they begin by stating that the expression denotes a
ἑρμαῖον (properispomenon), a 'heap of stones', and conclude their explanation with a reference to an aetiological story by a certain Anticlides (the
third-century historian?). The purpose of this story (which is also found
in the *Etymologicum Magnum* s.v. ἑρμαῖον) was to explain the Greek custom
of making stone-heaps (σωροὶ λίθων) and the habit of wayfarers to add still
more stones to those cairns, which, according to the author, were called
Ἑρμαῖοι λόφοι. Now stone-heaps actually existed—and still exist—in
Greece: Paus. for instance saw them, see ii 36. 3, iii 13. 3. Moreover, it
appears from Anticlides' story that these ἑρμαῖα (as the scholl. call them, cf.
also Hesych. s.v. ἑρμεών) consisted of an upright stone surrounded by a
heap of stones at its base, and in the 19th century such a monument was
actually found together with a slab inscribed 'of Hermes' (Guthrie, *Gods*,
90). These and similar considerations led Wilamowitz and Nilsson to
derive the name of the god (which has since been found on the Linear B
tablets in the form *e-ma-a₂*) from ἕρμα, in origin probably 'stone', cf.
Chantraine, *Dictionnaire* s.v. (the phonetical objection advanced by
Schwyzer, *Grammatik*, i 562 n. 1, need not be decisive because both the
noun and the name of the god are likely to be pre-Hellenic, see
Chantraine, ibid. s.v. Ἑρμῆς, Guthrie, op. cit., 88 and J. Chittenden (see
xv 319 n. and *Hesperia*, xvi (1947), 89–114). The relation of the Homeric
forms has been elucidated by Ruijgh, *Études*, 266 n. 154, see also Hainsworth on *Od.* v 28. Finally it is to be noted that the cairns which Frazer (on
Paus. ii 38. 7) identified with the 'herms' mentioned by the author, were
rather extensive, some 15 ft. in diameter.

It thus appears that the meaning of Ἑρμαῖος λόφος cannot be established beyond reasonable doubt. Anyhow, if the expression really was a
generic designation, there is no need to regard its use here as due to exact
local knowledge.

474. ἀμφιγύοισι: the translation 'with a double curved edge', utrimque
curvatus (de cuspide hastae utrimque in latitudinem aliquam extenta,
Doederlein), is not beyond all doubt, but preferable to 'double-pointed'

(i.e. with a spear-head and a butt-end, σαυρωτήρ), cf. Trümpy, *Fachausdrücke*, 59; see also *LfgrE* s.v. and O. Höckmann, *Archaeologia* i E ii 286 ff.   ἔγχεσιν ἀμφιγύοισι: also xxiv 527 and often in the *Iliad*, always at the verse-end.

475. οὐδέ: here used adversatively (cf. Denniston, *Particles*, 191) but at *Od.* iii 184 the same expression means 'and I do not know'.

476. ἱερὴ ἲς Τηλεμάχοιο: see xiii 20 n.

478–80. = *Il.* i 467–9 etc.

480. See xiv 453–4 n.

481. The end of the day is marked in a similar way at *Il.* vii 482 κοιμήσαντ' ἄρ' ἔπειτα καὶ ὕπνου δῶρον ἕλοντο (our line has a variant δὴ τότε κοιμήσαντο, cf. xix 427 ~ *Il.* ix 713). The phrase κοίτου τε μνήσαντο is likely to be a modification of an older *κοίτοιο μέδοντο (μέδηται, μέδεσθαι, cf. κοίτου τε μέδηται *Od.* ii 358, κοίτοιο μεδώμεθα iii 334), a verse-end formula: δόρποιο μέδοντο (*Il.* xxiv 2), δόρποιο μέδεσθαι (*Il.* xviii 245 etc., cf. xiv 251 with n.). *Od.* xx 138 ὅτε δὴ κοίτοιο καὶ ὕπνου μιμνήσκοιτο is also a modification.

INDEX

Greek words

General

Acastus, 217–18
accentuation, 53, 168, 276
Achaean-Aeolic dialect, 154, 226, 228, 249
Achaean dialect, Achaean stage of epic diction, 153–5, 181, 185, 246, 256, 267, 268, 269
Acheron, 70, 214
Achilles, 30, 67, 82, 109, 282; in Hades, 77, 100, 105, 106, 107, 109, 110; μῆνις, 284; shield, 115, 226; weeping, 274
adapatation of lines/expressions, 17, 22, 31, 37, 87, 89, 95, 98, 101, 120, 130, 173, 178, 194, 195, 196, 197, 202, 203, 205, 212, 215, 218, 220, 222, 223, 225, 226, 227, 228, 232, 233, 235, 237, 240, 243, 247, 250, 251, 253, 255, 256, 261, 262, 267, 268, 269, 270, 274, 275, 276, 278, 280, 282, 284, 285–6
Aeaea, 4, 15, 46, 48, 52, 54, 117
Aeetes, 52
Aegisthus, 11
Aeolia, 43, 44
Aeolic dialect, Aeolism, 34, 96, 152–5, 156, 166, 168, 173, 175, 181, 194, 209, 218, 224, 225, 226, 256, 264, 269, 271, 277, 280, 281, 282
Aeolus, 9, 10, 43, 46, 50; bag, 43, 44
Aeschylus, 165, 166, 226, 253, 283
Aethiopis, see Cyclic epics
Aethon, 163
Agamemnon, 77, 97, 100, 101, 102, 103, 104, 105, 109, 110, 186
Ajax, 77, 100, 105, 109–10
Alcaeus, 108, 152, 228, 253
Alcinous, 12, 39, 98–9
Alcmene, 93
Alexandrian scholarship, 25, 54, 79, 80, 120, 123, 139, 147, 229, 234, 251; *see also* Aristarchus, Aristophanes of Byzantium, Rhianus, Zenodotus
allegorical interpretation, Moly, 61; Sirens, 119–20

alliteration, 212, 220
amber, 260
Amphiaraus, 248
Amphinomus, 281, 282
Amphion, 93, 94
anachronisms, 180
anacoluthon, 37, 108, 186, 265
analytical interpretation, 5–6, 7, 9–10, 19, 35, 39, 40, 52, 54, 57, 59, 60, 64, 68, 69, 70, 72, 73, 75–6, 82–3, 84, 85, 86, 88, 91, 97, 101, 103, 121, 122, 135, 138, 139, 147, 164, 245, 249, 262, 273, 275, 285; *see also* interpolation
anaphora, 62, 82, 122, 128, 270
Andromache, 109, 199
animals, birds, 141, 169, 214, 261, 276; Circe's, 55; Cyclops', 21, 37; sense presence of a god, 272
Anthesteria, 71, 76
Anticleia, 77, 82, 86–7, 88, 89, 90, 91, 101
Antilochus, 105
Antinous, 282, 285
Apollo, 258; arrows of, 87; god of the birds of omen, 263; Lord of Ismarus, 25; priest of, 25
Apollonius Rhodius, 48, 49, 119, 121
apostrophe, 195–6
apposition, 169
ἀπρέπεια, τὸ πρέπον, 184, 229, 232, 234
Arcadian dialect, 152, 204, 207, 282
Arcado-Cypriot dialect, 154, 155, 194–5
Archilochus, 189
architecture, 241; ἀντίθυρον, 272; αὐλή, 24, 192–3; δῶ, 162; θύραι, 56; μέγαρον, 161, 239–40, 280, 283; μέσσαυλος, 67; οἶκος, 240; οὐδός, 267; πρόθυρον, 56, 272, 280; σταθμός, 283; τειχίον, 272; ὑπερῷα, 285
Ares, 208
Arete, 98, 100
Arethusa, 190
Argonauts, *Argonautica* (old), 4–5, 7, 47–8, 49, 51–2, 73, 76, 118–19, 121,

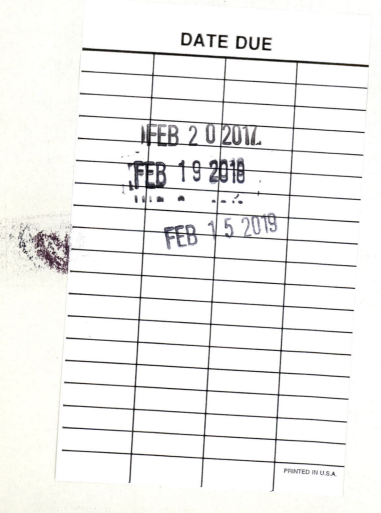